PRINCIPLES OF PATENT LAW

By

Roger E. Schechter
Professor of Law,
George Washington University

John R. Thomas
Professor of Law,
Georgetown University

CONCISE HORNBOOK SERIES®

Mat #40159786

610 Opperman Drive
P.O. Box 64526
St. Paul, MN 55164–0526
1–800–328–9352

Printed in the United States of America

ISBN 0–314–14751–9

In memory of my grandparents—Max, Ida, Jack and Bertha—
who invented a new life in America

R.E.S.

To Sayuri and Karen

J.R.T.

*

Preface

Over the past decade, perhaps no subject has migrated as quickly from the periphery to the heart of the law school curriculum as patent law. Not so very long ago the subject was not even taught at many law schools, or if taught at all, was given cursory coverage in a survey course treating all of intellectual property law. There were few casebooks, few full-time teachers and the material was considered the arcane province of the rare lawyer with a hard science background.

In recent years more and more schools have begun offering comprehensive courses in both basic and advanced patent law and more and more students have been clamoring to get into those courses. The speed of this development has, however, left something of a shortfall in the materials available to the conscientious student who seeks to cement his or her understanding of the field. We offer this small volume as a modest contribution towards filling that gap.

Readers familiar with our lengthier volume in the West Hornbook series will note significant similarities between the patent sections of that book and this new effort. While carrying forward the organizational scheme and much text from the Hornbook, however, this new format has permitted us to expand our treatment of numerous topics, provide many additional examples, clarify ambiguities and discuss the latest judicial opinions and statutory amendments. Liberated, somewhat, from space constraints, we hope that this volume is a comprehensive yet manageable and user-friendly treatment of a fascinating and fast-changing subject. While we have concentrated primarily on an exposition of doctrine, we have also tried to offer up the outlines of underlying policy disputes and, here and there, our own views on the wisdom of various cases.

Patent law is only likely to grow in importance in the years to come. The pace of technological innovation will surely continue to accelerate, increasing globalization will bring diverse national patent regimes into closer harmony, and an ever expanding scope of patentable subject matter will likely draw more firms and independent innovators into the patent system. We hope that with this effort we have made a small contribution towards preparing the next generation of lawyers who will be working in this dynamic field.

In that next generation of lawyers, we are especially grateful to Scott Cunning (GW '04) and Steven Purdy (Georgetown '05) for their thorough research assistance and meticulous proofreading. The opportunity to work with and be challenged by thoughtful and creative students like these, and so many others we have known through the years, is a constant source of inspiration and intellectual pleasure for us, and gives us great optimism that the legal challenges of the future will be met with skill and dedication. We also wish to thank Anna Selden and other members of the Georgetown Office of Faculty Support for their helpful assistance with our manuscript.

ROGER E. SCHECHTER
JOHN R. THOMAS

Washington, D.C.
May 2004

Summary of Contents

*

Table of Contents

*

PRINCIPLES OF PATENT LAW

*

Chapter 1

INTRODUCTION TO THE LAW OF PATENTS

Table of Sections

No matter what your role in the U.S. legal system, if you are interested in the patent law, you have come at a good time. By any conceivable measure, patents are more significant by an order of magnitude than a generation ago. More patents are sought and enforced than ever before; the attention paid to patents in business transactions and corporate boardrooms has dramatically increased; and the commercial and social importance of patent licenses, judgments and settlements is at an all-time high. Not only is the patent regime of newfound influence, it is also of increasing interest. The brisk pace of technological change has channeled a steady stream of intriguing legal issues towards the patent system. Jurists, academics and practitioners alike have in turn championed an intellectual revival of this venerable discipline. In sum, there has never been a better time to study patents. We hope that this introductory chapter, which provides an overview of the basic workings and policy aspirations of the patent system, provides a solid foundation for the more detailed treatment found in subsequent chapters.

§ 1.1 Brief Overview of the Patent Law

Since the first Congress enacted the Patent Act of 1790, the patent law has been a wholly federal, statutory subject. Today the patent law is governed by the Patent Act of 1952, found in Title 35 of the United States Code. The Patent Act allows inventors to obtain patents on processes, machines, manufactures and compositions of matter that are useful, novel, and nonobvious.[1] An invention is judged as useful if it is minimally operable towards some practical purpose.[2] To be considered novel within the patent law, an invention must differ from existing references that disclose the state of the art, such as publications and other patents.[3] The nonobviousness requirement is met if the invention is beyond the ordinary abilities of a skilled artisan knowledgeable in the appropriate field.[4]

In order to receive a patent, an inventor must file a patent application with a specialized government agency known as the United States Patent and Trademark Office, or PTO.[5] Patent applications must include a specification that so completely describes the invention that skilled artisans are enabled to practice it without undue experimentation.[6] The patent application must also contain distinct, definite claims that set out the proprietary interest asserted by the inventor.[7]

Trained personnel at the PTO, known as examiners, review all applications to ensure that the invention described and claimed in the application fulfills the pertinent requirements of the patent

§ 1.1

1. 35 U.S.C.A. §§ 101, 102, 103 (2000).

2. *See* Brenner v. Manson, 383 U.S. 519, 86 S.Ct. 1033, 16 L.Ed.2d 69 (1966).

3. 35 U.S.C.A. § 102 (2000).

4. 35 U.S.C.A. § 103(a) (2000).

5. 35 U.S.C.A. § 111 (2000).

6. 35 U.S.C.A. § 112 (2000).

7. 35 U.S.C.A. § 112 (2000).

law. An acquisition proceeding at the PTO is commonly known as "prosecution." If the PTO believes that the application fulfills the statutory requirements, it will allow the application to issue as a granted patent.[8] In such a case the PTO will assemble and publish the corresponding patent instrument, which includes the complete specification, claims, and prior art references considered during prosecution.[9] Each patent ordinarily enjoys a term of twenty years commencing from the date the patent application was filed.[10] Issued patents provide interested parties with notice of the patentee's proprietary rights and are also a valued source of technical information.

Granted patents give the patentee the right to exclude others from making, using, selling, offering to sell, or importing into the United States the patented invention.[11] Parties who engage in those acts without the permission of the patentee during the term of the patent can be held liable for infringement. The patentee may file a civil suit in federal court in order to enjoin infringers and obtain monetary remedies.[12] Although issued patents enjoy a presumption of validity, accused infringers may assert that the patent is invalid or unenforceable on a number of grounds.[13] Patents have the attributes of personal property and may be assigned or licensed to others.[14]

In addition to the usual sort of patent, technically known as a "utility patent," the intellectual property laws also provide for other sorts of patents and patent-like rights. Design patents are available for new, original, and ornamental designs.[15] A plant patent may be issued for a distinct and new variety of plant that has been asexually reproduced, through grafting, budding, or similar techniques.[16] Plant variety protection certificates are available for sexually reproduced plants, including most seed-bearing plants, provided they are stable and clearly distinguishable from known varieties.[17]

§ 1.2 Patent Law Norms

Several core concepts form the theoretical basis for the patent laws. An understanding of these concepts is highly useful in mastering the structure of the existing rules of the patent system, and can also help shed light on the proper resolution of new and

8. 35 U.S.C.A. § 151 (2000).
9. 35 U.S.C.A. § 154 (2000).
10. 35 U.S.C.A. § 154 (2000).
11. 35 U.S.C.A. § 271(a) (2000).
12. 35 U.S.C.A. § 281 (2000).
13. 35 U.S.C.A. § 282 (2000).
14. 35 U.S.C.A. § 261 (2000).
15. 35 U.S.C.A. § 171 (2000).
16. 35 U.S.C.A. § 161 (2000).
17. 7 U.S.C.A. § 2321 *et seq.* (2000).

controversial issues that are constantly being presented by the changing legal and technological landscape.

1.2.1 The Right to Exclude

Patents confer the right to exclude others from making, using, selling, offering to sell, and importing the protected invention.[1] Much like a deed of real property, patent instruments define the boundaries of the "technological territory" that is proprietary to the patent owner. The patent owner may bring suit to enjoin infringement by "trespassers" who exploit the patented invention without authorization. Put differently, others have a duty to avoid practicing a patented invention without the permission of the patent owner.

Patents do not affirmatively allow their owners to exploit the patented product on the marketplace, however.[2] The actual marketing of a patented product is subject to the constraints of property rights, consumer protection statutes, antitrust principles, and other laws. Because patents do not provide a positive right to practice a patented invention, some commentators refer to the patent right as a "negative" right to exclude.

Two examples can helpfully illustrate this principle. First, suppose that inventor Professor Gizmo develops a new pharmaceutical, files a patent application at the PTO, and subsequently obtains a patent. The fact that Gizmo owns a patent does not allow her to start dispensing the drug to patients. Because her invention deals with a regulated medicine, she is legally obligated to first obtain the approval of the Food and Drug Administration (FDA). If Gizmo actually began selling the drug without the necessary regulatory approvals, she might be criminally liable under the food and drug laws. Gizmo's patent would allow her to prevent her competitors from marketing that drug, however, whether those competitors had obtained FDA approval or not.

Consider a second situation. Imagine that five years ago Professor Mickey invented a new type of mousetrap and secured a patent on that invention. Now assume that some time this year Dr. Minnie develops an improved version of that mousetrap—perhaps one which is more humane in dispatching the trapped rodent. Dr. Minnie is entitled to apply for a patent on her improvement, and if the standards of patentability are met, that patent will be granted. However, that patent does not necessarily allow her to market her better mousetrap, because doing so would infringe the patent of Professor Mickey. Moreover, Professor Mickey cannot market the improved mousetrap without the permission of Dr. Minnie. Each

§ 1.2

1. 35 U.S.C. § 271(a) (2000).

2. *See* King Instruments Corp. v. Perego, 65 F.3d 941 (Fed. Cir. 1995).

can exclude the other from practicing the inventions covered by their respective patent, but neither patent confers an absolute right to practice the invention. The result is that without some sort of agreement between them, neither would be legally free to manufacture and sell the improved mousetrap.[3]

1.2.2 Intangible Property and the Exhaustion of Rights

Patent law does not create property rights in any particular material object in which an invention has been embodied. The patent system instead creates a more abstract proprietary interest that is independent of any specific physical good employing the patented invention.[4] The consequences of owning a patent are therefore quite different from those of owning an automobile or a piece of real estate, for example. A particular patent may be seen as a "private regulation," effective across the United States, that prevents others from unauthorized use of the patented invention.

The concept of exhaustion provides a vivid example of the difference between rights in intangible property and rights over a tangible object.[5] Once the patent owner has made an unqualified sale of a physical product embodying his or her invention, the patent owner cannot prohibit the subsequent resale of that particular product. Any patent rights in that specific physical product are said to have been "exhausted" by this initial sale. The exhaustion doctrine allows goods to move through the stream of commerce unhindered by multiple claims to proprietary interests. Sometimes the exhaustion principle is termed the "first sale" doctrine.[6]

For example, suppose that homeowner Hal Handy purchases an automatic screwdriver at a Block & Docker Company store. The screwdriver is subject to a patent owned by Block & Docker. Later, Handy sells the screwdriver to a neighbor at a garage sale. Ordinarily, Block & Docker would be able to prevent others from selling screwdrivers that embody its patented technology. In this case, however, the patent right in that particular screwdriver was exhausted when Block & Docker made its first sale to Handy. Handy, as well as any subsequent purchasers of that individual screwdriver, may freely sell it without concern for the Block & Docker patent. What Handy cannot do, however, is to examine the automatic screwdriver and then build a second one just like it. That

3. This situation is sometimes said to involve "blocking" patents. *See, e.g.*, Robert P. Merges, *Intellectual Property Rights and Bargaining Breakdown: The Case of Blocking Patents*, 62 Tenn. L. Rev. 75 (1994).

4. *See* A.S. Solomons v. United States, 21 Ct.Cl. 479, 483, *aff'd*, 137 U.S. 342 (1890).

5. *See, e.g.*, Anton/Bauer, Inc. v. PAG, Ltd., 329 F.3d 1343, 1349–50 (Fed. Cir. 2003).

6. For a detailed discussion of the first sale doctrine, *see* § 8.1.1.2, *infra*.

would violate Block & Docker's intangible property rights in the invention.

1.2.3 The Public Domain

Most inventors build on the work of those who have come before them. The ability of the current generation of inventors to advance technology depends, in large measure, on their ability to use older technology free from legal restraints. To insure that this is possible, the patent regime has numerous doctrines that limit the scope of patent protection, and declare certain material free for all to use. This material is said to be in the public domain. Free from the proprietary interests of others, the public domain provides a body of knowledge that supports further innovation.[7] A flourishing public domain not only aids inventors, but benefits consumers, competitors, and other members of the user community by permitting competition which can make innovative products available at lower cost.

The requirements that an invention be new and nonobvious to qualify for patent protection ensure that the patent system does not withdraw subject matter from the public domain.[8] Congress has reasoned that unless an inventor has contributed subject matter that is new and beyond the state of the art, he should not be awarded a patent. This principle makes good sense as a policy matter, for there is obviously little reason to offer the reward of a patent to an individual who merely discloses technical information already known to the public. The limited duration of patent rights—ordinarily twenty years from the date the patent application was filed—also contributes to the public domain.[9] Once a patent has expired, others may practice the patented invention without regard to that extinguished proprietary interest. Each year an enormous amount of technical information becomes freely available for others to exploit and build upon as various patents expire. In these ways, and in others we shall encounter further on, the patent system seeks both to preserve and to expand the public domain.

1.2.4 One Patent Per Invention

The patent system insists that only one patent issue per invention. Allowing the same inventor to repeatedly return to the Patent Office to obtain additional patents on the same invention would permit the inventor to extend the period of exclusivity beyond the specified statutory term, delaying the entry of the subject matter into the public domain, without any offsetting

7. *See, e.g.,* Jessica Litman, *The Public Domain*, 39 EMORY L.J. 965 (1990).

8. 35 U.S.C.A. § 103(a) (2000).

9. 17 U.S.C.A. § 302 (2000).

benefits to the public. Allowing different inventors all to receive patents on the same invention would require parties seeking permission to use the technology to deal with multiple right-holders, leading to uncertainty and wasteful transaction costs, and might actually prevent any of the patent holders from commercializing the invention out of fear that the others could sue for infringement. These ideas manifest themselves in several patent law principles. In addition to novelty and nonobviousness, the doctrine of "double patenting" prevents the same inventor from obtaining multiple patents to the same or similar inventions.[10]

1.2.5 Patent Award to the First Inventor

Every day, technological rivals across the globe compete to create valuable inventions. In many cases they will often develop similar or identical inventions at approximately the same time. In such circumstances, the patent system has developed a winner-take-all policy. Under U.S. law, the first person to have actually invented that technology obtains the patent. The timing of real-world events, such as the date a researcher conceived of a new chemical compound or a machinist constructed a new engine, is significant under this "first-to-invent" priority principle. The first inventor will be awarded a patent even though a rival may have been the first to prepare a patent application and submit it to the PTO. When multiple parties claim the right to a patent, the PTO conducts special administrative proceedings termed "interferences" to determine which party was the first actual inventor.[11]

The U.S. "first-to-invent" priority principle is very much the exception among the world's patent-granting states. All other jurisdictions follow a "first-to-file" priority principle, awarding the patent to the first person to file a Patent Office application, even though he may have not been the first actual inventor. Debate continues over whether the United States should adopt the "first-to-file" priority system that has become the global norm, or whether we should retain our traditional "first-to-invent" principle.

1.2.6 The Claims Define the Patented Invention

Every utility patent closes with at least one claim.[12] A patent claim is a single-sentence definition of the exact scope of the intangible property right asserted by the inventor. Claims play a dominant role in the patent project, for they precisely define the particular subject matter that has been patented. When PTO examiners decide whether to approve a patent application, the focus of their inquiry is the claims. When courts decide issues of validity

10. *See infra* § 7.4.2.

11. *See infra* § 4.3.2.1.

12. 35 U.S.C. § 112, ¶ 1 (2000).

and infringement, their central concern is the interpretation of the claims of the plaintiff's patent. Although patent claims are often not models of eloquent expression, they nonetheless should be read carefully when encountered in patent instruments and the judicial opinions that discuss them.

Because only the claims define the patented invention, it is inappropriate to rely upon any other materials to derive the scope of the patent owner's exclusive rights. Individuals who want to know the proprietary interest associated with a particular patent must read its claims, rather than rely upon the "heart," "gist," or any other notion of the subject matter that has been invented. Note, however, that the role of the claims is only to specify the scope of the patent owner's right to exclude, not to explain how to put the invention into practice. The remainder of the patent instrument, consisting of a "written description" that more broadly discloses the invention, serves this supporting role.[13] Through a discussion of the invention's general principles, working examples and drawings, the written description must teach others how to make and use the invention.

1.2.7 Territoriality

The nations of the earth have yet to agree upon a unified legal regime governing patent rights. There is no global patent. Innovators must secure and enforce patent rights within the particular jurisdiction where they desire protection. Further, the reach of a particular patent extends only so far as the nation or region recognizing the right. A patent recognized in the United States, for example, cannot be the basis of infringement litigation in Japan.[14]

The patent laws of the United States and its trading partners are nonetheless linked through a modest number of international agreements that, together, comprise the international intellectual property regime. The foundational treaty, the Paris Convention,[15] established the basic principle of "national treatment," which is a requirement that signatories treat nationals of other signatory states no worse than they treat their own citizens in intellectual property matters. More recently, the World Trade Organization Agreement on Trade–Related Aspects of Intellectual Property Rights,[16] the so-called TRIPS Agreement, required its signatories to provide minimum substantive standards of intellectual property

13. 35 U.S.C. § 112, ¶ 2 (2000).

14. *See, e.g.*, Opinion of the Comptroller General, 159 USPQ 298, 301 (1968) ("It is a fundamental concept that territorial limitations of sovereignty preclude a country from giving extraterritorial effect to its patent laws.").

15. Paris Convention For the Protection of Industrial Property, Mar. 20, 1883, 13 U.S.T. 2, 828 U.N.T.S. 107.

16. Agreement on Trade–Related Aspects of Intellectual Property Rights, Apr. 15, 1994, Annex 1C, 33 I.L.M. 1197 (1994).

protection and enforcement. Along with other treaties, these international agreements have eased the ability of innovators to enjoy intellectual property protection in foreign countries.

§ 1.3 Patent Policy

The United States functions for the most part as a "free market economy." Most people believe that vigorous competition among firms both promotes consumer freedom to choose goods and services in an open marketplace, and fosters opportunity for businesses by ensuring a level playing field among competitors. One consequence of our free market economy is that, absent government intervention, we are ordinarily all free to copy the ideas of others without paying for them and without fear of any legal liability. If someone operates an auction house on the Internet and it proves to be a big smash hit, you too can open an Internet-based auction site. If someone discovers that calcium channel blockers help treat hypertension, you too can use a calcium channel blocker to lower your blood pressure and can market those drugs to others by advertising their ability to accomplish this beneficial result.

It is plain to see that the patent system provides an exception from this fundamental principle of open competition. The grant of a patent allows a single firm to exclude all others from operating an Internet-based auction house or selling calcium channel blockers, depriving consumers and competitors of the benefits of competition. Why, then, does the U.S. government operate a patent system? Supporters of the patent system have generally appealed to instrumental rationales and, to a lesser extent, the natural rights of individuals to enjoy a proprietary interest in their inventions. These justifications are tempered by the recognition that individuals have sometimes abused the patent system, as well as the observation that no conclusive demonstration proves the patent system achieves its laudable goals.

1.3.1 Instrumental Rationales

Instrumental rationales are justifications for legal rules that are practical in nature. They purport to explain the law by demonstrating that it achieves concrete real world benefits. The patent system is often explained by reference to a number of public policies that are instrumental in character. Generally speaking, these theories view the patent system—and its key feature of exclusivity—as providing incentives for individuals to engage in desirable behavior.

Proponents of this view reason that absent a patent system, inventions could easily be duplicated or exploited by free riders, who would have incurred no cost to develop and perfect the technology involved, and who could thus undersell the original inventor. The resulting inability of inventors to capitalize on their inventions would lead to an environment where too few inventions are made.[1] On this logic, many commentators have argued that the patent system is necessary to encourage individuals to engage in inventive activity.

It is profitable to delve into the "incentive theory" of patent law a bit further. Like other goods, inventions may be analyzed in terms of two economic characteristics.[2] The first is whether the benefits of the good are "excludable." That is true where it is feasible for one person—usually the owner of the good—to deny other access to it, so that no one can use it without his permission. A good, and delicious example is a bottle of wine. Whoever holds the bottle, controls the wine. If Claude has possession of the wine, he can prevent or exclude his friend Dominique from drinking it. Now contrast the example of a clever new idea for a restaurant. If Claude comes up with the concept of a restaurant where all the dishes are made with garlic, and where the servers are dressed as snails, he does not have any practical way to prevent Dominique from using the same idea in a competitive restaurant across town or across the street. Absent some legal rule that he can invoke against Dominique, there is no inherent "excludability" in the case of the restaurant concept.

A second important trait is whether consumption of a given good is rivalrous. If one person's use of the good necessarily diminishes the ability of another to benefit from that same good, the good is said to be a rival good. Return to our bottle of wine. If Claude guzzles the wine, there is none left for Dominique to enjoy. For every sip one takes, there is less for the other. The wine is plainly a rival good. On the other hand, consider something like pleasing parkway scenery. No matter how many times Claude drives by and enjoys the view, it remains there for Dominique to enjoy as well. Because all may profit from the parkway scenery without diminishing the benefits of any others, we would characterize it as a non-rival good.

Goods differ in their degrees of excludability and rivalrousness. Those that are fully nonexcludable and nonrival are termed public goods. The production of public goods is subject to market failure, for their nonexcludable and nonrival traits suggest that they will be underproduced relative to social need. This follows because potential producers of public goods are uncertain whether they will

§ 1.3

1. *See* Rebecca S. Eisenberg, *Patents and the Progress of Science: Exclusive Rights and Experimental Use*, 56 U. Chi. L. Rev. 1017 (1989).

2. *See generally* William M. Landes & Richard A. Posner, *An Economic Analysis of Copyright Law*, 18 J. Legal Stud. 325 (1989).

benefit from the good sufficiently to justify their labors. To put the matter bluntly, they might conclude that there is no point in producing something if they have no assurance of being paid for their effort. No private party will plant beautiful parkway scenery at his or her own expense because there is no way to recoup the costs involved and make a profit. (That, incidentally is why parkway beautification tends to be undertaken by the government, if it is done at all.) The consequence is that individuals will therefore tend to produce goods with greater excludability and rivalrousness—like wine—and to underproduce public goods like parkway scenery.

The production of desirable public goods is thus said to present a problem of collective action. While society as a whole usually favors the development of certain public goods, ranging from military defense to flood control projects, to attractive parkways, private citizens may lack sufficient incentives to produce them. Left uncorrected, this would lead to suboptimal social outcomes.

Technological inventions are nonexcludable. Whether they consist of a new bowling ball, business method, or biotechnology, others may easily become imitators. The cost of developing a new machine or pharmaceutical may run in the millions of dollars, but such works may be copied extremely cheaply. Inventions are also nonrival, for competitive uses do not impact an inventor's personal ability to exploit the invention. Anyone can synthesize a new chemical compound repeatedly, for example, without exhausting that compound or depriving another of the ability to also synthesize it. These externalities are said to discourage innovation. As a result, absent legal intervention, many economists argue that few persons would invent. In such a world consumers would have access to few innovations.

Fortunately, government is uniquely suited towards solving collective action problems by modifying individual incentives to engage in desirable behavior. The patent law provides a good example of this sort of market intervention. The patent law ameliorates the risk of market failure by allowing individuals to obtain proprietary rights in their inventions. This property rule entitlement creates excludability, allowing innovators to prevent free riders from benefitting from their efforts. By diminishing the public goods aspects of inventions, the patent system encourages individuals to increase their investment in research and development. To put the point a bit less technically, if I know in advance that the law guarantees that I will reap all the profits from an invention, I am much more likely to give up time on the tennis court or in the wine cellar and to spend long hours in the lab, hoping to get rich.

In addition to the incentive theory, the courts have also suggested that absent a patent law, individuals would favor maintaining their inventions as trade secrets so that competitors could not exploit them. Trade secrets do not enrich the collective knowledge of society, however, nor do they discourage others from engaging in duplicative research. The patent system avoids these inefficiencies by requiring inventors to consent to the disclosure of their inventions in issued patent instruments as a condition of legal protection.[3]

There are still other instrumental explanations for the patent laws. For instance, the Patent Act is thought to stimulate technological advancement by inducing individuals to "invent around" patented technology. Issued patent instruments may point the way for others to develop improvements, exploit new markets or discover new applications for the patented technology. Moreover, the patent system may encourage patentees to exploit their proprietary technologies during the term of the patent. The protection provided by a patent's proprietary rights increases the likelihood a firm will continue to refine, produce, and market the patented technology.[4] Finally, the patent law has been identified as a facilitator of markets. Absent patent rights, an inventor may have scant tangible assets to sell or license, and even less ability to police the conduct of a contracting party. By reducing a licensee's opportunistic possibilities, the patent system lowers transaction costs and makes technology-based transactions more feasible.[5]

While these various explanations have an intuitive appeal and the support of a large body of theoretical scholarship, they have not been empirically validated. In other words, no one has conducted a study to demonstrate that we get more useful inventive activity with patents than we would without them. Indeed, it is almost impossible to imagine how such a study could be structured. Thus the instrumental justifications remain open to challenge by those who are unpersuaded by their internal logic.

1.3.2 *Natural Rights*

In contrast to the incentive theory, where inventor's rights are but a necessary means to an end, the "natural rights" school places the inventor front and center. The most celebrated proponent of natural rights, the seventeenth century English philosopher John Locke, posited that persons have a natural right of property in their

3. *See, e.g.*, Grant v. Raymond, 31 U.S. 218, 247, 6 Pet. 218, 8 L.Ed. 376 (1832).

4. F. Scott Kieff, *Property Rights and Property Rules for Commercializing Inventions*, 85 Minn. L. Rev. 697 (2000).

5. *See* Robert P. Merges, *Intellectual Property and the Costs of Commercial Exchange: A Review Essay*, 93 Mich. L. Rev. 1570 (1995).

bodies.[6] Reasoning from this premise, Locke further asserted that individuals should enjoy a property entitlement to the products of their labors. Lockean theory suggests that innovators too should be entitled to enjoy the fruits of their labors, by being granted an exclusive rights in their works.[7]

Some natural rights theorists take one step further in this context, additionally stressing the dignity and worth of inventors in their justifications for the patent law.[8] Under this approach, the relationship between inventors and their works is viewed as much more personal and intimate than the ordinary associations between individuals and objects. Inventions are seen as virtual extensions of the inventor herself. As such, inventors possess the fundamental right to control, and should be compensated for, uses of their works.

1.3.3 Criticism of the Patent System

In its long history, the patent system has inspired a great number of detractors. Some critics have asserted that the patent system is unnecessary due to market forces that already suffice to create an optimal level of invention. The desire to gain a lead time advantage over competitors, as well as the recognition that technologically backwards firms lose out to their rivals, may well provide sufficient inducement to invent without the need for further incentives.[9] Commentators have also observed that successful inventors all too often are transformed into complacent, established enterprises that use patents to suppress the innovations of others.[10] In many differing eras and industries, speculators have been accused of building vast patent portfolios that contribute little to technological advancement, but reportedly have been used merely to threaten legitimate manufacturers and service providers.[11] It is also undeniably true that the inventions that fueled some of today's most dynamic industries, such as early biotechnologies and computer software, arose at a time when patent rights were unavailable or uncertain for innovations in those fields.[12]

6. John Locke, Two Treatises of Government (Peter Laslett, ed., 2d ed. 1967).

7. *See* Wendy J. Gordon, *A Property Right in Self Expression: Equality and Individualism in the Natural Law of Intellectual Property*, 102 Yale L.J. 1533 (1993).

8. *See* Wendy Lim, *Towards Developing a Natural Law Jurisprudence in the U.S. Patent System*, 19 Santa Clara Computer & High Tech. L.J. 559 (2003).

9. *See* Frederic M. Scherer, Industrial Market Structure and Economic Performance 384–87 (1970).

10. *See* Robert P. Merges & Richard R. Nelson, *On the Complex Economics of Patent Scope*, 90 Colum. L. Rev. 839 (1990).

11. *See, e.g.*, Nicholas Varchaver, *The Patent King*, 143 Fortune no. 10 at 202 (May 14, 2001).

12. *See, e.g.*, Pamela Samuelson, Benson *Revisited: The Case Against Patent Protection for Algorithms and Other Computer Program–Related Inventions*, 39 Emory L.J. 1025, 1135–36 (1990).

Many of these criticisms are well taken, but they too suffer from the lack of a sound empirical foundation. Supporters and critics of the patent system alike agree that the nature of technological progress is at best poorly understood. The question of whether the patent system advances the interests of society is not yet within our abilities to answer precisely, and is perhaps unknowable. Most are content to recognize the realities that industry has become increasingly enthusiastic in its pursuit of patents, the number of patent professionals is at historically high levels, and the public interest in the patent system is virtually without precedent. While only a few are prepared to argue that the patent system should be abolished entirely, an elaborate debate rages over the proper scope of patent protection and the various rules of patent law that defines that scope. The devil, as usual, is in the details.

§ 1.4 History

1.4.1 Origins

Legal historians have been quick to seize upon venerable antecedents to our contemporary patent law regime. An ancient Greek system of rewarding cooks for excellent recipes,[1] exclusive privileges granted for innovations relating to Tyrolean mines in the fourteenth century,[2] and a Florentine patent granted in 1421 have been variously cited as predecessors to the modern patent law.[3] However, most observers consider legislation enacted on March 19, 1474, by the Venetian Republic as the first true patent statute.[4] With its requirements that the invention be new, useful, and reduced to practice; provision for a ten-year term; and registration and remedial scheme, the Venetian statute bears a remarkable resemblance to the modern law. By the seventeenth century, numerous European states had enacted similar legislation.[5] For purposes of the common law world, the most significant of these successors was the English Statute of Monopolies, an important commercial statute of the Jacobean era.

1.4.2 The Statute of Monopolies

By the start of the seventeenth century, the English Crown had a long history of awarding importation franchises and other

§ 1.4

1. *See* Bruce Bugbee, Genesis of American Patent and Copyright Law 166 n.5 (1967).

2. Erich Kaufer, The Economics of the Patent System (1989).

3. M. Frumkin, *The Origin of Patents*, 27 J. Pat. Off. Soc'y 143, 144 (1943).

4. *See* Giulio Mandich, *Venetian Patents (1450–1550)*, 30 J. Pat. Off. Soc'y 166 (1948).

5. F.D. Prager, *A History of Intellectual Property From 1545 to 1787*, 26 J. Pat. Off. Soc'y 711 (1944).

exclusive rights. But this practice had become subject to abuse during the reigns of Elizabeth I and James I, as favored subjects obtained grants of supervision or control over long-established industries. Parliament responded in 1624 by enacting the Statute of Monopolies.[6] Although the Statute was principally designed to proscribe monopolistic grants by the Crown, it did authorize the issuance of "letters patent" directed towards the "working or making of any manner of new manufacture" to "the true and first inventor or inventors." Such patents possessed terms of fourteen years and could not be "contrary to law" or "mischievous to the State."

1.4.3 The Constitution

The patent tradition established by the Statute of Monopolies continued in many of the New World colonies. For example, a Connecticut statute of 1672 outlawed the award of monopolies except for "such new inventions as shall be judged profitable for the country and for such time as the general court shall judge meet." As well, many colonial governments granted individuals privileges or rewards for their inventions very early in their histories.[7]

By 1787, state grants of patents were at their zenith, and the delegates to the Constitutional Convention apparently realized the possibility of interstate conflicts among competing inventors. As a result, Convention delegates unanimously agreed that the U.S. Congress should possess the power to:

> promote the Progress of Science and useful Arts by securing for limited Times to Authors and Inventors the exclusive Right to their respective Writings and Discoveries.

Article I, section 8, clause 8 of the Constitution houses this grant of authority. The language of this clause can be somewhat confusing to modern readers. Eighteenth century understanding of the term "Science" was broader than it is today, connoting knowledge and learning in the most general sense. In turn, the "useful Arts" meant the manual, mechanical, and industrial arts of the period, a concept analogous to the modern sense of the word "technology." As a result, the Intellectual Property Clause's use of the terms "Science," "Authors," and "Writings" refers to the domain of the copyright law, while the parallel use of the words "useful Arts," "Inventors," and "Discoveries" provides the constitutional basis for the patent law.

6. Chris R. Kyle, *"But a New Button to an Old Coat": The Enactment of the Statute of Monopolies*, 19 J. LEGAL HISTORY 203 (1998).

7. *See* Edward C. Walterscheid, *The Early Evolution of United States Patent Law: Antecedents (Part I)*, 78 J. PAT. & TRADEMARK OFF. SOC'Y 615 (1996).

1.4.4 *The 1790 and 1793 Acts*

The first Congress quickly acted upon this constitutional grant, and President George Washington signed the first U.S. patent statute into law on April 10, 1790.[8] The Act created a board, known as the "Commissioners for the Promotion of the Useful Arts," authorized to determine whether "the invention or discovery [was] sufficiently useful and important" to deserve a patent. The board consisted of the Secretary of State (Thomas Jefferson), the Secretary of War (Henry Knox), and the Attorney General (Edmund Randolph).[9]

This Heroic Age of the patent law proved short-lived, as examination duties proved too onerous for the three-member board—although it is amusing to imagine Colin Powell, Donald Rumsfeld, and John Ashcroft meeting daily to decide patent questions if the scheme had been continued to the present day. At all events, Congress responded by enacting the Patent Act of 1793,[10] which abandoned patent examination in favor of a registration scheme. Under the 1793 Act, the State Department was assigned the wholly administrative task of maintaining a registry of patents. Whether a registered patent was valid and enforceable was left solely to the courts.

1.4.5 *The 1836 and 1870 Acts*

Observing that the registration system of the 1793 Act had sometimes encouraged duplicative and fraudulent patents, Congress restored an examination system with the Patent Act of 1836.[11] The 1836 Act created a Patent Office within the Department of State and provided for the filing and formal examination of patent applications. The 1870 Act largely maintained the provisions of its predecessor,[12] but at several points stressed that patentees define their proprietary interest in a distinctly drafted claim. Litigation under these two statutes frequently culminated at the Supreme Court, resulting in opinions that established nonobviousness, enablement, experimental use, and other fundamental doctrines of contemporary patent law.[13]

8. Act of April 10, 1790, Ch. 7, 1 Stat. 109.

9. *See* KENNETH W. DOBYNS, THE PATENT OFFICE PONY: A HISTORY OF THE EARLY PATENT OFFICE (1994).

10. Act of Feb. 21, 1793, Ch. 11, 2 Stat. 318.

11. Act of July 4, 1836, Ch. 357, 5 Stat. 117.

12. Act of July 8, 1870, Ch. 230, 16 Stat. 198.

13. Prior to 1891, the Supreme Court had mandatory, rather than discretionary appellate jurisdiction, which explains the large volume of patent business which routinely came before the Court.

1.4.6 The 1952 Act

Although judicial postures towards patents varied with the U.S. economic climate throughout the nineteenth and early twentieth centuries, the Depression Era amounted to a Dark Age for the patent system. The vigorous anti-monopoly sentiments of that period were accompanied by an active dislike of patents. Although the U.S. patent system predated the Sherman Antitrust Act by more than a century, the courts were quick to find ordinary patent licensing and enforcement efforts to be violative of the antitrust laws and the related doctrine of patent misuse. Indeed, the Supreme Court's propensity to strike down patents in this era reached such proportions that Justice Jackson was compelled to lament in a 1949 dissent that "the only patent that is valid is one which this Court has not been able to get its hands on."[14]

The drafters of the Patent Act of 1952 sought to reverse this anti-patent trend; as events have borne out, it has become apparent that they dramatically succeeded. Among the innovations of the 1952 Act were the codification of the nonobviousness standard and the curtailing of the defense of patent misuse.[15] The 1952 Act is wholly codified into Title 35 of the United States Code and, with frequent amendments over the past half-century, remains the governing U.S. patent statute.

1.4.7 The Federal Courts Improvement Act of 1982

Another significant patent law reform was procedural in nature. The Evarts Act of 1891 established the familiar circuit courts of appeal, numbered and organized on a geographic basis.[16] In the decades that followed, experience demonstrated that the different regional courts of appeal held widely varying views of the patent system. While some circuits were not inhospitable to patents, others would only rarely find a patent valid and enforceable. These disparities undermined the uniformity of the federal patent system and led to an unseemly amount of forum shopping.

Law reform efforts ultimately led Congress to adopt the Federal Courts Improvement Act of 1982, which provided for the creation of a new intermediate appellate court called the United States Court of Appeals for the Federal Circuit.[17] The Federal Circuit hears, among other matters, appeals from the PTO and from the federal district courts in patent matters, regardless of where those federal district courts are located. These dual routes of appeal mean that most patent issues quickly darken the door of the Federal Circuit. As a result, any study of U.S. patent law largely concerns

14. *See* Jungersen v. Ostby & Barton Co., 335 U.S. 560, 572, 69 S.Ct. 269, 93 L.Ed. 235 (1949).

15. Act of July 19, 1952, Ch. 950, 66 Stat. 797.

16. Act of March 3, 1891, Ch. 517, 26 Stat. 826.

17. Pub. L. No. 97–164, 96 Stat. 25 (April 2, 1982).

the work product of the Federal Circuit. Federal Circuit decisions are subject to discretionary review by the Supreme Court, though the usual route of certiorari.

Proponents of the Federal Circuit believe that the court has brought stability and predictability to the patent law.[18] Detractors have questioned whether the patent law has prospered under the stewardship of a tribunal that considers a limited variety of cases and arguably has a vested interest in a robust patent system.[19] All observers agree that the Federal Circuit has dramatically expanded the range of patentable subject matter, liberally upheld large damages awards and preliminary injunctions, and strengthened the patent grant in comparison to many predecessor courts.

The Federal Circuit is housed in the Howard T. Markey Building, which sits just across Pennsylvania Avenue from the White House in Washington, D.C. The Federal Circuit consists of twelve active circuit judges and a number of senior circuit judges. Ordinarily a panel of three judges resolves appeals placed before the court. Occasionally, in order to resolve important issues, all of the active judges of the Federal Circuit convene in special *en banc* proceedings.[20]

1.4.8 The American Inventors Protection Act of 1999

Following several years of discussion, Congress gave final approval to the American Inventors Protection Act in 1999 (AIPA).[21] The AIPA worked numerous reforms to the U.S. patent law, including the creation of an infringement defense for first inventors of business methods which are later patented by another; the extension of the patent term in the event of processing delays at the PTO; the mandate for publication of certain pending patent applications; and the provision of optional *inter partes* reexamination procedures. Most of these matters are taken up elsewhere in this text in connection with the large topics to which they relate.

§ 1.5 International Patent Harmonization

Despite increasing international trade and the longstanding recognition that technology knows no borders, the nations of the earth have yet to agree to a global patent system. Patent prosecution and litigation therefore occur on a piecemeal, jurisdiction-by-

18. *See* Joan E. Schaffner, *Federal Circuit Choice of Law:* Erie *Through the Looking Glass,* 81 IOWA L. REV. 1173 (1996) (noting these aspirations for the Federal Circuit).

19. *See* Steven Anderson, *Federal Circuit Gets Passing Marks to Date But There's A Lot of Room for Improvement,* 10 CORPORATE LEGAL TIMES no. 10 at 86 (March 2000).

20. *See* South Corp. v. United States, 690 F.2d 1368, 215 USPQ 657 (Fed.Cir. 1982).

21. Pub. L. No. 106–113, 113 Stat. 1501 (Nov. 29, 1999).

jurisdiction basis. Still, the desire to facilitate multinational patent acquisition and harmonize national laws has been keenly felt, and has led to several international agreements concerning patents. The United States has joined three such agreements that are worthy of note here.

1.5.1 The Paris Convention

The 1883 Paris Convention for the Protection of Industrial Property is the foundational international agreement concerning patents (and trademarks).[1] The Paris Convention contains few provisions mandating particular legal requirements for the patent law, but it does obligate the signatory nations to provide for what is known as "national treatment". This means that member states must treat domiciliaries of Paris Convention signatory states in the same manner as their own domiciliaries.

Article 4 of the Paris Convention also allows an applicant to obtain a so-called "priority date" by filing a patent application in any signatory state. This applicant may then file a subsequent patent application in any other signatory state within twelve months and claim the benefit of the date of the original application. Each Paris Convention signatory has agreed to treat the subsequent application as if it were filed on the date of the original application. Among other benefits, this twelve-month grace period prevents unscrupulous individuals from copying the original patent application and becoming the first to claim the invention as their own in other countries, before the true inventor has the opportunity to file foreign applications.

1.5.2 The Patent Cooperation Treaty

The Patent Cooperation Treaty, or PCT,[2] was formed in 1970 and is open to any country that has joined the Paris Convention. This agreement provides an optional application procedure in order to simplify multinational patent acquisition. Over one hundred signatory nations have adopted the PCT filing mechanisms and a standardized application format.

1.5.3 The TRIPS Agreement

The Agreement on Trade–Related Aspects of Intellectual Property Rights, a component of the international agreement establishing the World Trade Organization (WTO),[3] has been joined by many

§ 1.5

1. Paris Convention for the Protection of Industrial Property, Mar. 20, 1883, 13 U.S.T. 1. For more on the Paris Convention, *see infra* § 12.1.

2. Patent Cooperation Treaty, June 19, 1970, 28 U.S.T. 7645. For more on the PCT, *see infra* § 12.2.

3. Agreement on Trade–Related Aspects of Intellectual Property Rights, General Agreement on Tariffs and

members of the world trading community. As the first treaty that extensively required signatory nations to maintain specified standards of substantive patent law, the so-called "TRIPS Agreement" was an impressive accomplishment. The TRIPS Agreement specifies that member states must observe certain requirements pertaining to patent-eligible subject matter, patent term, and standards of patentability such as novelty and nonobviousness. In order to comply with the TRIPS Agreement, the United States enacted the Uruguay Round Agreements Act in 1995. Among the changes worked by this legislation were the introduction of provisional patent applications, the change of patent term to twenty years measured from the date the patent application was filed, and the acceptance of evidence of dates of inventive activity performed in WTO member countries.

§ 1.6 Other Forms of Intellectual Property

Several other legal regimes are akin to the patent system in that they also give rise to proprietary rights in creations of the mind. Along with patents, the so-called "intellectual property" laws include trade secrets, copyrights and trademarks. This section very briefly reviews each of these fields. A comprehensive treatment of each of these areas can be found elsewhere.[1]

1.6.1 Trade Secrets

The principal intellectual property alternative to patents is trade secret law.[2] Valuable information that is not publicly known and that is subject to measures to preserve its secrecy may be granted trade secret rights under state statutory or common law. Unlike patents, no formalities are required to maintain trade secret protection. Trade secret law protects against industrial espionage and similar unscrupulous methods ferreting out the secret technology. It also provides remedies in cases involving breach of trust, such as when a former trusted employee leaves a firm and begins to use the secret in competition with his former employer. Trade secret protection is more limited than that offered by the patent law, however. Trade secret law does not prevent reverse engineering or independent discovery of the protected information, for example, while patent rights would. Trade secret rights endure for

Trade, Final Act Embodying the Results of the Uruguay Round of Multilateral Trade Negotiations, Apr. 15, 1994, Annex 1C, 33 I.L.M. 1197. For more on the TRIPS Agreement, *see infra* § 12.6.

§ 1.6

1. *See generally* Roger E. Schechter & John R. Thomas, INTELLECTUAL PROPERTY: THE LAW OF COPYRIGHTS, PATENTS AND TRADEMARKS (2003).

2. *See* RESTATEMENT (THIRD) OF UNFAIR COMPETITION §§ 39–45.

as long as the protected information is not known to the public. This text considers trade secrets at some length in Chapter 13.

1.6.2 Copyright and Related Rights

Copyright law provides protection for original works of authorship fixed in a tangible medium of expression.[3] The types of creations addressed by copyright range from traditional works of art, including literature, music, and visual art, to such modern forms of artistic expression as sound recordings, motion pictures, and even computer software.[4] Copyright protection arises automatically, as soon as the work has been fixed in tangible form.[5] Authors may register their works with the Copyright Office, however, and obtain certain procedural and substantive advantages during copyright enforcement.[6] The copyright law affords authors the exclusive right to reproduce, adapt, publicly distribute, publicly perform, and publicly display the protected work, subject to certain limitations such as the fair use privilege.[7] A variety of more specialized rights are provided to certain types of works or in certain specific situations. The term of copyright is ordinarily the life of the author plus seventy years.[8] Copyright is an exclusively federal statutory regime, and state laws equivalent to copyright are explicitly preempted by the federal copyright statute.[9]

Congress has supplemented the federal copyright statute with a number of related statutes. The Semiconductor Chip Protection Act provides copyright-like rights for the circuitry designs of semiconductor chips.[10] The Audio Home Recording Act established a royalty payment system for manufacturers of digital audio home recording devices.[11] Also notable is the Digital Millennium Copyright Act, which prohibits the circumvention of anti-piracy measures built into computer software and limits the copyright infringement liability of Internet service providers.[12]

A number of state law intellectual property rights are cousins of copyright law, and provide somewhat similar protection to different categories of subject matter. For instance, the right of publicity gives individuals control over the commercial use of their identities.[13] Another example are various common law principles protecting individuals who submit ideas—such as television program con-

3. 17 U.S.C.A. § 102(a) (2000).

4. *Id.*

5. *Id.*

6. 17 U.S.C.A. §§ 408–412 (2000).

7. 17 U.S.C.A. §§ 106, 107–122 (2000).

8. 17 U.S.C.A. § 302 (2000).

9. 17 U.S.C.A. § 301 (2000).

10. Pub. L. No. 98–6209, 98 Stat. 3347 (1984).

11. Pub. L. No. 92–140, 85 Stat. 391 (1971).

12. Pub. L. No. 105–304, 112 Stat. 2863 (1998).

13. *See* Restatement (Third) of Unfair Competition §§ 46–49.

cepts—to others when the recipient makes an uncompensated use of those ideas.[14]

1.6.3 *Trademark and Related Rights*

Trademarks consist of any word or symbol used by a merchant to identify its goods or services, and to distinguish them from those of others.[15] To be subject to protection under the trademark laws, a mark must successfully distinguish the origins of its associated goods, and not be confusingly similar to marks used by others or merely descriptive of the characteristics of those goods.[16] Trademark rights arise under state law as soon as the mark is used on goods in commerce.[17] However, trademarks may be registered with the PTO, a step that affords significant substantive and procedural advantages.[18] Trademark law also protects the appearance of product packaging and, in some cases, the actual physical configuration of the goods, if these serve as brand identifiers. A trademark owner may prevent others from using any mark that creates a likelihood of confusion as to the source or sponsorship of the associated goods or services.[19] Trademark rights persist so long as the mark continues to be used and retains its distinctiveness.[20]

Trademarks form one arm of the common law of unfair competition, a collection of principles that encourage the maintenance of honest practices in commercial affairs. A number of other doctrines are grouped under this heading, including passing off, reverse passing off, dilution, and false advertising.[21]

14. Nadel v. Play–By–Play Toys & Novelties, Inc., 208 F.3d 368 (2d Cir. 2000).

15. *Id.* at § 9.

16. *Id.*

17. *Id.* at § 18.

18. 17 U.S.C.A. § 1051 (2000).

19. *See* RESTATEMENT (THIRD) OF UNFAIR COMPETITION § 20.

20. *Id.* at § 30.

21. *See generally* RESTATEMENT (THIRD) OF UNFAIR COMPETITION.

Chapter 2

PATENT ELIGIBILITY

Table of Sections

---

§ 2.1 Basic Concepts

Section 101 of the Patent Code defines the categories of subject matter that may be patented. According to the statute, a person who "invents or discovers any new and useful process, machine, manufacture, or any composition of matter, or any new and useful improvement thereof, may obtain a patent therefore, subject to the conditions and requirements of this title." An invention that falls within one of the four itemized statutory categories—processes, machines, manufactures, and compositions of matter—may be entitled to a so-called "utility patent." A utility patent is the general sort of patent for innovative products and processes, and is by far the most frequently sought type of patent. As a result, when commentators refer to a patent, they are ordinarily referring to the legal instrument more technically known as a utility patent. Two more specialized kinds of patents, pertaining to industrial designs and botanical plants, are also available under U.S. patent law, and will be considered at the close of this chapter.

That an invention constitutes a process, machine, manufacture, or composition of matter is a necessary, but not sufficient condition for that invention to be the subject of a valid patent. Patentable inventions must also meet additional requirements imposed by the statute, in particular utility, novelty, and nonobviousness. In addition, the inventor must file an application at the U.S. Patent and Trademark Office (PTO) that fully discloses and distinctly claims the invention. An invention that is judged to be a process, machine, manufacture, or composition of matter is termed "patentable subject matter," or sometimes "patent-eligible subject matter" to reflect the notion that it may be patented if the other statutory requirements are met.

The four categories set forth in section 101 represent the current Congressional interpretation of the term "useful arts," which is the Constitutional expression of the subject matter appropriate for patenting. Historically, the useful arts were contrasted with the liberal and fine arts. This approach confined the patent system to inventions in the field of applied technology. Inventions that employed the natural sciences to manipulate physical forces fell within the useful arts. Those that relied upon such things as the social sciences, commercial strategy, or personal skill were judged unpatentable.[1]

In recent years, however, the patent system has demonstrated an increasing permissiveness towards patentable subject matter. In particular, the Federal Circuit has steadily dismantled earlier prohibitions upon patent eligibility, discarding rules that previously denied patents to subject matter ranging from computer software, to printed matter, to methods of doing business. In response to this trend, the PTO has issued patents involving inventions from a broad range of disciplines, including one on a method of executing a golf putt,[2] one for a new teaching method,[3] and one for a technique of psychological analysis.[4]

The present state of affairs suggests that few, if any restrictions limit the range of patentable subject matter. Once limited to natural scientists and engineers, the patent system now appears poised to embrace the broadest reaches of human experience. It is

§ 2.1

1. *See* John R. Thomas, *The Patenting of the Liberal Professions*, 40 Boston College L. Rev. 1139 (1999).

2. U.S. Patent No. 5,616,089 (Apr. 1, 1997) ("Method of putting"). *See also* Carl A. Kukkonen III, *Be a Good Sport and Refrain from Using My Patented Putt: Intellectual Property Protection for Sports Related Movements*, 80 J. Pat. & Trademark Off. Soc'y 808 (1998).

3. U.S. Patent No. 5,558,519 (Sept. 24, 1996) ("Method for instruction of golf and the like").

4. U.S. Patent No. 5,190,458 (Mar. 2, 1993) ("Character assessment method").

hardly an exaggeration to say that under current law, if you can name it, you can claim it. As a result, much of this chapter may appear to be solely of historical significance, with the abolition of earlier limitations upon patent eligibility by an increasingly lenient judiciary proving to be a recurring pattern. Still, patent eligibility continually proves itself to be an unsettled field. To understand our current state of affairs it is helpful to know how we got here.

Before proceeding further, the reader should note that section 101 twice employs the phrase "new and useful," first to modify the quartet of patent-eligible subject matter, namely "process, machine, manufacture or any composition of matter" and then again to modify the reference to "any improvement thereof." One might think, therefore, that some showing of novelty and utility would be required to bring material within the ambit of patent-eligible subject matter. Despite this wording, however, the courts have traditionally distinguished the requirement of patent eligibility from those of novelty and utility.[5] Thus, the issue of whether a particular invention is of the kind the patent laws were intended to protect has traditionally been considered a different matter from whether the invention possess novelty, and is useful, within the meaning of the patent law. Utility and novelty are addressed in Chapters 3 and 4 of this text respectively.

§ 2.2 Product and Process Claims

Patent attorneys typically speak of inventions as involving either a product or process.[1] Product claims concern tangible things, including objects and artifacts. In terms of § 101, product inventions consist either of machines, manufactures, or compositions of matter. A machine includes an apparatus or mechanical device.[2] Compositions of matter include such things as chemical compounds, mechanical or physical mixtures, and alloys.[3] Finally, a manufacture is a broadly oriented, residual category of manmade items.[4] When a product invention is presented in the fashion of a patent claim, it is defined in terms of its structural elements. A product claim directed towards an automobile, for example, would claim such parts as a frame, engine, tires, and fuel tank.

5. Brian P. Biddinger, *Limiting the Business Method Patent: A Comparison and Proposed Alignment of European, Japanese and United States Patent Law*, 69 FORDHAM L. REV. 2523 (2001).

§ 2.2

1. John R. Thomas, *Of Text, Technique and the Tangible: Drafting Patent Claims Around Patent Rules*, 17 JOHN MARSHALL J. OF COMPUTER & INFORMATION L. 219 (1998).

2. *See* Nestle–Le Mur Co. v. Eugene, Ltd., 55 F.2d 854 (6th Cir.1932).

3. Diamond v. Chakrabarty, 447 U.S. 303, 100 S.Ct. 2204, 65 L.Ed.2d 144 (1980).

4. *Id.*

In contrast, process inventions involve a series of acts performed in order to produce a given result. Processes, which are also commonly termed "methods" in patent parlance, concern techniques and behavioral engagements. When a process invention is drafted as a patent claim, the claim consists of a list of steps. A process claim directed towards a method of making cast iron, for example, might consist of the steps of (a) combining iron ore, coke, and limestone; and (b) heating these ingredients in a blast furnace.

Process inventions are commonly divided into two types, although this distinction is largely a matter of characterization rather than of substantive effect. These are termed "method of using" and "method of making" claims.[5] Suppose that a pharmaceutical chemist synthesizes a new compound and also discovers that the compound has a valuable therapeutic property, such as lowering a patient's blood pressure. The chemist may draft a "method of using" claim that recites a process for using the compound to treat hypertension. In addition, the inventor may obtain claims for a method of making the compound, stating the techniques he employed to synthesize the compound.

Some inventions can be claimed as both products and processes. In terms of the patent law, at least, many machines may be conceived as containing a process. When you turn on a washing machine, for example, it engages in a series of wash, rinse, and spin cycles, and that behavior can be claimed as a series of process steps. The inventor of the first washing machine could have sought a patent on a product, by claiming the physical apparatus that makes up the machine, and could have also sought a patent on a new process for washing clothes, by claiming the series of steps that describe the activity of the new washing machine once it begins to function. It is ordinarily the privilege of an inventor to claim the invention as she sees fit, and many patents in fact do present claims that describe the same invention in terms of (1) a product, (2) a method of using that product, and (3) a method of making that product.

2.2.1 Scientific and Mathematical Principles

Many judicial decisions recite the maxim that abstract concepts, mathematical algorithms, and scientific principles are not patentable. Under this rule, Georg Ohm could not patent V (voltage) = L (current) x R (resistance), nor could Albert Einstein patent the special theory of relativity. On the other hand, a practical application of an abstract concept, mathematical algorithm, or scientific principle may be patented. As the Supreme Court declared in the mid-nineteenth century, "a principle is not patentable. A

5. *See* In re Pleuddemann, 910 F.2d 823 (Fed.Cir.1990).

principle, in the abstract, is a fundamental truth; an original cause; a motive; these cannot be patented . . . "[6] The same point was made by Judge Jerome Frank of the Second Circuit, when he observed in 1944 that "epoch-making 'discoveries' or 'mere' general scientific 'laws,' without more, cannot be patented.... So the great 'discoveries' of Newton or Faraday could not have been rewarded with such a grant of monopoly."[7]

Thus, an inventor could not patent the broad optical principles that allow the generation of lasers, for example. On the other hand, if an inventor discovered a way to generate a laser beam; or a method for using a laser to align automobile wheels, generate a hologram, or "weld" detached retinas back into place without making an incision, then these inventions would be eligible for patenting within the meaning of § 101.

The policy reasons for this traditional exception to patentable subject matter have never been especially clear. Surely individuals who uncover fundamental principles of the natural world or mathematics provide a tremendous social benefit. Providing the incentive of proprietary rights for such discoveries might seem a wise public policy. One often-stated argument to the contrary is that scientific and mathematical principles have always existed, even if they were not previously recognized. Those who explain these principles have therefore merely discovered them, rather than engaged in the act of invention. A significant problem with this argument is that the Constitution and the Patent Act each expressly state that patents may issue for discoveries.[8]

Another broadly stated reason for excluding scientific and mathematical principles from the patent system is that patenting these broad ideas may slow technological progress. The courts have recognized that one scientific principle may potentially lead to thousands of applied technologies. Under this rationale, providing one individual with broad proprietary rights in an "upstream idea" may slow the dissemination of that idea through "downstream products" developed by others.[9]

This justification also has its shortcomings. Many specific products—such as cameras, computers, and telescopes, for example—have numerous, diverse uses. Yet § 101 has not been read to deny patents on any of these devices. In fact, virtually any sort of invention, be it an abstract principle or discrete apparatus, potentially leads to later improvements. Despite these apparent short-

6. Le Roy v. Tatham, 55 U.S. 156, 159 (1852).

7. Katz v. Horni Signal Mfg. Corp. 145 F.2d 961 (2d Cir. 1944), *cert. den.*, 324 U.S. 882, 65 S.Ct. 1029, 89 L.Ed. 1432 (1945).

8. *See* U.S. CONST., Art. I, § 8, cl. 8; 35 U.S.C.A. § 100(a) (2000).

9. *See O'Reilly v. Morse*, 56 U.S. 62 (1854) (Grier, J., dissenting).

comings, however, the maxim that patents protect applications of scientific and mathematical principles, rather than the principles themselves, remains a bedrock rule of patent law.

2.2.2 The Physical Transformation Requirement

Processes were traditionally required to achieve a physical transformation in order to be patentable. In its 1877 opinion in *Cochrane v. Deener*,[10] the Supreme Court explained that a process "is a mode of treatment of certain materials to produce a given result. It is an act, or a series of acts, performed upon the subject-matter to be transformed and reduced to a different state or thing." Under the physical transformation standard, an industrial process for manufacturing glass out of sand, soda, and lime would be eligible for patenting. This standard would exclude more abstract methods, however, such as a method of counting cards in order to improve your chances in a poker game or a technique of memory enhancement helpful for forgetful people.

Courts rarely, if ever, provided much explanation for the physical transformation requirement. Among its apparent effects is a tendency to confine the patent system to manufacturers, machinists, and other members of traditional industries, as compared to the public at large. A physical transformation requirement also tended to tie the patent system to tangible things, making determinations of property entitlements, infringements and remedies more straightforward. Everything else being equal, it is much easier to determine whether a glassworks is using a patented manufacturing method than to decide whether a law student used a proprietary mnemonic aid in order to ace a final exam. One academic commentator has further explained the rationale of the requirement in the following terms:

> Broadly speaking, the patent system is not directed to all developments of humankind, but rather only those that involve technology. The Constitutional provision, for example, expressly connects patenting with the "useful arts." The distinction between technological and non-technological subject matter essentially defines the boundary between the systems of patent and copyright. The desire to preclude patent rights over non-technological matters underlies many of the historical objections to extending the definition of statutory subject matter.
>
> One function of the physical transformation requirement has therefore been to provide a rough, rule-based mechanism for determining where this boundary between the technological and the non-technological existed in specific cases. By necessity a method that results in a physical resource being transformed

10. 94 U.S. 780, 24 L.Ed. 139 (1876).

must involve the use of technology at some level. Accordingly, it should be validly patentable. A method that does not leave such a transformation in its wake, in contrast, is likely to be non-technological and therefore outside the patent system's proper reach. In this way, requiring such a transformation enabled the system to block effectively the grant of patent protection over developments in the liberal arts and sciences.[11]

On the other hand, it can be argued that the patent incentive is needed to encourage the creation and public disclosure of both physical and abstract inventions alike, and that there is no compelling reason to discriminate among inventors based upon their field of endeavor.

As the technological community has moved from the industrial to the information age, the physical transformation requirement has become more lenient. For example, in its 1994 decision in *In re Schrader*,[12] the Federal Circuit considered an application for a patent on "a method for competitively bidding on a plurality of related items, such as contiguous tracts of land or the like." Although the Federal Circuit concluded that the invention in *Schrader* was not patentable, it observed that the "transformation or conversion" could occur with respect to subject matter that was merely "representative of" physical things. This language seemed to signal a new willingness to allow many inventions from the field of data processing to be eligible for patenting.

Five years later, in 1999, the Federal Circuit decided *AT & T Corp. v. Excel Communications*,[13] which completely laid to rest the notion that a process must achieve a physical transformation to be patentable. This appeal arose from AT & T's efforts to enforce a patent directed towards the composition of billing records used in telephone networks. The AT & T patent claimed a method for a phone company to determine whether both the caller and the recipient of a long-distance telephone subscribed to the company's network. If so, the phone company could provide a different billing treatment to such calls, most likely discounting the fee in order to encourage both individuals to subscribe to the same phone company.

The invention relied upon the fact that when a customer makes a long-distance telephone call, the telephone network contemporaneously maintains billing records. These records included such information as the originating and terminating telephone

11. R. Carl Moy, *Intellectual Property in an Information Economy: Subjecting Rembrandt to the Rule of Law: Rule-based Solutions for Determining the Patentability of Business Methods*, 28 Wm. Mitchell L. Rev. 1047, 1083–84 (2002).

12. 22 F.3d 290, 294–96, 30 USPQ2d 1455, 1459–60 (Fed.Cir.1994).

13. 172 F.3d 1352, 50 USPQ2d 1447 (Fed.Cir.1999), *cert. denied*, 528 U.S. 946, 120 S.Ct. 368, 145 L.Ed.2d 284 (1999).

numbers, as well as the length of the call. Also associated with the call was data indicating an individual's chosen "primary interexchange carrier," or long-distance service provider.

The claimed invention called for the addition of a discrete item of data, termed the "PIC indicator," to the billing record. The value of the PIC indicator was determined by applying the logical "AND" function to the data identifying the primary interexchange carriers of the originator and recipient of the long-distance call. If both customers have subscribed to the same phone company, the PIC indicator was set to a logical "one." Otherwise the PIC indicator remained at the value of "zero." The phone company could then apply its discounted rate to any call where the PIC indicator is set to one, without more extensive data processing at the time of billing.

The district court held that the AT & T patent was improvidently granted because the invention it claimed was not within § 101.[14] According to the district court, the patented invention merely retrieved and reorganized data known to the telephone company. Because the invention's only physical step involved data gathering for use in an algorithm, the district court concluded that it was not patentable subject matter.

Following an appeal, the Federal Circuit reversed. The Federal Circuit quickly disposed of Excel's argument that because AT & T's claims did not recite a physical transformation, they were not patentable subject matter. Upon its review of the precedents, the court concluded that physical transformation was not an absolute requisite for patentability. Instead, observing a tangible outcome was merely one way of determining whether the patented invention achieved a useful, concrete, and tangible result. Because AT & T's claimed process produced "a number which had a specific meaning," it could be employed in a discrete setting and was therefore patentable.

The case law thus reveals that, as the patent system has entered the twenty-first century, it is no longer appropriate to judge the patentability of processes solely by whether they work a physical transformation or not. The ultimate question is whether these processes achieve a useful, concrete, and tangible result. As the PTO and the courts apply this lenient standard, the patent system should continue to open its doors to inventions from the information sciences.

14. 1998 WL 175878 (D.Del.1998).

2.2.3 *Process Claims for New Uses*

Section 100(b) of the Patent Code notes that a process "includes a new use of a known process, machine, manufacture, composition of matter, or method." This definition allows inventors to obtain a proprietary interest in a newly discovered property of a known product. For example, suppose that doctors for many years knew that a chemical known as "Compound R" could be used as a heart medication. Later, inventor Harry Hirsute discovers that Compound R also relieves male pattern baldness. Hirsute could not seek a patent on Compound R itself, which is already known to the art. However, Hirsute could draft a claim towards a method of curing baldness. The claim towards this secondary medical indication for the known substance would be eligible for patenting under § 101, and Hirsute could obtain a patent on a method of using Compound R to treat baldness if the other requirements for patenting are met.

Although inventors are allowed to obtain process patents on newly discovered uses, the patent law limits the scope of protection to the particular method claimed. Also, like all patents, the use of a patented method is subject to the proprietary interests of others.[15] As a result, owners of patents on new uses may have to account for earlier patents. Suppose, for example, that Aaron Avon owns a patent claiming (1) a particular chemical compound and (2) a method of using that compound as a skin softening agent. Avon sells the patented chemical under the trademark SOFT–SKIN. An Avon customer, Gina Gardner, purchases a bottle of SOFT–SKIN and accidentally drops some of it in her garden. Gardner unexpectedly discovers that the Avon chemical makes a wonderful fertilizer for rose bushes. Gardner files a patent application claiming the use of SOFT–SKIN as a plant fertilizer.

In this example, Avon's product patent is termed the "dominant" patent, while Gardner's method of use patent is termed a "subservient" patent. In these circumstances, Gardner cannot practice her process without employing SOFT–SKIN, which is patented by Avon. On the other hand, Avon could not employ SOFT–SKIN as a lawn fertilizer (or license others to do so) without infringing Gardner's method of use patent. In these circumstances the holders of the dominant and subservient patents often possess incentives to cross-license one another.[16]

15. *See supra* § 1.2.1.

16. *See* Steven C. Carlson, *Patent Pools and the Antitrust Dilemma*, 16 Yale J. Reg. 359, 362–65 (1999).

§ 2.3 Biotechnology

2.3.1 Products of Nature

Patent eligibility principles pose few obstacles to the patenting of biotechnologies in the United States. The most significant restriction is that a "product of nature"—a naturally occurring substance discovered in the wild—may not be patented *per se*. Suppose, for example, that noted metallurgist and explorer Danny Steele travels to an uncharted region of the Himalayas. Steele then unearths a new mineral deposit on one of the highest peaks of Nepal. Even if this mineral had not been previously known to exist, longstanding case law establishes that Steele may not obtain a utility patent claiming the mineral itself.[1] As the Supreme Court has put it, a "new mineral discovered in the earth, or a new plant found in the wild is not patentable subject matter . . . Such discoveries are 'manifestations of . . . nature, free to all men and reserved exclusively to none.' "[2]

However, the same case law does provide that significant artificial changes to a product of nature may render it patentable.[3] To continue this hypothetical, suppose that our intrepid Mr. Steele discovers that certain compounds within the mineral have valuable heat-resistant properties. He then develops a purified form of these compounds. Steele may obtain a product patent on the isolated compounds. He may also obtain process claims towards any heat-resistant uses of the mineral that he discovers, and for his purification process as well, assuming that it is novel and nonobvious.

Judge Learned Hand's well-known decision in *Parke–Davis & Co. v. H.K. Mulford & Co.* applied these principles to a purified substance from a living organism.[4] Adrenaline is a hormone, produced by the adrenal glands, that doctors use as a heart stimulant and muscle relaxant. The inventor in *Parke–Davis*, Jokichi Takamine, determined how to obtain a purified adrenaline extract from living animals. Takamine claimed these compounds in "stable and concentrate form, and practically free from inert and associated gland-tissue." Further, although adrenaline salts—which consisted of a base and an acid—were known to the art, they had certain negative side effects when used for medical treatment. Takamine was able to isolate his extract in the form of a base, which proved superior for medical use. Judge Hand upheld the patentability of the claims at issue, explaining:

> Nor is the patent only for a degree of purity, and therefore not a new "composition of matter." [The claimed invention]

§ 2.3

1. *See, e.g.*, Ex parte Latimer, 1889 Comm'r Dec. 13 (1889).

2. Diamond v. Chakrabarty, 447 U.S. 303, 309 (1980).

3. *See, e.g.*, Amgen, Inc. v. Chugai Pharmaceutical Co., 927 F.2d 1200, 18 USPQ2d 1016 (Fed.Cir.1991) (claiming a purified and isolated DNA sequence encoding erythropoietin).

4. 189 F. 95 (S.D.N.Y. 1911), *aff'd*, 196 F. 496 (2d Cir. 1912).

> does not include a salt, and no one had ever isolated a substance which was not in salt form, and which was anything like Takamine's.... But, even if it were an extracted product without change, there is no rule that such products are not patentable. Takamine was the first to make it available for any use by removing it from the other gland-tissue in which it was found, and, while it is of course possible logically to call this a purification of the principle, it became for every practical purpose a new thing commercially and therapeutically. That was a good ground for a patent.[5]

The PTO has followed the *Parke–Davis* holding in analyzing more modern biotechnologies, and in particular in situations involving genetic materials. If a scientist discovers that a particular gene sequence performs a certain biological task, that scientist may claim the gene—so long as she specifies that the gene has been produced by artificial methods. For example, a claim towards an "isolated and purified DNA encoding a protein from Cyclotella cryptica" passes muster under the *Parke–Davis* reasoning.[6]

At this point in the story, some readers may have become concerned that the patenting of biological compounds by others may convert them into infringers. After all, the human body both produces adrenaline and houses thousands of genes. However, as produced within the body these products are neither isolated nor purified, and thus not covered by any patents. As a result, the same distinction that allows the invention of the purified substance to be eligible for patenting within the meaning of § 101—the fact that it is artificially generated—also constrains the scope of the patentee's proprietary interest, and frees us all from the obligation of paying a royalty every time we get a burst of adrenaline playing or watching football or taking a final exam in patent law.

The most notorious and confusing episode concerning the "product of nature" rule was the Supreme Court's 1948 opinion in *Funk Brothers Seed Co. v. Kalo Inoculant Co.*[7] The patented invention related to an innoculant for leguminous plants, such as soybeans or peanuts. As the Court explained, these innoculants consist of bacteria that are introduced into seeds, assisting the growth of plants. The inventor, Bond, had recognized a problem in the art: that only a specific strain of bacteria would work with each particular plant. Indeed, if a farmer used the wrong strain, even in

5. 189 F. at 103.

6. U.S. Patent No. 5,928,932. Curious readers may wish to know that "cyclotella cryptica" is a diatom, meaning that it is a microscopic, single-cell aquatic algae with cell walls containing silica. Scientists have considered cyclotella cryptica as an alternative fuel source, for its cells contain lipids that can be converted into a compound that could replace diesel fuels.

7. 333 U.S. 127, 68 S.Ct. 440, 92 L.Ed. 588 (1948).

combination with the right strain, the farmer might actually inhibit the growth of a particular crop. Bond discovered a combination of bacteria that were mutually non-inhibitive and that could thus be used to innoculate several groups of plants. After securing a patent for both the process of making the bacteria combination, and for the combination itself, he sought to enforce his patent against a competitor.

Writing for the majority, Justice Douglas struck down the patent as merely claiming "the discovery of some of the handiwork of nature." As he put it, "the ancient secrets of nature now disclosed" were "part of the storehouse of knowledge of all men." Consequently Bond was not entitled to a patent on his invention.

This reasoning is curious, however, because as Justice Douglas himself noted, the combination of bacteria that Bond brought together did not exist in natural form. Therefore, the view that Bond's invention went towards a true product of nature seems difficult to accept at face value. Perhaps more sense can be made of the Court's remark that "however ingenious the discovery of that natural principle may have been, the application of it is hardly more than an advance in the packaging of the innoculants." Here Justice Douglas seems more concerned with the question of technical advance. Of course, this concern more properly implicates the so-called "nonobviousness" requirement of § 103, rather than patent eligibility concerns under § 101.[8] Given this apparent confusion, the *Funk Brothers* majority opinion is of dubious precedential value today.

Justice Frankfurter wrote a concurring opinion that has better withstood the passage of years. He argued that exceptions to patentability based upon such terms as "laws of nature" are, outside of the obvious cases of discoveries from the wild, extremely dubious. Everything that happens does so in accordance with the "laws of nature," even if they are imperfectly understood. Justice Frankfurter would have struck down the claimed invention on an alternative ground. He noted that Bond's claims did not recite the specific combination of bacterial strains that he employed, but rather attempted to secure exclusive rights to any combination of bacteria that possessed non-inhibitive properties. According to the Justice Frankfurter, then, Bond's patent presented overly broad claims in comparison with his narrow technical disclosure.[9] In modern terms, these issues would be addressed in terms of whether

8. *See infra* Chapter Five for discussion of the nonobviousness requirement.

9. Two other Justices dissented. They agreed with Frankfurter that the majority's "product of nature analysis" was unpersuasive, but they considered Bond's claims adequately supported by his disclosures, and would have upheld the patent.

the patent provided a sufficiently full "enabling disclosure" under § 112 of the Patent Act.[10]

The Patent Office continues to adhere to the rule that a true product of nature cannot be patented, because it does not fall within any of the categories of subject matter listed in the patent statute. As it points out in the Manual of Patent Examining Procedure, "a thing occurring in nature, which is substantially unaltered, is not a 'manufacture.' A shrimp with the head and digestive tract removed is an example."[11] However, as Professor Chisum points out, "any significant alteration of the product from its natural state would seem to make the product a 'manufacture' and remove the product-of-nature problem."[12]

2.3.2 *Genetically Engineered Organisms*

When inventors design new forms of life never before known, there can be no argument that the resulting entity is a "product of nature" in the traditional sense. There remain, however, serious ethical and policy questions of whether the patent system should be available to protect inventions of this sort. The landmark case on this issues is the Supreme Court's 1980 opinion in *Diamond v. Chakrabarty,* which made short work of the matter. In that decision, the Court unequivocally declared that a genetically engineered microorganism was patentable.[13] *Diamond v. Chakrabarty* began when the PTO rejected Dr. Ananda Chakrabarty's claims towards an artificially generated bacterium with the ability to degrade crude oil. Among their other benefits, such bacteria would have great utility in cleaning up oil spills. Nonetheless, the PTO denied Chakrabarty's patent application. On appeal, the Court of Customs and Patent Appeals (CCPA)—the predecessor of the Federal Circuit—reversed, and the Supreme Court then affirmed the CCPA in sweeping terms.

The Supreme Court's decision initially addressed whether a microorganism constituted a "composition of matter" or "manufacture" within the meaning of § 101. According to Chief Justice Burger, either one of these categories would apply to Chakrabarty's bacterium. The Court indicated that these statutory terms should be broadly construed, in particular due to legislative history that indicated patentable subject matter should "include anything under the sun that is made by man."

10. *See infra* § 6.1.1.

11. *Manual of Patent Examining Procedure* § 706.03(a). The shrimp example is based on Ex parte Grayson, 51 USPQ 413 (Bd. App. 1941).

12. 1 D. Chisum, *Patents* § 1.02-[7][a].

13. 447 U.S. 303, 100 S.Ct. 2204, 65 L.Ed.2d 144 (1980).

The Patent Office offered two principal arguments opposing this conclusion. First, the Patent Office pointed to two plant-specific intellectual property statutes, the Plant Patent Act of 1930 and the Plant Variety Protection Act of 1970. These two statutes, addressed in § 2.9 of this text, authorize the award of proprietary rights for certain kinds of plants. According to the Patent Office, these acts reflected a Congressional understanding that the terms "manufacture" and "composition of matter" did not refer to living organisms. Chief Justice Burger swiftly rejected this argument. Congress had enacted the plant-specific statutes in order to make intellectual property protection more readily available to plant breeders, the Court reasoned, not to preclude them from obtaining utility patents.

The Patent Office also argued that because genetic technology could not have been foreseen at the time the patent statute was drafted, the resolution of the patentability of such inventions should be left to Congress. Again, the Court disagreed, observing that a "rule that unanticipated inventions are without protection would conflict with the core concept of the patent law that anticipation undermines patentability." The Court also quickly dismissed concerns over the possible perils of genetic research. Researchers would assuredly pursue work in biotechnology whether their results were patentable or not, the Court reasoned, and the regulation of genetic research was a task that also fell to the legislature.

Diamond v. Chakrabarty opened the doors of the patent system to the nascent field of biotechnology. In the quarter century since, the U.S. biotechnology industry has flourished under this holding and numerous patents have issued on all manner of living organisms. For instance, following the lead of the Supreme Court, in 1987 the PTO Board in *Ex parte Allen*[14] reasoned that certain claimed polyploid Pacific oysters constituted a non-naturally occurring manufacture or composition of matter. (The oysters there at issue, being sterile, had the virtue of being edible year round). Contemporaneously, then-PTO Commissioner, Donald Quigg issued a formal notice, stating that non-naturally occurring, non-human multicellular living organisms are patentable subject matter.[15] Among the notable patents the PTO issued in keeping with this notice was one for the so-called Harvard mouse.[16] Harvard mice are genetically engineered such that half the females developed cancer, making them highly useful in cancer research.

14. 2 USPQ2d 1425 (BPAI 1987), *aff'd*, 846 F.2d 77 (Fed.Cir.1988) (non-precedential).

15. *See* 1077 PTO Off. Gazette 24 (April 21, 1987).

16. U.S. Pat. No. 4,736,866 (Apr. 12, 1988).

In more recent years, other patents have issued on a method for breeding genetically altered pigs,[17] that might be used to develop strains that could gain weight more quickly; for a genetically altered cow[18] that will yield milk essentially identical to human breast milk; and on a method for breeding transgenic dwarf goats,[19] whose many uses we will leave to the reader's imagination. The Supreme Court's broad sense of patentable subject matter has also proven influential overseas,[20] as well as in disciplines far removed from biotechnology.

Lest all this conjure notions of patents on Frankenstein monsters, we should note that the Commissioner Quigg's 1987 PTO Notice did advise that "the grant of a limited, but exclusive property right in a human being is prohibited by the Constitution." Presumably Commissioner Quigg was referring to the Thirteenth Amendment, which provides that "[n]either slavery nor involuntary servitude, except as a punishment for crime whereof the party shall have been duly convicted, shall exist within the United States." The Commissioner further advised that claims directed to a non-plant multicellular organism which could include a human being within its scope should include the limitation "non-human" to avoid a § 101 rejection.

The subsequent expansion of the holding in *Chakrabarty* to all living organisms except humans is not to suggest that the reasoning of the case was inevitable or that it is immune from criticism. The Court's chief task in that case was an issue of statutory interpretation—namely to determine if a living organism fell within the statutory categories of "manufactures" or "compositions of matter." The Court first determined that the term "manufacture" meant "the production of articles for use from raw or prepared materials by giving to those materials new forms, qualities, properties, or combinations, whether by hand-labor or machinery." One might question whether a living being is well-described by the terms "article" or "material." Next, the Court explained that the term "composition of matter" included "all compositions of two or more substances and . . . all composite articles, whether they be the results of chemical union, or of mechanical mixture, or whether they be gases, fluids, powders or solids." Most observers would not likely limit their description of a living entity to merely that of a composition made out of multiple substances. Moreover, this broad definition of the term "composition of matter" would render the

17. U.S. Pat. No. 5,573,933 (Nov. 12, 1996).

18. U.S. Pat. No. 6,013,857 (Jan. 11, 2000).

19. U.S. Pat. No. 5,907,080 (May 25, 1999).

20. *But see Commissioner of Patents v. President and Fellows of Harvard College*, 2002 SCC 76 (decision of the Canadian Supreme Court).

terms "manufacture" and "machine" within § 101 redundant, in contravention of well-established rules of statutory construction.

Finally, although the Court relied on language in the legislative history of the patent statute declaring that "anything under the sun that is made by man" was amenable to patenting, Congress did not draft the actual language of § 101 that broadly. It instead provided four presumably more narrow categories—processes, machines, manufactures, and compositions of matter—none of which appears to logically encompass living organisms. *Diamond v. Chakrabarty* seems to be a case where the Supreme Court fit a square peg into a round hole, but with spectacularly successful results for the affected industry.

Chakrabarty can also be attacked on policy grounds. Observers have continued to question the morality of the patenting of living inventions. In the late 1990's, a team of inventors decided to place the issue of biotechnology patenting squarely before the PTO and the courts. In conjunction with biotechnology activist Jeremy Rifkin, cellular biologist Dr. Stuart Newman recently filed a patent application claiming a method for combining human and animal embryo cells to produce a single embryo. This embryo could then be implanted in a human or animal surrogate mother, resulting in the birth of a "chimera," or mixture of the two species. The Newman–Rifkin application specifically mentions chimeras made in part from mice, chimpanzees, baboons, and pigs. At the time this book goes to press, the PTO has rejected the application on several grounds, among them ineligible subject matter under § 101. No matter what the ultimate disposition of their application, Newman and Rifkin have renewed the debate on the extent, and the morality, of the patentability of living inventions.[21]

§ 2.4 Methods of Medical Treatment

The U.S. patent system has never questioned that inventors may patent medical devices. Patents have issued on such devices as surgical instruments, catheters, and artificial hearts. The propriety of patenting methods of medical treatment has proven more controversial, however. Although some have urged that such patents offered individuals incentives to invent and disclose new medical methods, others pointed to the possibility that patents might restrict access to life-saving techniques, lead to invasions of patient privacy, and override the culture of disclosure and peer review that pervades the medical community.[1]

21. *See* Barry S. Edwards, "*. . . And On His Farm He Had a Geep*": *Patenting Transgenic Animals*, 2 Minn. Intell. Prop. Rev. 89 (2001).

§ 2.4

1. *See* Scott D. Anderson, *A Right Without A Remedy: The Unenforceable*

One of the earliest judicial manifestations of these concerns, *Morton v. New York Eye Infirmary*,[2] involved the use of ether. That ether had an intoxicating effect when inhaled was a commonly known fact. Co-inventors Jackson and Morton had discovered that, when breathed in sufficient quantities, ether was also useful as an anaesthetic. Their invention allowed surgery to proceed with a great reduction in human suffering. Jackson and Morton obtained a method patent claiming the use of ether in surgical operations.

While acknowledging that this invention was among the "great discoveries of modern times," the New York Circuit Court nonetheless struck down the patent. The court's dated and rather enigmatic language leaves the modern reader in doubt over the precise basis for invalidity. For example, the court suggests both that the invention was merely a product of nature, and that the invention lacked novelty—both rather dubious grounds for invalidity under the facts. In other language, however, the *Morton* opinion suggested that inventions manipulating the "natural functions of an animal" were unpatentable. Subsequent nineteenth century decisions relied upon *Morton* to hold that methods of medical treatment were inappropriate for patenting.[3]

Later judicial opinions evidenced a more liberal posture towards patents on medical procedures. For example, the 1954 opinion of the PTO Board in *Ex parte Scherer*[4] allowed a patent on a claimed "method of injecting medicaments by pressure jet." The Board distinguished *Morton* on a rather dubious ground, stating that the invention there involved known methods and materials. Following the *Scherer* decision, medical practitioners obtained numerous U.S. patents on methods of medical treatment, ranging from administering insulin to treating cancer.

Traditionally, few owners of medical method patents had attempted to enforce their proprietary rights. But in the early 1990's a Dr. Samuel Pallin alleged that another physician infringed his patented cataract surgery procedure.[5] The lawsuit led to a raging debate that questioned the impact of patents upon medical ethics, patient care, and professional autonomy. Following the condemnation of patents on medical procedures by the American Medical Association House of Delegates, Congress chose to act. The result was legislation codified at § 287(c) of the Patent Act.

Medical Procedure Patent, 3 MARQ. INTELL. PROP. L. REV. 117 (1999).

2. 17 F.Cas. 879 (No. 9865) (S.D.N.Y.1862).

3. *See* Ex parte Brinkerhoff, 24 Off. Gaz. Pat. Off. 349 (Comm'r Pat. Off. 1883), *reprinted in* 27 J. PAT. OFF. SOC'Y 797 (1945) (denying patent on method for treating hemorrhoids).

4. 103 USPQ 107 (PTO Bd.1954).

5. *See* Pallin v. Singer, 36 USPQ2d 1050 (D.Vt.1995).

Section 287(c) is a complex provision that limits the scope of rights associated with patented medical methods. In essence, the legislation deprives patentees of all remedies, both monetary and injunctive, against medical practitioners and related health care entities engaged in infringing "medical activity."[6] The term "medical activity" is defined as "the performance of a medical or surgical procedure on a body," although patented products, compositions of matter, and biotechnologies are expressly excluded from this definition.[7] The effective result of the statute is that while medical methods remain statutory subject matter, a proprietor cannot enforce a medical method patent against those parties most likely to infringe it.

The actual impact of § 287(c) depends upon the nature of the invention. The majority of patentable medical methods probably involve a new apparatus or device as well. In such cases, the impact of § 287(c) is largely symbolic. For example, suppose that surgeon Dr. So invents a new kind of suture. In this case, Dr. So might obtain a patent with claims to both (1) the composition of the new suture itself and (2) a method of using the suture to seal wounds. Although § 287(c) applies to the method claims, it expressly excludes the composition of matter claims. As a result, Dr. So retains fully enforceable proprietary rights against others who use the patented suture.

On the other hand, suppose that a Dr. Bonn obtains a patent for a variation of the Heimlich maneuver. Like the Heimlich maneuver, Dr. Bonn's method involves thrusting one's fist slightly above the navel of a choking person. In this case, the patented method does not involve a product, composition of matter, or biotechnology, so § 287 applies in full. Dr. Bonn would be precluded from obtaining patent infringement remedies against a medical practitioner or related health care entity. Interestingly, because § 287(c) protects only licensed medical practitioners and related health care entities, Dr. Bonn might be able to obtain the usual remedies against lay persons who use his patented technique. This, of course, could put restaurant patrons in a bit of a dilemma, as they would have to decide whether to forego saving a choking companion in order to avoid liability for patent infringement.

§ 2.5 Computer–Related Inventions

The patentability of computer-related inventions proved extremely controversial. Dozens of reported cases, and hundreds of law review articles and other commentary, discussed and disputed

6. 35 U.S.C.A. § 287(c) (2000). *See* Gerald J. Mossinghoff, *Remdies Under Patents on Medical and Surgical Procedures*, 78 J. PAT. & TRADEMARK OFF. SOC'Y 789 (1996).

7. 35 U.S.C.A. § 287(c)(2)(A) (2000).

the merits of extending patent protection to software and other computer technologies. Events at the PTO and Federal Circuit have now outstripped this debate. There is now no doubt that patent protection is broadly available for computer-related inventions. Still, a review of the high points of this long saga is a familiar waystation in the patent law. The past debate over the patent eligibility of computer-related inventions may provide clues as to the scope of protection accorded such patents in the future, and its teachings provide general guidance as to the responses of the patent system to new technologies.

2.5.1 The Mental Steps Doctrine

Although the venerable doctrine of mental steps was developed long before the advent of the solid state transistor or semiconductor chip, it serves as an appropriate starting point in considering computer-related inventions. Under the mental steps doctrine, an invention that was principally a matter of human selection, interpretation, or decision-making was not patentable. Consider, for example, an improved method of "head and hand" judging of whether an apricot is of sufficient quality to purchase from a grocery store. The method might consist of steps such as picking up the apricot, holding it up to the light, turning it, and smelling the stem, all the while comparing the results to remembered sensations, such as the texture of a NERF® ball or the odor of a specified flower. Because this process is a matter of personal observation and discernment, not making use of any particular physical apparatus, it would be judged to consist solely of mental steps and therefore be unpatentable.

In one representative case, *In re Heritage*,[1] the Court of Customs and Patent Appeals considered a claimed method of coating a porous, sound-reducing fiber board. The method called for the progressive coating of individual boards. Heritage's application explained that a technician should periodically test the board in order to ensure that it maintained desirable acoustic properties. The CCPA affirmed the PTO's rejection of the application, explaining that the "mental process of making a selection of the amount of coating material to be used in accordance with a predetermined system" was not patentable. According to the CCPA, the claim called solely for human calculation and judgment, which as purely mental acts were not patentable subject matter.

The CCPA and other courts that applied the mental steps doctrine concluded that such inventions were no more than ab-

§ 2.5

1. 150 F.2d 554, 66 USPQ 217 (CCPA 1945).

stract ideas or mathematical algorithms. Because the claims of these patents were not tied to a discrete physical apparatus, courts made the armchair judgment that technological progress would be better served by preserving these broad principles within the public domain. They also sensed that such abstractions did not present completed inventions, and that granting and enforcing such rarefied objects of property would present practical difficulties.

The mental steps doctrine has not been the focus of many judicial decisions, and in recent decades the fate of the doctrine has grown uncertain. In its 1970 decision in *In re Musgrave*,[2] the CCPA effectively repudiated the mental steps doctrine, although its holding did not bind the other federal courts. Just two years later, however, the Supreme Court decision in *Gottschalk v. Benson*,[3] mentioned that "mental processes" were not patentable. Because the Supreme Court statement was so terse, and unaccompanied by a discussion of the contrary *Musgrave* decision, the state of the law was left rather unclear. At all events, the mental steps doctrine has not played a significant role in patent law at least since the creation of the Court of Appeals for the Federal Circuit in 1982.

At the dawn of the computer revolution, however, the mental steps doctrine seemed to enjoy a more robust existence. This legal situation proved problematic for the computer industry, for the advent of computer technology resulted in electronic execution of the process steps that had previously been performed by the human mind. When computer scientists inevitably turned to the patent system, they urged that their inventions comprised applied technology, not abstract mental steps. The PTO and courts were initially unpersuaded. Simply because the claimed process steps could also be performed by a machine did not render them patentable. Therefore, the policy concerns that animated the doctrines prohibiting patents on mental steps, abstract ideas, or mathematical algorithms were at first applied to computer technology.

2.5.2 Computer–Related Inventions at the Supreme Court

Representative of this early posture is the 1972 Supreme Court opinion in *Gottschalk v. Benson*.[4] There the applicant claimed a method of converting numerals from binary-coded decimal to pure binary format. The steps of the method comprised mathematical operations that shuffled a sequence of bits in order to express appropriately a particular number. The application contained claims both reciting the method as performed by a computer, and

2. 431 F.2d 882, 167 USPQ 217 (CCPA 1970).

3. 409 U.S. 63 (1972).

4. 409 U.S. 63, 93 S.Ct. 253, 34 L.Ed.2d 273 (1972).

the abstract performance of the method without regard to any particular physical means. The method had broad application in data processing tasks, ranging from "the operation of a train to verification of drivers' licenses to researching the law books" in the words of the Court.[5]

In a cryptic opinion, the Court upheld the Patent Office's rejection of the application. The Court first recited the traditional requirement that patentability hinged upon the "[t]ransformation and reduction of an article 'to a different state or thing.' "[6] Arguably, at least those claims reciting computer implementation of the numerical conversion method did involve some sort of physical conversion. Operation of the computer would not only manipulate those electrical signals representing the data, but generate electrical signals in order to instruct the computer to perform certain tasks. Yet the Court found this hardware insufficient, drawing its analysis to a close with a self-styled "nutshell":

> It is conceded that one may not patent an idea. But in practical effect that would be the result if the formula for converting BCD numerals to pure binary numerals were patented in this case. The mathematical formula involved here has no substantial practical application except in connection with a digital computer, which means that if the judgment below is affirmed, the patent would wholly pre-empt the mathematical formula and in practical effect would be a patent on the algorithm itself.[7]

Thus the Court held that computerization of mathematical equations could not shift them from the realm of ideas to that of industry. Internal circuitry operations were not enough to uphold even those claims reciting computer hardware, for barring the presence of an idiot savant or enormous mechanical device to perform the claimed conversions rapidly, a digital computer presented the only context in which the equations had meaning. The computer amounted only to nominal apparatus that placed no meaningful limitations upon the scope of the claims.

This early resistance to patents on computer-related inventions faded over time, however. By the early 1980's, PTO examiners found more favor in computer-related inventions, and the courts seemed more willing to uphold the issued patents.[8] While the omnipresence of computer technology and its significance to the United States economy may have carried the day, one suspects that both the PTO and the courts grew weary of the relentless argumen-

5. 409 U.S. at 68.

6. 409 U.S. at 70.

7. 409 U.S. at 71–72.

8. *See, e.g.*, In re Deutsch, 553 F.2d 689, 193 USPQ 645 (CCPA 1977); In re Chatfield, 545 F.2d 152, 191 USPQ 730 (CCPA 1976).

tation of a bar that has scant motivation to favor restraints upon the scope of patenting.

The first sense of this change of tack at the Supreme Court was its 1981 opinion in *Diamond v. Diehr.*[9] The *Diehr* applicants claimed a process for operating a rubber-molding press with the aid of a digital computer. Their computer continuously monitored the temperature within a press and employed the well-known Arrhenius equation[10] to calculate the amount of time required to cure rubber placed within the press. When the computer calculated that the elapsed time equaled the actual molding time, it signaled a device to open the press.[11]

At the Patent Office, the examiner concluded that the process steps that were implemented in computer software were not statutory subject matter for patents. The examiner further reasoned that the "remaining steps—installing rubber in the press and the subsequent closing of the process—were 'conventional and necessary to the process and cannot be the basis of patentability.' "[12] The CCPA reversed the rejection, however. Following a grant of *certiorari*, the Supreme Court affirmed, explaining that the applicants were not seeking to patent a mathematical formula, but instead an industrial process that involved a number of discrete steps, including installing rubber in a press, closing the mold, constantly determining the temperature of the mold, constantly recalculating the appropriate cure time through the use of a formula and a digital computer, and automatically opening the press at the proper time.[13]

Many observers have noted that the advancement offered by the *Diehr* applicants consisted not so much of rubber-making, but of mathematical computations. The physical steps on which so much depended—reading a thermometer and signaling a press door to open—appear trite. Allowing patentability to hinge upon the minimal recitation of these steps within the claims seems unfounded, for they merely stated the only valid technical context in which the mathematics would operate. They did not present meaningful limitations upon the scope of the claimed formula.[14] Still, *Diehr* signaled the PTO and the lower courts that, in appropriate circumstances, computer-related inventions were appropriate for patenting.

9. 450 U.S. 175, 101 S.Ct. 1048, 67 L.Ed.2d 155 (1981).

10. Your authors disagree on just how well-known this equation actually is. One of us (the political science major) had never heard of it before reading the opinion in *Diehr*. If you are curious, the equation is: $k=A*\exp^{(-Ea/R*T)}$. You can learn more about it and practice using it by visiting the following Internet page: <http://www.shodor.org/unchem/advanced/kin/arrhenius.html>.

11. 450 U.S. at 177–78.

12. 450 U.S. at 181.

13. 450 U.S. at 187.

14. Richard H. Stern, *Tales from the Algorithm War: Benson to Iwahashi, It's Deja Vu All Over Again,* 18 AIPLA Q.J. 371 (1991).

2.5.3 Computer-Related Inventions at the Federal Circuit

In response to these pronouncements by the Supreme Court, the predecessor to the Federal Circuit, the Court of Customs and Patent Appeals, formed the two-part *Freeman–Walter–Abele* test. First articulated in 1978 by the *In re Freeman*[15] decision, the court refined the test two years later in its 1980 opinion, *In re Walter*.[16] Following the Supreme Court's issuance of its *Diehr* decision, the court once again modified the standard in its 1982 decision, *In re Abele*.[17] As this test was later described by the Federal Circuit:

> It is first determined whether a mathematical algorithm is recited directly or indirectly in the claim. If so, it is next determined whether the claimed invention as a whole is no more than the algorithm itself; that is, whether the claim is directed to a mathematical algorithm that is not applied to or limited by physical elements or process steps. Such claims are nonstatutory. However, when the mathematical algorithm is applied in one or more steps of an otherwise statutory process claim, or one or more elements of an otherwise statutory apparatus claim, the requirements of section 101 are met.[18]

A representative case applying the *Freeman–Walter–Abele* standard is *Arrhythmia Research Technology, Inc. v. Corazonix Corp.*[19] The invention here involved a type of heart arrhythmia called ventricular tachycardia. This ailment afflicts many patients who have suffered heart attacks, and a surprisingly large number of characters on TV medical dramas, and essentially consists of abnormally rapid heart beats. It can be treated with certain drugs, but they bring with them attendant risks. The problem was to identify which heart attack victims had a propensity for ventricular tachycardia so that treatment could be more selective. Upon further research, a Dr. Simson learned that the hearts of those likely to suffer from ventricular tachycardia exhibit certain tell-tale signs: namely, their electrical signals have so-called "late potentials" in the "QRS" segment of the heart's signals. Simson then employed a signal processing technique termed the "Butterworth filter" to isolate the QRS segment.[20] The output of the process was then compared with a known value; if it was less than the predetermined level, the patient was judged prone to ventricular tachycardia.

15. 573 F.2d 1237, 197 USPQ 464 (CCPA 1978).

16. 618 F.2d 758, 205 USPQ 397 (CCPA 1980).

17. 684 F.2d 902, 214 USPQ 682 (CCPA 1982).

18. Arrhythmia Research Technology, Inc. v. Corazonix Corp., 958 F.2d 1053, 22 USPQ2d 1033 (Fed.Cir.1992).

19. 958 F.2d 1053, 22 USPQ2d 1033 (Fed. Cir. 1992).

20. This method does not, despite the name, involve the use of pancake syrup.

The PTO allowed a patent to issue on this invention. As granted, the Simson patent included both claims to methods of and apparatus for analyzing electrocardiographic signals. During enforcement litigation, however, a district court held that both sorts of claims were unpatentable under § 101. On appeal, the Federal Circuit reversed. Applying *Freeman–Walter–Abele*, the court concluded that the claimed invention included a mathematical formula. The court then proceeded to the second part of the *Freeman–Walter–Abele* test, in order to determine whether the claimed invention was otherwise statutory. As to the process claims, the court concluded that the invention consisted of tangible steps that transformed one electrical signal into another. The specificity and physicality of these steps brought them within the requirements of § 101. Similarly, the product claims described a particular combination of discrete machine elements, including an analog-to-digital converter, a high pass filter, and a minicomputer, that also made them eligible for patenting.

In *Arrhythmia*, the Federal Circuit effectively viewed the Simson invention as processing an electrical signal generated by the human heart. Seen this way, the Simson invention seemed to fall into a class of traditionally patentable technologies, including items ranging from radio receivers to electrical transformers, that use signal processing methods. And so the invention readily fulfilled the second part of the *Freeman–Walter–Abele* standard. However, a different characterization of the Simson invention might have led to a different outcome. Simson may well have been viewed as merely (1) discovering the scientific principle that the electrocardiographic signals of patients with ventricular tachycardia exhibited certain characteristics, and (2) employing well-known electrical engineering techniques to put that principle towards its only possible use. In that case, the policy reasons for disallowing patents on scientific principles seem to apply with full force against the patentability of the Simson invention.

As demonstrated by cases like *Arrhythmia*, the *Freeman–Walter–Abele* standard did little to answer the hard questions about patent eligibility issues under § 101. Rather, *Freeman–Walter–Abele* encouraged patent drafters to circumvent the issue by including some sort of apparatus in their claims. Simson made sure to include a converter and filter in his claims, for example, while the inventor in *Diamond v. Diehr* recited a thermometer and oven door opener. This nominal apparatus suggested that the claim recited more than just math and therefore fulfilled the second part of *Freeman–Walter–Abele*. Encouraged by *Freeman–Walter–Abele*, the patent bar became well-schooled in drafting computer-related claims that incorporated structural elements and therefore constituted patent-eligible subject under this judicial interpretation of § 101.

The Federal Circuit appeared to recognize these difficulties, and responded not by refining the *Freeman–Walter–Abele* standard, but by rejecting it. The occasion was the 1994 *en banc* decision in *In re Alappat.*[21] The *Alappat* case concerned a claimed apparatus useful for generating smooth and continuous lines for display on an oscilloscope, which is a device that provides a visual representation of variations in electrical current. To achieve this effect, Alappat's invention completed various mathematical computations in order to convert so-called "vector list data" into "pixel illumination intensity data." Stated more plainly, the function of the Alappat invention was to transform one set of numbers into another set of numbers.[22]

At first glance, an invention that converts one number into another would seem to fall squarely into the category of an excluded mathematical algorithm. However, Alappat had apparently hoped that drafting his claims in terms of a specific calculating machine would make the § 101 inquiry go more smoothly. As a result, Alappat had claimed his invention as a product, reciting various "means" for performing mathematical functions such as subtraction and normalization. Despite Alappat's best efforts, the PTO rejected his claims as consisting of a mathematical algorithm. In reaching this conclusion, the PTO in part observed that if Alappat's patent application was granted, it would cover a general purpose computer (such as a law student's laptop) that used software to perform the claimed mathematical functions. This observation confirmed the PTO's view that Alappat's invention did not relate to specific structure, such as the electrical hardware of any particular computer or programmable calculator. Rather, the PTO saw Alappat's invention as abstract mathematical principles that were independent of the hardware platform capable of performing the claimed functions.

On appeal, the Federal Circuit reversed. The majority approved of Alappat's artful claim drafting, concluding that the Alappat invention was "not a disembodied mathematical concept which may be characterized as an 'abstract idea,' but rather a specific machine to produce a useful, concrete, and tangible result."[23] The court further reasoned that the fact that Alappat's claims covered general purpose computers did not imperil its patentability. The Federal Circuit concluded that software "programming creates a new machine, because a general purpose computer in effect becomes a

21. 33 F.3d 1526, 31 USPQ2d 1545 (Fed.Cir.1994).

22. 33 F.3d at 1537–39, 31 USPQ2d at 1551–53.

23. 33 F.3d at 1544, 31 USPQ2d 1557.

special purpose computer once it is programmed to perform particular functions pursuant to instructions from program software."[24]

Alappat did not expressly reject the *Freeman–Walter–Abele* test, but plainly the Federal Circuit did not perform its usual two-part analysis. The view that any computer program effectively creates new hardware effectively means that every computer-related invention fulfills the second prong of *Freeman–Walter–Abele*, rendering that standard superfluous. In its 1999 decision in *AT&T Corp. v. Excel Communications, Inc.*,[25] the Federal Circuit confirmed that the *Freeman–Walter–Abele* test was all but dead. According to the Federal Circuit's analysis in *AT&T*, a § 101 analysis should not focus upon whether the claim recited physical limitations or not. Instead, it should be determined whether the claimed invention achieves a "useful, concrete and tangible result." Under the latest thinking of the Federal Circuit, then, virtually any invention that can be used to obtain a practical result is patentable subject matter.

Apparent to any reader of the more recent Federal Circuit opinions is that the "useful, concrete, and tangible result" standard is very lenient. Only a few computer-related inventions for which a patent is sought will not minimally achieve a functional or serviceable result. As a result, modern day computer scientists and engineers should rarely encounter statutory subject matter rejections at the PTO.

Computer technology has taken the patent system a long way from the mental steps doctrine. As we shall see, computer-related inventions also triggered the movement towards the patentability of two other subjects traditionally excluded from the patent system, printed matter and methods of doing business, subjects to which we turn in the following sections.

§ 2.6 Presentations of Information

Presentations of information traditionally did not comprise patentable subject matter. Under the printed matter doctrine, information inscribed upon a surface for purposes of presentation was held outside the scope of § 101. Courts viewed such inventions as no more than memorialized versions of abstract ideas. They reasoned that the mere act of recording information upon a surface—which patent lawyers sometimes call a "substrate" in this context—should not impart patentability. This rule also performed

24. 33 F.3d at 1545, 31 USPQ2d at 1558.

25. 172 F.3d 1352, 50 USPQ2d 1447 (Fed.Cir.1999), *cert. denied*, 528 U.S. 946, 120 S.Ct. 368, 145 L.Ed.2d 284 (1999).

a channeling function, diverting works of authorship from the patent law to the copyright law.

One significant exception to the printed matter doctrine arose in the case law. An invention was patentable if it included a physical structure that resulted in a functional relationship between the information and the surface it was written upon. The line between the printed matter rule and its exception did not sparkle with clarity, and the case law reflects some rather subtle distinctions between printed matter and patentable invention. For example, a system of blank checks and stubs useful in a combined checking/savings account was considered unpatentable printed matter.[1] But a railway ticket consisting of a base and separable attachment was judged a unique physical structure and therefore appropriate for patenting.[2]

Although the Federal Circuit has not expressly overturned the printed matter doctrine, its 1983 decision in *In re Gulack* offered the view that the rule "stands on questionable legal and logical footing."[3] Later, in *In re Lowry*,[4] the Federal Circuit reversed a PTO rejection based upon the printed matter rule. Lowry's patent application claimed a computer memory for storing data for access by a computer program. According to the Federal Circuit, Lowry's invention was not analogous to printed matter because it included "electronic structural elements which impart a physical organization on the information stored in memory."

PTO allowance of patents claiming encoded machine instruction further suggests the decline of the printed matter rule. Traditionally, software was claimed in method format, as a series of instructions to be performed by a computer. But applicants also have claimed computer programs as an article of manufacture, in terms of the computer-readable media on which the software has been stored. The following provides an example of this type of claim:

> A compact disk containing a set of computer-readable instructions, the set of instructions comprising:
>
> obtaining a password from an authorized user of the computer,
>
> requesting computer users to provide the password,
>
> comparing responses to said request with the password, and
>
> providing access to the computer only to users who know the password.

§ 2.6

1. In re Sterling, 70 F.2d 910 (CCPA 1934).

2. Cincinnati Traction Co. v. Pope, 210 F. 443 (6th Cir.1913).

3. In re Gulack, 703 F.2d 1381, 217 USPQ 401 (Fed.Cir.1983).

4. 32 F.3d 1579, 32 USPQ2d 1031 (Fed.Cir.1994).

The only formal treatment of claims of this sort, *In re Beauregard*,[5] consists of an unpublished decision from the PTO Board of Appeals. There, the PTO rejected a claim towards encoded computer instruction based upon the printed matter rule. Beauregard appealed to the Federal Circuit, but the court never heard oral argument. The position of the Solicitor of the Patent Office changed hands during the pendency of Beauregard's appeal, with the new incumbent quickly filing a motion to dismiss. According to the Solicitor, the Patent Office now accepted "that computer programs embodied in a tangible medium, such as floppy diskettes, are patentable subject matter." Following *Beauregard*, inventors of computer software commonly obtain claims directed towards encoded machine instruction alongside traditional method claims.

§ 2.7 Methods of Doing Business

Until recent years, whether business methods could be patented was not entirely certain. A number of decisions suggested that methods of doing business were not patentable *per se*. As early as 1868, the Patent Commissioner explained that "[i]t is contrary to the spirit of the law ... to grant patents for methods of bookkeeping."[1] Nineteenth century courts also opined that "a method of transacting common business"[2] or "a mere contract"[3] were unpatentable.

The best-known of these decisions was probably *Hotel Security Checking Co. v. Lorraine Co.*,[4] which concerned a "method and means for cash-registering and account-checking" designed to prevent fraud by waiters and cashiers. The system employed certain forms that tracked sales and ensured that waiters submitted appropriate funds at the close of business. The Second Circuit invalidated the patent on the basis of prior knowledge, finding that the patented technology "would occur to anyone conversant with the business." However, the court further observed that a "system of transacting business disconnected from the means of carrying out the system is not, within the most liberal interpretation of the term, an art" amenable to patenting.

Still, over the years the PTO allowed a number of patents to issue on inventions that could arguably be described as business methods.[5] At least one judicial opinion, *Paine, Webber, Jackson &*

5. 53 F.3d 1583, 35 USPQ2d 1383 (Fed.Cir.1995).

§ 2.7

1. Ex parte Abraham, 1868 Comm'r Dec. 59, 59 (Comm'r Pat. 1868).

2. United States Credit Sys. Co. v. American Credit Indemnity Co., 53 F. 818, 819 (S.D.N.Y.1893).

3. In re Moeser, 27 App.D.C. 307, 310 (1906).

4. 160 F. 467 (2d Cir.1908).

5. *See* William D. Wiese, *Death of a Myth: The Patenting of Internet Business Models After* State Street Bank, 4 MARQUETTE INTELL. PROP. L. REV. 17, 30–33 (2000).

Curtis v. Merrill Lynch,[6] also appeared to approve of patents on business methods. There the district court upheld a patent on a data processing methodology for a combined securities brokerage/cash management account. Because the *Paine, Webber* court stressed that the patent taught a method of operation on a computer, however, the extension of its reasoning to the broader category of business methods was uncertain.

Consistent with its sweeping view of patentable subject matter, the Federal Circuit ultimately rejected the methods of doing business exception. The occasion was the celebrated opinion in *State Street Bank v. Signature Financial Group*.[7] Signature Financial Group held the patent at suit. Directed to a "Data Processing System for Hub and Spoke Financial Services Configuration," it described a data processing system for implementing an investment structure known as a "Hub and Spoke" system. This system allowed individual mutual funds (Spokes) to pool their assets in an investment portfolio (Hub) organized as a partnership. According to the patent, this investment regime provided the advantageous combination of economies of scale in administering investments coupled with the tax advantages of a partnership.

Maintaining a proper accounting of this sophisticated financial structure proved difficult. Indeed, due to "the complexity of the calculations, a computer or equivalent device is a virtual necessity to perform the task." Signature's patented system purported to allow administrators to "monitor and record the financial information flow and make all calculations necessary for maintaining a partner fund financial services configuration." In addition, it tracked "all the relevant data determined on a daily basis for the Hub and each Spoke, so that aggregate year end income, expenses, and capital gain or loss can be determined for accounting and for tax purposes for the Hub and, as a result, for each publicly traded Spoke." Crucially, Signature's invention marked no advance in computer technology or mathematical calculations. The basis for patentability was the uniqueness of the investment package Signature claimed in its patent.

Following issuance of the patent, Signature entered into licensing negotiations with a competitor, State Street Bank, that ultimately proved unsuccessful. State Street then brought a declaratory judgment action against Signature, seeking to have the patent declared invalid. The district court granted summary judgment in

6. 564 F.Supp. 1358, 218 USPQ 212 (D.Del.1983).

7. State Street Bank and Trust Co. v. Signature Financial Group, Inc., 149 F.3d 1368, 47 USPQ2d 1596 (Fed.Cir.

favor of State Street under two alternative grounds.[8] First, the court applied the *Freeman–Walter–Abele* test, concluding that:

> At bottom, the invention is an accounting system for a certain type of financial investment vehicle claimed as means for performing a series of mathematical functions. Quite simply, it involves no further physical transformation or reduction than inputting numbers, calculating numbers, outputting numbers, and storing numbers. The same functions could be performed, albeit less efficiently, by an accountant armed with pencil, paper, calculator, and a filing system.

The court then buttressed its holding by turning to "the long-established principle that business 'plans' and 'systems' are not patentable." The court judged that "patenting an accounting system necessary to carry on a certain type of business is tantamount to a patent on the business itself. Because such abstract ideas are not patentable, either as methods of doing business or as mathematical algorithms," the patent was held invalid.

On appeal, the Federal Circuit reversed in a magisterial opinion. Writing for a three-judge panel, Judge Rich found the patent claimed not an abstract idea but a programmed machine that produced a "useful, concrete, and tangible result." "This renders it statutory subject matter, even if the useful result is expressed in numbers, such as price, profit, percentage, cost, or loss." According to the court, "[t]he question of whether a claim encompasses statutory subject matter should not focus on which of the four categories of subject matter a claim is directed to—process, machine, manufacture, or composition of matter—but rather on the essential characteristics of the subject matter, in particular, its practical utility." The court further trumpeted that:

> Today, we hold that the transformation of data, representing discrete dollar amounts, by a machine through a series of mathematical calculations into a final share price, constitutes a practical application of a mathematical algorithm, formula, or calculation, because it produces "a useful, concrete and tangible result"—a final share price momentarily fixed for recording and reporting purposes and even accepted and relied upon by regulatory authorities and in subsequent trades.

The Federal Circuit then turned to the district court's business methods rejection, opting to "take the opportunity to lay this ill-conceived exception to rest." According to Judge Rich, restrictions upon patents for methods of doing business were inappropriate

1998), *cert. denied*, 525 U.S. 1093, 119 S.Ct. 881, 142 L.Ed.2d 704 (1999).

8. State Street Bank and Trust Co. v. Signature Financial Group, Inc., 927 F.Supp. 502, 38 USPQ2d 1530 (D.Mass. 1996).

from the start and no longer the law under the 1952 Patent Act. Following issuance of the *State Street Bank* opinion, methods of doing business were to be subject only to the same patentability analysis as any other sort of process.

Whether or not the Federal Circuit reached the appropriate result in *State Street Bank*, the court's opinion includes some curious statements. At one point, for example, the court explains that the claimed invention achieves a useful result because it produces "a final share price." In fact, the claims of the patent-in-suit do not actually include the phrase "final share price," nor does the Signature invention calculate one. The Federal Circuit further stated: "After *Diehr* and *Chakrabarty*, the *Freeman–Walter–Abele* test has little, if any, applicability to determining the presence of statutory subject matter." As a matter of chronology this statement is plainly false: the Supreme Court issued *Chakrabarty* in 1980 and *Diehr* in 1981. The Court of Customs and Patent Appeals authored *Abele* in 1982.

It is also interesting to compare Judge Rich's opinion in *State Street Bank* with a pair of speeches he delivered almost forty years earlier. In those speeches he explained:

> Section 101, entitled "Inventions patentable," enumerates the categories of invention subject to patenting. Of course, not every kind of invention can be patented. Invaluable though it may be to individuals, the public, and the national defense, the invention of a more effective organization of the materials in, and the techniques of teaching a course in physics, chemistry, or Russian is not a patentable invention because it is outside of the enumerated [statutory] categories.... Also outside that group is one of the greatest inventions or our times, the diaper service.[9]

This earlier statement plainly conflicts with Judge Rich's subsequent declaration in *State Street Bank* that the 1952 Act placed business methods on the same statutory footing as other sorts of inventions. Any parent of a small child can especially appreciate that, in the language of the *State Street Bank* holding, a diaper service would surely be considered to achieve a "useful result" and therefore constitute patentable subject matter.

At all events, the *State Street Bank* decision has prompted many industries that never previously relied on patent protection to enter the patent system. Internet-based business models have been most quickly subject to appropriation via patents, given their close affinity to computer-related inventions. But few believe that com-

9. Giles S. Rich, *Principles of Patentability*, 28 George Wash. Univ. L. Rev. 393, 393–94 (1960) (based upon speeches delivered in September 1959 and December 1959).

puter hardware is an invariable requirement under the lenient patentability standard established in *State Street*. The financial, insurance, and service industries are also turning to the patent system. As the proprietors of these patents begin to commence litigation against their competitors, we should learn more about their enforceability and scope.

§ 2.8 Designs

Title 35 of the United States Code provides for design patents in a short series of provisions codified at §§ 171–173. Design patents may be awarded for "any new, original and ornamental design for an article of manufacture."[1] The surface ornamentation, configuration, or shape of an object form the most typical subjects of design patents. The design may be patented only if it is embodied in an article of manufacture, such as furniture, tools, or athletic footwear. The chief limitation on the patentability of designs is that they must be primarily ornamental in character. If the design is dictated by the performance of the article, then it is judged "primarily functional" and ineligible for design patent protection.[2]

Suppose, for example, that inventor Tori Irons invents a new golf club. The club features an sleek shaft and a broad, angular head. Suppose further that Irons seeks design patent protection on the club. In judging whether design patent protection is appropriate, a PTO examiner would consider whether the club's configuration is dictated by Irons' desire to lower the golf handicap of club users. If so, then the design is not principally directed towards ornamentation, and the award of a design patent would not promote the decorative arts. Irons should seek a utility patent in these circumstances. But if her design is principally directed towards giving the club a graceful and pleasing appearance, with the function of the club a secondary consideration, then a design patent is appropriate.

Because subsequent discussion within this text is largely limited to utility patents, some additional comments on design patents are appropriate here. An inventor must file an application at the PTO in order to obtain design patent protection. Design patents are generally subject to all provisions applicable to utility patents, in particular novelty and nonobviousness. The latter requirement is judged from the perspective of "the designer of ordinary capability who designs articles of the type presented in the application."[3] If

§ 2.8

1. 35 U.S.C.A. § 171 (2000).

2. *See* Best Lock Corp. v. Ilco Unican Corp., 94 F.3d 1563, 40 USPQ2d 1048 (Fed.Cir.1996).

3. In re Nalbandian, 661 F.2d 1214, 211 USPQ 782 (CCPA 1981).

the application matures into an issued design patent, the resulting design patent instrument is relatively straightforward. It principally consists of one or more drawings illustrating the proprietary design. The term of a design patent is fourteen years from the date of grant.[4]

Whether an accused design infringes the patented design is judged from the perspective of the ordinary observer. As explained by the Supreme Court in its 1871 opinion in *Gorham Mfg. v. White*:

> if, in the eye of an ordinary observer, giving such attention as a purchaser usually gives, two designs are substantially the same, if the resemblance is such as to deceive such an observer, inducing him to purchase one supposing it to be the other, the first one patented is infringed by the other.[5]

The lower courts have added one important refinement to this standard. In the words of the Federal Circuit, "the accused design must appropriate the novelty in the patented device which distinguishes it from the prior art."[6] Under this qualification, the accused design must include the novel features of the patented design to constitute an infringement.

The Federal Circuit opinion in *Avia Group International, Inc. v. L.A. Gear California, Inc.* illustrates the workings of these standards.[7] The patented design related to an athletic shoe sole. As compared to prior art sole designs, the patented design was notable for its use of a pivot point surrounded by a swirl effect. In approving the district court's finding of infringement, the Federal Circuit held both that (1) the patented and accused designs bore an overall similarity from the perspective of the ordinary observer, and (2) the accused design incorporated both novel features of the patented design, namely the pivot point and swirl effect.

§ 2.9 Plants

The days of Johnny Appleseed, who walked across the frontier dispensing seed free of charge, passed us by long ago. Nurseries, seed companies, and other members of the agricultural community are now both big businesses and full-fledged participants in the patent system. Plant breeders have long borne an uneasy relationship with the utility patent statute, however. First, even where bred under artificial conditions, plants seem readily classified as unpatentable products of nature.[1] Second, unlike other sorts of

4. 35 U.S.C.A. § 173 (2000).

5. 81 U.S. 511, 528, 20 L.Ed. 731 (1871).

6. L.A. Gear, Inc. v. Thom McAn Shoe Co., 988 F.2d 1117, 1125, 25 USPQ2d 1913, 1918 (Fed.Cir.1993).

7. 853 F.2d 1557, 7 USPQ2d 1548 (Fed.Cir.1988).

§ 2.9

1. *See* Mark D. Janis & Jay P. Kesan, *U.S. Plant Variety Protection:*

inventions, plants are not especially amenable to description in a written patent instrument. Diagrams or textual illustrations may fully convey the workings of a mechanical, chemical or electrical technology, but plant breeders usually require a sample of the plant in order to make use of it.[2] Although many inventors have managed to overcome these hurdles and obtain utility patents for plant-related inventions, Congress has nonetheless enacted two specialized statutes to level the patent playing field for agriculture and industry.

The first of these, the Plant Patent Act, is codified in sections 161 through 164 of Title 35. A plant patent may be issued for a distinct and new variety of plant that has been asexually reproduced, through grafting, budding, or similar techniques. Expressly excluded from the Plant Patent Act are tuberpropagated plants or plants found in an uncultivated state.[3] The other relevant statute is the Plant Variety Protection Act, or PVPA, which is codified at 7 U.S.C.A. § 2321 and subsequent sections. The PVPA provides for the issuance of plant variety protection certificates pertaining to sexually reproduced plants, including most seed-bearing plants. Fungi and bacteria are ineligible for certification. The plant must be clearly distinguishable from known varieties and stable, in that its distinctive characteristics must breed true with a reasonable degree of reliability.[4]

The key distinction between the two regimes is the manner in which the inventor has reproduced the protected plant. Asexual reproduction, which results in a plant genetically identical to its parent, forms the basis of plant patent protection. Certification under the PVPA instead depends upon sexual reproduction, which results in a distinct plant that combines the characteristics of its parents.

An example illustrates this distinction. Suppose that inventor Joanie Peachpit cultivates a unique orange tree growing in her orchard. The tree bears seedless oranges of excellent color and taste. Peachpit's nurturing of the tree is by itself insufficient to support a plant patent, and because the tree does not reproduce sexually it is ineligible for a PVPA certificate. But if Peachpit is able to reproduce the tree asexually, through the use of budwood or other techniques, then she would be able to pursue plant patent protection.

Sound and Fury ... ?, 39 HOUSTON L. REV. 727 (2002).

2. *See* Nicholas J. Seay, *Protecting the Seeds of Innovation: Patenting Plants*, 16 AIPLA Q.J. 418 (1989).

3. 35 U.S.C.A. § 161 (2000).

4. 7 U.S.C.A. § 2402(a) (2000).

Suppose further that Peachpit experiments with soybeans, eventually arriving at a variety that grows well in cooler climates. Because soybeans reproduce sexually, Peachpit may be able to obtain a plant variety certificate under the PVPA. She would have to show that her soybean variety demonstrated at least one distinct, uniform and stable trait.

The key features of these two statutes are worth noting here. Plant patents are issued by the PTO provided that the novelty and nonobviousness requirements are met. Applicants must submit an application featuring color drawings that disclose all the distinctive characteristics of the plant capable of visual representation. Importantly, the Plant Patent Act provides that these applications need only include a written description that "is as complete as is reasonably possible."[5] A plant patent enjoys a term of twenty years from the date of filing,[6] and is infringed if any other party asexually reproduces the plant, or uses or sells the plant so reproduced.

In contrast, the PVPA is administered by the Department of Agriculture. The holder of a plant variety certificate obtains the right to "exclude others from selling the variety, or offering it for sale, or reproducing it, importing, or exporting it, or using it in producing (as distinguished from developing) a hybrid or different variety therefrom."[7] The term of a PVPA certificate is twenty years (twenty-five years for trees and vines).[8]

The PVPA contains two notable limitations to the exclusive rights awarded to owners of plant variety protection certificates. First, the PVPA contains a research exemption.[9] This provision allows competitors of the certificate holder to engage in certain research activities safe from infringement liability. Second, the PVPA grants farmers a limited right to save and sell seeds that are protected by a plant variety protection certificate.[10] Importantly, the utility patent statute incorporates neither of these exceptions. Both the competitor who used the protected plant in research, and the farmer who saved descendants of seed he purchased from the certificate holder for replanting, could qualify as an infringer under the utility patent statute. As a result, the rights granted under the PVPA are more limited than under the utility patent statute.

Plant breeders understandably have historically preferred utility patent protection over a plant variety protection certificate because the PVPA offers more limited rights. Some legal uncertainty existed, however, as to whether utility patents were available for seed-bearing plants given the availability of plant-specific legisla-

5. 35 U.S.C.A. § 162 (2000).

6. 35 U.S.C.A. §§ 161, 154(a)(2) (2000).

7. 7 U.S.C.A. § 2483(a) (2000).

8. 7 U.S.C.A. § 2483(b) (2000).

9. 7 U.S.C.A. § 2544 (2000).

10. 7 U.S.C.A. § 2543 (2000).

tion. In *J.E.M. AG Supply, Inc. v. Pioneer Hi–Bred International, Inc.*,[11] the Supreme Court settled the issue by holding that a plant protected under the PVPA may also be claimed in a utility patent. Justice Thomas rejected arguments that congressional enactment of this more specialized legislation evidenced the congressional intent that living plants could not be the subject of utility patents. He observed that the PTO had a long history of granting utility patents towards plants and that the Court's own precedent had interpreted § 101 quite broadly. The Court also explained that a particular legal or property interest is often the subject of multiple statutes. For example, computer software may qualify for protection under both the copyright and patent laws. The Supreme Court concluded that merely because these laws may be of different scope does not suggest that they are invalid or mutually inconsistent.

One effect of the *J.E.M. v. Pioneer* case is that farmers must be increasingly aware of the possibility of patent protection on the seed they plant. They must also comply with so-called "bag tags"—label licenses that place conditions upon the use of patented seed—or risk becoming patent infringers.[12] *J.E.M. v. Pioneer* also seems to relegate the PVPA to the status of a second-class intellectual property statute. Plant breeders are unlikely to settle solely for a plant protection certificate if they can also obtain the more robust rights associated with a utility patent. The PVPA risks becoming something of a "petty patent" regime, reserved as a backup for utility patent protection or for seeds that lack commercial significance.

§ 2.10 Closing Thoughts on Patent Eligibility

If our experience with the patent law has taught us one thing, it is that the scope of patentable subject matter will inevitably broaden. This trend has accelerated to the point that few cognizable restraints appear to limit the scope of patenting. With the patent system poised to impact a range of activities as broad as human experience itself, we may justly question why the law of patent eligibility has become a one-way ratchet. A review of structural aspects of the U.S. patent system goes a long way to offering an explanation for this historical trend.

First, most accused infringers are patentees themselves. Although the defendant in a patent infringement suit ordinarily encourages the court to strike down the asserted patent, the preferred grounds for invalidity are ones that do not endanger the defendant's own patent portfolio. With these incentives understood,

11. 534 U.S. 124, 122 S.Ct. 593, 151 L.Ed.2d 508 (2001).

12. *See* Monsanto Co. v. McFarling, 302 F.3d 1291, 64 USPQ2d 1161 (Fed. Cir. 2002).

it is easy to see that the adversary system often provides only a lackluster exchange of views on patent eligibility.

Second, the structure of the patent bar encourages attorneys to urge a robust sense of patent eligibility. The organization of the patent bar differs starkly from that of attorneys in other disciplines, such as the labor bar. There, attorneys tend to represent exclusively either management or employees. This organization tends to generate healthy discussion on issues of moment in labor law. But patent attorneys most often establish long-term relationships with particular clients, whether they are asserting a patent against a competitor or themselves stand accused of infringement. As a result, the structure of the bar fails to create a constituency opposed to patents on methods of doing business or other inventions previously thought to be outside the patent system.

Finally, broad notions of patent eligibility appear to be in the best interest of the patent bar, the PTO, and the Federal Circuit. Workloads increase and regulatory authority expands when new industries become subject to the appropriations authorized by the patent law. Noticeably absent from this private, administrative, and judicial structure is a high regard for the public interest.

On the other hand, many plausible arguments may be raised in favor of broad notions of patentable subject matter. The focus of the U.S. economy has moved beyond the industrial, mechanical, and manual arts that have been traditionally patented. Why shouldn't the law respond to these changing conditions? If innovators have devoted significant intellectual or economic resources to come up with a new and inventive idea, why shouldn't they be awarded a proprietary right regardless of their discipline? The benefits associated with the patent system—incentives to innovate, invest, and engage in transactions—may apply with equal force to inventions from developing industries as well. It should also be noted that in many fields where patents remain controversial, including computer software, biotechnology, and business methods, skeptics typically remain hard-pressed to point to any specific harms done by the patent system.

Regardless of one's views, all should agree that determining the appropriate subject matter for patenting is important because there are few other constraining doctrines that limit the scope of proprietary rights associated with granted patents. As discussed in subsequent chapters of this book, an alleged infringer need not have derived the patented invention from the patentee, as liability rests solely upon a comparison of the text of the patent instrument with an accused infringement.[1] The patent law as well lacks a

§ 2.10

1. *See* J.H. Reichman, *Legal Hybrids Between the Patent and Copyright Paradigms*, 94 COLUM. L. REV. 2432 (1994).

meaningful experimental use exemption in the nature of copyright law's fair use privilege.[2] The decision to subject particular areas of endeavor to the patent system is therefore of great moment, in effect subjecting entire industries to a private regulatory environment with constantly shifting contours. As you make your way through this material, you might pause to think about the impact of the patent system upon traditionally patent-free industries such as services or finance, and to ponder whether every aspect of human endeavor is appropriately subjected to, in the words of Thomas Jefferson, the "embarrassment" of exclusive patent rights.

2. *See* Maureen O'Rourke, *Towards a Doctrine of Fair Use in Patent Law*, 100 Colum. L. Rev. 1177 (2000).

Chapter 3

UTILITY

Table of Sections

Sec.

---

§ 3.1 Basic Concepts

Section 101 of the Patent Act mandates that patents issue only to "useful" inventions. This utility requirement is rarely an obstacle to a patent. It requires only a minimal showing that the invention capable of achieving a pragmatic result.[1] To satisfy the requirement patent applicants only have to demonstrate a single, operable use of the invention that is credible to persons of ordinary skill in the art. Although the utility requirement is readily met in most fields, it presents a more significant hurdle to patentability in the disciplines of chemistry and biotechnology. In these fields, inventors sometimes synthesize new compounds without a precise knowledge of how they may be used to achieve any particular practical working result. When patent applications are filed claiming such compounds, they may be rejected as lacking utility within the meaning of the patent law.

As demonstrated by Justice Story's 1817 instructions to the jury in *Lowell v. Lewis*[2] and *Bedford v. Hunt*,[3] the notion of utility is a longstanding feature of United States patent law. In *Lowell*, Justice Story remarked:

> All that the law requires is, that the invention should not be frivolous or injurious to the well-being, good policy, or sound morals of society. The word "useful", therefore, is incorporated into the act in contradistinction to mischievous or immoral.... But if the invention steers wide of these objections, whether it

§ 3.1

1. Mitchell v. Tilghman, 86 U.S. (19 Wall.) 287, 396, 22 L.Ed. 125 (1873).

2. 15 F.Cas. 1018, 1019 (No. 8568) (C.C.D.Mass.1817).

3. 3 F.Cas. 37 (No. 1217) (C.C.D.Mass.1817).

> be more or less useful is a circumstance very material to the interest of the patentee, but of no importance to the public. If it be not extensively useful, it will silently sink into contempt and disregard.

In *Bedford*, Justice Story further explained that the patent law "does not look to the degree of utility; it simply requires that [the invention] shall be capable of use, and that such use is such as sound morals and policy do not discountenance or prohibit.... "[4]

These early remarks suggest two roles for utility requirement. The first is that the invention actually work, in that it has a pragmatic, real-world use, rather than being some mystery object that just "sits there." This concept is often called "practical utility." The second role, frequently termed "moral utility," is meant to captures the idea that the use of the patented invention should comport with a sense of the public order. As will be seen, although the practical utility requirement persists much as Justice Story outlined it, the notion of moral utility has nearly disappeared from U.S. law. These two components of the utility requirement are discussed in turn below.

§ 3.2 Inoperable Inventions

As explained by Justice Story, any invention that minimally works fulfills the requirement of practical utility. This utility requirement does not mandate that the invention be superior to existing products and processes in order to qualify for a patent. Justice Story rejected this proposed standard of "general utility" nearly two centuries ago,[1] and the patent law has retained this result ever since. Put succinctly, then, the patent law wants inventors to come up with something new and different, not necessarily better. Once the patent issues, the competitive market will determine if the invention is an advance on available devices or a second-rate product.

Newcomers to the patent system may be surprised to learn that a patented invention need not be superior to the state of the art. Many of us have seen advertisements touting the fact that a particular product is subject to a patent. Some lay persons may believe that the patent grant reflects a government determination that the product is better than others available on the market. More informed individuals, however, know that the PTO does not judge the degree of utility of patented invention when assessing utility under § 101.[2] In order to ascertain compliance with the

4. 3 F. Cas. At 37.

§ 3.2

1. 3 F. Cas. at 37.

2. Although an invention need not be superior to the state of the art to fulfill the utility requirement of § 101, or indeed any other patentability re-

utility requirements, PTO examiners instead simply confirm that the invention may be put to one plausible, real-world use.

The utility requirement therefore plays a quite limited role in most technical fields. The utility requirement merely sifts out utterly incredible inventions from the domain of patentability. As one might expect, the utility requirement is not often used as a defense in patent infringement proceedings. The fact that the defendant is accused of using the patented invention suggests that the invention is capable of at least one functional use.

Disagreements over the utility requirement more often arise in patent acquisition proceedings at the PTO. Citing the utility requirement, the PTO has disallowed patents on such purported wonders as a perpetual motion machine[3] or a method of slowing the human aging process.[4] While such inventions would, no doubt, be great boons to humanity, they suffered from one problem—they didn't work! The PTO has also issued Utility Guidelines for use by its examiners. The guidelines explain that an invention fulfills the utility requirement if it has a well-established use in the art or the applicant has disclosed a specific utility that is credible to a person of ordinary skill in the art.[5] The PTO will also reject obviously trivial assertions of utility, such as the use of a particular chemical compound as a paperweight or ship ballast.

It is important to note that the PTO does not operate laboratories or test facilities. PTO examiners ordinarily judge the utility of a claimed invention based upon their understanding of scientific and technical principles. If necessary, PTO examiners will ask patent applicants to submit test results or more detailed information explaining the practical utility an invention is alleged to possess, although even here the Federal Circuit has observed that "there is no per se requirement for clinical evidence to establish the utility of any invention."[6]

A relationship exists between the utility requirement of § 101 and the so-called "enablement" requirement of § 112. As discussed in Chapter 6 of this book, the first paragraph of § 112 of the Patent Act requires that patent instruments contain a full and clear description of the patented invention. This description must be sufficiently complete as to enable others to use the patented inven-

quirement, evidence that the invention is in fact superior to known technologies may support a conclusion of nonobviousness under § 103. *See infra* § 5.5.3.

3. Newman v. Quigg, 877 F.2d 1575, 11 USPQ2d 1340 (Fed.Cir.1989).

4. Ex parte Heicklen, 16 USPQ2d 1463 (BPAI 1990).

5. 64 Fed. Reg. 71440 (Dec. 21, 1999).

6. In Re Cortright, 165 F.3d 1353, 1355 (Fed. Cir. 1999) (holding a patent claim for method of treating baldness by applying a product used for softening cow udders to the scalp was not inherently unbelievable and thus not lacking utility).

tion. Plainly, one cannot describe how to use an invention if that invention is useless. As a result, arguments about the lack of usefulness of the invention are often made both in the context of the utility requirement of § 101 and the enablement requirement of § 112.[7]

More complex issues of practical utility can arise in cases where a patent claims a range of subject matter. In some cases, the entire range of claimed subject matter may not achieve a useful result. The question then arises whether the entire claim is invalid for lack of utility. This situation most often arises in cases where a patent claims a broad group of related chemicals, usually called a "chemical genus," and some of the particular chemicals within that genus are inert. In such circumstances, the courts have resolved this issue on a case-by-case basis.[8]

Suppose, for example, that a patent claims a refrigerant consisting of 20–40% chlorine, 20–40% fluorine, and 20–60% carbon. Testing demonstrates that although most of the possible combinations of the three ingredients serve as a useful refrigerant, the precise combination of 22% chlorine, 28% fluorine, and 50% carbon is in fact an inert compound—that recipe yields a substance that does nothing but take up space. In this case, the court will likely compare the number of inoperative and operative combinations overall; consider whether the patent instrument explains how to select which combinations in fact produce a refrigerant; and determine whether it is already known to the field how to choose a functional combination. If the number of inoperable combinations is relatively large, and no guidance exists concerning the selection of a working combination, then the claimed range as a whole may fall short of the utility requirement.

Straightforward policy reasons explain the lenient utility standard. If the invention is not especially useful, then society will bear a low cost if a patent issues on that invention. Few people will want to pay a premium to use an invention that is inferior to what is already publicly available. Further, society is better served by access to a library of issued patents describing as many inventions as possible, even if many of them do not achieve better results than technology that is already known. This liberal view of utility allows subsequent inventors access to a greater variety of previous technologies, some of which may yet be judged the superior solution when employed within a different context.[9] For example, some

7. In re Brana, 51 F.3d 1560, 34 USPQ2d 1436 (Fed. Cir. 1995).

8. Atlas Powder Co. v. E.I. du Pont De Nemours & Co., 750 F.2d 1569, 224 USPQ 409 (Fed.Cir.1984). *Atlas Powder* was resolved as an enablement case under § 112, but its principles apply equally to utility. *Atlas Powder* is discussed later in this text at § 6.1.1.

9. Vornado Air Circulation Systems Inc. v. Duracraft Corp., 58 F.3d 1498, 1508, 35 USPQ2d 1332, 1340 (10th Cir. 1995).

patented inventions may be inferior to known technology because they consume vast amounts of electrical power. If scientists ever perfect room-temperature superconductivity—possibly years in the future after these patents have expired—then the use of these inventions will become much more feasible. In sum, a minimal utility requirement imposes low short-term costs but holds potential long-term benefits.

Taking this rationale one step further, one might argue that the utility requirement is itself useless. If a patent issues on a wholly inoperative invention, then the invention can obviously never be used, and as a result the patent will never be infringed. Moreover, no one would ever buy something that does not work and has no purpose, so the public will not suffer the burden of paying higher prices for the patented object. This view is correct, however, only to the extent that a patented invention lacks utility throughout the entire term of the patent. If a patent was granted on an invention with no known function, then the existence of the patent might discourage others from learning how to put that invention to use. Anyone who actually discovered a use for the invention would be unable to exploit that discovery without fear of patent infringement liability, possibly delaying the introduction of a beneficial product to the marketplace.

For example, suppose that inventor Fred Furst obtained a patent on a chemical compound even though he had no idea what use could be made of the compound. Later, another inventor, Paula Post, discovers that the compound reverses male pattern baldness. Under these circumstances Post would be unable to sell the compound without Furst's permission. The two parties may possess strong incentives to deal, of course, assuming that transaction costs are low and that Furst is amenable to granting a license (he may well be selling an alternative product and be unwilling to authorize a competitor). Knowing all of this in advance, Post might not even wish to experiment with the substance, recognizing that she would be legally unable to exploit any resulting discoveries. These facts demonstrate the utility of the utility requirement—it helps determine the appropriate point in technological progress at which a patent application may be filed. Scenarios such as these have arisen most frequently in the fields of chemistry and biotechnology, to which we now turn.

§ 3.3 Utility in Chemistry and Biotechnology

In modern practice, the utility requirement most often comes into play in the fields of chemistry and biotechnology. In these disciplines, inventors often synthesize a new compound, or a method of making a new compound, without a preexisting knowledge of a particular use for that compound. They may generate the compounds based on their knowledge of the behavior of related compounds, or may wish to explore a class of compounds for which some application may develop in the future. However, at the time the inventor generates the compound, he might have no precise knowledge of the compound's utility.

The utility requirement should be viewed in light of the considerable incentives chemists and biotechnicians possess to obtain patent protection on compounds of interest as soon as possible. For example, in the case of pharmaceutical compounds, food and drug authorities require considerable product testing before the pharmaceutical can be broadly marketed. Before investing further time and effort on laboratory testing and clinical trials, actors in the pharmaceutical field desire to obtain patent rights on promising compounds even where their particular properties are, as yet, not well understood. But when patent applications are filed too soon on the heels of the initial synthesization of the substance, chemists and biotechnicians have discovered that the ordinarily dormant utility requirement has posed considerable obstacles.

The Supreme Court opinion in *Brenner v. Manson* addressed such a situation.[1] The inventor Manson filed a patent application claiming a new method of making a known steroid compound. Although the particular compound Manson was concerned with was already known to the art, chemists had yet to identify any setting in which it could be gainfully employed. However, because those working in the field knew that another steroid with a very similar structure had tumor-inhibiting effects in mice, Manson's new method of making the compound was a research tool of interest to the scientific community.

The PTO Board of Appeals affirmed the examiner's rejection of the application. The Board reasoned that because Manson could not identify a single use for the steroid produced by his new process, the utility requirement was not satisfied. In their view, he had come up with a novel way of doing something that was useless. The Board was unimpressed that a similar compound did have beneficial effects, noting that in the unpredictable art of steroid chemistry, even minor changes in chemical structure often lead to significant and unforeseeable changes in the performance of the compound. Manson then appealed to the CCPA, which reversed. Key to the CCPA's reasoning was that the sequence of process steps claimed by Manson would produce the steroid of interest. Ac-

§ 3.3

1. 383 U.S. 519, 86 S.Ct. 1033, 16 L.Ed.2d 69 (1966).

cording to the CCPA, because the claimed process worked to produce a compound, the utility requirement was satisfied.

The Supreme Court granted certiorari and once more reversed. The Court took issue with Justice Story's understanding that the utility requirement is fulfilled so long as the claimed invention is not socially undesirable. At least within the context of scientific research tools, the Court imposed a requirement that an invention may not be patentable until it has been developed to a point where "specific benefit exists in currently available form." Chief among the Court's concerns was the breadth of the proprietary interest that could result from claims such as those in Manson's application. "Until the process claim has been reduced to production of a product shown to be useful, the metes and bounds of that monopoly are not capable of precise delineation.... Such a patent may confer power to block whole areas of scientific development, without compensating benefit to the public." The Court closed by noting that "a patent is not a hunting license. It is not a reward for the search, but compensation for its successful conclusion. 'A patent system must be related to the world of commerce rather than to the realm of philosophy.' "

The merits of *Brenner v. Manson* have been roundly debated. As noted by Justice Harlan in dissent, the argument that a now-useless substance might subsequently be found to have utility ought not to carry much weight because patented products and processes often are later found to possess additional, more valuable uses. In such cases advance knowledge of one particular use does not somehow restrain the patentee's proprietary interest in those additional applications. For example, the chemical compound nitroglycerine, originally developed as an explosive, was later found to be useful as a heart medication. If an inventor had obtained a patent on the nitroglycerine compound itself (plainly useful in the demolition of old buildings), then he would continue to possess a proprietary interest in that compound no matter what applications were discovered for it (such as its new utility as a heart medication). Indeed, whether characterized as a basic research tool or an applied technology, any invention potentially serves as the basis for later developments.

That the influence of *Brenner v. Manson* may be waning is suggested by the leading Federal Circuit opinion on utility, *In re Brana*.[2] Like Manson, Brana claimed chemical compounds and stated they were useful as antitumor substances. The scientific community knew that structurally similar compounds had shown antitumor activity during both *in vitro* testing, done in the laboratory using tissue samples, and during *in vivo* testing using mice as

2. 51 F.3d 1560, 34 USPQ2d 1436 (Fed.Cir.1995).

test subjects.[3] The latter tests had been conducted using cell lines known to cause lymphocytic tumors in mice.

The PTO Board rejected the application for lack of utility, but on appeal the Federal Circuit reversed. Among the objections of the PTO was that the tests cited by Brana were conducted upon lymphomas induced in laboratory animals, rather than real diseases. The Federal Circuit responded that an inventor need not wait until an animal or human develops a disease naturally before finding a cure. The PTO further protested that Brana cited no clinical testing, and therefore had no proof of actual treatment of the disease in live animals. The Federal Circuit countered that proof of utility did not demand tests for the full safety and effectiveness of the compound, but only acceptable evidence of medical effects in a standard experimental animal.

Incredibly, the *Brana* opinion fails to discuss or even cite *Brenner v. Manson*. This lapse certainly suggests that the Federal Circuit will adopt a more liberal approach to the utility requirement than the Supreme Court did in *Brenner v. Manson*. The Federal Circuit did indicate that, in cases where the invention lacks a well-established use in the art, the applicant must disclose a specific, credible use within the patent's specification. Beyond this minimal statement, however, neither tribunal has set forth a statement of the utility standard notable for its clarity. The extent to which a particular chemical or pharmaceutical invention will suffice to fulfill the utility requirement remains a matter to be decided on a case-by-case basis.

While *Brenner v. Manson* and *Brana* continue to generate heated discussion, the PTO has struggled to apply the utility requirement in the context of applications claiming genetic materials. Inventors often seek patent protection on biological compounds soon after they have been synthesized. Such compounds include complementary DNA ("cDNA"), which corresponds to proteins used by human cells, and expressed sequence tags ("ESTs"), DNA sequences that correspond to a small portion of each cDNA. Because this nascent field is highly unpredictable, the functions of cDNA fragments and ESTs are usually unknown at the time they are discovered. Yet they remain extraordinarily valuable for their potential uses, and scientists from private industry, government facilities and university laboratories alike have marketed these research tools for commercial sale.

3. The phrase "in vitro" literally means "in glass," and refers to testing in a test tube, or more generally in a laboratory setting. The phrase "in vivo" means in a live subject and usually implicates human or animal trials of a chemical or pharmaceutical.

The patentability of these genetic materials has proven controversial. While *Brenner v. Manson* holds that serious scientific interest alone does not fulfill the utility requirement, *Brana* and other Federal Circuit opinions suggest a more lenient posture. Some legal and scientific commentators have expressed concern that proprietary interests in scientific knowledge will impede research efforts overall. They have also suggested that inventors of cDNA sequences and ESTs have been seeking an overly broad scope of patent protection, out of proportion with their relatively modest technical achievements. Others have urged that originators of cDNA sequences, like other inventors, also require a return on investment, and that allowing patents only on final products would merely further industry concentration.[4] Both the patent bar and the scientific community await judicial resolution of the legal protectability of these crucial technologies, a decision that will hopefully lead to a further clarification of the precise scope of the patent law's utility requirement.

§ 3.4 Immoral, Fraudulent and Incredible Inventions

Historically, courts also employed the utility requirement to strike down patents concerning inventions that were judged to be useful only for immoral, fraudulent, or inappropriate purposes, For example, a handful of early decisions invalidated patents on inventions intended for use in gambling or other disfavored activities. Most of these dour opinions originated in the nineteenth century or the early part of the twentieth. For example, various courts in that era held a patented automatic toy race course,[1] lottery devices,[2] and a slot machine[3] to lack utility because their functions were judged unwholesome. Inventions that were designed to mislead consumers were similarly invalidated. This latter class of inventions included a patented process that would permit lower quality tobacco to simulate high-quality tobacco by artificially causing spots to form on the leaf. In stern, scolding language, the Court of Appeals for the Second Circuit believed the sole purpose of the invention was to practice deception and fraud upon the public.[4] This aspect of the utility requirement has been termed "moral utility."

The modern view is that so long as the invention may be put to a single lawful use, it possesses utility within the patent statute.

4. *See generally* Rebecca S. Eisenberg, *Intellectual Property at the Public–Private Divide: The Case of Large–Scale DNA Sequencing,* 3 U. Chi. L. Sch. Roundtable 557, 560 (1996).

§ 3.4

1. National Automatic Device Co. v. Lloyd, 40 F. 89 (N.D.Ill.1889).

2. Brewer v. Lichtenstein, 278 F. 512 (7th Cir.1922).

3. Schultze v. Holtz, 82 F. 448 (N.D.Cal.1897).

4. Richard v. Du Bon, 103 F. 868, 873 (2d Cir.1900).

That the invention might also be put to an illegal purpose does not make it unpatentable. This position recognizes that public mores are susceptible to change, and that once reviled race tracks, lotteries and birth control devices have moved from a position of illegality to one of widespread adoption by the state and members of the public. It also avoids subjective judicial judgments as to the moral worth of a particular technology.[5]

Similarly, inventions that allow manufacturers to make cheaper substitutes for more expensive products are now judged to possess utility. Representative of the contemporary position is the Federal Circuit opinion in the delightfully named case of *Juicy Whip, Inc. v. Orange Bang, Inc.*[6] The reader of this opinion learns much about beverage displays in shopping mall food courts. It seems that so-called "post-mix" dispensers maintain beverage syrup concentrate and water in separate locations, only combining the two ingredients immediately before the beverage is dispensed. While post-mix dispensers have a large capacity and are quite sanitary, they do not allow vendors to promote impulse purchases by displaying a frothing, succulent beverage for all to see. In contrast, "pre-mix" dispensers hold a combination of syrup concentrate and water at the ready, but suffer from limited storage capacity and are prone to bacterial contamination, which can leave the consumer as well as the beverage frothing after the purchase has been consumed.

The plaintiff, Juicy Whip, held a patent for a post-mix dispenser that included a transparent bowl. According to the patent, the bowl was filled with a liquid that appeared to be the beverage available for purchase. While the bowl was arranged in such a way that it seemed to be the source of the beverage, in fact no fluid connection existed between the bowl and the beverage dispenser at all. Instead, the beverage was mixed on the fly, immediately prior to each beverage sale. The district court struck Juicy Whip's patent on the ground of lack of utility, reasoning that the patented invention acted only to deceive consumers. The court stated that the purpose of the invention "was to create an illusion, whereby customers believe that the fluid contained in the bowl is the actual beverage they are receiving, when of course it is not."

The Federal Circuit reversed on appeal, concluding that the fact that one product can be altered to make it look like another is, in itself, a specific benefit sufficient to satisfy the statutory requirement of utility. The appeals court noted that many valued products, ranging from cubic zirconium (a common inexpensive substitute for

5. *See* Robert A. Choate et al., Cases and Materials on Patent Law 375–76 (3d ed. 1987).

6. 185 F.3d 1364, 51 USPQ2d 1700 (Fed.Cir.1999).

diamonds in jewelry) to synthetic fabrics, are designed to appear as something that they are not.[7] Because the claimed post-mix dispenser possessed the features of a post-mix dispenser while imitating the visual appearance of a pre-mix dispenser, the utility requirement was met. The Federal Circuit also noted that simply because some customers might believe they are receiving fluid directly from the display tank did not defeat utility. The Federal Circuit took the view that the utility requirement does not direct the PTO or the courts to resolve issues of deceptive trade practices as part of the patent granting process, and that these issues should be left to such agencies as the Federal Trade Commission or the Food and Drug Administration, or perhaps to private litigation instigated by competitors.

That the defendant in *Juicy Whip* mounted a utility argument seems particularly odd. It was accused of patent infringement, yet chose to argue that the patent should be struck down because use of the dispenser was a deceptive trade practice! Indeed, had the patent been invalidated, any merchant would have apparently been free to use such a dispenser as well. The awkwardness of this situation suggests that few accused infringers would be willing to make such an argument, a state of affairs that in part explains the paucity of moral utility notions in U.S. law.

Notably, the principal international intellectual property treaty, the so-called "TRIPS Agreement," allows its signatories to exclude from patent protection those inventions that offend notions of morality.[8] Article 27, paragraph 2 of the TRIPS Agreement provides:

> Members may exclude from patentability inventions, the prevention within their territory of the commercial exploitation of which is necessary to protect *ordre public* or morality, including to protect human, animal or plant life or health or to avoid serious prejudice to the environment, provided that such exclusion is not made merely because the exploitation is prohibited by their law.

The patent statutes of numerous foreign countries, as well as regional agreements such as the European Patent Convention,[9] include provisions that are in line with the TRIPS Agreement. Experience reveals, however, that foreign courts and patent offices

7. Note, however, that most purchasers of cubic zirconium rings and polyester shirts know at the time of purchase that those items are not, respectively, real diamonds or real silk, while the purchaser of a beverage from the patentee's machine would not know that the beverage was not the same as the one on display in the visible tank.

8. *See supra* § 1.5.3.

9. *See* Donna M. Gitter, *Led Astray by the Moral Compass: Incorporating Morality Into European Union Biotechnology Patent Law*, 19 BERKELEY TECH. L.J. 1 (2001).

have rarely, if ever, actually rejected a patent application or invalidated an issued patent on these grounds. Even in jurisdictions possessing a firm statutory basis for injecting notions of morality into patentability determinations, the prevailing view domestically and abroad remains that the patent system is not the appropriate vehicle for determining the moral worth of new technologies.[10]

10. *See* Cynthia M. Ho, *Splicing Morality and Patent Law: Issues Arising from Mixing Mice and Men*, 2 WASH. U. J. L. & POL'Y 247 (2000).

Chapter 4

NOVELTY

Table of Sections

---

§ 4.1 Introduction

Novelty is the core value of the patent system. To obtain the proprietary rights granted by the patent system, an inventor must create something new. There are at least two important policy bases for demanding novelty as a prerequisite for a patent. First, little gain would result from granting a patent on a technology that is already known to the public,[1] while such a patent would actually limit competition and raise prices on known devices and methods. The novelty requirement therefore preserves the public domain by preventing individuals from appropriating its contents. Second, the novelty standard promotes efficiency, by discouraging technologists from engaging in duplicative development efforts. Cognizant that they may obtain patent rights only when they advance the state of the art, researchers will be motivated to turn first to libraries, not laboratories, in order to gain needed technology.[2]

It should be noted here that the novelty requirement is not the only one based upon the prior art. Novelty is complemented by the requirement of nonobviousness. Not only must a patentable invention not be strictly described by a single reference, it must not have been obvious to persons of ordinary skill in the art at the time it was made in light of the prior art taken as a whole. The nonobviousness standard allows courts to consider whether combinations of prior art references, viewed in light of the knowledge of skilled practitioners, should prevent an invention from being patented. Thus, in order to merit a patent, not only must the invention be new, but it must be more than a banal or self-evident advance over the existing state of technology. In practice, novelty presents the first stage of a prior art-based analysis, with nonobviousness conducted next. Nonobviousness will be taken up in Chapter 5 of this text.

A determination of novelty requires two distinct inquiries. First, the current state of the art must be assessed as a basis for comparison. This step requires a determination of which sources from the universe of available knowledge are pertinent to the novelty inquiry. The Patent Act defines the materials—usually called "references"—that may be used to judge the novelty of the claimed invention in § 102. Typical references under § 102 include such documentary materials as patents and publications, as well as evidence of actual uses or sales of a technology within the United States. The sum of these references is denominated the "prior art." Once the full scope of the prior art has been identified, the second inquiry is whether the invention described in a patent application is identical to any one of those prior art references. If so, the purported invention lacks novelty and no patent will issue.

§ 4.1

1. Pfaff v. Wells Electronics, 525 U.S. 55, 119 S.Ct. 304, 310, 142 L.Ed.2d 261 (1998), *reh'g denied*, 525 U.S. 1094, 119 S.Ct. 854, 142 L.Ed.2d 707 (1999).

2. *See* Brett Frischmann, *Innovation and Institutions: Rethinking the Economics of U.S. Science and Technology Policy*, 24 Vermont L. Rev. 347 (2000).

Making one's way through § 102 is not an easy task. The authors of this complex statute cobbled it together by augmenting the often dated language of venerable predecessor statutes with terse summaries of complex and highly nuanced case law. This drafting effort proved difficult even for the leading experts of the day. Furthermore, the statute cannot be read in isolation from the subsequent half century of judicial precedent that has interpreted nearly each of its words.

The Long March through § 102 will be appreciably assisted, however, by considering the seven subsections of the provision in two groups. Paragraphs (a), (e), (f), and (g) deal directly with novelty, while paragraphs (b), (c), and (d) concern a related, but distinct problem known as "statutory bar." The difference between these two ideas is largely a matter of chronology. Novelty provisions deal with events that occurred prior to the date the applicant claims to have *invented* the alleged patentable technology. The statutory bar provisions, by contrast, deal with events that occurred prior to the date an applicant *filed* her patent application. Some quick reflection on the inventive process will help make this distinction more vivid.

Inventors do not always file for patents immediately upon conceptualizing their invention. They may delay for a wide variety of reasons. For instance they may wish to further refine the invention, they may want to see if anyone would be willing to invest in commercializing the invention, or they may have difficulty in finding a patent lawyer, who in turn may be busy and may not be able to complete a patent application for many months. Thus an inventor may invent something in say, May 15, 2000, but not file for a patent until October 1, 2002, almost two and a half years later. Qualifying events that occur prior to May 15, 2000, are said to defeat novelty—they predate the invention and demonstrate that it was not really new as of the date it was finalized by the patent applicant. Those events that occur before October 1, 2002, are those that can give rise to a statutory bar—they may have come after the invention, but because they come before the date the patent application was filed, they may suggest that no patent should issue for policy reasons. Either type of problem will result in a denial of the patent application, but the logic differs.

Let us first consider the notion of the statutory bar, and take a quick overview look at the three provisions that deal with it. These provisions are generally designed to encourage reasonably prompt application for a patent after the inventive work is completed, and they do that by penalizing undue delay. Consistent with that objective, the statutory bars are tied to the date the inventor filed an application at the PTO. In practice, § 102(b) is the most important and frequently invoked source of a statutory bar. Under

§ 102(b), the point in time one year prior to the filing date is termed the "critical date." In the example in the preceding paragraph, that would be October 1, 2001. If certain statutorily specified activities—such as sales of the device described in the patent application, or the publication of written materials describing it—have occurred before the critical date, there will be a "bar" preventing the applicant from obtaining a patent. Not surprisingly, the the one-year period generated by § 102(b) is commonly termed the "grace period."

The other two statutory bar subsections are less important and less frequently litigated. Section 102(d) creates a statutory bar if the U.S. application has not been filed within one year of a foreign application on the same invention, but only where the foreign application timely matured into a granted patent. The remaining provision in our first group, § 102(c) offers a broadly stated, if little used, provision denying patentability when the invention has been abandoned to the public.

Turning to the second cluster of sub-sections in section 102, we find a variety of rules that deal with the requirement of novelty pure and simple. The novelty provisions mandate that one who is not the first inventor of a technology cannot obtain a patent, regardless of when or even whether another patent application has been filed. Crucial to this set of provisions is the invention date. Sections 102(a) and (g) implement the first-to-invent rule by declaring public knowledge of an earlier invention to be a form of prior art. Section 102(g) also serves as the basis for the PTO priority contests known as interferences, which determine who among several competing inventors should be entitled to a patent.

Section 102(e) deals with a special situation that arises when another party, who we can call Early, has filed a patent application prior to date of invention of a patent applicant, who we can call Apollo. The contents of Early's application would not normally be known either to Apollo, or anyone else besides Early and his lawyer, because patent applications are kept secret for at least 18 months after they are filed. If, however, Early's application described, but did not claim, the same invention as the one for which Apollo now seeks a patent and if Early's application eventually is published or results in an issued patent, section 102(e) makes Early's patent application prior art that will defeat the novelty of the Apollo's application.

Finally, section 102(f) prevents a patent from issuing to an applicant who did not himself invent the claimed invention. If all of this seems a bit arcane or even daunting, not to worry. We will unravel the complexities of these provisions in the pages to follow.

Regrettably, the world's patent laws do not exhibit a great deal of uniformity in their definitions of the prior art. The United States in particular has gone its own way by maintaining a unique "first-to-invent" system. In the United States, when more than one patent application is filed claiming the same invention, the patent will be awarded to the applicant who establishes the earliest acts of invention. Other countries have opted for a "first-to-file" rule under which entitlement to a patent is established by the earliest effective filing date of a patent application. Although inventors around the world have long maligned the interface problems created by the first-to-invent system, the United States has yet to muster the political will to harmonize its patent law with global norms.[3]

As mentioned earlier, once we have identified all possible references that might give rise to novelty or statutory bar issues, the second determination is whether any of those references fully describes the claimed invention. When an invention has been described in a prior art reference, it is said to be anticipated. The standard of anticipation is a strict one. Each and every element of the claimed invention must be disclosed in a single prior art reference. In addition, that reference must enable persons of skill in the art to put the disclosed information into practice.

The two novelty inquiries—determining the scope of the prior art, and identifying whether any one prior art reference fully anticipates the claimed invention—may be taken up in either order. In order to build from basic concepts into the more sophisticated material, this text begins in § 4.2 by reviewing the fundamental standard of novelty. Section 4.3 of this text then reviews the statutory bars of paragraphs (b), (c) and (d) of § 102. Section 4.4 concludes the chapter by presenting the remaining paragraphs of § 102–(a), (e), (f) and (g)—each of which concerns prior invention.

§ 4.2 The Novelty Standard

The black letter rule concerning novelty is straightforward: An invention is judged novel unless a single prior art reference discloses every element of the challenged claim and enables one skilled in the art to make the invention.

4.2.1 The Strict Identity Requirement

Anticipation requires the presence in a *single* prior art disclosure of *each and every element* of the claimed invention.[1] Although

3. *See* Charles L. Gholz, *First-to-File or First-to-Invent*, 82 J. PAT. & TRADEMARK OFF. SOC'Y 891 (2000).

§ 4.2

1. See In re Robertson, 169 F.3d 743, 49 USPQ2d 1949 (Fed. Cir. 1999).

older cases suggest a looser standard, allowing courts to find anticipation where a single reference includes the equivalents of all of the claimed elements,[2] in more recent decisions the Federal Circuit has rigidly upheld a standard of literal identity.[3] As that court put it not too long ago, "A judgment of invalidity for anticipation requires that a single prior art reference disclose every limitation in a patent claim."[4] Even the presence of minor or insubstantial differences between the claimed invention and the reference will mean that there is no anticipation, and will allow us to conclude that the invention meets the test of novelty. It is important to note, however, that in such circumstances, a nonobviousness analysis might well prove fatal to the patentability of the claimed invention.[5] In order to demonstrate that a claimed invention is anticipated, attorneys often construct so-called "claim charts" that contrast claim language with the properties of the prior art reference.

The anticipation inquiry thus involves an exercise in comparison, in which patent claims sought by an applicant are compared with a given prior art reference. This comparative inquiry is quite similar to the analysis undertaken by courts when confronted with claims of literal patent infringement, except in that case they compare the plaintiff's patent claims with the attributes of the defendant's device or process. The difference between the two inquiries is largely a matter of timing, which has led to one of the more frequently invoked aphorisms of patent law, namely "that which would literally infringe if later in time anticipates if earlier than the date of invention."[6] Suppose, for example, that the manufacturer of an unpatented chemical compound learns that a competitor has obtained a patent on that exact compound. If the manufacturer's earlier activities serve as prior art against the patent, then the patent is invalid because it has been anticipated. On the other hand, if the manufacturer's activities do not count as prior art, its continued production of the compound will infringe the patent.

In contrast to pertinent prior art for nonobviousness, an anticipating reference need not originate from a so-called "analogous art"—that is to say, a field of endeavor that is akin to the subject

2. *See* RCA Corp. v. Applied Digital Data Sys., Inc., 730 F.2d 1440, 221 USPQ 385 (Fed.Cir.1984) (Kashiwa, J., dissenting).

3. *E.g.,* PPG Indus., Inc. v. Guardian Indus. Corp., 75 F.3d 1558, 1566, 37 USPQ2d 1618, 1634 (Fed.Cir.1996).

4. General Elec. Co. v. Nintendo Co., Ltd., 179 F.3d 1350, 50 U.S.P.Q.2d 1910, (Fed.Cir. 1999).

5. *See* Continental Can Co. USA v. Monsanto Co., 948 F.2d 1264, 1267, 20 USPQ2d 1746, 1748 (Fed.Cir.1991).

6. Lewmar Marine Inc. v. Barient Inc., 827 F.2d 744, 3 USPQ2d 1766 (Fed. Cir.1987), *cert. denied,* 484 U.S. 1007, 108 S.Ct. 702, 98 L.Ed.2d 653 (1988).

matter of the claimed invention.[7] While nonobviousness is conducted from the perspective of the skilled artisan, the novelty inquiry is far more open-ended. A reference might originate from a technical discipline far removed from the field of interest to the inventor yet still constitute an anticipation.

The obscure Federal Circuit decision in *In re Runion* offers an amusing application of this principle.[8] Runion filed a patent application in 1990 claiming a bird feeder consisting of a pan coated with an abrasive substance, such as sand. According to Runion, the feeder's rough surface automatically trimmed the beaks of birds that ate from the pan. Because chickens instinctively peck at each other with their beaks, Runion explained that well-trimmed beaks would decrease injuries and improve yields within the poultry industry.

The PTO rejected Runion's application due to a U.S. patent that issued in 1915 to an inventor named Wolff. The Wolff patent disclosed a pan that was coated with vegetable grit to form a coating "of a rough or pebbled character." Wolff explained that dough would not stick to such a surface. As a result, bakers could readily remove bread loaves simply by turning the pan upside down. According to the PTO, the Wolff patent fully anticipated Runion's claimed invention.

Having issued sixty-five years prior to Runion's filing date, the Wolff patent plainly qualified as prior art under § 102(b). One might wonder, however, whether the Wolff reference should properly be imposed against Runion. The problem that Runion attempted to solve—the failure of chickens to trim their own beaks and their unpleasant habit of pecking their comrades—was much different than the dilemma of bread sticking to baking utensils, which was faced by Wolff, despite the similarity of their solutions. Baking also appears to be a remote discipline to participants within the poultry industry. Poultry farmers would not likely consult the baking literature when determining whether their needs could be resolved by existing technologies. Put differently, the Wolff patent appears to be a bird of a different feather than Runion.

Although these arguments possess a certain persuasiveness, the patent law has long contemplated a more strict anticipation inquiry. When a claimed product has already been described in a prior art reference, the mere suggestion that the product could be used in a new way provides an insufficient benefit to justify the issuance of a patent on the product. Such a patent might also place the risk of patent infringement upon individuals using technologies believed to belong to the public domain. This is not entirely unfair

7. Ex parte Lee, 31 USPQ2d 1105, 1110 n. 1 (Bd.Pat.App. & Int'f 1993).

8. 989 F.2d 1201 (Fed. Cir. 1993) (nonprecedential opinion).

because the second comer in such cases may be able to obtain a method patent directed towards the new use of a known product or process, as described previously at § 2.2.3.

To complete the story of *In re Runion*, connoisseurs of *coq au vin* and other sympathetic readers may be pleased to learn that the PTO's rejection over the Wolff patent did not stick. The Federal Circuit ultimately decided that the "vegetable grit" surface described in the Wolff patent was not sufficiently abrasive so as to be able to trim bird beaks. The court reversed the PTO's rejection, and a persevering Runion ultimately obtained his patent. Interested readers may locate U.S. Patent No. 5,235,934 on the PTO website (www.uspto.gov).

4.2.2 Genus and Species

Sometimes a patent application will claim a set or group of technological things, such as an entire class of chemical compounds. The PTO may then learn of a prior art reference that describes a subordinate member of that group, such as a discrete compound within the claimed class. In the patent law, these sorts of problems are referred to as those of "genus" and "species," with the former term referring to the over-all class or category in question, and that latter referring to one specific substance or compound within the class. Genus-species relationships create logical difficulties for the anticipation analysis of the patent law, but they have been resolved as follows.

When a species disclosed by the prior art literally falls within a claimed genus, the claimed genus will be considered anticipated. The Federal Circuit opinion in *Titanium Metals Corp. v. Banner* illustrates this concept.[9] The application at issue, which had been assigned to Titanium Metals, claimed a "titanium base alloy consisting essentially by weight of about 0.6% to 0.9% nickel, 0.2% to 0.4% molybdenum, up to 0.2% maximum iron, balance titanium, said alloy being characterized by good corrosion resistance in hot brine environments." Cited against the claim as a prior art reference was an article written in the Russian language. The Russian article included a chart that showed a compound consisting of 0.75% nickel, 0.25% molybdenum, and 99% titanium. The court recited "an elementary principle of patent law that when, as by a recitation of ranges or otherwise, a claim covers several compositions, the claim is 'anticipated' if one of them is in the prior art."

Things are a bit trickier when we turn the problem around and try to decide if a genus described in the prior art should anticipate a species subsequently claimed in a patent application. For example, suppose that in 1970 chemist Nate Nimrod patented a process

9. 778 F.2d 775, 227 USPQ 773 (Fed. Cir.1985).

of making high-strength synthetic fibers useful in the manufacture of bulletproof vests. Among other steps, the Nimrod patent called for the use of a polymer that is treated with sulfuric acid for a period of at least 5 minutes at a temperature less than 50 degrees. The Nimrod patent expired in 1987. In 2005, inventor Anne Archer discovers that if she uses a specific polymer known as a polyamide; employs a solvent of sulfuric acid with a 98% concentration; and treats the compound for a period of exactly 12 minutes at precisely 27 degrees, then she obtains dramatically superior results. The fiber is unexpectedly stronger than using other, variant processes, and the costs of production are lower. The question then arises whether the Nimrod patent should be considered to anticipate the Archer invention.

In these kinds of cases, in one sense an earlier disclosed genus may be automatically considered to encompasses all of the species within that genus. Under this reasoning, the Archer invention would be considered fully anticipated by the expired Nimrod patent. However, the courts and the PTO have not gone this route. They have instead reasoned that a reference that describes a genus does not necessarily anticipate later claims to a species. Particularly in biotechnology and the chemical arts, a genus can sometimes encompass millions of species, and a particular reference may not suggest that any particular species should be employed.[10] In cases where the prior art discloses a genus, the usual mechanism for evaluation is nonobviousness. The selection of an optimum value within a range of parameters is normally within the realm of ordinary skill.[11] But where the number of possibilities is vast, or the results yielded by one combination with the range turn out to be unexpectedly good, the discovery of the optimal species might not have been obvious to a skilled artisan.

4.2.3 The Enablement Requirement

The Supreme Court has long recognized that anticipation cannot occur unless a prior art reference is "enabling"—that is, it contains "a substantial representation of the patented improvement in such full, clear, and exact terms as to enable any person skilled in the art or science to which it appertains to make, construct, and practice the invention to the same practical extent as they would be enabled to do so if the information was derived from a prior patent."[12] In plain English this means that the prior art

10. *See* In re Deuel, 51 F.3d 1552, 1558–59, 34 USPQ2d 1210, 1215–16 (Fed.Cir.1995).

11. *See* L'Esperance v. Nishimoto, 18 USPQ2d 1534, 1539–40 (Bd.Pat.App. & Int'f 1991).

12. Seymour v. Osborne, 78 U.S. (11 Wall.) 516, 20 L.Ed. 33 (1870).

reference must not merely describe the results of a technical innovation, it must also provide information about how to build it. This so-called "enablement" requirement finds anticipation, and thus denies patentability, only where earlier efforts have truly enriched the technological arts. Consequently, such references as technological forecasts or works of speculative fiction cannot ordinarily serve as anticipations. Although the phrase "Beam me up, Scotty" has inspired millions of devoted Trekies, the *Star Trek* television series would be of little moment to the inventor of an operative personal teleportation device. Because Captain Kirk, Spock, and the other members of the *Enterprise* crew neglected to explain how their transporter actually worked in between their struggles with the Romulans, Gorn, and the dreaded Horta, the enablement requirement of anticipation has not been met.

That a reference must be enabling to anticipate a patent is entirely sensible as a policy matter. The patent system encourages the development of downstream products, not upstream ideas. If a prior art reference is merely theoretical or speculative, without explaining how the disclosed subject matter can actually be practically accomplished, then society has yet to gain an operable technology. Indeed, the patent incentive may well be needed to encourage someone to actually put an earlier theory into practice.

The *Titanium Metals* case also serves as a useful illustration of the enablement requirement. There, the prior art Russian article offered no instruction on how to synthesize the claimed titanium alloy. Nor did it disclose that the compound had special corrosion resistance properties. The court readily dismissed the argument of Titanium Metals that the Russian article was nonenabling, however. Expert testimony established that skilled metallurgists could readily generate the compound. Indeed, the patent application at issue itself presumed that skilled artisans could prepare the claimed alloy. Moreover, that the Russian article did not mention the corrosion resistance properties of the compound was also beside the point. According to the court, Congress had not authorized the patenting of an old alloy by one who had merely discovered some of its useful properties.

The holding of *Titanium Metals* may initially seem troubling. That a point on a graph in a foreign language publication could deny patentability may seem a poor outcome, particularly since the U.S. patent applicant had discovered a valuable property of the alloy. The applicant was not left without any patent position, however. Titanium Metals could freely seek process patent protection by claiming its invention as a "new use of a known ... composition of matter."[13] And had the field of titanium metallurgy

13. 35 U.S.C.A. § 101 (2000).

been less well understood, then the Russian article would assuredly have had to contain further teachings in order for it to anticipate the Titanium Metals application.

4.2.4 Inherency and Accidental Anticipation

Difficult policy questions and some fine distinctions arise in cases of accidental anticipations. Suppose the proprietor of a patented chemical compound brings an infringement suit against a competitor. The competitor would like to defend the suit by challenging the validity of the patent. If it can show that the patent was anticipated, it would be void for lack of novelty. So the accused infringer undertakes a painstaking search and eventually learns that a third party had unknowingly synthesized the patented chemical compound years before. Should the third party's unintended, unappreciated technology serve as an anticipation? Plainly the compound had been earlier invented in a technical sense. Yet this prior effort cannot be said to have enriched the public domain, for others were unable to profit from the original inventor's effort.

In 1880 the Supreme Court addressed this situation in *Tilghman v. Proctor*.[14] That case involved Tilghman's patented process for manufacturing fat acids and glycerine from fatty bodies by the action of water at a high temperature and pressure. The fat acids produced by the process could be used to manufacture candles and soap. The accused infringers alleged several different anticipations, ranging from a steam cylinder to a water barometer. During the operation of each of these earlier devices, fat acids had likely been generated as later claimed by Tilghman. But in each case this technical effect was incidental to other purposes and had not been understood by the earlier inventors. The Court held that these prior uses did not destroy the novelty of Tilghman's patent. "If the acids were accidentally and unwittingly produced, whilst the operators were in pursuit of other and different results, without exciting attention and without it even being known what was done or how it had been done, it would be absurd to say that this was an anticipation of Tilghman's discovery."

The decision of the Court of Customs and Patent Appeals in *In re Seaborg* applies these principles to a more advanced technology.[15] The applicant there claimed a new element, Americium, that had been generated via a nuclear reaction. The Patent Office rejected the claim based upon the prior art Fermi patent. The Fermi patent, which described the operation of several nuclear reactors, did not expressly disclose Americium. The Patent Office nonetheless con-

14. 102 U.S. 707, 26 L.Ed. 279 (1880).

15. 328 F.2d 996, 140 USPQ 662 (CCPA 1964).

cluded that the use of Fermi's process would have necessarily resulted in the production of Americium.

On appeal, Seaborg argued that no evidence actually demonstrated that the use of the Fermi reactors generated Americium. According to Seaborg, theoretical calculations revealed that at best, the Fermi reactors would have produced trace amounts of Americium that were diluted with many tons of intensely radioactive uranium fuel. Seaborg took the position that an unidentified, unidentifiable presence of Americium should not count as an anticipation. The CCPA agreed and overturned the Patent Office rejection. Judge Smith concluded that "the claimed product, if it was produced in the Fermi process, was produced in such minuscule amounts and under such conditions that its presence was undetectable."

Other cases of alleged "inherent anticipations" have reached different results under varying circumstances. The Federal Circuit decision in *Continental Can Co. v. Monsanto Co.*[16] is illustrative. The asserted patent claimed a plastic bottle with a sturdy, ribbed bottom structure. The claims of the patent required that the ribs of the bottom structure be hollow. The basis for the defendant's invalidity argument was the prior art Marcus patent, which also described a sturdy plastic bottle. On its face, the Marcus reference did not expressly state whether ribs on the bottom of the bottle were hollow or not. The defendant argued that because the ribs of the Marcus reference were formed by injection blow molding, they necessarily would have been hollow. The trial court granted summary judgment in favor of the defendant, holding the patent invalid as anticipated by the Marcus reference.

On appeal, the Federal Circuit vacated the summary judgment and remanded the matter for trial. Because a genuine dispute existed over whether the Marcus reference inherently disclosed hollow ribs or not, it held that it was inappropriate for the trial court to declare summarily that the patent was anticipated. The Federal Circuit offered some guidance for the trial court to follow, explaining that inherency must not be a matter of possibility or probability. Conjecture or the possibility of making slight modifications to known technology would not do. Instead, the subject matter asserted to be present via inherency must necessarily form part of the reference's technical disclosure. The court further instructed that inherency is to be judged from the perspective of a person of ordinary skill in the art.

This line of cases suggests that accidental technical effects will not defeat the novelty of a later patent where they are sporadic and unappreciated. Paradigmatic of such circumstances are technologies

16. 948 F.2d 1264 ,20 USPQ2d 1746 (Fed.Cir.1991).

momentarily formed through mistake or unusual conditions, for "[c]hance hits in the dark will not anticipate an invention."[17] However, where a technical effect was consistently obtained, detectable and reproducible, even though incidental to what was deliberately intended and not fully understood by the inventor, then it will be accorded anticipatory effect through the inherency doctrine.

§ 4.3 Prior Art for Novelty: The Statutory Bars

The presence of a single, enabling, fully anticipatory reference is a necessary, but insufficient condition to demonstrate that a claimed invention lacks novelty. That reference must also qualify as "prior art" as defined by § 102. Because they are fundamental to all patent systems, the so-called "statutory bar" provisions of § 102 are an appropriate starting point. As we have noted above, there are three paragraphs in this section that relate to the statutory bar: the public use, on sale, patented, and printed publication bars of § 102(b); the public abandonment bar of § 102(c); and the delayed U.S. filing bar of § 102(d). We can consider them in alphabetical order.

4.3.1 Introduction to § 102(b)

Of the three statutory bars, § 102(b) is by far the most frequently employed. Section 102(b) denies a patent where "the invention was patented or described in a printed publication in this or a foreign country or in public use or on sale in this country, more than one year prior to the date of the application for patent in the United States." The statute focuses attention on the so-called "critical date," defined as one year before the date the patent application was filed. Section 102(b) bars patentability where, before the critical date, the invention was in public use or on sale in the United States; or either patented or described in a printed publication anywhere in the world.

Section 102(b) acts in the nature of a statute of limitation. It can be triggered either by activities performed by the patent applicant himself, or by activities performed by others. Thus, once the inventor publishes an article describing his invention, or otherwise engage in the other activity specified by § 102(b), he must file a patent application at the PTO within one year or forfeit his U.S. patent rights. In addition, the inventor must also be concerned with the activities of others. Should another individual have also come up with the same invention, and performed acts specified by § 102(b) prior to the critical date, then the statutory bar is also triggered.

17. United Chromium, Inc. v. International Silver Co., 60 F.2d 913, 917 (2d Cir.1932).

The Federal Circuit has identified § 102(b) as serving the following purposes:

> First, there is a policy against removing inventions from the public which the public has justifiably come to believe are freely available to all as a consequence of prolonged sales activity. Next, there is a policy favoring prompt and widespread disclosure of new inventions to the public. The inventor is forced to file promptly or risk possible forfeiture of his [patent] rights due to prior sales. A third policy is to prevent the inventor from commercially exploiting the exclusivity of his invention substantially beyond the statutorily authorized [20–year] period. The on-sale bar forces the inventor to choose between seeking patent protection promptly following sales activity or taking his chances with his competitors without the benefit of patent protection. The fourth and final identifiable policy is to give the inventor a reasonable amount of time following sales activity (set by statute as 1 year) to determine whether a patent is a worthwhile investment. This benefits the public because it tends to minimize the filing of [patent applications concerning inventions] of only marginal public interest.[1]

Unhappily, the major patent statutes of the world diverge with regard to the grace period, with the U.S. approach being the most lenient or generous to the procrastinating inventor. Indeed, the American approach stands in marked contrast to the "absolute novelty" provisions of the European Patent Convention. Under the European regime, disclosure of an invention even one day before the filing date bars patentability.[2] The Japanese system lies in between, providing for a six-month grace period that applies only to the inventor's own activities.[3] Under the Japanese patent law, then, disclosure by a third party at any time prior to the filing date acts as a bar. Thus, while pre-filing date activities may not prejudice the ability of an inventor to get a U.S. patent under § 102(b), so long as they are not before the "critical date," they may seriously compromise the possibility of obtaining patents abroad—a reality that counsels in favor of prompt filing of patent applications.

Opinion differs as to the wisdom of a grace period. Proponents of the grace period urge that because inventors often labor under the "publish or perish" principle, they face pressure to publish

§ 4.3

1. General Electric v. United States, 654 F.2d 55, 61–64, 211 USPQ 867, 873–75 (Ct.Cl.1981) (en banc).

2. Convention on the Grant of European Patents, Oct. 5, 1973, Art. 54 (2), 13 I.L.M. 286 (1974).

3. *See* William LaMarca, *Reevaluating the Geographical Limitation of 35 U.S.C.A. § 102(b)*, 22 Univ. Dayton L. Rev. 25, 43–44 (1996).

their results promptly—often long before a patent application can be drafted and filed. Thus, a grace period comports with the norms of the scientific community and promotes a more prompt disclosure of inventions. It further avoids the prospect of forfeiture, where inventors have inadvertently disclosed their inventions to the public shortly before a patent application was filed. Finally, a grace period is said to benefit inventions that require testing in a "real world" environment. In contrast, supporters of the European absolute novelty regime have argued that a grace period increases legal uncertainties. They suggest that an inventor's ability to delay the filing of a patent application until after a full year of commercial activity has elapsed is unjustified, for it slows the inventor's entry into the patent system. According to the supporters of an "absolute novelty" regime, education on the existing requirements to obtain a patent presents the most effective way of avoiding forfeitures.[4]

Although views vary on the propriety of a grace period, most would admit that the choice of a one-year period within § 102(b) is an arbitrary one. That there is nothing inviolate about one year is demonstrated by that fact that prior to 1939, the grace period under U.S. law was two years. And as noted, the Japanese patent statute, which provides a grace period solely for cases of pre-filing use by the patent applicant, is currently set at six months. At least we can be grateful for the ease of calculation that the statute presently provides.

Turning to the details, § 102(b) itemizes four kinds of events that will trigger the bar, provided they take place before the critical date. Two of those deal with events that take place only "in this country"—namely that the invention was either "in public use" or "on sale" here. The other two events—description of the invention in a patent, or in a printed publication—can trigger bar if they have taken place "in this or a foreign country." Also bear in mind the requirement of strict identity we have discussed above. The thing that is "on sale" in the United States, or the thing that is described in a French printed publication, must be exactly identical to the applicant's proposed invention in order to raise an obstacle to patentability. Because each of the four anticipatory events listed in § 102(b) has been the subject of great judicial scrutiny, the various terms have taken on detailed, and somewhat counterintuitive meanings. It is thus necessary to explore them closely, and one by one.

4. *Compare* Jan E.M. Galama, *Expert Opinion on the Case For and Against the Introduction of a Grace Period in the European Patent Law* (April 30, 2000), *with* Joseph Straus, *Expert Opinion on the Introduction of a Grace Period in the European Patent Law* (May 8, 2000).

4.3.2 "Public Use" Under § 102(b)

One event that will raise a statutory bar is "public use" of the technology in question by either the patent applicant or anyone else, within the United States more than one year prior to the date of the application. The concept of "public use" owes its origins to the Supreme Court's 1829 opinion in *Pennock v. Dialogue*.[5] The plaintiff's patent was for a method for manufacturing a type of rubber hose useful for conveying air and fluids. The invention had been built by 1811, but the inventor did not file a patent application until seven years later. In the meantime, the inventor had licensed a third party to market the hose and enjoyed considerable sales. The inventor later asserted his patent against a competitor. The defendant urged that the patent should be struck down based upon section 1 of the Patent Act of 1793, which provided that an invention must be one that was "not known or used before the application" to be patentable.

Writing for the Supreme Court, Justice Story affirmed a judgment for the defendant. Story reasoned that the words "not known or used before the application" did not refer to knowledge or use by inventors themselves. Because inventors must know of their own work product, a literal interpretation of section 1 would lead to a rejection of every patent application. In addition, Story reasoned, Congress could not have meant to deny patents where the inventor merely employed others to assist in the construction or use of the invention, or in cases where the invention had been used without the inventor's consent. Instead, the Court held that the "true meaning" of the statute was to deny patents to inventions "known or used by the public before the application." As Justice Story put it, if the inventor "shall put [the invention] into public use, or sell it for public use before he applies for a patent, ... this should further [a] bar to his claim."

Subsequent patent statutes codified the concept of "public use" pioneered in *Pennock v. Dialogue*. The courts have interpreted the term broadly, holding that even a limited use that results in negligible public exposure will trigger the "public use" bar. Such activities are known as "non-informing uses" in patent parlance. *Egbert v. Lippmann*,[6] long the target of feeble classroom wit, well illustrates this point. There, a Samuel H. Barnes invented an improved corset spring (or "steel") after hearing complaints from a young lady friend, Frances Lee, as well as a Miss Cugier. Samuel gave one set to Frances in 1855 and another to her in 1858. Frances wore the springs within some of her corsets for a "long time," even inserting them into different corsets when the original garment wore out. Samuel and Frances later "intermarried." Sometime in 1863, a Mr. Sturgis visited the couple and received an explanation

5. 27 U.S. 1, 7 L.Ed. 327 (1829).

6. 104 U.S. 333, 26 L.Ed. 755 (1881).

of the working of the corset springs from Frances, suggesting a curious sort of dinner table conversation at the Barnes home. At all events, a patent application was finally filed in 1866 and in due course a patent issued. After Samuel passed away and Frances remarried, she brought a patent infringement suit against another vendor of corset springs. Among the defenses raised by the alleged infringer was that the Barnes corset spring was in public use before the critical date, and that the patent was thus invalid.

The Supreme Court held that Frances' employment of the corset springs was a "public use" in the sense of the patent law. The Court judged that the "public use" standard could be satisfied by the inventor's gift of a single patented article to one person. Noting that "some inventions are by their very character only capable of being used where they cannot be seen or observed by the public eye," the Court further concluded that "if its inventor sells a machine of which his invention forms a part, and allows it to be used without restriction of any kind, the use is a public one." Accordingly, the patent-at-suit was held invalid.

The dissenting opinion by Justice Miller observed that the majority's holding seemed to remove the term "public" from the statute: "If the little steep spring inserted in a single pair of corsets, and used by only one woman, covered by her outer-clothing, and in a position always withheld from public observation, is a public use of that piece of steel, I am at a loss to know the line between a public and a private use." Although the dissent's reading of the statute initially seems persuasive, modern technologies increasingly justify the holding of the majority. Like the corset springs of *Egbert v. Lippmann*, inventions in disciplines ranging from biotechnology to electronics often exhibit a non-informing character. For example, members of the public remain unable to discern the inner workings of new electronic circuitry even after listening to the radio of which those circuits form a part. A contrary holding in *Egbert* would have rendered the public use provisions of § 102(b) substantially irrelevant to inventors within such technical fields, and restricted the scope of the statute to relatively simple mechanical inventions that are ordinarily employed in plain view of the user. A better ground for dissent may have been the unwillingness of the seemingly scandalized Court, which took pains to note that Samuel "slept on his rights for seven years," to imply a relationship of confidentiality between Samuel and Frances. A more modern view might be that Frances was not really a member of the "public" at all, but a colleague and inventive (as well as romantic) collaborator of Samuel Barnes.

The treatment of prior, secret uses of an invention has also lead to some strained interpretations of the term "public use." Although the text of § 102(b) does not differentiate between patent applicants and third parties, the courts have nonetheless drawn distinctions between these two categories of actors when determining the prior art effect of secret uses. In particular, the courts have held that secret activity comprises a "public use" within the meaning of § 102(b) when performed by the patent applicant. However, the identical use, when performed by a third party, will not serve as prior art against an unrelated applicant. In so doing, the courts have sought to balance two of the chief policies undergirding § 102, preservation of the public domain and maintenance of the statutory patent term.

The Federal Circuit's early opinion in *Gore v. Garlock*[7] exemplifies third party secret use cases. Gore obtained a patent including process claims for quickly stretching crystalline, unsintered polytetrafluroethylene (commonly known under the trademark "Teflon"). During later enforcement litigation, a competitor learned that a John Cropper, living in New Zealand, had earlier invented the same technology. Prior to the critical date, Cropper both sent a letter describing the invention to a Massachusetts company, and sold his machine to Budd. Budd employees were told to maintain the Cropper machine in confidence, and at some later point Budd practiced the process.

If the activities of Budd and Cropper were considered "public use" of the invention, they would have rendered the patent invalid because they occurred before the critical date. However, the Federal Circuit described the Budd and Cropper commercializations as secret and not a "public use" under § 102(b). Chief Judge Markey noted that if Budd had sold anything, it was stretched Teflon, and not the process used in producing it. Further, Budd's use of the machine did not enrich the public domain, because an observer of the machine could not determine such parameters as the stretching speed or traits of the stretched material. The court concluded that "[a]s between a prior inventor who benefits from a process by selling its product but suppresses, conceals, or otherwise keeps the process from the public, and a later inventor who promptly files a patent application from which the public will gain a disclosure of the process, the law favors the latter."[8]

Judge Learned Hand's decision in *Metallizing Engineering Co. v. Kenyon Bearing & Auto Parts*,[9] demonstrates that a court will reach a different holding where the secret use is made by the applicant himself. The technology there concerned a process for

7. W.L. Gore & Associates v. Garlock, Inc., 721 F.2d 1540, 220 USPQ 303 (Fed.Cir.1983), *cert. denied*, 469 U.S. 851, 105 S.Ct. 172, 83 L.Ed.2d 107 (1984).

8. 721 F.2d at 1550, 220 USPQ at 310.

9. 153 F.2d 516, 68 USPQ 54 (2d Cir.), *cert. denied*, 328 U.S. 840, 66 S.Ct. 1016, 90 L.Ed. 1615 (1946).

reconstructing machine parts known as "metallizing." The inventor, Meduna, maintained the process as a trade secret. Only the reconditioned parts could be viewed by the public, for Meduna kept the process itself under lock and key. He finally filed a patent application on August 6, 1942, but had been practicing the process before the critical date. During a subsequent patent infringement suit brought by Meduna, the district court held that Meduna's concealed process did not comprise a "public use" within the statute.

Following an appeal, the Second Circuit panel reversed the trial court. Judge Hand identified a distinction in secret use cases between "(1) [t]he effect upon his right to a patent of the inventor's competitive exploitation of his machine or of his process" and "(2) the contribution which a prior use by another person makes to the art."[10] Judge Hand agreed that in the second set of circumstances, a secret use by a third party did not constitute a "public use" under the predecessor statute to § 102(b), because it did not enrich the public's level of technical knowledge. Citing his earlier opinion in *Gillman v. Stern*, Judge Hand concluded that the issue in third party cases "was whether a prior use which did not disclose the invention to the art was within the statute, and it is well settled that it is not."[11]

Judge Hand went on to explain, however, that a different policy concern arose in the event of secret uses by the inventor. He noted that secret uses allow inventors to delay filing a patent application beyond the grace period and thus "extend the period of monopoly."[12] Concerning an inventor who secretly exploited his technology for a time longer than the grace period, Hand concluded that if "he goes beyond that period of probation, he forfeits his right regardless of how little the public may have learned about the invention."[13]

Hand's observations bear further discussion. The statute currently limits the patent term to twenty years from the date a patent application is filed at the PTO. Section 102(b) also offers inventors the privilege of a one-year grace period in which to put the invention to public use before filing that application. The maximum period from the initial commercialization to expiration of an associated patent, then, is ordinarily twenty-one years. An inventor who practiced a technology as a trade secret for many years before filing an application could disrupt this scheme, however, in effect delaying the patent expiration date. Declaring the inventor's own secret use to be a "public use" within § 102(b) prevents this abuse. In

10. 153 F.2d at 520, 68 USPQ at 58.

11. 153 F.2d at 519, 68 USPQ at 58.

12. 153 F.2d at 520, 68 USPQ at 58.

13. *Id.*

effect this scheme forces the inventor to choose between patent law and trade secret law as the desired legal regime to protect the commercially operable invention.[14] Yet because this policy concern is not present when the secret commercial use was not made by the inventor, the more natural reading of the term "public use" should prevail in third party cases like *Gore v. Garlock*.

To summarize, then, if the patent applicant or owner makes a use that is not merely non-informing but entirely secret, those activities will nonetheless qualify as a "public use" within the meaning of § 102(b). For others, however, while a non-informing use may constitute a "public use," a secret use does not. As the dividing line between a non-informing and secret use is not always a sharp one, third party use cases often depend on the manner in which the use is characterized.

Baxter International v. COBE Laboratories, Inc. provides an example of this situation.[15] Baxter sued COBE for infringement of a patent relating to a sealless centrifuge useful for separating blood into its components. In turn, COBE asserted that the Baxter patent was invalid because the centrifuge had been in "public use" prior to the critical date. More specifically, a Dr. Suaudeau had used an identical centrifuge while working at the National Institutes of Health (NIH) more than a year before the application that lead to the Baxter patent was filed.

The Federal Circuit majority held that Suaudeau's earlier use sufficed to invalidate the Baxter patent. Judge Lourie observed that Suaudeau's laboratory was located in a public building on the NIH campus, that co-workers and other visitors were free to observe the centrifuge, and that Suaudeau had also made no effort to maintain the centrifuge in confidence. As a result, the § 102(b) "public use" bar applied.

Judge Newman responded with a vigorous dissent. In her view, Suaudeau's laboratory work amounted to a secret third-party use that should not raise a § 102(b) bar. Judge Newman characterized Suaudeau's laboratory use as internal and private, and therefore difficult even for the most diligent prior art searcher to uncover. The result of the holding, the dissent predicted, was a "perpetual cloud on any issued patent" due to the existence of "secret prior art."

The dissenting decision makes many valid points. However, uses such as Suaudeau's are likely no more difficult for members of the innovative community to determine than other sources that unquestionably constitute prior art. As we shall soon learn, even a single text, written in an obscure language and available only in an

14. For more on trade secrets, *see infra* Chapter 13.

15. 88 F.3d 1054, 39 USPQ2d 1437 (Fed. Cir. 1996).

isolated library overseas, may trigger the "printed publication" bar of § 102(b).[16] The holding of *Baxter v. COBE* also serves one of the purposes of § 102(b), the encouragement of the prompt filing of patent applications. Aware that the nonsecret but obscure uses may defeat patentability, inventors should be encouraged to turn to the PTO in a timely fashion.

4.3.3 "On Sale" Under § 102(b)

Another patent-defeating event specified by § 102(b) is that the invention was placed "on sale" in the United States by anyone, more than one year before the filing of the patent application. This event is distinct from "public use," although judicial opinions sometimes do not carefully distinguish between the two events. The statutory language calls for the invention merely to be "on sale," not necessarily sold. Consequently even a single offer to sell may suffice to bar patentability.[17] The on-sale bar may be triggered by anyone,[18] so long as the sales activities occur in the United States.

The on-sale bar may be triggered even where the parties to the sale were unaware that the invention was the subject of a commercial transaction. The Federal Circuit's 1999 decision in *Abbott Laboratories v. Geneva Pharmaceuticals,*[19] is illustrative. In that case, brand-name drug manufacturer Abbott sued Geneva and two other generic drug companies for infringement of U.S. Patent No. 5,504,207. The '207 patent concerned a chemical compound known as terazosin hydrochloride, useful in the treatment of prostate disease and high blood pressure. Terazosin hydrochloride exists in four anhydrous crystalline forms,[20] and claim 4 of the '207 patent specifically claimed the Form IV anhydrate. As a challenge to the validity of Abbott's patent under § 102(b), Geneva pointed to the activities of Byron Chemical Company, a firm that was not involved in the lawsuit. Byron had made at least three sales of Form IV terazosin hydorchloride in the United States more than one year before the filing date of the '207 patent.

At first glance, the fact that a third party had completed sales of the claimed invention in the United States prior to the critical date would call for a straightforward application of the § 102(b) bar. Patentee Abbott offered an interesting argument, however. It seems that prior to the litigation, nobody actually knew that Byron had sold the particular crystalline form of terazosin hydrochloride

16. *See infra* § 4.3.5.2.

17. Intel Corp. v. United States Int'l Trade Comm'n, 946 F.2d 821, 20 USPQ2d 1161 (Fed.Cir.1991).

18. J.A. LaPorte, Inc. v. Norfolk Dredging Co., 787 F.2d 1577 , 299 USPQ 435 (Fed.Cir.1986).

19. 182 F.3d 1315, 51 USPQ2d 1307 (Fed. Cir. 1999).

20. An "anhydrous" crystal is one that does not have any water.

that was later claimed in the '207 patent. The sales transactions spoke generically to anhydrous terazosin hydrochloride, without specifying that the Form IV anhydrate crystal had been sold. Only testing of these samples, performed many years later for purposes of the '207 patent litigation, revealed that the patented compound had been on sale some years before the patent was sought. Under these facts, Abbott urged that the on-sale bar of § 102(b) should not apply. According to Abbott, because the parties were wholly ignorant of the true nature of the compounds they sold, the compound should not be considered "on sale" within the meaning of the Patent Act.

The district court rejected Abbott's argument, and on appeal the Federal Circuit affirmed. According to Judge Lourie, offers for sale need not identify all the characteristics of an invention to trigger the on-sale bar. Nor do the parties to the transaction need to recognize the significance of all of these characteristics. If the product offered for sale inherently possesses all the limitations of the claims, then the on-sale bar applies.

Although § 102(b) speaks of the "invention" being on sale in the United States, the courts have interpreted the statute to require sales activity with respect to a physical embodiment of the invention, as compared to more abstract patent rights in the invention.[21] Thus, an offer to license patent rights or the transfer of patent rights from an employee to an employer does not trigger the bar. The on-sale bar would apply to sales activity involving commercial embodiments of the invention, however.

The Federal Circuit has recognized a notable exception to the on-sale bar. The on-sale bar must involve separate and unrelated parties. Where the parties are related, the courts may disregard the sale provided that "the seller so controls the purchaser that the invention remains out of the public's hands."[22] Factors pertinent to determining whether the on-sale bar applies to transactions between related parties include whether there was a need for testing by other than the patentee; the amount of control exercised; the stage of development of the invention; whether payments were made and the basis thereof; whether confidentiality was required; and whether technological changes were made.[23]

A recurring issue under § 102(b) has been whether sales activity may trigger the on-sale bar where the invention has not yet been physically constructed. Some opinions, such as *Timely Products*

21. Moleculon Research Corp. v. CBS, Inc., 793 F.2d 1261, 229 USPQ 805 (Fed.Cir.1986).

22. Ferag AG v. Quipp Inc., 45 F.3d 1562, 33 USPQ2d 1512 (Fed.Cir.), *cert. denied*, 516 U.S. 816, 116 S.Ct. 71, 133 L.Ed.2d 31 (1995).

23. Continental Can Co. v. Monsanto Co., 948 F.2d 1264, 20 USPQ2d 1746 (Fed.Cir.1991).

Corp. v. Arron,[24] held or assumed that the on-sale bar was inapplicable where the invention was not ready "on hand" at the time of sale. Others, most notably the controversial opinion in *UMC Electronics Co. v. United States*,[25] concluded that there was no strict requirement that the invention be "reduced to practice" for the on-sale bar to apply. A choice between these competing positions requires a weighing of the common sense view that something cannot be sold if it has not yet been constructed; an awareness of everyday commercial practices, such as the "vaporware" phenomenon in the software industry;[26] and the desire to provide inventors with a definite standard for determining when they must file a patent application.

The recent Supreme Court opinion in *Pfaff v. Wells Electronics*[27] resolved the "reduction to practice" issue, as it relates to the on-sale bar of § 102(b). Pfaff was the named inventor on a patent directed towards a computer chip socket. Prior to the critical date, Pfaff presented his inventive concept to representatives of Texas Instruments. Although Pfaff had not yet constructed even a single prototype, the Texas Instruments representatives nonetheless placed a large purchase order for the sockets. A third party manufacturer ultimately produced a working embodiment of the invention after the critical date. Following the issuance of the chip socket patent, Pfaff brought suit against a competitor, which argued that the claims were invalid due to the on-sale bar.

The Court agreed with the defendant that the on-sale bar applied under the facts. Justice Stevens set forth a two-part test to determine whether an invention was "on sale" within the meaning of § 102(b). "First, the product must be the subject of a commercial offer for sale." The Court believed that this test satisfied the inventive community's desire for certainty, because inventors could "both understand and control the timing of the first commercial marketing of the invention." Here, Pfaff had accepted the Texas Instruments purchase order before the critical date.

The second part of the test was that "the invention must be ready for patenting." The Court recognized at least two ways to satisfy this condition. The invention may have been physically constructed: an "actual reduction to practice" in the language of the patent law. Alternatively, "drawings or other descriptions of

24. 523 F.2d 288, 187 USPQ 257 (2d Cir.1975).

25. 816 F.2d 647, 2 USPQ2d 1465 (Fed.Cir.1987), *cert. denied*, 484 U.S. 1025, 108 S.Ct. 748, 98 L.Ed.2d 761 (1988).

26. Vaporware has been defined as a "new computer hardware or software product that is not ready for market at the time it is announced to the public by the producer." J. Thomas McCarthy, *Desk Encyclopedia of Intellectual Property* (2d ed. 1995).

27. 525 U.S. 55, 119 S.Ct. 304, 142 L.Ed.2d 261 (1998), *reh'g denied*, 525 U.S. 1094, 119 S.Ct. 854, 142 L.Ed.2d 707 (1999).

the invention sufficiently detailed to enable a person skilled in the art to practice the invention" would also suffice. Pfaff's delivery of detailed engineering specifications and diagrams to the manufacturer prior to the critical date demonstrated that he had fulfilled this second prong.

The Supreme Court hoped that its *Pfaff* standard would eliminate the uncertainties of the Federal Circuit's earlier "all the facts and circumstances" approach. Subsequent treatment of the *Pfaff* rule suggests, however, that when jurists announce a blunt rule, they should fully consider its consequences. Interestingly, while the facts of *Pfaff* provided the Court ample opportunity to consider the second part of the test, there was little need to discuss the first.[28] In the circumstances presented to the Supreme Court, Pfaff had sold sockets before he fabricated even a single prototype of his invention, not to mention tested them to see whether they were functional or practical. Pfaff's remarkable technical abilities, as well as the confidence of his contracting partner, gave the Court ample opportunity to discuss whether an invention was "ready for patenting" when it had yet to advance beyond a sketch pad.

The facts of *Pfaff* provided far less fertile ground for discussing the new requirement that the product must be the subject of a commercial offer for sale. Because there was no question that Pfaff had accepted a purchase order prior to the critical date the Supreme Court was able to give the first prong of its test short shrift and quickly move to the "ready for patenting" issue. The *Pfaff* decision is notable for its absence of discussion of conflicting Federal Circuit case law that suggested the opposite holding concerning the first half of the test: that commercial activity not rising to the level of a formal offer for sale could nonetheless trigger the on-sale bar.[29]

Subsequent decisions have suggested that *Pfaff's* requirement of a commercial offer for sale has fallen prone to a common failing of bright-line rules: promoting strategic behavior that extends just to the limit of the rule. In the context of the on-sale bar, the *Pfaff* holding seems to encourage inventors to skirt the policies of the on-sale bar by engaging in any number of activities that fall just short of a formal offer for sale. For example, in one subsequent case, the inventor of an integrated circuit had, prior to the critical date, distributed advertisements, data sheets and promotional information to customers, and had also received requests from sales repre-

28. *See* Linear Tech. Corp. v. Micrel Inc., 275 F.3d 1040, 1048, 61 USPQ2d 1225, 1229 (Fed. Cir. 2001).

29. *See, e.g.*, RCA Corp. v. Data Gen. Corp., 887 F.2d 1056, 1062, 12 USPQ2d 1449, 1454 (Fed. Cir. 1989) (noting that the requirement of a definite offer does not mandate "a definite offer in the contract sense," but merely excludes "indefinite or nebulous discussions about a possible sale").

sentatives for product samples.[30] The Federal Circuit held these activities did not trigger the on-sale bar because none of them constituted an offer for sale. Surely these activities implicated the policies underlying the on-sale bar, in particular concern for manipulation of the patent term and the reliance interest of competitors. Simple as the *Pfaff* rule is, by failing to probe into the broader circumstances under which an invention can be injected into the public domain, it may give inadequate weight to some of the innovation policies that should inform a sound patent law.

4.3.4 "In this Country"

Under § 102(b), the fact that an invention is in "public use" or "on sale" is significant only if those events occur "in this country." The policy behind this exclusion appears to be based on the judgment that information about uses and offers for sales that take place overseas would be very difficult for U.S. inventors to obtain. Notably, the "in this country" limitation does not apply to patents and printed publications. As a result, U.S. inventors are charged with knowledge of documentary information no matter where that information is available.

Commentators have questioned the wisdom of maintaining a geographical distinction between the various provisions of § 102(b).[31] Although the likely motivation for this statutory language was the perceived difficulty of obtaining evidence of foreign activity, modern conveniences of communication and transportation mitigate against this concern. More recently drafted patent statutes, most notably the European Patent Convention, do not restrict the prior art territorially. Additionally, the "in this country" limitation of § 102 also appears as a rare instance of discrimination against those members of the technological community based in the United States. Activity that would not prejudice foreign actors acting in their home markets may deleteriously impact U.S. inventors, a seemingly unsound result as a matter of U.S. patent policy.

The authors of one of the more troubling decisions on point, *Ex parte Thomson*,[32] seem to have been aware of these criticisms of the geographical distinctions within the Patent Act, for they appear to have ignored the "in this country" language of § 102 altogether. In *Thomson*, the PTO Board of Appeals affirmed the rejection of a claimed cotton cultivar[33] known as Siokra under the "printed

30. *See* Linear Tech. Corp. v. Micrel Inc., 275 F.3d 1040, 1044, 61 USPQ2d 1225, 1226–27 (Fed. Cir. 2001).

31. President's Commission on the Patent System, To Promote the Progress of ... Useful Arts in an Age of Exploding Technology 2, 3 (1966).

32. 24 U.S.P.Q.2d 1618 (PTO BPAI 1992).

33. A "cultivar" is a variety of a plant developed from a natural species and maintained through cultivation.

publication" bar of § 102(b). The Board cited three technical documents, each published more than one year before the filing date of the rejected application. According to the Board, these disclosures suggested to a skilled cotton grower to purchase Siokra seeds and use conventional breeding techniques to obtain the claimed cultivar.

The difficulty with the Board's reasoning is that a mere written description of a plant, by itself, does not allow others to grow that precise plant. An actual sample of the plant is needed to reproduce it. The "printed publication" bar of § 102(b) should not have applied, therefore, because the cited documents failed to provide enabling disclosures.[34] The "public use" bar also would not have applied, for no evidence of record indicated that Siokra had ever actually been grown in the United States. The documented use of the plant actually appears to have been confined to Australia—which plainly is not "in this country" within the meaning of § 102(b). As a result, even if the *Thompson* decision implemented the sound policy of denying a patent to an invention that was readily available to interested parties in the United States prior to the critical date, it appears to have been wrongly decided in view of the actual language of the U.S. Patent Act.

4.3.5 Experimental Use

The concept of experimental use further refines the meaning of the statutory term "public use" in § 102(b). If a use is judged as experimental, then it is not a "public use" within the meaning of § 102(b). The experimental use doctrine also appears to apply to inventions placed "on sale" prior to the critical date, although far less precedent addresses this situation.

The doctrine of experimental use essentially provides inventors with additional "tinker time" beyond the one-year grace period. In deciding experimental use cases, courts must balance two competing policies. The first, a principal focus of § 102(b), is to allow inventors sufficient time to determine whether an invention is suitable for its intended purposes and worth the bother of patenting. The second is a concern for the integrity of the statutory patent term. Overbroad application of the experimental use doctrine would allow an inventor to delay filing a patent application and, consequentially, delay the date of patent expiration.

The 1877 Supreme Court opinion in *City of Elizabeth v. American Nicholson Pavement Co.*[35] remains the most significant experimental use case. There, Nicholson invented an improved wooden pavement. In 1848, Nicholson installed the pavement on a portion

34. *See supra* § 4.2.2.

35. 97 U.S. 126, 24 L.Ed. 1000 (1877).

of a toll road owned by his company. The road was open to the public and subject to continuous use through 1854, when Nicholson filed a patent application. During this time, Nicholson regularly inspected the pavement to determine its durability under various traffic and weather conditions. Nicholson later brought suit against the city of Elizabeth, New Jersey, which had laid allegedly infringing pavement.

The Court decided that because Nicholson's use was experimental in nature, it was not a "public use" within the meaning of the predecessor statute to § 102(b). The Court reasoned that the public interest supported the filing of applications on "perfect and properly tested" inventions, as compared to less refined technologies. Where an inventor has made "a bona fide effort to bring his invention to perfection, or to ascertain whether it will answer the purpose intended," the Court held that the public use bar should not apply.

City of Elizabeth may be subjected to ready criticism. One wonders why the statutory grace period did not suffice for Nicholson's testing purposes, particularly since he did not appear to make a single change to the pavement during a seven-year period. Moreover, testing in a laboratory or otherwise more secluded environment—say, a factory grounds where the employees could have been subjected to a confidentiality agreement—might have fulfilled Nicholson's purposes. If the Court was so moved by Nicholson's desire to build a long-lasting pavement, then seemingly every patent applicant would do well to stress that durability was among the aims of the invention. Perhaps the weakness of the concept of a procrustean grace period of varying length for each patent applicant has lead to only infrequent findings of experimental use in modern patent cases.

More recently, the precedent of the Federal Circuit has called for an analysis of the totality of the circumstances to determine whether the inventor has engaged in an experimental use. Among the numerous indicia of experimentation identified by the court are:

(1) the number of prototypes and duration of testing;

(2) the attention to records or reports during the testing;

(3) the existence of a confidentiality arrangement;

(4) the receipt of any commercial advantage by the patentee;

(5) the inventor's control over the testing;

(6) the tailoring of the sort of testing with respect to the specific features of the invention; and

(7) whether the invention allowed the testing to be conducted without public access, through concealment of the technology or other means.[36]

The Federal Circuit applied these seven factors in *Lough v. Brunswick Corp.*[37] The plaintiff in that case, boat repairman Steven Lough, worked at a Florida marina. Observing a consistent corrosion problem with upper seal assemblies used in marine motors, in 1986 he invented an improved device. Lough then filed a patent application on June 8, 1988, and was granted a patent on July 18,1989. Lough subsequently brought an infringement suit against Brunswick. A jury awarded Lough damages of $1.5 million after concluding that Lough's invention was not in "public use" prior to the critical date of June 8, 1987.

Following an appeal, the Federal Circuit reversed. The Court of Appeals initially observed that neither party contested the fact that the patented invention had been publicly accessible prior to the critical date. It seems that Lough had constructed six usable prototypes of the invention in the spring of 1986. He then installed prototypes on his own boat, as well as the boat of his employer and a marina customer, and gave the other prototypes to friends for installation on their own boats. The central issue in the case, then, was whether these uses were experimental in nature. The *Lough* panel concluded that they were not. The Federal Circuit observed that Lough had neither asked for nor received any comments about the operability of the prototypes; kept no records of his supposed testing; did not inspect the seal assemblies after they had been installed by others; and ultimately failed to maintain any supervision or control over the seals during the alleged testing. Because Lough could not rely upon the experimental use doctrine, his patent was held invalid.

The Federal Circuit has also stressed that any putative experimentation must go towards the technical features of the invention.[38] Testing to predict whether the invention will enjoy marketplace success does not constitute experimental use within the meaning of § 102(b). One early Federal Circuit case, *In re Smith*,[39] considered a test in which 76 consumers were given samples of "Carpet Fresh" rug deodorizer. Following consumer use of "Carpet Fresh" in their homes, the consumers were questioned about their reactions to the product. The Federal Circuit held that this test constituted a "public use" and declined to apply the experimental

36. Lough v. Brunswick, 86 F.3d 1113, 39 USPQ2d 1100 (Fed.Cir.1996), *reh'g denied*, 103 F.3d 1517 (Fed.Cir. 1997).

37. 86 F.3d 1113, 40 USPQ2d 1100 (Fed. Cir. 1996).

38. *See* In re Smith, 714 F.2d 1127, 218 USPQ 976 (Fed.Cir.1983).

39. 714 F.2d 1127, 218 USPQ 976 (Fed. Cir. 1983).

use doctrine. According to the court, the dominant purpose of the test was to determine whether potential consumers would buy "Carpet Fresh" and how much they would be willing to pay, rather than to assess the product's technological aspects. The *Smith* decision suggests that consumer marketing tests will ordinarily not qualify as experimental uses that negate the "public use" bar of § 102(b).

4.3.6 Patents and Printed Publications

Section 102(b) denies patentability to inventions that have been "patented" or described in a "printed publication" before the critical date anywhere in the world. As with the terms "public use" and "on sale," each of these terms has been subjected to a detailed construction by the courts and PTO. An overview of this interpretative project is necessary to achieve a proper understanding of § 102(b). Review of these terms is appropriate for a second reason. Several of these terms also appear in other parts of § 102, in particular paragraphs (a), (d) and (g). Because the courts have generally interpreted these terms consistently within § 102, their introduction here will be of appreciable assistance in future reading.

4.3.6.1 "Patented"

An invention that has been "patented" one year before the date of filing under § 102(b) will bar a later U.S. application. Issues over the term "patented" ordinarily arise with respect to patents granted abroad. Global legal regimes yield an exotic array of intellectual property rights that can differ significantly from familiar domestic patents. The courts have been left to determine which of these rights constitutes a "patent" within the terms of § 102.

The Federal Circuit opinion in *In re Carlson* is illustrative.[40] The PTO became aware of several pieces of prior art pertinent to Carlson's claimed dual compartment bottle. One of them was a so-called Geschmacksmuster (GM), a German design registration. Registration of the GM was effective at the time it was deposited at a local government office in Germany. Lists of registered designs were published shortly thereafter in the German Federal Gazette. The Gazette provided a general description of the design, the class of articles deposited, identifying numbers of the deposited designs, the name and location of the registrant, the date and time of registration, and the city location of the registered design.

Following PTO rejection of the claim of his design patent based in part upon the GM, Carlson appealed to the Federal Circuit. Carlson proposed that under § 102 "the embodiment of foreign

40. 983 F.2d 1032, 25 USPQ2d 1207 (Fed.Cir.1992).

protection must take a form that fully discloses the nature of the protected design in a medium of communication capable of being widely disseminated." Arguing that the Gazette entry did not fulfill this standard, Carlson urged that the GM could not be considered "patented" within the meaning of § 102(a).

Writing for a three-judge panel, Judge Clevenger upheld the PTO rejection. The court reasoned that the Gazette entry sufficed to alert readers that a multiple bottle design had been registered. An interested reader could then proceed to the appropriate German office to obtain the actual design, either in person or through an agent. Although cognizant of the difficulties entailed for a U.S. applicant to scrutinize a particular GM, the court concluded that this burden was imposed by statute.

As suggested by *Carlson*, a second complexity with regard to foreign rights is the determination of the precise date an invention has been "patented." In the United States this analysis is straightforward. U.S. patents are granted on the same day that notice of their issuance is published in the PTO Official Gazette. This single date also marks the time when the exclusive rights associated with the patent become effective, and also the point at which interested members of the public may obtain a complete copy of the patent instrument and the prosecution history. In foreign patent systems these events may occur on different dates. Where some occur more than one year before the applicant filed in the United States and some less than a year, the choice of the key date becomes crucial to patentability.

The moment at which an invention becomes "patented" within the meaning of § 102 is subject to a case-by-case determination. The prevailing view, however, is that an invention is patented at the time the sovereign bestows a formal grant of legal rights to the applicant.[41]

4.3.6.2 Printed Publications

The term "printed publication" has been afforded a liberal construction. A document need not be formally typeset nor published to serve as a source of prior art under § 102. Instead, the courts have accounted for "ongoing advances in the technologies of data storage, retrieval and dissemination."[42] Any document available to the public, no matter where located, constitutes a "printed publication" within § 102. Thus, such documents as handwritten notes, papers distributed at a conference, or advertising circulars may all

41. In re Monks, 588 F.2d 308, 200 USPQ 129 (CCPA 1978).

42. In re Hall, 781 F.2d 897, 228 USPQ 453 (Fed.Cir.1986).

constitute printed publications.[43] On the other hand, documents distributed to a small group under circumstances of confidentiality would not.[44]

The effective date of a publication is the date it becomes accessible to the public. The document comprises prior art under § 102 whether or not anyone has actually reviewed its contents. The text of the printed publication need not be written in the English language to be effective prior art.

The Federal Circuit opinion in *In re Hall*, offers an instructive application of these principles. There, the PTO cited a doctoral thesis available at the library of the University of Freiburg, Germany, which had been written more than one year before the applicant applied for a patent, as a bar to granting the patent. Although the applicant argued that the reference was invalid because the exact date of cataloging and shelving was unknown, the court recognized that ordinary business practices do not always call for the memorialization of such information. Judge Baldwin was satisfied that general practices of the Freiburg library would have rendered the doctoral thesis publicly accessible well before the critical date.

The applicant next urged that even if catalogued, a single thesis in one university library should not constitute prior art. According to the applicant, the Freiburg thesis was not sufficiently accessible so as to inform interested practitioners about the technology. The Federal Circuit agreed that a printed publication must be publicly accessible, but held that the Freiburg thesis was sufficiently available to diligent individuals interested in the art. That an unpublished foreign language thesis sitting in obscurity on the shelves of a German university library should serve as prior art against a domestic applicant may trouble some readers. Yet Congress fashioned § 102 out of the apparent belief that U.S. inventors should be held accountable for knowledge that had been reduced to a tangible form, even where that knowledge has been memorialized abroad. In an era of increasing technical harmonization and access to information, this judgment seems sound.

Three years later, the Federal Circuit went the other way in *In re Cronyn*.[45] The reference at issue there was a senior thesis deposited in the library of Reed College, a solely undergraduate institution located in Portland, Oregon. Although the library was open to the public, the thesis was neither generally catalogued nor

43. *See* In re Wyer, 655 F.2d 221, 210 USPQ 790 (CCPA 1981).

44. *See* Northern Telecom, Inc. v. Datapoint Corp., 908 F.2d 931, 15 USPQ2d 1321 (Fed.Cir.1990).

45. 890 F.2d 1158, 13 USPQ2d 1070 (Fed.Cir.1989).

indexed. Instead, all student theses were listed on a special index of cards available for public examination, both at the main college library and in a shoebox stored in the chemistry department. Identifying "dissemination and public accessibility" as the pertinent indicia of whether a prior art reference was "published" or not, the court held that the latter standard was not fulfilled here. The fact that the theses were distinctly filed, as well as the sorting of individual cards only via the name of the author, led to the conclusion that the theses "had not been catalogued or indexed in a meaningful way." Comparison of *Cronyn* with *Hall* suggests that the decision whether a particular reference rises to the level of a "printed publication" is an intensely factual one.

The courts and the PTO have yet to rule on whether an Internet posting is a "printed publication" within the meaning of § 102. Several commentators, relying upon progressive judicial attitudes towards the term, have concluded that Internet postings would qualify.[46] Others have expressed the concern that Internet postings are not sufficiently indexed to fulfill the requirement of public accessibility.[47] We project that the status of Internet postings as "printed publications" should be resolved on a case-by-case basis. Information that could be readily located via the major search engines should enjoy the status of a "printed publication" under § 102. On the other hand, such postings as instant messages or e-mail correspondence to a single colleague, even if archived, would lack the traits of public dissemination and accessibility that are the hallmarks of a printed publication.

4.3.7 Abandonment Under § 102(c)

The second provision that gives rise to a statutory bar is § 102(c),which bars a patent where the applicant "has abandoned the invention." By definition one cannot abandon something that does not yet exist. Consequently this provision does not relate to conduct that pre-dates the invention. Necessarily, the abandonment issue can only arise based on conduct that takes place after the invention has been made, but before the patent application has been filed.

At the outset, the reader should bear in mind that § 102(c) does not refer to disposal of a physical embodiment of the invention itself—for example, by tossing a model of the invention into the nearest dumpster. Rather, it concerns the intentional surrender of

46. *See, e.g.*, Neal P. Perotti, *Does Internet Information Count as a Printed Publication*, 42 IDEA 249 (2002); G. Andrew Barger, *Lost in Cyberspace: Inventors, Computer Piracy and "Printed Publications,"* 71 U. Det. Mercy L. Rev. 353 (1994).

47. Max Oppenheimer, In Vento Scribere: *The Intersection of Cyberspace and Patent Law*, 51 Fla. L. Rev. 229 (1999).

an invention *to the public*. Once an inventor has donated the technology to the public, she will be barred from seeking a patent. Older Supreme Court opinions instruct that abandonment may occur where an inventor expressly dedicates it to the public, through a deliberate relinquishment or conduct evidencing an intent not to pursue patent protection.[48] The circumstances must be such that others could reasonably rely upon the inventor's renunciation.[49]

Human nature being what it is, few individuals expressly cede their patentable inventions to the public without seeking compensation. As a result, a paucity of recent precedent considers § 102(c) in any meaningful way. Perhaps the only circumstance implicating this statute would involve an express public statement by an inventor dedicating a technology to the public. If a subsequent call from the inventor's creditors led to second thoughts and the filing of a patent application, § 102(c) might then come into play.

It is important not to confuse the use of the term "abandonment" in § 102(c) with other uses of the term in the patent law. In particular, § 102(g) refers to individuals who have "abandoned, suppressed or concealed" the invention itself, for example, by suspending work on a project before developing a working model. Section 102(c) instead concerns abandonment of the right to obtain a patent. This statute also does not prevent inventors from withdrawing applications from the PTO, an action that is also termed an "abandonment." The Patent Act allows inventors to retract patent applications from the PTO without necessarily prejudicing their right ultimately to obtain a patent. Inventors who earlier abandoned applications are always free to file again. Although these applicants will lose the benefit of their earlier filing date, and thus may expose themselves to bars under §§ 102(b) or (d), they will not be impacted by § 102(c) if all the circumstances do not indicate abandonment of the invention to the public.

4.3.8 Delayed United States Filing Under § 102(d)

The final statutory bar provision contained in the statute is § 102(d). It bars a U.S. patent when (1) an inventor files a foreign patent application more than twelve months before filing the U.S. application, and (2) a foreign patent issues from that application prior to the U.S. filing date. The requirements are conjunctive: both requirements must be met in order to trigger § 102(d) and bar the issuance of a patent. By encouraging prompt filing in the United

48. *See* Beedle v. Bennett, 122 U.S. 71, 7 S.Ct. 1090, 30 L.Ed. 1074 (1887); Agawam Woolen Co. v. Jordan, 74 U.S. (7 Wall.) 583, 19 L.Ed. 177 (1868); Kendall v. Winsor, 62 U.S. (21 How.) 322, 16 L.Ed. 165 (1858).

49. *See* Mendenhall v. Astec Indus., Inc., 13 USPQ2d 1913, 1937 (E.D.Tenn. 1988), *aff'd*, 887 F.2d 1094 (Fed.Cir. 1989); Macbeth–Evans Glass Co. v. General Electric Co., 246 F. 695 (6th Cir. 1917).

States, § 102(d) ensures that the term of U.S. patents will not appreciably extend past the expiration date of parallel foreign patents.[50]

An example illustrates the application of § 102(d). Suppose that Orlanth, the inventor of a new method for curing herring, files an application at the Swedish Patent Office on May 25, 2002. The Swedish application matures into a granted Swedish patent on August 1, 2003. If Orlanth has not filed his U.S. patent application at the PTO as of August 1, 2003, the date of the Swedish patent grant, the § 102(d) bar would be triggered. Note that this bar would not apply if Orlanth filed his U.S. application on May 30, 2003, even though that is (just a bit) more than one year after his Swedish patent application because as of that date, no Swedish patent has issued. Similarly, if the Swedish Patent Office acted with blazing speed because of the significance of herring-related inventions to that country's citizens, and had issued Orlanth a patent on June 15, 2002, just three weeks after he filed for the Swedish patent, he would still have until May 25, 2003, to file in the U.S., because any such filing would not be more than 12 months after his foreign filing.

Commentators have often approached § 102(d) with some distaste.[51] Because inventors may choose to file a patent application only in the United States, the policy goal of assuring that the U.S. market will become patent-free contemporaneously with foreign markets seems poorly served via the § 102(d) bar. More telling is that § 102(d) almost exclusively works against foreign inventors. Individuals based in the United States seldom encounter problems with § 102(d), for inventors the world over tend to file applications in their home patent offices first. And while this statute comports with the letter of Article 27 of the TRIPS Agreement, which requires that "patents shall be available . . . without discrimination as to the place of the invention," § 102(d) in practice derogates from the principle of national treatment of foreign inventors.

The leading Federal Circuit decision applying § 102(d) is *In re Kathawala*.[52] Kathawala, the inventor of cholesterol-inhibiting compounds, filed patent applications in the United States, Greece, and Spain. The three applications included substantially the same specifications but contained differing claims. The Greek patent claimed compounds, pharmaceutical compositions, methods of use, and methods of making. The U.S. patent contained all but the method claims. The Spanish patent claimed only the method of making the compound. Not only was the U.S. application filed more than one

50. *See* Ex parte Mushet, 1870 Comm'r Dec. 106.

51. *See* Donald S. Chisum, *Foreign Activity: Its Effect on Patentability under United States Law*, 11 INT'L REV. INDUS. PROP. & COPYRIGHT L. 26 (1980).

52. 9 F.3d 942, 28 USPQ2d 1785 (Fed.Cir.1993).

year after the Greek and Spanish applications were filed, each of these foreign applications actually led to granted patents before the U.S. filing date.

Appealing the PTO's imposition of a § 102(d) bar before the Federal Circuit, Kathawala offered two arguments worthy of note here. First, Kathawala asserted that because the Spanish patent contained only method of making claims, which were not claimed in the U.S. application, the invention claimed in the United States had not been previously "patented" in a foreign country within the meaning of § 102(d). Kathawala also urged that the claims of the Greek patent were invalid because, at the time the patent issued, the Greek patent law actually disallowed patents directed to pharmaceuticals.

The Federal Circuit had little trouble rejecting these arguments. According to Judge Lourie, § 102(d) should not be given a constrained reading. It was enough that Kathawala's Spanish application disclosed and provided the opportunity to claim all aspects of his invention, including the compounds themselves. Allowing dilatory inventors to obtain U.S. patents on others aspect of the same "invention" patented too long ago abroad would frustrate the policy of the statute, according to the court. The court also dismissed Kathawala's arguments regarding the Greek patent, declining to speculate on the patent eligibility law of Greece. Both Greek and U.S. patents included claims towards the same subject matter because Kathawala had put them there, and their validity was irrelevant to whether the subject matter was "patented" in accordance with § 102(d).

Not only was the *Kathawala* court's unwillingness to consider Greek patent law surprising, its generous view of patented subject matter seems questionable. Few members of the patent community would say that disclosed but unclaimed subject matter is patented, for as we shall see in some detail in a subsequent chapter, the claims—not the specification—are the measure of patentee rights. Perhaps *Kathawala* should have been an obviousness case. But given the expansive holding in *Kathawala*, applicants should be particularly wary of how they take advantage of foreign patent registration regimes. Under some of those systems, the foreign patent offices may not fully examine applications for compliance with the patent law, leading to short processing times and prompt issuances of foreign patents, which may, in turn, act as a bar to obtaining a more valuable U.S. patent under the provisions of § 102(d).

§ 4.4 Prior Art for Novelty: Prior Invention

The remaining provisions of § 102, paragraphs (a), (e), (f) and (g), do not concern the date an inventor filed a patent application at the PTO. They instead pertain to a real world event: the date on which the subject matter sought to be patented was actually invented. These provisions are all based on the premise that the first individual to invent a particular technology should be awarded the patent. At we write these words, the United States faces mounting pressure to switch to the world norm of a first-to-file patent system, where novelty is assessed solely based on the filing date. But at least for the near future, the first-to-invent system appears firmly fixed within the U.S. patent regime. As with the case of the trio of statutory bar provisions, it is necessary to take a close look at each of the quartet of novelty provisions separately to understand the details of their operation.

4.4.1 Prior Invention Under § 102(a)

Section 102(a) states the essential first-to-invent rule unique to the U.S. patent system. An invention "known or used by others in this country, or patented or described in a printed publication in this or a foreign country, before the invention thereof by the applicant for a patent" may not be patented. Under this rule, in order to obtain a patent, an applicant must prove that he actually invented a claimed invention prior to the date of an anticipatory reference. For example, suppose that Professor Connie Cool files a patent application on December 1, 2003, claiming a new refrigeration technology. During prosecution of the application, a PTO examiner discovers that another person, Charlie Chilly, had used the same technology claimed by Cool as of October 12, 2003. Because Charlie used the invention less than one year before Cool's filing date, the § 102(b) bar does not apply. Nonetheless, to obtain a patent, Cool must demonstrate that she invented the subject matter of her patent application prior to Charlie's use. Two concepts are critical here: the meaning of the term "known or used" within § 102(a), and the precise activity sufficient to demonstrate a date of invention. Let us consider those in sequence.

In our hypo, it is possible that Charlie might have used the refrigeration in technology secretly, without in any way allowing others an opportunity to learn about it. Should that suffice to defeat novelty under § 102(a)? The literal language of § 102(a) requires only that the prior invention be "known or used:" unlike § 102(b), § 102(a) does not include the word "public." The courts have nonetheless interpreted § 102(a) to require some form of public accessibility to the first inventor's invention before the second inventor's patent application will be rejected. We turn again to Judge Learned Hand, whose opinion in *Gillman v. Stern* remains a leading case on this point.[1]

§ 4.4

1. 114 F.2d 28, 46 USPQ2d 430 (2d Cir. 1940).

In *Gillman*, one Wenczel obtained a patent on a pneumatic machine for quilting fabric. The patent was later asserted during infringement litigation. The accused infringer learned of a third party, Haas, who had employed a substantially similar machine. Because Wenczel had filed his application in 1931, uses by Haas in 1929 and 1930 did not trigger a statutory bar under the two-year grace period of the day. In contemporary terms, the issue before the court was whether the prior use by Haas rendered the quilting machine "known or used by others" as provided in § 102(a). If so, that would mean that Wenczel was not the first inventor and his patent would thus be invalid under the U.S. first to invent rules. However, the controlling fact was that Haas maintained the machine as a trade secret. Haas sold quilted fabric, not the pneumatic machine, and the fabric he produced appeared the same as any other.

After canvassing the precedents, Judge Hand concluded that an inventor who kept his technology as a trade secret could not be judged the first inventor in terms of the patent law. Inventors like Haas had chosen not to augment the store of public knowledge, and therefore their efforts should not prejudice later patent applicants. In contrast to Haas, Wenczel had brought about the publication of a patent instrument and the enrichment of the art. The bottom line that emerges from *Gillman* is that the trade secrets of others are not prior art that defeat novelty.

In dicta, Judge Hand also noted that the patent law distinguished between secret and non-informing uses. According to Judge Hand, the precedent had afforded non-informing uses the status of prior art. Judge Hand observed that this scheme might potentially lead to anomalous results where the public was unable to profit from the non-informing use.

The holding in *Gillman* has the merit of reading §§ 102(a) and (b) identically with regard to the prior art status of secret and non-informing uses. For example, opinions like *Gore v. Garlock* have lent consistent interpretations to the term "public use" in cases of third party secret uses. This happy harmony may have actually originated from an oversight: in the later case of *Metallizing Engineering*, Judge Hand candidly admitted to confusing §§ 102(a) and (b), as demonstrated by his frequent reference to the term "public use" in *Gillman*. Subsequent opinions have nonetheless been persuaded by the reasoning of *Gillman* and upheld its result.

National Tractor Pullers Association v. Watkins[2] presents one of the more unusual factual circumstances in which a court applied the *Gillman* rule. There, the declaratory judgment plaintiff assert-

2. 205 USPQ 892 (N.D.Ill.1980).

ed that a patented device useful in tractor pulling contests was invalid under § 102(a). The plaintiff pointed to earlier drawings made by a third party on the underside of a tablecloth in his mother's kitchen. The drawings had never been publicized, nor had the depicted device been commercialized. The court concluded that these drawings did not comprise prior art, declaring: "Prior knowledge as set forth in 35 U.S.C. § 102(a) must be prior public knowledge, that is knowledge which is reasonably accessible to the public."

Note, however, that even a modest degree of public accessibility will allow an earlier invention to qualify as a prior art reference under § 102(a). If the invention has not been purposefully concealed or kept as a trade secret, then the courts will ordinarily find that it was sufficiently accessible to comprise prior art. The well-known decision of the Court of Appeals for the Fifth Circuit in *Rosaire v. Baroid Sales Division, National Lead Co.* is illustrative.[3] That case involved two patents issued to Rosaire and Horvitz for methods of prospecting for oil. Horvitz sold his interest to Rosaire, who subsequently brought an infringement suit against National Lead. Among the accused infringer's defenses was that the patents were invalid due to the earlier work of one Teplitz. Teplitz had both conceived of the patented methods, and used them in Texas oil fields, prior to the earliest dates of invention claimed by Rosaire and Horvitz. Importantly, the "work was performed in the field under ordinary conditions without any deliberate attempt at concealment or effort to exclude the public and without any instructions of secrecy to the employees performing the work."

The Fifth Circuit held that Teplitz's activities sufficed to trigger § 102(a). The court concluded that "where such work was done openly and in the ordinary course of the activities of the employer," it was sufficiently accessible to constitute prior art. *Rosaire* and later cases thus establish the basic rule that an earlier invention is "known or used" within the meaning of § 102(a) so long as it is not secret. This result holds even if the actual amount of public access is likely to have been minimal or even nonexistent. It is enough that interested persons could have discerned this information had they tried, even though nobody actually did so.

The holding of *Rosaire* is debatable. One of the goals of the patent system is the public dissemination of innovative products and processes. Although the work of Teplitz in the *Rosaire* case was not secret, it may well have been quite obscure. As between Teplitz and the team of Rosaire and Horvitz, it was the latter duo who actually made an effort to disclose their invention to the public, by filing a patent application which necessarily contained full informa-

3. 218 F. 72, 104 USPQ 100 (5th Cir. 1955).

tion about the details of the technology and how to practice it. Invalidating the Rosaire and Horvitz patents hardly seems to advance this important policy goal.

The *Rosaire* holding is perhaps better explained by a fact that the court mentions, but does not stress. Teplitz's employees were not obliged to hold the oil prospecting methods in confidence. They were free to transfer this information to new employers or to colleagues working in the field. On a more theoretical level, the patent law has never required first inventors to undertake significant affirmative efforts in order to preserve their right to use their own invention. After all, Teptlitz was not the defendant in this patent infringement lawsuit, but he might have been in the next one. The current rule allows the Teplitzes of the world to dedicate the invention to the public domain without going to the expense of filing a patent application or engaging in a publicity campaign. However, the patent law has less solicitude for individuals who deliberately conceal their inventions. In cases like *Gillman* and *National Tractor Pullers*, the law more comfortably assigns patent rights to individuals who publicly disclosed an invention against earlier inventors who suppressed their knowledge.

The other key aspect of § 102(a) is determining an applicant's date of invention. The nature of the activity that comprises the applicant's invention date is, alas, not elaborated in § 102(a). The statute merely states the phrase "the invention thereof by the applicant for a patent" without further definition. However, the drafters of the 1952 Act relied upon extensive case law concerning predecessor statutes to § 102(a). This precedent set forth an elaborate definition of the level of activity that amounted to an "invention date" in the patent law. This definition involves three terms of art: conception, reduction to practice and diligence.

For present purposes, a working definition of each of these terms suffices. Conception concerns the mental act of invention. It occurs when the inventor has formed "a definite and permanent idea of the complete and operative invention, as it is hereafter to be applied in practice."[4] Reduction to practice ordinarily follows conception. An actual reduction to practice consists of a demonstration that the invention is suitable for its intended purpose.[5] Actual reduction to practice involves the construction of a working model of the invention and often some minimal testing. Constructive reduction to practice consists of the filing of a patent application at

4. Burroughs Wellcome Co. v. Barr Labs., Inc., 40 F.3d 1223, 1228, 32 USPQ2d 1915, 1919 (Fed.Cir.1994), *cert. denied,* 516 U.S. 1070, 116 S.Ct. 771, 133 L.Ed.2d 724 (1996).

5. Coffin v. Ogden, 85 U.S. (18 Wall.) 120, 21 L.Ed. 821 (1873).

the PTO. Lastly, diligence involves the showing of continuous and reasonable efforts towards the reduction to practice of an invention.

These concepts help us define the time of "invention" noted in § 102(a) in the following way. An actual reduction to practice presents the most straightforward way to demonstrate that an inventor was possessed of the invention prior to the date of a reference. That is, if an inventor can show that he constructed an operable, proven prototype of the invention prior to the effective date of a reference, then that reference is disregarded under the terms of § 102(a).

Even if the applicant has not reduced the invention to practice prior to the reference date, however, he still has the opportunity to remove the reference. First, he must demonstrate that he conceived of the invention prior to the date of the reference. Second, he must show that he acted diligently from the reference date until a subsequent reduction to practice. Such a reduction to practice may be actual or constructive.[6]

That an actual reduction to practice, achieved before the effective date of a reference, demonstrates possession of an invention to the satisfaction of the patent law should be unsurprising. But that the combination of conception and diligence should allow an inventor to avoid a § 102(a) reference may at first appear elusive. In this regard the patent law recognizes that although anyone can have a good idea, not everyone has a lot of money. In contrast, a reduction to practice usually demands that an inventor marshal significant resources, whether he attempts to construct a working prototype or chooses to file a patent application. So long as he remains diligent in working towards either sort of reduction to practice, however, § 102(a) will not deny him the patent just because an intervening party comes up with the same invention before he is able to reduce the invention to practice. The statute may thus be seen as promoting an equality of opportunity between actors in the technological community with different levels of financial means.

It is important to note that in the 1952 Act, Congress expressly articulated the concepts of conception, reduction to practice, and diligence within § 102(g). Although the terms are not used explicitly in § 102(a), the concepts still govern in determining the date of invention under that provision as well. We will return in further depth to the concepts of conception, reduction to practice, and diligence when we take up § 102(g) in § 4.3.2 below.

Another point worth mentioning is that § 102(a) applies only to activities by persons other than the inventor herself. Obviously,

6. Mahurkar v. C.R. Bard, Inc., 79 F.3d 1572, 38 USPQ2d 1288 (Fed. Cir. 1996).

you can't out-invent yourself, so the first-to-invent principle of § 102(a) makes prior art only out of knowledge, use, patents, or publications originating from someone other than the patent applicant (in cases of acquisition proceedings at the PTO) or patentee (in cases of infringement litigation). For example, suppose that Dr. Barleybean uses a method of canning shrimp in the United States on March 1, 2004. Barleybean then files a patent application at the PTO on June 1, 2004. Barleybean's use does not count as prior art under § 102(a) because it was not "by others," as § 102(a) compels. Of course, if Barleybean made a public use of her invention more than one year before her filing date, then the statutory bar of § 102(b) would apply.

An important procedural aspect of § 102(a) involves the use of Rule 131 at the PTO. This rule allows patent applicants to declare an invention date prior to the date of a prior art reference. This declaration is typically accompanied by a detailed factual showing, such as diagrams or laboratory notebooks, that demonstrate sufficient inventive activity to pre-date the reference. The need for Rule 131 arises because inventors need not attest to their date of inventive activity when they file patent applications. Instead, they reveal their invention date on an *ad hoc* basis only when the examiner produces a pertinent prior art reference. Use of Rule 131 is informally known as "swearing behind" or "antedating" a reference.

A brief example best illustrates the workings of § 102(a) and Rule 131. Suppose that a patent examiner discovers a technical journal article published one month before a particular application's filing date. That article fully discloses the claimed invention and would anticipate the application if it serves as prior art under § 102(a). Note that because the article was published within the one-year grace period established under § 102(b), the application is not subject to a statutory bar.

The examiner may issue a rejection under § 102(a), however. Without any knowledge of the true invention date, the examiner must assume that the applicant invented the claimed technology on the same date the application was filed. The examiner's § 102(a) rejection is in the nature of an invitation, however. The applicant may file a Rule 131 affidavit showing sufficient inventive activity prior to the effective date of the reference. In particular, the applicant must show either (1) an actual reduction to practice prior to the publication date of the journal article, or (2) conception of the invention prior to the publication date, coupled with diligence from the publication date until a subsequent reduction to practice. This reduction to practice may be either actual, which would involve the construction and testing of a prototype, or constructive, which would rely upon the filing date of the patent application. If the examiner is satisfied with the applicant's showing, she will withdraw the rejection.

By its own terms, Rule 131 applies only to §§ 102(a) and (e). Rule 131 does not apply to statutory bars such as § 102(b), which are keyed to the filing date of the patent application. Further, the use of Rule 131 should not be confused with a true interference proceeding under § 102(g). If two patents or patent applications claim the same subject matter, then the rival inventors must engage in a priority contest to determine which is entitled to a patent.

The following hypothetical sums up the working of § 102(a) and Rule 131. Suppose that Dr. Quark conceived of a new machine for making shatterproof glass on March 1, 2003. He then diligently works on building a working model of his device, at last building a working prototype on May 15, 2003. Quark then files a patent application at the PTO on December 12, 2003. During the prosecution of the application, the PTO examiner discovers a Finnish patent application, published on April 20, 2003, that fully anticipates the invention claimed in Quark's application. The § 102(b) bar does not apply because the patent application was published less than one year before the date Quark filed his application. However, the PTO examiner may reject Quark's application based upon the published Finnish application and § 102(a). In such cases, the examiner's rejection is subject to a rebuttal by the applicant. Quark has the opportunity to overcome the rejection by showing that, within the technical meaning of the patent law, he invented his glass-making machine prior to the date the Finnish application was published.

In this case, assuming that all of his dates of inventive activity are properly corroborated, Quark will be able to overcome the examiner's § 102(a) rejection. Because Quark did not reduce his invention to practice until May 15, 2003, almost one month after the publication date of the Finnish application, Quark cannot rely upon his reduction to practice date alone. However, Quark may submit evidence that (1) he conceived of the invention on March 1, 2003, prior to the April 20, 2003, publication date of the Finnish patent application; and (2) he was diligent from April 20th (the date of the reference in question) until his own actual reduction to practice on May 15, 2003. Upon receipt of this evidence via a Rule 131 affidavit, the PTO examiner will withdraw this rejection and, absent any other objections, allow Quark to obtain his patent.

Curious readers may wonder why the PTO examiner does not further pursue the dates of invention concerning the Finnish patent application. After all, someone—presumably someone in Finland—invented the same glass-making machine as Quark, and almost certainly did so prior to the date the Finnish application was published. Given that administrative processing must have delayed the publication of the Finnish application, why doesn't the PTO examiner telephone Helsinki in order to determine when that application was filed at the Finnish Patent Office or, better yet, learn when the Finnish applicant actually invented the glass-making machine? The short answer is that activities such as merely inventing a machine, or filing a patent application, do not necessarily result in public disclosure of that machine. Besides, while such activity might mean that the glass-making technology was "known or used," no evidence suggests that this knowledge or use occurred in the United States, as § 102(a) requires. Patents and printed publications are the only foreign references that count under § 102(a). As a result, the day the Finnish application was published is the first permissible date that the examiner may employ under § 102(a).

4.4.2 Prior Invention Under § 102(g)

Section 102(g) consists of two sub-paragraphs. The second of these, § 102(g)(2), expressly states the rule that the first inventor be awarded a patent: "A person shall be entitled to a patent unless . . . before the applicant's invention thereof the invention was made in this country by another. . . . " Section 102(g)(2) then states an important exception to this rule. If the first inventor has "abandoned, suppressed or concealed" the technology at issue, then he has essentially forfeited his special status in accordance with § 102(g)(2). Section 102(g)(2) goes on to instruct that "[i]n determining priority of invention there shall be considered not only the respective dates of conception and reduction to practice of the invention, but also the reasonable diligence of one who was first to conceive and last to reduce to practice, from a time prior to conception by the other."

As suggested by its division into sub-paragraphs, § 102(g) serves two principal purposes in the patent law. Like § 102(a), § 102(g)(2) provides a source of prior art that may be used as the basis of a rejection for anticipation. Section 102(g) serves a second function, provided in § 102(g)(1). This provision also provides a mechanism for resolving disputes relating to so-called "priority of invention." In this second situation, one party seeks more than merely the denial of another's entitlement to patent rights on a particular technology. She also seeks to obtain patent rights for herself. We need to review both of these concepts in turn, and then move on to a more detailed review of § 102(g) policy and practice.

4.4.2.1 Prior Art Under § 102(g)

As with § 102(a), § 102(g)(2) defines prior art that may be used to demonstrate that an invention lacks novelty. In these circumstances, the party asserting a § 102(g) reference is not claiming the invention for itself, but arguing that the issued patent is invalid. This effort usually involves the identification of a third party that allegedly invented first. In this sense, § 102(g) functions similarly to § 102(a).

At least two important distinctions exist between § 102(a) and (g), however. First, § 102(g) applies only to inventions "made in this country." Under § 102(a), patents and printed publications may originate "in this or a foreign country."

Second, we have seen that the courts have interpreted § 102(a) to require knowledge or use that was publicly accessible at the time the patented invention was made.[7] Section 102(g) has not been similarly construed, however. Instead, as explained by the Court of Claims in *International Glass Co. v. United States*, "prior invention under 102(g) requires only that the invention be complete, i.e., conceived and reduced to practice, and not abandoned, suppressed or concealed."[8] Thus, under § 102(g) a completely private invention may serve as prior art against a later inventor. It is important to note, however, that such private inventors may well be judged to have "abandoned, suppressed or concealed" the invention at issue, typically by maintaining the technology as a trade secret. In such cases these earlier, private inventions will not be considered within the prior art. The sorts of conduct that cause an invention to be judged "abandoned, suppressed or concealed" are discussed in § 4.4.2.8 below.

Some examples illustrate the difference between § 102(a) and § 102(g). First, suppose that Professor Terra publishes an article on March 1, 2004, describing a miniature earthmover. Although the article describes the earthmover and its construction in considerable detail, Terra never actually builds a working model. Without knowledge of the Terra invention, Dr. Gaia files a patent application claiming the same earthmover on April 1, 2004.

Under these facts, a patent examiner may cite the Terra article against the Gaia application under § 102(a), but not under § 102(g). Section 102(a) applies because the invention was described in a printed publication. However that printed publication will only defeat novelty if it came before Gaia "invented" the earthmover. Gaia can file a Rule 131 to "swear behind" Terra's article by showing relevant conduct (either reduction to practice, or conception plus diligence) prior to the date of the article. Note,

7. *See supra* § 4.3.1.

8. International Glass Co. v. United States, 408 F.2d 395, 161 USPQ 116 (Ct.Cl.1969).

however, that section 102(g) does not apply because it requires that the invention "was made in this country by another inventor. . . ." Although Terra wrote an article, she never reduced the invention to practice, either actually (by building a working model) or constructively (by filing a patent application).

Alternatively, suppose that Professor Terra builds a working prototype of a diatomaceous earth filter[9] on March 1, 2004. Terra discloses the invention only to a laboratory assistant who has signed a confidentiality agreement, and in fact neither Terra nor her assistant disclose the filter to anyone else. Without knowledge of the Terra invention, Dr. Gaia invents the identical filter on April 1, 2004, and files a patent application claiming the same filter on April 15, 2004.

In this case, § 102(g) might apply, but § 102(a) would not. Terra's activities serve as prior art under § 102(g) because Terra "made" or invented the filter prior to Gaia in the United States.[9.5] However, section 102(a) would not apply because Terra did not disclose her invention to the public, even within the generous interpretation of § 102(a) provided in such cases as *Gillman v. Stern.*

4.4.2.2 Priority Under § 102(g)

Section 102(g) serves a second function, by virtue of the language of § 102(g)(1). This provision also provides a mechanism for resolving disputes relating to so-called "priority of invention." In this class of cases, an alleged earlier inventor is not only trying to prevent another party from obtaining patent rights on a particular technology, but is also seeking to secure those patent rights for herself.

The need to determine priority of invention should be clear. As rivals across the globe compete to develop valuable technologies, they will often develop similar or identical inventions at approximately the same time. In such circumstances, the U.S. patent system has adopted a winner-take-all policy. Only the person or persons that first developed a particular technology will be awarded a patent. This policy is implemented through the rules set forth in § 102(g), which determine which actor will be judged the first inventor in terms of the patent law.

9. Diatoms are a type of single cell marine algea. Diatomaceous earth is an extremely fine soil made up of the fossil remains of diatoms, and useful as filter which can remove extremely small particles. A diatomacous earth filter will really make the water in your swimming pool sparkle!

9.5 We say § 102(g) "might" apply because we would still have to consider if Terra "abandoned, suppressed or concealed" the invention after building the prototype.

Section 102(g)'s function both as a rule of priority and as a source of novelty-destroying prior art can be confusing at first blush. Professors Merges has proposed a helpful framework for coming to grips with these distinct roles. He suggests that students consider patent priority contests as cases in which each competing inventor attempts to defeat the other's claim of novelty. The first inventor at law is awarded the patent once she removes the last obstacle to patentability, namely her rival's claim to an earlier invention date under § 102(g).[10]

It should be noted that until 1999, § 102(g) consisted of only a single paragraph that was nearly identical to present-day § 102(g)(2). The American Inventors Protection Act of 1999 recast existing § 102(g) as § 102(g)(2) and added a new § 102(g)(1). This legislation was intended only to clarify the rules for determining priority of invention during interference proceedings. The new, expanded version of § 102(g) more clearly demonstrates that the statute serves both as a source of prior art and a mechanism for resolving interferences.

Most § 102(g) priority contests are resolved at the PTO via so-called "interference" practice. A patent interference is a complex administrative proceeding that ordinarily results in the award of priority to one of its participants. These proceedings are not especially common. One estimate is that less than one-quarter of one percent of patents are subject to an interference.[11] This statistic may mislead, however, because the expense of interference cases may lead to their use only for the most commercially significant applications.[12] In any event, because many § 102(g) cases involve interferences, a word on their special procedures and terminology is appropriate at the start.

Interferences may occur between two pending applications, or between a pending application and an issued, unexpired patent. Section 135 requires the PTO to call for an interference when "an application is made for a patent which . . . would interfere with any pending application, or with any unexpired patent." An examiner may declare an interference when she learns of two conflicting applications without any activity by the applicants. Alternatively, an applicant may initiate an interference upon discovering an issued patent, or an application published prior to its formal issuance, that claims the same invention.

10. Robert Patrick Merges, Patent Law and Policy 395 (2d ed. 1997).

11. Clifford A. Ulrich, *The Patent Systems Harmonization Act of 1992: Conformity at What Price?*, N.Y.L. Sch. J. Int'l & Comp. L. 405, 415 (1996).

12. *See* Gerald D. Malpass, Jr., *Life After the GATT TRIPS Agreement—Has the Competitive Position of U.S. Inventors Changed?*, 19 Houston J. Int'l L. 207 (1996).

Patent interference procedures typically involve some particular terminology. Many cases will refer to so-called "senior" and "junior" parties: "A senior party is the party with the earliest effective filing date.... A junior party is any other party."[13] Interferences also make use of a concept called a "count," which corresponds to a claim which the interfering parties share. The counts of an interference define what the dispute is about; this is the subject matter which each of the parties asserts that it invented first.

When an application for an interference is filed, a primary examiner makes a preliminary determination "whether a basis upon which the applicant would be entitled to a judgment relative to the patentee is alleged and, if a basis is alleged, an interference may be declared."[14] If the primary examiner preliminarily determines that the application meets that requirement, the application is referred to an examiner-in-chief to determine whether an interference should go forward.[15] If the examiner-in-chief determines that a prima facie case for priority has been established, the interference proceeds.[16] If however, the examiner-in-chief concludes that a prima facie case has not been shown, the examiner-in-chief declares an interference but "enter[s] an order stating the reasons for the opinion and directing the applicant, within a time set in the order, to show cause why summary judgment should not be entered against the applicant."[17] If such an order to show cause issues, the applicant "may file a response to the order and state any reasons why summary judgment should not be entered."[18]

If the interference continues, next comes the filing of the applicant's preliminary statements. These statements contain allegations of the dates of various inventive activities the parties believe they can establish during an interference. After preliminary statements have been filed, the parties may submit various motions to the Board of Patent Appeals and Interferences, raising issues that will be contested during the interference.[19] The trial phase of the interference follows. The parties are given the opportunity to present affidavits, declarations, and exhibits such as laboratory notebooks and publications. After the trial comes a final hearing before a three-member panel of the Board of Patent Appeals and Interferences, consisting solely of oral argument by the parties. The Board then issues its decision, typically awarding priority of invention to one of the interfering parties. The unsuccessful party may then appeal to the Federal Circuit.

13. 37 C.F.R. § 1.601(m).

14. 37 C.F.R. § 1.608(b).

15. 37 C.F.R. §§ 1.609 & 1.610(a).

16. 37 C.F.R. § 1.617(a).

17. Id.

18. 37 C.F.R. § 1.617(b).

19. 37 C.F.R. § 1.633.

Interferences may be resolved in other ways, however. One party may assert ordinary grounds for patent invalidity; for example, that the patent claims subject matter ineligible for patenting. This effort tends to be rather uncommon, as often a defense which invalidates one application or patent will be effective for them all; but sometimes the result that no one obtains a patent is a satisfactory conclusion for one of the parties to the interference. Settlement between the parties is another option, although Congress has recognized the possibility of collusive arrangements with anticompetitive effects. The result is 35 U.S.C.A. § 135(c), which requires that the parties file copies of agreements reached in contemplation of termination of an interference. The filed agreements are available for public inspection.

Occasionally the Patent Office and applicants remain unaware of interfering applications, with the result that two patents directed towards the same inventive concept issue. Section 291 of the Patent Act, entitled "Interfering Patents," addresses these hopefully rare circumstances. Owners of interfering patents may have their respective rights determined by a federal district court following the filing of a civil suit.

4.4.2.3 Inventive Activity in Foreign Countries

Before considering the statutory language of § 102(g) in greater detail, a review of the special rules regarding inventive activity performed abroad is necessary. Historically, § 104 provided that an inventor could not rely upon activity in a foreign country to establish dates of conception, reduction to practice, or diligence. The only exception, which the statute continues to provide, is for persons "serving in any other country in connection with operations by or on behalf of the United States." Although § 104 was arguably motivated by concerns over the quality of evidence of inventive activity that might be obtained from overseas, its effect was to shut foreign inventors out of the first-to-invent system. Inventors based overseas were typically left to rely upon the priority date of a foreign patent application as provided by the Paris Convention and § 119(a).[20]

In the face of stern international opposition to § 104, Congress twice amended the statute. In 1993, in connection with the North American Free Trade Agreement Act (NAFTA), § 104 was amended to allow proof of inventive activity in a NAFTA country. The effective date of the NAFTA amendment to § 104 is December 8, 1993. In 1994, in connection with the Uruguay Round Agreements Act (URAA), § 104 was amended to allow proof of inventive activity

20. *See* Fujikawa v. Wattanasin, 93 F.3d 1559, 1561, 39 USPQ2d 1895, 1896 (Fed.Cir.1996).

in WTO member countries. Although the URAA legislation appears confused as to the effective date of the § 104 amendment, observers generally agree that it is January 1, 1996.[21]

The final episode in this saga concerns the enactment of the American Inventors Protection Act of 1999. That statute designated the existing § 102(g) as § 102(g)(2) and added § 102(g)(1). New § 102(g)(1) specifies that "during the course of an interference" inventors may establish dates of inventive activity "to the extent permitted in section 104." This express reference to § 104 allows parties to an interference to introduce dates of inventive activity performed in the United States as well as in NAFTA and WTO member countries. Since the vast majority of the world's nations are members of the WTO, this means that inventive activity virtually anywhere ought to be relevant in determining priority of invention under § 102(g)(1).

So much for interferences. Section 102(g) also serves as a source of prior art, however, as specified in § 102(g)(2). The discerning reader of § 102(g) will note that § 102(g)(2) continues to require that the "invention was made in this country." Although § 102(g)(1) recognizes NAFTA- and WTO-based amendments to § 104, § 102(g)(2) appears to suffer from a disconnect. Of what use could the newfound ability to prove dates of inventive activity under § 104 be to foreign inventors if, when they seek to apply these dates to the substantive law of § 102(g)(2), these dates have no prior art effect? Until this issue is the subject of judicial resolution or further legislative reform efforts, the prior art status of dates of foreign inventive activity remains clouded.[22]

Having offered the context of interference proceedings and foreign inventive activity, we can now turn to a more detailed consideration of those acts that rise to invention within § 102(g).

4.4.2.4 Conception

Conception is the formation in the mind of the inventor of a definite and permanent idea of the complete and operative invention, as it is to be applied in practice. The conception must include every feature of the claimed invention.[23] The conception is complete when a person of ordinary skill in the art could practice the invention without undue experimentation.[24] Although conception is a purely mental act, the courts have held that inventors may not demonstrate their date of conception solely through their own,

21. *See* Thomas L. Irving & Stacey D. Lewis, *Proving a Date of Invention and Infringement After GATT/TRIPS*, 22 AIPLA Q.J. 309, 313 (1994).

22. *See* Harold C. Wegner, *TRIPS Boomerang: Obligations for Domestic Reform*, 29 VAND. J. TRANSNAT'L L. 535, 549 (1996).

23. Kridl v. McCormick, 105 F.3d 1446, 41 USPQ2d 1686 (Fed.Cir.1997).

24. Sewall v. Walters, 21 F.3d 411, 30 USPQ2d 1356 (Fed.Cir.1994).

uncorroborated testimony. Inventors must instead provide evidence of a conception date with such proofs as models, documentation, and the testimony of others. We will consider this requirement of corroboration more extensively in § 4.4.2.7 below.

Oka v. Youssefyeh,[25] decided on appeal by the Federal Circuit following an interference, illustrates the requirement of conception. The senior party, Oka, had invented the enzyme inhibitor compounds of the count in Japan. Because § 104 at that time prohibited the entry of evidence relating to inventive acts performed abroad, Oka was left to rely upon the filing date of his Japanese application, October 31, 1980, under § 119(a), to establish his priority.

The junior party, Youssefyeh, worked in the United States. Youssefyeh sought to rely upon § 102(g) to displace Oka as the first inventor. He wished to show that he conceived of the invention prior to October 31, 1980. If Youssefyeh could make this preliminary showing, and also demonstrate diligence at the appropriate times, he could become the first inventor in terms of § 102(g).

The Federal Circuit held that Youssefyeh had conceived of the invention during the last week of October 1980. At that point, work had begun on actually synthesizing compounds within the scope of the count. The court dismissed the earlier date selected by the PTO Board, October 10, 1980, at which point Youssefyeh was in possession of a method of making a compound outside the scope of the count. Chief Judge Markey recognized the general rule that, within the chemical arts, conception of a species within a genus may constitute conception of the genus. But even Youssefyeh acknowledged that the compound he had invented as of October 10th was in fact a different species, not a genus.

Having decided that Youssefyeh had conceived during the last week of October, the court was faced with an interesting priority problem. Precedent established that the actual date associated with the "last week of October" was the final date of the period, October 31, 1980. In essence, then, the parties had tied, for Youssefyeh's conception date was the same as Oka's filing date. Chief Judge Markey decided the case on procedural grounds. Because Oka was the senior party, he was presumptively entitled to the patent. As Youssefyeh could not show an *earlier* conception date, Oka was entitled to priority. Although this result appears questionable in light of PTO interference rules, which only place the burden on the junior party to demonstrate entitlement to an interference in the first instance, it appears eminently fair. Oka had undoubtedly conceived of the invention prior to filing a Japanese application and, had § 104 not barred him from demonstrating his inventive

25. 849 F.2d 581, 7 USPQ2d 1169 (Fed.Cir.1988).

activity in Japan, could have shown he was the first inventor in fact.

4.4.2.5 Reduction to Practice

An inventor may reduce an invention to practice in two ways: (1) constructively, by filing a patent application, and (2) actually, at a minimum by constructing a working physical embodiment of the invention. If the reduction to practice is constructive, the filed application "must be for the same invention as that defined in the count in an interference, and it must contain a disclosure of the invention sufficiently adequate to enable one skilled in the art to practice the invention defined by the count, with all the limitations contained in the count, without the exercise of inventive faculties."[26]

The doctrine of constructive reduction to practice strikes many observers as an odd policy choice. The very term "reduction to practice" suggests real world engineering, not the filing of papers at the PTO. Yet the patent law does not require that applicants build working models in order to participate in the first-to-invent system. A constructive reduction to practice theory also comports with the requirement that the patent instrument fully explain to skilled artisans how to practice the claimed invention. The enabling disclosure required at the time the application is filed ensures that the technology is ripe for implementation.

An actual reduction to practice involves the construction of a physical embodiment that includes all the elements of the claimed invention. The prototype need not be entirely perfected and ready for commercial development. Slight deficiencies that can be readily solved by skilled artisans will not prevent a showing of an actual reduction to practice, so long as the prototype manifests the invention in an operative form.[27] The courts have also required the inventor to show that the invention successfully performs its intended function. Typically this demonstration involves some sort of testing or actual use. *Scott v. Finney*,[28] a newfound source of risqué humor for patent law instructors and treatise authors alike, presents the Federal Circuit's mature views on the amount of testing required to achieve an actual reduction to practice.

Scott, the junior party, filed a patent application relating to a penile implant exactly one year after Finney did. The implant employed two reservoirs connected through a manipulable valve. In order to show that he actually reduced the invention to practice

26. Travis v. Baker, 137 F.2d 109, 58 USPQ 558 (CCPA 1943).

27. Hildreth v. Mastoras, 257 U.S. 27, 34, 42 S.Ct. 20, 66 L.Ed. 112 (1921).

28. 34 F.3d 1058, 32 USPQ2d 1115 (Fed.Cir.1994).

prior to Finney's invention date, Scott submitted a video tape. The tape showed Scott at the operating table simulating the operation of a prototype that had been implanted into an anesthetized patient. An expert testified that the video demonstrated that the prototype produced sufficient rigidity for intercourse. The PTO Board disagreed, however, asserting that Scott must show testing "under actual use conditions or testing under conditions that closely simulate actual use conditions for an appropriate period of time."[29]

Scott appealed to the Federal Circuit, which reversed. The court held that the Board had applied an overly rigid standard of reduction to practice.[30] According to the court, "[t]esting need not show utility beyond a possibility of failure, but only utility beyond a probability of failure."[31] Further, the nature of testing required depended upon "the character of the invention and the problems it solves."[32] While complex inventions might require laboratory testing that accurately duplicate actual working conditions, the mere construction of simpler inventions may be sufficient to demonstrate successful operation. The invention of the *Scott v. Finney* count, a relatively uncomplicated mechanical device, fell in this latter class. In light of the videotape and expert testimony, Scott had made "a reasonable showing that the invention will work to overcome the problem it addresses."[33]

Another Federal Circuit decision, *DSL Dynamic Sciences Ltd. v. Union Switch & Signal*, Inc.,[34] involves a more mundane technology but covers much the same ground. This appeal resulted from interfering patent applications claiming a "coupler mount assembly," a device used to attach various equipment to a railway car coupler without interfering with the coupler's ability to attach one railway car to another. Union Switch contended that it had actually reduced the invention to practice prior to September 9, 1983, the earliest date to which DSL was entitled, and as a result should be declared the winner of the interference.

In order to demonstrate reduction to practice, Union Switch relied upon tests performed in April and May of 1983 in which the inventors tested the prototype on moving trains. DSL in turn argued that these tests did not sufficiently demonstrate an actual reduction to practice. DSL observed that the tested prototype had been attached to cabooses, rather than freight cars. Not only was the invention intended to be used with freight cars, according to

29. 34 F.3d at 1060–61, 32 USPQ2d at 1117.

30. We said that the humor was risqué, not that it was particularly clever.

31. 34 F.3d at 1062, 32 USPQ2d at 1118.

32. 34 F.3d at 1062, 32 USPQ2d at 1119.

33. 34 F.3d at 1063, 32 USPQ2d at 1119.

34. 928 F.2d 1122, 18 USPQ2d 1152 (Fed. Cir. 1991).

DSL, cabooses placed less demanding operating conditions on the prototype than freight cars would. DSL also pointed to the unsatisfactory performance of several coupler mount assemblies that Union Switch sold to a third party in 1985. DSL's position was that if the couplers were inoperable in 1985, they could not have been reduced to practice in 1983.

Both the PTO and the district court had awarded the patent to Union Switch, and on appeal the Federal Circuit affirmed. Judge Rich concluded that even if DSL was correct that the coupling switches were to be used on freight cars rather than cabooses, the Union Switch tests sufficiently simulated the conditions present on a freight car. Extensive Union Switch testing, involving long distances, high speeds, and considerable vibration, showed that the invention worked for its intended purpose. The Federal Circuit also discounted evidence concerning the sale of unsatisfactory devices in 1985. Judge Rich explained that an invention need not be in a commercially satisfactory stage of development to be considered reduced to practice.

4.4.2.6 Diligence

An inventor who is first to conceive, but last to reduce to practice, will be entitled to priority by showing "reasonable diligence" toward reduction to practice. The required period of diligence for the inventor who was first to conceive, but last to reduce to practice, begins at the time "prior to the conception by the other" and ends when the inventor who was first to conceive reduces the invention to practice. Diligence which begins after the other's conception date, or occurs after reduction to practice has taken place, does not bear upon the priority contest. The diligence standard balances the interest in rewarding the first inventor with the public's interest in obtaining prompt disclosure of the invention.[35]

It is important to remember that the patent law never sponsors a diligence race.[36] Only one party's diligence is ever relevant in a priority contest between two inventors. That party is the inventor who was first to conceive, but second to reduce to practice. The inventor who is both first to conceive and first to reduce an invention to practice wins the priority contest without having to show diligence at all. If the first inventor to reduce the invention to practice overly delays in employing the invention commercially or filing a patent application, however, she may well have been considered to have "abandoned, suppressed, or concealed" the invention, a topic discussed here at § 4.4.2.8.

35. Griffith v. Kanamaru, 816 F.2d 624, 2 USPQ2d 1361 (Fed.Cir.1987).

36. Steinberg v. Seitz, 517 F.2d 1359, 1364, 186 USPQ 209, 212 (CCPA 1975).

The level of inventor activity that constitutes diligence must necessarily be judged on a case-by-case basis. In general, the courts have judged inventors quite strictly. Inventors must show "a continuous course of activity, carried on without significant interruption and accomplished in reasonably prompt manner, considered in light of all the attendant circumstances."[37] The inventor must account for the entire period mandated by § 102(g), specifically demonstrating either diligent efforts or excused activities. Although older precedent recognizes several justifications for lapses in inventive activity, including poverty, illness and employment demands,[38] more contemporary decisions have seldom excused activities unrelated to the invention.

Gould v. Schawlow[39] reflects this exacting posture. Gould, the junior party in an interference, was the first to conceive but the second to reduce to practice. The other party to the proceedings, Schawlow, had filed his patent application on July 30, 1958, and relied upon this date as his constructive reduction to practice. To obtain an award of priority, Gould needed to show diligence from a time prior to Schawlow's filing date of July 30, 1958, until the date of Gould's constructive reduction to practice, April 6, 1959.[39.5] Gould provided ample evidence of significant inventive efforts, including his departure from Columbia University for the private sector, authorship of a grant proposal, discussions with colleagues, and maintenance of a "laser notebook." The court nonetheless held that Gould had not demonstrated sufficient diligence. According to the court, Gould had not correlated his efforts with particular times, and much of his testimony consisted of general assertions. *Gould v. Schawlow* demonstrates that inventors may show diligence only with difficulty, and only if particularized evidence of inventive activities at definite times can be produced.

Sometimes an inventor wishes to show a constructive, rather than an actual, reduction to practice. Because only the filing of a patent application constitutes a constructive reduction to practice, often the diligence of a patent attorney is called into question. Perhaps due to the federal judiciary's fuller appreciation of the demands of legal practice, the courts have been decidedly more lenient towards patent attorneys than to inventors in diligence cases. Patent attorneys need not drop all other cases when they receive an inventor's disclosure. The attorney need only show

37. Diasonics, Inc. v. Acuson Corp., 1993 WL 248654, *16 (N.D.Cal.1993).

38. *See* Courson v. O'Connor, 227 F. 890 (7th Cir.1915); Christie v. Seybold, 55 F. 69, 77 (6th Cir.1893).

39. 363 F.2d 908, 150 USPQ 634 (CCPA 1966).

39.5 As the first to conceive, Gould had to show diligence prior to Schalow's date of reduction to practice until the date of Gould's own reduction to practice.

reasonable diligence in taking up the cases on her docket. Ordinarily, if the attorney takes up the cases in the order they are received, the courts will consider the diligence standard to have been met.[40]

4.4.2.7 Corroboration

An inventor may rely on the various inventive activities—conception, reduction to practice, and diligence—only if they have been corroborated. The corroboration requirement serves to prevent fraud.[41] Particularly in the case of conception, a purely mental act, the acceptance of the inventor's unsupported testimony would offer great temptation to perjury and provide the adverse party scant opportunity to rebut such evidence.[42] As the Federal Circuit has concisely concluded, "the mere unsupported evidence of the alleged inventor ... can not be received as sufficient proof of ... prior conception."[43]

The Federal Circuit applies a so-called "rule of reason" analysis to determine whether an inventor has corroborated his testimony. This analysis calls for review of all pertinent evidence in order to reach a sound determination of the credibility of the inventor.[44] Corroborating evidence typically consists of laboratory notebooks and statements of witnesses. Only the inventor's testimony need be corroborated. If the inventor submits physical exhibits to demonstrate inventive activity, the trier of fact can conclude for itself what those exhibits show.[45] Factors bearing on whether an inventor's testimony has been adequately corroborated include:

(1) the relationship between the corroborating witness and the alleged prior user,

(2) the time period between the event and trial,

(3) the interest of the corroborating witness in the subject matter in suit,

(4) contradiction or impeachment of the witness' testimony,

(5) the extent and details of the corroborating testimony,

(6) the witness' familiarity with the subject matter of the patented invention and the prior use,

(7) the probability that a prior use could occur considering the state of the art at the time, and

40. *See* Bey v. Kollonitsch, 806 F.2d 1024, 231 USPQ 967 (Fed. Cir. 1986).

41. Berry v. Webb, 412 F.2d 261, 267, 162 USPQ 170, 174 (CCPA 1969).

42. Price v. Symsek, 988 F.2d 1187, 26 USPQ2d 1031 (Fed.Cir.1993).

43. 988 F.2d at 1195.

44. Holmwood v. Sugavanam, 948 F.2d 1236, 1239, 20 USPQ2d 1712, 1714 (Fed.Cir.1991).

45. Mahurkar v. C.R. Bard, 79 F.3d 1572, 38 USPQ2d 1288 (Fed.Cir.1996).

(8) the impact of the invention on the industry, and the commercial value of its practice.[46]

In its 1998 decision in *Woodland Trust v. Flowertree Nursery, Inc.*,[47] the Federal Circuit considered these factors in a case involving uncorroborated oral testimony of prior use. Woodland Trust owned a patent claiming a method and apparatus for protecting plants from freezing. The PTO issued the patent in 1988 based upon an application filed in 1983. When Woodland brought an infringement suit, Flowertree Nursery defended in part on the ground of patent invalidity. According to Flowertree, two nurseries—including one that belonged to Hawkins, who also was an owner of Flowertree—had used the patented invention during the 1960's and 1970's. Flowertree presented no written evidence of this putative prior use, other than two grainy, undated photographs that the courts discounted. Instead, four witnesses, comprised of relatives, friends and business associates of Hawkins, presented oral testimony to this effect. The district court accepted the oral testimony and held the Woodland patent invalid under § 102(a).

On appeal, the Federal Circuit reversed. After extensively reviewing pertinent Supreme Court precedent, Judge Newman observed that the use of oral evidence of interested persons was a disfavored mechanism for proving patent invalidity. According to several venerable Supreme Court cases, even honest witnesses can be tempted to remember facts favorable to the cause of one's relative or friend, particularly when these events purportedly took place many years ago. Judge Newman found this line of reasoning even more persuasive in the modern business environment, where some sort of written record ordinarily accompanies business activity. Given the absence of such a record in this case, as well as the relationship between the witnesses and the many years that had passed between the alleged dates of prior use and the date of the testimony, the Federal Circuit concluded that the accused infringer had not shown that the Woodland patent was invalid by clear and convincing evidence.

4.4.2.8 Patent Award to the Second Inventor

Section 102(g) provides that a first inventor may forfeit priority where she "abandoned, suppressed, or concealed" the invention. Congress intended this language, which appeared for the first time in the 1952 Patent Act, to codify the existing case law concerning priority. These early cases typically involved a first inventor who opted to withhold a technology, either by maintaining it as a trade secret or simply neglecting it. At some later point, a second individ-

46. Price v. Symsek, 988 F.2d 1187, 1195 n. 3, 26 USPQ2d 1031, 1037 n.3 (Fed.Cir.1993).

47. 148 F.3d 1368, 47 USPQ2d 1363 (Fed. Cir. 1998).

ual independently invented the same technology. Still later, the first inventor learned of this second invention, often through the grant of a patent to the second inventor. "Spurred" into action by the second inventor, the first inventor filed a patent application and claimed priority of invention as being the first inventor in fact.

In such cases the courts declined to award priority to the first inventor. The second inventor, who had made efforts to disclose the technology, had acted consistently with sound patent policy. Had the second inventor not acted, the first inventor might never have disclosed the invention at all, either continuing to neglect it or preferring instead to exploit it indefinitely as a trade secret. Although expressed in three words, the phrase "abandoned, suppressed, or concealed" captures this single concept.

Dunlop Holdings, Ltd. v. Ram Golf Corp.[48] presented the Seventh Circuit with an interesting question as to the sorts of activity that amount to an abandonment, suppression, or concealment. This opinion resulted from Dunlop's assertion of its patent on a material called Surlyn, useful as a golf ball cover. The alleged infringer, Ram Golf Corporation, knew of the use of the same material by a third party, Butch Wagner. Prior to Dunlop's date of invention, Wagner had not only made the identical invention, but distributed numerous golf balls embodying the invention to friends and potential customers. However, Wagner arguably took efforts to conceal the precise material he used as a golf ball cover, and at least one expert in the field was unable to determine the content of the cover following a thorough examination.

Although Dunlop was not the first inventor in fact, it argued that it should be considered the first inventor at law. According to Dunlop, Wagner had "abandoned, suppressed or concealed" the use of Surlyn as a golf ball cover because he did not disclose to the public the reason his golf ball cover was so durable. The trial court rejected the argument and struck down Dunlop's patent under § 102(g).

Following an appeal, the Seventh Circuit affirmed. Judge Stevens, as he was then, offered three reasons why Wagner's public, non-informing use demonstrated that he had not "abandoned, suppressed or concealed" the invention. First, the public still had the benefit of the invention because the golf balls had entered the stream of commerce. Similarly, potential competitors would likely be able to discern the nature of the invention through reverse engineering. Finally, Judge Stevens viewed inventors such as Wagner as public benefactors, who should not themselves be impeded from marketing their inventions by a later inventor's patent.

48. 524 F.2d 33, 188 USPQ2d 481 (7th Cir.1975).

Commentators have criticized *Dunlop Holdings*. The evidence suggested that competitors were not nearly as able to determine the composition of the cover as the court assumed. Many competitors take their chances on maintaining their innovations as a secret for as long as they can, and one wonders why their efforts should bar a later patent applicant.[49] Still, *Dunlop Holdings* stands for the proposition that if one commercially exploits an invention, there is no abandonment, suppression, or concealment even if the underlying technology cannot be readily deduced by examination or reverse engineering.

The Federal Circuit has had numerous occasions to interpret the phrase "abandoned, suppressed, or concealed" in § 102(g), including the interesting case of *Apotex USA, Inc. v. Merck & Co., Inc.*[50] Plaintiff Apotex owned two patents relating to a process for making a stable solid formulation of enalapril sodium, a product useful in the treatment of high blood pressure. Defendant Merck manufactured enalapril sodium as the active ingredient in certain of its own anti-hypertensive drugs. In the United States this product was termed Vasotec; in some other countries it was known as Renitec. Merck had done so continuously since 1983, and in fact owned several U.S. and Canadian patents covering the enalapril sodium composition itself. Merck did not own a patent covering its process of making Vasotec, however.

Merck disclosed the ingredients used in its Vasotec manufacturing process on at least two occasions. In 1992, Merck published a monograph in Canada listing the ingredients used to make Vasotec. Four years earlier, the 1988 edition of the Dictionnaire Vidal, a French pharmaceutical dictionary, also disclosed the ingredients used to make Renitec.

Merck also explained how it made Vasotec during a patent litigation against Apotex. In 1991, Merck sued Apotex in Canada for patent infringement. During the 1994 trial, a Merck official explained how the company manufactured Vasotec. Supposedly, within days of hearing this testimony, an Apotex official named Dr. Bernard Sherman conceived of a new process of making enalapril sodium. Apotex subsequently obtained two patents claiming the Sherman method.

Apotex later filed suit against Merck in the U.S. District Court for the Northern District of Illinois. According to Apotex, Merck's process of manufacturing Vasotec infringed both patents. Following a summary judgment motion, the trial court held that both patents

49. 1 Martin J. Adelman, Patent Law Perspectives § 2.3[8–4] at 2–270.2 to 2–270.3 (2d ed. 1992).

50. 254 F.3d 1031 (Fed. Cir. 2001).

were invalid, reasoning that Apotex was not actually the first inventor of the process.

On appeal, Apotex advanced two principal arguments. First, Apotex contended that Merck had failed to show that it had not "abandoned, suppressed or concealed" the invention. According to Apotex, due to the wording of § 102(g), Merck would have to show that it had not "abandoned, suppressed or concealed" the invention based on activities performed within the United States. Second, Apotex argued that even if the Canadian monograph, French dictionary and Canadian trial could be considered, they did not teach key information about Merck's manufacturing method. According to Apotex, Merck had in fact "abandoned, suppressed or concealed" its manufacturing method.

The Federal Circuit rejected both of Apotex's arguments. First, Judge Lourie determined that the language "in this country" in § 102(g) applied only to the country where "the invention was made." As a result, evidence negating a conclusion that an inventor "abandoned, suppressed or concealed" his invention is not limited to activities occurring within the United States. As applied to this case, the result was that the Canadian monograph, French dictionary, and Canadian trial could be considered to negate abandonment, suppression or concealment by Merck.

Second, Judge Lourie reasoned that Sherman invented the patented manufacturing methods before 1994. The question before the court was whether Merck had taken any steps to make the benefits of the invention known to the public prior to 1994. Judge Lourie concluded that Merck had taken such steps. Crediting the Canadian monograph, French dictionary, and Canadian trial, Judge Lourie concluded that these disclosures made the invention publicly known before Apotex entered the field.

The Federal Circuit disagreed with Apotex that such disclosures did not adequately describe Merck's method of manufacturing. Judge Lourie observed that Sherman had admitted that a skilled chemist could have determined how to make Vasotec from a review of the Canadian monograph, along with an inspection of the Vasotec tablets themselves. This combination of Merck's disclosures, alongside Sherman's admissions, provided the public with knowledge of the invention. As a result, Merck could not be said to have "abandoned, suppressed or concealed" the invention within the meaning of § 102(g). The Federal Circuit concluded by affirming the trial judge's summary judgment that the Apotex patents were invalid.

Apotex USA, Inc. v. Merck & Co., Inc. provides a helpful discussion of the phrase "abandoned, suppressed or concealed" in section 102(g). Along with predecessor cases, the *Apotex* ruling suggests that an individual that actually distributes a product to the public is unlikely to be found to have "abandoned, suppressed or concealed" any inventions associated with that product. It will be interesting to observe if the Federal Circuit reaches this result in cases where the manufacturing process is not so readily determined by skilled individuals as in *Apotex*.

Paulik v. Rizkalla is another important § 102(g) case from the Federal Circuit.[51] Rizkalla was the senior party in an interference, having filed a patent application on March 10, 1975. Paulik had actually reduced the invention to practice as early as November 1970 and filed an invention disclosure form with his employer's patent department at that time. The patent department initially opted not to pursue patent protection on the invention, but began to draft an application in January or February 1975. Paulik's application was filed on June 30, 1975. The PTO Board awarded priority of invention to Rizkalla. According to the Board, Paulik's conduct fell within the language of § 102(g) denying priority of inventorship to those who have "abandoned, suppressed or concealed" the invention.

Following Paulik's appeal to the Federal Circuit, the *en banc* court reversed. The majority of the court held that an inventor, after taking no action for years, could renew inventive activities and recover from a charge of abandonment. Paulik could obtain priority if, on remand, he could "demonstrate that he had renewed activity on the invention and that he proceeded diligently to file his patent application, starting before the earliest date to which Rizkalla is entitled." Writing for the majority, Judge Newman reasoned that a contrary result would discourage inventors "from working on projects that had been 'too long' set aside, because of the impossibility of relying, in a priority contest, on either their original work or their renewed work."[52]

A vigorous dissent authored by Judge Friedman urged that the majority's view could not be squared with the plain language of § 102(g). According to the dissent, the statute provided only that one who has abandoned, suppressed, or concealed an invention has forfeited priority, with no opportunity for redemption. The dissent also questioned whether Paulik, whose deliberate suppression of the invention caused it to be the junior party, was truly deserving of priority over Rizkalla. Finally, the dissent charged the majority with adding an additional complexity to interference proceedings.

As a technical matter, the terms "diligence" and "abandoned, suppressed or concealed" present distinct legal concepts under § 102(g). Diligence is limited to instances when an inventor is

51. 760 F.2d 1270, 226 USPQ 224 (Fed.Cir.1985).

52. 760 F.2d at 1276, 226 USPQ at 228.

second to reduce to practice, but first to conceive of the invention. The concept of inventor abandonment, suppression, and concealment instead concerns the conduct of the first individual to reduce the invention to practice. In practice, however, both notions involve similar acts and intentions on behalf of an inventor.

4.4.2.9 First Inventor Defense

The First Inventor Defense Act of 1999 created an infringement defense for an earlier inventor of a method of doing business that is subsequently patented by another. The defendant must have reduced the infringing subject matter to practice one year before the effective filing date of the patent and made commercial use of that subject matter in the United States before the effective filing date.

The impetus for this provision lies in the rather complex relationship between the law of trade secrets and the patent system. Trade secrecy protects individuals from misappropriation of valuable information that is useful in commerce. One reason an inventor might maintain an invention as a trade secret rather than seek patent protection is that he may feel that the subject matter of the invention is not of a type that is patentable. Such material as customer lists or data compilations have traditionally been regarded as amenable to trade secret protection but not to patenting. Inventors might also maintain trade secret protection due to ignorance of the patent system or because they believe they can keep their invention secret longer than the period of exclusivity granted through the patent system.[53]

It is important to note from the outset that the patent system has not favored trade secret holders. As we have already seen, well-established patent law establishes that an inventor who makes a secret, commercial use of an invention for more than one year prior to filing a patent application at the PTO forfeits his own right to a patent.[54] This policy is principally based upon the desire to maintain the integrity of the patent term. The Patent Act grants patents a term of twenty years commencing from the date a patent application is filed.[55] If the trade secret holder could make commercial use of an invention for many years before choosing to file a patent application, he could disrupt this regime by delaying the expiration date of his patent.

53. *See* David D. Friedman, et al., *Some Economics of Trade Secret Law*, 5 J. Econ. Persps. 61, 64 (1991).

54. *See* Metallizing Eng'g Co. v. Kenyon Bearing & Auto Parts, 153 F.2d 516, 68 USPQ 54 (2d Cir.), *cert. denied*, 328 U.S. 840, 66 S.Ct. 1016, 90 L.Ed. 1615 (1946).

55. 35 U.S.C.A. § 154 (2000).

On the other hand, settled patent law principles also establish that prior secret uses will not defeat the patents of later inventors.[56] Moreover, if an earlier inventor made secret commercial use of an invention, and another person independently invented the same technology later and obtained patent protection, then the trade secret holder could face liability for patent infringement. This policy was based upon the reasoning that issued, published patent instruments fully inform the public about the invention, while trade secrets do not. As between a subsequent inventor who patented the invention, and had disclosed the invention to the public, and an earlier trade secret holder who did not, the law favored the patent holder.

Although all these principles have been long settled, legal developments in the late 1990's concerning the patentability of methods of doing business focused renewed attention upon the relationship between patents and trade secrets. Inventors of methods of doing business traditionally relied upon trade secret protection because such inventions had long been regarded as unpatentable subject matter. As a result, until recently inventors of innovative business methods obtained legal advice not to file applications at the PTO. This advice was sound under the patent law as it then stood.

The 1998 Federal Circuit opinion in *State Street Bank and Trust Co. v. Signature Financial Group*[57] altered this traditional principle. In the *State Street Bank* opinion, the Federal Circuit overturned the historical bar denying patents on methods of doing business. As a consequence, inventors in such sectors as finance, insurance, and services began to seek legal protection for their inventions through the patent system. Patent experts recognized, however, that this change in background principles dealt a harsh blow to individuals who invented business methods prior to the issuance of the *State Street Bank* opinion. Many of these inventors had maintained their innovative business methods as trade secrets for many years. As a result, they were unable belatedly to obtain patent protection on their business methods—they would be barred under § 102(b) because their own long use, albeit secret, triggered a statutory bar. Moreover, because trade secrets did not constitute prior art against the patent applications of others, a subsequent inventor would be able to obtain patent protection. Under these circumstances, a trade secret holder could find himself an adjudi-

56. *See* W.L. Gore & Assocs. v. Garlock, Inc., 721 F.2d 1540, 220 USPQ 303 (Fed.Cir.), *cert. denied*, 469 U.S. 851, 105 S.Ct. 172, 83 L.Ed.2d 107 (1984).

57. 149 F.3d 1368, 47 USPQ2d 1596 (Fed.Cir.1998), *cert. denied*, 525 U.S. 1093, 119 S.Ct. 851, 142 L.Ed.2d 704 (1999).

cated infringer of a patented business method that he actually invented first, and that he had been practicing for many years.

The First Inventor Defense Act reconciles these principles by providing an infringement defense for an earlier inventor of a method of doing business that was later patented by another. As detailed in § 273 of the Patent Act, this infringement defense is subject to several qualifications. First, the defendant must have reduced the infringing subject matter to practice at least one year before the effective filing date of the patent application. Second, the defendant must have commercially used the infringing subject matter prior to the effective filing date of the patent. Finally, any reduction to practice or use must have been made in good faith, without derivation from the patentee or persons in privity with the patentee.

Looking forward, it would seem a rather straightforward matter to alter the first inventor defense to embrace a more expansive range of patentable subject matter. In this regard the first inventor defense could evolve into a doctrine quite similar to that which prevails in other countries.[58] These statutes are commonly referred to as creating "prior user rights." Unlike the more limited regime created by the First Inventor Defense Act of 1999, prior user rights abroad are not limited to methods of doing business. They instead apply to any sort of invention. Experience with the First Inventor Defense Act of 1999 might provide a basis for deciding whether Congress should consider a more full-fledged prior user rights regime, or maintain the current system as a limited cure of a specific problem.

4.4.3 Disclosure in U.S. Patent Applications Under § 102(e)

Section 102(e) provides a complex rule that governs the prior art status of published patent applications and issued patents. Under § 102(e)(1), a published U.S. patent application that discloses, but does not claim the invention, constitutes prior art as of its filing date. Section 102(e)(2) works similarly: an issued U.S. patent that discloses, but does not claim the invention, constitutes prior art as of its filing date.

In approaching § 102(e) for the first time, one should remember procedures followed at the PTO. The PTO's current practice is to publish some pending patent applications eighteen months after the filing date. Not all applications are published, however. Specifically, where an applicant certifies that he will not seek foreign

58. *See* The Advisory Commission on Patent Law Reform, A Report to the Secretary of Commerce 48 (1992).

patent rights pertaining to that invention, the PTO will not publish the U.S. application. As a result, some patent applications are published eighteen months after they are filed. Other patent applications are never published at all, and their contents become publicly accessible only if the PTO allows them to issue as granted patents.

The purpose of § 102(e) is to define the point at which these published applications and issued patents serve as prior art against others. Our discussion of § 102(a) and (b) has shown that the patent law usually does not allow references that are not available to the public, such as trade secrets, to have patent-defeating effect. Consequently, the most appropriate date for a published application or issued patent to have prior art effect might seem to be the date it actually issues from the PTO.

In the famous 1926 opinion in *Alexander Milburn Co. v. Davis–Bournonville Co.*,[59] however, Justice Holmes reached a different conclusion. He determined that the disclosures of the patent instrument should have the status of prior art as of their filing date. Since Congress subsequently codified the *Alexander Milburn* rule in § 102(e)(2), a review of the opinion of Justice Holmes will help explain how the patent law came to this seemingly counterintuitive result.

In the *Alexander Milburn* case, Clifford filed a patent application on January 31, 1911, that disclosed, but did not claim, a welding and cutting apparatus. On March 4, 1911, Whitford filed a patent application claiming the apparatus that Clifford had disclosed but not claimed. Apparently Whitford lacked sufficient evidence to demonstrate any invention date earlier than the date of his patent application. The Patent Office granted Clifford's patent on February 6, 1912, while Whitford's patent issued on June 4, 1912. Subsequently, an accused infringer of Whitford's patent argued that Clifford's disclosure of the apparatus served as anticipatory prior art against Whitford. Note that because Clifford had not claimed the same apparatus as Whitford, priority of invention was not an issue in the case.

During arguments before the Supreme Court, Whitford asserted that Clifford's patent could not be considered prior art until the date of its issuance. According to Whitford, Clifford's application disclosed nothing to the public at the time of filing, for the Patent Office maintained it in secrecy until the date of issuance. Although Whitford's characterizations were undoubtedly correct, Justice Holmes nonetheless disagreed in a pithy opinion. According to Holmes, "Clifford had done all that he could do to make his

59. 270 U.S. 390, 46 S.Ct. 324, 70 L.Ed. 651 (1926).

description public" by filing a patent application.[60] Clifford merely waited for the Patent Office to approve his application. In such circumstances, Patent Office delays in processing applications should not control the content of the prior art.

Justice Holmes' reasoning has some apparent flaws. At the time he was writing, the grace period provided by the predecessor statute to § 102(b) was two years.[61] If indeed the Patent Office was a model of rapidity, granting patents on the day they were filed, then Whitford would seemingly be able to avoid the Clifford reference by filing before January 31, 1913. Nor could Clifford's application be available as prior art under the earlier version of § 102(a), for his prior knowledge or use was of a totally private character.[62]

Yet the *Alexander Milburn* holding, and its codification in § 102(e), present a sensible compromise. Inventors file hundreds of applications at the PTO on a daily basis. These patent applications paint a telling portrait of the state of the art. It would seem anomalous for the PTO to disregard earlier filed applications when making patentability decisions, particularly since PTO officials are adept at cataloguing and retrieving patent-related documents.

Justice Holmes authored *Alexander Milburn* at a time when the PTO maintained patent applications in secrecy. Under the American Inventors Protection Act of 1999 the PTO will now publish pending patent applications eighteen months following the filing date, unless the applicant certifies that he will not file a parallel application abroad. When Congress provided for the publication of patent applications, it opted to apply the reasoning of *Alexander Milburn* in this new context. As a result, under § 102(e)(1), published patent applications count as prior art as of the date they are filed. Section 102(e)(1) therefore creates an eighteen-month period in which a pending application has prior art effect, but is not available to the public.

The PTO applies § 102(e) in the following manner. If an examiner becomes aware of a granted patent that discloses, but does not claim, the invention claimed in a pending application, she may issue a § 102(e) rejection. The applicant may elect to respond with a Rule 131 affidavit.[63] That affidavit must demonstrate sufficient inventive activity prior to the filing date associated with the granted patent. The applicant must show either (1) an actual reduction to practice prior to the patent's filing date, or (2) conception of the invention prior to the patent's filing date, coupled with diligence from the filing date until a subsequent reduction to practice.

60. 270 U.S. at 400.

61. Rev. Stat. § 4486, as amended March 3, 1897, ch. 391, 29 Stat. 692.

62. *See supra* § 4.3.1.

63. *See supra* § 4.3.1.

Alternatively, suppose that an examiner encounters two co-pending applications filed by different inventors.[64] Further assume that the earlier application discloses subject matter that would anticipate the later filed application. Because the examiner is obliged to preserve the confidentiality of each application in this situation, the examiner must wait until one of two events occurs before dispensing a rejection under § 102(e): Either the earlier application is published, under § 102(e)(1); or, for those applications the PTO will not publish, the issuance of the application as a granted patent under § 102(e)(2).[65]

Section 102(e) differs from § 102(g) in that the invention must be described in the patent's specification, but not claimed. In cases where two patents or applications claim the same invention, the inventors are subject to a priority contest, either through an interference proceeding or in the courts. By its own terms, § 102(e) speaks to patents or applications "by another." Therefore § 102(e) does not apply to patents or applications belonging to the same inventor.

Section 102(e) expressly applies only to U.S. patents. For foreign patents, their date of effectiveness as prior art is the first date they are publicly disclosed. Although different patent systems overseas include varying provisions, generally speaking the first date foreign patent offices publish a patent document is either (1) the date on which the foreign patent actually issues, or (2) an earlier date, mandated by foreign patent statutes, on which pending patent applications are published (in most countries this date is approximately 18 months after the application is filed). For example, suppose that Dr. Nanuck files a Canadian patent application on May 1, 2004. The Canadian Patent Office publishes that application 18 months later, on November 1, 2005, and eventually grants Nanuck an issued Canadian patent on September 12, 2006. Because § 102(e) does not apply, the first date that the Canadian patent can serve as prior art under U.S. law is November 1, 2005, the date the Canadian Patent Office published Nanuck's application.

The courts have read the requirement that § 102(e) applies to applications "filed in the United States" quite literally. Even though a patent application may have obtained foreign priority through § 119(a) and the Paris Convention, the issued patent that results has prior art effect only at the time of the actual U.S. filing date.[66]

64. The PTO allows examiners to issue provisional rejections of applications where they share common inventors or ownership.

65. *See* MANUAL OF PATENT EXAMINING PROCEDURE § 706.02(f).

66. *See* In re Hilmer, 359 F.2d 859, 149 USPQ 480 (CCPA 1966). *See infra* § 12.1.4.

An example demonstrates the basic workings of § 102(e). Suppose that Professor Gizmo conceives of a new X-ray machine on July 7, 2004, actually reduces the machine to practice on October 13, 2004, and files an application directed towards the machine at the PTO on February 28, 2005. During prosecution, the PTO examiner discovers an issued U.S. patent to Gizmo's rival, Dr. Nefarious. The Nefarious patent discloses, but does not claim, the same X-ray machine that Gizmo claims. The Nefarious patent issued on March 17, 2007, based upon an application filed on November 1, 2004. Assume further that the PTO did not publish the pending application of Nefarious eighteen months after its filing date because Nefarious sought patent rights only in the United States.

Under these facts, the PTO examiner may issue a § 102(e) rejection to Gizmo based upon the Nefarious patent. Assuming that Gizmo has sufficient corroboration of her dates of inventive activity, Gizmo may file a Rule 131 affidavit demonstrating that prior to the filing date of the Nefarious patent (Nefarious filed on November 1, 2004), Gizmo reduced her invention to practice (Gizmo did so on October 13, 2004). If the PTO examiner harbors no further objections, then Gizmo will be awarded a patent.

Concerned readers may be troubled about the status of Dr. Nefarious in this situation. After all, the PTO did not contact Nefarious concerning the Gizmo application, and Gizmo will obtain a patent that may be quite similar to that of Nefarious. The answer is that because Nefarious did not expressly claim the X-ray machine, but instead merely disclosed it in his patent, he is not deemed to possess a sufficient interest in that invention. That Gizmo later claimed that X-ray machine is, on this view, of no moment to Nefarious. Of course, if Nefarious had expressly claimed the X-ray machine that Gizmo later claimed, then the PTO would have declared an interference and awarded a patent only to the party that was the first inventor. If Gizmo does procure a patent, and Nefarious belatedly wishes to appropriate the X-ray machine invention, Nefarious may be able to file a so-called "reissue application" at the PTO in order to claim the X-ray machine expressly. Nefarious must meet certain requirements to invoke the mechanism of reissue, however, the details of which are discussed in § 7.5.3 of this volume.

Before we leave § 102(e), it should be noted that this provision makes reference to § 351(a) of the Patent Act. In so doing § 102(e) obliquely refers to the provisions of the Patent Cooperation Treaty (PCT). The PCT is discussed fully in Chapter 12 but a few words on the subject may be helpful at this stage of the game. In short, the PCT allows applicants to file an "international application" at one qualified patent office that designates all signatory countries in which patent protection is sought. By operation of the treaty, that single application is deemed to have the same legal effect as the filing of multiple applications in all signatory countries designated by the applicant. Because over 100 states have joined the PCT, the filing of one international application can do the work of many regular national filings. All international applications are published 18 months after they are filed.

When acceding to the PCT, the United States had to adapt the *Alexander Milburn* rule to international applications. Following 2002 amendments to § 102(e), the basic prior art rules are as follows. Publications of international applications that designate the United States and are published in the English language fall within § 102(e)(1), and are accorded prior art effectiveness as of the date of their filings. Similarly, § 102(e)(2) states that a U.S. patent shall enjoy prior art effect as of the filing date of the international application if that application designated the United States and was published in the English language. Neither of these provisions changes the basic *Alexander Milburn* rule with respect to non-PCT applications filed in the United States.

4.4.4 Derivation Under § 102(f)

The final novelty defeating provision in the statute is section 102(f), which prevents a patent from issuing to an applicant who "did not himself invent the subject matter sought to be patented." If an individual derived the invention from another, simple equity and common sense dictate that no patent should result from his application. Section 102(f) thus presents something of a standing requirement, reinforced by § 101 and the Constitution itself, mandating that only the true inventor apply for the patent. A prima facie case of derivation entails a showing of another's prior conception of the claimed subject matter along with an awareness of that conception to the applicant or patentee.[67]

The courts have not employed § 102(f) with great frequency. Because a predicate to derivation is that another first invented the subject matter sought to be patented, § 102(a) ordinarily will also apply to such cases. Parties adverse to the patent generally will find proofs of patent invalidity more straightforward under § 102(a), which does not entail the nettlesome issues of communication and copying. Section 102(f) is most often employed in those factual circumstances where § 102(a) does not apply. In particular, § 102(f) is not limited to inventions conceived "in this country,"

67. *See* Price v. Symsek, 988 F.2d 1187, 26 USPQ2d 1031 (Fed.Cir.1993); Campbell v. Spectrum Automation Co., 513 F.2d 932, 185 USPQ 718 (6th Cir. 1975).

nor have courts imposed a requirement of public knowledge as they have in § 102(a).[68]

For example, suppose that on May 27, 2004, Dr. Nefarious is enjoying a poolside drink in an Ensenada, Mexico resort. Nefarious overhears Professor Gizmo's oral description of her latest invention to an academic colleague. Nefarious rushes back to the United States and files a patent application at the PTO on May 29, 2004, claiming Gizmo's invention. Under these circumstances, the § 102(b) statutory bar does not apply because Gizmo's invention has neither been "on sale" nor in "public use" in the United States. Section 102(a) also does not apply because Gizmo's invention was not "known or used" in the United States either. Under these facts, assuming Gizmo can prove that Nefarious derived his claimed invention from her, then § 102(f) would apply and serve as the basis for rejection of the Nefarious patent application.

68. *See generally* OddzOn Products, Inc. v. Just Toys, Inc., 122 F.3d 1396, 43 USPQ2d 1641 (Fed.Cir.1997).

Chapter 5

NONOBVIOUSNESS

Table of Sections

---

§ 5.1 Introduction

Section 103(a) denies patentability "if the differences between the subject matter sought to be patented and the prior art are such that the subject matter as a whole would have been obvious at the time the invention was made to a person having ordinary skill in the art to which said subject matter pertains." The patent community employs the awkward term "nonobviousness" to express this requirement. As we shall see, nonobviousness descends from the historical and more ephemeral standard of "invention." In practice, nonobviousness is the most significant hurdle to patentability. Much of the dialogue between an applicant and a PTO examiner typically concerns nonobviousness, and it is the most common validity defense raised by accused infringers in court.

Section 103(a) requires jurists and PTO examiners to decide whether an inventor's work product differs from the state of the art enough to be patent-worthy. In resolving this issue, the nonobviousness analysis proceeds in the same fashion as the novelty inquiry. First, the class of technology relevant to the assessment of obviousness must be identified. The relevant prior art for nonobviousness generally is the same as that for novelty, with a few exceptions. Notably, not only must the reference fall into a § 102 category to be recognized as a source of prior art for § 103(a), the reference must also be considered analogous to what is claimed in the patent or patent application. In addition, Congress created a special rule, codified in § 103(c) of the Patent Act, addressing the prior art status of collaborative research efforts. Prior art for nonobviousness is addressed in § 5.2 below.

Once the apposite prior art has been determined, then the claimed invention must be found to be nonobvious with respect to those references. This Chapter considers that issue in § 5.3. Section 103(a) requires that the knowledge possessed by a typical scientist or engineer working within the relevant technical area must form the yardstick for the nonobviousness decision. In contrast to the novelty requirement, multiple references may be considered together when analyzing nonobviousness. As this text will discuss, however, a skilled artisan must have been motivated to combine the references, with the expectation that this combination would have a reasonable probability of success.

Closely akin, if not identical to nonobviousness is the standard of "inventive step" employed overseas. For example, Article 56 of the European Patent Convention provides that "[a]n invention shall be considered as involving an inventive step if, having regard to the state of the art, it is not obvious to a person skilled in the art."[1] Notwithstanding the near synonymous quality of this terminology, as we shall see, the U.S. patent bar possesses such a collective bad memory over the historical standard of "invention" that use of the term "inventive step" should be avoided domestically. Further, to reflect the fact that the nonobviousness analysis is based upon the prior art, rather than employing today's hindsight, the U.S. patent community frowns upon the use of the present

§ 5.1

1. Convention on the Grant of European Patents, Oct. 5, 1973, 13 I.L.M. 268 (1974).

tense when describing nonobviousness. It is good practice to employ the language "*would have been* obvious" when discussing or writing about § 103(a) problems.[2]

Those new to the patent system should not lose sight of the impact of the nonobviousness requirement. It allows the PTO and the courts to deny or invalidate a patent even where it claims a product that has never been previously made, or a process that has never been previously performed. Section 103(a) therefore reflects the policy that not all novel inventions should be patentable.

Writers and judges have offered numerous justifications for this "novelty plus" requirement. Most readily apparent is that nonobviousness creates a "patent-free" zone around the state of the art. Section 103(a) allows skilled technicians to complete routine work such as the straightforward substitution of materials, the ordinary streamlining of parts and technical processes, and the usual marginal improvements that occur as a technology matures, without concern that they may infringe a patent.[3] Because skilled artisans engage in this sort of day-to-day work out of necessity, there also seems to be little reason to offer the reward of a patent for such routine accomplishments.

The nonobviousness requirement may also arise out of recognition of the practical limitations of the PTO and interested private parties who wish to invalidate a patent. As we have seen, in order to show that a claimed invention has been anticipated, a prior art reference must provide an enabling disclosure of every element of that invention. Finding an earlier publication, patent, public use or offer for sale that is completely identical to the claimed invention is sometimes difficult, however. PTO examiners and interested individuals have only so many resources to devote towards sifting through the enormous volume of technical information that exists in our modern, global society. If several references can be found that, in combination, indicate that the invention would have been obvious, there is at least some chance that the invention wasn't really novel either.

Economic studies have advanced a more theoretical justification for demanding nonobviousness as a condition of patentability. Legal economists have urged that an optimal patent system would only grant patents to inventions that have been induced by the patent system itself. If ordinary market forces provided sufficient incentives to invent and disclose new technologies, then the award

2. Panduit v. Dennison Mfg., 774 F.2d 1082, 1088 n. 7, 227 USPQ 337, 340 n.7 (Fed.Cir.1985), *judgment vacated on other grounds*, 475 U.S. 809, 106 S.Ct. 1578, 89 L.Ed.2d 817 (1986), *on remand* 810 F.2d 1561, 1 USPQ2d 1593 (Fed.Cir.1987).

3. Martin J. Adelman *et al.*, Patent Law: Cases and Materials 310 (2d ed. 2003).

of a patent would be unnecessary to promote innovation. In such cases, the public should not be made to suffer the inconvenience of having a patent issue. Although the patent system does not attempt to discern the motivation of individual inventors, it does employ the proxy of nonobviousness. Under this view, the nonobviousness requirement encourages individuals to pursue projects that, because they require expansion of the state of the art, are of uncertain success.[4]

§ 5.2 Prior Art for Nonobviousness

Section 103(a) requires the patent community to determine "the differences between the subject matter sought to be patented and the prior art." But the statute nowhere defines the term "prior art." The courts have filled in this gap by declaring that all of the materials that are relevant in determining novelty and statutory bar questions under § 102 should be considered as prior art for nonobviousness inquiry as well.[1]

There is, however, one important difference between the scope of the prior art for the purposes of § 102 on the one hand, and with regard to the nonobviousness inquiry of § 103 on the other. Where the issue is nonobviousness, the technology must also originate within an "analogous art," a technical discipline relevant to the claimed invention or concerning a problem pertinent to the claimed subject matter. The Patent Act also exempts from consideration certain prior art that arose due to joint research efforts. Under § 103(c), when the prior art and the claimed invention are, at the time of invention, owned by a single entity, then they may not be considered in a nonobviousness analysis. These topics are taken up in turn below.

4. *See generally* Rebecca Eisenberg, *Patents and the Exclusive Progress of Science: Exclusive Rights and Experimental Use*, 56 U. Chi. L. Rev. 1017 (1989).

§ 5.2

1. Whether subject matter available under §§ 102(c) or 102(d) applies as well to § 103(a) has yet to be conclusively determined. This circumstance is likely due to the relatively infrequent use of either provision. Both the CCPA, in In re Bass, 474 F.2d 1276, 1290, 177 USPQ 178, 189 (CCPA 1973), and the Federal Circuit, in OddzOn Products, Inc. v. Just Toys, Inc., 122 F.3d 1396, 1403, 43 USPQ2d 1641, 1645–46 (Fed.Cir.1997), have stated in dicta that neither provision serves as a source or prior art to § 103(a). This result is questionable with regard to § 102(c). If an inventor has truly abandoned an invention to the public, sound patent policy would suggest that his dedication should apply to obvious variations of that technology as well. And given the breadth accorded to the § 102(d) bar by the Federal Circuit in In re Kathawala, 9 F.3d 942, 28 USPQ2d 1785 (Fed. Cir.1993), the fact that foreign patents within § 102(d) do not input into § 103(a) may be of little moment.

5.2.1 Analogous Arts

The fact that a reference falls into one of the categories itemized in § 102 is not enough to render it applicable to the nonobviousness determination. The technology must also issue from a technical area judged sufficiently germane to that of the claimed invention. Such areas are known as "analogous arts." This doctrine, which does not apply to novelty determinations, follows from the requirement of § 103(a) that nonobviousness be judged from the perspective of "a person having ordinary skill in the art." Thus, although a person of skill in a given technical area is presumed to have access to all of the technical knowledge comprising the state of the art, this knowledge can only be employed within the constraints of the abilities and expertise of practitioners within that field.

A simple example illustrates both the general implications of this doctrine, and the kinds of problems that can arise on its fringes. Assume that Professor Cutler has devised a new method for manufacturing a knife blade that never needs sharpening, and is now seeking patent protection for his invention. If the examiner at the PTO discovers a previously issued French patent concerning methods for producing knife blades, and a previously published scientific article in the *Alabama Knife Blade Production Journal*, the examiner could rely on the combined teachings of those two references to conclude that Cutler's invention is obvious. Both of these references plainly come from the same technical field as Cutler's—knife blade production. Now imagine that the second reference was an article in the *Alabama Toy and Game Technology Review* describing how to make exceptional sharp edges on scary Freddy Kruger-type gloves for children's Halloween costumes. Before using this reference in a nonobviousness analysis, the examiner would have to be satisfied that toy manufacturing is an "analogous art" to knife production. If it is not, the reference would be ignored for purposes of applying § 103.

The Federal Circuit's 1992 decision in *In re Clay*[2] presents a thorough explanation of its view of analogous arts. Clay's application concerned a process for storing refined liquid hydrocarbon product in a storage tank having a dead volume between the tank bottom and its outlet port. The process involved the placement of a gelation solution into a tank's dead volume and later allowing the solution to gel. According to Clay, the addition of a gel-degrading agent would allow the gel to be readily removed from the tank. The PTO had rejected Clay's application under § 103(a) in part due to the Syndansk reference. Syndansk called for the introduction of a similar gel into an underground, natural, oil-bearing formation in

2. 966 F.2d 656, 23 USPQ2d 1058 (Fed.Cir.1992).

order to better channel oil flow during extraction. The Marathon Oil Company owned both Syndansk's patent and Clay's application.

Judge Lourie first noted that a two-part standard governed whether prior art is analogous. The first determination was "whether the art is from the same field of endeavor, regardless of the problem addressed."[3] If so, then the art should be considered analogous and within the § 103(a) inquiry. Even if this first step was not met, however, the reference could still be deemed analogous if "reasonably pertinent to the particular problem with which the inventor is involved."[4] Such a reference "logically would have commended itself to the inventor's attention in considering his problem."[5]

According to Judge Lourie, the Syndansk reference fulfilled neither test. With regard to the field of endeavor, Syndansk addressed the use of gel in unconfined, irregular volumes of natural subterranean formations, in extreme operating conditions. Clay instead manipulated the confined, dead volume of an artificial storage tank under ordinary atmospheric conditions. And concerning the pertinence of the problem, the court reasoned that Syndansk dealt with the removal of oil from rock, while Clay with oil from a storage tank. As the problem concerning Clay involved dissimilar structures and working conditions, a person of ordinary skill would not have been led to consult the Syndansk patent for information bearing on the problem that Clay was trying to solve.

Although the second aspect of the inquiry seems correctly decided, the *Clay* court appeared to give lip service to the first part of its analogy test. That both the Clay and Syndansk inventions dealt with the use of gel in oil extraction, and were owned by the same company, suggests that both fell within the same field of endeavor. The Federal Circuit also seemingly collapsed the first part of its analogy standard into the second, for the same facts guided its reasoning for each.

Despite *Clay*, the trend is towards a broadening of the prior art that courts consider pertinent.[6] The Federal Circuit opinion in *In re Paulsen*,[7] decided just two years after *Clay*, is representative. There, the court held prior art "directed to hinges and latches as used in a desktop telephone directory, a piano lid, a kitchen cabinet, a washing machine cabinet, a wooden furniture cabinet, or a two-part housing for storing stereo cassettes" to be analogous to the problem of devising a hinge and latch closing means for a portable

3. 966 F.2d at 659, 23 USPQ2d at 1060.

4. *Id.*

5. 966 F.2d at 659, 23 USPQ2d at 1061.

6. *See* Twin Disc, Inc. v. United States, 231 USPQ 417, 427 (Cl.Ct.1986).

7. 30 F.3d 1475, 31 USPQ2d 1671 (Fed.Cir.1994).

computer. According to the court, the problems addressed in the patent application were not unique to the computing field. They instead concerned how to connect and secure the two parts of a clamshell-style portable computer, a problem well known to the simple mechanical arts.

Recall that under § 102, it is a necessary, but not sufficient condition of anticipation that a single reference describe all the elements of the claimed invention. That single prior art reference must also explain to skilled persons in the art how to put the invention into practice. This standard is termed the "enablement" requirement.[8] Importantly, no such requirement exists for obviousness under § 103. Even if a reference does not fully disclose how a technology works by itself, it may be employed for all that it teaches in the context of obviousness.[9]

Suppose, for example, that the inventor Dr. Knies files a patent application claiming a combination of a detachable automobile seat and baby stroller. The U.S. PTO patent examiner discovers a journal article, written by Goldmann and published more than one year before the date of the Knies patent application, that briefly describes the concept of a combination detachable automobile seat/ baby stroller. The Goldmann reference qualifies as prior art under the "publication" bar of § 102(b). However, Goldmann describes the combination detachable automobile seat/baby stroller concept in only a cursory fashion, and in particular provides no details on how the two features can be workably combined and secured to the floor of an automobile interior. As a result, the Goldmann reference is not an enabling one, and the examiner would be unable to make an anticipation rejection under § 102(b).

The examiner could use the Goldmann reference in the context of an obviousness analysis under § 103, however. Suppose that the examiner discovers two additional prior art references. One of the references provides an enabling description of the combination of an ordinary seat and a baby stroller. The other reference also provides an enabling description of the same mechanical means employed by Knies to secure a detachable seat to the floor of an automobile interior. Although these two references describe all the elements of the Knies invention and are enabling, they do not suggest that the references should be combined. The examiner would be able to make a § 103 rejection by citing the Goldmann publication in order to demonstrate the motivation to combine these two reference—even though Goldmann is by itself nonenabling.

8. *See supra* § 4.2.3.

9. Symbol Technologies, Inc. v. Opticon, Inc., 935 F.2d 1569, 19 USPQ2d 1241 (Fed.Cir.1991).

5.2.2 Section 103(c)

Congress amended § 103 in 1984 by adding a new provision now codified at § 103(c).[10] As subsequently amended in 1999, § 103(c) exempts prior art arising from "one or more of subsections (e), (f), and (g)" of § 102 from consideration in the nonobviousness inquiry under § 103(a), if certain conditions are met. Specifically, the putative prior art under § 102(e), (f), or (g), as well as the claimed invention, must either be owned by, or subject to an obligation of assignment to, a single entity at the time the invention was made.

A knowledge of the history of § 103(c) may aid understanding of this rather technical provision. Congress enacted § 103(c) in response to the CCPA's decision in *In re Bass.*[11] There, co-inventors Bass, Jenkins, and Horvat had applied for a patent on an air control system for carding machines (these are machines that clean and straighten textile fibers so that they can be spun into thread). Their effective filing date was October 11, 1965. The PTO rejected their claims on the ground of nonobviousness, a rejection which the CCPA affirmed on appeal. Among the references cited by the PTO as demonstrating the obviousness of the invention were two patents: a patent granted to Bass and Horvat, which had matured from an application filed on August 23, 1965; and a patent issued to Jenkins, based upon an October 13, 1964, application.

The correspondence of inventor surnames between the application and the prior art patents was not a coincidence—the prior art patents had been granted to the same Bass and Horvat, in the one case, and the same Jenkins in the other, as were seeking the new patent. This meant that the PTO and CCPA cited these inventors' own earlier work against them to establish obviousness. Ordinarily, the patent statute makes it clear that an inventor's own prior inventive efforts may not anticipate her own subsequent patent application. For example, in § 102(g), the invention must be made by "another" to serve as prior art. However, the *Bass* court reasoned that an opposite approach was permissible in this case because of a traditional patent law principle that treats each new combination of joint inventors as a distinct "inventive entity." This rule applies even where these combinations share individual inventors. Under this rule, the team of Bass, Jenkins and Horvat are considered a different inventive entity than the team of just Bass and Horvat. Each group of natural persons essentially acquires its own legal identity; they, as a whole, constitute "the inventor" of that technology. On this view, the two prior art patents at issue in

10. Patent Law Amendments of 1984, Pub. L. No. 98–622, § 104, 98 Stat. 3385.

11. 474 F.2d 1276, 177 USPQ 178 (CCPA 1973).

the *Bass* litigation were, as matter of legal technicality, the work of a different inventor than the one seeking the present patent, and thus relevant prior art.

Whatever the merits of *In re Bass* in a world where most inventions are made by individual putterers in their garage, it is a dubious approach in today's world, where most technology development is conducted by corporate entities. Such corporations usually employ numerous technologists to engage in collaborative research and development efforts, and there may be a constant shifting in the composition of inventive teams working on different projects. Applying the rule of *In re Bass* in this setting could lead to harsh results and unjustified findings of obviousness, because it would permit a rejection even if only a slight change in personnel occurs. In a particularly fertile and interactive corporate research department, inventors could find themselves unable to obtain patents due to "in-house" rejections for obviousness based upon efforts by their peers, and even in part by themselves!

Congress intended § 103(c) to solve the problem highlighted in *In re Bass* by exempting § 102 (e), (f), and (g) prior art from the obviousness analysis in joint research and development settings. The workings of § 103(c) can prove elusive, but an example should lend some clarity to its provisions. Suppose that two inventors, Roger and Joy, each work for the Coif Corporation. As part of their employment contracts, Roger and Joy have agreed to assign inventions that they develop to the Coif Corporation. Roger conceives of a new electromagnetic generator on November 1, 2002. He immediately informs Joy about his idea. Working diligently in his laboratory, Roger reduces the invention to practice on December 22, 2002. The Coif Corporation files a patent application on Roger's behalf on February 12, 2003. The Roger patent issues on January 19, 2004.

On April 10, 2003, Joy realizes that she can improve upon Roger's generator. Because of her workload, she does not start on the project until May 3, 2003. Without further consulting Roger, she ultimately completes her improved generator on June 1, 2003. However, although Joy's invention represents an improvement over Roger's work, assume that it would have been obvious in light of the Roger generator. At all events, the Coif Corporation files a patent application on behalf of Joy on October 1, 2003.

Under these facts, the Roger patent cannot serve as prior art against Joy. The statutory bars of § 102(b) and (d) are not triggered here.[12] There is also no indication that Roger's invention was

12. Section 102(b) does not apply because the inventions claimed in the Roger and Joy patent applications were not in public use or on sale in the United States, or described in a patent or printed publication anywhere in the world, more than one year before their respective filing dates. Section 102(d) does not

"known or used by others" within the meaning of § 102(a), given the judicial requirement of a public knowledge or use.[13] If § 103(c) were not available, the Roger patent would constitute prior art under § 102(e) because Joy's invention date (April 10, 2003) occurred after the Roger application was filed (February 12, 2003). Absent § 103(c), the Roger patent would also serve as prior art under § 102(f) because Joy derived an obvious variation of her invention from Roger. Further, without § 103(c) Roger's work would be available under § 102(g), because Roger both conceived and reduced his invention to practice prior to Joy's conception date. However, both of these patents have been (or will be assigned) to the Coif Corporation, the employer of both Roger and Joy. Thus, because § 103(c) exempts § 102(e), (f) and (g) art from the nonobviousness inquiry where the inventions were subject to a common obligation of assignment, the Roger patent may not be employed as a prior art reference against the Joy application.

Section 103(c) is a narrowly worded provision. If a reference is otherwise available as prior art, such as under § 102(a) or (b), then it remains pertinent to § 103(a). Also recall that § 103(c) solely concerns nonobviousness. It does not affect the availability of prior art for purposes of anticipation.

§ 5.3 The Nonobviousness Inquiry

Having identified the set of permissible prior art that applies to a claimed invention, a decision maker must next determine whether that invention would have been obvious to a person of skill in the art. The current legal framework for addressing nonobviousness issues is the product of a rich historical heritage. Without a sense of that history, a full grasp of the nonobviousness standard will prove difficult. This chapter therefore first reviews the leading Supreme Court precedents dealing with nonobviousness and its historical predecessor, the standard of invention. It then turns to more recent refinements of the nonobviousness standard announced by the Federal Circuit.

5.3.1 The Historical Standard of Invention

The Supreme Court's 1850 opinion in *Hotchkiss v. Greenwood*[1] proved to be the seminal decision regarding a prior art-based patentability requirement that exceeded novelty. The patent there concerned a door knob constructed of potter's clay or porcelain. Others had constructed similar knobs out of metal or wood, but the

apply because no foreign patents have been sought or acquired under the facts of the hypothetical.

13. *See supra* § 4.4.1.

§ 5.3

1. 52 U.S. 248, 11 How. 248, 13 L.Ed. 683 (1850).

patented door knobs could be produced "better and cheaper."[2] Having lost at trial following a jury verdict, the patentee appealed to the Supreme Court. The chief argument on appeal was the propriety of a jury instruction that the patent was void if it called for "the mere substitution of one material for another" such that "no other ingenuity or skill [was] necessary to construct the knob than that of an ordinary mechanic acquainted with the business."[3] The Court upheld the instruction, stating that unless the knowledge required to construct the knob exceeded that "possessed by an ordinary mechanic acquainted with the business, there was an absence of that degree of skill and ingenuity which constitute essential elements of every invention. In other words, the improvement is the work of the skillful mechanic, not that of the inventor."[4]

Although the *Hotchkiss* standard took the abilities of the "skillful mechanic" as its point of reference, it also employed the rhetoric of "invention" and "ingenuity." The latter language seemed to many courts to suggest a more subjective standard, in particular one which favored the Romantic inventor who conceived of the invention in a "flash of creative genius."[5] Over time this latter vision seemed to prevail. Courts demanded that inventors demonstrate "a substantial discovery and a substantial invention,"[6] "something new, unexpected and exciting,"[7] and even "that impalpable something."[8] Judge Learned Hand was led to comment that the so-called "invention" standard was "as fugitive, impalpable, wayward and vague a phantom as exists in the whole paraphernalia of legal concepts."[9]

The anti-monopoly sentiments that arose during the Depression era lead to extreme public and judicial skepticism towards patents. During this era courts began to apply an increasingly stringent "invention" standard that found most patents wanting. In 1941, the Supreme Court declared that "[s]ince *Hotchkiss* . . . it has been recognized that if an improvement is to obtain the privileged position of a patent more ingenuity must be involved than the work of a mechanic skilled in the art . . . That is to say, the new device, however useful it may be, must reveal the flash of creative genius, not merely the skill of the calling."[10] By 1949,

2. *Id.* at 264.

3. *Id.* at 265.

4. *Id.* at 267.

5. *See* Cuno Eng'g Corp. v. Automatic Devices Corp., 314 U.S. 84, 91, 62 S.Ct. 37, 86 L.Ed. 58 (1941).

6. *See* Bradley v. Eccles, 122 F. 867, 870 (C.C.N.D.N.Y.1903).

7. *See* Thurber Corp. v. Fairchild Motor Corp., 269 F.2d 841, 849, 122 USPQ 305, 311 (5th Cir.1959).

8. *See* McClain v. Ortmayer, 141 U.S. 419, 427, 12 S.Ct. 76, 35 L.Ed. 800 (1891).

9. Harries v. Air King Products Co., 183 F.2d 158, 162, 86 USPQ 57, 61 (2d Cir.1950).

10. Cuno Engineering Corp. v. Automatic Devices Corp., 314 U.S. 84 (1941).

Justice Jackson was moved to observe with some frustration that "the only patent that is valid is one which this Court has not been able to get its hands on."[11] The apex of this movement was to occur one year later, in the Court's 1950 decision in *Great A & P Tea Co. v. Supermarket Equipment Corp.*[12]

The patent in *Great A & P* concerned a cashier's counter for use in grocery and other stores. The two lower courts had upheld the patent, but the Court granted certiorari and struck the patent down. According to Justice Jackson himself, the disputed invention claimed a combination of known elements and, as such, must be judged under the so-called "synergy" test. "The conjunction or concert of known elements must contribute something; only when the whole in some way exceeds the sum of its parts is the accumulation of old devices patentable." This demand for "unusual or surprising consequences" seemed to call for the downfall of nearly every patent claim, for nearly every invention may be cast as a combination of old elements. The patent community sought relief from this unfavorable precedent, ultimately prevailing with the enactment of the nonobviousness standard in § 103 in the 1952 Patent Act.

5.3.2 The Modern Standard of Nonobviousness

Dissatisfaction with such arduous standards as "synergy" and the "flash of genius" led Congress to include a statutory basis for invention within the 1952 Patent Act. Section 103(a) does not refer to the historical "invention" standard, but instead to an objective nonobviousness standard founded upon the knowledge of a person of ordinary skill in the art. To emphasize this point, the final sentence of § 103(a) provides that "[p]atentability shall not be negatived by the manner in which the invention was made." This language was meant to overturn precedent requiring that the invention be realized in a "flash of genius." Methodological, persistent investigation and long months of trial and error may just as readily yield a patentable invention as an instantaneous burst of creative insight.[13] Indeed, the Federal Circuit has held that lengthy periods of research preceding a claimed invention actually support, rather than negate, a conclusion of nonobviousness.[14]

Although the 1952 Patent Act took effect on January 1, 1954, the Supreme Court did not have the opportunity to interpret § 103(a) for many years. Only in 1966 did the Supreme Court turn its attention to the new statutory provision. In that year it issued

11. Jungersen v. Ostby & Barton Co., 335 U.S. 560, 572, 69 S.Ct. 269, 93 L.Ed. 235 (1949).

12. 340 U.S. 147, 71 S.Ct. 127, 95 L.Ed. 162 (1950).

13. In re Dow Chemical Co., 837 F.2d 469, 5 USPQ2d 1529 (Fed.Cir. 1988).

14. *Id.*

three opinions of such importance that the patent bar commonly refers to them simply as "The Trilogy." The three cases, *Graham v. John Deere*, *Calmar, Inc. v. Cook Chemical Co.*, and *United States v. Adams*, are notable for establishing a framework for conducting nonobviousness analyses commonly termed the "*Graham* factors."

5.3.2.1 The Graham Factors

In *Graham v. John Deere Co.*,[15] the Court presented a lengthy exposition of the constitutional framework for the nonobviousness requirement, judicial development of the invention standard, as well as the impact of § 103 and the requirement of nonobviousness. In the most frequently cited passage of the opinion, the Court then set forth the often-quoted "Graham factors":

> While the ultimate question of patent validity is one of law, . . . [§ 103] lends itself to several basic factual inquiries. Under § 103, the scope and content of the prior art are to be determined; differences between the prior art and the claims at issue are to be ascertained; and the level of ordinary skill in the pertinent art resolved. . . . Such secondary considerations as commercial success, long felt but unresolved needs, failure of others, etc., might be utilized to give light to the circumstances surrounding the origin of the subject matter sought to be patented. As indicia of obviousness or nonobviousness, these inquiries may have relevancy.[16]

Stated succinctly, then, the *Graham* test calls for the determination of four factual issues:

(1) The scope and content of the prior art.

(2) The differences between the prior art and the claims at issue.

(3) The level of ordinary skill in the pertinent art.

(4) Secondary considerations (e.g., commercial success).

The resulting conclusion of nonobviousness depends upon these factual inquiries but is ultimately an issue of law.

After announcing this framework for nonobviousness analyses under § 103, the Court then proceeded to the facts at hand. William T. Graham was concerned with the construction of a plow that would not break upon striking soil obstructions such as rocks. In 1950, he obtained the '811 patent, directed towards a plow with a spring clamp. The device featured an upper plate secured to the lower flange of the H-beam of a plow frame. A hinge plate was pivoted to the upper plate, with one end of the plow shank resilient-

15. 383 U.S. 1, 86 S.Ct. 684, 15 L.Ed.2d 545 (1966).

16. *Id.* at 17–18.

ly and frictionally held between the upper and hinge plates. An opening in the shank allowed a rod to extend through it. A coil spring was placed around the rod and seated on the upper plate. When the plow hit an obstruction, the shank moved downward against the tension of the coil spring and pivoted the hinge plate. This pivoting action allowed the plow to pass over obstructions and increased the resiliency of the shank.

Three years later, in 1953, Graham obtained a second patent that he eventually asserted in his lawsuit against the John Deere Company, and which was the subject of the Supreme Court's non-obviousness analysis. That was the '798 patent, which improved upon his earlier effort. The two inventions differed in that (1) the '798 invention featured a stirrup and bolted connection of the shank to the hinge plate and (2) the '798 invention placed the shank below the hinge plate. This distinction shifted the point of wear from the bottom of the upper plate to the top of the stirrup of the hinge plate, a more easily replaced part. The patentee also argued that the reversal allowed the shank to flex away from the hinge plate when the plow encountered an obstruction.

Graham lost. Both lower courts to consider the issue held the '798 patent invalid, and the Supreme Court ultimately affirmed. Justice Clark concluded that the '798 patent would have been obvious due to the teachings of two references: Graham's own '811 patent[17] and a reference not before the Patent Office examiner, a device marketed by the Glencoe Manufacturing Company. The Glencoe device included a stirrup, and the Court judged that any skilled artisan would have immediately sought to reverse the shank and the plate in order to improve the flex. As a result, the Court concluded that the invention of the '798 patent would have been obvious under § 103.

The opinion in *Graham* involved a second case, *Calmar, Inc. v. Cook Chemical Co.* This litigation arose from a falling out between two former contracting parties, Calmar and Cook Chemical. The technical problem here was how to keep a spray insecticide bottle from leaking during shipment. To prevent leaking during shipment, the prior art often detached the pumping unit from the bottle of insecticide itself. The consumer needed to remove the cap from the bottle and then attach the pumping unit in order to spray the insecticide. Apparently this arrangement was difficult to package,

17. Graham's own, earlier '811 patent served as prior art against the '798 patent-in-suit under § 102(b). More specifically, the Patent Office issued the '811 patent on January 10, 1950, more than one year before the August 27, 1951 filing date of the '798 patent. As a result, even though the '811 patent represented Graham's own work, the Patent Office and courts appropriately considered the '811 patent for purposes of the obviousness analysis because it met the § 102(b) definition.

and in addition thieves were making off with the pumping units. So Cook, which made the insecticide, asked its pump maker, Calmar, to develop a leak-proof pump.

After several failures by Calmar, Cook decided to enter the pump-making market itself. Cook ultimately developed the invention described in the patent at suit, the so-called "Scroggin patent," by adding a tiny lip to help seal the insecticide during shipment. In essence, Scroggin invented a finger-operated, leak-proof sprayer top. This arrangement allowed the consumer simply to remove the overcap and start killing insects immediately. Conveniently enough, Calmar later marketed a pump similar to that of Cook. Cook then sued its former supplier for patent infringement.

The trial court held the Scroggin patent not invalid and infringed, and the Eighth Circuit affirmed. The Supreme Court reversed, finding that the Scroggin patent would have been obvious in light of three prior art patents to Lohse, Mellon, and Livingstone, respectively. The Lohse and Mellon patents both taught the use of shipper-sprayers similar to that of Scroggin. The Livingstone patent, which was not before the examiner, concerned a seal designed to cover and protect pouring spots that functioned without the use of a gasket or washer. The Court rejected the argument that the Livingstone patent should be disregarding as nonanalogous art: "Closure devices in such a closely related art as pouring spouts for liquid containers are at the very least pertinent references."[18]

The Court then considered the proper scope of the Scroggin patent claims. Turning to the patent's prosecution history, or record of the dialogue between the examiner and applicant, the Court found that the examiner had originally imposed rejections based upon the Lohse and Mellon patents. In response, Scroggin accepted claim limitations that confined the scope of his invention to two features. In the view of the Court, the first feature, "the space between the skirt of the overcap and the container cap," was taught by Mellon. Livingstone taught the second feature, "the substitution of a rib built into the collar to achieve a seal for a washer or gasket." Finally, the Court was unpersuaded that secondary considerations supported the patentability of the Scroggin patent. The patent rested on a narrow advance, already disclosed by Livingstone and available to anyone who had conducted a patent search. Consequently, the Court concluded that the Scroggin patent would have been obvious under § 103.

Although both *Graham v. John Deere* and *Calmar v. Cook* are extremely well-known cases still considered authoritative today, their application of the law to the particular patents at issue seems problematic. In neither case did the Court seem overly concerned

18. *Id.* at 35.

with its newly announced analytical framework for conducting nonobviousness analyses. Not only was there no remand for determination of the required factual issues, some *Graham* factors, such as the level of skill in the art, receive no discussion whatsoever. The statement in the *Graham v. John Deere* opinion that "all the elements of the '798 patent are present in the Glencoe structure" suggests that the Court believed this was little more than an anticipation case. In *Calmar v. Cook*, the Court did explicitly mention the "secondary consideration" of long-felt need, but quite quickly concluded that this factor did not weigh in favor of the patentee.

Due to these deficiencies—and perhaps because it is the only one of the Trilogy to uphold, rather than strike down, an asserted patent—*United States v. Adams*[19] is the patent bar's favorite Supreme Court decision on nonobviousness. The final installment of the Trilogy concerned the invention by Adams of a battery employing cuprous chloride and magnesium. This combination of electrodes had never been previously placed in a single battery. The prior art did teach the use of zinc and silver chloride as electrode material in batteries, however. The prior art further disclosed that cuprous chloride and silver chloride, as well as magnesium and zinc, were equivalent electrode materials. The Adams battery nonetheless possessed quite desirable characteristics over the prior art, to the extent that experts in the field initially expressed skepticism over its claimed abilities.

As part of the wartime effort, Adams notified the U.S. government about his battery. The Government ultimately employed Adams' battery design without notifying him. Years later, Adams learned of the use of his battery and brought suit in the predecessor to the Court of Federal Claims against the federal government to receive compensation for the use of his invention. The Court of Claims held the patent not invalid and infringed.

Following a grant of certiorari, the Government primarily relied upon six references to argue to the Supreme Court that Adams' invention was obvious and that his patent was therefore invalid. The Niadudet treatise and the Hayes patent taught a battery with a zinc anode and a silver chloride cathode that could work in an electrolyte of pure water. The Wood patent described the possibility of substituting magnesium for zinc on the anode, while the Codd treatise indicated that magnesium was a theoretically desirable electrode. The Wensky patent taught a battery with zinc and copper electrodes, with cuprous chloride added as a salt in an electrolyte solution. Finally, the Skrivanoff patent described the use of a magnesium anode; a cathode pasted with, among other

19. 383 U.S. 39, 86 S.Ct. 708, 15 L.Ed.2d 572 (1966).

compounds, cuprous chloride; and an electrolyte of alcoline, chlorochromate, or a permanganate strengthened with sulphuric acid. An expert for Adams testified, however, that he met with first a fire, and then an explosion, when he attempted to assemble the Skrivanoff battery.

After disposing of several preliminary issues, the Court concluded that the invention claimed by Adams would not have been obvious in light of the six Government references. Although it noted the extreme structural similarities between the claimed invention and the prior art, the Court was moved by the many advantages of the Adams battery. The Adams battery could be stored while dry and activated with ordinary water or salt water. It also operated well at extreme temperatures and delivered a constant voltage regardless of the rate at which current was withdrawn. Secondary considerations, such as the initial disbelief and ultimate acknowledgment of experts, as well as the inability of the Patent Office to find a single pertinent reference within the crowded battery art, also supported the nonobviousness of the Adams patent.

As we leave the Trilogy, it should be noted again that they comprise central opinions within the modern patent law. Moreover, the Federal Circuit has accorded them great significance. Arguably the Supreme Court itself did not comprehend the importance of the Trilogy because, in subsequent cases decided in the 1960's and 1970's, such as *Anderson's–Black Rock v. Pavement Salvage Co.*[20] and *Sakraida v. Ag Pro, Inc.*,[21] the Court seemed to apply its earlier "invention" standard. Upon the consolidation of patent appeals to the Federal Circuit, however, that court opted to follow the *Graham* test for nonobviousness. Indeed, the Federal Circuit has simply ignored without comment these intervening opinions, holding fast to the *Graham* test.

5.3.2.2 The Person of Ordinary Skill in the Art

Section 103(a) mandates the assessment of nonobviousness from the perspective of "a person having ordinary skill in the art." The Federal Circuit has provided the following list of factors to be considered in determining the level of ordinary skill in the art:

(1) the educational level of the inventor;

(2) type of problems encountered in the art;

(3) prior art solutions to those problems;

(4) rapidity with which inventions are made;

(5) sophistication of the technology; and

20. 396 U.S. 57, 90 S.Ct. 305, 24 L.Ed.2d 258 (1969).

21. 425 U.S. 273, 96 S.Ct. 1532, 47 L.Ed.2d 784 (1976).

(6) educational level of active workers in the field.[22]

Surprisingly few judicial opinions actually reach a specific determination of the level of ordinary skill in the art. For example, neither *Graham v. John Deere*, nor any of the other opinions comprising the Trilogy, actually tell us whether the level of skill in the art was that of a high school graduate or Ph.D. with post-doctoral studies and ten years of industry experience. In practice, the concept of "a person of ordinary skill in the art" seems more designed to remind judges to put themselves in the shoes of a skilled artisan, rather than to compel a specific factual finding.

All things being equal, however, accused infringers typically seek to prove a high level of skill in the art. In developed arts with expert practitioners, many inventions would be routine. In contrast, patentees prefer that the level of ordinary skill in the art be that of a neophyte, to whom very little would be obvious.

5.3.2.3 Motivation to Combine

Although a conclusion of nonobviousness may be founded upon a single prior art reference, most nonobviousness analyses concern multiple references. The Federal Circuit has spoken in length about the circumstances in which teachings from multiple references may be combined in order to produce the claimed invention. The most significant requirement is that some reason, suggestion, or motivation must have provided a person of ordinary skill in the art cause to combine the references to produce the claimed invention with a reasonable probability of success. In *Pro–Mold & Tool Co. v. Great Lakes Plastics, Inc.*,[23] the Federal Circuit explained that the "reason, suggestion, or motivation" can come from one of three sources:

(1) the references themselves,

(2) knowledge of those skilled in the art, or

(3) "the nature of the problem to be solved, leading inventors to look to references relating to possible solutions to that problem."

Note, however, that the suggestion to combine references need not be explicit—an implicit suggestion may be enough. As the Federal Circuit put it, there is "no requirement that the prior art contain an express suggestion to combine known elements to achieve the claimed invention."[24]

22. Environmental Designs, Ltd. v. Union Oil Co., 713 F.2d 693, 696, 218 USPQ 865, 868 (Fed.Cir.1983), *cert. denied*, 464 U.S. 1043, 104 S.Ct. 709, 79 L.Ed.2d 173 (1984).

23. 75 F.3d 1568, 37 USPQ2d 1626 (Fed.Cir.1996).

24. Motorola, Inc. v. Interdigital Tech. Corp., 121 F.3d 1461, 1472, 43 USPQ2d 1481 (Fed. Cir. 1997).

An example illustrates the requirement of a "reason, suggestion, or motivation" to combine references. Suppose that Professor Gadget invents a combination lawn mower-metal detector device. Gadget reasons that homeowners will want to hunt for "buried treasure" as they periodically mow their lawns. On January 1, 2005, Professor Gadget files a patent application claiming that combination. During prosecution, the PTO examiner discovers a March 21, 2003, article in the *Journal of Beachcombing* that provides a full disclosure of the metal detector employed by Gadget. The PTO examiner also discovers a German patent, issued on December 13, 2002, that provides a detailed disclosure of a lawn mower of the type claimed by Gadget. Because both references were publicly available more than one year before the filing date of Gadget's application, they both qualify as prior art under § 102(b). The references also arise from analogous arts and, as such, may be considered for purposes of § 103. Without more, however, the PTO examiner cannot issue a proper rejection for obviousness. There must be some reason, suggestion, or motivation to combine the disclosures of the journal article and German patent. If the examiner found a third reference, say a textbook that generally suggested the possibility of installing metal detectors on lawn mowers, then the examiner could appropriately reject Gadget's application for obviousness.

In imposing this requirement, the Federal Circuit seeks to guard against the use of hindsight. The inventor's specification should not be used as a blueprint in deciding nonobviousness.[25] "Care must be taken to avoid hindsight reconstruction by using 'the patent in suit as a guide through a maze of prior art references, combining the right references in the right way so as to achieve the result of the claims at suit.' "[26] To similar, but rather more abstract effect, the Federal Circuit counsels that in nonobviousness analyses, "the invention must be considered as a whole."[27] A proper nonobviousness analysis judges the claimed invention holistically, not by cobbling together the teachings of different references to match different claim limitations in a piecemeal fashion.

Although these policy goals are admirable, sometimes the Federal Circuit seems too demanding in its search for a reason, suggestion or motivation to combine prior art references. Consider, for example, the Federal Circuit's 1999 decision in *In re Dembic-*

25. Interconnect Planning Corp. v. Feil, 774 F.2d 1132, 1138, 227 USPQ 543, 547 (Fed.Cir.1985).

26. Grain Processing Corp. v. American Maize–Products Co., 840 F.2d 902, 907, 5 USPQ2d 1788, 1792 (Fed.Cir. 1988).

27. Rockwell Int'l Corp. v. United States, 147 F.3d 1358, 47 USPQ2d 1027 (Fed.Cir.1998).

zak.[28] The *Dembiczak* invention consisted of a plastic trash or leaf bag that, when filled, simulated the appearance of a Halloween pumpkin. The PTO rejected the application on the basis of the combination of (1) references that described children's crafts projects resulting in paper bags decorated with Jack–O–Lantern faces and (2) conventional plastic bags. According to the PTO, it would have been a routine design choice to substitute plastic for paper to produce the claimed invention. The Federal Circuit disagreed and reversed. According to Judge Clevenger, the PTO Board had made no particularized findings of any specific reason, motivation, or suggestion to combine the children's crafts references with conventional trash and lawn bags.

With respect to the Federal Circuit, in cases such as *Dembiczak* the court's reasoning seems excessively mechanical. As a trip to the checkout counter at most grocery stores will reveal, the selection of "paper or plastic" is a quite routine set of alternative materials for bagging purposes. In most fields, practitioners are seldom such dullards as to require detailed step-by-step instructions to accomplish basic tasks. Yet here, and in other cases,[29] the Federal Circuit seems to state that an invention would not have been obvious unless its precise recipe existed in the prior art. It is also worth noting that *Graham v. John Deere* did not require a reason, motivation, or suggestion to combine references in order to make a rejection for obviousness. Worse, the current Federal Circuit approach risks diluting the nonobviousness requirement to little more than an anticipation test conducted over multiple references. Although avoiding hindsight is a worthy goal, the courts and PTO should also ensure that a meaningful nonobviousness requirement preserves a robust public domain.

5.3.2.4 The Prima Facie Case of Obviousness

The Federal Circuit often speaks of a "prima facie" case of obviousness. The prima facie case is a procedural tool of patent examination at the PTO.[30] During prosecution, the PTO examiner bears the burden of producing a prima facie case of obviousness, or some other ground for denying patentability. If the examiner makes that showing, then the burden of going forward shifts to the applicant. Once the applicant produces rebuttal evidence, the examiner must determine the patentability of the invention on the totality of the record.[31] A prima facie case of obviousness ordinarily involves a showing that the teachings of the prior art would have

28. 175 F.3d 994, 50 USPQ2d 1614 (Fed. Cir. 1999).

29. In re Sang–Su Lee, 277 F.3d 1338, 61 USPQ2d 1430 (Fed. Cir. 2002).

30. In re Piasecki, 745 F.2d 1468, 223 USPQ 785 (Fed.Cir.1984).

31. In re Oetiker, 977 F.2d 1443, 24 USPQ2d 1443 (Fed.Cir.1992).

suggested the claimed invention to a person of ordinary skill in the art.[32]

5.3.2.5 *Disfavored Frameworks for Nonobviousness*

The Federal Circuit has cautioned against the use of two different frameworks when conducting a nonobviousness inquiry. The first is the so-called "*Winslow* Tableau." This standard, first depicted by the CCPA in *In re Winslow*,[33] called for the decisionmaker to picture "the inventor as working in his shop with the prior art references—which he is presumed to know—hanging on the walls around him." The decisionmaker would then determine whether the inventor would have readily achieved the combination that comprised the claimed subject matter.

The difficulty with this image is that it visualized the inventor in physical possession of only the most pertinent prior art, making a conclusion of obviousness of the claimed invention all too readily reached. Judge Rich recognized this difficulty in *In re Antle*,[34] where he noted that the *Winslow* tableau ignored the reality that helpful references would be interspersed alongside numerous unhelpful sources, and perhaps even references that taught away from the solution. *Winslow* is also problematic because it obscures the fact that the nonobviousness inquiry should be conducted from the perspective of a person of ordinary skill in the art, not of the actual inventor herself.

A second disapproved framework is the standard of "obvious to try," sometimes called "obvious to experiment."[35] An "obvious to try" situation exists when prior art references may be of interest to a skilled artisan who is attempting to achieve a desired result, but rather than sufficiently teaching how to obtain that result, the references simply invite further experimentation.[36] Where no suggestion indicates which of many possibilities was likely to be successful, it is inappropriate to conclude that a claimed invention would have been obvious simply because the inventor could have tried each of numerous possible choices until he eventually arrived at a successful result.[37]

For example, suppose that a reference suggests that a broad class of chemical compounds might prove useful for achieving a particular technical effect. However, the class of compounds has millions of individual members, and the reference offers no sugges-

32. In re Rijckaert, 9 F.3d 1531, 20 USPQ2d 1955 (Fed.Cir.1993).

33. 365 F.2d 1017, 151 USPQ 48 (CCPA 1966).

34. 444 F.2d 1168, 170 USPQ 285 (CCPA 1971).

35. In re Dow Chemical Co., 837 F.2d 469, 5 USPQ2d 1529 (Fed.Cir. 1988).

36. In re Eli Lilly & Co., 902 F.2d 943, 14 USPQ2d 1741 (Fed.Cir.1990).

37. In re O'Farrell, 853 F.2d 894, 7 USPQ2d 1673 (Fed.Cir.1988).

tion about which compound will prove successful. Such a reference is not germane to § 103(a), for it merely made each of the particular compounds "obvious to try" rather than obvious to the skilled artisan.

5.3.3 The Secondary Considerations

In *Graham*, the Court noted that such "secondary considerations as commercial success, long felt but unresolved needs, failure of others, etc., might be utilized to give light to the circumstances surrounding the origin of the subject matter sought to be patented."[38] The Court recognized that the secondary considerations "focus attention on economic and motivational rather than technical issues and are, therefore more susceptible of judicial treatment than are the highly technical facts often present in patent litigation."[39] The secondary considerations are believed to provide objective evidence of how interested industry actors perceived the claimed invention.[40]

The *Graham* Court noted that the secondary considerations were "indicia of obviousness or nonobviousness" that "may have relevancy" in particular cases.[41] Arguably the Federal Circuit has more eagerly employed them than this Supreme Court language would suggest.[42] According to the Federal Circuit, which appears to prefer the label "objective evidence of nonobviousness,"[43] the term "secondary" does not refer to the importance of the considerations. The term instead indicates that these considerations necessarily arise second in time, after the invention has been introduced in the market, in contrast to the other *Graham* factors which focus upon the "time the invention was made."[44] Accordingly, the Federal Circuit has instructed that secondary considerations must be considered in every case, both by the courts and PTO.[45]

For a secondary consideration to be accorded probative value, its proponent must establish a "nexus" between the evidence and the merits of the claimed invention.[46] The nexus requirement means that there must be a showing of a legally and factually

38. 383 U.S. at 17–18.

39. *Id.* at 36.

40. Heidelberger Druckmaschinen AG v. Hantscho Commercial Products, Inc., 21 F.3d 1068, 30 USPQ2d 1377 (Fed.Cir.1994).

41. 383 U.S. at 18.

42. *See* Robert P. Merges, *Commercial Success and Patent Standards: Economic Perspectives on Innovation*, 76 CAL. L. REV. 805 (1988).

43. *See* Minnesota Mining & Mfg. Co. v. Johnson & Johnson Orthopaedics, Inc., 976 F.2d 1559, 24 USPQ2d 1321 (Fed.Cir.1992).

44. Truswal Sys. Corp. v. Hydro–Air Eng'g, 813 F.2d 1207, 1212, 2 USPQ2d 1034, 1038 (Fed.Cir.1987).

45. Custom Accessories, Inc. v. Jeffrey–Allan Industries, Inc., 807 F.2d 955, 1 USPQ2d 1196 (Fed.Cir.1986).

46. Ashland Oil, Inc. v. Delta Resins & Refractories, Inc., 776 F.2d 281, 227 USPQ 657 (Fed.Cir.1985), *cert. denied*, 475 U.S. 1017, 106 S.Ct. 1201, 89 L.Ed.2d 315 (1986).

sufficient connection between the commercial success and the claimed invention.[47] The sorts of showings that will fulfill the nexus requirement accompany the following review of the usual secondary considerations.

5.3.3.1 Commercial Success

The Federal Circuit views an invention's commercial success as presenting strong evidence of nonobviousness. In such circumstances the marketplace is presumed to have provided others with ample incentive to perfect the invention, and their failure to do so suggests nonobviousness. The commercial success may occur abroad[48] and may even have been enjoyed by an infringer.[49] Note, however, that mere evidence showing that the patentee sold a large number of goods supposedly embodying the claimed invention does not sufficiently demonstrate that the invention enjoyed commercial success.[50] The success must be due to the claimed features of the invention, rather than factors such as advertising, superior workmanship, or other features within the commercialized technology, in order to fulfill the nexus requirement.

The Federal Circuit decision in *Hybritech, Inc. v. Monoclonal Anitbodies, Inc.* reflects these principles.[51] The patented invention consisted of a "sandwich" immunoassay using monoclonal antibodies. Antibodies are components of the immune system, while a monoclonal antibody is an antibody of exceptional purity and specificity. Monoclonal antibodies are able to recognize and bind to a specific foreign molecule, called an antigen. The patented invention used this technology as a diagnostic tool, allowing doctors to identify particular infectious agents.

When Hybritech brought an infringement suit against a competitor, the district court invalidated the patent under, among other grounds, the nonobviousness requirement of § 103. On appeal, the Federal Circuit reversed. Judge Rich concluded that the prior art references, viewed in their best light, were at most merely invitations to experiment with monoclonal antibodies in immunoassays. In reaching this conclusion, the court also took account of a number of secondary considerations, including the commercial success enjoyed by Hybritech diagnostic kits. According to the Federal Circuit, this marketplace success resulted from the technical advan-

47. Demaco Corp. v. F. Von Langsdorff Licensing Ltd., 851 F.2d 1387, 7 USPQ2d 1222 (Fed.Cir.1988).

48. Lindemann Maschinenfabrik GmbH v. American Hoist & Derrick Co., 730 F.2d 1452, 221 USPQ 481 (Fed. Cir. 1984).

49. Syntex (U.S.A.) Inc. v. Paragon Optical Inc., 7 USPQ2d 1001 (D. Ariz. 1987).

50. In re Baxter Travenol Labs., 952 F.2d 388, 21 USPQ2d 1281 (Fed. Cir. 1991).

51. 802 F.2d 1367, 231 USPQ 81 (Fed. Cir. 1986).

tages of the claimed invention. The record revealed that the Hybritech diagnostic competed with numerous others for the trust of highly trained medical professionals who wished to make fast, accurate, and safe diagnoses. "This is not the kind of merchandise that can be sold by advertising hyperbole," Judge Rich concluded.

On the other hand, suppose that Macrosoft, a software company with a huge share of the market for personal computer operating systems, begins selling data compression software. Macrosoft files a patent application and, in response to an examiner's rejection for obviousness, argues that it has sold several million copies of the software. However, it may be that many consumers simply bought the data compression software along with their operating system due to Macrosoft's general reputation, the assurance that the program would function with the Macrosoft operating system, or an irresistible Macrosoft advertising campaign. With no nexus between the claimed features of the invention and the commercial success, Macrosoft's impressive sales would not weigh in favor of patentability.

5.3.3.2 Copying

If others copy the patented invention, then the courts have inferred that the invention would not have been obvious.[52] Otherwise the copyists would have copied a noninfringing prior art technology, or could have developed their own, noninfringing technology. Although copying may be a high form of flattery, other motivations may have inspired a copyist. For example, the copyist may have reasonably believed that the invention was unpatentable because it lacked novelty or would have been obvious. In such cases, this secondary consideration will not be accorded weight during the analysis.

Suppose, for example, that an inventor is awarded a patent on a new fuel filter. A large automobile manufacturer with ample resources precisely copies the patented filter. If the patentee can show that many different fuel filters were available within the public domain and that a noninfringing substitute could have readily been developed, a court would likely find that copying supports a conclusion of nonobviousness.

5.3.3.3 Licenses

The existence of licenses under the patented invention suggests that other industry actors believed the invention to be nonobvious.[53] Otherwise, they would have challenged the validity of the

52. Diamond Rubber Co. v. Consolidated Rubber Tire Co., 220 U.S. 428 (1991).

53. Eibel Process Co. v. Minnesota & Ontario Paper Co., 261 U.S. 45 (1923).

patent in the courts or at the PTO. In enforcing the nexus requirement, the courts will ensure that the competitors did not take a relatively inexpensive license simply to avoid costly litigation, as part of a larger cross-licensing arrangement, or for other reasons that do not support the nonobviousness of the claimed invention.

Consider the hypothetical Pervasive Polymers, Inc., a company that enjoys a 70% market share in the polymer market. No other company in that market has more than a 2% market share. During infringement litigation, Pervasive Polymers argues that it has licensed the asserted patent to 20 different competitors. Twenty is an impressive number of patent licenses, but suppose the facts further indicate that these licenses involved not just the patent which is the subject of the litigation, but rather the entire Pervasive Polymers portfolio of over 1200 patents. In addition, the terms of the licenses called for extremely reasonable royalty rates. In such a case, the aggressive licensing activities of Pervasive Polymers are not likely to be given weight during the nonobviousness analysis. Without further evidence, the court cannot assume that the licensees sought permission to use the asserted patent, as compared to another patent within the vast Pervasive Polymers portfolio. Perhaps the licensees simply wanted their much larger rival to leave them alone. On the other hand, if a number of competitors paid higher royalties in order to practice the subject matter of a particular patent, then such evidence is pertinent to nonobviousness.

5.3.3.4 Long–Felt Need

Sometimes an industry faces a technical problem that remains unresolved despite efforts to improve the situation. That the claimed invention solved this problem suggests that the invention was nonobvious.[54] The expressed need must correlate with the problem solved by the claimed invention in order to satisfy the nexus requirement.

For example, suppose that for several decades the semiconductor industry sought a way to mass produce inexpensive transistors. The concept of packaging the transistors in plastic held great promise, but for many years was hindered by various technical problems. If a patented invention solved these problems by providing an inexpensive method of packaging transistors in plastic, then the secondary consideration of long-felt need suggests the invention would not have been obvious.[55]

54. Graham v. John Deere, 383 U.S. at 17–18.

55. *See* Texas Instruments, Inc. v. U.S. Int'l Trade Comm'n, 988 F.2d 1165, 26 USPQ2d 1018 (Fed. Cir. 1993).

5.3.3.5 *Praise and Skepticism*

The skepticism of skilled artisans that the claimed invention could ever be achieved bolsters the case for nonobviousness.[56] Evidence that others initially doubted that the invention would produce the asserted results, or that the solution achieved by the invention was illogical or impossible, would support the patentability of the claimed invention. On the other hand, recognition of the merits of the claimed invention by skilled artisans, varying from product evaluations to industry awards, also suggests the invention is patentable.[57] For example, in one case various representatives of multinational corporations referred to the patented product as "magical," "bewitching," and "remarkable"—high accolades indeed, suggesting that the claimed invention would not have been obvious.[58] Both the praise and doubt must relate to the technical features of the claimed invention for the nexus requirement to be satisfied.

Sometimes skepticism of the invention occurs before the invention is ever conceived. In this class of cases, patent lawyers say that the prior art "teaches away" from the solution realized by the inventor. This information would discourage a person of ordinary skill in the art from pursuing the path taken by the inventor. The presence of prior art that "teaches away" supports the nonobviousness of the claimed invention.[59] For example, in *Arkie Lures, Inc. v. Gene Larew Tackle, Inc.*,[60] the patented invention consisted of a salt-impregnated plastic fishing lure. Some fish are apparently attracted to salt, but prior to the invention no salty fishing lure had ever been successfully commercialized. During the period the invention was developed, manufacturers told the inventor that salt was an undesirable additive for plastic lures because salt reduced the plastic's strength, roughened its texture, and possibly caused violent explosions during the manufacturing process! The Federal Circuit concluded that the invention fulfilled the § 103(a) standard, citing the fact that the inventor persisted against the conventional wisdom as potent evidence of the nonobviousness of the invention.

5.3.3.6 *Prior Failures of Others*

Prior failures by skilled artisans who attempted to achieve the claimed invention also suggests nonobviousness.[61] For example,

56. Environmental Designs, Ltd. v. Union Oil Co., 713 F.2d 693, 218 USPQ 865 (Fed. Cir. 1983).

57. Akzo N.V. v. U.S. Int'l Trade Comm'n, 808 F.2d 1471, 1481, 1 USPQ2d 1241, 1247 (Fed. Cir. 1986).

58. W.L. Gore & Associates, Inc. v. Garlock, Inc., 721 F.2d 1540, 220 USPQ 303 (Fed. Cir. 1983) (patent for process of stretching PTFE, commonly known by the trademark Teflon).

59. Arkie Lures, Inc. v. Gene Larew Tackle, Inc., 119 F.3d 953, 43 USPQ2d 1294 (Fed.Cir.1997).

60. 119 F.3d 953, 43 USPQ2d 1294 (Fed. Cir. 1997).

61. Graham v. John Deere, 383 U.S. at 17–18.

suppose that several teams of accomplished scientists had previously tried to invent a method of achieving room-temperature superconductivity, but failed. Ultimately an inventor discovers a way to achieve this effect. Demonstration that others had unsuccessfully tried where the inventor succeeded will bolster the case for nonobviousness. Because industrial demands often provoke individuals to research and experiment, the prior failures of others often enters into the obviousness analysis along with another secondary consideration, long-felt need.

This secondary consideration would seem to present potent proof of nonobviousness. Rather than hypothesizing about what skilled persons might have done years in the past, evidence of the prior failure of others seems to provide an actual glimpse into real-world capabilities. By demonstrating the prior failures of others, the proponent of the patent offers direct proof of facts that some of the other secondary considerations, such as commercial success and long-felt need, merely assume.

The relevance of the prior failures of others to the nonobviousness inquiry can be misleading, however. The standard of nonobviousness is judged from the perspective of the hypothetical person of ordinary skill in the art, not an actual individual. One especially salient difference between a person of ordinary skill and an actual individual is that the former is judged to know of the full contents of the prior art. Such knowledge is not likely attributable to any living person, or even an interdisciplinary team of inventors. As a consequence, evidence of the prior failures of others should be carefully scrutinized to ensure that it does not unfairly tip the obviousness analysis towards patentability.

5.3.3.7 Unexpected Results

The law does not require that an invention exhibit unexpected results to be patentable. But a finding that the invention does demonstrate superior and unexpected properties suggests nonobviousness.[62] For example, suppose that manufacturers produce "safety glass" by coating ordinary glass with a protective layer of chemicals. The field has long operated under the assumption that the thicker the coating of protective layer applied to the glass, the stronger the resulting glass. By demonstrating that the use of thinner coatings led to dramatically stronger automobile glass, an inventor has bolstered her case for patentability by showing unexpected results.

62. *American Hoist & Derrick Co. v. Sowa & Sons*, 725 F.2d 1350, 220 USPQ 763 (Fed. Cir. 1984).

The policy rationale for use of this secondary consideration is straightforward: Something that would have been surprising to a person of ordinary skill in a particular art would probably not have been obvious. Whether a result is unexpected or not is judged from the perspective of the person of ordinary skill in the art.

5.3.4 *Nonobviousness in Chemistry and Biotechnology*

The law of nonobviousness applies with just as much force to inventions from the chemical and biotechnological arts as it does to inventions from other disciplines.[63] The distinct technical landscape of these fields has lead to unique issues of nonobviousness, however, resulting in a body of doctrine specific to this branch of applied science. It will be profitable to consider three areas of particular importance for nonobviousness determinations in chemistry and biotechnology. First, we will address the use of structural similarities as evidence of chemical obviousness, with emphasis upon the leading case of *In re Dillon.*[64] We will then turn to issues of nonobviousness involving genetic materials, and in particular the well-known decision of *In re Deuel.*[65] Finally, we will take up the relationship between product and process claims as discussed in the leading cases of *In re Durden*[66] and *In re Ochiai.*[67]

5.3.4.1 *Structural Similarities as Evidence of Obviousness*

One recurring problem in making obviousness determinations concerning chemical inventions is that a newly-synthesized chemical composition may possess a very similar structure to compounds well known to the art. In other words, the claimed and prior art compounds may have nearly identical chemical formulae. Yet the two compounds may display widely varying behaviors, technical effects, or properties, because in chemistry, subtle structural differences may implicate major practical consequences. Whether newly synthesized compounds of this sort should be judged nonobvious in the sense of § 103(a) is an issue that has long plagued the courts. This issue has also arisen in terms of PTO practice. The extent to which a prima facie case must consider the chemical properties of the prior art and claimed compounds, in addition to their structure, has been of great procedural importance.

63. *See* In re Johnson, 747 F.2d 1456, 1460, 223 USPQ 1260, 1263 (Fed. Cir.1984).

64. 919 F.2d 688, 16 USPQ2d 1897 (Fed.Cir.1990), *cert. denied,* 500 U.S. 904, 111 S.Ct. 1682, 114 L.Ed.2d 77 (1991).

65. 51 F.3d 1552, 34 USPQ2d 1210 (Fed. Cir. 1995).

66. 763 F.2d 1406, 226 USPQ 359 (Fed.Cir.1985).

67. 71 F.3d 1565, 37 USPQ2d 1127 (Fed.Cir.1995).

In 1990, the Federal Circuit took up these issues *en banc* in *In re Dillon*.[68] Dillon had claimed compositions containing tetra-orthoesthers useful as fuel additives to reduce fuel emissions. The PTO had rejected her application based upon prior art that disclosed structurally similar tetra-orthoestheters. The prior art taught that these compounds should be added to fuels, but in order to obtain the benefit of dewatering, rather than for pollution control. The majority held that a prima facie case of obviousness was created when there was "structural similarity between claimed and prior art subject matter, proved by combining references or otherwise, where the prior art gives reason or motivation to make the claimed compositions." The applicant or patentee then possessed the burden of rebutting the prima facie case, and would be able to submit evidence that the claimed compound possessed new properties or improved properties that were unexpected. The ultimate question of nonobviousness depended upon consideration of the structure and all of the properties of the claimed composition.

The dissenting decision by Judge Newman severely criticized the majority's holding. According to the dissent, the *Dillon* majority had effectively held that structurally similar chemical compounds are prima facie obvious. The case law had suggested this principle many years earlier, where it was known as the *"Hass–Henze* Doctrine,"[69] the dissent stated, but subsequent decisions (notably *In re Papesch*[70]) had discarded it. Judge Newman instead advocated a prima facie obviousness standard that considered not only chemical structures, but also their properties.

An example may help illuminate the distinction between the approaches of the majority and dissent in *Dillon*. Suppose that Mikalos Myrmex synthesizes a particular chemical compound that is useful for killing fire ants. Myrmex timely files a patent application claiming the compound, which he calls "Compound M," and disclosing its use as a fire ant poison. During a prior art search, the PTO examiner discovers a prior art patent that discloses a compound that is structurally similar to Compound M. This earlier patent explains that claimed compound—which we will call "Compound P"—acts as an anti-bacterial agent.

Under the standard employed by the *Dillon* majority, Compound M is prima facie obvious. The structural similarities of Compounds M and P leads to a presumption they possess similar

68. 919 F.2d 688, 16 USPQ2d 1897 (Fed.Cir.1990), *cert. denied*, 500 U.S. 904, 111 S.Ct. 1682, 114 L.Ed.2d 77 (1991).

69. *See In re Henze*, 181 F.2d 196, 85 USPQ 261 (CCPA 1950); *In re Hass*, 141 F.2d 122, 60 USPQ 544 (CCPA 1944) (establishing that, in cases where a claimed compound is structurally similar to a prior art compound, the claimed compound is unpatentable unless the applicant can show that the claimed compound possesses a property or advantage that the prior art compound does not).

70. 315 F.2d 381, 137 USPQ 43 (CCPA 1963).

properties. An inventor of ordinary skill in the art would therefore be motivated to make a compound similar to Compound P in the hopes that the new compound would also be harmful to other living organisms, such as fire ants. Myrmex would then be able to rebut the prima facie case by showing, for example, that Compound P did not kill fire ants or that Compound M possesses greatly superior fire ant-slaying properties than Compound P.

Proceedings would advance much more quickly under the standard proposed by the *Dillon* dissent, however. Compound M would not be prima facie obvious at all under the standard advocated by Judge Newman. Because the prior art did not suggest that Compound P would be useful for killing fire ants, the examiner could not make an obviousness rejection based upon the prior art patent.

Given that the distinction between the majority and dissenting approaches is subtle, newcomers to this debate may question what all the shouting was about. After all, Dillon would have been able to obtain claims to a *method* of using the tetra-orthoesther compound to reduce fuel emissions, even if her *product* claim would have been obvious. Similarly, in our example, Mikalos could always obtain a method of using Compound M to kill fire ants, even if the PTO would be unwilling to grant a patent on Compound M itself in light of Compound P.[71]

The answer lies in the perception among members of the chemical industry that product claims are more valuable than process claims. After all, if Myrmex obtains a product claim on Compound M, then he would be able to exclude others for making, using, selling, offering to sell, or importing Compound M for any purpose. However, the method claims would only prevent others from making, using, selling, offering to sell, or importing Compound M for the purpose of killing fire ants. Cases like *Dillon* present an issue of policy: should the Dillons of the world be entitled to product protection for the compound, or be limited to more modest process claims? The majority approach in *Dillon* attempts to temper the inventor's desire for sweeping patent protection by taking greater account of the relatively modest technical advance the inventor has actually contributed.

5.3.4.2 Nonobviousness and Genetic Materials

Federal Circuit case law concerning the nonobviousness of genetic materials has proved particularly controversial, as suggested by the leading case of *In re Deuel*.[72] Here, the invention of Thomas F. Deuel and his colleagues (collectively "Deuel") related to DNA molecules encoding for human and bovine heparin-binding

71. *See supra* § 4.2.2.

72. 51 F.3d 1552, 34 USPQ2d 1210 (Fed. Cir. 1995).

growth factor, known as HBGFs. HBGFs are proteins that are useful for tissue repair. Deuel's inventive activity resulted in the purification and sequencing of the cDNA[73] of both bovine and human HBGF. Deuel also predicted the complete amino acid sequence of both bovine and human HBGF.

Deuel followed the following steps in order to complete his invention:

1. Isolate and purify bovine HBGF from bovine uterine tissue.

2. Determine the first 25 N-terminal amino acids in bovine HBGF.

3. Deduce a set of degenerate DNA probes from the partial amino acid sequence of bovine HBGF.

4. Screen a bovine cDNA library for hybridization with a probe of the set.

5. Clone the resulting bovine gene.

6. Predict the amino acid sequence of bovine HBGF.

7. Screen a human cDNA library for hybridization with a probe deduced in step 3.

8. Clone the resulting human gene.

9. Predict the amino acid sequence of human HBGF.

As amended, Deuel's patent application consisted of four claims numbered 4–7. Each was drafted in independent format.[73.5] The claims read as follows:

> 4. A purified and isolated DNA sequence consisting of a sequence encoding human heparin-binding growth factor of 168 amino acids having the following amino acid sequence: [sequence omitted].
>
> 5. The purified and isolated cDNA of human heparin-binding growth factor having the following nucleotide sequence: [sequence omitted].
>
> 6. A purified and isolated DNA sequence consisting of a sequence encoding bovine heparin-binding growth factor of 168 amino acids having the following amino acid sequence: [sequence omitted].

73. cDNA, or "complementary DNA," is produced by reverse transcribing the messenger RNA transcript of genomic DNA. *See* DAVID FREIFELDER & GEORGE M. MALACINSKI, ESSENTIALS OF MOLECULAR BIOLOGY 278 (2d ed. 1993).

73.5 For a discussion of the distinction between independent and dependent claims, *see* § 6.2.2 in the following chapter.

7. The purified and isolated cDNA of bovine heparin-binding growth factor having the following nucleotide sequence: [sequence omitted].

The PTO examiner relied upon only two prior art references during prosecution. The first reference, Bohlen, disclosed a partial amino acid sequence of heparin-binding brain mitogens (HBBMs). HBBMs are homologous (that is, similar in structure) to HBGF, and both substances are herapin-binding proteins. HBBMs are found in different tissues of the body than HBGFs, however: Deuel purified HBGF from uterine tissue, while the Boheln reference declared HBBMs to be "brain-specific." The second reference, Maniatis, consisted of a handbook including a general method for cloning a gene. Maniatis taught how to screen a DNA or cDNA library with a gene probe in order to isolate DNAs or cDNAs. However, Maniatis did not describe how to isolate a particular DNA or cDNA molecule.

Based upon the Bohlen and Maniatis references, the PTO examiner rejected claims 4–7 for obviousness. The examiner concluded that, applying these references, it would have been obvious for a person of ordinary skill in the art to clone a gene for HBGF. More specifically, Bohlen disclosed a heparin-binding protein and its N-terminal sequence. Maniatis disclosed a method for cloning genes. According to the examiner, a person of ordinary skill in the art would have been motivated by Bohlen to clone a gene for HBGF, a useful protein, in order to allow for its recombinant production. The examiner further reasoned that a skilled artisan could have designed a gene probe based on Bohlen's disclosed N-terminal sequence, then screened a DNA library in accordance with the Maniatis method to isolate a gene encoding an HBGF.

Deuel appealed the examiner's decision to the Board of Patent Appeals and Interferences, which affirmed. The Board stated the issue as "whether or not knowledge of the partial amino acid sequence of a protein, in conjunction with a reference indicating a general method of cloning, renders the invention as a whole, i.e., the gene, prima facie obvious." Asserting that cloning techniques were routine, the Board concluded that "when the sequence of a protein is placed into the public domain, the gene is also placed into the public domain." Dissatisfied with the Board's decision, Deuel appealed to the Federal Circuit.

Judge Lourie began by observing that, within the chemical arts, a prima facie case of obviousness is ordinarily established through structural similarity between the claimed compound and a compound within the prior art. Judge Lourie noted that in this case, neither Maniatis nor Bohlen disclosed any cDNA molecules that were relevant to the claimed inventions of Deuel. As a result,

Judge Lourie stated that: "The PTO's theory that one might have been motivated to try to do what Deuel in fact accomplished amounts to speculation and an impermissible hindsight reconstruction of the invention." Judge Lourie viewed the prior art as providing no more than a general motivation to search for some gene, and that was not enough to render obvious the genes specifically claimed by Deuel.

Judge Lourie next addressed the ramifications of the redundancy of the genetic code upon nonobviousness in the patent law. He stated:

> The genetic code relationship between proteins and nucleic acids does not overcome the deficiencies of the cited references. A prior art disclosure of the amino acid sequence of a protein does not necessarily render particular DNA molecules encoding the protein obvious because the redundancy of the genetic code permits one to hypothesize an enormous number of DNA sequences coding for the protein. No particular one of these DNAs can be obvious unless there is something in the prior art to lead to the particular DNA and indicate that it should be prepared.[74]

In a frequently quoted line from the *In re Deuel* opinion, Judge Lourie stated: "the existence of a general method of isolating cDNA or DNA molecules is essentially irrelevant to the question whether the specific molecules themselves would have been obvious, in the absence of other prior art that suggests the claimed DNAs." Judge Louie then provided some suggestions as to what sort of prior art would suffice for the PTO to reach a conclusion of obviousness:

> A prior art disclosure of a process reciting a particular compound or obvious variant thereof as a product of the process is, of course, another matter, raising issues of anticipation under 35 U.S.C. Section 102 as well as obviousness under Section 103. Moreover, when there is prior art that suggests a claimed compound, the existence, or lack thereof, of an enabling process for making that compound is surely a factor in any patentability determination. There must, however, still be prior art that suggests the claimed compound in order for a prima facie case of obviousness to be made out....[75]

Judge Lourie then concluded that, because the prior art references did not teach or suggest the claimed cDNA molecules, the PTO's rejection of claims 5 and 7 should be reversed. He next turned to claims 4 and 6, which encompassed DNA sequences encoding human and bovine HBGFs. Here the court also overturned the PTO rejection. Judge Lourie observed that the Bohlen

74. 51 F.3d at 1558–59, 34 USPQ2d at 1215.

75. 51 F.3d at 1559, 34 USPQ2d at 1215–16.

reference disclosed only a partial amino acid sequence. According to Judge Lourie, the PTO could have reached a conclusion of obviousness only if the prior art described or more completely suggested the complete amino acid sequence of the protein.

In re Deuel attracted a great deal of criticism from skeptical commentators who believed the Federal Circuit was too lenient in allowing biotechnology inventions to be patented. Some observers contended that the Federal Circuit erred in ruling that DNA sequences encoding the protein were nonobvious because the court focused on the structure of the chemical claimed in Deuel's patent application.[76] "Instead of acknowledging the specificity of the technology involved, the court focused on a criterion familiar to old time chemists whose main way to design new compounds was molecular modification—structural similarity."[77] The court concluded that since proteins are chemically different from nucleic acids, they cannot be considered as their structural analogs.

However, molecules such as DNA and proteins are related via information that is transferred between them.[78] Some commentators declared the Federal Circuit's reasoning to be faulty because it compared DNA and proteins to structures of simple organic compounds in chemical cases. Although traditional chemical practice distinguished compounds based upon their structure, biotechnology does not necessarily call for the same reasoning.

A second basis of criticism of *In re Deuel* has been that the Federal Circuit focused upon the "consequences of genetic code's redundancy on DNA's obviousness, asserting that it precludes contemplation and conception of the exact structure of cDNA molecules."[79] Judge Lourie concluded that because of the redundancy in the genetic code, countless possible DNA sequences could code for the protein. As a result, the Federal Circuit concluded that a person of ordinary skill in the art could not have determined the DNA sequence without actually doing the experiment performed in Deuel.

However, while knowledge of a protein sequence does not provide immediate knowledge of the corresponding DNA sequence, many commentators believe that skilled artisans can readily deter-

76. Anita Varma & David Abraham, *DNA Is Different: Legal Obviousness and the Balance Between Biotech Inventors and the Market*, 9 Harvard Journal of Law and Technology53 (1996).

77. Phillipe Ducor, *Recombinant Products and Nonobviousness: A Typology*, 13 Santa Clara Computer & High Technology Law Journal 1, 43 (1997).

78. Sara Dastgheib–Vinarov, *A Higher Nonobviousness Standard for Gene Patents: Protecting Biomedical Research from the Big Chill*, 4 Marquette Intellectual Property Law Review 143 (2000).

79. Phillipe Ducor, *The Federal Circuit* and In re Deuel: *Does § 103 Apply to Naturally Occurring DNA?*, 77 J. Pat. & Trademark Off. Soc'y 871, 886 (1995).

mine the DNA through the use of standard techniques.[80] Specifically, a skilled biotechnician may employ a routine hybridization procedure using a cDNA or genomic library in order to fill the informational gap between a protein and the corresponding DNA that codes for that protein. The Federal Circuit has been accused of overlooking the fact that if a protein sequence is known, the DNA/RNA sequence can easily be found.

Some observers believe that, following *In re Deuel*, the nonobviousness standard may be of diminished significance where certain inventions regarding genetic materials are concerned. One analyst stated that the holding of *In re Deuel* could have been reduced to a simple statement: "35 U.S.C. § 103 does not apply to newly retrieved natural DNA sequences."[81] Another commentator explained that "as a result of this decision, patents may be issued for DNA molecules even if the applicant discovered the DNA by using an 'obvious' scientific method."[82]

On the other hand, *In re Deuel* may be of decreased significance today. Deuel filed his application in the very early days of the biotechnology industry. The prior art references at issue in *In re Deuel* were published in the 1980's. Since that time, the biotechnology industry has experienced many dramatic advances. Most notable was the June 26, 2000, announcement by U.S. President Bill Clinton and U.K. Prime Minister Tony Blair that the first phase of the Human Genome Project was completed.[83] Although their announcement was largely symbolic, it does evidence the reality that the amount of sequenced human DNA has increased dramatically from the body of information that was available in the prior art at the time of *In re Deuel*.

Other sequencing efforts have also proceeded apace, including the fruit fly, nematode and bacterial genomes.[84] The sequencing of nonhuman DNA is significant because DNA can be conserved between species. As such, a sequence from one species can provide information about the genome of a different species.[85] As each DNA sequence enters the public domain, the likelihood of encountering homologous strands increases.[86]

80. Dastgheib–Vinarov, *supra* note 78, at 155.

81. Ducor, *supra* note 79, at 883.

82. Lisa A. Karczewski, Comment, *Biotechological Gene Patent Applications: The Implications of the USPTO Written Description Requirement Guidelines on the Biotechnology Industry*, 31 McGeorge Law Review 1043, 1057 (2000).

83. *See* Richard J. Berman, *Gene Sequences*, National Law Journal B7 (Sept. 4, 2000).

84. *See Green Genes: The First Plant Genome: The First Plant Genome Has Just Been Announced*, The Economist (Dec. 16, 2000).

85. *Id.*

86. *See* Rick Weiss, *Surprises Abound as Scientists Genetically Decode a Plant*, Seattle Times (Dec. 14, 2000).

There have been many less celebrated advancements as well. The number of DNA isolation, sequencing and cloning techniques has increased, as has the speed and accuracy of these methods.[87] For example, it is much easier to create an appropriate probe than in earlier days, given the contemporary ability to synthesize short DNA sequences artificially as well as improved fluorescent detection technology.[88] Although the reasoning of *In re Deuel* states that these general isolation methodologies would not by themselves render a DNA sequence obvious, in combination with other prior art, they are relevant to an obviousness analysis.

As a result, although some may believe that the impact of *In re Deuel* was quite important, its influence may largely be historical. The prior art has increased dramatically over the set of references available in *In re Deuel*. As a result, the repercussions of *In re Deuel* will likely be felt only for those applications for biotechnology patents that were filed several years ago.

5.3.4.3 Product and Process Claims

Method claims have also raised perplexing issues with regard to chemistry and biotechnology. It is often the case that skilled artisans would have been readily able to generate a new chemical compound or biotechnological product, using well-known, conventional processes, once they were told the precise composition of a given end product. However, they would have lacked motivation to perform this process without knowledge of the special properties of the new product.

In terms of the patent law, the question is whether claims directed towards such a method of making would have been obvious. In one sense, since the method is being used to produce a novel and nonobvious product, the method too must be novel and nonobvious. But on the other hand, if the process is used in a conventional way to generate a product, perhaps we should view the process as novel but not necessarily nonobvious. In appropriate cases, the same reasoning applies not just to end products, but also to starting materials.

A simple analogy may focus attention on the nub of this problem.[89] Consider a team of botanists which jointly invents a new sort of fruit hybrid, such as a fanciful "appleberry." They file an application at the PTO claiming both the appleberry and a method of making an appleberry pie. Plainly the applicants' appleberry pie

87. *See* Michael Lasalandra, *Scientists joyfully announce gene sequencing completion*, BOSTON HERALD (June 27, 2000).

88. *See* Andrew Pollack, *DNA Chip May Help Usher In New Era of Product Testing*, NEW YORK TIMES ABSTRACTS (Nov. 28, 2000).

89. *See* ROBERT PATRICK MERGES & JOHN FITZGERALD DUFFY, PATENT LAW AND POLICY: CASES AND MATERIALS 838 (3d. ed. 2002).

recipe is novel. Indeed, it could not have possibly existed prior to the invention of the appleberry. But should the mere substitution of a new filling entitle the botanists to a patent on a method of making a fruit pie? The rejection of the botanists' method claims on the ground of nonobviousness amounts to the policy judgment that it should not.

The Federal Circuit addressed these issues in *In re Durden.*[90] There, the applicants had filed applications claiming oxime compounds, insecticidal carbamate compounds, and a process for producing the carbamate compounds using the oxime compounds as starting materials. Patents had issued on the oxime and carbamate compounds, but the PTO had rejected the process claims over a prior art patent.

On appeal, the applicants conceded that "the claimed process, apart from the fact of employing a novel and unobvious starting material and apart from the fact of producing a new and unobvious product, is obvious." The Federal Circuit stated the issue to be resolved as "whether a chemical process, otherwise obvious, is patentable *because* either or both the specific starting material employed and the product obtained, are novel and unobvious." The court affirmed the rejection, concluding that:

> Of course, an otherwise old process becomes a *new* process when a previously unknown starting material, for example, is used in it which is then subjected to a conventional manipulation or reaction to produce a product which may also be *new*, albeit the *expected* result of what is done. But it does not necessarily mean that the whole process has become *unobvious* in the sense of § 103. In short, a *new* process may still be obvious, even when considered "as a whole," notwithstanding the specific starting material or resulting product, or both, is not to be found in the prior art.[91]

Durden proved burdensome precedent for actors in the recombinant biotechnology industry. Broadly speaking, recombinant technologies involve the alteration of a host cell so that it produces a desirable protein. The resulting products, including erythropoietin, interferon, and tissue plasminogen activator (tPA), are identical or similar to naturally occurring products. As such, the valuable protein product is often not patent eligible in and of itself.[92] Biotechnologists do claim the transformed host cells as a sort of "machine" capable of producing a desirable protein. They also seek to claim the method of making the end product. Biotechnologists

90. 763 F.2d 1406, 226 USPQ 359 (Fed.Cir.1985).

91. 763 F.2d at 1410, 226 USPQ at 362.

92. *See supra* § 2.3.1.

discovered significant opposition to such method claims within the PTO, however. Based upon *Durden*, many examiners rejected such claims because the process of obtaining desirable protein products from transformed host cells is ordinarily well understood by skilled artisans. This set of skills applies even to host cells that are themselves patentable starting materials.[93]

Congress responded by enacting the Biotechnological Process Patents Act of 1995.[94] This legislation created § 103(b), a complex statute that applicants may elect to employ. Section 103(b) provides that a "biotechnological process" that uses or results in a novel, nonobvious composition of matter will be considered nonobvious if (1) the inventor files an application or applications claiming the process and the composition of matter at the same time; and (2) the process and composition of matter were owned by the same person at the time they were invented. The term "biotechnological process" is elaborately defined to tie the statute to contemporary biotechnology research, including such processes as "cell fusion procedures yielding a cell line that expresses a specific protein, such as a monoclonal antibody."

The Federal Circuit opinion in *In re Ochiai*,[95] issued just a few weeks after Congress enacted § 103(b), suggests that this legislative effort may have been unnecessary. Claim 6 of Ochiai's application recited a process for preparing a cephem compound (which has antibiotic properties). Although the cephem compound generated by this process was novel and nonobvious, the PTO reasoned that the process recited in claim 6 would have been obvious. Several prior art references taught the use of an extremely similar process to create a slightly different final product than claimed by Ochiai. The PTO concluded that the holding of *Durden* mandated the rejection of claim 6.

On appeal, the Federal Circuit reversed the PTO rejection. The court reasoned that the claimed starting material was unknown to skilled artisans prior to the filing of Ochiai's application. The court then concluded that although the claimed method was extremely similar to teachings of the prior art, the prior art nonetheless offered no suggestion or motivation to perform the claimed process. According to the *Ochiai* panel, "[s]imilarity is ... not necessarily obviousness." The court distinguished *Durden*, stating that it presented no more than an application of the general rule "that section 103 requires a fact-intensive comparison of the claimed process with the prior art rather than the mechanical application of another *per se* rule." Because nonobviousness cases involve complex

93. *See* Jeremy (Je) Zhe Zhang, In re Ochiai, In re Brouwer *and the Biotechnology Process Patent Act of 1995: The End of the* Durden *Legacy?*, 37 IDEA: J.L. & TECH. 405, 415 (1997).

94. Pub. L. 104–41, 109 Stat. 351.

95. 71 F.3d 1565, 37 USPQ 1127 (Fed.Cir.1995).

factual issues and "applications of a unitary legal regime to different claims and fields of art to yield particularized results," reasonable persons could well disagree about the outcome of a particular nonobviousness determination.

The PTO Commissioner responded to *Ochiai* with a Notice that resembled a sigh of relief. Recognizing the holding of *Ochiai*, the Commissioner discouraged use of § 103(b) and additionally announced that the PTO would not issue regulations to implement that statute. Instead, applicants wishing to employ the statute were invited to petition the Commissioner. The Notice further instructed examiners that "language in a process claim which recites making or using an unobvious product must be treated as a material limitation."

Although difficult to reconcile with *Durden*, *Ochiai* has been favorably received by most commentators. Nonetheless, its consistency with the congressional intent underlying § 103(b) may be questioned. Congress enacted § 103(b) as a narrow provision that solved a specific problem for a single industry. More broadly worded proposals that would have applied to all technologies had been considered and rejected. For example, because Ochiai's application involved a chemical technology, it would not be considered a "biotechnological process" under the statute ultimately enacted. Plainly *Ochiai*'s holding considerably opens up what Congress had crafted as a narrow exception to the prevailing case law.

5.3.5 Synopsis

The following example summarizes the key nonobviousness concepts we have canvassed in this chapter. Assume that an inventor, Bramer, files a patent application claiming an electrical circuit on July 1, 2005. The circuit is used as a digital signal processor in home stereo systems. It consists of two sub-circuits: an amplifier, followed by a filter.

The PTO examiner first considers Bramer's application on February 15, 2006. The examiner immediately locates two pertinent references. The first, a magazine article authored by Haas and published on March 21, 2003, describes the identical amplifier claimed by Bramer. The Haas article states that this amplifier is useful in high-voltage electrical power systems. The second is a U.S. patent that issued to Cline on February 1, 2006. The Cline patent matured from an application filed on April 1, 2005, and describes, but does not claim, the identical filter claimed by Bramer. Cline's patent also concerns home stereo systems.

Although the Haas and Cline references describe the components of Bramer's claimed invention, the examiner determines that neither reference suggests the desirability of combining the two elements. The examiner therefore cites a third reference, an engineering textbook authored by Jones and published on September 1, 1997. The Jones book concerns the design of signal processing circuits and generally discusses the desirability of combining amplifiers with filters to process digital signals. With these references available under § 102, the examiner has generated a prima facie case of obviousness under § 103(a).

Although Bramer may offer a number of responses to the examiner's rejection, two options suggest themselves in particular.[96] First, Bramer may attempt to demonstrate that at least one of the references cited by the examiner is not pertinent prior art for nonobviousness. If Bramer can remove any of the three references as prior art, then the examiner must withdraw the entire nonobviousness rejection. Both Haas and Jones are prior art under § 102(b), as they were both published before Bramer's critical date of July 1, 2004 (one year before he filed the patent application). However, the Cline patent is available as prior art only under § 102(e). Bramer may be able to antedate Cline by filing a Rule 131 affidavit. He would have to prove that he invented the claimed subject matter prior to Cline's filing date of April 1, 2005.[97]

Bramer may also argue that the Haas reference comprises nonanalogous art. Bramer could urge that high-voltage electrical power systems do not arise from the same field of endeavor as home stereo systems, nor was Haas reasonably pertinent to the particular problem faced by Bramer. The success of this argument would depend on additional development of the factual record by Bramer.

If Bramer cannot remove any of the references as prior art, his second option is to offer a substantive argument of nonobviousness. In the language of the patent community, such arguments on the merits are termed a "traverse." These arguments typically invoke an expert's opinion that skilled artisans would not have found the claimed invention obvious in light of the prior art. Bramer may also submit evidence of any secondary considerations that support the nonobviousness of his invention. Given the close correspondence between the prior art and the claimed invention here, Bramer's attempt to traverse the examiner's rejection seems unlikely to prevail, but his arguments must be judged in light of a full consideration of the *Graham* test and § 103(a).

96. Bramer could also amend the claims of the application, narrowing them so as to avoid the combined teachings of the prior art references. Of course, Bramer could also abandon the application.

97. *See supra* § 4.4.1. Note that § 103(c) does not serve to remove the Cline reference, because the Cline patent and Bramer's application are not owned by the same person or subject to an obligation of assignment to the same person. If Cline and Bramer both work for the same corporation, the Cline reference would then cease to be available as prior art for nonobviousness. On this point, *see supra* § 5.2.2.

Chapter 6

THE PATENT INSTRUMENT

Table of Sections

Patents may be distinguished from other intellectual property rights in that they can only arise after a formal application process and governmental review. There is no such thing as a common law patent, or a patent that arises instantaneously by operation of law. Individuals must present written applications to the PTO in order to secure proprietary interests in their inventions. These applications may ultimately mature into issued patent instruments, the documents that form the basis of individual patent rights. The Patent Code itemizes in detail the contents of each patent instrument in § 112, a statute comprised of six unnumbered paragraphs. The first two of these paragraphs are of central significance to the patent project.

The first paragraph of § 112 requires that the patent instrument disclose the invention. The patent community commonly refers to that portion of the patent instrument disclosing or describing the invention as the "specification" or "description." Section 112 ¶ 1 subjects the specification to three requirements. First, the specification must enable skilled artisans to make and use the invention. Second, the specification must contain a "written description" of the invention, sufficient to show that the inventor had accomplished the invention at the time he filed the application. Finally, the specification must detail the "best mode" contemplated by the inventor. We will take a closer look at these three requirements in § 6.1 below.

The second paragraph of § 112 requires that the specification "conclude with one or more claims particularly pointing out and distinctly claiming the subject matter which the applicant regards as his invention." Although the claims technically form part of the specification, patent practitioners commonly refer to the specification and claims as distinct portions of the patent instrument. This is so because the claims are the most important part of the patent instrument, setting forth the exact scope of the proprietary rights possessed by the patentee. Section 112 ¶ 2 contains a requirement of definiteness, a mandate that claims be sufficiently precise so that others may have notice of the extent of the patentee's proprietary interest.

The remaining paragraphs of § 112 also concern the claims. The third through fifth paragraphs of § 112 set interpretational standards for the construction of so-called "dependent claims." As we shall see later in this chapter, dependent claims recite the contents of an earlier, independent claim, but then continue to provide further limitations. In addition, § 112 ¶ 6 concerns a particular sort of claim format, so-called "means-plus-function" claims. The various detailed rules governing patent claims are reviewed in § 6.2 below.

§ 6.1 The Specification

Each patent instrument must include a specification that explains the invention in detail. Although the patent statute does not mandate a particular format for the specification, the PTO has promulgated regulations setting forth certain required elements, and the order in which they must be set out, including such components as a title, abstract, and a detailed textual description of the invention.[1] Drawings should be included "where necessary to the understanding of the subject matter sought to be patented."[2]

§ 6.1

1. 37 C.F.R. § 1.77.

2. 35 U.S.C. § 113 (2000).

The statute does require that the specification fulfill three essential requirements, however: enablement, written description, and best mode, each of which is discussed at length below.

6.1.1 Enablement

Section 112 ¶ 1 provides that the specification must "enable any person skilled in the art to which it pertains, or with which it is most nearly connected, to make and use" the claimed invention. Some commentators have viewed the enablement requirement as reflecting or embodying a contract between the inventor and the public.[3] In exchange for the exclusive rights granted by a patent, an inventor must enrich the art such that other persons may practice his invention. A detailed example of a specific embodiment of the invention, along with a more general description of its mode of operation or technical principles, typically suffices to fulfill the enablement requirement.

6.1.1.1 The **Wands** *Factors*

The courts have traditionally read the enablement requirement to mandate that the patentee disclose sufficient information so that a skilled artisan would be able to practice the claimed invention without undue experimentation.[4] Courts base the enablement requirement upon the exercise of ordinary skill and the reasonableness of the efforts needed to practice the claimed invention. In *In re Wands*,[5] the Federal Circuit cited a number of factors that should be considered in determining if the patent has provided enough detail to satisfy the enablement requirement, including:

(1) The quantity of experimentation necessary.

(2) The amount of direction or guidance provided.

(3) The presence or absence of working examples.

(4) The nature of the invention.

(5) The state of the prior art.

(6) The relative skill of those in the art.

(7) The predictability or unpredictability of the art.

(8) The breadth of the claims.

For example, suppose that noted software tycoons Gil Bates and Steve Hobbes obtain a patent relating to a computerized inventory control system. Among the elements of the claimed

3. *See* Orin S. Kerr, *Rethinking Patent Law in the Administrative State*, 42 Wm. & Mary L. Rev. 127 (2000).

4. In re Vaeck, 947 F.2d 488, 20 USPQ2d 1438 (Fed.Cir.1991).

5. 858 F.2d 731, 8 USPQ2d 1400 (Fed. Cir. 1988).

invention is a computer program that coordinates suppliers, warehousers, and retailers. Suppose further that the patent does not disclose a detailed, line-by-line listing of software code written in a particular programming language. Bates and Hobbes instead set forth high-level flow charts and a more abstract description of the program expressed in English.

So long as the Bates and Hobbes disclosure would allow a skilled computer programmer to develop functional software through ordinary efforts in a reasonable amount of time, their patent will be judged enabling. Although a disclosure of a complete, line-by-line program within the Bates and Hobbes specification would render the matter more certain, it is not required provided that the description sufficiently allows persons of ordinary skill to practice the invention. That different programmers might work out the details of the disclosed software in different ways is irrelevant to whether Bates and Hobbes met the enablement requirement. Similarly, that a highly skilled computer scientist might be able to generate software superior to that described in the specification has no bearing on the enablement inquiry.[6]

The Bates and Hobbes example also illustrates that patents need not disclose information well understood by knowledgeable artisans. As patent specifications are directed towards persons of skill in the art, they need not, and for purposes of brevity preferably do not, start from the most elementary principles and work their way to the claimed technology.[7] The Federal Circuit has also held that patent specifications need not constitute detailed production documents. Exacting manufacturing data concerning the dimensions, tolerances and other parameters of mass production need not be disclosed.[8]

One of the *Wands* factors speaks to the predictability of the art. The enablement requirement rule does not often present significant problems for inventors operating in predictable fields like mechanics or electronics. Using well-known physical laws and the knowledge of these disciplines, skilled artisans may not only construct alternative embodiments, but foresee their performance without difficulty. In unpredictable arts such as biotechnology and

6. *See* Northern Telecom, Inc. v. Datapoint Corp., 908 F.2d 931, 15 USPQ2d 1321 (Fed.Cir.1990); White Consolidated Indus., Inc. v. Vega Servo–Control, Inc., 713 F.2d 788, 218 USPQ 961 (Fed.Cir. 1983).

7. Hybritech Inc. v. Monoclonal Antibodies, Inc., 802 F.2d 1367, 231 USPQ 81 (Fed.Cir.1986), *cert. denied*, 480 U.S. 947, 107 S.Ct. 1606, 94 L.Ed.2d 792 (1987). In this regard, the patent specification stands in stark contrast to the typical law review article, which assumes the reader knows nothing and which spends dozens of pages laying out the fundamentals of a field of law before finally, in the last few paragraphs, laying out the germ of a new idea.

8. Christianson v. Colt Industries Operating Corp., 822 F.2d 1544, 3 USPQ2d 1241 (Fed.Cir.1987).

some branches of chemistry, however, the courts have been more strict in judging whether a particular disclosure supports a broadly drafted claim. In these less certain fields, small changes to the structure of the invention may lead to vastly different behaviors.

For example, a very minor alteration to a functional chemical compound may render it inert or useless for a particular purpose. As such, patent specifications within unpredictable arts must provide more than just a few illustrations in order to support a broadly drafted, generic claim. Instead, the specification must show with reasonable specificity how to practice the invention across the entire scope of the claim.[9]

The influence of the predictability of an art in the enablement analysis is well illustrated by *In re Wright*,[10] a biotechnology case. Wright filed an application claiming processes for producing live, non-pathogenic vaccines against RNA viruses, as well as methods for their use. The description within Wright's specification was much more narrow, however, detailing only the use of a recombinant vaccine that conferred immunity in chickens against the Prague Avian Sarcoma Virus, a development which no doubt caused rejoicing by the chickens of the Czech Republic but which provided little guidance to those wishing to combat other viruses. The Federal Circuit affirmed the allowance of claims directed towards the specifically disclosed process, but disallowed much broader claims reciting methods of protecting living organisms against RNA viruses. Based upon the level of skill in the art as of the February 1983 filing date, Judge Rich reasoned that Wright's application offered skilled artisans no more than an invitation to engage in lengthy experimentation. According to the court, Wright's success against a particular strain of an avian RNA virus could not be extrapolated with a reasonable expectation of success to the subject matter of the rejected claims. In other words, there was insufficient information in the specification to inform others how they might make a vaccine against Budapest Feline Virus, or Vienna Canine Virus.[10.5]

The final *Wands* factor states that the "breadth of the claims" is relevant to enablement. Whether a particular specification is enabling must always be understood in relationship to what has been claimed. Courts often state that patented subject matter must be enabled to the full breadth of a particular claim.[11] Consequently, in some cases, the scope of the claim is so broad in comparison to

9. PPG Industries, Inc. v. Guardian Industries Corp., 75 F.3d 1558, 37 USPQ2d 1618 (Fed.Cir.1996).

10. 999 F.2d 1557, 27 USPQ2d 1510 (Fed.Cir.1993).

10.5 These are fanciful viruses that we made up for illustrative purposes only.

11. In re Wright, 999 F.2d 1557, 27 USPQ2d 1510 (Fed.Cir.1993).

its disclosure that the claim will be struck down for lack of enablement.

The venerable 1854 Supreme Court decision in *O'Reilly v. Morse* illustrates this principle.[12] The Morse in the caption of this case was Samuel Morse, the inventor of the telegraph. The final claim of his telegraphy patent provided:

> Eighth. I do not propose to limit myself to the specific machinery, or parts of machinery, described in the foregoing specifications and claims; the essence of my invention being the use of the motive power of the electric or galvanic current, which I call electro-magnetism, however developed, for making or printing intelligible characters, letters, or signs, at any distances, being a new application of that power, of which I claim to be the first inventor or discoverer.

The Court held the claim invalid:

> Indeed, if the eighth claim of the patentee can be maintained, there was no necessity for any specification, further than to say that he had discovered that, by using the motive power of electro-magnetism, he could print intelligible characters at any distance. We presume it will be admitted on all hands, that no patent could have issued on such a specification. Yet this claim can derive no aid from the specification filed. It is outside of it, and the patentee claims beyond it.

This rejection would today be cast in terms of enablement: Morse had simply claimed far more than he had invented.

A more recent decision, *In re Fisher*, presents similar circumstances.[13] In *Fisher*, the applicant appealed the rejection of his application from the PTO to the Court of Customs and Patent Appeals. Fisher's application disclosed a method of producing adrenocorticotrophic hormones (ACTH) useful for treating arthritis. According to the application, the Fisher method resulted in dramatically improved potencies of ACTH. Specifically, while prior art methods produced products with 0.5 International Units of ACTH activity per milligram, the Fisher method resulted in substances with 1.11 to 2.30 International Units of ACTH activity per milligram.

The claims of the Fisher patent were quite broader than this disclosed potency range, however. The claims recited merely an ACTH preparation "containing at least 1 International Unit of ACTH per milligram"—with no upper potency limit specified. What this means in practical terms is that if someone else developed a way to make preparations with 5.0 International Units of ACTH

12. 56 U.S. (15 How.) 62 (1854).

13. 427 F.2d 833, 166 USPQ 18 (CCPA 1970).

activity per milligram, and began doing so, they would be held to infringe the recited claim of Fisher's patent. Even though Fisher's patent did not in any way explain how to produce products with greater than 2.30 International Units of ACTH activity per milligram, the open-ended wording of his claims would result in a judgment of infringement. Just like Samuel Morse, Fisher appeared to be claiming much more than he invented, or, at a minimum, claiming more than he was willing to explain to the public in his patent instrument.

Following an appeal, the CCPA agreed that Fisher's claims had been properly rejected. The court concluded that an inventor who discovered how to achieve a potency of greater than 1 should not be allowed to obtain patent rights over all such compositions having potencies greater than 1, including potential future compositions having potencies far in excess of those obtainable from his teachings. As the Federal Circuit summarized just a few years ago, the "enablement requirement ensures that the public knowledge is enriched by the patent specification to a degree at least commensurate with the scope of the claims. The scope of the claims must be less than or equal to the scope of the enablement. The scope of enablement, in turn, is that which is disclosed in the specification plus the scope of what would be known to one of ordinary skill in the art without undue experimentation."[14]

Regrettably, no precise equation allows us to determine whether a particular patent claim suffers from "undue breadth" in view of the disclosure of the patent's specification. Most patents include claims that are broader than the specific working examples that are disclosed. Courts recognize that limiting the scope of patent protection to these particular embodiments could render patent protection meaningless, as skillful competitors could design products that deviated slightly from the details of their construction. On the other hand, allowing inventors to obtain excessively broad, generic claims might provide rights out of proportion to the patent's contribution and discourage future innovation. As informed by the *Wands* factors, the enablement requirement provides a solid starting point, but unfortunately not an easily applied rule, for assessing when a particular patent claim exceeds its appropriate scope.

6.1.1.2 The Timing of the Enablement Inquiry

The specification must be enabling at the time the inventor filed his application. Subsequent progress in the state of the art should not be considered in determining whether an earlier filed application or patent fulfills the enablement requirement.[15] The

14. National Recovery Technologies, Inc. v. Magnetic Separation Systems, Inc., 166 F.3d 1190, 1195–96, 49 USPQ2d 1671 (Fed. Cir. 1999).

15. *See* In re Goodman, 11 F.3d 1046, 29 USPQ2d 2010 (Fed.Cir.1993).

unusual facts in *Gould v. Hellwarth*,[16] which involves one of the famous series of applications on laser technology filed by Gordon Gould, illustrate this principle. This appeal resulted from an interference declared between Gould and a Dr. Hellwarth.[17] The count of the interference related to a so-called "Q-switch," a device for controlling laser emissions.

Interestingly, neither party submitted the usual evidence of inventive activity common to interferences. With both sides relying solely upon their filing dates, one would suspect that Gould, the senior party, would prevail. But Hellwarth offered another argument: that although the Q-switch disclosure was adequate in and of itself, as of Gould's 1959 filing date neither Gould nor anyone else could build an operable laser. As a result, Hellwarth urged that Gould's application did not meet the enablement requirement. This contention was a clever one for Hellwarth, because he had filed his application in 1961 after Hughes Aircraft, Bell Laboratories, and other entities had constructed operating lasers.

The Board of Interferences agreed with Hellwarth, and on appeal the Court of Customs and Patent Appeals affirmed. Writing for the court, Judge Lane agreed that Gould's application did not contain a set of parameters sufficient to construct a laser. Although Gould did list ruby as a possible laser medium, a forecast that proved accurate, necessary data such as the type, size, and orientation of the ruby crystal were absent. The fact that numerous actors, including leading members of the U.S. technological community, failed to produce a laser until 1960 further supported the conclusion that the Gould application offered insufficient guidance. This result may seem harsh, particularly since we know that Gould's Q-switch actually worked quite well once the industry finally generated a functioning laser. But Gould's broad claims did plainly recite laser activity, which in 1959 fell more in the realm of speculative fiction than scientific reality.

6.1.1.3 The Role of Working and Prophetic Examples

Patent specifications typically describe so-called "working examples" that correspond to results actually achieved by the inventor. However, specifications may also contain simulated or predicted illustrations. Known in the patent law as "prophetic examples," such "paper experiments" may contribute to enablement so long as they actually aid those of ordinary skill in the art to achieve the invention.

16. 472 F.2d 1383, 176 USPQ 515 (CCPA 1973).

17. For a discussion of "interference" practice, see § 4.4.2.2, *supra*.

One of the more explosive opinions in patent law, *Atlas Powder Co. v. E.I. du Pont De Nemours & Co.*,[18] exemplifies the effect of prophetic examples and the workings of the enablement requirement more generally.[19] Atlas obtained a patent claiming water-resistant blasting agents and sought to enforce it against DuPont. The claim called for the mixture of such ingredients as salts, fuels, and emulsifiers to form an emulsion. The patent's specification then offered numerous particular examples of each sort of ingredient, which could be combined in different ways to form thousands of different emulsions.

Among DuPont's defenses was that the patent was invalid for lack of enablement. It seems that if a particular salt, fuel, and emulsifier were chosen indiscriminately, the resulting mixture wouldn't necessarily achieve an explosive with the desired properties. Indeed, DuPont claimed that 40% of the time, combining ingredients disclosed in the Atlas specification did not yield a successful product. Further, although Atlas scientists had performed approximately 300 experiments while perfecting the emulsion, Atlas described additional experiments that it had actually not conducted.

Initially, the combination of numerous failures and prophetic examples would suggest a finding of insufficient enablement, because of the need for others to engage in undue experimentation. The Federal Circuit nonetheless affirmed the finding of the district court that the Atlas patent contained an enabling disclosure. Both courts agreed that the prophetic examples were closely tied to actual experiments, with slight modifications introduced with the expectation of achieving better outcomes. Judge Baldwin further noted that patents need not teach optimal results in order to fulfill the enablement requirement, but instead must provide enough description to enable the invention to work for its intended purpose. Because the combination of compounds that were described worked most of the time, the Atlas patent met this requirement. Additionally, the Federal Circuit found that a skilled chemist would know how to modify unsatisfactory compounds in order to form a superior emulsion. In sum, skill in the art in this predictable field readily bridged any gaps in the Atlas patent disclosure.

6.1.1.4 Exhibits and Biological Samples

Although previous patent practice required applicants to prepare models or exhibits to accompany the specification, the PTO today strongly discourages these submissions. While the PTO re-

18. 750 F.2d 1569, 224 USPQ 409 (Fed.Cir.1984).

19. It perhaps also exemplifies the tendency of law teachers to generate bad puns from the facts of important opinions.

tains the authority to require applicants to submit specimens for purposes of exhibit or inspection, it exercises that power only in rare cases.[20]

An exception to the rule disfavoring the submission of samples exists with regard to biological inventions. When an invention depends upon the use of living materials such as microorganisms or cultured cells, a mere written account within a patent specification may not suffice to enable others conveniently to make and use the invention. A sample of the biological material itself is needed. As the Federal Circuit has explained, "[w]hen an invention relates to a new biological material, the material may not be reproducible even when detailed procedures and a complete taxonomic description are included in the specification. Thus the . . . Patent Office established the requirement that physical samples of such material be made available to the public as a condition of the patent grant."[21] In such cases the patent applicant must submit these materials to a public facility that acts as a biological depository. Upon request, the depositories distribute samples to interested members of the public.[22]

The United States is a signatory to the Budapest Treaty on the International Recognition of the Deposit of Microorganisms for the Purposes of Patent Procedure. The Budapest Treaty recognizes certain facilities as "international depository authorities." If an inventor makes a deposit with any one of these authorities, the deposit is recognized as valid for patent purposes by the United States and all other Budapest Treaty signatories where patent protection is sought. The World Intellectual Property Organization (WIPO), which administers the Budapest Treaty, includes more information on this international agreement on the www.wipo.org website.

6.1.2 Written Description

A U.S. patent must include a "written description" of the invention claimed therein under § 112 ¶ 1. The written description requirement has been recognized as distinct from enablement, which considers whether the patent instrument allows persons of skill in the art to practice the claimed invention without undue experimentation. The written description requirement instead concerns whether the inventor had possession, as of the filing date of the application, of the subject matter that he claims.

20. 35 U.S.C. § 114.

21. In re Lundak, 773 F.2d 1216, 1220, 227 USPQ 90, 93 (Fed. Cir. 1985).

22. *Id. See also,* Elizabeth R. Hall & T. Ling Chwang, *Deposit Requirements for Biological Materials*, 14 Hous. J. Int'l L. 565 (1992).

6.1.2.1 Traditional Views of the Written Description Requirement

The majority of written description cases involve amendments to claims made during the course of prosecution at the PTO. When claims are amended after the original filing date—either in their entirety or through alterations to earlier claims—the "written description" test seeks to determine if the additional material was disclosed somewhere in the original application. The written description requirement ensures that inventors do not improperly augment their patents by including subsequent technical advances in a previously filed application.

The written description requirement is best understood in the context of other conditions that an applicant must fulfill to obtain patent protection. Most prominent of these is 35 U.S.C. § 102(b), which bars a patent if the invention was in public use, on sale, or subject to other specified events more than one year prior to the filing date.[23] Under § 102(b), the filing date of a particular application is thus crucial. But if applications could be freely amended after filing, then inventors might be sorely tempted to file prematurely, keep tinkering, and then tack late developments onto earlier filed applications by amending the wording of their claims. This subterfuge would allow inventors to take unfair advantage of an early filing date, avoiding the impact of § 102(b). Similarly, because an application's filing date is considered a constructive reduction to practice, this tactic would allow inventors to unfairly avoid prior art references and obtain priority of invention under § 102(a), (e) and (g).[24]

The written description requirement guards against these abuses by ensuring that later amendments find support in earlier filings. If the amendments in fact contain information that was not previously disclosed, the amendment will be judged for prior art and other purposes as of the date it was actually filed. Most importantly, the benefit of the filing date of an earlier patent application will not be awarded.

Application of Barker,[25] a 1977 Court of Customs and Patent Appeals case, demonstrates the impact of the written description requirement. Barker filed an application directed towards a method of making prefabricated panels of shingles. Barker's invention concerned the construction of shingle panels with a length of 48 inches. As industry standards called for 16-inch gaps between roofing studs, prefabricated panels could then be easily used to cover three successive gaps during housing construction. The speci-

23. *See supra* § 4.3.1.

24. *See supra* § 4.4.

25. 559 F.2d 588, 194 USPQ 470 (CCPA 1977).

fication called for the construction of panels comprised of either eight or sixteen shingles. At some point following his initial filing, Barker filed an amendment with the PTO adding claim 18 to his application. Claim 18 recited a method of making prefabricated shingle panels with "at least six shingles." The PTO Board rejected claim 18 as not within the written description of the original application.

The CCPA affirmed the decision of the Board. According to the majority opinion of Judge Miller, the specification and drawings showed only panels consisting of eight or sixteen shingles. The use of a different number of shingles simply was not articulated until the filing of claim 18, and as such the written description requirement was not fulfilled.

Barker keenly illustrates the differences between enablement and written description. As urged by Judge Markey in his vigorous dissent, this invention was clearly enabled by the disclosure. A person with expertise in the construction trade, and indeed even one of little skill, could have readily prefabricated a panel using any number of shingles upon reviewing Barker's patent application. The only practical constraint was that the combined shingles needed to reach a total length of 48 inches. Yet because Barker disclosed only the use of eight or sixteen shingles, he could not later claim a panel comprised of at least six shingles. Note that Barker was not left entirely without recourse with respect to claim 18. If he opted to follow the appropriate procedural steps at the PTO, claim 18 could be judged as of the date Barker entered his amendment for novelty and other purposes.

Written description cases such as *Barker* often refer to the concept of "new matter." This phrase appears in § 132 of the patent statute, which provides that "[n]o amendment shall introduce new matter into the disclosure of the invention."[26] Although new matter and written description present closely related concepts, they are not interchangeable. Section 132 prohibits the introduction of new matter into the disclosure of an application via amendment. Section 112 ¶ 1 requires that claim language be supported by a written description in the specification. The proper basis for rejection of a claim amended to recite elements thought to be without support in the original disclosure is § 112 ¶ 1, not § 132.[27]

The notable Federal Circuit decision in *Vas–Cath Inc. v. Mahurkar* further explains the policy and practice of the written description requirement.[28] That case concerned Mahurkar's two

26. 35 U.S.C. § 132 (2000).

27. In re Rasmussen, 650 F.2d 1212, 211 USPQ 323 (CCPA 1981).

28. 935 F.2d 1555, 19 USPQ2d 1111 (Fed. Cir. 1991).

U.S. utility patents relating to double lumen catheters. Vas–Cath and its licensee sought a declaratory judgment that Mahurkar's patents were invalid under § 102(b). The declaratory judgment plaintiffs pointed to a Canadian design patent that Mahurkar had obtained on August 9, 1982. The plaintiffs observed that Mahurkar had not filed his U.S. utility patent applications until October 1, 1984, more than a year after the issue date of the Canadian patent, thereby triggering the "patented" bar of § 102(b).

Mahurkar in turn argued that his utility applications were entitled to a filing date on March 8, 1982, which happened to be well before the date the Canadian design patent issued. It seems that on that date in 1982 Mahurkar had filed an application for a U.S. design patent that included the same drawings that Mahurkar later included in his utility patent applications. Mahurkar contended that because earlier design applications provided adequate support for his later utility patent applications, the 1982 filing date applied to both applications.[29] The issue before the courts was whether the 1982 design patent application demonstrated that Mahurkar was in possession of the subject matter claimed within the later utility patent applications.

At trial, Circuit Judge Easterbrook of the Court of Appeals for the Seventh Circuit, sitting by designation as the trial judge, held that the Mahurkar utility patents were not entitled to the 1982 filing date. Judge Easterbrook was not persuaded that the 1982 design patent application, which consisted solely of drawings, supported the combination of features and specific parameters that Mahurkar claimed in 1984. Following an appeal, the Federal Circuit reversed and remanded. Judge Rich concluded that drawings alone could indeed convey an adequate written description of an invention. The Court of Appeals also observed that unopposed expert testimony established that persons of ordinary skill in the art would be aware that only certain parameters would actually result in a functioning catheter. As a result, the summary judgment disposition that the 1982 drawing had not conveyed the invention to skilled artisans was inappropriate. On remand, Judge Easterbrook subsequently decided that the 1982 design patent application provided an adequate written description for each of Marhurkar's claims.

6.1.2.2 Recent Developments in Written Description Law

Although most written description cases concern amendments to claims during prosecution at the PTO, a handful of Federal

29. *See* 35 U.S.C. § 120 (2000) (describing requirements for filing a continuing application and the legal consequences thereof); *see also infra* § 7.2.4 of this text.

Circuit opinions have found written description violations even where the claims were originally filed with an application. Most of these opinions have involved biotechnological inventions.[30] Representative of this line of cases is *Regents of the University of California v. Eli Lilly and Co.*,[31] which concerned a pioneering patent directed to the recombinant production of insulin.

The University of California filed the application that led to the patent-in-suit in 1977. The University based the application upon its cloning of the rat insulin gene. At this point, the University had determined and isolated the appropriate complementary DNA sequences found in rats, but not in humans. Although the University patent included a prophetic example describing a method that could be used to isolate human insulin-encoding complementary DNA, University researchers did not actually accomplish this feat until nearly two years after the 1977 filing date. As originally filed, the patent included both broad claims directed towards complementary DNA encoding vertebrate or mammalian insulin, as well as a narrower claim specifically reciting complementary DNA encoding human insulin. When the University brought suit against Eli Lilly for patent infringement in 1990, among Eli Lilly's defenses was that the patent did not contain a written description of the claimed invention.

The Federal Circuit agreed that the University patent did not comply with the written description requirement. According to Judge Lourie, the patent's failure to describe the claimed complementary DNA through its relevant structural or physical characteristics amounted to a fatal defect. The fact that the patent defined the claimed complementary DNA functionally, by the insulin it could be used to produce, was more a statement of result rather than a description of what the patented invention was. The court noted that many possible gene sequences might achieve this outcome. The court suggested that in order to fulfill the written description requirement, the University should have disclosed the complete and correct nucleotide sequence comprising the complementary DNA.

Regents v. Eli Lilly and other cases in its line have proven controversial.[32] Commentators have urged that the written description requirement should not concern originally-filed claims, which

30. *See* Fiers v. Revel, 984 F.2d 1164, 25 USPQ2d 1601 (Fed.Cir.1993); Amgen, Inc. v. Chugai Pharmaceutical Co., 927 F.2d 1200, 18 USPQ2d 1016 (Fed.Cir.1991).

31. 119 F.3d 1559, 43 USPQ2d 1398 (Fed.Cir.1997), *cert. denied*, 523 U.S. 1089, 118 S.Ct. 1548, 140 L.Ed.2d 695 (1998).

32. *See, e.g., Enzo Biochem, Inc. v. Gen–Probe Inc.*, 323 F.3d 956, 63 USPQ2d 1609 (Fed. Cir. 2002) (Rader, J., dissenting from denial of petition to rehear the case *en banc*).

under § 112 ¶ 2 form part of the specification.[33] In addition, the requirement that patents must expressly specify the nucleotide sequence of any claimed DNA arguably places a higher standard of disclosure for the protection of genetic materials than exists for other sorts of inventions. The Federal Circuit might have achieved the same result in this case by concluding that the University had not constructively reduced the claimed invention to practice by the 1977 filing date, or perhaps by finding that the patent did not fulfill the enablement requirement. In any event, this new interpretation of the written description requirement appears entrenched in the patent law, as evidenced by PTO attempts to develop guidelines so that examiners may follow *Regents v. Eli Lilly* and related precedent.[34]

6.1.3 Best Mode

The final requirement of § 112 ¶ 1 is that the specification "set forth the best mode contemplated by the inventor of carrying out his invention." The best mode requirement ensures that the public receives the most advantageous implementation of the technology known to the inventor, allowing competitors to compete with the patentee on equal footing after the patent expires. Typically the best mode requirement compels inventors to disclose information that might otherwise be maintained as a trade secret.

The leading case on the best mode requirement is *Chemcast Corp. v. Arco Industries Corp.*[35] The inventor, Rubright, formerly worked for the accused infringer, Arco. He later left to start his own company, Chemcast, the eventual plaintiff. While at Chemcast, Rubright invented and obtained a patent on a grommet designed to seal an opening in a sheet metal panel. When Chemcast asserted that Arco infringed the Rubright patent, Arco contended that the patent failed to disclose the best mode known to Rubright. Specifically, Arco urged that the absence of a description of the type, hardness, supplier, and trade name of material used to make the locking portion of the grommet was fatal to the patent.

The Federal Circuit agreed with Arco, and concluded that Chemcast's patent rubbed it the wrong way. The court initially set forth an influential two-part test for determining whether a patent specification fulfills the best mode requirement. The first inquiry was whether the inventor knew of a mode of practicing the claimed

33. *See* Janice M. Mueller, *The Evolving Application of the Written Description Requirement to Biotechnological Inventions*, 13 Berkeley Tech. L.J. 615, 633 (1998).

34. *See* Department of Commerce, Patent and Trademark Office, *Request for Comments on Interim Guidelines for Patent Applications Under the 35 U.S.C. 112–1 "Written Description" Requirement*, 63 Fed. Reg. 32639 (June 15, 1998).

35. 913 F.2d 923, 16 USPQ2d 1033 (Fed.Cir.1990).

invention that he considered superior to any other. If this first, subjective standard was met, then a court should enter into a second, objective inquiry: does the specification disclose sufficient information to enable persons of skill in the art to practice the best mode?

Considering the first, subjective inquiry, the *Chemcast* court affirmed the finding that Rubright preferred a rigid PVC composition, available under the trade name R–4467, for use in the locking portion of the grommet. Indeed, as this material had been developed specifically for Chemcast at some expense, Rubright likely found his knowledge of a best mode difficult to deny. Proceeding to the second prong of the best mode inquiry, the court also found Rubright's specification wanting. His patent failed to disclose R–4467, its supplier in the marketplace, or even the hardness of the preferred material. Although the inventor did discuss the use of PVC at 70 or higher on the Shore A hardness scale, this material was three hardness scales away from his preferred material hardness and was manifestly inferior. The reader of the opinion is left with the impression that the fact that the best grommet would result from the use of R–4667 was a very valuable trade secret and that the inventor's specification almost misled those who wished to practice the invention.

The two-part test articulated in *Chemcast* demonstrates that the best mode requirement is distinct from enablement. Enablement forms an objective standard that focuses upon knowledge of persons of ordinary skill in the art, while the best mode requirement includes a subjective component that stresses the knowledge of the inventor. As can be readily appreciated, a patent may contain an enabling disclosure yet not provide the best mode.

For example, suppose that the noted food chemist Rhonda Ramon obtains a patent claiming a method of making fried instant noodles. The application discloses sufficient information to allow skilled artisans to make the noodles without undue experimentation. However, Ramon does not explain that numerous experiments have shown that her process achieves unexpectedly superior results when performed at a temperature of 137.5° C. Ramon's patent would fulfill the enablement requirement. However, by failing to disclose the optimal temperature, Ramon has concealed the best mode of her invention, and as a result her patent should be held invalid.

The inventor must disclose the best mode known to him at the time he files a patent application. Technical understandings gained subsequent to the filing date need not be disclosed, even if the application is still pending at the PTO. This rule holds even if the inventor files a so-called "continuing application," a technique of extending PTO prosecution discussed in the following chapter of this text.[36]

Additionally, the best mode requirement applies only to the inventors named in the patent application. The controversial Federal Circuit opinion in *Glaxo Inc. v. Novopharm Ltd.*[37] illustrates this point. That case concerned an anti-ulcer medication invented by a Dr. Crookes during his employment with Glaxo. Consistent with an employment contract, Glaxo filed a patent application on behalf of Crookes. The application ultimately matured into a patent claiming the compound and disclosing a method of making it. While Glaxo management was aware that other employees had invented a better technique for making the medication originally discovered by Crookes, they never informed Crookes prior to the filing of the application.

Under these circumstances, the Federal Circuit held that no best mode violation occurred. Concluding that the wording of the statute expressly limited the best mode requirement to knowledge held by the inventor, the court saw no evidence that suggested Crookes himself knew of a better way to manufacture the medication. A vigorous dissent by Judge Mayer urged that the best mode requirement should not be given such a pinched reading. Judge Mayer concluded that because Glaxo both directed the prosecution and enjoyed the proprietary rights afforded by the issued patent, the district court should have further inquired into whether Glaxo had deliberately concealed a superior mode of practicing the invention from Crookes.

Whether the best mode requirement pertains to the invention as expressly claimed, or to the entire disclosed invention, depends upon the particular circumstances of the case. In general, the inventor's obligation to disclose the best mode relates to the invention *as claimed*. As a result, if an inventor does not expressly claim certain subject matter, ordinarily there is no best mode disclosure obligation with respect to that subject matter. There is an exception to this rule, however, in cases where the undisclosed subject matter has a material effect upon the properties of the claimed invention. For this class of cases, the Federal Circuit applies the best mode requirement to the entire *disclosed* invention, even where some of the elements of the invention that are described within the patent instrument have not been explicitly claimed.

36. *See* Transco Products, Inc. v. Performance Contracting, Inc., 38 F.3d 551, 32 USPQ2d 1077 (Fed.Cir.1994), *cert. denied*, 513 U.S. 1151, 115 S.Ct. 1102, 130 L.Ed.2d 1069 (1995).

37. *See* Glaxo Inc. v. Novopharm Ltd., 52 F.3d 1043, 34 USPQ2d 1565 (Fed.Cir.1995), *cert. denied*, 516 U.S. 988, 116 S.Ct. 516, 133 L.Ed.2d 424 (1995).

Two Federal Circuit cases illustrate these propositions. In *Bayer AG v. Schein Pharmaceuticals, Inc.*,[38] Bayer's patent claimed the chemical compound commonly known as the antibiotic Cipro, much in the news as a treatment for anthrax infection. The inventor, Dr. Grohe, preferred to synthesize Cipro by starting with another chemical compound and performing certain additional chemical reactions. Observing that the Bayer patent did not specify the starting material preferred by Grohe, an accused infringer alleged a violation of the best mode requirement. The Federal Circuit disagreed and held the patent not invalid. It explained that the only preferences that must be disclosed to comply with the best mode requirement are (1) a preferred embodiment of the invention or (2) preferences that have a material effect on the properties of the claimed invention. In this case neither of these triggering events occurred. The Bayer patent simply did not claim any starting materials, and the selection of Grohe's preferred starting material did not affect the characteristics of Cipro.

In another case, *Dana Corp. v. IPC Ltd. Partnership*,[39] the Federal Circuit took the more expansive view of the best mode requirement. Here the patent-in-suit claimed a valve stem seal useful in internal combustion engines. One of the limitations of the claimed invention called for a "portion of elastomeric material atop said valve guide...." Prior to filing a patent application, the inventor learned that treating the surface of the elastomeric material with fluoride was necessary to prevent the seal from leaking. The inventor considered a fluoride surface treatment as the best way of practicing the invention, and his employer did in fact sell seals that had been so treated. This information did not make its way into the patent application, however. The Federal Circuit held that the patent was invalid even though the patent claims did not expressly recite that the elastomeric material had been subject to a surface treatment. Because the failure to disclose the fluoride surface treatment directly impacted the operation of the claimed invention, the court judged that the inventor did not fulfill the best mode requirement.

The best mode requirement has encountered severe criticism in recent years. A 1992 Presidential Commission urged that Congress eliminate the best mode requirement, reasoning that the enablement requirement already compels sufficient technical disclosures and that the best mode at the time of filing is unlikely to remain the best mode when the patent expires.[40] Because many foreign patent laws include no analog to the best mode requirement in U.S.

38. 301 F.3d 1306, 64 USPQ2d 1001 (Fed. Cir.2002).

39. 860 F.2d 415, 8 USPQ2d 1692 (Fed. Cir. 1988).

40. *See* The Advisory Commission on Patent Law Reform, A Report to the Secretary of Commerce 102–03 (1992).

law, inventors based overseas have also disfavored disclosing their best mode. At the time this book goes to press, however, scant effort has been directed towards legislative reform of the best mode requirement.

§ 6.2 The Claims

The claims form the most significant part of the entire patent instrument, for it is the claims themselves that set forth the proprietary technological rights possessed by the patentee. When considering patentability and infringement issues, courts and PTO examiners turn to the particular wording of the invention as claimed.[1] Because the claims define the invention for purposes of the patent law, it is inappropriate to rely upon another portion of the specification, such as a drawing or the abstract of the invention, for this purpose.

The U.S. patent system employs what is known as a peripheral claiming system. Under this regime the claims mark out the outer boundaries of the technology considered proprietary to the patentee.[2] Like a real property deed, a claim in a patent sets the "metes and bounds" of the rights associated with that instrument.[3] Patentability and infringement issues should also focus upon a careful reading of a claim, rather than some more conceptual sense of the "heart," "gist" or "essence" of the invention.

Although claims hold a central place in the patent system, they are difficult texts to draft properly.[4] Claim drafting requires considerable analytic, research and writing skills, as well as scientific and technical competence. Claims submitted to the PTO must reduce sophisticated technical concepts to a single sentence, and yet present an accurate description of the invention. They must also be written with a keen awareness of the technical field in which the invention lies. Often only a few carefully chosen words of limitation mark a patentable distinction between the claimed invention and prior technical knowledge.

Claims drafters must also bear in mind the legal standards for properly drafted claims. The most significant statutory provision governing claiming is the second paragraph of § 112. That provision calls for the patent specification to close with "one or more

§ 6.2

1. *See* In re Van Geuns, 988 F.2d 1181, 1184, 26 USPQ2d 1057, 1058 (Fed. Cir.1993).

2. Ex parte Fressola, 27 USPQ2d 1608 (PTO Bd.1993), *aff'd*, 17 F.3d 1442 (Fed.Cir.1993).

3. *See* Corning Glass Works v. Sumitomo Elec. U.S.A., Inc., 868 F.2d 1251, 1257, 9 USPQ2d 1962, 1966 (Fed.Cir. 1989).

4. *See* Advanced Cardiovascular Sys., Inc. v. C.R. Bard Inc., 144 F.R.D. 372, 25 USPQ2d 1354, 1357 (N.D.Cal.1992).

claims,'' and in practice most U.S. patents contain multiple claims.[5] Under this regime each claim presents a separate statement of the patented invention. It is quite possible for some claims of a patent to be invalid on prior art grounds, while others are valid. Similarly, a competitor may infringe some claims of a patent but not others, depending upon the precise formulation of each claim. Individual claims effectively afford distinct proprietary interests that must be judged on their own merits.[6]

Section 112 ¶ 2 also requires that the claims particularly point out and distinctly claim the subject matter which the applicant regards as his invention. Before turning to this requirement of definiteness in claim language, it will be profitable to take up the basic mechanics of claim drafting and formatting in U.S. patent practice.

6.2.1 Basic Claim Drafting

Although patent applicants enjoy a great deal of discretion in setting forth the substance of a claim,[7] years of PTO interpretation and judicial precedent have resulted in a standardized drafting protocol. Among the most notable practices is that each claim must be expressed in a single sentence. Often this rule results in a lengthy sentence with stilted language, dependent clauses, and an abundance of adverbs. Nonetheless, the one-sentence format has been upheld as contributing to the efficient processing of patent applications.[8] The PTO further directs that claims be stated in three parts: a preamble, transition phrase, and body.

6.2.1.1 The Preamble

The preamble, or introductory words of a claim, provides the general nature of the invention. Sometimes the preamble simply recites an apparatus, article of manufacture, composition of matter, or method, tracking the categories of statutory subject matter of § 101. Most preambles are more specific, however, stating such things as "a packaged semiconductor," "a steering wheel unit for mounting on a steering column of a motor vehicle," or "a method of preparing Factor VIII pro-coagulant activity protein."

A recurring issue concerning the preamble is whether the subject matter it recites should act as a limitation upon the scope of

5. It should be noted that patent application fees are assessed on a per-claim basis. At this writing, the basic filing fee is $770 (with special reduced fees for "small entities"). That permits a party to file up to three claims. For each claim in excess of three there is a further fee of $86. For the entire fee schedule, *see* 37 C.F.R. § 1.16 (2003).

6. *See* Continental Can Co. USA, Inc. v. Monsanto Co., 948 F.2d 1264, 20 USPQ2d 1746 (Fed.Cir.1991).

7. *See* Ex parte Tanksley, 37 USPQ2d 1382, 1386 (PTO Bd. 1994).

8. *See* Fressola v. Manbeck, 36 USPQ2d 1211 (D.D.C.1995).

the claim. Unlike the elements of the invention listed in the body of the claim, which define the invention and therefore limit the scope of claim coverage, the preamble often does no more than name the invention's intended purpose. As a result, the courts ordinarily do not consider the preamble as a claim limitation. Therefore, a prior art reference could anticipate the claimed invention under § 102 even though the subject matter of the preamble was not disclosed by the reference. Similarly, during enforcement litigation, an accused technology need not embody the language of the preamble in order to be judged a literal infringement.

Sometimes a preamble will be held to rise to the level of a claim limitation, however. The Federal Circuit has stated that if a preamble breathes "life and meaning" to the claim, it should be considered a claim limitation.[9] More concretely, if the preamble is necessary to define the claimed invention, then it will usually be held to limit the scope of the claim.

An illustration may lend some clarity to this distinction. Consider the following hypothetical patent claims:

1. A diagnostic medical imaging system comprising:

   an ultrasound image generator; and

   a flat panel display capable of displaying an ultrasound image generated by said ultrasound generator.

2. A diagnostic medical imaging ultrasound system capable of being housed on a portable support, comprising:

   an ultrasound image generator integrated with said support; and

   a flat panel display integrated with said support, capable of displaying an ultrasound image generated by said ultrasound generator.

In claim 1, the body of the claim completely defines the invention without reference to the preamble. The preamble simply notes that the intended field of use of the invention is medical diagnostics. This intended use would not limit the scope of the claims. In claim 2, however, both elements recited in the body of the claim expressly refer to subject matter introduced in the preamble (note the cross-reference in the words "said support" which refers back to the "portable support" mentioned in the preamble). A court would likely consider not merely a support, but a portable support as a necessary limitation of claim 2. A consequence of this reading of the claim is that a party who manufactured an ultrasound diagnostic

9. Catalina Marketing Int'l v. Coolsavings.com, Inc., 289 F.3d 801, 62 USPQ2d 1781 (Fed. Cir. 2002).

device of this sort which was connected to an immovable support would not be liable for infringing claim 2.

6.2.1.2 The Transition Phrase

The transition phrase connects the preamble to the body of the claim. In practice, the drafter must choose from one of three transition phrases: "comprising," "consisting of," or "essentially consisting of." This humble choice of words actually has significant substantive effect upon the scope of the claim. The transition phrase determines whether the claim is limited to structures with only those elements (closed terminology) or is open to structures containing at least those elements, and possibly others (open or hybrid terminology).

The use of the term "comprising" encompasses technologies with all the elements described in the body of the claim. Whether the technology incorporates additional elements is irrelevant.[10] Consider, for example, a claim reciting "a composition of matter *comprising* element A; element B; and element C." The term "comprising" renders the claim open to additional ingredients. This open claim covers any composition with at least the elements A+B+C. Thus, both the combination of A+B+C and A+B+C+D are encompassed by the claim.

In contrast, a claim which employs the term "consisting of" is closed to additional ingredients. Infringement can occur only when the accused technology has exactly the same elements recited in the claim—no more or no less. Thus, a competitor's sale of a composition with ingredients A+B+C+D is outside the literal scope of a claim towards "a composition of matter *consisting of* element A; element B; and element C."[10.5]

Why would anyone want to employ such a limiting transitional phrase? Sometimes the nature of an invention lies in the elimination of certain components or process steps known to the prior art. "Closed" claim language allows an inventor to avoid an anticipation rejection. For example, suppose that prior art match heads consist of four elements: (1) a fuel, such as sulfur; (2) an oxidizer, such as potassium chlorate, to make the match head burn more strongly; (3) a dilutant, such as starch, to control the burning rate; and (4) a binder, such as glue, to hold the ingredients of the match head together and bind the match head to the stick. Later, inventor John Storm discovers that a certain combination of fuels and

10. Mannesmann Demag Corp. v. Engineered Metal Products Co., Inc., 793 F.2d 1279, 230 USPQ 45 (Fed.Cir. 1986).

10.5 The reference to the "literal" scope of the claims is important because, as we shall see, a patentee may sometimes invoke something called the "doctrine of equivalents" to secure relief against parties for non-literal infringement. The subject is taken up in § 8.2.2.

oxidizers allows match heads to be manufactured without the use of a dilutant—a streamlining step that significantly reduces costs. Storm would be able to draft a claim reading: A match head, *consisting of* a fuel, an oxidizer, and a binder. In this example, Storm's use of "closed" claim language would allow him to avoid an anticipation rejection over the prior art, even though the prior art discloses all of the elements of his invention (albeit with a dilutant).

As one can imagine, however, claims drafters do not favor this extremely restrictive "consisting of" transition phrase. They are well aware that their competitors may easily avoid the claim by adding a superfluous element to an otherwise infringing technology. In such circumstances, drafters prefer to use the phrase "consisting essentially of," which is a hybrid transition. This terminology renders the claim open to additional elements, so long as they do not materially affect the basic and novel characteristics of the claimed combination. Suppose that a claim recited "a composition of matter *consisting essentially of* element A; element B; and element C." If element D would not materially change the composition, then A+B+C+D lies within the literal scope of this hybrid claim. In appropriate situations, most often in the chemical arts, this form of transition can be very powerful.

Note that the words "the steps of" are ordinarily added to the transition phrase when the claim is directed towards a process or method.

6.2.1.3 The Body

The body of the claim provides the elements of the invention, as well as how these elements cooperate either structurally or functionally. Claims ordinarily devote one clause to each of the primary elements of the invention, often separating them with a semicolon. These clauses may be given a reference label, such as "(a)," "(b)," "(c)," and so on, to allow readers to refer to their language more readily. The drafter should also indicate how one element interacts with the others to form an operative technology, employing such language as "attached to," "operated by," or "positioned above."

Elements of an invention are ordinarily introduced with an indefinite article, such as "a" or "an," as well as terms such as "one," "several," or "a plurality of." When that element is noted later in the claim, claims drafters ordinarily employ the definite article "the" or the term "said." If an element appearing for the first time is accompanied by "the" or "said," then it will ordinarily be rejected by an examiner as lacking so-called "antecedent basis." The following claim employs these articles correctly:

An ion source comprising:

a housing which defines a discharge chamber;

a wave guide transmitting a microwave to generate plasma within said discharge chamber; and

a matching tube having a cross-sectional form that gradually varies in a direction of propagation of the microwave.[11]

This claim also illustrates a peculiarity of the patent law: the reluctance to claim an empty space, such as a chamber, hollow, hole, or gap, directly. Instead, drafters usually define such spaces in terms of the structures that form them. This rule may seem vacuous, but it is commonly observed in modern patent practice. Apparently patent drafters believe that claims should recite structure—not the absence of structure![12]

Courts routinely state that the patent applicants are allowed to coin their own terms for use in claims. As expressed in the vernacular of the patent law, "a patentee is free to be his or her own lexicographer."[13] However, newly minted terms may not be misdescriptive, nor should the applicant employ such banal terms as "gadget" or "widget." The courts and PTO have been even more hostile to the use of trademarks or trade names within patent claims. Typical of such cases is *Ex parte Bolton*,[14] which rejected a claim reciting the trademark "FORMICA." The PTO Board of Appeals reasoned that the manufacturer was free to change the composition of FORMICA as it pleased, rendering Bolton's claim of indefinite scope.

6.2.2 Claim Formats

Beyond these basic tenets of claim drafting lie a great number of refining principles. In particular, a number of claim formats are either described in the Patent Act or have been the subject of extensive judicial treatment. Each of these formats provides an understood protocol that may be advantageous for the drafter, perhaps providing the optimal way to claim a particular invention. The most important claim formats are reviewed next.

6.2.2.1 Dependent Claims

Section 112, paragraphs 3–5 allow the use of so-called "dependent" patent claims. The statute mandates that dependent claims must recite an earlier claim and provide additional limitations. For example, following independent claim 1, dependent claim 2 might

11. This claim is based upon U.S. Patent No. 5,925,886 (July 20, 1999).

12. Robert C. Faber, Landis on Mechanics of Patent Claim Drafting § 26 (4th ed. 1996).

13. Hormone Research Foundation, Inc. v. Genentech, Inc., 904 F.2d 1558, 1563, 15 USPQ2d 1039, 1043 (Fed.Cir. 1990), *cert. denied*, 499 U.S. 955, 111 S.Ct. 1434, 113 L.Ed.2d 485 (1991).

14. 42 USPQ 40 (Pat.Off.Bd.App. 1938).

provide: "A tape cassette handling system as recited in claim 1, further comprising ... " Such claims are interpreted to include all of the previous limitations as well as those which are newly recited. Claims may also be multiple dependent format, as in a claim which recites "a tape cassette handling system as recited in claims 1 or 2, further comprising ... " The statute instructs readers to "incorporate by reference all the limitations of the particular claim in relation to which it is being considered."[15]

The possibility of dependent claims presents a drafting convenience for patent applicants. They enable drafters to express claims of increasingly narrow scope in a succinct fashion. The result of this system is that claims drafters typically craft a series of claims in each application, forming a "reverse pyramid" of successively narrower claims. The first, independent claim of the patent is the most broad and abstractly written. The most narrow, dependent claim usually describes a product the inventor would actually consider putting into commercial practice. Intermediate claims are set to varying levels of abstraction, each taking a place on the spectrum of technologies surrounding the narrowly focused commercial embodiment of the invention.

Skilled drafters employ this technique because they recognize the patentee may wish to enforce the narrowest possible claim against an accused infringer. After all, the narrower the claim, the higher the likelihood that such a claim will withstand a defense of invalidity. That is because the greater the number of limitations in a claim, the more unlikely it is that prior art will render that claim anticipated under § 102 or obvious under § 103. Importantly, not all the pertinent prior art may be known to the applicant, and the claims drafter must speculate as to the sorts of references that may bear upon the claimed invention. Also, the narrower the claim, the greater the difficulty an accused infringer will have in attacking it based upon lack of enablement.

On the other hand, the patentee also wants the broadest claim possible in order to have the possibility of reaching as many competitors as possible. Where claims are broad and contain few limitations other industry actors will find efforts to design competing technologies that do not fall within the scope of those broad or sweeping claims more difficult, and thus would be able avoid literal infringement less easily. That reality may encourage them to negotiate a license rather than risk a lawsuit. So a claims drafter will attempt to write the broadest claim the PTO will allow, allowing a range of potential technological protection in each patent instrument.

15. 35 U.S.C. § 112 ¶ 4 (2000).

The following hypothetical illuminates the workings of dependent claims. Suppose that Moe Jackson is the proprietor of a patent with the following claims:

1. A method of forming a porous surface for use with an orthopaedic implant, said method comprising the steps of:

   providing a plurality of metallic particles; and

   mixing a water-soluble protein compound with said metallic particles.

2. The method of claim 1, wherein said protein compound comprises gelatin.

3. The method of claim 2, where said metallic particles comprise titanium.

4. The method of claim 3, where said mixing is performed at a temperature of 421.6° C.[16]

Jackson brings an enforcement action against Leon Sanders, alleging infringement of claims 1–4. During trial, Sanders introduces into evidence an article from a medical journal. That article, a § 102(b) reference not discovered by the PTO examiner, explained that a mixture of chromium particles and gelatin formed a superior coating for use with artificial hip implants. The court concludes that, in view of the reference, claims 1 and 2 were anticipated and claim 3 would have been obvious, because those skilled in the art were aware that chromium and titanium have similar properties in this context. However, the court holds that the invention defined in claim 4 would not have been obvious to one of skill in the art because performing the method with titanium at 421.6° C produced unexpectedly good results.

In this case, the more narrowly drafted claim 4 is not invalid even though it formally depends on an invalid claim. For the sake of convenience, claim 4 could be viewed in independent form as follows:

4. A method of forming a porous surface for use with an orthopaedic implant, said method comprising the steps of:

   providing a plurality of titanium particles; and

   mixing gelatin with said titanium particles;

   whereby said mixing is performed at a temperature of 421.6° C.

16. This hypothetical is loosely based on U.S. Pat. No. 5,926,685 (July 20, 1999). An orthopaedic implant is typically inserted within the human body during surgery, serving as a replacement for the knees, hips or other skeletal joint.

To the extent that Sanders practices the method recited in claim 4, he has committed patent infringement. Jackson would be able to obtain remedies for patent infringement as provided by the statute.

6.2.2.2 Functional Claims

Functional claims define an invention in terms of what it does rather than in terms of its structure. Patent practitioners generally term such claims as "means-plus-function" claims, a reference to the final paragraph of § 112. Section 112 ¶ 6 provides that an element in a combination claim may be expressed as a means or step for performing a specified function. It further directs that such a claim shall be construed to cover the corresponding structure, material, or acts described in the specification and equivalents thereof.

In the following simplified claim, elements (a) and (b) are expressed structurally, while element (c) is drafted in means-plus-function form.

1. A hammer, comprising:

(a) a head;

(b) a handle; and

(c) means for attaching said head and said handle.

To determine the literal scope of element (c), § 112 ¶ 6 directs that the reader turn to the patent's specification. Assume that the patent's specification explained that the "handle and head may be attached through the use of a nail or bolt." In this case claim 1 should be literally read to cover the following combination:

1. A hammer, comprising:

(a) a head;

(b) a handle; and

(c) [a nail, bolt and equivalents thereof] for attaching said head and said handle.

Because § 112 ¶ 6 refers to "a claim for a combination," a claim that consists of a single means for accomplishing a particular task is improper.[17] Thus a claim reading "A tool comprising means for driving a nail into a board" would be invalid.

Section 112 ¶ 6 owes its origin to increasing judicial hostility to functional claiming in the first half of the twentieth century. This trend culminated in the 1946 Supreme Court decision *Halliburton Oil Well Cementing Co. v. Walker.*[18] Walker's patent claims, directed towards an apparatus for measuring the depth of oil wells, included

17. *See* In re Hyatt, 708 F.2d 712, 218 USPQ 195 (Fed.Cir.1983).

18. 329 U.S. 1, 67 S.Ct. 6, 91 L.Ed. 3 (1946).

a number of limitations cast in means-plus-function format. These included "means communicating with said well for creating a pressure impulse in said well" and "echo receiving means." The Court struck down Walker's claims, reasoning that because they were not tied to the specific structures Walker had invented they were overbroad and indefinite. According to the Court, "unless frightened from the course of experimentation by broad functional claims like these, inventive genius may evolve many more devices to accomplish the same purpose."[19]

The patent bar protested mightily against *Halliburton Oil*, which cast great doubt upon a large number of issued patents that had employed a functional claiming style. In response Congress amended the patent statute by adding the provision now codified at § 112 ¶ 6.[20] The intent of Congress was to establish clear parameters within which functional claims could be written and interpreted.[21]

Three principal issues have arisen concerning the operation of § 112 ¶ 6. The first is whether the rule that means-plus-function elements should be interpreted in light of the disclosures in the specification applies to PTO determinations of patentability, or only to claim interpretation in subsequent infringement litigation. A second issue concerns which claims should be read as invoking § 112 ¶ 6, and hence the mandatory statutory procedure for interpreting them. Finally, the precise parameters of the closing phrase of § 112 ¶ 6, "and equivalents thereof," is of paramount concern during the interpretation of means-plus-function claims. We can consider each of these problems in turn.

The Federal Circuit addressed the first of these issues in its *en banc* opinion in *In re Donaldson*.[22] Although § 112 ¶ 6 does not by its own terms distinguish between prosecution and litigation, PTO policy prior to 1994 was not to read means-plus-function claims as limited by the language of the specification. The PTO took the position that it was to give claims their broadest reasonable meaning. Therefore, claims in means-plus-function were read literally, covering all possible means for performing the stated function, even means that were not described in the specification. Because broader claims read upon a greater range of prior art references, this policy resulted in the rejection of claims that would have been approved had § 112 ¶ 6 been applied. For instance, in our hammer example above, the PTO would read the element "means for attaching said

19. 329 U.S. at 12.

20. Warner–Jenkinson Co. v. Hilton Davis Chem. Co., 520 U.S. 17, 117 S.Ct. 1040, 137 L.Ed.2d 146 (1997).

21. Dawn Equip. Co. v. Kentucky Farms, Inc., 140 F.3d 1009, 46 USPQ2d 1109 (Fed.Cir.1998) (Plager, J., additional views).

22. 16 F.3d 1189, 29 USPQ2d 1845 (Fed.Cir.1994).

head and said handle" to encompass all possible attachment means, not merely the use of bolts, nails, or their equivalents. Thus, if the examiner located a prior art reference describing a hammer in which the head was attached to the handle by glue, that reference would render the claim anticipated and the patent would not issue.

This disharmony between PTO practice and the statute came to a head in *In re Donaldson*. Donaldson's claims concerned an industrial dust collector. The dust collector's filter featured flexible, diaphragm-like walls. When the filter required cleaning, an operator needed only to reverse the air pressure, causing the walls to flex in the opposite direction which would dislodge caked dust into a bin below. Claim 1 of Donaldson's application claimed this element of the invention in the following terms: "means, responsive to pressure increases in said chamber caused by said cleaning means, for moving particulate matter in a downward direction." The PTO rejected the application based on the Swift prior art reference. Swift, which also performed a cleaning function with reverse air pulses, had sloped rather than flexible walls. Donaldson appealed to the Federal Circuit, arguing that had the PTO interpreted his claims in accordance with § 112 ¶ 6, the Swift reference would not have rendered the claimed invention obvious.

The Federal Circuit heard Donaldson's appeal *en banc*. Writing for the unanimous court, Judge Rich reasoned that nothing in the statute exempted the PTO from following § 112 ¶ 6. No statutory language or legislative history supported this conclusion, and Judge Rich was quick to point out that § 112 is found in Chapter 11 of Title 35, titled "Application for Patent." The court further found that fidelity to the statute would do no harm to the PTO's policy of giving claims their broadest reasonable interpretation. The PTO could continue to give claims their broadest fair reading so long as it followed § 112 ¶ 6 when construing functional claims. The Federal Circuit also rejected the PTO's argument that § 112 ¶ 6 raised issues of indefiniteness because that statute required limitations to be exported from the specification into the claims. If an inventor opted to employ means-plus-function language in a claim, then he must set forth in the specification an adequate disclosure showing what was meant by that language. Failure to do so would constitute a violation of § 112 ¶ 2. Concluding that Donaldson's claims were patentable over the Swift reference when properly interpreted, the court reversed the PTO rejection.

With the statutory procedures of § 112 ¶ 6 now applying to both prosecution and litigation, both examiners and courts now require mechanisms for determining which claims should be considered to be written in means-plus-function format. The Federal Circuit has held that the use of the word "means" triggers a presumption that the inventor used this term to invoke the statutory mandates for means-plus-function clauses.[23] However, not every use of the term "means" indicates that the claim is a means-plus-function claim. The presumption of invoking § 112 ¶ 6 can be rebutted if the claim language does not link the term "means" to a recited function.

Cole v. Kimberly–Clark Corp.[24] demonstrates how courts determine whether a particular claim is drafted in means-plus-function format. There the Federal Circuit construed a claim involving disposable diapers with sides that easily tear open to facilitate removal of a soiled diaper. Among the claim elements was "perforation means extending from the leg band means to the waist band means through the outer impermeable layer means for tearing the outer impermeable layer means for removing the training brief in the case of an accident by the user." The district court determined on summary judgment that a "perforation means" is merely a "perforation" and that the bonded tearable side seams on the defendant's allegedly infringing diapers were not perforations.

The Federal Circuit affirmed on appeal, also declining to apply § 112 ¶ 6. According to the court, the "perforation means . . . for tearing" element of Cole's claim was not a true "mean-plus-function" claim within the scope of the statute because it recited not only perforations, the structure supporting the tearing function, but also their location (extending from the leg band to the waist band) and range (extending through the impermeable layer). The court reasoned that a claim that cited such detailed structure should not qualify as functional.

On the other hand, the term "means" is not the only one which will invoke § 112 ¶ 6. In *Mas–Hamilton Group v. LaGard, Inc.*,[25] the Federal Circuit considered a claim that recited a "lever moving element." The court held that § 112 ¶ 6 applied to this claim element as well, despite its failure to use the usual catch word "means." The court recognized that many devices take their name from the functions they perform, such as a screwdriver, brake, or lock, and that the use of these terms in a claim would count as a structural, rather than functional definition. However, the phrase "lever moving element" lacked a well-understood structural meaning in the art. As a result, the court held that the claim defined this element functionally rather than structurally, just as if the drafter had used the phrase "means for moving a lever." Consequently, its literal scope was restricted to structures disclosed

23. York Products Inc. v. Central Tractor Farm & Family Center, 99 F.3d 1568, 40 USPQ2d 1619 (Fed.Cir.1996); Greenberg v. Ethicon Endo–Surgery, Inc., 91 F.3d 1580, 1584, 39 USPQ2d 1783, 1786–87 (Fed.Cir.1996).

24. 102 F.3d 524, 531, 41 USPQ2d 1001, 1006 (Fed.Cir.1996).

25. 156 F.3d 1206, 48 USPQ2d 1010 (Fed.Cir.1998).

in the specification and equivalents thereof that performed the identical function, rather than to any conceivable device for moving a lever. Similarly, a PTO Board decision has found claim language reciting "a jet driving device" to invoke § 112 ¶ 6.[26]

Section 112 ¶ 6 also refers to process or method claims, providing that "an element in a claim for a combination may be expressed as a ... step for performing a specified function without the recital of ... acts in support thereof." Step-plus-function claim elements describe a step, or generic description of a portion of a process, without reciting more specific acts about how that step or function should be accomplished. According to the statute, such claims should be construed as covering the corresponding "acts described in the specification and equivalents thereof." For example, suppose that one of the elements of a process claim was "the step of raising the temperature to 300 degrees." If the patent's specification described the use of an oven to raise the temperature to 300 degrees, the literal coverage of the claim would extend to the use of an oven and equivalent acts, but not, perhaps, to the process of using a laser beam to do so. The Federal Circuit has acknowledged the propriety of step-plus-function claims,[27] but scant case law has thus far been devoted towards interpreting them. That court has, however, been quick to point out that not every claimed process step invokes the interpretational method of § 112 ¶ 6.

A final issue concerning § 112 ¶ 6 is the operation of its equivalency provision. The statute calls for functional claim language "to cover the corresponding structure, material, or acts described in the specification and equivalents thereof." The Federal Circuit has interpreted this provision to hold that for a means-plus-function limitation to read on an accused device, the accused device must employ means identical or equivalent to the structures, material, or acts described in the patent specification. The accused device must also perform the identical function as specified in the claims.[28]

The Federal Circuit has provided that, for purposes of § 112 ¶ 6, an equivalent results from an insubstantial change which adds nothing of significance to the structure, material, or acts disclosed in the patent specification.[29] The court often expresses this concept through the succinct phrase "structural equivalency."[30] For exam-

26. Ex parte Stanley, 121 USPQ 621 (PTO Bd.1959).

27. *See* O.I. Corp. v. Tekmar Co., 115 F.3d 1576, 42 USPQ2d 1777 (Fed. Cir.1997).

28. King Instruments Corp. v. Perego, 65 F.3d 941, 36 USPQ2d 1129 (Fed. Cir.1995), *cert. denied,* 517 U.S. 1188, 116 S.Ct. 1675, 134 L.Ed.2d 778 (1996).

29. Valmont Indus., Inc. v. Reinke Mfg. Co., 983 F.2d 1039, 25 USPQ2d 1451 (Fed.Cir.1993).

30. Laitram Corp. v. Rexnord, Inc., 939 F.2d 1533, 19 USPQ2d 1367 (Fed. Cir.1991).

ple, recall that in the hammer example above, the specification explained that "the handle and head may be attached through the use of a nail or bolt." A screw would likely be considered a structural equivalent to a nail or bolt, but the use of glue to secure the head and the handle would probably not be judged structurally equivalent.

The court has often stressed that structural equivalency under § 112 ¶ 6 differs from equivalency under the doctrine of equivalents.[31] The doctrine of equivalents will be further discussed in Chapter 8. For present purposes, it is enough to recognize that despite their demands for clear claiming, the courts have been willing to find liability even where an accused infringer diverges slightly from a strict reading of the claims. An equivalent under the doctrine results from an insubstantial change which, from the perspective of persons of ordinary skill in the art, adds nothing of significance to the claimed invention. An equivalent under the doctrine, though not literally meeting the claims, still infringes the patent.[32]

As can be imagined, the contrast between structural equivalency and equivalency under the doctrine has proven a rather subtle affair. As this text will discuss further in § 8.2.2.5, the difference between the statutory equivalency provision of § 112 ¶ 6 and the judicially created doctrine of equivalents is principally a matter of timing. An equivalent under § 112 ¶ 6 is at the time the patent issues, which is the moment the PTO has fixed the literal meaning of the claims. However, the proper time for assessing infringement under the doctrine of equivalents is at the time of infringement. Therefore, an "after-arising" technology could infringe under the doctrine of equivalents without being considered a § 112 ¶ 6 equivalent.

6.2.2.3 Product-by-Process Claims

Sometimes an inventor realizes that she has arrived at a new composition, but cannot specify that composition either by name or structure. In these cases the inventor cannot define the composition directly. But she is able to describe the composition as the product of the process she used to make the composition. So-called "product-by-process" claims reflect these circumstances. The following claim is representative:

> A diamond-bearing material prepared by a process comprising the steps of

31. *See* Endress + Hauser, Inc. v. Hawk Measurement Sys.Pty. Ltd., 122 F.3d 1040, 43 USPQ2d 1849 (Fed.Cir. 1997).

32. *See* Warner-Jenkinson Co. v. Hilton Davis Chem. Co., 520 U.S. 17, 117 S.Ct. 1040, 137 L.Ed.2d 146 (1997).

detonating a charge consisting essentially of a carbon-containing explosive having a negative oxygen balance to form a detonation product; and

cooling the detonation product at a rate of about 200 to 6,000 degrees/minute.

For example, suppose that amateur inventor Steven Serendip is working in his makeshift basement laboratory one evening. Serendip accidentally mixes together equal portions of three chemical compounds with which he has been experimenting—alpherion, beterium and gammanium. There is an immediate puff, and a blue rubbery mass forms at the bottom of his beaker. Serendip realizes that the resulting compound, which he immediately names "flabber," possesses incredible strength and elasticity. Serendip's formal chemistry education is modest and he only possesses a vague notion of the chemical reactions that must have occurred to produce flabber. Nor does he own a spectroscope or other expensive equipment to find out the precise composition of flabber. These circumstances will not prevent him from filing a patent application claiming flabber, however, if he defines his invention via the process he used to produce it. In other words he could file a claim for "a strong, highly elastic substance prepared by a process comprising the step of mixing together equal portions of alpherion, beterium, and gammanium."

Product-by-process claims are not mentioned in the patent statute, but have been the subject of a modest number of judicial and PTO decisions.[33] These claims are most common in chemical practice but sometimes arise in other fields. Some inventors employ this claim format even when they are able to claim the product directly, usually as a supplementary claim.[34]

A recurring issue regarding product-by-process claims concerns the extent of their claim coverage. One school of thought is that these claims cover the resulting product no matter how it is made. To further the above example, suppose that Serendip were issued a patent containing the single product-by-process claim towards flabber hypothesized above. Under this line of reasoning, Serendip's claim would cover competitor sales of flabber even though others employed different manufacturing techniques. In the 1991 opinion *Scripps Clinic & Research Foundation v. Genentech, Inc.*,[35] a three-judge panel of the Federal Circuit adopted this view.

33. *See* In re Thorpe, 777 F.2d 695, 697, 227 USPQ 964, 965–66 (Fed.Cir. 1985).

34. *See* Ex parte Edwards, 231 USPQ 981 (PTO Bd.1986).

35. 927 F.2d 1565, 18 USPQ2d 1896 (Fed.Cir.1991).

Another possibility, however, is that product-by-process claims are restricted to the method of making recited in the claims. Under this outlook, Serendip's competitors would be able to avoid his product-by-process claim by using another method to make flabber. Just one year after *Scripps Clinic*, a different three-judge panel of the Federal Circuit issued its opinion in *Atlantic Thermoplastics Co. v. Faytex Corp.*,[36] adopting this reasoning. According to the *Atlantic Thermoplastics* panel, both binding Supreme Court precedent and sound claiming practice indicated that product-by-process should be given a more restrictive interpretation. *Scripps Clinic* was distinguished because that panel had "ruled without reference to the Supreme Court's previous cases involving product claims with process limitations."[37]

Atlantic Thermoplastics proved a controversial opinion, particularly given the Federal Circuit's self-described "obligation of promoting uniformity in the field of patent law."[38] Judge Rich went so far to describe *Atlantic Thermoplastics* as "mutiny," "heresy," and "illegal."[39] But the *Atlantic Thermoplastics* panel did seem to have the better reading of the earlier cases, and at least one subsequent district court opinion opted to limit product-by-process claims to the actual process recited therein.[40]

6.2.2.4 Jepson Claims

A "Jepson claim" defines an invention in two parts: a preamble which recites the admitted prior art, followed by an "improvement" clause which recites what the applicant regards as his invention. Jepson claims may be identified by the transition phrase "where the improvement comprises," or words to that effect. The following claim was drafted in Jepson format:

> An improved polarized sunglass lens laminate comprising a first lens portion, a second lens portion, a polarizing film disposed between the first and second lens portions, and an adhesive binding the two lens portions and the polarizing film together,

36. 970 F.2d 834, 23 USPQ2d 1481 (Fed.Cir.1992).

37. *Id.* at 839 n.2, 23 USPQ2d at 1492 n.2.

38. Midwest Industries, Inc. v. Karavan Trailers, Inc., 175 F.3d 1356, 1360, 50 USPQ2d 1672, 1676 (Fed.Cir.1999), *cert. denied*, 528 U.S. 1019, 120 S.Ct. 527, 145 L.Ed.2d 409 (1999).

39. Atlantic Thermoplastics Co. v. Faytex Corp., 974 F.2d 1279, 23 USPQ2d 1801 (Fed.Cir.1992) (Rich, J., dissenting from the denial of rehearing en banc).

40. *See* Tropix, Inc. v. Lumigen, 825 F.Supp. 7, 10, 27 USPQ2d 1475, 1478 (D.Mass.1993).

> the improvement of which comprises incorporating sufficient ultraviolet absorber into the adhesive to block substantially all of the UVA radiation in sunlight.[41]

Jepson claims take their name from an early Patent Office Board opinion, *In re Jepson*,[42] which approved this format. Although Jepson was not the first inventor to employ this style of claim, the fact that his application was associated with this seminal opinion has provided him a measure of fame in the patent community.

The use of the Jepson format has two primary effects. First, the preamble unquestionably acts as a limitation upon the scope of the claims in a Jepson claim.[43] The second, and more important effect is that any subject matter recited in the preamble presumptively constitutes prior art even if not available under a § 102 category.[44] This presumption may be rebutted by a showing that the preamble recites the inventor's own work product and is not otherwise prior art under § 102.[45]

PTO examiners highly favor the use of Jepson claims. In the event that no anticipatory reference is available, the task of generating nonobviousness rejections is greatly simplified when an applicant opts to admit that everything in the claim but the "improvement" clause constitutes prior art. With regard to the previous example, the PTO examiner would take as a given that the combination of a sunglass lens, polarizing film, and adhesive binding is known to the art. The examiner need only show that it would have been obvious to incorporate ultraviolet absorber into the adhesive binding in order to reject the claim under § 103. However, suppose alternatively that this claim had been drafted in the usual style, as a combination of elements. In this case the examiner would have to demonstrate that a skilled artisan would have been motivated to combine references to produce each of the elements of the claimed invention, a task likely more difficult than had a Jepson format been employed.

Given that Jepson claims tend not to portray inventions in a favorable light, the fact that applicants continue to use them may appear puzzling. One reason Jepson claims remain popular is that foreign patent offices, and in particular the European Patent Office, strongly encourage the use of this claim format.[46] Many applicants based abroad simply file the same set of claims at the PTO that they did abroad. Foreign applicants are ordinarily well advised to

41. U.S. Patent No. 5,926,248 (July 20, 1999).

42. 1917 Comm. Dec. 62, 243 O.G. 525 (Ass't Comm'r Pat. 1917).

43. Pentec, Inc. v. Graphic Controls Corp., 776 F.2d 309, 227 USPQ 766 (Fed.Cir.1985).

44. In re Fout, 675 F.2d 297, 213 USPQ 532 (CCPA 1982).

45. Reading & Bates Construction Co. v. Baker Energy Resources Corp., 748 F.2d 645, 223 USPQ 1168 (Fed.Cir. 1984).

46. *See* Arthur L. Plevy, *Some Important Differences Between Patent Practice in Europe and the United States*, 209 N.J. LAW. 40, 41–42 (June 2001).

avoid the Jepson format in the United States, however, simply by reformatting their claims. Absent special circumstances, domestic inventors would be wise to avoid Jepson claims entirely.

6.2.2.5 Markush Claims

So-called "Markush" claims are common only in chemical practice. Like Jepson, Eugene Markush was not the first inventor to employ this style of claim. But because his application was concerned with the important Patent Office opinion approving this claiming protocol, his name has become associated with it both in the United States and abroad.[47] Drafters employ the Markush format when no commonly accepted generic term is commensurate in scope with the invention the applicant wishes to claim.[48]

Markush groups usually claim a family of compounds by defining the structure common to all members of that family, along with one or more alternatives selected from a set consisting of named chemical compounds. A letter, most often "R," typically represents this latter set of alternatives. A sample Markush claim appears as follows:

> A compound of the formula OH–CH–R, where R is selected from the group consisting of chlorine, bromine, and iodine.

Although this simple example neatly illustrates the Markush format, it may not fully convey the desirability of this type of claim. In this case, if the Markush format were unavailable an inventor could simply draft three claims individually reciting chlorine, bromine and iodine. But in the real world of chemistry the relevant alternatives often constitute chemical radicals that may themselves consist of hundreds of closely related compounds. Inventors in such fields as pharmacology, ceramics, and metallurgy would be sorely pressed if required to draft dozens or hundreds of claims to define each and every member of the alternative group. They would also incur prohibitive filing fees at the PTO, which charges additional fees when applications contain a large number of claims.

A proper Markush group claims a set of substances that share at least one common trait.[49] For example, the chemical compounds claimed above must have the same use, perhaps as a dye or detergent, in order to be arranged in a Markush format.

Unlike Jepson claims, Markush claims are not construed as including an admission concerning the prior art. In particular, use of the Markush format does not amount to an admission that the claimed alternatives comprise obvious variations of one another. To

47. *See* Ex parte Markush, 1925 C.D. 126, 340 O.G. 839 (Comm'r Pat. 1924).

48. U.S. Department of Commerce, Patent and Trademark Office, Manual of Patent Examining Procedure § 803.02 (7th ed. July 1998).

49. *See* In re Harnisch, 631 F.2d 716, 206 USPQ 300 (CCPA 1980).

continue the above example, suppose that an examiner discovers a scientific journal article available under § 102(a). That article describes the nucleus of the claimed compound along with chlorine. Unless the examiner can additionally demonstrate that the other claimed alternatives were anticipated or would have been obvious within the terms of § 103, the applicant would be allowed to narrow the claim to bromine and iodine, unprejudiced by the fact that a Markush grouping was employed.[50]

6.2.3 Definiteness

Section 112 ¶ 2 requires that the claims particularly point out and distinctly claim the subject matter which the applicant regards as his invention. Patent attorneys more succinctly refer to this requirement as one of definiteness.[51] The Federal Circuit has interpreted the statute as calling for such precision in claim language that the subject matter they encompass is clearly articulated.[52] Definite claims allow examiners to determine whether the invention fulfills the strictures of patentability or not. The requirement also insures that once the patent issues, interested parties may also obtain clear warning of which technologies will infringe the claim.[53]

A claim meets the standard of § 112 ¶ 2 if it has a clear and specific meaning to persons of skill in the art. Claims are not to be read in the abstract, but in view of the disclosure of the entire patent instrument. If a claim, when read in view of the remainder of the specification, reasonably apprises skilled artisans of the scope of the patented invention, then the definiteness requirement is satisfied.[54]

The definiteness standard is distinct from the requirements governing a patent's disclosure in § 112 ¶ 1. In particular, a claim need not teach others how to practice the patented invention. The enablement standard applies to the patent specification as a whole, not to the claims in particular.[55]

A leading opinion on definiteness in claim language is *Orthokinetics, Inc. v. Safety Travel Chairs, Inc.*[56] The patent-at-suit concerned a collapsible wheelchair that facilitated the placement of wheelchair-bound persons in and out of an automobile. Each of its

50. Application of Ruff, 256 F.2d 590, 118 USPQ 340 (CCPA 1958).

51. *See* Miles Labs., Inc. v. Shandon Inc., 997 F.2d 870, 874–75, 27 USPQ2d 1123, 1126 (Fed.Cir.1993).

52. *See* In re Borkowski, 422 F.2d 904, 909, 164 USPQ 642, 645–46 (CCPA 1970).

53. *See* Leeds v. Commissioner of Patents and Trademarks, 955 F.2d 757, 759, 21 USPQ2d 1771, 1773 (D.C.Cir. 1992).

54. Morton Int'l, Inc. v. Cardinal Chem. Co., 5 F.3d 1464, 1470, 28 USPQ2d 1190, 1194 (Fed.Cir.1993).

55. *See* Miles Labs., Inc. v. Shandon Inc., 997 F.2d 870, 874, 27 USPQ2d 1123, 1126 (Fed.Cir.1993).

56. 806 F.2d 1565, 1 USPQ2d 1081 (Fed.Cir.1986).

claims required the front part of the wheelchair to be "so dimensioned as to be insertable through the space between the doorframe of an automobile and one of the seats thereof." The accused infringer argued that this claim language was fatally indefinite, an argument accepted by the trial court.

On appeal, the Federal Circuit reversed. Chief Judge Markey reasoned that because automobiles come in various sizes, calling for a portion of the wheelchair to be "so dimensioned" was "as accurate as the subject matter permits." Expert testimony demonstrated that, upon reviewing the patent's specification, persons of ordinary skill could have easily measured the interior dimensions of a particular automobile in order to build a functioning wheelchair. In such circumstances, the patent law did not require the applicant to claim all possible lengths corresponding to the dimensions of hundreds of different automobiles. Because Orthokinetic's claims were sufficiently distinct such that skilled artisans could understand their meaning, they fulfilled the definiteness requirement.

Patent claims often employ words of degree, such as "about," "approximately," "close to," "substantially equal," or "closely approximate." Such terms can raise perplexing issues of definiteness. The courts have usually assumed a lenient posture towards their use in claims, provided that the claims reasonably define the invention under § 112 ¶ 2 standards.[57] The Federal Circuit will turn to other portions of the specification, the prior art, prosecution history, and understandings of persons of skill in the art to identify some standard for measuring the precise limits of a word of degree.[58]

57. *See* Andrew Corp. v. Gabriel Electronics, 847 F.2d 819, 6 USPQ2d 2010 (Fed.Cir.1988).

58. *See* Amgen, Inc. v. Chugai Pharmaceutical Co., 927 F.2d 1200, 18 USPQ2d 1016 (Fed.Cir.1991).

Chapter 7

PATENT PROSECUTION

Table of Sections

Patents come into existence only through the intervention of the government. The entity assigned the task of approving patent applications is an agency within the U.S. Department of Commerce called the United States Patent and Trademark Office, or PTO. The administrative process through which an inventor acquires a patent from the PTO is known as prosecution. The most frequent professional duty of patent practitioners, prosecution is also the task assigned to most entry-level patent lawyers. However, even those engaged exclusively in patent litigation need to be thoroughly familiar with the events at the PTO that lead to the grant of any patent which is sued upon or defended against, because those events can greatly affect the scope of protection afforded to the patent and the availability of various defenses. Attorneys who do not routinely practice patent law may also find themselves more frequently approached by inventors wishing to obtain a patent than by patent proprietors who wish to enforce their intellectual property rights by suing an alleged infringer. For all these reasons, a basic grasp of prosecution mechanisms is crucial to a full understanding of the patent law.

§ 7.1 Introduction to the Patent and Trademark Office

The Patent and Trademark Office, or PTO, is an administrative agency of the federal government.[1] The PTO is organized within the Department of Commerce and is under the policy direction of the Secretary of Commerce. A Director, who is appointed by the President with the consent of the Senate, heads the PTO. The Secretary of Commerce also appoints a Commissioner of Patents with the specific responsibility of managing the PTO's patent operations.[2] The PTO is currently housed in northern Virginia, near Washington, DC. There is a wealth of information about the PTO on its web site, which can be found at <www.uspto.gov>.

Most of the employees of the PTO are patent examiners, who are charged with scrutinizing applications to determine if a patent should issue. The examining corps itself is organized into various Examining Groups, which are further divided into Group and Individual Art Units. A Group Director heads each of the Examining Groups, while the various Group Units are directed by a senior official designated the Supervisory Primary Examiner, or SPE. Front-line examiners are classified as either primary or assistant. Primary examiners possess considerable experience and are authorized to make decisions pertinent to patentability on an independent

§ 7.1

1. 35 U.S.C.A. § 1 (2000).

2. 35 U.S.C.A. § 3 (2000). As you would suspect, there is also a Commissioner of Trademarks.

basis. Each primary examiner acts, in a sense, like a one-person patent office. Assistant examiners tend to be more recent hires who work under the supervision of primary examiners. At the time this book went to press, the PTO employed over 3000 patent examiners. Patent examiners need not be attorneys.

Several additional entities within the PTO are worthy of note here. The PTO maintains a Board of Patent Appeals and Interferences.[3] The Board consists of approximately sixty administrative patent judges. The Board hears appeals in panels of three, although sometimes the PTO convenes expanded panels to hear important cases. The PTO also maintains an Office of the Solicitor. The PTO Solicitor and his or her staff of attorneys represent the PTO in judicial proceedings, in particular appeals to the Federal Circuit by aggrieved applicants. Finally, the American Inventors Protection Act of 1999 established a Patent Public Advisory Committee.[4] The Committee has nine voting members appointed by the Secretary of Commerce for three-year terms. The Committee meets to discuss policies, goals, performance, budget and user fees that bear upon the PTO's patent operations, and prepares an annual report.

The PTO is virtually unique among federal agencies in its licensing of practitioners. Before someone may prepare and prosecute patent applications on behalf of others, he must pass a difficult test administered by the PTO, known colloquially as the "patent bar exam." The PTO waives the testing requirement for former patent examiners with sufficient experience. PTO registration and practice is open to lawyers and nonlawyers alike. Registered nonlawyers are termed patent agents.[5]

§ 7.2 The Mechanics of Prosecution

7.2.1 Preparation of Applications

An inventor who wishes to obtain patent protection must first prepare an application. Although inventors may represent themselves before the PTO, the vast majority engage the services of a patent attorney or agent for this purpose. Applicants may chose to prepare either a provisional or nonprovisional application. We will take a brief look at the nature and purposes of provisional applications a bit further on in this chapter. Most inventors, however, opt for nonprovisional, or regular applications. In this text, as in patent practice generally, a reference to a patent application should be taken as referring to a nonprovisional application unless the context plainly indicates otherwise.

3. 35 U.S.C.A. § 6 (2000).

4. 35 U.S.C.A. § 5 (2000).

5. *See* Michelle J. Burke & Thomas G. Field, Jr., *Promulgating Requirements for Admission to Prosecute Patent Applications*, 36 IDEA: J. L. & Tech. 145 (1995).

An application must include a specification, at least one claim, and the proper filing fee. The filing fee as of January 1, 2003, was $770.[1] The Patent Act also requires that the applicant submit an oath or declaration stating that he believes himself to be the original and first inventor of the invention for which he seeks a patent.[2] Drawings should be included when necessary.[3] PTO regulations further provide that the elements of a patent application should appear in the following order:

(1) the title of the invention;

(2) a cross-reference to any related applications;

(3) a reference to a microfiche appendix containing a computer program;

(4) a brief summary of the invention;

(5) a brief description of any drawings;

(6) a detailed description;

(7) at least one claim;

(8) an abstract;

(9) a signed oath or declaration; and

(10) any drawings.[4]

Inventors possess no duty to perform a prior art search prior to filing a patent application. However, if an applicant does know of a prior art reference that is material to the patentability of the claimed invention, he must disclose it to the PTO.[5] Any prior art that the applicant wishes the PTO to consider should be listed in a so-called Information Disclosure Statement, or IDS.[6] An IDS includes a copy of all patents, publications, or other information submitted for consideration. References not available in the English language must be accompanied by a concise English explanation.

7.2.2 Provisional Applications

Commencing on June 8, 1995, the PTO began to accept provisional patent applications. The fee associated with a provisional application is only $160,[7] considerably less than that required to file a nonprovisional application. Provisional applications also need not include claims, nor must they be accompanied by an inventor oath or declaration.[8] Although provisional applications are less expensive and simpler to prepare than nonprovisional applications, they also

§ 7.2

1. 37 C.F.R. § 1.16 (2002).
2. 35 U.S.C.A. § 115 (2000).
3. 35 U.S.C.A. § 113 (2000).
4. 37 C.F.R. § 1.77 (2002).
5. 37 C.F.R. § 1.56 (2000).
6. 37 C.F.R. §§ 1.97, 1.98 (2000).
7. 35 U.S.C.A. § 41(a)(1)(C) (2000).
8. 35 U.S.C.A. § 111(b) (2000).

provide fewer benefits. The PTO does not examine provisional applications. In addition, the PTO will consider the applicant to have abandoned a provisional application twelve months after it is filed.

The value of filing a provisional application is that the applicant may gain the benefit of its filing date. If an applicant files a nonprovisional application within twelve months of the provisional application, the nonprovisional application will be treated as if it were filed on the date of the provisional application. This special treatment may disqualify certain events—such as the inventor's own sales or public uses—as § 102(b) prior art that would defeat the application. Importantly, the pendency of a provisional application does not subtract from the term of any subsequent nonprovisional application that matures into an issued patent.

An example may illustrate the workings of the provisional application scheme. Suppose that inventor Wyatt Wingfoot filed a provisional application on December 1, 2002. Unless Wingfoot filed a nonprovisional patent application by December 1, 2003, claiming the benefit of the earlier filing, the PTO will consider the provisional application to have been abandoned. If Wingfoot met this deadline by filing a nonprovisional application on November 1, 2003, and if the PTO issues a patent based on that application, that patent will expire on November 1, 2023—twenty years from the filing date of the nonprovisional application.

This example illustrates one benefit of provisional applications. Provisional applications delay both the start and the end of the patent term. If Wingfoot had filed a nonprovisional application on December 1, 2002, then the patent would have expired on December 1, 2022. By first filing a provisional application, Wingfoot has managed to postpone the date the patent expires by a year. Of course, the date the patent will issue has likely also been delayed, for almost one additional year has passed before the Wingfoot's application will be put into queue to be considered by a PTO examiner. But such delays may be of little concern to visionary inventors who do not believe the market is quite ready for their inventions yet. On the other hand, if the invention is ready for marketing immediately, then the use of a provisional application is not a sound strategy.

As provisional applications are cheaper to file than nonprovisional applications, inventors who are short on funds may also wish to file provisional applications. Hopefully, they will have acquired additional resources by the one-year anniversary of their provisional application filing date—perhaps by finding foward-thinking investors or perhaps by commercializing their inventions—so that they may be able to afford a nonprovisional application.

Sometimes time pressures also render provisional applications an attractive alternative to nonprovisional applications. Because provisional applications need not include claims, which are often time-consuming to draft, they may be prepared more quickly than nonprovisional applications. This advantage looms large in a patent system that, with its § 102(b) bars and favoritism towards the first inventor, is very sensitive to questions of timing. For example, suppose that on September 15, 2004, a patent attorney receives a call at 4:30 PM from a client who wishes to file a patent application. The client further explains that she published an article describing the invention exactly one year ago, on September 15, 2003. The patent attorney should recognize that a "printed publication" bar under § 102(b) is looming. A patent application must be filed on September 15, 2004, or the application will be rejected based upon the published article. Given the tight time frame, the only practical way for the patent attorney to prepare and submit the application may be in provisional format. A nonprovisional application can then be filed up to twelve months later, allowing more reflection upon how the patent's claims should be drafted.

Notably, provisional applications may not claim priority from any other application. An inventor could not, for example, file a series of provisional applications and claim the benefit of earlier provisional application filing dates. Amendments to the patent statute in 1999 clarified that if the twelve-month pendency period of a provisional application ends on a holiday, the applicant may file a corresponding nonprovisional application on the next working day.

7.2.3 *Examination of Applications*

Once an inventor has completed a patent application, he should forward it to the PTO for further consideration. It is important to note from the outset that the prosecution of a patent at the PTO is an *ex parte* procedure. Members of the public, and in particular the patent applicant's competitors, do not participate in patent acquisition procedures. Moreover, PTO examiners do not possess a competing interest relative to the applicant. Instead, they assist the applicant in fulfilling the statutory requirements for obtaining a patent grant.[9]

Once the PTO receives a patent application, PTO staff will forward it to the examining group bearing responsibility for that sort of invention. A supervisory primary examiner then assigns the application to an individual examiner. The examiner will review the application and conduct a search of the prior art. The examiner

9. *See* Russell E. Levine *et al.*, *Ex Parte Patent Practice and the Rights of Third Parties*, 45 American Univ. L. Rev. 1987 (1996).

then judges whether the application properly discloses and claims a patentable invention.

The examiner must notify the applicant of her response to the application.[10] Termed an Office Action, this response may either allow the application to issue or reject it in whole or in part. The Office Action must identify each claim, indicate whether it has been rejected or allowed, and offer the examiner's reason for her actions. If the claim is to be rejected, the examiner ordinarily must establish a *prima facie* case of unpatentability by a preponderance of the evidence.

If a rejection has resulted, the attorney will usually respond by either amending the claims or by asserting that the rejection was improper. Under the first option, the attorney introduces changes to the claims, typically modifying or augmenting the claim language in order to overcome a rejection founded on the prior art or lack of claim definiteness. Alternatively, the attorney may argue on the merits that the rejection was improper. The patent bar refers to this sort of substantive argument as a "traverse."

Applicant attempts to traverse an examiner's rejection often involve the use of affidavits. Two PTO rules describe the kinds of affidavits an applicant is most likely to file. Rule 131 affidavits, which declare dates of inventive activity such as conception or reduction to practice, are employed to circumvent rejections based upon 35 U.S.C.A. §§ 102(a) or (e). You may recall that we took up Rule 131 affidavits earlier in this volume, in § 4.4.1. Most of the other affidavits an applicant might wish to file at the PTO fall under Rule 132. This rule provides applicants with the broad ability to offer affidavits for consideration by the examiner. Rule 132 affidavits are typically prepared by technical experts, who express opinions or report laboratory tests that support the patentability of the claimed invention.

If the examiner remains unconvinced by the applicant's response, she will issue a second Office Action titled a "Final Rejection." Although this sort of rejection is termed "final," applicants in fact retain a number of options. They may submit a response to the final rejection, which the examiner may accept if the response places the application in condition for allowance. Applicants can also request an interview with the examiner, conducted in person or over the telephone, in order to discuss how the examiner's rejection can be overcome. If an applicant remains unsuccessful in securing allowance, he ordinarily has three alternatives. He may abandon the application,[11] file a so-called "continuing applica-

10. 35 U.S.C.A. § 132 (2000).

11. 35 U.S.C.A. § 133 (2000).

tion,"[12] or seek review of the examiner's actions by filing a petition to the Commissioner or appeal to the Board of Patent Appeals and Interferences.[13] The latter two options are discussed below. Alternatively, if the examiner agrees that the application should mature into a granted patent, she will issue a Notice of Allowance.[14] The payment of an issuance fee will then result in a granted patent, along with the publication of its abstract, a selected drawing, and its broadest claim in the PTO's Official Gazette. Along with the patent itself, the "prosecution history" or "file wrapper," comprising the application and all subsequently generated documents, is then made available to the public.

7.2.4 Continuing Applications

Continuation application practice exists out of the recognition that the path to a Final Rejection can be a short one. The filing of an ordinary application usually purchases the applicant a scant two Office Actions by the examiner. Agreement often cannot be reached by this point, however, leaving the applicant with only the alternatives of abandonment of patent protection or the filing of an appeal. By filing a continuation application, an applicant essentially purchases an additional period of prosecution.[15] This time allows additional further dialogue between the applicant and examiner, with the goal of more accurate and proper claiming of a previously disclosed invention without the necessity of an appeal.

The notion of the continuing application traces its roots back to the mid-nineteenth century case of *Godfrey v. Eames*.[16] In that case a party named Lewis had filed a patent application in 1855. The Commissioner of Patents rejected the application following an examination. In response Lewis withdrew his application in April, 1857, but on that very same day filed a new application for essentially the same invention. Because Lewis had put his invention on sale in 1854, this new application would have been barred because it was filed beyond the then-applicable two-year grace period. However, if the new application were treated as if it had been filed on the same date as the original, namely 1855, the statutory bar would not apply. The Court declared that "if a party choose[s] to withdraw his application for a patent ... intending at the time of such withdrawal to file a new petition, and he accordingly do[es] so, the two petitions are to be considered as parts of the same transaction, and both as constituting one continuous application within the meaning of the law." Congress effectively codified this doctrine in section 120 of the 1952 patent statute.

12. 35 U.S.C.A. § 120 (2000).

13. 35 U.S.C.A. § 134 (2000).

14. 35 U.S.C.A. § 151 (2000).

15. 35 U.S.C.A. § 120 (2000); 37 C.F.R. § 1.60 (2000).

16. 68 U.S. 317 (1864).

An example can help illustrate how continuing application practice works in the context of modern patent prosecution. Suppose that inventor Pete Perry files a patent application claiming a stain-resistant fabric on June 7, 2004. The PTO examiner issues a First Office Action rejecting all the claims for obviousness under § 103 and lack of definiteness under § 112, first paragraph. In turn, Perry files a Response to First Office Action, in which Perry amends the claims. The PTO examiner responds by issuing a Final Office Action again rejecting all the claims. Further discussion between Perry and the examiner reveals a difference of views that cannot be immediately resolved. Rather than filing an appeal, Perry may instead file a continuation application. If Perry elects this option, prosecution would continue on the basis of the same application and administrative record.

The chief benefit of a continuation application is the one we noted in *Godfrey v. Eames*, namely that it is awarded the constructive filing date of a qualifying predecessor application. To continue the above example, suppose that Perry filed a continuation application on April 1, 2006. For purposes of determining the filing date, that continuation application is treated as having been filed on June 7, 2004—the filing date of the "parent" application. If the PTO examiner ultimately relents and allows Perry's application to issue, then the term of the Perry patent is also based upon the earliest priority date to which Perry is entitled. The expiration date of the Perry patent would therefore be June 7, 2024, twenty years from the date of his earliest application.

Section 120 establishes certain conditions that an application must fulfill to qualify as a continuation application. A valid continuation application must: (1) expressly refer to the prior application; (2) be filed prior to the patenting, abandonment, or termination of proceedings of the prior application; (3) identify at least one inventor included in the prior application; and (4) consist of the same written description as the prior application, with no new subject matter added to the continuation.

Inventors can file multiple continuing applications. Many patents have issued based upon chains of continuation applications involving a parent, grandparent, and even more remote predecessor applications.

PTO practice also allows for so-called "continuation-in-part," or CIP applications. A CIP application repeats a substantial portion of an earlier application, but adds new matter not disclosed in the original application. Inventors sometimes file CIP applications in order to add improvements they have made to the invention after the filing of their original patent application. Claims that are dependent upon the latter-added new matter are entitled only to the filing date of the CIP.[17]

Again, an example will be helpful. Suppose that on January 5, 2004, inventor Martha Mason files a patent application claiming an improved method of manufacturing acetylsalicylic acid, better known as aspirin. Mason's application contains a single claim that specifies a particular chemical reaction that results in the production of acetylsalicylic acid. Mason then continues to work in her laboratory and, on June 12, 2004, Mason unexpectedly discovers that the use of a catalyst dramatically improves the process. On August 1, 2004, Mason files a patent application that (1) expressly refers to her prior application; (2) was filed prior to the patenting, abandonment, or termination of proceedings of her prior application; (3) and identifies her as the inventor. However, the August 1st application includes additional information about the use of the catalyst, as well as a claim 2 reciting the use of the catalyst.

In this case, the August 1st application will be treated as a CIP. For purposes of patent term, the filing date of the entire application is treated as January 5, 2004, the earliest priority date to which the application is entitled. However, in terms of relevant prior art, the patent is now subject to two filing dates. The contents of the parent application, including claim 1, will be entitled to the January 5, 2004, filing date. However, claim 2 and the additional disclosure concerning the catalyst will be accorded their actual filing date of August 1, 2004. This means that certain references, such as scientific articles published during the first seven months of 2004, could be cited against the claim involving the catalyst (i.e., the one accorded the August filing date), but not against the method claimed in the original application (i.e., the one filed in January).

7.2.5 The Restriction Requirement and Divisional Applications

If one application concerns multiple independent and distinct inventions, the PTO may require the applicant to select one invention for further prosecution in that application.[18] This procedure is known as a restriction. Although the applicant must elect only a single invention for further prosecution in the original application, he may opt to file so-called divisional applications relating to the remaining inventions. The word "divisional" in this context simply reflects the idea that the Patent Office can make the applicant "divide up" the application so that discrete inventions can be considered separately. If the applicant pays the noted fees and

17. *See* Cecil D. Quillen, Jr. & Ogden H. Webster, *Continuing Patent Applications and Performance of the U.S. Patent and Trademark Office*, 11 Fed. Cir. B.J. 1 (2001).

18. 35 U.S.C.A. § 122 (2000).

follows the appropriate procedures, all applications will continue to benefit from the filing date of the original application.

For example, suppose that inventor Kenneth Cline files a patent application on August 1, 2003. Cline's application discloses and claims both a novel type of dental floss and a heat-seeking missile. The PTO will likely impose a restriction requirement, forcing Cline to elect either the floss or the missile for further prosecution with regard to that application. Suppose Cline elects to continue prosecuting the missile. PTO procedures would then allow Cline to file a divisional application directed towards the dental floss. If both applications resulted in issued patents, they would each be accorded a filing date of August 1, 2003, and would ordinarily expire on August 1, 2023.

The restriction requirement serves several purposes. Easily the most important is the maintenance of the PTO fee structure. Otherwise, applicants would be sorely tempted to cut their prosecution costs by claiming several distinct inventions in one application. The restriction requirement also better enables the PTO to classify applications and to assign a qualified examiner to consider the application.[19]

Restriction is not an absolute requirement. Section 121 of the Patent Act merely authorizes the PTO to compel applicants to elect a single disclosed invention.[20] If the PTO opts not to do so, the resulting patent is valid even though it concerns more than one invention.

7.2.6 Publication of Applications

The Domestic Publication of Foreign Filed Patent Applications Act of 1999 requires the PTO to publish pending patent applications eighteen months from the earliest filing date to which they are entitled.[21] However, if an applicant certifies that the invention disclosed in the application will not be the subject of a patent application in another country that requires publication of applications 18 months after filing, then the application will not be published.

Some background about international and comparative patent law will assist understanding of this provision. First, there is no global patent system. Patent rights must be applied for and secured separately in each nation on earth. In a world where technology knows no borders and international trade is of ever increasing

19. *See* Applied Materials, Inc. v. Advanced Semiconductor Materials America, Inc., 98 F.3d 1563, 40 USPQ2d 1481 (Fed.Cir.1996) (Archer, C.J., dissenting), *cert. denied*, 520 U.S. 1230, 117 S.Ct. 1822, 137 L.Ed.2d 1030 (1997).

20. 35 U.S.C.A. § 121 (2000).

21. 35 U.S.C.A. § 122(b) (2000).

importance, patent protection in a single country is often insufficient to protect inventors.

In recognition of these realities, the United States has long been a signatory of the Paris Convention for the Protection of Industrial Property, an international agreement dating back to the late nineteenth century.[22] This treaty attempts to ease the burdens of maintaining patent rights in many jurisdictions. Among the chief provisions of the Paris Convention is the so-called priority right. The priority right allows patent applicants to benefit from an earlier filing date in a foreign country. So long as an inventor files abroad within one year of his first filing and complies with certain formalities, his subsequent foreign filings will be treated as if they were made as of the date of his initial filing.

A second important background principle is that foreign patent offices ordinarily publish patent applications eighteen months after their first effective filing date. As an example, suppose that an inventor filed an application at the U.S. PTO on June 1, 2003. Suppose further that the inventor sought patent rights in Germany, which is also a signatory to the Paris Convention. If the inventor files a German patent application by June 1, 2004, his German application will be treated as if it had filed on June 1, 2003, which was his U.S. filing date. Consequently, the German Patent Office would publish the German application on December 1, 2004, eighteen months after the first effective filing date to which the inventor is entitled, but, in this illustration, a mere six months after the filing in Germany.

In contrast to overseas regimes, the U.S. patent system traditionally maintained filed applications in secrecy. This approach advantaged patent applicants because it allowed them to understand exactly what the scope of any allowed claims might be prior to disclosing an invention. Thus, if the applicant was wise enough to maintain the invention that was subject to a patent application as a trade secret, then he could choose between procuring the allowed patent claims or retaining trade secret status. If, late in the prosecution process, the applicant realized that the claims had been narrowed to such a degree that the economic value of a patent would be minimal, he could just abandon the application, and continue to practice the invention as a trade secret.

However, this secrecy regime has been perceived as imposing costs as well. Others might well engage in duplicative research efforts during the pendency of a patent application, unaware that

22. Paris Convention for the Protection of Industrial Property, Mar. 20, 1883, art. 6 bis, 21 U.S.T. 1629, 828 U.N.T.S. 305 (revised July 14, 1967). For a detailed discussion of the provisions of the Paris Convention, see § 12.1, *infra*.

an earlier inventor had already staked a claim to that technology. Holding patent applications in secret also allows inventors to commence infringement litigation on the very day a patent issues, without any degree of notice to other members of the technological community.

The Domestic Publication of Foreign Filed Patent Applications Act of 1999 attempts to strike a middle ground between these competing concerns. Effective November 29, 2000, U.S. patent applications have been published approximately eighteen months after the date of filing. However, where the inventor represents that he will not seek patent protection abroad, then the U.S. PTO will retain the application in confidence until it is issued as a granted patent.

Sometimes inventors seek more robust patent protection in some countries than in others. This step may be taken for business reasons or due to differences in the patent or competition laws in varying jurisdictions. The Act therefore contains a provision allowing applicants to "submit a redacted copy of the application filed in the Patent and Trademark Office eliminating any part or description of the invention in such application that is not also contained in any of the corresponding application filed in a foreign country."[23] As a result, if an applicant seeks broader patent protection in the United States than in other countries, only the more limited version of the application will be published here.

The Domestic Publication of Foreign Filed Patent Applications Act of 1999 also provides for so-called provisional rights. Provisional rights entitle the patent applicant to recover damages, equal to a reasonable royalty, from persons who employ the invention as claimed in the published patent application after the date of publication.[24] Provisional rights are subject to a number of qualifications, most importantly that the patent actually issue; that the claims in the issued patent are substantially identical to the ones in the published application; and the person using the invention as claimed in the published application had actual notice of that application. We will take up provisional rights at greater length in § 9.2.4.

Some commentators upon the Domestic Publication of Foreign Filed Patent Applications Act of 1999 have quipped that the legislation essentially does nothing. Because the statute only makes available applications that were already published by foreign patent offices,[25] no more or less information is made available at any

23. 35 U.S.C.A. § 122(b)(2)(B)(v) (2000).

24. 35 U.S.C.A. § 154(d) (2000).

25. This follows because if a party files in the United States first, and then in a foreign patent office within the one year Paris Convention grace period, the

particular time than was before. The only advantage of this legislation would lie in convenience. Inventors may find the U.S. PTO more accessible than foreign counterparts, and the published applications would be available in the English language.

Detractors also note that this legislation might antagonize our trading partners. Inventors ordinarily file patent applications in their home jurisdictions first and only thereafter turn to the task of filing abroad. As a practical matter, then, the only applications that will not be published under this statute are those filed by U.S. inventors (namely, U.S. inventors who assert they have no intention of filing abroad, or whose applications are finally rejected before 18 months elapse). This domestic favoritism strikes against the principle of national treatment, a pledge the United States made when it signed the Paris Convention to treat domestic and foreign inventors equally.

Perhaps the most that can be said in support of the current state of U.S. law on publishing patent applications is that it hopefully marks a transition period in U.S. patent law, providing a first step towards an ecumenical publication system, like that used by foreign patent offices, where all applications will be published at the same point regardless of the identity of the applicant or the existence of foreign filings.

7.2.7 Petition and Appeal

If an applicant reaches an impasse with the examiner, he may either appeal to the Board of Patent Appeals and Interferences,[26] or file a petition with the PTO Director. The forum of review depends upon the nature of the issue in dispute. It is often said that substantive issues may be resolved through appeal, while procedural matters may be petitioned.[27] Although this expression is more of a rule of thumb than a wholly accurate precept, as a general matter decisions of the examiner directly relating to the rejection of claims are appealable. The Board therefore considers such issues as statutory subject matter, utility, novelty, nonobviousness, enablement, and claim definiteness.

foreign application is treated as if filed on the U.S. application date. That means that the application will be published by the foreign office 18 months after the U.S. filing, the very same date on which it will now be published by the U.S. PTO, under the 1999 law discussed in the text. Similarly, if a party files abroad first, and then in the United States within a year, the U.S. PTO will treat the application as if filed on the foreign application date. Again, both offices would thus wind up publishing the application on the same date. The only time this situation does not apply is when a party does not seek foreign patent protection—but that is the one case where U.S. patent applications will not be published under the 1999 legislation.

26. *See* 35 U.S.C.A. § 134 (2000).

27. *See* In re Searles, 422 F.2d 431, 435, 164 USPQ 623, 626 (CCPA 1970).

In contrast, petitions to the Director involve such issues as expediting examination, requesting an extension of time, reviving an abandoned application or reviewing a restriction requirement. Petitions are usually resolved by Group Directors within the PTO. As compared with appeals practice, the pursuit of a petition within the PTO is much more informal and summary in character.

Dissatisfied applicants may ordinarily seek judicial review of appeals or petitions. If the applicant receives an adverse decision from the Board, he may opt to bring a civil action against the Director. This action must be filed in either the United States District Court for the District of Columbia[28] or the Court of Appeals for the Federal Circuit.[29] The primary advantage of the former route is that the applicant may submit new evidence into the record, an option unavailable at the Federal Circuit. Appeals from suits lodged in the D.C. District Court go to the Federal Circuit as well. In contrast, an unsuccessful petitioner may seek judicial review through a number of mechanisms, including the Administrative Procedure Act,[30] the All Writs Act,[31] or a civil action against the Commissioner.[32] Such actions may be brought in any United States district court, with the Federal Circuit designated as the forum for appellate review.

7.2.8 Invention Secrecy Orders

The Invention Secrecy Act, which has been codified in §§ 181–188 of the Patent Act, stipulates that whenever the publication or disclosure of the invention by the granting of a patent "would be detrimental to the national security," the Commissioner of Patents shall issue an invention secrecy order.[33] The notice compels the inventor not to publish or disclose the invention to anyone not aware of the invention prior to the date of this order. The PTO will also withhold both the issuance of a U.S. patent on that invention, and the grant of foreign filing license,[34] which allows inventors to seek patent rights overseas. The inventor may seek compensation for damages caused by the secrecy order.[35] Government officials periodically review the secrecy order and may rescind it when disclosure of the invention is no longer deemed detrimental to national security.

§ 7.3 Inventorship

A topic conveniently taken up alongside prosecution is that of inventorship. A patent application ordinarily must be made, or

28. 35 U.S.C.A. § 145 (2000).

29. 35 U.S.C.A. § 141 (2000).

30. 5 U.S.C.A. §§ 701–706 (2000).

31. 28 U.S.C.A. § 1651 (2000).

32. 28 U.S.C.A. § 1338(a) (2000).

33. 35 U.S.C.A. § 181 (2000).

34. *See infra* § 12.3.

35. 35 U.S.C.A. § 183 (2000).

authorized to be made, by the inventor.[1] Even if the inventor has assigned his invention to his employer or other entity, the inventor himself must ordinarily sign a declaration or oath stating that he believes he is the first inventor.

Inventorship determinations have many other consequences in the patent law. Inventors are presumptively the owners of a patent, so a defendant's successful assertion of joint inventorship serves as a fine infringement defense. In addition, inventorship determinations influence the definition of many of the categories of prior art under § 102. For example, paragraph (a) refers to prior knowledge or use "by others," while paragraph (e) makes prior art out of patent applications filed "by another" in appropriate circumstances.[2] Without knowledge of the inventors appropriately associated with the patent or application under consideration, these prior art categories cannot be properly defined.

Many patented inventions are conceived and reduced to practice by a single individual. But in addition to individual inventors, joint inventors are also recognized by the patent statute. Amendments introduced in 1984 to § 116 specify that individuals may be joint inventors "even though (1) they did not physically work together or at the same time, (2) each did not make the same type or amount of contribution, or (3) each did not make a contribution to the subject matter of every claim of the patent." Although this negative definition is of some use in inventorship determinations, the statute does not affirmatively specify the nature of the technical contributions that cause an individual to rise to the level of an inventor. Courts agree that to qualify as an inventor, an individual must have contributed to the conception of the invention, and that the conceiver's status as inventor is not defeated if he employs the services of others to perfect the invention. But beyond these simple defining principles, inventorship cases tend to be highly fact specific and seldom provide firm guidance on resolving future disputes.

An illustrative inventorship decision is *Ethicon, Inc. v. United States Surgical Corp.*[3] Here, a Dr. Yoon was named as the inventor of a patent relating to surgical tools called trocars.[4] Along with his licensee, Ethicon, Yoon brought an infringement suit against U.S. Surgical. U.S. Surgical subsequently learned that Choi, an electronics technician, had collaborated with Yoon and made some contributions to the patented invention. U.S. Surgical then promptly ob-

§ 7.3

1. *See* 35 U.S.C.A. § 115 (2000).

2. *See* 35 U.S.C.A. § 102(a), (e) (2000).

3. 135 F.3d 1456, 45 USPQ2d 1545 (Fed. Cir. 1998).

4. Trocars are sharp-pointed instruments used to puncture a body cavity in order to aspirate fluid from the body.

tained a license from Choi and then asked the court to name Choi as a co-inventor of the patent-in-suit.

The reason U.S. Surgical took these steps may not be especially obvious at first glance. U.S. Surgical was well aware, however, that if Choi were judged an inventor of the patent-in-suit, he would also enjoy the status of co-owner. In turn, § 262 of the Patent Act allows each co-owner of a patent to exploit the invention "without the consent of and without accounting to the other owners." As a result, if Choi was indeed a co-inventor, U.S. Surgical would enjoy the status of authorized licensee and be able to preempt the lawsuit altogether.

U.S. Surgical's gamble paid off before the district court. The district judge ruled that Choi was a co-inventor of two of the fifty-five claims of the patent-in-suit and therefore was a joint owner of the entire patent. Ethicon's appeal to the Federal Circuit resulted in an affirmance. Pointing to drawings in Choi's notebook, the Federal Circuit majority found that Choi had at least contributed to the device recited within the two patent claims. The Court of Appeals also cited a number of circumstantial factors in finding Choi's claim of joint inventorship corroborated. For instance, the court highlighted (1) Yoon's need for a person with electronics expertise, (2) Choi's electronics expertise, (3) Yoon's proposal that the two work together, (4) their informal business relationship, (5) the length of time they worked together, (6) the absence of pay to Choi, (7) the similarity between the patent figures and the notebook drawings, and (8) Choi's letter saying he could no longer be a "member" of Yoon's business.

A dissenting opinion by Judge Newman protested the elevation of Choi to a joint inventor due to his contribution to only two of the fifty-five claims of the patent-in-suit. Judge Newman observed that prior to the 1984 amendments to § 116, Choi would not have been considered a joint inventor because he had not contributed to each of the patent's claims. She interpreted § 116 as merely permitting the naming of additional persons as inventors on a patent instrument. Being named as an inventor should not necessarily result in full status as a co-owner, she explained, because the concepts of inventorship and ownership are conceptually distinct.[4.5] In her view, ownership rights in a patent are based on the notion that both inventors had shared equally in the invention. In such circumstances, a "joint tenancy" system where each inventor owns an undivided share of the entire patent is appropriate. According to Judge Newman, given the 1984 changes to the law of joint inventorship, the law of joint patent ownership deserved reassessment.

4.5 For more on patent ownership, see § 11.1 of this text.

Hess v. Advanced Cardiovascular Systems, Inc. is another significant Federal Circuit decision, but in this case the court rejected the claim of co-inventorship.[5] There, two surgeons named Simpson and Robert received a patent on a balloon angioplasty catheter. When their assignee brought an infringement suit, the defendant produced declarations by Hess asserting that he should have been named a co-inventor. It seems that while working for a tubing supply company, Hess had discussed the catheter project with Simpson and Robert. Some of the contributions of Hess made their way into the patented product following further development by Simpson and Robert.

Following the rejection of his assertion of co-inventorship, Hess appealed to the Federal Circuit. The appeals court agreed that the contributions of Hess did not rise to the level of an inventor. According to the Federal Circuit, the contributions of Hess were known to the art and available on the marketplace. Hess was seen as no more than a skilled salesman who explained how his employer's products could be used to meet the technical requirements of Simpson and Robert.

The Federal Circuit's opinion does not provide an exhaustive explanation of the technical contributions of Hess towards the catheter project. Still, the outcome of the opinion appears subject to doubt given that Simpson and Robert had themselves stated that Hess was responsible for significant portions of the patented catheter. One supposes that although Simpson and Robert were superlative surgeons, their skills in the art of plastics manufacturing were less developed. It seems unlikely that the catheter project could have gotten off the ground without Hess, who should have been valued as more than merely a walking, talking catalogue of the prior art. The reader of the *Hess* opinion senses that the Federal Circuit distrusted Hess's tardy claims of inventorship and questioned the standing of a rather humble sales engineer against the qualifications of two highly skilled surgeons.

Some hypotheticals further illustrate the implications of *Hess*. Suppose that Professor Gizmo asks her laboratory technician, Steve Schlep, to combine certain chemicals in such a way as to form Compound X. Gizmo further asks Schlep to determine, using standard testing methodologies well known in the field, whether or not Compound X functions as an adhesive at high temperatures. If Schlep merely follows Gizmo's instructions, making no inventive contribution to the project, then Schlep will not qualify as an inventor even though Schelp was literally the first person to synthesize Compound X. The courts have long held that inventors may

5. 106 F.3d 976, 41 USPQ2d 1782 (Fed.Cir.1997), *cert. denied*, 520 U.S. 1277, 117 S.Ct. 2459, 138 L.Ed.2d 216 (1997).

employ others to help them achieve a reduction to practice without making co-inventors out of their assistants, much as an author may dictate the words of a story to a stenographer without making the latter into a co-author.

In contrast, suppose that Gizmo had the idea of Compound X but did not possess an operative way of synthesizing it. Upon explaining her idea to Schelp, Schlep discovers a new, nonobvious way to formulate Compound X. Or, alternatively, suppose that Gizmo tells Schlep precisely how to fabricate Compound X, but she has no idea to what uses the new compound can be put. After trial and error at the laboratory bench, Schlep identifies an unexpected application for Compound X—say, as a depilatory, after noting that all of the hair on his arms has fallen off when some of the new compound got onto his skin. In either of these alternative hypotheticals, Schlep would likely qualify as a co-inventor. He has made an inventive contribution to the development of Compound X and should be named on any patent instrument that claims that invention.

As inventors named in a patent often receive benefits ranging from financial rewards from their employers to recognition from the technical community, intracorporate disputes over inventorship are not uncommon. Patent attorneys must often demonstrate persistence and tact in order to ensure that the appropriate individuals are named in a given patent. They should also be aware of corporate technical disclosure forms and other documents that label a person as the "inventor," for such determinations are often made without awareness of the strictures of the Patent Act.[6]

§ 7.4 Duration of Rights

The term of U.S. patents was traditionally measured from the date the PTO issued the patent. The Act of 1790 allowed the issuance of patents "for any term not exceeding fourteen years." The Act of 1861 increased this term to "seventeen years from the date of issue." That durational scheme remained in effect for nearly 135 years. However, on June 8, 1995, the U.S. patent system shifted to a term based upon the filing date. Consequently U.S. patent law is now in a transition period regarding patent term.

For patents resulting from applications filed after June 8, 1995, the patent term is ordinarily twenty years from the date the patent application was filed. For patents issued prior to June 8, 1995, as well as for patents resulting from applications pending at the PTO

6. *See generally* W. Fritz Fasse, *The Muddy Metaphysics of Joint Inventorship*, 5 HARV. J. L. & TECH. 153 (1992).

as of that date, the patent endures for the greater of twenty years from filing or seventeen years from grant.[1]

Although the life of the patent is now measured from the filing date, the patentee gains no enforceable rights merely by filing a patent application. These rights accrue only if and when a patent issues, and include the power to enjoin infringers and obtain an award of damages.[2] If the application was published in accordance with the Domestic Publication of Patent Applications Abroad Act of 1999, discussed earlier in this chapter, then the patentee also obtains provisional rights equivalent to a reasonable royalty, as of the date the application is published. In such a case, however, the patentee may not assert these provisional rights until the patent issues.

While the distinction between a patent term based on the date of issue and one based on the date of the application may not appear to loom particularly large, significant consequences flow from the decision of the United States to adopt a twenty-year patent term measured from the filing date. Prior to June 8, 1995, the filing of continuing applications did not affect the length of the effective patent term. Once the patent issued, it endured for a seventeen-year term from the date of issue, even if it had been pending at the patent office for 5, 10, or even 20 years, due to a lengthy string of continuing applications. Moreover, during this era, patent applications were not published, but rather were held in secrecy by the PTO throughout the entire period of prosecution. These rules permitted applicants to manipulate the patent prosecution system to the detriment of their competitors.

This is because during an extended period of patent prosecution competitors would sometimes eventually hit upon the same invention, and invest resources in exploiting it, without any knowledge of the pending patent application. When the patent finally issued to the applicant many years later, competitors would be forced to either abandon their investments at great cost, or pay royalties to the patentee on pain of being found liable for infringement. Patents that issued after long delays of this sort came to be called "submarine" patents,[3] because they emerged from a series of concealed continuation applications to "torpedo" industries that had developed in ignorance of the pending applications.

§ 7.4

1. *See* Mark A. Lemley, *An Empirical Study of the Twenty–Year Patent Term*, 22 AM. INTELL. PROP. L. Q.J. 369 (1994).

2. We will take up the subject of remedies for patent infringement in considerable detail in Chapter 9, *infra*.

3. *See* Steve Blount & Louis S. Zarfas, *The Use of Delaying Tactics to Obtain Submarine Patents and Amend Around A Patent That A Competitor Has Designed Around*, 81 J. PAT. & TRADEMARK OFF. SOC'Y 11 (1999).

The current durational scheme eliminates the possibility of submarine patents, because no matter how many continuing applications are filed, the duration of the patent is now measured from the date of the first application in the series. (Moreover, in cases where an applicant also plans to seek patent protection abroad, the application will be published 18 months after filing, putting competitors on notice.) As a result, an applicant who files multiple continuing applications that unduly delay the prosecution process at the PTO is merely shortening his own term of eventual patent protection.

While the current patent duration scheme is thus relatively straightforward and has several advantages, there are three significant qualifications that may alter the basic twenty-year term. First, the term of a patent may be extended under § 156, a provision of the Hatch–Waxman Act. This complex statute authorizes increased patent terms on inventions that have been subject to a lengthy premarket approval process under the Federal Food, Drug and Cosmetic Act. The notion here is that drug companies should not be deprived of the full period of exclusivity in which to exploit a patented medication because regulatory requirements delay the point at which they can begin selling the drug to the public. The maximum period of patent term extension under § 156 is five years, however. To the extent that regulatory review periods exceed the authorized period of patent term extension, the patent proprietor must bear the shortfall.

Second, enjoyment of the full patent term is subject to the payment of maintenance fees. Currently, a patent expires after four, eight, or twelve years if maintenance fees are not timely paid on each occasion. As of January 1, 2003, the amounts due are $890 by the fourth year, $2,050 by the eighth year, and $3,150 by the twelfth year. These sums are due 6 months prior to the deadline, although the PTO will accept late maintenance fee payments in some circumstances.[3.5] As only about thirty-three percent of the patents issued in the United States are maintained beyond their eleventh year,[4] maintenance fees effectively dedicate a great deal of patented technology into the public domain.

Finally, the Patent Term Guarantee Act of 1999 provides certain deadlines that, if not met by the PTO, result in an automatic extension of the term of individual patents.[5] The most significant of these deadlines appear to be fourteen months for a First Office Action and four months for a subsequent Office Action. In addition, the prosecution of an original patent application must be complete

3.5 35 U.S.C.A. § 41(b) (2000).

4. *See* Charles E. Van Horn, *Practicalities and Potential Pitfalls When Using Provisional Patent Applications*, 22 AIPLA Q.J. 259, 296 (1994).

5. 35 U.S.C.A. § 154(b) (2000).

within three years of the actual U.S. filing date, with exceptions granted for continuing applications and appeals. As might be expected, each day of PTO delay beyond these limits results in one additional day of patent term. The Director is charged with calculating any patent term extensions that might result from missed PTO deadlines.

§ 7.5 Post-Grant Proceedings

The Patent and Trademark Office's involvement in the United States patent system does not necessarily end when it formally grants a patent. The law has long recognized the numerous possibilities for mistakes, ranging from minor typesetting errors to significant substantive flaws, that can make their way into the patent instrument. The patent statute thus provides the PTO with several different mechanisms for correcting these inevitable errors. The magnitude of the mistake largely determines which procedure will be employed.

7.5.1 Certificates of Correction

The least onerous and most frequently used of these procedures is a certificate of correction.[1] Patentees employ a certificate of correction to address minor typographical errors. Such errors typically include misspelled words, omission of the name of an assignee or the printing of a claim in original rather than amended form. Mistakes incurred through the fault of the PTO may be corrected free of charge. Most of these mistakes occur during the formatting and typesetting of the formal copy of the patent instrument. Otherwise, the petitioner must submit a fee along with proof that he made the error in good faith.

The PTO may also issue a certificate correcting the inventors named on a particular patent instrument.[2] When the correct inventors are not named in an issued patent, through error and without deceptive intent, the parties and assignees may petition the PTO to amend the patent. Provided that a sufficient factual showing is made, the PTO will issue a certificate correcting the error in inventorship.

7.5.2 Disclaimers

The Patent Act provides for two sorts of disclaimers.[3] Applicants employ the first kind, terminal disclaimers, in order to avoid double patenting rejections. Terminal disclaimers are discussed in section 7.7.2 of this Chapter. Patentees file the second kind, statu-

§ 7.5

1. 35 U.S.C.A. §§ 254, 255 (2000).
2. 35 U.S.C.A. § 256 (2000).
3. 35 U.S.C.A. § 253 (2000).

tory disclaimers, in order to eliminate invalid claims from otherwise sound patents. A statutory disclaimer effectively cancels the claim from the patent. Failure to file a statutory disclaimer does not render the remaining claims of a patent invalid or unenforceable. The Patent Act merely provides that a patentee may not recover costs for a litigation unless he filed a disclaimer of any invalid claims with the PTO prior to commencing litigation.[4]

Suppose, for example, that Carol Kinkead is the proprietor of U.S. Patent No. 6,797,617. As issued, the '617 patent contained ten claims. Suppose that Kinkead brought suit against a competitor. During this litigation, the court held that claim 1 of the '617 patent was invalid due to obviousness. If, sometime later, Kinkead wished to commence a second litigation against another alleged infringer, she should file a statutory disclaimer of claim 1 at the PTO. Taking this step prior to filing the second suit would allow her to recover costs from the defendant should she prevail.

7.5.3 Reissue

A patentee may employ the reissue proceeding to correct a patent that he believes to be inoperative or invalid. In contrast to certificates of correction or disclaimers, which are quite limited in scope, reissues allow for a comprehensive dialogue between the patentee and examiner. The reissue proceeding thus provides a powerful mechanism for preparing a patent for litigation or licensing negotiations. The current patent statute allows for reissue when a patent is "deemed wholly or party inoperative or invalid, by reason of a defective specification or drawing, or by reason of the patentee claiming more or less than he had a right to claim in the patent."[5]

7.5.3.1 The Error Requirement

In order to be reissued, a patent must be defective due to an "error without any deceptive intention."[6] Towards this end, the PTO requires that the applicant file a reissue oath or declaration stating at least one error that forms the basis for reissue. Although the term "error" appears straightforward, it has developed into a term of art in the patent law.

The Federal Circuit has interpreted the reissue statute to require a patentee to show two different types of error in order to be entitled to reissue. First, there must be an error in the patent

4. 35 U.S.C.A. § 288 (2000).

5. 35 U.S.C.A. § 251 (2000).

6. *Id.* This requirement can be traced back to the Supreme Court's 1832 decision in *Grant v. Raymond*, 31 U.S. 218 (1832), where the court sustained the validity of a reissued patent if "by an innocent mistake, the instrument introduced to secure [the] privilege fails in its object ... "

instrument itself, a requirement that we will explore in just a moment. In addition, there must also be a showing that the problem with the patent was due to an "error in conduct." This second requirement means that the patentee must show that the problem with the patent was due to inadvertence or mistake rather the result of a deliberate or strategic decision made during the original prosecution.[7]

With respect to the first requirement of an error in the patent, not every sort of mistake constitutes an error within the meaning of the reissue statute. The Patent Act explains that reissues may be obtained where the patent contains "a defective specification or drawing," or if the patentee claimed "more or less than he had a right to claim."[8] In practice, most reissue proceedings seek to amend the patent claims. For example, the patentee might recognize that the claims contain an ambiguity that might render them invalid under the definiteness requirement of § 112 ¶ 1. Alternatively, subsequent to the issuance of a patent, the patentee may learn of prior art that would invalidate the claimed invention due to anticipation or obviousness. Indeed, the Federal Circuit has noted that "[t]he basis for seeking narrowing reissue has generally been the belated discovery of partially-invalidating prior art."[9] By incorporating additional limitations into the claim through reissue, the patentee may yet be able to define a patentable advance over the newly discovered prior art.

Suppose, for example, that Dr. Tinker obtains a patent claiming a new radiator cap on December 1, 2003, based upon an application filed on August 12, 2000. While Dr. Tinker is reviewing some back issues of the *Radiator Review* monthly magazine, she discovers an article in the May 1996 issue that describes a radiator cap almost identical to her claimed invention. Tinker realizes that the magazine article counts as prior art under § 102(b)—it was published more than one year before her filing date—and that it might render her invention obvious within the meaning of § 103. Because her patent already issued and administrative proceedings with the PTO have closed, Tinker cannot simply telephone the PTO and ask an examiner to narrow the scope of her claims. Tinker may wish to file a reissue application, however, in order to add further language of restriction to her patent's claims. Tinker may be able to distinguish successfully her patented radiator cap from the prior art and turn an invalid patent into a valid, albeit more circumscribed one.

7. In re Wilder, 736 F.2d 1516, 1518 222 U.S.P.Q. 369 (Fed.Cir. 1984).

8. 35 U.S.C.A. § 251 (2000).

9. In Re Amos, 953 F.2d 613, 616 21 USPQ2d 1271 (Fed. Cir. 1991).

A third possibility is that the patentee claimed less than he had a right to claim. In such cases, although the written description of the patent may cover particular commercial embodiments of the disclosed invention, the patent claims might not have been drafted to read upon these embodiments. Consider the example of Herr Budd, who hypothetically obtains a patent concerning a method of brewing beer. Assume that the specification of the Budd patent includes two "working examples" discussing the brewing of lager- and pilsner-style beers. However, the claims of the Budd patent are specifically restricted to the making of lager-style beer. If Doktor Weiser, a competitor of Budd, began brewing pilsner-style beer, then the Budd patent would not literally cover his competitor's activities. Nor would Budd be able to employ the doctrine of equivalents against Weiser because under the "public dedication doctrine" subject matter that is disclosed, but not claimed in a patent is disclaimed.[10] To get around this dilemma Budd may be able to pursue a so-called broadening reissue, in order to broaden the scope of his claims. Broadening reissues are subject to special restrictions described in § 7.6.3.3 below.

Although the grounds for reissue listed in the statute appear extensive, the Federal Circuit has stated on numerous occasions that reissue is not a universal curative for all patent prosecution problems. Some flaws are simply too grave to be corrected through the use of a reissue proceeding. These include a specification that does not fulfill the requirements of § 112; cases where the applicant has engaged in inequitable conduct during the original prosecution; and cases where the invention has been entirely anticipated under § 102. None of these sorts of mistakes constitutes an error cognizable by the reissue statute.

The courts have also specified that other sorts of mistakes are uncorrectable simply because they are not the sort the reissue statute was designed to remedy. Jurists have uniformly reasoned that if the error requirement did not serve as a gatekeeper, unlimited access to reissue would diminish incentives for applicants to get things right during initial prosecution. But beyond this fundamental principle of administrative efficiency, the courts have lacked mechanisms for determining what sort of conduct amounts to an error within the reissue statute. The result has been some varying case law and fine reasoning about the precise scope of the error requirement.

Moreover, the patentee seeing reissue must also show the right kind of "error in conduct" during the initial patent prosecution. The precise contours of this requirement are also a bit fuzzy around the edges. Illustrative of this uncertainty is the 1989

10. *See infra* § 8.2.2.3.4.

opinion of the Federal Circuit in *Hewlett–Packard Co. v. Bausch & Lomb Inc.*[11] Bausch & Lomb (B&L) had purchased the '950 patent, which was directed towards a plotter—a type of device in which a large piece of paper or chart moves underneath a marking pen. The '950 patent contained nine claims. Prior to commencing enforcement litigation against Hewlett–Packard (H–P), B&L realized that only the broadest '950 patent claim, claim 1, read on an H–P plotter. But this same broad claim was likely invalid over the prior art. While claims 2–9 of the '950 patent were likely not invalid, they also were too narrow to cover H–P's product.

B&L opted to file a reissue application at the PTO. To show error in conduct, its affidavits represented that the drafter of the '950 patent application had limited contact with the inventor and did not realize which limitations were significant in light of the prior art. After some wrangling with PTO officials, B&L ultimately obtained a reissue of the '950 patent that included three additional claims. These three claims were of intermediate scope and specifically covered the H–P plotter. When B&L commenced infringement litigation, H–P argued that the initial failure of B&L to include multiple dependent claims of varying scope was insufficient in itself to establish error warranting reissue. Following an appeal, the Federal Circuit agreed.

As the court saw it, B&L was not alleging that its patent was inoperative

> by reason of the patentee claiming either too much or too little in scope, but because he included, in a sense *too few* claims.... [T]he practice of allowing reissue for the purpose of including narrower claims as a hedge against the possible invalidation of a broad claim has been tacitly approved, at least in dicta, in our precedent ... For purposes of this case, we will assume that that practice is in accordance with the remedial purpose of the statute, although B&L clearly did not allege an "error" in the patent which meets the literal language of the statute. We need not decide here whether omission of narrow claims which more specifically cover a broadly claimed invention meets the first prong of the requirement for error, that is, error in the patent, because B&L clearly did not establish the second prong, namely, inadvertent error in conduct. Contrary to B&L's position, a reissue applicant does not make a prima facie case of error in conduct merely by submitting a sworn statement which parrots the statutory language.... The reissue statute was not enacted as a panacea for all patent prosecution problems, nor as a grant

11. 882 F.2d 1556, 11 USPQ2d 1750 (Fed.Cir.1989).

> to the patentee of a second opportunity to prosecute de novo his original application.[12]

As a result, the Federal Circuit held the new, narrower, claims added during the reissue proceeding invalid.

The reasoning of the *Hewlett–Packard* opinion may be justly criticized. The patent law employs dependent claims to ameliorate the principle that limitations may not be read from the specification into the claims in order to preserve their validity. The failure to include appropriate dependent claims in the '950 patent appears to have been a simple lack of foresight, rather than some sort of strategic calculation. Perhaps the Federal Circuit was influenced by the affidavits filed by B&L at the PTO, some of which appeared inaccurate and even bordered on the fraudulent. In any event, B&L would have been better advised simply to confess to the PTO its actual suspicion that claim 1 was invalid, and simply have disclaimed it when filing the reissue application.

7.5.3.2 *Reissue Procedures at the PTO*

A patentee commences reissue proceedings by filing a reissue application. The PTO requests that reissue applicants include the originally issued patent instrument, usually known as the "ribboned copy," along with the other paperwork. This requirement is in keeping with the statute's mandate that the patentee surrender the original patent in order to obtain a reissued patent. Although a patentee may ultimately abandon a reissue proceeding and arrange for the return of her patent, she should be reluctant to do so: the cloud this abandoned application would cast upon the patent will be duly noted by courts and competitors.

Once the PTO accepts a reissue application, it oversees the customary procedures of patent prosecution. The standard sequence of Office Actions and responses occurs, and applicants may also file continuation and divisional applications as necessary. Note that continuation-in-part applications are not allowed during reissue proceedings: this step would involve the introduction of new matter, which is prohibited by the first paragraph of § 251. The second paragraph of § 251 also allows several patents to issue from a single reissue application.

In stark contrast to the usual prosecution process, reissue proceedings are open to the public. To this end, the PTO Official Gazette announces the filing of reissue applications each week. PTO regulations then mandate that the reissue proceeding not commence for at least two months, in order to allow third parties to

12. *Id.* at 1565.

submit evidence and arguments relating to the patentability of the reissue application.

Reissue proceedings therefore expose the patentee to some risk. Although he may have carefully calculated the steps he needs to take to move through the reissue proceeding, these plans may be thrown off by interested parties. Competitors and licensees in particular may vigorously contest the reissue of the patent by submitting additional prior art or arguments against patentability. If the patent reissues, however, the patentee has likely strengthened his patent for use in licensing negotiations or during litigation.

Reissued patents receive a new number, but their term is set to the remaining term of the original patent. Suppose, for example, that a patent application was filed on January 19, 1997, resulting in an issued patent on March 15, 1999. The patentee then filed a reissue application on December 1, 1999, which led to a reissued patent on August 1, 2000. The expiration date of the reissued patent would ordinarily be January 19, 2017, twenty years from the filing date of the original patent.

7.5.3.3 Broadening Reissues

A patentee may employ a reissue to expand the scope of his claims so that they cover all the technologies that he disclosed in his original specification. The fourth paragraph of § 251 sets forth a two-year statute of limitations for seeking such a broadening reissue.[13] Suppose, for example, that Ed Alva obtains a patent directed towards a method of grating cheese. The PTO issues the Alva patent on July 5, 2004. Although the specification of the Alva patent discloses the use of the method with regard to American, Swiss, and Gouda cheese, the patent's claims recite only the grating of American cheese. If Alva wishes to obtain additional claims that specifically recite the grating of Swiss or Gouda cheese, then he must file a reissue application no later than July 5, 2006. Otherwise the claims can never be broadened through the use of the reissue proceeding.

Meeting this deadline has proved a somewhat subtle affair, as suggested by two cases, *In re Doll*[14] and *In re Graff*.[15] In *Doll*, the patentee filed a reissue application containing broadened claims within the two-year statutory period. The claims were further broadened during the course of prosecution after the two-year period had expired, prompting a rejection by the examiner under the fourth paragraph of § 251. The Court of Customs and Patent

13. 35 U.S.C.A. § 251 (2000).

14. 419 F.2d 925, 164 USPQ 218 (CCPA 1970).

15. 111 F.3d 874, 42 USPQ2d 1471 (Fed.Cir.1997).

Appeals reversed in a terse opinion, holding that the reissue oath was proper.

Graff involved an applicant who filed a reissue application approximately twenty-two months after the issuance date. The initial reissue application was solely directed towards an erroneous drawing and contained no changes to the claims whatsoever. During the course of prosecution and following the expiration of the two-year period, however, Graff introduced broadened claims. The examiner rejected these claims as untimely under the fourth paragraph of § 251. On appeal, the Federal Circuit affirmed. The court distinguished the holding in *Doll* by noting that "the public was placed on notice of the patentee's intention to enlarge the claims by the filing of a broadening reissue application within the two year statutory period." According to the Federal Circuit, because the public lacked notice that Graff sought a broadening reissue within the statutory period, any enlarged claims were properly rejected.

7.5.3.4 *The Recapture Rule*

Along with the two-year statute of limitations, the courts have developed another significant restriction on broadening reissues know as the "recapture" rule. The recapture rule prevents a patentee from acquiring, through reissue, claims of the same or broader scope than those canceled from the original application.[16] This doctrine typically arises when an examiner rejected an original claim based upon the prior art. If, during the initial prosecution, the patentee then opted to narrow that claim to avoid the cited prior art reference (or references), he cannot use the reissue proceeding to recapture the abandoned subject matter. As the Federal Circuit has summarized, this " 'rule prevents a patentee from regaining through reissue ... subject matter that he surrendered in an effort to obtain allowance of the original claims.' ... The rule is rooted in the 'error' requirement in that such a surrender is not the type of correctable 'error' contemplated by the reissue statute."[17]

The Federal Circuit opinion in *Mentor Corp. v. Coloplast, Inc.*[18] demonstrates the recapture rule. Mentor had obtained a patent claiming a condom catheter that transferred an adhesive from its outer to its inner surfaces upon unrolling. A review of the prosecution history indicated that Mentor had inserted this limitation into the claims following the examiner's prior art rejection. Mentor later

16. *See* Ball Corp. v. United States, 729 F.2d 1429, 221 USPQ 289 (Fed.Cir. 1984).

17. Hester Industries, Inc. v. Stein, Inc. 142 F.3d 1472, 1480, 46 USPQ2d 1641 (Fed. Cir. 1998).

18. 998 F.2d 992, 27 USPQ2d 1521 (Fed.Cir.1993).

learned of Coloplast's competing product, a catheter with adhesive applied directly to its inner surface. Aware that its patent claims did not read directly on the Coloplast product, Mentor initiated a reissue proceeding at the PTO. After Mentor submitted detailed evidence of commercial success, the examiner reissued the patent. Notably absent from the reissued claims were limitations calling for adhesive transfer.

Mentor then sued Coloplast for infringement of both the original and reissue patents. Coloplast denied infringement of the original patent claims because its catheters did not transfer adhesive from the outer to the inner surface. Coloplast admitted infringement of the reissue patent but asserted that Mentor had improperly invoked the reissue statute by recapturing what it had deliberately surrendered during the original prosecution in response to a prior art rejection. The jury disagreed, and the trial judge denied Coloplast's motion for judgment as a matter of law after the adverse verdict.

On appeal, the Federal Circuit reversed. The court concluded that Mentor could not use the reissue proceeding to modify its deliberate actions during the original prosecution. Because Mentor had purposefully added claim language requiring adhesive transfer following the examiner's prior art rejection, the court reasoned, Mentor should not be allowed to recapture that subject matter by deleting these claim limitations during reissue. In so doing, the court justified the recapture rule both upon the requirement of error as well as concerns for the reliance interests of third parties. The Federal Circuit did not consider Mentor's deliberate decision to narrow its claims, instead of filing a continuation application or appealing to the Board, to be the sort of error comprehended by the reissue statute. Additionally, the court sympathized with a hypothetical third party that might have reviewed the prosecution history and made commercial decisions based upon Mentor's express surrender of subject matter that had originally been claimed.

Neither of these grounds provides an entirely satisfactory explanation for the recapture rule. Reissue is a broad-reaching curative mechanism that corrects many sorts of mistakes that patentees made deliberately, albeit ill advisedly. For example, patentees commonly use reissue to rectify claims of inappropriate scope, even though each word of those claims was purposefully written. The court's notice rationale is entirely circular: if there was no recapture rule, third parties would not be inclined to rely upon the prosecution history. In addition, the reissue statute's provisions for intervening rights, which are discussed immediately below, provide an adequate mechanism for addressing the reliance interests of others.[19] On the other hand, there is a certain rough justice in preventing a patentee from having it "both ways" by giving up certain subject matter to secure the original patent, only to return to the PTO to reclaim that subject matter during a reissue. In any event, the venerable recapture rule remains a fixed part of the law of reissue at the Federal Circuit.

7.5.3.5 Intervening Rights

Congress recognized that third parties may have made commercial decisions based upon the precise wording of the claims of an issued patent. If that patent is later reissued with different claims, this reliance interest could be frustrated. In order to protect individuals who may have relied upon the scope of the claims of the original patent, the second paragraph of § 251 provides for so-called intervening rights.[20] There are two sorts of intervening rights: absolute and equitable.[21]

Absolute intervening rights are set forth in the first sentence of the second paragraph of § 251. According to that provision,

> A reissued patent shall not abridge or affect the right of any person ... who, prior to the grant of a reissue, made, purchased, offered to sell, or used within the United States, or imported into the United States, anything patented by the reissued patent, to continue the use of, to offer to sell, or to sell to others to be used, offered for sale, or sold, the specific thing so made, purchased, offered for sale, used, or imported unless the making, using, offering for sale, or selling of such thing infringes a valid claim of the reissued patent which was in the original patent.

Under this provision, if prior to reissue a third party made items that did not infringe the original patent, but that do infringe the reissued patent, the third party is free to continue selling off its inventory of those items even after the effective date of the reissued patent. Similarly, if it built a machine that did not infringe original claims, it could continue using it after the date of the reissue. Note that absent this statutory language, the described activities would infringe the reissued patent. Note also that these rights are limited to the sale or continued use of individual machines, manufactures or products covered by the reissue patent, and do not encompass any right to make new products or machines after the effective date of the reissued patent. Moreover there is one further significant limitation to the rights defined by this statutory language—if the

19. *See* John R. Thomas, *On Preparatory Texts and Proprietary Technologies: The Place of Prosecution Histories in Patent Claim Interpretation*, 47 UCLA L. Rev. 183. 237–40 (1999).

20. 35 U.S.C.A. § 252 (2000).

21. *See Seattle Box Co. v. Industrial Crating & Packaging, Inc.*, 756 F.2d 1574, 225 USPQ 357 (Fed. Cir. 1985).

infringed claim of the reissue patent was also within the original patent, then no absolute intervening right arises.

The second sentence of the second paragraph of § 251 provides for equitable intervening rights. This statute allows a court to authorize the continued practice of an invention claimed in a reissue patent "to the extent and under such terms as the court deems equitable for the protection of investments made or business commenced before the grant of the reissue." To qualify for equitable intervening rights, an infringer must have made at least substantial preparations to practice the patented invention. As with the absolute intervening right, equitable intervening rights apply only when a valid, infringed claim appears solely in the reissue patent.

That intervening rights may apply to broadening reissues should be apparent. Less intuitive is that intervening rights may also arise when the claims are narrowed during reissue. This follows because prior to a narrowing reissue, a defendant may have believed the original, broader claims to be invalid. Such grounds as anticipation, nonobviousness, indefiniteness, or lack of an enabling disclosure may have convinced competitors that the claims of the original patents were invalid, yet be inapplicable to narrower claims that result from a reissue. For instance, assume that Professor Swingline obtains a patent with a single broad claim for a stapler. Other parties might justifiably conclude that such a patent could not possibly be valid because it has been fully anticipated by the prior art. They might thus begin manufacturing various types of staplers that fall within Swingline's claim, confident that if sued they could have the patent declared invalid. Thereafter, however, Swingline might seek a reissue to narrow his claims so that they relate only to particular type of improved stapler—perhaps one that operates merely with a puff of breath, rather than one that requires the user to pound down upon a lever. If other already have made some puff-of-breath type staplers, they might need the protection of the intervening rights doctrine. It is likely that they would have it because the better view is that intervening rights may apply during any reissue, not just a broadening one.

There is a paucity of case law considering either sort of intervening right. This dearth of authority is likely due to artful reissue practice on behalf of patentees. Wise to the wording of the reissue statute, most patentees transfer as many claims from the original patent to the reissued patent as possible without amendment. Of course, if the defendant infringes a claim that appears in both the original and reissued patents, then no intervening rights are possible.

7.5.4 *Reexamination*

Reexamination proceedings were introduced into the U.S. patent law in 1980.[22] The Reexamination Act of 1999 renamed the traditional sort of reexamination as an "*ex parte* reexamination" and also introduced the possibility of an "*inter partes* reexamination." The principal purpose of either sort of reexamination is to provide third parties with an avenue for resolving validity disputes more quickly and less expensively than litigation. Indeed, prior to the adoption of the reexamination statute, third parties were ordinarily unable to challenge the validity of an issued patent at all unless they had been accused of infringement.

The chief limitation upon reexamination is that the cited grounds for invalidity must constitute a patent or printed publication.[23] Other grounds for patent invalidity, such as the on-sale bar of § 102(b), may not be considered during reexamination. The reason for this restriction is that the PTO is much more able to assess patents or printed publications than other sorts of prior art. Full consideration of such issues as public use, offers to sell, inventorship, and fraud ordinarily entails examination of witnesses and other techniques of litigation—procedures that are time-consuming, expensive, and of a sort not customarily overseen by the PTO.

7.5.4.1 *Ex parte Reexamination*

Under the *ex parte* reexamination regime, any individual, including the patentee, a licensee, and even the PTO Director himself, may cite a patent or printed publication to the PTO and request that a reexamination occur.[24] The reexamination request must be in writing and explain the relevance of the cited reference to every claim for which reexamination is requested. The request must also be accompanied by the appropriate fee, which as of January 1, 2003, was $2,520. Although the PTO does not keep the identity of the requester confidential, individuals desiring anonymity may authorize a patent agent or attorney to file the request in the agent's own name.

A PTO examiner then must determine whether the patents or printed publications cited in the request raise "a substantial new question of patentability."[25] This standard is met when there is a significant likelihood that a reasonable examiner would consider the reference important in deciding whether the claim is patentable. If the PTO determines that the cited reference does not raise "a substantial new question of patentability," then it will refund a large portion of the requestor's fee. The PTO's denial of a reexami-

22. 35 U.S.C.A. §§ 301, 302 (2000).

23. *See* 35 U.S.C.A. § 302 (2000).

24. *See* 35 U.S.C.A. § 302 (2000).

25. 35 U.S.C.A. § 303(a) (2000).

nation request may not be appealed.[26] On the other hand, if the PTO determines that the cited reference does present a substantial new patentability question, then it will issue an order for reexamination.[27] Under § 304, the patentee is given the opportunity to file a preliminary statement for consideration in the reexamination. If the patentee does so, then the requestor may file a reply to the patentee's statements. As a practical matter, because most patentees do not wish to encourage further participation by the requestor, few preliminary statements are filed.

Following this preliminary period, the PTO will essentially reinitiate examination of the patent. Because the PTO has determined that a substantial new question of patentability exists, ordinarily the First Office Action includes a rejection of at least one of the claims. As the PTO's determination of whether a substantial new question of patentability must be based upon a patent or printed publication, this rejection will ordinarily be based upon anticipation, obviousness, or double patenting. To the extent that the owner of the reexamined patent adds new claims or otherwise amends the application, then the examiner may also raise issues pertaining to § 112.

Prosecution then continues following the usual rules for examination of applications.[28] However, several special rules apply to reexaminations. First, the PTO conducts reexaminations with special dispatch.[29] Examiners must give priority to patents under reexamination, and will set aside their work on other patent applications in favor of the reexamination proceeding. To further ensure their timely resolution, patentees may not file a continuation application in connection with a reexamination.[30] Second, no new matter may be introduced into the patent during reexamination.[31]

If the reexamined claims are upheld in original or amended form, the PTO will issue a certificate of conformation. Once this certificate has issued, the reexamined patent once more enjoys the statutory presumption of validity.[32] The doctrine of intervening rights, discussed at section 7.5.3.5 in connection with reissue, also applies to claims that survive reexamination.[33] If the PTO judges the claims to be unpatentable over the cited reference, then it will issue a certificate of cancellation.[34] Patentees adversely affected by

26. 35 U.S.C.A. § 303(c) (2000).

27. 35 U.S.C.A. § 304 (2000).

28. 35 U.S.C.A. § 305 (2000).

29. 35 U.S.C.A. § 305 (2000).

30. *Id.*

31. *Id.*

32. 35 U.S.C.A. § 307(a) (2000).

33. *See* 35 U.S.C.A. § 307(b) (2000).

34. *See* 35 U.S.C.A. § 307(a) (2000).

a reexamination may appeal to the Board or to the courts as necessary.[35]

Frequently a defendant accused of infringement before a court files a reexamination request at the PTO. If the PTO accepts the request, the PTO and the relevant court will find themselves in the awkward situation of simultaneously considering the validity of the same patent. In *Ethicon, Inc. v. Quigg*,[36] the Federal Circuit concluded that because the Patent Act required reexaminations to be conducted with "special dispatch," the PTO may not stay reexamination proceedings due to ongoing litigation. Whether a court will stay litigation in favor of the reexamination lies within the discretion of the judge. Such factors as the technical complexity of the invention, the overall workload of the court, and whether the reexamination request was filed early or late in the litigation typically influence this determination.

7.5.4.2 Inter partes Reexamination

As traditionally structured, the *ex parte* reexamination statute encountered criticism. As the title "*ex parte* reexamination" suggests, the role of the reexamination requestor is very limited in these proceedings. Only the patentee may participate in the dialogue with the examiner, and only the patentee may appeal the matter to the Board or to the courts if the PTO reaches an unsatisfactory conclusion. Many third parties did not believe the limited role provided for them offered a viable alternative to validity challenges in court. As a result, the ability of *ex parte* reexamination to provide an expert forum as a faster, less expensive alternative to litigation of patent validity was compromised. Data supported these observations, for far fewer *ex parte* reexaminations were requested than had been originally anticipated.[37]

The Optional Inter Partes Reexamination Procedure Act of 1999 responded to these concerns by providing third-party requesters with an additional option.[38] They may employ the traditional reexamination system, which has been renamed an *ex parte* reexamination, or they may opt for a considerable degree of participation in the newly minted *inter partes* reexamination. Under this legislation, third-party requesters may opt to submit written comments to accompany patentee responses to the PTO. The requester may also appeal PTO determinations that a reexamined patent is not invalid to the Board and the courts. To discourage abuse of *inter partes* reexamination proceedings, the statute provides that

35. *See* 35 U.S.C.A. § 306 (2000).

36. 849 F.2d 1422, 7 USPQ2d 1152 (Fed.Cir.1988).

37. *See* Mark D. Janis, *Rethinking Reexamination: Toward a Viable Administrative Revocation System for U.S. Patent Law*, 11 HARV. J. L. & TECH. 1 (1997).

38. 35 U.S.C.A. §§ 311–318 (2000).

third-party participants are estopped from raising issues that they raised or could have raised during reexamination during subsequent litigation. The filing fee for *inter partes* reexaminations is also quite steep; it was $8,800 as of January 1, 2003.

We have little experience with these procedures thus far. It will be interesting to observe the willingness of the patent bar to engage in these proceedings and the ability of the PTO to step out of its ordinarily *ex parte* mindset.[39] This expansion of the scope of reexamination also suggests that the rule limiting reexamination to consideration of only patents and printed publications may also be deserving of reconsideration in the near future.

7.5.4.3 Reexamination versus Reissue Review

The difference between a reexamination and a reissue may appear elusive to newcomers to the patent system. The following points may help illuminate the distinctions between the two post-grant proceedings:

- A request for reexamination may be filed by "any person," while a reissue must be filed with the approval of the patentee.
- A request for reexamination need not assert an "error" without deceptive intent, while a reissue application must do so.
- A reexamination is directed towards prior art patents and printed publications, while a reissue is directed towards any issue that is pertinent to the original application. Where the patentee amends matter in the patent, however, ancillary issues concerning compliance with § 112 and other statutes may arise in a reexamination as well.
- A reexamination cannot be employed to broaden the patent's claims, nor may it be abandoned by the patentee. An applicant may employ a reissue to secure broadened claims if the reissue application is filed within two years from the date of the patent grant, and may also choose to abandon the reissue and have the PTO return its original patent.
- Claims may be copied from a reissue application in order to place the application into an interference. Reexaminations do not give rise to interferences.

§ 7.6 Other PTO Proceedings

7.6.1 Interferences

Sometimes two or more inventors seeks to obtain patent rights for the same invention. In such circumstances, the PTO may

39. *See* Mark D. Janis, *Inter Partes Reexamination*, 10 Fordham Intell. Prop. Media & Ent. L.J. 481 (2000).

conduct an interference proceeding in order to determine which claimant was the first inventor within the meaning of the patent law. These contests over priority of inventorship are termed interferences. They are discussed in this text at § 4.3.2.1.

7.6.2 Protests

Members of the public are allowed to enter a protest against a patent application.[1] The protest must specifically identify the application and be served upon the applicant. The protest must also include a copy and, if necessary, an English translation, of any patent, publication or other information relied upon. The protester also must explain the relevance of each item.

The rights of the protester are extremely limited. The only PTO acknowledgment of the protest will occur if the protestor opts to include a self-addressed stamped postcard along with the protest papers. In that case the PTO will simply mail the postcard upon receipt of the protest papers. The PTO possesses complete discretion in deciding whether the patent applicant must respond to the protester's contentions. The protester will learn of the disposition of the protest only upon the issuance of the patent and the opening of the prosecution history to the public.

Protest proceedings have traditionally played a small role in PTO practice. Until Congress enacted the Domestic Publication of Foreign Filed Patent Applications Act of 1999, the PTO maintained applications in secrecy. Therefore, the circumstances in which members of the public would learn of a patent application were relatively limited. With the PTO commencing publication of some pending patent applications as of November 30, 2000, protests would seem far more likely. However, the Domestic Publication of Foreign Filed Patent Applications Act of 1999 nipped this prospect in the bud, providing that the PTO shall "ensure that no protest or other form of pre-issuance opposition ... may be initiated after publication of the application without the express written consent of the applicant."[2] Of course, this provision essentially confines the protest mechanism to its previous trivial status, because it eliminates the possibility of protest in exactly that class of cases where the public is most likely to have actual information about the content of a pending application.

§ 7.6

1. 37 C.F.R. § 1.291 (2000).

2. 35 U.S.C.A. § 122(c) (2000).

7.6.3 *Citation of Prior Art*

In lieu of filing a protest or provoking a reexamination, individuals may simply cite patents or printed publications to the Patent and Trademark Office.[3] If accompanied by a written explanation of the relevance of the cited prior art to the patent, this submission will be included in the patent's official record. Section 301 allows competitors to place prior art on the record, ensuring that it will be considered if a reexamination is declared. Of course, particularly pertinent prior art will undoubtedly hamper the patentee's enforcement or licensing efforts, and may even encourage another party to file a reexamination itself.

7.6.4 *Public Use Proceedings*

Individuals (other than the patent applicant himself) may also file a petition with the PTO showing that an invention described in a pending patent application had been in public use or on sale more than one year prior to the filing of the patent application or before the date of invention.[4] Such a petition must be filed prior to the day the patent applicant receives a notice of allowance from the PTO. Otherwise, the PTO will reject the petition as untimely.[5]

If the PTO determines that this petition makes a prima facie case of anticipation or obviousness, it may institute public use proceedings. If the PTO concludes that a public use bar exists, then the claims will be rejected. Although the outcome of a public use proceeding may not be appealed, the application will be returned to *ex parte* prosecution at the close of the proceeding. The applicant may then appeal an adverse examiner decision to the Board.

As with protests, public use proceedings have traditionally not been of great moment in patent practice. The PTO's former practice of keeping applications secret meant that few persons, other than the patent applicant, knew of most pending applications. Public use proceedings are more likely to occur in connection with reissue applications. As noted previously, reissue applications are published in the PTO Official Gazette. Such publicity readily allows interested individuals to identify the application and institute public use proceedings. With a partial publication regime now in place following the Domestic Publication of Foreign Filed Patent Applications Act of 1999, public use proceedings may play a greater role in the future.

§ 7.7 Abuses of the Patent Acquisition Process

Experience has taught us that the patent prosecution system is susceptible to abuse by applicants. The judiciary has responded by

3. 35 U.S.C.A. § 301 (2000).

4. *See* 37 C.F.R. § 1.292 (2000).

5. U.S. PTO, MPEP § 720.

developing various doctrines to curb the worst of these misuses. The most significant of these doctrines, which concern inequitable conduct, double patenting, and prosecution laches, are considered in turn below.

7.7.1 *Inequitable Conduct*

Because the usual advantages of an adversarial system do not attach to the *ex parte* prosecution process, the patent system relies to a great extent upon applicant observance of a duty of candor and truthfulness towards the PTO. However, the applicant's obligation to proceed in good faith may be undermined by the great incentive applicants possess not to disclose prior art or to misrepresent facts that might deleteriously impact their prospective patent rights. The patent law therefore imposes a draconian penalty for those who stray from honest and forthright dealings with the PTO. Under the doctrine of inequitable conduct, if an applicant intentionally misrepresents a material fact or fails to disclose material information, then the resulting patent will be declared unenforceable.[1]

Most inequitable conduct cases involve an applicant's knowing failure to disclose material prior art to the PTO. But numerous other circumstances have also caused courts to find inequitable conduct and judge the asserted patent unenforceable. These include deceitful statements in affidavits, the submission of misleading test results, and dishonest inventor's oaths. Although this doctrine applies to a number of factual circumstances, the case law unfailingly requires two elements to exist before a court will decide that the applicant has engaged in inequitable conduct. First, the patentee must have misrepresented or failed to disclose material information to the PTO in the prosecution of the patent. Second, such nondisclosure or misrepresentation must have been intentional.[2]

7.7.1.1 *Materiality*

A misrepresented or undisclosed fact must be "material" to serve as the basis for a finding of inequitable conduct. One of the PTO rules of practice, Rule 56, offers a definition of this standard. Entitled "Duty to Disclose Information Material to Patentability," Rule 56 is a basic provision governing ethical representation of inventors at the PTO. From 1977 to 1992, Rule 56 provided that "information is material where there is a substantial likelihood that a reasonable examiner would consider it important in deciding whether to allow the application to issue as a patent." The PTO promulgated a new Rule 56 in 1992. The new rule states that a

§ 7.7

1. *See* Robert J. Goldman, *Evolution of the Inequitable Conduct Defense in Patent Litigation*, 7 HARV. J. L. & TECH. 37 (1993).

2. *Id.*

reference is judged material if it either (1) establishes, by itself or in combination with other information, a prima facie case of unpatentability of a claim; or (2) is inconsistent with a position taken by the applicant.

The precise relationship between the judicial standard of "materiality" and Rule 56 remains somewhat fuzzy. The courts are not bound by either the new version or old version of Rule 56, of course, and so they are free to draw their own conclusions about the appropriate standard for inequitable conduct. However, when deciding whether particular information is material or not, the courts have often relied upon the Rule 56 definition.

A leading Federal Circuit case discussing the materiality standard is *Molins PLC v. Textron, Inc.*[3] There, the U.K. enterprise Molins filed patent applications relating to a batch machining process in many countries, including the United States. During prosecution overseas, several foreign patent examiners discovered the Wagenseil prior art reference. A member of the Molins patent department, Whitson, concluded that Wagenseil anticipated the batch process claims. However, Whitson never informed Molins's U.S. patent representative about the Wagenseil reference. As a result, the PTO examiner did not know of Wagenseil during the original prosecution. Although Molins eventually abandoned all of its foreign applications, it obtained two U.S. patents pertaining to the batch process.

Following Whitson's retirement, his successor, Hirsch, reviewed the U.S. patent files and realized that the PTO had not been informed of Wagenseil. Hirsch quickly filed a prior art statement that listed the Wagenseil reference. Later, based in part on Wagenseil, a competitor filed a reexamination request directed towards one of Molins's patents. Although the PTO granted the request, none of the claims were rejected based upon Wagenseil during the reexamination. Seemingly emboldened by this successful outcome, Molins then filed an infringement suit against several competing corporations.

The trial court easily found that Molins had violated its duty of candor towards the PTO. The court concluded that Whitson had engaged in inequitable conduct by failing to disclose Wagenseil to the PTO even though he knew it was highly material. As a result, both of Molins's patents were unenforceable. Following an appeal, the Federal Circuit affirmed. The court agreed that the Wagenseil reference was material under the "reasonable examiner" standard. According to Judge Lourie, extensive evidence demonstrated that many foreign patent examiners considered Wagneseil significant; that Whitson had amended many claims in light of rejections based

3. 48 F.3d 1172, 33 USPQ2d 1823 (Fed.Cir.1995).

upon Wagenseil overseas; and that Whitson had indicated during several foreign patent examinations that Wagenseil was the most pertinent reference of which he was aware.

The court did recognize a significant problem with the application of the "reasonable examiner" standard to these facts. One PTO examiner had actually considered the Wagnseil reference during reexamination, and interestingly, did not call for a single change to any of Molins's patent claims based on his review of that reference. However, Judge Lourie noted that the materiality standard is not concerned with whether the particular examiner assigned to the application at issue believed the reference to be important. According to the court, materiality instead rested upon the view of a hypothetical, reasonable examiner. More persuasive was the court's point that a reference is not immaterial simply because the claims are eventually deemed to be allowable over that reference.

Molins strongly suggests that patent applicants should err on the side of disclosure when considering whether or not to submit a reference to the PTO. An important point mentioned, but not further discussed in *Molins*, is that applicants have no duty to disclose an otherwise material prior art reference if the reference is cumulative to, or less material than, references already before the examiner. Applying this concept in *Halliburton Co. v. Schlumberger Technology Corp.*,[4] the Federal Circuit overturned the district court's holding of inequitable conduct by reasoning that references discovered by the examiner were more pertinent to the claimed invention than those that were known but not cited by the applicant. Although this opinion appears to allow examiner competence to excuse an unscrupulous applicant, the courts have reasoned that cumulative prior art adds nothing to what is already of record and therefore need not be disclosed.

Another important Federal Circuit opinion concerning the issue of materiality in the context of inequitable conduct is *Critikon Inc. v. Becton Dickinson Vascular Access Inc.*[5] Critikon filed suit against Becton Dickinson for infringement of the Lemieux patent, which was directed to an intravenous (IV) catheter. The patented catheters included a needle guard that prevented health care workers from accidental needle sticks. They featured a needle guard that automatically moved into position over the tip of the needle as the needle is withdrawn from the IV catheter.

After Critikon filed a motion seeking a preliminary injunction, Becton Dickinson raised several grounds in defense. Among Becton Dickinson's arguments was that Critikon had engaged in inequita-

4. 925 F.2d 1435, 17 USPQ2d 1834 (Fed.Cir.1991).

5. 120 F.3d 1253 (Fed. Cir. 1997).

ble conduct. In particular, Becton Dickinson argued that Critikon failed to cite the so-called "McDonald patent" to the PTO examiner during the prosecution of the Lemieux application. The district court rejected these arguments and granted Critikon's motion for a preliminary injunction. According to the district court, the McDonald device operated in an substantially different fashion from Lemieux's invention and therefore would not have been material during prosecution.

Following the award of a preliminary injunction to Critikon, the plot thickened. As litigation progressed, Critikon amended its complaint to assert that Becton Dickinson infringed two additional patents: the Dombrowski patent and the so-called "Lemieux reissue patent." Subsequent to Critikon's initiation of infringement proceedings against Becton Dickinson, the PTO concluded reissue proceedings on the Lemieux patent.[6] Once the Lemieux patent had reissued, Critikon added the Lemieux reissue patent to the district court action.

In response to Critikon's amended complaint, Becton Dickinson made several additional contentions. First, Becton Dickinson argued that, as was the case during the original prosecution of the Lemieux patent, Critikon had failed to disclose the McDonald patent to the PTO during the reissue proceedings. Becton Dickinson also pointed to Critikon's failure to disclose the ongoing Critikon–Becton Dickinson litigation to the PTO during the reissue proceedings. Finally, Becton Dickinson offered additional evidence that Critikon's attorneys had cited the McDonald patent to the PTO in other proceedings. Despite these additional arguments, the district court nonetheless again held that Critikon had not engaged in inequitable conduct.

Becton Dickinson then appealed to the Federal Circuit, which reversed. Judge Rich began his analysis of the materiality issue by noting that the "starting point in determining materiality" was the standard set out in PTO Rule 56, and he quoted the prong of the then-effective rule that defined a reference as material if it is inconsistent with the position taken by the applicant. Elsewhere in his discussion, however, he seemed to rely on the pre–1992 Rule 56 formula, by focusing on whether the McDonald reference "would have been material to a reasonable patent examiner."

Whatever the precise standard of materiality he had in mind, he went on to explain that the McDonald patent disclosed two features that were significant during the prosecution of the Lemieux patents. Crucial to the PTO examiner's decision to allow the Lemieux patents to issue was the use of a "retaining means" and an automatically engaged protective housing that, in combination,

6. *See supra* § 7.5.3.

covered the needle in order to prevent accidental needle pricks. The Federal Circuit was not impressed with Crtikon's arguments that the McDonald device operated differently, did not highlight the use of automatic positioning, and required a two-step operating procedure in comparison to the one-step process of the Lemieux patents. Even though the McDonald patent might have operated differently, it nonetheless disclosed highly pertinent features. As well, both the McDonald and Lemieux devices could be operated with one hand. As a result, Judge Rich concluded that the McDonald patent was material to patentability and should have been disclosed.

7.7.1.2 Intent

An applicant's misrepresentation or nondisclosure of a material fact is a necessary, but not sufficient, component of a finding of inequitable conduct. The applicant must also have affirmatively sought to mislead the PTO. In *Kingsdown Medical Consultants, Ltd. v. Hollister, Inc.*,[7] the Federal Circuit overturned earlier decisions that had found inequitable conduct based upon grossly negligent behavior by the applicant. According to the *en banc* court, the involved conduct, viewed in light of all of the evidence, must indicate sufficient culpability to require a finding of an intent to deceive.

In the *Kingsdown* case, Kingsdown was in the midst of prosecuting an application directed towards a two-piece ostomy appliance[8] when Hollister introduced a similar product to the marketplace. Kingsdown opted to file a continuation application in order to obtain claims that tracked Hollister's device. Unfortunately, when Kingsdown took the ministerial step of copying its lengthy claims from the original to the continuation application, it accidentally transferred an earlier, unamended version of one of the claims into the continuation. Once the patent issued, Kingsdown sued Hollister for infringement. The district court found inequitable conduct on two grounds. First, the court concluded that Kingsdown's miscopying evidenced gross negligence, sufficient to support a finding of inequitable conduct. Second, the district court held that Kingsdown's tactics in seeking tight claim coverage against the Hollister device evidenced an intent to deceive.

The Federal Circuit reversed on appeal. The court noted that even if Kingsdown's conduct could be characterized as gross negligence, that level of scienter was insufficient to support a conclusion of inequitable conduct. Nor does an applicant's effort to obtain claims that read upon a competitor's product constitute deceit, whether the applicant first learned of that product during or prior

7. 863 F.2d 867, 9 USPQ2d 1384 (Fed.Cir.1988).

8. This is a medical device used by patients with openings in their abdominal walls, for release of waste.

to prosecution. The court instead held that challenged conduct would be judged inequitable only where all the circumstances indicate that the applicant affirmatively maintained a fraudulent intent towards the PTO.

Of course, courts seldom encounter direct evidence of an applicant's intent to deceive. They must instead infer the applicant's mental state based on circumstantial evidence. A pattern of deliberately withholding or mischaracterizing information would be most probative of fraudulent intent, particularly if the patentee cannot provide a believable, good faith explanation for its repeated conduct. Some judicial opinions also speak towards a balancing of materiality and intent. In cases where an applicant knowingly withheld prior art references, for example, courts have reasoned that the more material the references to the patentability of the claimed invention, the more likely the applicant intended to deceive the PTO.

Suppose, for example, that Dr. Nefarious files an application at the PTO directed towards a new machine for making dental floss. Nefarious does not disclose an article published two years earlier in the well-known journal *Fiendish Fluoridators Fortnightly*. Because that article includes many of the elements claimed in the patent application of Nefarious, it is highly material. Although no direct evidence of the intent of Nefarious may exist, a court would put great weight on the fact that Nefarious had cited the article in numerous earlier writings, had discussed the article extensively in a speech given about the same time as he filed his patent application, and had even written a letter to the editor of *Fiendish Fluoridators Fortnightly* discussing the article in question. In such an extreme case, a court could readily assume that Nefarious was very much aware of the importance of the journal article and harbored an intent to deceive the PTO.

The Federal Circuit decision in *Critikon v. Becton Dickinson*,[9] discussed immediately above, also considered the intent requirement of inequitable conduct. Recall that in that case, Critikon sought to enforce its Lemieux patents against Becton Dickinson. As discussed previously, the Federal Circuit held that the prior art McDonald patent, which disclosed a retaining means for use in an intravenous catheter, was material to the prosecution of the Lemieux patents. The remaining issue for purposes of inequitable conduct, then, was whether Critikon representatives possessed the intent to mislead or deceive the PTO.

Although the district court held that Critikon representatives lacked such an intent, the Federal Circuit viewed matters differently and reversed. According to Judge Rich, the requisite level of

9. 120 F.3d 1253, 44 USPQ2d 1666 (Fed. Cir. 1997).

intent for a finding of inequitable conduct could be inferred from the facts of record. It seems that one Critikon attorney had reviewed the McDonald patent and left handwritten notations on his copy. Another Critikon attorney had likely received those notes, and at all events had cited the McDonald patent to the PTO during several other proceedings. Further, the retaining means taught by the McDonald patent was quite material to the prosecution of the Lemieux patents. Despite these facts and circumstances, Critikon had both failed to disclose the McDonald patent during prosecution of both the original and reissue Lemieux patents, and failed to disclose the district court action during the reissue proceedings. This circumstantial evidence sufficed to demonstrate an intent to mislead the PTO and led to the conclusion that the Lemieux patents were unenforceable.

There is one final point to bear in mind. The patent statute does not impose any duty on applicants actually to undertake a prior art search. Consequently one cannot be found guilty of inequitable conduct for failure to discover a prior art reference. The only obligation imposed on a patent applicant is to cite those pieces of material prior art of which he or she is already aware. It is the task of the PTO, and eventually adversaries in court, to ferret out all pertinent art. The inequitable conduct doctrine penalizes the devious, not the lazy or the ignorant.

7.7.2 Double Patenting

The patent system envisions the issuance of only a single patent per invention. Allowing inventors to obtain multiple patents on a single invention could disturb the integrity of the twenty-year patent term and confront accused infringers with the possibility of paying multiple damages for a single infringing act.[10] The following example illustrates these difficulties.

Suppose that inventor Carla Complement files a patent application claiming a photocopier on March 21, 2000. That patent issues as U.S. Patent No. 6,789,123 on August 1, 2002. On August 1, 2003, Complement files a second patent application. Complement's 2003 application contains a disclosure and claims identical to that of the '123 patent. The harms that might result from the issuance of Complement's 2003 application as a separate patent are apparent. The '123 patent will expire on March 21, 2020, but the patent resulting from the 2003 application would provide Complement with over three years of additional patent protection. Further, if Complement brought suit against a competitor, that individual would face the possibility of twofold infringement liability.

10. *See* Applied Materials Inc. v. Advanced Semiconductor Materials America, Inc., 98 F.3d 1563, 1568, 40 USPQ2d 1481, 1484 (Fed.Cir.1996), *cert. denied,* 520 U.S. 1230, 117 S.Ct. 1822, 137 L.Ed.2d 1030 (1997).

Despite the conspicuous drawbacks of double patenting, the prior art definition provided by § 102 contains no express statutory mechanism for addressing this abuse of the patent acquisition process. Many activities must be performed by "another" to be patent-defeating under § 102, including the secret prior art established by § 102(e). Only the statutory bars of § 102(b) and (d) generate prior art from the applicant's own work.[11] Thus, in the absence of other activities that disclose the invention to the public, an inventor could extend the statutory protection period through a simple policy: file an application no later than one year after an earlier, related application has matured into a patent.[12]

As a result, the courts have been left to develop the law of double patenting on their own. They have identified two sorts of double patenting. The first kind, which occurs when both patents have claims of identical scope, is known as "same-invention double patenting." If the claims of the later patent could not be literally infringed without literally infringing the claims of the earlier patent, then a court will strike down the later patent for double patenting. Courts have sometimes based the prohibition against same invention doubling patenting on § 101, which allows an applicant to "obtain *a* patent" on an invention. Two patents on the same invention are thus more than the statutory language contemplates. As a result, this doctrine is sometimes referred to as statutory double patenting.

When two patents do not claim the identical invention, but instead obvious variations of each other, the later patent will also be invalidated due to so-called "obviousness-type double patenting." In contrast to same invention double patenting, judges may employ prior art references in combination with the claims of the earlier patent to determine whether the later patent claims an invention that would have been obvious to those of skill in the art. Because no provision of the Patent Act concerns obviousness-style double patenting, courts sometimes refer to this doctrine as non-statutory double patenting.

Double patenting may occur when the same inventor obtains two issued patents directed towards the same inventive concept, in which case it will be up to a court to strike down the duplicative patent when and if it is asserted in infringement litigation. However, the PTO also considers the double patenting doctrine during prosecution. As a result, an applicant may face a double patenting rejection based upon either a granted patent or another pending

11. 35 U.S.C.A. § 102 (b), (d) (2000).

12. This is why Carla, in our hypothetical above, filed the second patent application on August 1, 2003, exactly one year after the first patent issued. This timing would permit her to argue that the earlier patent was not a pertinent reference under § 102(b).

application. *In re Vogel,*[13] one of the meatier decisions in the patent law, was such a case. There the PTO imposed a double patenting rejection based upon a granted patent that claimed a method of preparing pork products for long term storage. Claims 7 and 10 of Vogel's pending application recited an analogous process applied to meat, while claim 11 was directed towards a similar process on beef products.

Vogel appealed to the CCPA, contending that the double patenting rejection was improper. The court first considered whether this was a case of same invention double patenting. The court thought not: the patent claims concerned pork, while the claims of Vogel's second application recited beef and meat. Beef is not the same as pork, and many processes that would infringe claims 7 and 10 of the application would not infringe the patented claims, which were limited to pork.

The CCPA then turned to obviousness-style double patenting. Turning first to claim 11 of Vogel's application, the court found no evidence of record that beef and pork exhibited similar characteristics for purposes of long-term storage. With nothing to suggest that beef and pork were obvious variants of one another, the court overturned the PTO's double patenting rejection. The CCPA next considered whether claims 7 and 10 were appropriately rejected for double patenting. The court observed that the term "pork" was literally covered by the term "meat." As a result, allowance of Vogel's pending application would effectively extend the term of the already patented pork preparation process. The court therefore affirmed the PTO's double patenting rejection with respect to those claims.

The reader of *Vogel* obtains the fortunately rare privilege of simultaneously learning about the making of both law and sausages. But beyond being tempted into vegetarianism by the rather graphic claim language in that case, most readers of *Vogel* find it easy to scoff at the court's reasoning regarding the relationship of beef and pork. Most cooks would freely substitute beef for pork in the majority of recipes if no pork was on hand.[14] As well, the meat packing industry likely knew the spoilage characteristics of both beef and pork quite well. Still, the PTO always possesses the burden of presenting evidence that opposes patentability, and its failure to present proof may well have allowed Vogel to avoid a double patenting rejection at the CCPA with regard to claim 11 of his second application.

13. 422 F.2d 438, 164 USPQ 619 (CCPA 1970).

14. *See* Johnston, *On the Validity of Double Patents*, 54 J. PAT. OFF. SOC'Y 291, 303 (1972).

Vogel also reminds us that double patenting focuses upon the claims. The double patenting doctrine rejects attempts of an inventor to claim the same inventive concept twice. If a later patent discloses but does not claim the same or similar invention as an earlier patent, then double patenting issues do not arise. Section 121 of the Patent Act also provides that "[t]he validity of a patent shall not be questioned for failure of the Director to require the application to be restricted to one invention."[15] The practical effect of this language is that the double patenting doctrine does not apply when the two patents at issue resulted from a PTO restriction requirement.

Courts have authorized the use of a "terminal disclaimer" to overcome obviousness-style double patenting rejections.[16] A terminal disclaimer causes a patent granted to a given inventor to expire on the same date as an earlier patent. By arranging for all related patents to elapse at the same time, the patentee overcomes the concerns of extended patent protection for the same inventive concept. The terminal disclaimer technique allows inventors to file applications claiming obvious variants on a single inventive idea, in order to create prior art against other applicants and to obtain a tight fit for potential infringements.

Patents that issue due to terminal disclaimers may be subject to abuse. Suppose that the owner of several closely related patents—all but one valid due to the filing of terminal disclaimers—sells one patent each to different, unrelated entities. This scenario would potentially subject an accused infringer to multiple infringement suits based on patents to the same invention. Such concerns led the PTO to mandate that terminal disclaimers include a provision that any subsequent patent shall be enforceable only while it is commonly owned with the application or patent which formed the basis for the double patenting rejection.[17]

Terminal disclaimers may not be used to overcome same invention double patenting rejections. The courts have reasoned that the use of terminal disclaimers in overcoming an obviousness-style double patenting is in the public interest because it encourages the disclosure of additional developments, the earlier filing of applications, and the earlier expiration of patents.[18] Because none of these benefits appears to flow when two patents claim the identical subject matter, however, neither the courts nor the PTO will allow the use of terminal disclaimers in such cases.

15. 35 U.S.C.A. § 121 (2000).

16. *See* In re Robeson, 331 F.2d 610, 141 USPQ 485 (CCPA 1964).

17. 37 C.F.R. § 1.321(c)(3) (2003).

18. *See* In re Berg, 140 F.3d 1428, 1436, 46 USPQ2d 1226, 1233 (Fed.Cir. 1998).

Sometimes events that occur during prosecution at the PTO can cause the double patenting doctrine to work a hardship against patent owners. In some cases, a PTO restriction requirement can result in one patent application leading to multiple issued patents, which may be on suspect ground with regard to double patenting. In other circumstances involving different patents on a genus and species, the order of patent issuance may also lead to some unfortunate double patenting consequences. Courts have responded to these scenarios by developing ameliorating doctrines to address these particular circumstances.

Let us first consider the restriction requirement. As discussed in § 7.2.5 above, the PTO may impose a restriction requirement when an applicant claims more than one invention in a single patent application. The applicant must elect which of those inventions he wishes to retain in the original application. The other inventions must either be abandoned or pursued in separate divisional applications, each of which is entitled to the filing date of the original application.

At first blush, this scenario may not seem to pose much of an issue with respect to double patenting. If the PTO concluded that the original application claimed two distinct inventions, for example, then there should be little chance that the two resulting patents would constitute grounds for double patenting. As with other determinations such as nonobviousness and enablement, however, PTO decisions in this context may be contested by third parties. Without a protective principle at the ready, it would be possible for an applicant to comply with a PTO restriction requirement, only to be accused of double patenting because two patents issued on the same invention!

Fortunately, the courts have interpreted § 121 of the Patent Act to provide some relief in this circumstance. Section 121 in part states that: "A patent issuing on an application with respect to which a requirement for restriction under this section has been made, or on an application filed as a result of such a requirement, shall not be used as a reference either in the Patent and Trademark Office or in the courts against a divisional application or against the original application or any patent issued on either of them, if the divisional application is filed before the issuance of the patent on the other application."[19] The courts have interpreted this language to prevent the use of the double patenting doctrine when the PTO has imposed a restriction requirement. This immunization is subject to one caveat: the claims in the patent in the divisional

19. 35 U.S.C. § 121 (2000).

application must not have been changed in material respects from the claims subject to the restriction requirement.[20]

For example, suppose that inventor Perry Winkle files a patent application claiming (1) a chemical reaction for producing nitrous oxide and (2) a catalyst for increasing the reaction time. The PTO imposes a restriction requirement. Winkle opts to prosecute the chemical reaction invention in the original application, and files a divisional application claiming the catalyst. Both patents issue. So long as the claims of the divisional patent have not been materially changed from the claims subject to the restriction requirement, Winkle may not be accused of double patenting with respect to the two patents. However, if Winkle amends the divisional patent to "cross back over the line" of the restriction requirement—for example, by once more claiming the chemical reaction—then double patenting may apply.

Another circumstance that may lead to an anomalous result in the double patenting context is when the PTO does not issue two patents in the same order in which they were filed. These cases usually involve two patents that claim inventions with a genus-species relationship. The anomaly arises because a genus is ordinarily not patentable over a species, but a species may be patentable over the genus.[21] In such cases, the order of issuance matters to the double patenting analysis.

Consider the following example. Suppose that Jon Stark files a patent application disclosing a genus of chemical compounds ("Application A"). Stark continues his research and later discovers that one particular member of that genus is particularly effective. Because the selection of the species would not have been obvious, and that species produces unexpectedly good results, the species would be patentable over the genus. Stark then files a second patent application claiming that species ("Application B").

If the PTO allows the applications to issue in the order Stark filed them, then no double patenting issues arise. A demonstration of obviousness-type double patenting would require a showing that prior art references in combination with the Patent A would render the species obvious. Because the selection of the species would not have been obvious, and the species produces unexpectedly strong results, there is no double patenting problem here.

However, suppose that the PTO allows Application B to issue as a granted patent first, even though Stark filed it second. Many reasons might explain Patent B's shorter prosecution time, including the varying workloads of different PTO examiners and the fact

20. *See Gerber Garment Technology, Inc. v. Letra Systems*, 916 F.2d 683, 16 USPQ2d 1436 (Fed. Cir. 1990).

21. *See supra* § 4.2.1.

that Application B claimed a narrow species to which little prior art applied, as compared with the more expansive genus of Application A. In that case, Patent A could be invalid for double patenting. The reason is that, as a general principle of patent law, the disclosure of even a single species of a genus invalidates later claims to that genus.[22] In this case, the species claims of Patent B would be judged to anticipate fully the genus claims of Patent A.

The courts long ago sensed that PTO processing times should not dictate whether patents are subject to the double patenting doctrine or not. In response they developed a doctrine that possesses one of the most confusing names in all of patent law, the "two-way double patenting doctrine." Under a two-way analysis, double patenting will not apply unless the claims of each patent would have been obvious in view of the claims of the other patent. To continue the example, then, under a two-way analysis the court would first check to see if the claims of Patent A would have been obvious in view of Patent B; and then see if the claims of Patent B would have been obvious in view of Patent A. In our example, this second condition would not be met, and as a result Stark would not be subject to the double patenting doctrine.

Although complex, the two-way double patenting technique has the merits of making the order of issuance irrelevant in genus-species cases. To make matters even more baroque, however, the Federal Circuit has placed a significant restriction upon the use of the two-way double patenting test. According to *Eli Lilly and Co. v. Barr Laboratories, Inc.*, the two-way double patenting test does not apply unless the PTO is "*solely* responsible for the delay in causing the second-filed application to issue prior to the first."[23] This means that if inventors do not pursue their applications expeditiously, they may lose the benefit of the two-way double patenting doctrine.

7.7.3 Prosecution Laches

Patent prosecution sometimes takes a long time. Most often this delay is due to legitimate differences between the applicant and PTO officials over the scope of patentable subject matter. Sometimes, however, applicants make a strategic decision to delay the issuance of their patents. By filing a series of continuation applications, certain inventors have kept their applications pending for decades before choosing to allow them to issue.[24]

Patents that issue after such an extended period of prosecution have been informally termed "submarine" patents. Submarine patents are viewed as especially harmful when an industry has

22. *Ibid.*

23. 251 F.3d 955, 968 n.7 (Fed. Cir. 2001), 58 USPQ2d 1869, 1878 n.7 (citing In re Berg, 140 F.3d 1437, 46 USPQ2d 1226 (Fed. Cir. 1998)).

24. *See supra* § 7.2.4.

become heavily reliant upon a technology that is believed to lie within the public domain. When a submarine patent covering a foundational technology unexpectedly emerges from the PTO, firms may find themselves in a poor bargaining position with the patent proprietor.

As the patent law presently stands, two principal legal mechanisms discourage the issuance of submarine patents. The first is the current twenty-year patent term based upon the date of filing. Generally speaking, each day spent in the PTO truncates the patent term, reducing the possible impact of a submarine patent.[25] In the most extreme, albeit fanciful, case a patent which issues 20 years after the filing date of the application would expire on the same day it issued! The second is the pre-grant publication of pending patent applications. The PTO publishes many, but not all U.S. patent applications approximately 18 months after they are filed.[26] Savvy competitors are therefore able to monitor pertinent patent applications and plan accordingly.

These two mechanisms are relatively recent additions to U.S. law, however. The twenty-year patent term, based upon the filing date, took effect on June 8, 1995. Applications claiming a priority date prior to June 8, 1995, enjoy the longer of two terms: either 20 years from the date of filing, or 17 years from the date the patent issues.[27] Similarly, pre-grant publication only applies to patent applications filed on or after November 29, 2000. Further, if the inventor states that she is filing only in the United States, no pre-grant publication will occur at all.[28] In cases where an application was filed before June 8, 1995, and patent protection is sought only in the United States, the traditional "submarine" patent strategy remains possible.

For example, suppose that inventor Terry Tortoise filed an application at the PTO on January 19, 1978. Tortoise sought protection only in the United States. After an extended series of continuation applications, the Tortoise patent issued on April 1, 2003. Because Tortoise has sought patent protection exclusively in the United States, the PTO did not previously publish the contents of any of the continuation applications. And because Tortoise enjoys a priority date prior to June 8, 1995, the Tortoise patent has a 17–year term based upon the issue date. The expiration date of the Tortoise patent is therefore April 1, 2020. However, in the 25 years that the patent application was pending (1978 to 2003) the technology in question has become common knowledge and is widely practiced by all firms in the industry. The result is that Tortoise

25. *See supra* § 7.4.

26. *See supra* § 7.2.6.

27. *See supra* § 7.4.

28. *See supra* § 7.2.6.

could now either suppress the technology or hold all of his rivals hostage by demanding exorbitant royalties.

This potential for abusive delays in prosecution has led to what has so far been a very limited judicial response. A small number of opinions have invoked the doctrine of "prosecution laches" to prevent the enforcement of patents that issue after unreasonable delay. Among these is the 2002 decision of the Federal Circuit in *Symbol Technologies, Inc. v. Lemelson Medical, Education & Research Foundation.*[29] *Symbol Technologies* addressed certain patents filed by the late inventor Jerome Lemelson. The patents at issue matured from applications that Lemelson filed in 1954 and 1956. In 1998, over four decades after these applications were filed, the Lemelson Foundation began to send letters to bar code scanner customers claiming these devices infringed his patents. Among the recipients of these letters was Symbol Technologies, which filed a declaratory judgment action against the Lemelson Foundation. Before the trial court, Symbol Technologies contended that the Lemelson Foundation was barred from enforcing its patents due to the doctrine of prosecution laches. The district court sided with the Lemelson Foundation, however, dismissing the declaratory judgment after the court concluded that prosecution laches was not a valid defense to patent infringement. Symbol Technologies appealed.

Given this procedural background, the issue on appeal was a narrow one: whether "the equitable doctrine of laches may be applied to bar enforcement of patent claims that issued after an unreasonable and unexplained delay in prosecution even though the applicant complied with pertinent statutes and rules."[30] The Federal Circuit confirmed that the doctrine of prosecution laches was an available defense and reversed the judgment of the district court. According to Chief Judge Mayer, two Supreme Court cases from the 1920's created the prosecution laches doctrine, and Congress had not seen fit to abolish it when enacting the 1952 Patent Act.

Given the few facts developed on the record—the only salient fact we learn is that the Lemelson patents took a long time to prosecute—as well as the court's narrow statement of the legal issue, the Federal Circuit had little opportunity to discuss prosecution laches further. The Court of Appeals in essence stated that the doctrine exists but said almost nothing about its scope and application.[31] Judge Newman's dissenting opinion feared the worst, however. Observing that continuation applications are commonplace in

29. 277 F.3d 1361, 61 USPQ2d 1515 (Fed. Cir. 2002).

30. 277 F.3d at 1363, 61 USPQ2d 1516.

31. *See* Jennifer C. Kuhn, Symbol Technologies*: The (Re)Birth of Prosecution Laches*, 12 Fed. Cir. B.J. 611 (2002–2003).

patent practice, she expressed concern that the doctrine of prosecution laches could condemn statutorily authorized acts of prosecution because they should have been accomplished sooner than the Patent Act requires. Only time will tell whether prosecution laches is of such broad application to justify the fears of the dissent, or whether use of the doctrine is in fact reserved to exceptional cases.[32] Moreover, as we get further and further into the regime of the 20–year term and eighteen-month publication, there will be fewer and fewer cases in which the doctrine can plausibly be raised.

32. *See* Digital Control Inc. v. McLaughlin Mfg. Co., 248 F. Supp. 2d 1015 (W.D. Wash. 2003).

Chapter 8

PATENT INFRINGEMENT

Table of Sections

The patent statute addresses infringement at section 271. Its opening paragraph, § 271(a), provides:

> Except as otherwise provided in this title, whoever without authority makes, uses, offers to sell, or sells any patented invention, within the United States or imports into the United States any patented invention during the term of the patent therefor, infringes the patent.

Surprisingly for many, beyond providing a list of infringing acts and offering a fleeting reference to the "patented invention," the statute does not further define how one should determine whether a patent has been infringed or not. This challenging task has fallen to the courts, who have faced a number of perplexing issues along the way.

§ 8.1 Scope of Rights

Broadly speaking, an individual may face liability for patent infringement in two ways. He may himself engage in one of the acts that the statute exclusively grants to the patentee, a practice termed direct infringement. Alternatively, a person may have engaged in indirect or dependent infringement. In such cases liability rests not upon the direct practice of the patented invention, but the successful encouragement of others to do so.

8.1.1 Direct Infringement

A patent confers the right to exclude others from making, using, selling, offering for sale, or importing into the United States the patented invention.[1] An individual need only perform one of these acts to be liable as an infringer. One who manufactures a patented product, but never sells or personally uses it, merely leaving it on a table as an object of adoration, is nonetheless guilty of patent infringement.

This definition reveals that patent infringement concerns behavior. Patent rights become relevant when an individual engages in one of the five noted activities. However, the patent community commonly employs such phrases as the "accused device" or the "infringing method." This terminology is a concise way of expressing the concept that an individual has engaged in acts forbidden by the patent statute with respect to that product or process.

A defendant's intent is irrelevant to the outcome of an infringement inquiry. Even an individual who has never previously known of the asserted patent or even of the entire patent system may be found to be an infringer. Infringement analyses thus have a *quasi in rem* flavor, as they focus upon a comparison of the patent claims to the accused technology.[2]

Importantly, the exclusive patent rights do not provide an affirmative right for the patentee to employ the invention himself.[3]

§ 8.1

1. 35 U.S.C.A. § 271(a) (2000).

2. *See* Jurgens v. CBK, Ltd., 80 F.3d 1566, 1570 n. 2, 38 USPQ2d 1397, 1400 n. 2 (Fed.Cir.1996). Under the doctrine of willful infringement, an adjudicated infringer's state of mind may be relevant to the amount of damages awarded. *See infra* § 10.2.4.

3. Leatherman Tool Group Inc. v. Cooper Industries, Inc., 131 F.3d 1011,

For example, the fact that an individual obtained a patent on a pharmaceutical compound does not allow him to market this medication to others. Approval of the appropriate food and drug authorities must first be obtained.

In addition, the patents of others might also interfere with a patentee's ability to practice his own patented invention.[4] For example, suppose that Admiral Motors obtains a patent on an internal combustion engine for use in automobiles. Later, Betty Beta purchases an automobile marketed by Admiral Motors that embodies the patented invention. Beta experiments with her new car and develops a dramatically improved fuel injector usable only in the patented Admiral Motors engine. Even if Beta patents her improved fuel injector, she cannot practice that technology without infringing Admiral's basic patent. In this case, the Admiral Motors patent is said to be a blocking, or dominant patent over Beta's improvement or subservient patent. Unless one of the parties licenses the other, Beta must wait until Admiral Motors' patent expires before practicing her own patented improvement invention. Of course, Admiral itself could not use Beta's fuel injector without obtaining a license from her.

The rights provided by U.S. patents are effective only in the United States.[5] They provide no protection against acts occurring in foreign countries. Individuals must obtain patent protection in each nation where they wish to guard against unauthorized uses of their inventions.

As has been discussed here previously,[6] patent rights ordinarily extend for a period of twenty years from the date the patent application was filed. This term may be modified based upon events at the PTO or at other regulatory agencies. Further, the patentee may not exercise his exclusive rights until such time as the patent has been granted by the PTO.

8.1.1.1 Process Patents

When a patent claim is expressed as a series of steps, it is known as a method or process claim.[7] Traditionally the patent law held that a process claim could be directly infringed only by the

1015, 44 USPQ2d 1837, 1841 (Fed.Cir. 1997). *See supra* § 1.2.1.

4. *See* Bio–Technology General Corp. v. Genentech, Inc., 80 F.3d 1553, 1559, 38 USPQ2d 1321, 1325 (Fed.Cir.), *cert. denied*, 519 U.S. 911, 117 S.Ct. 274, 136 L.Ed.2d 197 (1996).

5. *See* Dowagiac Mfg. Co. v. Minnesota Moline Plow Co., 235 U.S. 641, 650, 35 S.Ct. 221, 59 L.Ed. 398 (1915).

6. *See supra* § 7.4.

7. John R. Thomas, *Of Text, Technique and the Tangible: Drafting Patent Claims Around Patent Rules*, 17 John Marshall J. Computer & Info. L. 219 (1998).

performance of those steps.[8] Suppose, for example, that a manufacturer sold a device capable of performing a patented process. Such a manufacturer could not be liable for directly infringing the process unless it also performs the steps of this process. That manufacturer could face liability for contributing to or inducing the infringement of others, however.

This general principle was altered to some degree in the Process Patent Amendments Act of 1988. As codified in § 271(g), Congress provided process patent owners with the right to exclude others from using or selling in the United States, or importing into the United States, products made by a patented process. For example, suppose that an enterprise based in Italy manufactures chocolate employing a process patented in the United States. If the Italian company exports chocolate into the United States, it may face liability even though it performed every step of the patented process abroad, and even though the U.S. patentee does not have a patent on the chocolate itself, but merely on the method of making it.

A number of exceptions limit liability under the Process Patent Amendments Act. In particular, § 271(g) provides that if the product is materially changed by subsequent processes, or becomes a trivial or nonessential component of another product, then there is no infringement.[9] For instance, in the previous example, if the Italian firm added a very small amount of the chocolate made by the patented process to a cough syrup to disguise its bitter taste, the importation of the cough syrup would not infringe the U.S. patentee's rights. The Process Patents Amendment Act also created a new § 287(b), a complex statute that modifies the usual scheme of remedies available for patent infringement. Among other provisions, § 287(b) provides a grace period for individuals unaware of the patent implication of a particular process. Such persons may, upon receiving notice of infringement, dispose of products that would infringe under § 271(g) and avoid liability.

The Process Patents Amendment Act also introduced § 295 into the Patent Act. Congress enacted this provision out of the recognition that patentees may face great difficulties in proving that a particular product resulted from the performance of the patented process. Section 295 creates a presumption that a product has been made by a patented process if two conditions are met. First, there must be a substantial likelihood that the product was made by the patented process. Second, the plaintiff must have made a reasonable effort to determine the process actually used in the

8. United States v. Studiengesellschaft Kohle, m.b.H., 670 F.2d 1122, 212 USPQ 889 (D.C.Cir.1981).

9. *See* Eli Lilly & Co. v. American Cyanamid Co., 82 F.3d 1568, 38 USPQ2d 1705 (Fed.Cir.1996).

production of the product and have been unable to so determine. The effect of the presumption is that the accused infringer bears the burden of showing that the accused product was not made by the patented process.

8.1.1.2 The First Sale Doctrine

Under the "first sale" or "exhaustion" doctrine, an authorized, unrestricted sale of a patented product depletes the patent right with respect to that physical object.[10] As a result of this doctrine, the purchaser of a patented good ordinarily may use, charge others to use, or resell the good without further regard to the patentee. The courts have reasoned that when a patentee sells a product without restriction, it impliedly promises its customer that it will not interfere with the full enjoyment of that product.[11] The result of the first sale doctrine is that the lawful purchasers of patented goods may use or resell these goods free of the patent.[12] This is why it is not infringement for you to use your cell phone or computer, or to sell or give away those devices to others when you tire of them.

Often a patentee will restrict a sale or license of the patented invention upon certain conditions. For example, a sales contract might stipulate that the purchaser only use the patented goods in a named geographical location; resell the goods at specified prices; or purchase replacement parts from the patentee. It is in the nature of things for purchasers to violate these restrictions, and patentees have sometimes pursued charges of patent infringement against them.[13] The reasoning of the patentee is typically that the purchaser's use of the patented invention is unauthorized and therefore an infringement.

Although early Supreme Court opinions were reluctant to employ the patent law to police these infractions,[14] Federal Circuit case law has strongly upheld a cause of action for patent infringement where the sale was conditional, despite the first sale doctrine.[15] According to the Federal Circuit, restricted sales by the

10. *See* Intel Corp. v. ULSI System Technology, 995 F.2d 1566, 1568, 27 USPQ2d 1136, 1138 (Fed.Cir.1993), *cert. denied*, 510 U.S. 1092, 114 S.Ct. 923, 127 L.Ed.2d 216 (1994).

11. *See* B. Braun Medical, Inc. v. Abbott Laboratories, 124 F.3d 1419, 1426, 43 USPQ2d 1896, 1901 (Fed.Cir.1997).

12. *See* Intel Corp. v. ULSI System Technology, 995 F.2d 1566, 27 USPQ2d 1136 (Fed.Cir.1993), *cert. denied*, 510 U.S. 1092, 114 S.Ct. 923, 127 L.Ed.2d 216 (1994).

13. Of course, a patentee in such a case could also allege a breach of contract, but the availability of special remedies for patent infringement makes the patent claim more appealing.

14. *See, e.g.*, United States v. Univis Lens Co., 316 U.S. 241, 62 S.Ct. 1088, 86 L.Ed. 1408 (1942); Keeler v. Standard Folding–Bed Co., 157 U.S. 659, 15 S.Ct. 738, 39 L.Ed. 848 (1895); Adams v. Burke, 84 U.S. (17 Wall.) 453, 21 L.Ed. 700 (1873).

15. *See* Mallinckrodt, Inc. v. Medipart, Inc., 976 F.2d 700, 24 USPQ2d 1173 (Fed.Cir.1992).

patentee do not allow the inference that the patentee intended customers to enjoy unrestricted use of the invention. As a result, contractual conditions will generally be enforced through the patent law unless the court determines they violate some other law or policy, such as the antitrust law or the doctrine of patent misuse.

The Federal Circuit decision in *Monsanto Co. v. McFarling* is a case in point.[16] Monsanto had obtained patents claiming seeds and plants that were resistant to glyphosate herbicides such as ROUNDUP brand. Farmers that used the patented plants could therefore broadly spray these herbicides in their fields, killing weeds but not harming the resistant crops. Monsanto required that purchasers of its patented seed submit to a "Technology Agreement" that Monsanto styled as a license under the patents. The agreement in part stipulated that the patented seeds were to be used "for planting a commercial crop only in a single season" and further directed purchasers not to "save any crop produced from the seed for replanting."

McFarling, a soybean farmer, purchased Monsanto seeds in 1997 and 1998, both times submitting to the license. McFarling disregarded the agreement's terms, however. He saved seeds from earlier harvests and planted them in subsequent years instead of purchasing additional Monsanto seed. Monsanto sued McFarling for both patent infringement and breach of contract. The trial court awarded Monsanto a preliminary injunction and, following an appeal, the Federal Circuit affirmed. Judge Newman reasoned that the Technology Agreement required purchasers to use the seed only for the purpose of growing crops and not for the purpose of growing new seed. Absent a countervailing principle from antitrust, contract or other law, these provisions were enforceable. Judge Newman further reasoned that the exhaustion doctrine did not apply to the case: "The original sale of the seeds did not confer a license to construct new seeds, and since the new seeds were not sold by the patentee they entailed no principle of patent exhaustion."

The Federal Circuit's effective characterization of plants as self-replicating machines may cause readers to raise an eyebrow. Cases such as *Monsanto Co. v. McFarling* nonetheless epitomize the Federal Circuit viewpoint that starts with the proposition that patentees can ordinarily refuse to sell or license their intellectual properties altogether. As a result, the reasoning continues, patentees can freely impose conditions upon these transactions that, absent special circumstances such as an antitrust violation, will generally be enforced.

16. 302 F.3d 1291, 64 USPQ2d 1161 (Fed. Cir. 2002).

8.1.1.3 Repair and Reconstruction

A corollary of the right to use a patented product under the first sale doctrine is the right to repair the product as necessary for continued use. The patent law provides customers of the patentee with an implied license to repair or even replace parts of a patented product without paying further compensation. However, the customer may not reconstruct the patented product without violating the patentee's exclusive right to make the patented invention.[17] As you might anticipate, the courts have learned that the line between a repair and a reconstruction is often not a clear one, although most opinions lean towards finding a permissible repair rather than an infringing reconstruction.

A good illustration of the repair and reconstruction cases is the 2001 decision of the Federal Circuit in *Jazz Photo Corp. v. United States International Trade Commission*.[18] This litigation involved a patented disposable camera owned by Fuji Photo Film Co. Readers who are enthusiastic, but somewhat absent-minded photographers, or frequent attendees of weddings, may already be familiar with the basics of disposable cameras. After consumers snap the desired number of photographs using a disposable camera, they return the camera to a film developer. The developer actually cuts the camera open in order to remove the film. Given this physical cutting of the camera case, Fuji plainly intended that its cameras be disposed of following their use. However, other firms acquired the used cameras and refurbished them for an additional use. Fuji responded by accusing these firms of violating its patent rights before the International Trade Commission. The Commission held that the respondents had engaged in an impermissible reconstruction of the cameras, rather than a permitted repair, and therefore concluded that Fuji's patents had been infringed.

The Federal Circuit reversed on appeal. Judge Newman first explained that the patentee's unilateral intent regarding reuse of the patented article did not control the repair/reconstruction inquiry. The court instead entered into a detailed analysis of the activities of the accused infringers. The court concluded that the accused infringers were principally engaged in replacing the film, while the remaining portions of the camera remained as originally sold. According to Judge Newman, the replacement of unpatented parts with a shorter life than the combination as a whole was characteristic of a repair, rather than a reconstruction. As a result, the Federal Circuit concluded no patent infringement occurred under the facts of the case.

17. *See* Mark D. Janis, *A Tale of the Apocryphal Axe: Repair, Reconstruction, and the Implied License in Intellectual Property Law*, 58 Md. L. Rev. 423 (1999).

18. 264 F.3d 1094, 59 USPQ2d 1907 (Fed. Cir. 2001).

In assessing the persuasiveness of the *Jazz Photo* holding, a comparison of the claimed invention with the precise activity of the accused infringers is illuminating. Claim 1 of the asserted '087 patent in that case included six elements: (a) a film casing, (b) rolled film, (c) a film container, (d) a winding means, (e) a winding control means and (f) a frame counter. To refurbish the patented camera, the accused firms (1) removed the cover, (2) cut open the casing, (3) inserted new film and a film container, (4) replaced the winding wheel, (5) replaced the flash battery, (6) reset the counter, (7) resealed the case, and (8) added a new cover. A glance at these two lists reveals that the accused firms replaced three of the six claimed elements, and rebuilt or modified the other three!

The commercial circumstances of *Jazz Photo* also suggest that the accused infringers were not engaged in the business of repair. This was not a case where purchasers took a legitimately purchased patented product in for repairs, expecting to recover the product when the job was complete. Rather, the consumers wholly surrendered the cameras when they were returned for film development. As a result, the usual rationale for exempting activities from infringement via the repair doctrine—respect for legitimate owners of patented goods—seems less compelling here. *Jazz Photo* demonstrates that drawing a crisp distinction between repairs and reconstructions remains an elusive inquiry.

The right of repair does not arise if the owner of the combination patent also obtains patents separately claiming the individual component at issue. For example, suppose that Fuji had also obtained patent claims towards the film used inside the disposable camera. In that hypothetical case, Jazz Photo and the other accused infringers would have directly infringed these narrow components claims. Jazz Photo would also have been judged a contributory infringer of Fuji's combination claims. In reaching this conclusion, the courts have recalled that the right of repair is founded upon the existence of an implied license between the patentee and its customers. No such license should be presumed where the patentee also obtains a proprietary interest in the replaced component itself.[19]

8.1.1.4 Experimental Use

A handful of older cases recognize a limited "experimental use" defense to patent infringement. In his 1813 opinion in *Whittemore v. Cutter*,[20] Justice Story explained that "it could never have been the intention of the legislature to punish a man, who constructed such a machine merely for philosophical experiments, or

19. *See* R2 Medical Sys., Inc. v. Katecho, Inc., 931 F.Supp. 1397, 1444–45 (N.D.Ill.1996).

20. 29 F.Cas. 1120, 1121 (C.C.D.Mass.1813) (No. 17,600).

for the purpose of ascertaining the sufficiency of the machine to produce its described effects." To similar effect was the 1861 decision in *Poppenhusen v. Falke*, which explained "that an experiment with a patented article for the sole purpose of gratifying a philosophical taste, or curiosity, or for mere amusement is not an infringement of the rights of the patentee."[21]

Subsequent decisions have interpreted this defense extremely narrowly. Where a commercial purpose animated the accused infringer even in part, courts have universally refused to apply the experimental use defense. Perhaps because of the limited applicability of this doctrine, or simply because patentees have only rarely sued pure philosophers, the number of cases in which an accused infringer has successfully pled an experimental use defense are few indeed.[22] The fact that a general experimental use defense has never achieved codification in the Patent Act also betrays its quite limited nature.

Madey v. Duke University presents the Federal Circuit's latest thinking on the experimental use exception.[23] Duke University employed Madey as a research professor and director of a laser laboratory. After Madey resigned and moved to another university, he brought suit against his former employer, accusing it of infringement of two patents relating to the operation of specialized equipment used in the Duke laser laboratory. In response, Duke sought to take advantage of the experimental use defense to patent infringement. Duke pointed out that it was a non-profit institution that served educational objectives, and that its exploitation of the patented technology should therefore be shielded by the experimental use doctrine. The district court agreed and granted summary judgment in favor of Duke. On appeal, the Federal Circuit reversed and remanded, explaining that:

> major research universities, such as Duke, often sanction and fund research projects with arguably no commercial application whatsoever. However, these projects unmistakably further the institution's legitimate business objectives, including educating and enlightening students and faculty participating in these projects. The projects also serve, for example, to increase the status of the institution and lure lucrative research grants, students and faculty.
>
> In short, regardless of whether a particular institution or entity is engaged in an endeavor for commercial gain, so long

21. *Poppenhusen v. Falke*, 19 F.Cas. 1048, 1049 (C.C.S.D.N.Y.1861) (No. 11,-279).

22. *See* Note, *Experimental Use as Patent Infringement: The Impropriety of a Broad Exception*, 100 Yale L.J. 2169 (1991); Richard E. Bee, *Experimental Use as An Act of Patent Infringement*, 39 J. Pat. Off. Soc'y 357 (1957).

23. 307 F.3d 1351, 64 USPQ2d 1737 (Fed. Cir. 2002).

as the act is in furtherance of the alleged infringer's legitimate business and is not solely for amusement, to satisfy idle curiosity, or for strictly philosophical inquiry, the act does not qualify for the very narrow and strictly limited experimental use defense. Moreover, the profit or non-profit status of the user is not determinative.[24]

From one perspective, *Madey* merely extends a line of judicial opinions taking an ever more cabined view of the experimental use defense. On the other hand, few patent proprietors have been so bold to sue universities for their fundamental research activities. After *Madey*, perhaps patentees will be less circumspect. We suppose this is a price that universities must pay in an era where these institutions have become increasingly aggressive in developing and marketing sophisticated patent portfolios. The broader implications of *Madey* are nonetheless troubling. Even philosophers must eat, and to the extent they form organized centers of research and education, they now possess the duty to account to the patent system. As our copyright and patent regimes increasingly overlap, most notably with regard to the protection of computer software, the patent law threatens to detract from freedoms long recognized within the copyright system under its fair use doctrine. With society becoming increasingly dependent on complex technology, and with the swift rate of technological advance increasingly at odds with the 20–year patent term, perhaps it is time to recognize that a broader right to tinker might better serve the policy goals that animate the patent law.

Bear in mind as well that if experimentation results in an improved version of the patented device, the experimenter would likely be unable to practice that improvement commercially without the permission of the patentee, so that any harm to the original innovator from a broad experimental defense seems modest. Put the other way around, a stingy experimental defense doctrine essentially preserves to the patentee—and no one else—the right to continue to tinker with the invention, make it better, and patent improvements.

The experimental use defense to patent infringement should be contrasted with the experimental use principles relating to the statutory bars. Recall that courts and PTO examiners will toll the one-year grace period under § 102(b) if they are satisfied that the inventor engaged in legitimate experimentation beyond the statutory period.[25] Although this concept is also termed "experimental use," it is a patent validity principle that does not relate to the infringement analysis. The distinction is easy enough to keep clear

24. 307 F.3d at 1362, 64 USPQ2d at 1746.

25. *See supra* § 4.3.1.

if you recall that arguable experimentation *by the inventor* may bear on patent validity in the first instance, while arguable experimentation *by third parties* may bear on defenses to liability for patent infringement.

A very limited form of the experimental use exception, relating to patents on pharmaceuticals and medical devices, is found in the Patent Act. Congress added this provision because of the time-consuming Food & Drug Administration (FDA) approval process these products must undergo prior to marketing. When generic drug manufacturers and other competitors grow interested in marketing a medical product patented by another, they often wish to complete product testing and obtain regulatory approval during the term of the patent, so that on the day the patent expires, the generic manufacturer can begin to sell its own version of the product. Of course, such testing would be a forbidden "use" of the patented drug if done before the patent expires, allowing the patentee to commence an infringement suit to preclude any such competitor testing. Through such a strategy the patentee hopes to prevent the generic manufacturer from even beginning the regulatory approval process until the close of the patent term, which would tend to keep generic competitors out of the market for several additional months or years.

In its 1984 opinion in *Roche Products, Inc. v. Bolar Pharmaceutical Co.*,[26] the Federal Circuit resolved these competing positions in a manner consistent with the limited nature of the experimental use defense. The court held that even restricted uses of a patented drug, made solely for testing in order to obtain regulatory approval, were infringements. The court reasoned that because such tests were pursued for business purposes, rather than to amuse or satisfy curiosity, the experimental use defense was inapplicable. The practical effect of *Roche v. Bolar* was to extend the term of patents on drugs by the length of the FDA approval process.

Congress responded to *Roche v. Bolar* by enacting Title II of the Drug Price Competition and Patent Term Restoration Act of 1984, commonly known as the Hatch–Waxman Act.[27] This statute was intended to eliminate the *de facto* extension of patent term resulting from regulatory approval delays and to embody a compromise between innovative developers of so-called "pioneer drugs" and generic manufacturers. In favor of the generic manufacturers, Congress enacted § 271(e)(1), which exempts from infringement "uses reasonably related to the development and submission of

26. 733 F.2d 858, 221 USPQ 937 (Fed.Cir.), *cert. denied*, 469 U.S. 856, 105 S.Ct. 183, 83 L.Ed.2d 117 (1984).

27. Pub. Law. No. 98–417, Title II, 98 Stat. 1585 (Sept. 28, 1984).

information under a Federal law which regulates the manufacture, use, or sale of drugs." Cases such as *Intermedics, Inc. v. Ventritex, Inc.* have interpreted this exemption generously.[28] According to Magistrate Judge Brazil, "[w]here it would have been reasonable, objectively, for an accused infringer to believe that there was a decent prospect that the use in question would contribute (relatively directly) to the generation of information that was likely to be relevant in the processes by which the FDA would decide to approve the product," then the court should apply the § 271(e)(1) infringement exemption.

Indicative of the fact that this provision is not of limitless scope, however, is the recent Federal Circuit case, *Integra Lifesciences, I, Ltd. v. Merck*,[29] which declined to apply the Hatch–Waxman Act's experimental use exemption to the facts before the court. Here, Integra sued Merck for infringement of several patents relating to compounds thought to eliminate tumor growth and for treating a variety of other diseases. A Merck and Scripps Research Institute ("Scripps") partnership had conducted several *in vivo* and *in vitro* experiments on certain compounds. Integra alleged that this activity infringed its patents. In turn, Merck asserted § 271(e)(1) as a defense. The district court held that the Scripps–Merck activity did not fall under the § 271(e)(1) exemption.

The Federal Circuit affirmed the district court on appeal. To resolve the case the court needed to interpret the statutory language defining the scope of the exemption as limited to those activities conducted "solely for purposes reasonably related to the development and submission of information under federal law." In construing the meaning of the phrase "reasonably related," the court referred to legislative history, which stated that the underlying purpose and intended effect of the statute was to permit "a limited amount of testing so that generic manufacturers can establish the bioequivalency of a generic substitute" while at the same time having a minimal effect on the patentee's rights.

Judge Rader reasoned that the term "reasonably related" tied the exempt activities to the submission of information to the FDA. He explained that while infringing activities that enjoy the safe harbor of § 271(e)(1) need not directly produce data that is submitted to the FDA, activities that do not directly produce such data "strain the relationship to the central purpose of the statute." In particular, the Federal Circuit stated that the "FDA has no interest in the hunt for drugs that may or may not later undergo clinical testing for FDA approval." If the court reached a contrary result,

28. 775 F.Supp. 1269, 20 USPQ2d 1422 (N.D.Cal.1991), *aff'd*, 991 F.2d 808, 26 USPQ2d 1524 (Fed.Cir.1993).

29. 331 F.3d 860 (Fed. Cir. 2003).

Judge Rader reasoned, it would vitiate the exclusive rights of a whole class of patentees owning biotechnology tool patents, in direct conflict with the legislative intent that the exempt activity have only an minimal effect on patent owners' rights. Following the *Integra Lifesciences* case, therefore, a firm seeking to rely upon the § 271(e)(1) exception must have least identified a clinical drug candidate.

Congress also provided for two sorts of expedited FDA applications for generic drug manufacturers who seek regulatory approval to market generic equivalents of previously approved pioneer drugs. Rather than submit extensive data concerning the safety and effectiveness of the drug, the generic drug manufacturers may employ more easily garnered information. So-called abbreviated new drug applications (ANDAs) may employ data demonstrating that the pioneer and generic drugs are bioequivalents, while "paper new drug applications" (paper NDAs) may rely upon published literature to show the safety and effectiveness of the generic drug.

On the other side of the ledger, two provisions of the Hatch–Waxman Act favor patentees of pioneer drugs. First, as provided in § 156, the patent terms of products subject to regulatory approval by the FDA were extended. Thus, the initial developer of a new medicine is not itself penalized by a shortened term of patent protection due to a prolonged FDA approval process, preventing it from marketing the drug for the first several years of the patent term.

Second, Congress established a specialized patent registration and infringement regime. Under the Hatch–Waxman Act, pioneer drug manufacturers must file with the FDA the number and expiration date of any patent concerning the pioneer drug. When a generic manufacturer files an ANDA or paper NDA, it must include one of four certifications with respect to each pertinent patent: (1) that the manufacturer of the pioneer drug has not filed this information; (2) that the patent has expired; (3) the date on which such patent will expire; or (4) that such patent is invalid or will not be infringed by the generic drug.

If the generic manufacturer opts for the fourth sort of certification—a so-called "paragraph 4 certification"—it must notify the patentee. Section 271(e)(2) of the Patent Act then allows a patentee to launch infringement litigation against the would-be generic manufacturer immediately. This forces the generic manufacturer to be explicit about its intentions. Without such a rule, the generic company could conduct all necessary experiments and clinical tests for FDA approval early in the patent term, shielded from infringement liability by the provisions we discussed above. That would obligate the patentee to wait until the generic substitute was actually on the market in order to commence infringement litigation, putting it at a commercial and perhaps even legal disadvantage.

A charge of infringement under § 271(e)(2) is technical in nature. The generic manufacturer has done nothing more than request FDA approval to market a drug. If the patentee's charge of infringement is successful, however, he may prevent the marketing of that generic equivalent until the date the patent expires. Further, if the patentee brings such an infringement suit, the FDA may not issue a final marketing approval to the ANDA applicant until 30 months have passed from the date the patentee received notice of the paragraph 4 certification. Congress intended that this 30–month period, which is commonly termed the "30–month stay," would give the parties sufficient time to resolve their patent dispute before the ANDA applicant introduced its generic product to the market. Of course, if the patent is held invalid, unenforceable, or not infringed prior to the expiration of 30 months, then the FDA may issue a marketing approval at this earlier time.

8.1.1.5 Exports and Imports

Under U.S. patent law, the unauthorized exportation of patented goods does not by itself constitute an infringing act.[30] However, it is often the case that the exporter has manufactured or sold the exported goods as well. In such cases the exporter would obviously have violated the patentee's exclusive right to make or sell the patented invention in the United States.[31] Unauthorized importations are addressed more straightforwardly: § 271(a) expressly declares that a patentee possesses the exclusive right to import the patented invention into the United States.

The legal situation regarding the parallel importation of patented goods remains somewhat clouded. The term "parallel imports" refers to patented products that are legitimately manufactured abroad, and then sold in the United States without the permission of the authorized U.S. dealer. Because parallel imports occur outside the distribution channels arranged by the patentee, they are sometimes called "grey market goods." In such circumstances, the U.S. patent proprietor may attempt to use its intellectual property rights to block the importation of unauthorized goods. The patentee will take the position that the U.S. patent is fully enforceable against the importer because no sale occurred under the U.S. patent. The importer will instead assert that because the imported goods are authentic and were lawfully purchased, the U.S.

30. *See* Johns Hopkins University v. CellPro Inc., 152 F.3d 1342, 47 USPQ2d 1705 (Fed.Cir.1998).

31. *See* Amgen, Inc. v. Elanex Pharmaceuticals, Inc., 1996 WL 84590, *4 (W.D.Wash.1996).

patent right is subject to "international exhaustion" due to the foreign sale.

In its 2001 decision in *Jazz Photo Corp. v. United States International Trade Commission*,[32] the Federal Circuit devoted precisely two sentences towards the legal status of parallel imports. The entirety of the court's discussion comprised the following statement:

> United States patent rights are not exhausted by patent rights of foreign provenance. To invoke the protection of the first sale doctrine, the authorized first sale must have occurred under the United States patent. *See Boesch v. Graff*, 133 U.S. 697, 10 S.Ct. 378, 33 L.Ed. 787 (1890).

Although admirably succinct, this holding does not appear to be supported by the cited case. In the venerable *Boesch* decision, the plaintiff owned a U.S. patent for a lamp burner. An individual named Hecht, who was not a party to the litigation, enjoyed a "prior user right" pertaining to the lamp burners under German law. It seems that the German patent statute allowed individuals who had used an invention prior to the date of another's patent application the privilege of continuing to exploit the invention commercially, without regard to the patent. Hecht had met the conditions for this prior user right to apply, and as a result could sell the burners in Germany. Hecht eventually sold some burners to the defendants, who in turn imported them into the United States and commenced sales. The plaintiff brought suit to enjoin the sale of the imported burners in the United States. In opposing the injunction, the defendants argued that they had lawfully purchased the burners and that the U.S. patent should be subject to the exhaustion doctrine. The Supreme Court rejected the defendant's arguments, holding:

> The right which Hecht had to make and sell the burners in Germany was allowed him under the laws of that country, and purchasers from him could not be thereby authorized to sell the articles in the United States in defiance of rights of patentees under a United States patent.... The sale of articles in the United States under a United States patent cannot be controlled by foreign laws.[33]

The facts and holding of *Boesch* suggest that its precedential reach is quite limited. In *Boesch*, it was a prior user, rather than the patentee or its licensee, which made the foreign sale. Indeed, the patentee neither consented to the sale of the invention for purposes of sale in the U.S. nor received compensation for any such

32. 264 F.3d 1094, 59 USPQ2d 1907 (Fed. Cir. 2001).

33. 133 U.S. at 703.

sales. This is a much different state of affairs than the typical parallel importation case, where either the patentee or an authorized overseas distributor makes a sale as part of an arms-length commercial transaction.[34] Given this shaky precedential foundation, as well as the limited consideration of the issue in *Jazz Photo*, it is at least questionable whether this apparent absolute ban on parallel importation will survive further judicial scrutiny.[35]

At least one recent district court case suggests a somewhat different outcome that the blanket statement provided in *Jazz Photo*. In *Kabushiki Kaisha Hattori Seiko v. Refac Technology Development Corp.*,[36] the Southern District of New York suggested that the U.S. patent will be considered exhausted if the owner of both the U.S. and foreign patents makes an unrestricted sale abroad. But where the sale is restricted, or if the holders of the U.S. and foreign patent rights are distinct entities, then the U.S. patent may be employed to block a parallel import. With luck, further litigation will likely lead to judicial clarification of this important issue in the near future

The issue of parallel importation of patented goods is likely to be particularly important in the field of pharmaceuticals. Often prescription drug prices in other nations are lower than those in the United States. This can be due to nationalized health systems in those foreign countries that are able to buy vast quantities of medications in bulk; it can be due to different labor costs in those countries; it can be due to different regulatory obligations in those countries; or to a combination of all those factors. Obviously, as health care costs rise in the United States, there is a strong incentive for both individuals and firms to attempt to import comparable medications from abroad in order to realize cost savings.[37] Rather than wait for the courts, it is likely that Congress will directly address the question of international exhaustion of patent rights in the drug context in the near future.

8.1.1.6 Government Infringers

Sometimes a patentee learns of the unauthorized use or manufacture of the patented invention by an agency of the federal or state government. Where the federal government commits the infringing acts, 28 U.S.C.A. § 1498 authorizes the patentee to file suit in the United States Court of Federal Claims in order to obtain "reasonable and entire compensation." The patentee ordinarily

34. *See* Sanofi, S.A. v. Med–Tech Veterinarian Products, Inc., 565 F. Supp. 931, 220 USPQ 416 (D.N.J. 1983).

35. *See* PCI Parfums Et Cosmetiques International v. Perfumania, Inc., 35 USPQ2d 1159 (S.D.N.Y.1995).

36. 690 F. Supp. 1339, 9 USPQ2d 1046 (S.D.N.Y. 1988).

37. *See, e.g.*, Shubha Gosh, *Pills, Patens and Power: State Creation of Gray Markets as a Limit on Patent Rights*, 14 Fla. J. Int'l L. 217 (2002).

may recover the equivalent of a reasonable royalty from the federal government. However, injunctive relief is not available. Although § 1498 litigation is based upon the government's eminent domain taking of a patent license, these suits are otherwise quite similar to ordinary infringement actions against private parties.

If the infringing entity is a state government or agency of a state, then the patentee's ability to obtain relief is considerably less clear. Most observers believe that the states are, or should be, subject to the patent rights of private parties. However, the U.S. Constitution places a significant jurisdictional hurdle before a patentee seeking to vindicate its rights against a state. The Eleventh Amendment provides that a federal court is without power to entertain a suit by a private person against a state. As a result, aggrieved inventors must seek redress for patent infringement in that state's own courts. Because the federal courts possess exclusive jurisdiction over patent infringement litigation,[38] this state of affairs creates a dilemma—the only statutorily authorized forum is Constitutionally unavailable, and the only Constitutional forum is statutorily unavailable, at least for the assertion of a conventional patent infringement claim. This means that a patentee's only option would be a state court suit charging the state government with a taking, or asserting general unfair competition principles, in order to vindicate his patent rights.

Cognizant of this state of affairs, Congress attempted to abrogate the Eleventh Amendment immunity of states to patent infringement suits in 1992. The Patent and Plant Variety Protection Remedy Clarification Act introduced § 271(h) into the statute.[39] That provision specified not only that the states were subject to patent infringement suits in the federal courts, but that they were liable for any remedies that could be had against a private party.[40] However, the 1999 opinion of the Supreme Court in *Florida Prepaid Postsecondary Education Expense Board v. College Savings Bank* found that Congress lacked the authority to abrogate state immunity to patent infringement litigation in the federal courts under the Eleventh Amendment.[41]

Over the past several years, Congress has considered various mechanisms to overcome this stalemate, but to date has not been able to come to a final agreement on new legislation. Whether the Supreme Court will sanction a different mechanism for providing

38. 28 U.S.C.A. § 1338(a) (2000) ("The district courts shall have original jurisdiction of any civil action arising under any Act of Congress relating to patents.... Such jurisdiction shall be exclusive of the courts of the states in patent ... cases.")

39. Pub. L. No. 102–560, 106 Stat. 4230 (Oct. 28, 1992).

40. 35 U.S.C.A. § 271(h) (2000).

41. 527 U.S. 627, 119 S.Ct. 2199, 144 L.Ed.2d 575 (1999).

private actors with redress against the states for patent infringement remains of extreme importance for enterprises which compete against universities, laboratories, highway administrations, and other entities associated with state governments. The alternative—allowing patentees to sue states in state court—could lead to inconsistent rulings on a wide variety of patent-related issues, which would seem counter to the interests of just about everyone with a stake in the patent system.

8.1.2 Indirect Infringement

The patent law has long considered persons who encourage the unauthorized practice of another's patented invention to have engaged in culpable conduct. Such individuals face liability for patent infringement even if they never directly employ the patented invention themselves.[42] The patent law terms this sort of conduct "indirect" or "dependent" infringement.

The 1952 Act was the first U.S. patent statute to codify the indirect infringement doctrines that had been developed by the courts. Sections 271(b) and (c) are complementary provisions that Congress intended to lend clarity to the law of active inducement and contributory infringement. Section 271(b) addresses so-called "active inducement" by reciting in broad terms that one who aids and abets an infringement is likewise an infringer. Section 271(c) is a more specific provision that concerns a common circumstance in which indirect infringement occurs: the sale of a nonstaple component that is specially adapted for use in the patented invention. This sort of indirect infringement is termed "contributory infringement."

A direct infringement must occur for a party to face liability as an indirect infringer.[43] However, most courts do not require the patentee to prove another's actual act of direct infringement during litigation. It is enough that the patentee demonstrates that a customer of the accused indirect infringer would infringe if she used her purchase in its intended way.[44]

8.1.2.1 Active Inducement

Section 271(b) provides that "[w]hoever actively induces infringement of a patent shall be liable as an infringer." This broadly worded statute was intended to codify existing case law that extended infringement liability to persons who encouraged and assist-

42. *See* American Cotton–Tie Co. v. Simmons, 106 U.S. (16 Otto) 89, 1 S.Ct. 52, 27 L.Ed. 79 (1882).

43. Aro Mfg. Co. v. Convertible Top Replacement Co., 365 U.S. 336, 341–42, 81 S.Ct. 599, 5 L.Ed.2d 592 (1961).

44. *See* Standard Oil Co. v. Nippon Shokubai Kagaku Kogyo Co., 754 F.2d 345, 224 USPQ 863 (Fed.Cir.1985).

ed the infringement of others. Although § 271(b) does not expressly refer to the inducer's knowledge or purposes, the courts have consistently required that the defendant intended to cause the acts which it had reason to know were infringing of a patented device or method and thus knowingly induced the infringement.[45]

Subject to this requirement of intent, courts have found active inducement of infringement in varying circumstances. A typical case of active inducement occurs when a supplier sells a product that is capable of both infringing and noninfringing uses. If the supplier provides instructions, distributes advertising or offers training that promotes an infringing use, then it may be found to have violated § 271(b).[46] For instance, assume Delta Corp. manufactures and sells thin threads made of tungsten, which can be used in a variety of industrial applications. Assume that one possible use for these tungsten threads is as a component in a thermostat patented by Professor Climato. If Delta's advertising boasts that its threads can be used to build a Climato thermostat, or if its sales personnel teach purchasers how to use its threads to build Climato thermostats, Delta can be held for active inducement of infringement.

The courts have also found an active inducement of infringement when a defendant designed an infringing apparatus that another subsequently manufactured.[47] Finally, the courts have sometimes found active inducement where one party repairs or maintains another's infringing good, on the theory that such activities perpetuate the infringing use.[48]

8.1.2.2 Contributory Infringement

In contrast to § 271(b), § 271(c) is a narrowly focused provision. It concerns the specific situation where one party sells a specially manufactured component that the customer intends to employ in the practice of a patented invention. Section 271(c) renders such a seller liable for contributory infringement subject to three important qualifications. First, the component must constitute a material part of the patented invention and be especially made or adapted for use in the infringement. Second, the component must not constitute a staple article of commerce suitable for noninfringing uses. Finally, the alleged contributory infringer must

45. Hewlett–Packard Co. v. Bausch & Lomb Inc., 909 F.2d 1464, 1469, 15 USPQ2d 1525, 1529 (Fed.Cir.1990); Water Technologies Corp. v. Calco, Ltd, 850 F.2d 660, 668, 7 USPQ2d 1097 (Fed. Cir. 1988).

46. *See* Chiuminatta Concrete Concepts, Inc. v. Cardinal Industries Inc., 145 F.3d 1303, 46 USPQ2d 1752 (Fed. Cir.1998).

47. *See* Preemption Devices, Inc. v. Minnesota Mining & Mfg. Co., 803 F.2d 1170, 231 USPQ 297 (Fed.Cir.1986).

48. *See* National Tractor Pullers Ass'n, Inc. v. Watkins, 205 USPQ 892 (N.D.Ill.1980).

have known of the patent and that the use of the component would constitute an infringement.

For example, suppose that one Rod Cohen manufactures and sells button-shaped pieces of a particular sort of plastic.[49] The plastic buttons are purchased by independent cutting laboratories and made into contact lenses. Cohen is well aware that a competitor, Terri Tarsal, holds a patent claiming contact lenses made of the same plastic composition. Under these circumstances, it is likely that the cutting laboratories directly infringe the Tarsal patent and that Cohen is a contributory infringer. In addition, because the cutting laboratories may be present or potential customers of Tarsal, Tarsal will likely prefer to sue Cohen. Cohen may be able to argue that the plastic buttons constitute staple articles of commerce that are capable of noninfringing uses, such as on shirts or blouses. In so doing, Cohen should be aware that courts are wary of the farfetched, illusory, or theoretical alternative uses often proposed by accused contributory infringers.[50]

If you sense that sections 271(b) and (c) are redundant, or at least overlapping, your instincts are sound. All conduct falling under § 271(c), involving the sale of non-staple items for use in patented machines or processes, could be construed as a form of active inducement of infringement which is condemned by § 271(b). Courts typically apply § 271(b) to situations where the technology has multiple uses, only one of which infringes, reserving § 271(c) for situations where the only legitimate use of a sold component is an infringing one. However, the principal reason that Congress adopted § 271(c) as a separate category of patent infringing conduct is revealed by § 271(d).

That provision, in part, declares that when the patentee himself engages in the activities declared to be "contributory infringement" in § 271(c), the patentee cannot be denied relief or deemed guilty of "patent misuse." In other words, by giving the conduct a special label in § 271(c), Congress was able to use that label in § 271(d) to grant the patentee certain other privileges. This means that in the foregoing hypo, if Tarsal, the patentee, sells the unpatented button-shaped bits of plastic uniquely suited for use in his invention, and gets injunctions against every other vendor of those bits of plastic, thereby securing a monopoly on the unpatented component, he cannot be accused of abusing his patent monopoly. In addition, § 271(d) also specifies that a patentee may not be denied relief even if it refused to license or use its patent, if it conditioned a patent license on the acquisition of another patent

49. *See* Syntex (U.S.A.) Inc. v. Paragon Optical Inc., 7 USPQ2d 1001 (D.Ariz.1987).

50. *See* D.O.C.C. Inc. v. Spintech Inc., 36 USPQ2d 1145, 1155 (S.D.N.Y. 1994).

license, or if it required a patent licensee to also purchase non-patented products from it. At one time, all of these categories of behavior had been thought to constitute "patent misuse" which renders a patent unenforceable. We will return to § 271(d) and the doctrine of patent misuse in somewhat more depth in § 11.5 of this volume.

The well-known decision in *C.R. Bard, Inc. v. Advanced Cardiovascular Systems*[51] considered claims of infringement under paragraphs (b) and (c) of § 271. The Bard patent claimed a method of using a catheter in coronary angioplasty, a surgical procedure in which clogged arteries in the heart are re-opened by inserting a balloon and inflating it slightly.[52] The claimed method in part specifically required the surgeon using the catheter to "fluidly connect locations within [the] coronary artery...." The accused infringer marketed the only perfusion catheter approved by the FDA for use in coronary angioplasty.[53] The accused catheter featured a number of inlets, or side openings, running along its length. The inlets allow blood to circulate through the catheter during surgery. The district court had granted summary judgment in favor of the patent owner, finding that the accused infringer had actively induced or contributed to infringement of the patent.

The defendants appealed to the Federal Circuit. There, Judge Plager recognized that, as an appeal from summary judgment, the Court of Appeals was required to view the evidence in a light most favorable to the defendant. The court then observed that uncontested evidence in the record showed that the accused device could be used in ways that did not infringe the method patent. In particular, although the patented method required that the catheter's inlets be located in the coronary artery, surgeons could instead insert the catheter so that all the inlets were in the aorta. As a result, a reasonable jury could find that the accused catheter was capable of substantial noninfringing uses, thereby foreclosing a finding of contributory infringement under § 271(c). In addition, because the evidence of record was ambiguous as to surgeons' use of the accused catheter, a finding of active inducement under § 271(b) was also inappropriate. The Federal Circuit therefore reversed the summary judgment and remanded the case to the district court for further proceedings.

51. 911 F.2d 670, 15 USPQ2d 1540 (Fed Cir. 1990).

52. This case was litigated before the 1996 legislation which effectively eliminated patent protection for methods of performing medical procedures, now codified as § 287(c). *See* § 2.4 for a full discussion of the history and operation of this provision.

53. A catheter is a tubular medical device that can be inserted into a part of the body, including veins and arteries. A profusion catheter is a type of catheter that is used to inject fluid.

C.R. Bard, Inc. v. Advanced Cardiovascular Systems illustrates that in circumstances where multiple uses of a patented product exist, and at least one of them amounts to a substantial noninfringing use, the sale of the product will not result in liability so long as the seller does not encourage buyers to use the product in an infringing fashion. This conclusion fits the statutory scheme. The absence of encouragement negates liability under § 271(b), while the multiple uses prevent liability under § 271(c).

8.1.2.3 **Deepsouth** *and § 271(f)*

Prior to the 1984 amendments to the Patent Act, the manufacture and exportation of the unassembled components of a patented article was not considered an infringing act. Exemplifying this rule was the 1972 decision of the Supreme Court in *Deepsouth Packing Co. v. Laitram Corp.*[54] There, the defendant Deepsouth manufactured all the components of a patented shrimp peeler and shipped them in an unassembled state to clients abroad. The defendant's customers could assemble the machine parts in less than one hour. Obviously with this option available foreign customers had no reason to buy the fully constructed patented machine from Laitram, the patentee. Displeased, Laitram sued Deepsouth for infringement and the case found its way up to the Supreme Court. The Court, in a 5–4 decision, held that no infringement occurred in the United States because the defendant had neither made nor sold the combination of elements as claimed in the patent.

Congress responded to *Deepsouth* by adding paragraph (f) to § 271 of the Patent Act. The two subparagraphs of § 271(f) specify that the export of unassembled components of a patented invention may constitute an infringing act. Section 271(f)(1) parallels § 271(b) by stating that the supply of all or a substantial portion of the components of a patented invention for combination abroad is an active inducement of infringement. Section 271(f)(2) corresponds to § 271(c) by specifying conduct that is considered a contributory infringement. Under § 271(f)(2), the exported component must constitute a material part of the patented invention that is especially made or adapted for use in the infringement and must not be a staple article of commerce suitable for noninfringing uses. The accused infringer must also have known that the component would be combined outside the United States in a manner that would infringe a U.S. patent if such combination took place in the United States.

54. 406 U.S. 518, 92 S.Ct. 1700, 32 L.Ed.2d 273, 173 USPQ 769 (1972).

§ 8.2 Claim Interpretation

The Patent Act consistently bases the patentee's exclusive rights upon the "patented invention."[1] Modern courts have judged this phrase to refer to the invention as recited in the claims. Interpretation of the text of the claims is thus a central issue of contemporary patent law. When construing claims, courts consider their express language along with the specification, drawings and prosecution history associated with the patent.

Once the claims have been construed, they are compared to the product or process that the accused infringer has made, used, sold, placed on sale, or imported into the United States.[2] If the defendant's device or method is identical to a claim of the patent and if the defendant has performed one of the activities reserved to the patentee, then the court will find infringement. The burden falls to the patentee to prove infringement by a preponderance of the evidence. The defendant may assert a number of defenses to the charge of infringement, including invalidity, unenforceability, and various equitable defenses.[3]

If the accused product or process embodies every limitation of the claim, the claim is said to "read on" that product or process. In such cases the defendant has literally infringed the patent. The patentee's exclusive rights are not necessarily limited to the express language of the claims, however. Under the doctrine of equivalents, if the accused technology presents insubstantial differences from the claimed invention, then the court may find infringement even though the claim language is not literally met.

Before we take up the topics of literal and equivalent infringement, a preliminary word on claim interpretation is in order. Those new to the patent law may be pleased to learn that, unlike other intellectual property disciplines, individuals must define their patent interests expressly in a government-approved instrument before filing an infringement suit. Further, although patent claims employ notoriously stilted language, they are at bottom quite humble texts. Each claim is but a single sentence that verbally portrays a product or process. As compared to the ambiguous substantial similarity analysis found in copyrights, or vague likelihood of confusion standard of the trademark law, patent infringement analyses might appear at first blush to be entirely straightforward.

Experience has unfortunately taught us that infringement analyses in the patent law are as nettlesome as in any intellectual property discipline. Few claims prove so clear as to withstand the withering gaze of high stakes litigation without the exposure of an ambiguity or uncertainty. Claim interpretation issues recur so

§ 8.2

1. *E.g.*, 35 U.S.C.A. § 271(a) (2000).

2. *See* Cybor Corp. v. FAS Techs., Inc., 138 F.3d 1448, 1454, 46 USPQ2d 1169, 1172 (Fed.Cir.1998) (*en banc*).

3. 35 U.S.C.A. § 282 (2000).

frequently because these texts are exceptionally difficult to draft. Patent practitioners must marshal considerable legal and technological skills to write claims that capture the inventor's contribution, avoid subject matter known to the prior art, and anticipate future embodiments that others might employ. Yet financial limitations and marketplace demands for timely issuance weigh against comprehensive preparatory efforts. With each patent claim tied to a unique specification and prosecution history, the search for meaning becomes contextual and resort to the precedents unavailing. Claim drafters and interpreters have found certainty an elusive goal, but they have also encountered a set of intriguing issues that form the core of the patent project.

8.2.1 Literal Infringement

A patent is literally infringed if the accused product or process includes every element exactly as recited in at least one of its claims. Courts often compare literal infringement to the standard of anticipation. If the claimed subject matter existed within the public domain as defined in § 102, prior to the date of patentee's invention then the claim is anticipated; but if the claimed subject matter is employed after the date the patent is granted, then the claim is literally infringed.[4] To ensure that the claim precisely reads upon the accused technology, patent practitioners commonly prepare a claim chart comparing the claimed and accused subject matter.

Under this standard of absolute identity, if an accused product or process includes fewer elements or steps than were recited in the claims, there can be no literal infringement. Whether the accused technology can include more than the listed elements depends upon which transition phrase appears in the claims. Most claims employ the "comprising" transition phrase, which is open to additional elements beyond those recited in the claims. Other claims employ a closed or hybrid transition phrase, which may preclude a finding of infringement if the accused technology includes elements beyond those included in the claim.[5]

8.2.1.1 Markman v. Westview Instruments

Although the standards for literal infringement analysis are straightforward, they provide scant assistance in determining the meaning of particular claim terms. For example, suppose that a composition of matter claim calls for "approximately 20% vegetable paste." The accused compound consists of 18.86% tomato paste. Whether a content of 18.86% amounts to "approximately 20%"

4. *See* Lewmar Marine, Inc. v. Barient, Inc., 827 F.2d 744, 3 USPQ2d 1766 (Fed.Cir.1987), *cert. denied,* 484 U.S. 1007, 108 S.Ct. 702, 98 L.Ed.2d 653 (1988).

5. *See supra* § 6.2.1.2.

within the meaning of this claim will be subject to interpretation in the courts. A second issue is whether tomato paste qualifies as vegetable paste. Botanists have long classified tomatoes as fruits, but even today most lay persons would look for tomatoes in their grocer's vegetable section.[6]

In answering questions such as these, the courts traditionally faced two basic questions. The first is the determination of the materials that may be appropriately considered during claim interpretation. Beyond the asserted patent claim itself, litigants have offered such evidence as the prosecution history, prior art documents, learned treatises, dictionary definitions and the testimony of inventors, technical experts and legal experts. As these sources often provide conflicting evidence of meaning, the courts have been forced to develop a basic interpretational protocol for construing patent claims. Second, courts had to resolve whether the issue of claim interpretation was one of fact or law, which would determine whether juries or judges should decide the meaning of the claims, as well as the standard of review on appeal.

The *en banc* opinion of the Federal Circuit in *Markman v. Westview Instruments, Inc.*[6.5] provided answers to these fundamental questions. As such, it has become the governing precedent on both the substance and procedure of contemporary claim interpretation. The patented invention at issue there was a rather humble one, an inventory tracking system for a dry cleaning shop. Markman combined computer and bar code technology to minimize lost garments and employee theft during the dry cleaning process. His claimed "inventory control and reporting system" allowed the detection of "spurious additions to inventory as well as spurious deletions therefrom."

Markman's assertion of the patent against a competitor led to a jury trial. Although the jury had found for Markman, the trial judge instead directed a verdict of noninfringement. Asserting that claim interpretation was a matter of law for the court, the trial judge determined that the term "inventory" referred exclusively to articles of clothing. Because the defendant's accused device merely maintained a listing of invoices, it could not track the location of individual garments as they moved about the shop and therefore, on this reading of the claims, could not infringe.

On appeal, the Federal Circuit affirmed. In so doing, the court established two categories of evidentiary inputs for use in claim interpretation. The first, so-called "intrinsic evidence," consisted of the claims, the specification, and the prosecution history. Courts

6. This example is drawn from the well-known Supreme Court opinion in Nix v. Hedden, 149 U.S. 304, 13 S.Ct. 881, 37 L.Ed. 745 (1893), a statutory interpretation case.

6.5 52 F.3d 967 (Fed.Cir.1995).

were required to consider all of the intrinsic evidence of record to determine the meaning of the claims. All other sources, ranging from dictionary definitions to expert testimony, was classified as "extrinsic evidence." The trial court judge possessed discretion to consider extrinsic evidence, but need not do so if the intrinsic evidence established the proper interpretation of the claim.

The Federal Circuit also held that claim interpretation was a matter of law solely for the judge to decide. The majority reasoned that patents, like other written instruments, had traditionally been subject to interpretation by the courts. Further, participants in the patent system were best served by an articulated, reasoned analysis of the claim scope by a trained jurist. As a result, in a jury trial, it is the responsibility of the judge to resolve the meaning of the claims and to so instruct the jury. On appeal, the Federal Circuit would review claim interpretation holdings *de novo*, without deference to the findings of the trial court.

Applying these principles to the case at hand, the court concluded that the claim term "inventory" should be construed to mean "articles of clothing" rather than money or receipts. The claims, specification, and prosecution history all referred to movement of inventory throughout a dry cleaning establishment, an event that does not occur to dollars or slips of paper. The Federal Circuit also discounted the testimony of a patent attorney and Markman himself during the trial. According to the court, this testimony amounted to a legal opinion, a matter that lies solely within the province of the trial court. The court also reasoned that extrinsic evidence should not control the interpretation of the claims in the face of consistent intrinsic evidence as to claim meaning.

The Supreme Court affirmed the Federal Circuit in an opinion principally devoted towards Seventh Amendment concerns.[7] Justice Souter's review of early patent precedents revealed that judges, not juries, had interpretative responsibilities at the time the Seventh Amendment was enacted. The Court further reasoned that, as compared to juries, judges were the more able claims-interpreters due to their training and experience. Finally, the Court concluded that assigning claim interpretation tasks to judges would encourage uniformity through the application of stare decisis and the publicity of articulated judgments.

The outcome of the *Markman* opinions appears sensible. Unless Markman was running a money laundering establishment, his patent instrument simply could not logically be read to embrace cash within the term "inventory." Yet the courts' conclusion that a patent claim should be subjected solely to judicial construction

7. 517 U.S. 370, 116 S.Ct. 1384, 134 L.Ed.2d 577 (1996).

seems questionable. Patent claims are replete with technical terms ranging from electrodes to polypeptides to moments of inertia, words which lawyers are not well trained to construe. On the other hand, the proposition that lay jurors are better situated to interpret these terms is even more debatable.

One also wonders how the decision that claim interpretation is a matter of law squares with the venerable patent law principle that claims are directed towards persons of ordinary skill in the art. If the trial judge hears one skilled artisan testifying in favor of the plaintiff's proposed interpretation of a technological term of art, and another testifying in favor of the defendant's construction, surely the determination of which expert is more credible amounts to a question of fact. As Judge Schwartz memorably remarked in *Lucas Aerospace, Ltd. v. Unison Industries, L.P.*:

> As I understand *Markman,* because claim construction presents a purely legal question, trial judges must ignore all non-transcribable courtroom occurrences such as a witness's body language, inability to maintain eye contact when confronted with a telling question, hesitance or delay in giving an answer, an affirmative answer in a voice revealing the truthful answer is "no," or the changing demeanor of a witness when shifting from sure to treacherous footing. All of the preceding occurred in this trial. When two experts testify differently as to the meaning of a technical term, and the court embraces the view of one, the other, or neither while construing a patent claim as a matter of law, the court *has* engaged in weighing evidence and making credibility determinations. If those possessed of a higher commission wish to rely on a cold written record and engage in *de novo* review of all claim constructions, that is their privilege. But when the Federal Circuit Court of Appeals states that the trial court does not do something that the trial court does and must do to perform the judicial function, that court knowingly enters a land of sophistry and fiction.[8]

Although neither *Markman* opinion devotes much attention to trial procedures, these decisions have considerably impacted the conduct of patent litigation. Viewing claim interpretation as a pure issue of law promotes a sort of summary judgment procedure in which the trial judge resolves the meaning of the claims. The district courts have differed on the timing of these so-called "*Markman* hearings." Some courts conduct *Markman* hearings early in the litigation. These courts hope to narrow issues and promote settlement, but often must make decisions with scant evidence before them. Other courts hear evidence of claim meaning at the same time as the infringement trial and instruct the jury on the

8. 890 F. Supp. 329, 333 n.7 (D. Del. 1995).

appropriate construction just before it retires. Although this technique allows the court to receive evidence after discovery has been completed and litigation positions have been fully formed, it may prevent parties from offering testimony and argument concerning the judge's claim interpretation at the trial level.

The Federal Circuit's *de novo* standard of review on claim interpretation issues has also been keenly felt. If district court claim interpretations are reviewed without deference, then trial court proceedings become a mere waystation to appeal. Predictably, the Federal Circuit has demonstrated a high reversal rate following *Markman*. Indeed, in some celebrated cases, the Federal Circuit reached a claim interpretation that neither the district court, nor the accused infringer, nor the patentee had adopted. The jurists of the Federal Circuit have been admirably receptive of the views of the patent community, however, and their opinions will continue to refine the ubiquitous question of claim interpretation in the post-*Markman* era.

8.2.1.2 Canons of Claim Construction

Beyond the basic principles of claim interpretation delineated in *Markman*, Federal Circuit cases have intoned that "a number of canons ... guide our construction of all patent claims."[9] A review of the Federal Circuit's jurisprudence reveals a modest set of these interpretational protocols. Although commentators have doubted whether these universal rules of interpretation are of much use in deciding actual cases, Federal Circuit decisions persist in relying upon them to interpret claims. The more significant canons are described below.

Numerous decisions explain that patentees are free to be their own lexicographers.[10] By this the courts mean that patentees are allowed to coin their own words for use in claims. In such cases the patent's specification or prosecution history should clearly state that word's meaning. The lexicographic privilege arises because patent claims necessarily concern novel technologies for which established descriptive terms may not yet exist. For instance, the inventor of the telephone may want to designate the component of the device into which a user speaks as the "receiver" and to use that term in his claims. He is free to do so. However, any newly minted words should not be misleading, nor should the patentee employ such banal terms as "gadget" or "widget."

9. Athletic Alternatives, Inc. v. Prince Mfg., Inc., 73 F.3d 1573, 1578, 37 USPQ2d 1365, 1370 (Fed.Cir.1996).

10. *E.g.*, Vitronics Corp. v. Conceptronic, 90 F.3d 1576, 1582, 39 USPQ2d 1573, 1576 (Fed.Cir.1996).

Another fundamental canon of construction is that a claim term should be accorded a consistent meaning.[11] A particular term should be accorded the same meaning even though it has been used in different claims. Similarly, a claim cannot be interpreted narrowly in order to distinguish a claimed invention from the prior art, but then be accorded a broad construction in order to achieve a finding of infringement.

Patent specifications often include a detailed example of the invention that is termed the "preferred embodiment." The preferred embodiment typically supplies information about the most advantageous way the inventor knows to put the invention into practice, in keeping with the "best mode" requirement of the Patent Act.[12] The Federal Circuit has stated that an interpretation of a claim that would not include the preferred embodiment is "rarely, if ever, correct."[13] This canon recognizes that it is very unlikely that inventors would wish to define their inventions in a way that excludes the preferred embodiment, or that persons of skill in the art would read the claims that way.

The canon of claim differentiation has also been frequently invoked. Under this doctrine, the reader should presume that each claim of a patent conveys a different meaning. In an illustrative decision applying the claim differentiation doctrine, *Transmatic, Inc. v. Gulton Industries, Inc.*,[14] the Federal Circuit considered a patented light fixture for buses and other public transit vehicles. Claim 1 of the asserted patent called for a "light housing" but recited no other structural limitations on that claim element. In contrast, claim 3 of the patent-in-suit, which depended from claim 1, required that the light housing have "a horizontal wall with an inward securement formation" for securing the light fixture to a vehicle. The Federal Circuit applied the doctrine of claim differentiation to hold that claim 1 did not require the specific structure recited in claim 3.

The seminal *Markman* decision itself explained that claims are to be interpreted in light of the specification. The courts have also stressed, however, that limitations from the specification should not be imported into the claims. The Federal Circuit opinion in *Unique Concepts, Inc. v. Brown* illustrates the tension between these two competing canons.[15] Unique Concepts held an exclusive license on a patented assembly of border pieces used to fasten fabric wall coverings to walls. The patent's claims included a limitation calling

11. Fonar Corp. v. Johnson & Johnson, 821 F.2d 627, 632, 3 USPQ2d 1109, 1113 (Fed.Cir.1987).

12. 35 U.S.C. § 112 ¶ 1 (2000). *See supra* § 6.1.3.

13. Vitronics, 90 F.3d at 1583.

14. 53 F.3d 1270, 35 USPQ2d 1035 (Fed.Cir.1995).

15. 939 F.2d 1558, 19 USPQ2d 1500 (Fed.Cir.1991).

for "linear border pieces and right angle corner border pieces." Unique Concepts brought a patent infringement suit against Brown, but lost at trial after the district court held that Brown's assembly did meet this limitation. The trial court noted that Brown's assembly provided only mitered[16] linear pieces. Brown apparently formed border pieces simply by joining the linear pieces together on the fly during the installation of the wall coverings. Unique appealed to the Federal Circuit, which affirmed over a dissent by Judge Rich.

The majority opinion of the Federal Circuit agreed with the trial court that Brown did not infringe. According to Judges Lourie and Mayer, the claim limitation referred to two distinct parts of the assembly: "linear border pieces" and "right angle corner border pieces." The majority viewed the specification as demonstrating that the claim language "right angle corner border pieces" referred to a single preformed piece. The fact that linear border pieces could be arranged to form a right angle corner did not convert them into "right angle corner border pieces."

The dissenting opinion of Judge Rich viewed the patent's written description differently. Judge Rich pointed to language in the patent's written description that provided: "Instead of using preformed right-angle corner pieces of the type previously disclosed, one may improvise corner pieces by miter-cutting the ends of a pair of short linear border pieces placed at right angles to each other.... " According to Judge Rich, the specification demonstrated that mitered, linear pieces could be placed at right angles and joined to form borders.

In sum, the majority contended that it interpreted the claim term "right angle corner border pieces" in light of the specification. The dissent instead charged the majority with importing limitations from the specification into the claims. At the end of the day, *Unique Concepts* demonstrates that the difference between using the specification to interpret a claim term and importing claim scope from the specification is a subtle one.

The Federal Circuit has also established a "heavy presumption" that a word used in a claim carries its ordinary meaning.[17] Dictionaries may establish the commonly understood definition of a particular term. However, the Federal Circuit has noted at least four circumstances where a claim term will not be accorded its customary meaning.[18] First, as noted above, patentees may have

16. Mitered pieces are cut at an angle other than ninety degrees, so that they are beveled, and those pieces are then joined together.

17. *See* CCS Fitness, Inc. v. Brunswick Corp., 288 F.3d 1359, 62 USPQ2d 1658 (Fed. Cir. 2002).

18. *Ibid.*

acted as their own lexicographers and established their own meanings of particular terms within the patent instrument.

Second, assertions made by the patentee, either within the patent instrument or during prosecution, may cause the claim term to be interpreted more restrictively than usual. For example, during prosecution a patentee may have asserted that a claim term has a narrower meaning than usual in order to distinguish the claim from the prior art. During infringement litigation, the courts will hold the patentee to that more limited interpretation.[19]

Third, if a particular term is used in step- or means-plus-function format, then the claim term will be construed as mandated by § 112 ¶ 6.[20] Assume, for example, that the term "attachment means" is included in a claim, and that the patent discloses the use of glue to perform the attachment. Suppose further that a court would determine that the claim is drafted in means-plus-function format. Under these circumstances, the court would limit the meaning of the term "attachment means" to cover glue "and equivalents thereof" as required by § 112 ¶ 6—rather than covering any sort of attachment means whatsoever.

Finally, a claim term will be accorded less scope than its ordinary meaning if that term so deprives the claim of clarity that "there is no means by which the scope of the claim may be ascertained from the language used."[21] For example, in *Ethicon Endo–Surgery, Inc. v. U.S. Surgical Corp.*,[22] the Federal Circuit interpreted a claim reciting a surgical stapler. Among the elements of the claim was "a pusher assembly comprising one or more pusher bars" along with "a restraining structure." Although the term "pusher assembly" appeared in the asserted claim, it was not used or defined anywhere else in the entire patent instrument. Nor did the claim itself define the makeup of the "pusher assembly" other than through the two specific recited structures. As a result, the Federal Circuit did not grant the phrase "pusher assembly" a meaning that would encompass any device for pushing staples. Rather, the court limited the literal meaning of "pusher assembly" to the specific combination of pusher bars and a restraining mechanism.

8.2.2 Doctrine of Equivalents

The exclusive rights provided by a patent are founded upon, but not exclusively limited to, the text of its claims. Although the

19. *E.g.*, Spectrum Int'l, Inc. v. Sterilite Corp, 164 F.3d 1372, 1378, 49 USPQ2d 1065, 1069 (Fed. Cir. 1998).

20. *See supra* § 6.2.2.2.

21. Johnson Worldwide Associates, Inc. v. Zebco Corp., 175 F.3d 985, 990, 50 USPQ2d 1607, 1610 (Fed. Cir. 1999).

22. 93 F.3d 1572, 40 USPQ2d 1019 (Fed. Cir. 1996).

courts have long recognized the value of clear and certain claims, they have refused to confine the infringement inquiry to their precise choice of words. Instead, the scope of protection associated with a patent may be expanded beyond the literal wording of the claims under the doctrine of equivalents. Under the current formulation of the doctrine, an accused product or process that presents insubstantial differences from the claimed invention will be judged an equivalent and therefore an infringement.[23]

The doctrine of equivalents arose from judicial efforts to stop competitors who would introduce insignificant modifications into the claimed invention in order to avoid literal infringement.[24] However, courts have not limited use of the doctrine to cases of bad faith, copying, or piracy. Every patent infringement case potentially involves the doctrine of equivalents. When courts apply the doctrine of equivalents, they attempt to balance fair protection for the patentee with appropriate notice to competitors of the scope of the patentee's exclusive rights.

Four principal limitations restrict the scope of the doctrine of equivalents. The first, prosecution history estoppel, prevents patentees from receiving a scope of protection that they have surrendered at the PTO in order to persuade the examiner to allow the claim. Second, patentees are also restricted by the prior art, and may not obtain a claim construction that would embrace technologies known to the art or their obvious variants. Third, the doctrine of equivalents may not extend to subject matter that is disclosed within a patent but not expressly claimed—a principle known as the public dedication doctrine. Finally, under the All Elements Rule, each element recited in the claim is considered material to defining the invention. As such, the doctrine of equivalents is applied not to the invention as a whole, but to the individual elements recited within the claim.

8.2.2.1 Graver Tank and the Function–Way–Result Test

The 1950 decision of the Supreme Court in *Graver Tank v. Linde Air Products Co.*[25] stood as the most important doctrine of equivalents decision for most of the latter half of the twentieth century. Although the Supreme Court would revisit the doctrine in its 1997 *Warner–Jenkinson* decision,[26] the dialogue between the

23. *See* Toro Corp. v. White Consol. Industries, 266 F.3d 1367, 1370, 60 USPQ2d 1437, 1438 (Fed.Cir.2001).

24. Martin J. Adelman & Gary L. Francione, *The Doctrine of Equivalents in Patent Law: Questions that* Pennwalt *Did Not Answer*, 137 U. PA. L. REV. 673 (1989).

25. 339 U.S. 605, 70 S.Ct. 854, 94 L.Ed. 1097 (1950).

26. Warner–Jenkinson Co., Inc. v. Hilton Davis Chemical Co., 520 U.S. 17, 117 S.Ct. 1040, 137 L.Ed.2d 146 (1997).

majority and dissenting justices in *Graver Tank* continues to inform legal and policy discussions concerning patent infringement. *Graver Tank* thus remains an appropriate starting point for consideration of the doctrine of equivalents.

The patent at issue in *Graver Tank* concerned an electric welding composition termed a "flux." When applied to the surfaces to be joined through welding, a flux assists in the fusing of the two metals. The claimed flux consisted of calcium fluoride and alkaline earth metal silicate. The defendant's accused flux was known under the trademark Lincolnweld 660. It consisted of silicates of calcium and manganese. Manganese is not an alkaline earth metal. The question on which the case turned, therefore, was whether manganese was equivalent to an alkaline earth metal silicate for purposes of the welding arts. Relevant to that issue was the fact that the patentee marketed a flux composition known as Unionmelt Grade 20 consisting of silicates of calcium and magnesium, as well as the fact that prior art patents employed manganese as a welding composition.

The Court began its opinion by reviewing basic policies underlying the doctrine of equivalents. The Court observed that confining patent rights to cases of literal infringement would merely encourage competitors to make unimportant substitutions to the invention as claimed. Such a hollow grant of rights would discourage inventors from seeking patents and thwart a principal purpose of the patent system, the disclosure of new inventions. In sum, the "essence" of the doctrine of equivalents was to prevent "fraud on a patent."[27]

Quoting from its earlier opinion in *Sanitary Refrigerator Co. v. Winters*,[28] the Court next confirmed the famous tripartite test of the doctrine of equivalents. When an accused product or process performed "substantially the same function in substantially the same way to obtain the same result," an infringement occurred under the doctrine. The known interchangeability of the claimed and substituted ingredients was an important factor in an equivalency determination, according to the Court. The Court also stated that a finding of equivalence was a question of fact, provable through the use of experts, learned texts, and the disclosures of the prior art.[29]

Applying these principles to the facts at hand, the Court affirmed the finding of infringement under the doctrine of equivalents. According to the Court, chemists had testified that magnesium and manganese were equivalents in the welding art, and the trial court had properly found that the Lincolnweld and Unionmelt

27. 339 U.S. at 608.

28. 280 U.S. 30, 42, 50 S.Ct. 9, 74 L.Ed. 147 (1929).

29. 339 U.S. at 608–10.

fluxes were in all respects equivalent. The Court also saw no evidence that the defendant had engaged in independent development of the Lincolnweld flux. The Court found it "difficult to conceive of a case more appropriate for application of the doctrine of equivalents."[30]

Justices Black and Douglas each dissented. Justice Black principally urged that the Court should have pointed the plaintiff to the reissue statute rather than freely apply the doctrine of equivalents.[31] He reminded the majority that Congress had expressly provided procedures for obtaining broader claims through a reissue proceeding. To balance the interest of patentees and their competitors, the Patent Act subjects broadening reissues to a two-year statute of limitations and intervening rights. According to Justice Black, judicial readiness to find infringement through equivalency would ignore these sound safeguards and ultimately emasculate the reissue statute. Fifty years later, Justice Black's criticisms remain substantially unanswered.

The pithy dissent of Justice Douglas observed that the asserted patent had originally included broad, generic claims that would have read upon the Lincolnweld flux.[32] These claims had been struck down during infringement litigation due to lack of enablement. Justice Douglas urged that the doctrine of equivalents should not be used to resurrect claims that had been invalidated.

Although the premises of Justice Douglas are sound, most observers have reached exactly the opposite conclusion from them.[33] By obtaining generic claims from the PTO, Jones, the patentee in *Graver Tank*, had expressly declared a proprietary interest in the combination later embodied in the Lincolnweld flux. PTO policies of the day also prevented Jones from separately claiming more than three species of the distinctly claimed genus. Because technical reasons limited Jones' opportunity to obtain a valid claim covering the Lincolnweld flux, the case for the equivalent infringement was strong.

The patent community took from *Graver Tank* the function-way-result test for equivalency. Hundreds of subsequent equivalency opinions proceeded to apply it. Experience did not assist the courts in refining this standard, however, but instead demonstrated that its extraordinary vagueness was of scant use in resolving most infringement cases. Litigants placed vastly different meanings upon the terms "function," "way," and "result," with patentees reading

30. 339 U.S. at 612.

31. 339 U.S. at 612–18. For a thorough discussion of reissue practice, *see* § 7.5.3 of this volume.

32. 339 U.S. at 618.

33. *See, e.g.,* Hilton Davis Chem. Co. v. Warner–Jenkinson Co., 62 F.3d 1512, 1535, 35 USPQ2d 1641, 1659–60 (Fed. Cir.1995) (*in banc*) (Newman, J., concurring).

these terms broadly and accused infringers narrowly. And often this standard simply collapsed into a test of "way": if the accused technology did not perform the same function to achieve the same result, it ordinarily would not be the subject of a patent infringement suit at all. As stated more succinctly by Judge Learned Hand in *Claude Neon Lights, Inc. v. E. Machlett & Son*:

> Each case is inevitably a matter of degree, as so often happens, and other decisions have little or no value. The usual ritual, which is so often repeated and which has so little meaning ... does not help much in application; it is no more than a way of stating the problem.[34]

This experience led to considerable unrest in the lower courts, culminating 45 years later in a revisiting of the doctrine of equivalents by the Supreme Court.

8.2.2.2 **Warner–Jenkinson** ***and the Insubstantial Differences Test***

The Supreme Court's 1997 opinion in *Warner–Jenkinson Co. v. Hilton Davis Chemical Co.* provides a full-featured discussion of contemporary doctrine of equivalents issues.[35] Both the plaintiff-patentee, Hilton Davis, and the accused infringer, Warner–Jenkinson, manufactured dyes. The patent-in-suit claimed a method of removing impurities by filtering the dye through a porous membrane. As originally presented to the PTO, the claims did not speak towards the pH level at which this ultrafiltration process should be performed. Later during prosecution, in order to distinguish a prior art patent that operated at a pH above 9.0, Hilton Davis added the limitation "at a pH from approximately 6.0 to 9.0." The accused process operated at a pH of 5.0. A jury trial resulted in a finding of infringement under the doctrine of equivalents. The jurists of the Federal Circuit agreed to hear the case *en banc* and affirmed in a set of lengthy, deeply divided opinions. The Supreme Court then granted *certiorari* and offered a sweeping review of the doctrine of equivalents.

Warner–Jenkinson's first series of arguments contended that the doctrine of equivalents did not survive the enactment of the 1952 Patent Act—effectively arguing that hundreds of cases over the previous 45 years had been misguided. Its position was that the doctrine of equivalents was inconsistent with the statutory requirements for definite claims and broadening reissue proceedings, as well as the role of the PTO in determining claim scope. The Court tersely responded that each of these points had been raised and

34. 36 F.2d 574, 3 USPQ 220 (2d Cir.1929), *cert. denied*, 281 U.S. 741, 50 S.Ct. 347, 74 L.Ed. 1155 (1930).

35. 520 U.S. 17, 117 S.Ct. 1040, 137 L.Ed.2d 146 (1997).

rejected in *Graver Tank*, and there was no basis for overturning that decision today.[36]

Another, more interesting argument was that Congress had wholly codified the doctrine of equivalents when it authorized functional claiming in the sixth paragraph of § 112. This statute allows applicants to draft so-called "means plus function" claims that are "construed to cover the corresponding structure, material, or acts described in the specification and equivalents thereof."[36.5] According to Warner–Jenkinson, congressional authorization of an equivalency provision for functional claims amounted to the rejection of a general doctrine of equivalents for other sorts of claims. Justice Thomas rejected this position as well, reasoning that Congress specifically intended § 112 ¶ 6 to overturn the Supreme Court's 1946 opinion in *Halliburton Oil Well Cementing Co. v. Walker*, which had cast grave doubts on the validity of functional claiming. He concluded that such limited congressional action could not be seen to have such sweeping consequences for the venerable doctrine of equivalents.[37]

Warner–Jenkinson also urged that equivalents should be limited to variants described in the patent's specification or, alternatively, to those variants known at the time the patent issued. Justice Thomas quickly dismissed both of these positions, reasoning that the perspective of the person of ordinary skill in the art placed sufficient limits on the doctrine. The Court also upheld the ample precedent proclaiming equivalency to be a factual determination, to be decided by the jury in a jury trial.[38]

The Court went on to address a position that had been gaining increasing currency in the patent community: that the doctrine of equivalents should apply only to cases where the accused infringer engaged in bad faith efforts such as copying. It readily rejected this proposal as well. Although the *Graver Tank* opinion had reasoned that the doctrine of equivalents discourages piracy and the "unscrupulous copyist," the Court did not read *Graver Tank* as limiting the doctrine to cases involving defendants of that unsavory ilk. Ample precedent had described the doctrine in more neutral terms and had not limited equivalency to actors in bad faith. Following *Warner–Jenkinson*, then, intent is not an element of a doctrine of equivalents analysis.[39]

The final portion of the Supreme Court's *Warner–Jenkinson* opinion addressed the appropriate standard for the doctrine of equivalents. Concerned that the function-way-result test usually

36. 520 U.S. at 25–27.

36.5 A full discussion of this provision can be found in § 6.2.2.2 of this text.

37. 520 U.S. at 27–28.

38. 520 U.S. at 37.

39. 520 U.S. at 34–36.

associated with *Graver Tank* did not easily apply to sophisticated, nonmechanical technologies, the *en banc* Federal Circuit had engaged in a thorough rereading of the *Graver Tank* opinion. Observing that *Graver Tank* had several times described cases of "insubstantial differences" as appropriate for a finding of equivalency, the Federal Circuit explicitly held that "the application of the doctrine of equivalents rests on the substantiality of the differences between the claimed and accused product or processes, assessed according to an objective standard."[40]

The Supreme Court was surprisingly nonchalant towards the Federal Circuit's reinterpretation of *Graver Tank*. Declining to select the appropriate standard of equivalency, the Court observed that "[d]ifferent linguistic frameworks may be more suitable to different cases, depending on their particular facts." According to Justice Thomas, the essential inquiry was whether the accused product or process contained elements identical or equivalent to each element recited in the patent claim. The Court left for the Federal Circuit the further refinement of appropriate equivalency standards on a case-by-case basis.[41]

Given the Court's detached view of the appropriate standard of equivalency, Justice Thomas did not elaborate upon the newly approved insubstantial differences standard. However, the *Warner–Jenkinson* opinion and subsequent Federal Circuit opinions have suggested several mechanisms for determining whether insubstantial differences exist between the claimed invention and accused technology. As in *Graver Tank*, known interchangeability of substitutes for an element of the patented invention and independent experimentation by the accused infringer might be probative.[42] The familiar nonobviousness analysis may also be pertinent to the equivalency inquiry.[43] That a skilled artisan would have found the substitution of one ingredient of the claimed invention for the ingredient appearing in the accused product is probative of insubstantial differences. Finally, the function-way-result test is not dead after *Warner–Jenkinson*, but has evolved into one formula for articulating whether the differences between the claimed and accused technologies are insubstantial.

8.2.2.3 Limitations on the Doctrine of Equivalents

The insubstantial differences test is the starting point for the doctrine of equivalents, but the fulfillment of this standard does not necessarily compel a conclusion of infringement. Four significant

40. 62 F.3d 1512, 1518, 35 USPQ2d 1641, 1645 (Fed.Cir.1995).

41. 520 U.S. at 39–40.

42. 520 U.S. at 36.

43. Roton Barrier, Inc. v. Stanley Works, 79 F.3d 1112, 1128, 37 USPQ2d 1816, 1828 (Fed.Cir.1996) (Nies, J., concurring).

constraints place limits upon the application of the doctrine of equivalents. These are the All Elements Rule, the prior art, prosecution history estoppel and the public dedication doctrine. These limiting principles are frequently tested in patent infringement litigation and are worthy of further discussion here.

8.2.2.3.1 The All Elements Rule

In *Warner–Jenkinson*, the Supreme Court confirmed the principle that "[e]ach element contained in a patent claim is deemed material to defining the scope of the patented invention, and thus the doctrine of equivalents must be applied to individual elements of the claim, not the invention as a whole."[44] This principle is known as the All Elements Rule.[44.5] In applying it, a finding of infringement may arise only if each element of a claim is present in the accused device or process, either literally or equivalently. The doctrine of equivalents is thus not oriented to the patented invention as a whole, but instead is more strictly employed with respect to each element of a patent claim.

Although the All Elements Rule arguably has ancient origins in U.S. law, the Federal Circuit's 1987 *en banc* decision in *Pennwalt Corp. v. Durand–Wayland, Inc.*[45] provides its fullest articulation. Pennwalt's '628 patent bore the title "Sorter for Fruit and the Like." The '628 patent disclosed a mechanism that rapidly sorted fruit or other items based upon color, weight, or a combination of these traits. A hard-wired network, including hardware registers, followed each piece of fruit as it moved down a track. Among the claimed elements were first and second "position indicating means" that shifted the data corresponding to the fruit as it was conveyed along the sorting mechanism.

Pennwalt brought an infringement suit against Durand–Wayland, asserting that its '628 patent claims read on the defendant's accused Microsizer product. The district court held for the defendants. According to the trial judge, the Microsizer lacked the claimed "position indicating means" because it never shifted data. The Microsizer instead employed random access memory that stored the color and weight data in a discrete location. Thus, rather than shuffling data down a queue to match the progression of a piece of fruit, the Microsizer managed queue pointers. According to the trial court, because the accused device wholly lacked a claimed element of the '628 patent, it could not infringe either literally or under the doctrine of equivalents.

44. 520 U.S. at 29.

44.5 Some jurists call this doctrine the "All Limitations Rule." Cooper Cameron Corp. v. Kvaerner Oilfield Prods., Inc., 291 F.3d 1317, 1321, 62 USPQ2d 1846, 1849 (Fed.Cir.2002).

45. 833 F.2d 931, 4 USPQ2d 1737 (Fed.Cir.1987).

The majority of the Federal Circuit agreed with the trial court that the Microsizer's lack of a "position indicating means" was fatal to Pennwalt's contention of infringement. According to the majority, an accused technology must contain every element of a claimed invention, either literally or equivalently, to be judged an infringement. To hold otherwise would disconnect the infringement inquiry from the language of the claims themselves. A lengthy opinion offering the "additional views" of Judge Nies dubbed this canon the All Elements Rule.

A dissenting opinion from Judge Bennett and supplementary "commentary" from Judge Newman stridently disagreed with the All Elements Rule. According to the dissenters, the majority had devised an analytical framework for the doctrine of equivalents that was little more than a redundant literal infringement inquiry. The dissenters viewed the doctrine of equivalents as an equitable creation designed to work justice in individual cases, a goal that would be undone by such a restrictive and inflexible canon of construction.

The All Elements Rule is of great practical significance to claims-drafters. Consider the example of the following, simplified claims:

1. A fork comprising:

   a cylindrical handle; and

   four tines attached to said handle.

2. A fork comprising:

   a cylindrical handle;

   a first tine attached to said handle;

   a second tine attached to said handle;

   a third tine attached to said handle; and

   a fourth tine attached to said handle.[46]

These claims appear to provide the same scope of protection in terms of literal infringement. Yet suppose a competitor markets a fork with three tines. The holding of *Pennwalt* would permit a finding of equivalent infringement with regard to claim 1 if a court were willing to conclude that a three-tine structure was equivalent to the four-tine structure recited in the second element. But with respect to claim 2, the accused device would lack the final recited element—"a fourth tine attached to said handle"—either literally or in the form of an equivalent structure. Thus, to hold it infringing would violate the All Elements Rule and prove fatal to the case of equivalency.

46. *See* Martin J. Adelman et al., Patent Law: Cases and Materials 947 (1998).

Although this example is straightforward enough, application of the All Elements Rule has proven rather more difficult in the litigated cases. The most notorious episode concerning this canon arose a mere two years after *Pennwalt*, in the Federal Circuit's 1989 opinion in *Corning Glass Works v. Sumitomo Electric USA, Inc.*[47] That appeal concerned a patented fiber optic cable. This technology was designed to guide light through a glass fiber by ensuring that the refractive index of the glass is higher than the refractive index of the material surrounding the glass. The patentee, Corning Glass Works, developed a glass fiber that consisted of a silica core and an outer cover termed a "cladding." The core was "positively" doped so that its refraction index was higher than the surrounding cladding.[48] The claim read in part as follows:

> An optical waveguide comprising
>
> (a) a cladding layer . . . , and
>
> (b) a core formed of fused silica to which a dopant material on at least an elemental basis has been added to a degree in excess of that of the cladding layer so that the index of refraction thereof is of a value greater than the index of refraction of said cladding layer. . . . [49]

In what proved to be a fascinating set of circumstances, the defendants obtained the appropriate index of refraction differential by negatively doping the cladding. In other words, instead of making the core of their optic cable more reflective than the cladding, they just made the cladding less reflective. The district court found the defendants liable for infringement. The defendants appealed, citing the *Pennwalt* rule, and with a rather surprising opinion, the Federal Circuit affirmed. According to Judge Nies, the defendants misunderstood the sense of the term "element" in the All Elements Rule:

> "Element" may be used to mean a single limitation, but it has also been used to mean a series of limitations which, taken together, make up a component of the claimed invention. In the All Elements Rule, "element" is used in the sense of a limitation of a claim. . . . [T]he determination of equivalency is not subject to a rigid formula. An equivalent must be found for every limitation of the claim somewhere in the accused device,

47. 868 F.2d 1251, 9 USPQ2d 1962 (Fed.Cir.1989).

48. The term "doping" refers to the introduction of an impurity into silica glass in order to change its optical properties, and in particular its refraction index. Some impurities, including titanium oxide, are termed "positive dopants" and increase the refractive index of the glass. Other impurities, such as fluorine and boron oxide, are "negative dopants" used to decrease the refractive index of the glass.

49. 868 F.2d at 1256, 9 USPQ2d at 1965.

but not necessarily in a corresponding component, although that is generally the case.[50]

Many commentators have doubted whether *Pennwalt* and *Corning Glass* can be reconciled.[51] *Pennwalt* pronounces an element-by-element equivalency standard, while *Corning Glass* seemingly reverts to a holistic view of the doctrine of equivalents. And while these cases reach differing results, each concerned claims that were written too restrictively. The claims for the fruit sorter in *Pennwalt* included too many elements. A watchful drafter likely would have been able to define a patentable advance with a less comprehensive depiction of the invention. In *Corning Glass*, the claims were too narrow in a different sense. Rather than expressly call for the addition of dopant to the core, the claims-drafter could have more abstractly provided for the "addition of dopant to change the refraction index" or simply the "alteration of the refraction index differential."

Some observers have attempted to distinguish *Corning Glass* as involving unusual facts. For example, Judge Lourie's subsequent opinion in *Ethicon Endo–Surgery, Inc. v. United States Surgical Corp.*[52] speaks of *Corning Glass* as involving a special case: the "simultaneous substitution of two reciprocal limitations (cladding for core and negative dopant for positive)."[53] As well, the *Corning Glass* court was plainly impressed with Corning's landmark invention. Perhaps *Corning Glass* suggests that the doctrine of equivalents will be used more generously and with less attention to the All Elements Rule to correct claim scope in the case of pioneering advances.

Whatever the merits of the All Elements Rule, the Supreme Court opinion in *Warner–Jenkinson* broadly upheld it.[54] Interestingly, the facts of *Warner–Jenkinson* did not provide an apt vehicle for the approving statement of Justice Thomas. Recall that the crucial claim limitation there identified the pH at which a dye purification process should be performed. No one doubted that the accused process occurred at some acidity—it could hardly be otherwise. *Warner–Jenkinson* simply wasn't a case of a missing claim limitation. Nor did the Court see fit to discuss or even cite the crucial *Pennwalt* and *Corning Glass* opinions. The lower courts have always found the dicta of the Supreme Court extremely persuasive, however, and the All Elements Rule remains with us as a significant constraint upon the doctrine of equivalents.

50. 868 F.2d at 1259, 9 USPQ2d at 1968.

51. *E.g.*, Toshiko Takenaka, Interpreting Patent Claims: The United States, Germany and Japan 124–25 (1995).

52. 149 F.3d 1309, 47 USPQ2d 1272 (Fed.Cir.1998).

53. 149 F.3d at 1319, 47 USPQ2d at 1279.

54. 520 U.S. at 28–30.

8.2.2.3.2 *Prior Art Limitations*

The prior art also restrains the application of the doctrine of equivalents. Sound patent policy dictates that patentees should not be able to obtain a construction of their claims that would reach technologies that have entered the public domain. Those who practice a technology known to the prior art, or its obvious variant, are immune from a finding of infringement under the doctrine of equivalents.

Suppose, for example, that Lance Lumen files a patent application on July 4, 2003, directed towards a light bulb. The Lumen patent specifically claims a light bulb with a tungsten filament. That application matures into a U.S. patent granted on November 12, 2005. Lumen brings an infringement lawsuit against Arthur Aurelius. Because Aurelius manufactures light bulbs using a carbon filament, there is no literal infringement. Lumen's infringement case is based upon the doctrine of equivalents and the argument that a carbon filament is equivalent to a tungsten filament. At trial, Aurelius produces an article published in the January 1, 2000, issue of *Bright Ideas*, extensively discussing the use of carbon filaments in light bulbs. That article, published more than one year before Lumen's filing date, is prior art against the Lumen patent under § 102(b). Because Aurelius is merely practicing a technology that is disclosed by the prior art, Lumen cannot successfully assert a claim of equivalent infringement against him.

All of this makes good sense as a policy matter. Had Lumen's patent literally claimed the use of carbon filaments in light bulbs, those claims would have been anticipated by the *Bright Ideas* article and therefore invalid. Lumen should not, through the doctrine of equivalents, obtain a proprietary interest to which he is not entitled.[54.5] Of course, where the accused infringer practices a technology that is not precisely identical to a prior art reference, but is said to be an obvious variant of it, the analysis becomes rather more treacherous.

The leading case limiting the doctrine of equivalents on the basis of prior art is *Wilson Sporting Goods Co. v. David Geoffrey & Associates.*[55] That litigation concerned Wilson's assertion of a patent involving a golf ball cover dimple arrangement. The dimples were placed in such a manner as to allow the ball to fly higher and farther. In particular, the claims required that no dimples intersect

54.5 Indeed, in a case like this it is likely that Lumen's patent would be invalid under an obviousness analysis. After all, if Lumen argues that tungsten and carbon filaments are equivalent (i.e., insubstantially different) and if the prior art disclosed carbon filaments, the substitution of tungsten recited in patent would have been obvious to those schooled in the relevant art.

55. 904 F.2d 677, 14 USPQ2d 1942 (Fed.Cir.1990).

with six "great circles," or arcs of circles that passed completely around the widest part of the ball.

The defendant, Dunlop, marketed golf balls with a dimple configuration similar to that of the patent. The great circles of Dunlop's balls were not dimple-free as the claims literally required, however. Approximately 14% of the dimples intersected a great circle. At trial, the jury found that the accused golf balls infringed under the doctrine of equivalents.

On appeal, Dunlop pointed to evidence in the record regarding a prior art golf ball marketed by Uniroyal. According to Dunlop, the range of equivalency accorded to the Wilson patent should have been constrained by the Uniroyal ball, which featured a 12% dimple intersection rate. With such a slight distinction between the Dunlop and Uniroyal balls, Dunlop urged that a finding of infringement was improper.

The Federal Circuit agreed with Dunlop and reversed in a much-discussed opinion. Judge Rich set forward a new methodology for considering prior art restraints upon the doctrine of equivalents:

> Whether prior art restricts the range of equivalents of what is literally claimed can be a difficult question to answer. To simplify analysis and bring the issue onto familiar turf, it may be helpful to conceptualize the limitation on the scope of equivalents by visualizing a *hypothetical* patent claim, sufficient in scope to *literally* cover the accused product. The pertinent question then becomes whether that hypothetical claim could have been allowed by the PTO over the prior art. If not, then it would be improper to permit the patentee to obtain that coverage in an infringement suit under the doctrine of equivalents. If the hypothetical claim could have been allowed, then *prior art* is not a bar to infringement under the doctrine of equivalents.[56]

Under this methodology, a hypothetical claim that would have literally encompassed Dunlop's product would have recited a cover in which "no more than 14% of the dimples intersected a great circle on the surface of the ball." If Wilson had drafted the claim in that fashion, however, the court held that it would have been obvious in light of the prior art Uniroyal ball, with its 12% dimple rate. Because the distinction between a 12% and 14% dimple intersection rate was not a principled difference, Wilson's claim could not be accorded a range of equivalents broad enough to capture the accused golf balls.

56. 904 F.2d at 684–85, 14 USPQ2d at 1948.

Notable about the *Wilson Sporting Goods* decision is the seeming discomfort the Federal Circuit experienced about the analytical technique it had just announced. The court did not set out the hypothetical claim it presumably drafted when reaching its decision—the example in the previous paragraph is our speculation and not derived from Judge Rich's opinion. In addition, the court's analysis of the obviousness of the differences between the prior art and this unrevealed hypothetical claim was not an especially rigorous one. Not only did the court not remand for an analysis of the *Graham* factors under the law of obviousness—the prior art, the differences between the claimed invention and the prior art, the level of ordinary skill in the art, and the pertinent secondary considerations—the court did not even discuss them in a systematic way.

Although practitioners have criticized the hypothetical claim methodology as burdensome and confusing, particularly in jury trials, the Federal Circuit has emphasized in its more recent opinions that *Wilson Sporting Goods* did not establish rules of patent trial procedure.[57] *Wilson Sporting Goods* instead offered substantive guidance on the extent to which the prior art restrains the scope of equivalency. With or without hypothetical claims, numerous Federal Circuit cases have recognized that the prior art influences the permissible range of equivalents.[58] Where the circumstances allow, most accused infringers simply argue that they are practicing a technology that is available as prior art against the asserted patent, without the cumbersome apparatus of the hypothetical claim.

Wilson Sporting Goods also has the merit of bringing some analytical rigor to the enduring maxim of the patent law that claims towards pioneering inventions are entitled to a broader range of equivalents than patents claiming a narrow improvement in a crowded art.[59] This often recited canon of claim construction recognizes that the prior art is unlikely to restrain the scope of equivalents on patents that claim revolutionary advances. However, where the patented invention presents a more humble advance, then the prior art may restrain the range of equivalency to those claims.

57. *See* Conroy v. Reebok Int'l, Inc., 14 F.3d 1570, 1576–77, 29 USPQ2d 1373, 1378 (Fed. Cir.1994); Key Mfg. v. Microdot, Inc., 925 F.2d 1444, 1449, 17 USPQ2d 1806, 1810 (Fed. Cir.1991).

58. *See,* e.g., Baxter Healthcare Corp. v. Spectramed, Inc., 49 F.3d 1575, 34 USPQ2d 1120 (Fed.Cir.1995), *cert. denied,* 516 U.S. 906, 116 S.Ct. 272, 133 L.Ed.2d 194 (1995); We Care, Inc. v. Ultra-Mark Int'l Corp., 930 F.2d 1567, 18 USPQ2d 1562 (Fed.Cir.1991).

59. *See* Westinghouse v. Boyden Power-Brake Co., 170 U.S. 537, 561–62, 18 S.Ct. 707, 42 L.Ed. 1136 (1898).

8.2.2.3.3 Prosecution History Estoppel

The principle of prosecution history estoppel precludes a patentee from obtaining a claim construction before a court that would include subject matter surrendered at the PTO during prosecution. It is named for the "prosecution history" or "file wrapper," the publicly available papers that document the dialogue between the inventor and examiner during the patent acquisition. If the court concludes that an applicant relinquished certain subject matter in order to secure the allowance of her claims then, as a patentee, she may not employ the doctrine of equivalents to recapture the renounced subject matter.[60]

For example, suppose that Professor Gadget filed a patent application claiming a vaccine.[61] As filed, Gadget's claims contain no limitations concerning the number of times the vaccine should be administered in order to provide an effective immunization. During prosecution, the examiner cites a prior art reference that discloses a vaccine similar to Gadget's invention, which requires two administrations one month apart in order to protect a patient. In response, to distinguish his vaccine from the prior art, Gadget inserts a limitation into his claims. As amended, Gadget's claims recite a "single administration vaccine" such that "said patient may be effectively immunized with one dose." Satisfied that Gadget's vaccine presents a patentable advance over the prior art, the examiner allows the claims to issue.

Suppose further that Gadget later sues a competitor, Rue Bella, for patent infringement. Bella manufactures a vaccine very similar to that of Gadget, but the accused vaccine must be administered in two separate doses at least one month apart. Bella may order a copy of the prosecution history of the Gadget patent from the PTO and place it into evidence before the trial court. The court would then realize that Gadget expressly limited his claims to a single administration vaccine in order to avoid the prior art. Bella would further assert that as a result, the "one dose" limitation should not be expanded to "two doses" via the doctrine of equivalents. Because there is no literal infringement and prosecution history estoppel bars the application of the doctrine of equivalents, the court should dismiss Gadget's infringement suit.

In addition to estoppel through claim amendment, courts have also recognized estoppel by argument.[62] If an applicant makes an argument to the examiner characterizing the claimed invention or

60. *E.g.*, Loral Fairchild Corp. v. Sony Corp., 181 F.3d 1313, 50 USPQ2d 1865 (Fed.Cir.1999), *cert. denied*, 528 U.S. 1075, 120 S.Ct. 789, 145 L.Ed.2d 666 (2000).

61. This example is loosely based upon Intervet America, Inc. v. Kee–Vet Laboratories, Inc., 887 F.2d 1050, 12 USPQ2d 1474 (Fed.Cir.1989).

62. *See* Cybor Corp. v. FAS Technologies, Inc., 138 F.3d 1448, 46 USPQ2d 1169 (Fed.Cir.1998) (*in banc*).

distinguishing it from the prior art, then prosecution history estoppel may apply as well. No claim need be amended in these circumstances. Courts consider whether a competitor reading the administrative record would reasonably believe the applicant surrendered subject matter. Absent a strong indication to the contrary from the prosecution history, PTO examiners are assumed to rely upon applicants' arguments when deciding whether to allow patents to issue.

The doctrine of prosecution history estoppel formally differs from the use of prosecution histories as intrinsic evidence of the meaning of a claim. As described in the *Markman* opinion, prosecution histories complement the patent instrument as an essential input towards resolving the meaning of claim terms.[63] Prosecution history estoppel is a more rigid doctrine that comes into play only when the patentee resorts to the doctrine of equivalents. Thus, if a claim recited the use of a liquid with a pH of "approximately 5.0," the prosecution history would be relevant in a subsequent infringement suit to interpret the claim to determine if it literally covered a liquid with a pH of 4.5. Alternatively, if the patentee then claimed infringement under the doctrine of equivalents against a party using a liquid with a pH of 4.5, the prosecution history would be consulted to determine if the patentee had given up rights to a liquid of that acidity during the proceedings at the PTO.

In practice, however, these two uses of the prosecution history are complementary. Whether employed in the context of the initial task of interpretation, or in a subsequent infringement inquiry under the doctrine of equivalents, resort to the prosecution history ensures that claims may not be construed one way in order to obtain their allowance and in another way against accused infringers.

The Supreme Court's opinion in *Warner–Jenkinson* explained the procedural aspects of prosecution history estoppel. According to Justice Thomas, when the prosecution history shows that the patentee amended the claims during prosecution, the burden fell to the patentee to explain the reason for the amendment. The court must then "decide whether that reason is sufficient to overcome prosecution history estoppel as a bar to application of the doctrine of equivalents to the element added by that amendment."[64] If the patentee failed to offer a suitable explanation, "the court should

63. *See* Markman v. Westview Instruments, Inc., 52 F.3d 967, 34 USPQ2d 1321 (Fed.Cir.1995) (*in banc*), *aff'd*, 517 U.S. 370, 116 S.Ct. 1384, 134 L.Ed.2d 577 (1996).

64. *Warner–Jenkinson*, 520 U.S. at 33.

presume that the patent applicant had a substantial reason related to patentability for including the limited element added by amendment" and that prosecution history estoppel should apply.[65]

Courts have struggled over the extent to which prosecution history estoppel impacts the doctrine of equivalents. The following example, using dated technology, illustrates these difficulties. Suppose that, prior to the invention of the transistor, an inventor presents a claim reciting a computer that in part uses an "electric switch." The PTO examiner rejects the claim based upon prior art. The inventor then narrows the claim by deleting the term "electric switch" and replacing it with the term "vacuum tube." The PTO examiner then approves the claim. Subsequently, near the end of the patent's term, the inventor brings suit against a competitor that manufactures computers using a new, state-of-the-art device—the transistor, which did not exist at the time the patent was examined or issued.

The case law provides two alternative approaches for determining the scope of equivalents left to an amended claim limitation, known respectively as the "strict bar" and the "flexible bar." Under the strict bar approach, if a claim limitation has been amended during prosecution, then no range of equivalents exists for that amended limitation. In the above example, because transistors can act as electric switches, the patentee is deemed to have confined his invention to vacuum tubes and purposefully disclaimed transistors. Prosecution history estoppel would therefore completely defeat the patentee's charge of infringement. The strict bar approach has the advantage of providing a "bright line" rule, but may hold harsh consequences for patentees.

In contrast, applying the flexible bar, a court would assess the reason for the claim amendment to determine the remaining scope of the doctrine of equivalents. Prosecution history estoppel would apply only where the court concluded that a person skilled in the art would reasonably believe that the patentee had surrendered subject matter during prosecution. To continue the previous example, no reasonable competitor would believe that the patentee had surrendered subject matter by amending the claims because at the time the patentee made the amendment, the transistor had yet to be invented! As a result, the court would likely hold that prosecution history estoppel did not apply, and proceed to the doctrine of equivalents analysis.

The Federal Circuit has traditionally employed a flexible bar approach. In *Festo Corp. v. Shoketsu Kinzoku Kogyo Kabushiki Co.*,[66] however, the Federal Circuit abruptly announced its shift to a

65. *Id.*

66. 234 F.3d 558, 56 USPQ2d 1865 (Fed.Cir.2000) (*en banc*).

strict bar approach, only to be reversed by the Supreme Court. Here the plaintiff, Festo, owned the Stoll and Carroll patents. Each patent involved a magnetic rodless cylinder, which is typically used to operate a conveyer belt. The cylinder consists of a tube that contains a piston, along with a sleeve. Magnets are mounted on both the tube and the sleeve. The piston can be moved back and forth through the use of hydraulic fluid. Magnetic attraction then causes the sleeve to move along with the piston. In turn, the sleeve is attached to the conveyer belt, or whatever else should be moved.

During prosecution, Festo amended the claims of both the Stoll and Carroll patents to require a pair of sealing rings. The Carroll patent was additionally amended to require a sleeve made of magnetizable material. The accused infringer, SMC, produced a device employing a single, two-way sealing ring (not a "pair" of rings as recited in the amended claim) and a sleeve made of nonmagnetizable material (not a magnetizable material, as recited in the amended claim).

Although the Stoll and Carroll patents were not literally infringed, Festo argued that infringement existed under the doctrine of equivalents. SMC in turn contended that prosecution history estoppel barred Festo from resorting to the doctrine. Festo's position was that, following *Warner–Jenkinson*, an explanation existed for the two claim amendments. Festo characterized the sealing ring amendment as relating to the examiner's rejection based on § 112, pertaining to claim definiteness. Festo further described the sleeve material amendment as wholly voluntary.

Festo prevailed in the trial court and SMC appealed to the Federal Circuit, which reversed. The Federal Circuit applied the strict bar rule and held that prosecution history estoppel creates a complete bar to the doctrine of equivalents. "When a claim amendment creates prosecution history estoppel with regard to a claim element, there is no range of equivalents available for the amended claim element," the court explained.[67] The Federal Circuit reasoned that the need for certainty as to the scope of patent protection was paramount. It reasoned that amendments should be treated as disclaimers and construed against the inventor, and in favor of the public.

A unanimous Supreme Court vacated and remanded the case, rejecting the Federal Circuit's strict bar approach in favor of its own version of the flexible bar approach.[68] Justice Kennedy explained that prosecution history does not bar the inventor from asserting infringement against every equivalent to the narrowed element. The Court instead mandated a specific determination of

67. 234 F.3d at 569, 56 USPQ2d at 1872.

68. 535 U.S. 722, 122 S.Ct. 1831, 152 L.Ed.2d 944 (2002).

the range of subject matter surrendered by a narrowing amendment. The Court followed the approach established in *Warner–Jenkinson* by confirming the presumption that any territory surrendered through claim amendment is an equivalent of the territory claimed. Patentees can rebut this presumption, however, by showing that at the time of the amendment one skilled in the art could not reasonably be expected to have drafted a claim that would literally encompass the alleged equivalent. As Justice Kennedy explained:

> There are some cases, however, where the amendment cannot reasonably be viewed as surrendering a particular equivalent. The equivalent may have been unforeseeable at the time of the application; the rationale underlying the amendment may bear no more than a tangential relation to the equivalent in question; or there may be some other reason suggesting that the patentee could not reasonably be expected to have described the insubstantial substitute in question. In those cases the patentee can overcome the presumption that prosecution history estoppel bars a finding of equivalence.[69]

Apparent from this language is that although the Supreme Court rejected the strict bar approach of the Federal Circuit, the Court provided only a very modest number of ways for patent proprietors to avoid prosecution history estoppel. Following the Supreme Court opinion in *Festo*, patentees who have amended their claims possess only three opportunities to rebut the presumption of prosecution history estoppel due to a claim amendment.

The first of these three rebuttal criterion is that the alleged equivalent would have been unforeseeable. As Judge Lourie explained upon remand of the case to the Federal Circuit, "[u]sually, if the alleged equivalent represents later-developed technology (*e.g.*, transistors in relation to vacuum tubes, or Velcro® in relation to fasteners) or technology that was not known in the relevant art, then it would not have been foreseeable. In contrast, old technology, while not always foreseeable, would more likely have been foreseeable."[70] The Federal Circuit has stated that foreseeability presents a factual issue based upon the state of the art and the understanding of a hypothetical person of ordinary skill in the art at the time the claim amendment was made.[71]

The second possibility is that the reason for the narrowing amendment was "tangential," or not directly relevant, to the alleged equivalent. Although the lower courts have yet to apply this factor squarely since the Supreme Court's *Festo* decision, the Fed-

69. 535 U.S. at 740–41.

70. 344 F.3d 1359, 68 USPQ2d 1321 (Fed. Cir. 2003).

71. 344 F.3d at 1369, 68 USPQ2d at 1328.

eral Circuit has stated that an amendment made to avoid prior art that contains the equivalent in question does not qualify as tangential. The Federal Circuit has further stated that determinations of whether the second rebuttal criterion apply should be based upon an examination of the patent's prosecution history, rather than expert testimony or other extrinsic evidence.[72] The third category—"some other reason suggesting that the patentee could not reasonably be expected to have described the insubstantial substitute in question"—allows for the possibility that some reason, such as the shortcomings of language, prevented the patentee from describing the alleged equivalent when it narrowed the claim. The Federal Circuit has indicated that to the extent possible, application of this third criterion should also be based upon the patent's prosecution history, as opposed to extrinsic evidence.[73]

In *Festo*, the Supreme Court did agree with the Federal Circuit that amendments to satisfy § 112 also could trigger prosecution history estoppel.[74] Most prosecution history estoppel cases concern amendments made to distinguish prior art, and therefore involve §§ 102 or 103 of the Patent Act. But sometimes applicants change claims in order to make them more definite, a requirement under § 112. An examiner might ask the patentee to clarify an ambiguous word, for example, or provide more detail on how the different parts of the invention interact with each other. The Court reasoned that inventors make such amendments in order to procure a patent, and that as a result prosecution history should apply in the context of § 112 as well.

The use of prosecution histories in the task of claim interpretation has been criticized.[75] Like legislative histories or parol evidence, prosecution histories consist of preparatory documents of uncertain relation to the text ultimately approved. Unlike succinct, integrated patent instruments, these episodic and often lengthy compilations of correspondence can be time-consuming and costly to understand. Some academic commentary has consequently called for the abandonment of the principle of prosecution history estoppel in favor of an objective analysis of prior art and patentability constraints upon the scope of equivalents. However, the Federal Circuit cases have increasingly relied upon the prosecution history despite this critique. It follows that patent practitioners must heed the consequences of the prosecution history both during enforcement proceedings and while corresponding with examiners during prosecution.

72. *Id.*

73. 344 F.3d at 1370, 68 USPQ2d at 1328–29.

74. 122 S.Ct. at 1839–40.

75. *See* John R. Thomas, *On Preparatory Texts and Proprietary Technologies: The Place of Prosecution Histories in Patent Claim Interpretation*, 47 UCLA L. Rev. 183 (1999).

8.2.2.3.4 The Public Dedication Doctrine

In its 2002 decision in *Johnson & Johnston Associates, Inc. v. R.E. Service Co., Inc.*,[76] the *en banc* Federal Circuit recognized an additional limit upon the doctrine of equivalents. Under the *Johnson & Johnston* "public dedication doctrine," subject matter that is disclosed in a patent, but not claimed, may not subsequently be appropriated in infringement litigation through the doctrine of equivalents. Such unclaimed subject matter is considered to have been deliberately disclaimed and therefore dedicated to the public.

The *Johnson & Johnston* case involved a recurring situation: sometimes the claims of a patent are not as broad as the technical disclosure contained in that patent's written description. The patent at issue in that case, owned by Johnson & Johnston, concerned a printed circuit board. A printed circuit board is a thin plate on which computer chips or other electronic components are placed. The patent's specification explained that the substrate of the circuit board could be manufactured of a number of materials, including aluminum, steel and nickel. However, the patent's claims were limited to a substrate made of aluminum. Accused infringer R.E. Service manufactured printed circuit boards with a steel substrate.

Prior to *Johnson & Johnston*, competing views existed as to the impact of described, yet unclaimed subject matter upon the doctrine of equivalents. One possibility is that disclosure within the patent instrument acts in favor of a finding of equivalency. Under this perspective, the patent as a whole provides notice to interested competitors as to what the patentee regarded as an equivalent at the time the patent was granted.

At the other extreme, as represented by the 1996 Federal Circuit decision in *Maxwell v. J. Baker, Inc.*,[77] is the position that subject matter disclosed but not claimed in a patent application is, as a matter of law, dedicated to the public. Under this view, by failing to claim the full extent of the disclosed subject matter, an applicant deprives the PTO of the opportunity to consider whether this subject matter is patentable. This is because only the precise claim language is evaluated against the prior art. Allowing an applicant to obtain narrow claims from the PTO, and then to assert broader protection for unclaimed alternatives described in the specification, would defeat the fundamental principle that a patent's claims define its scope of proprietary rights.

76. 285 F.3d 1046, 62 USPQ2d 1225 (Fed.Cir.2002).

77. 86 F.3d 1098, 39 USPQ2d 1001 (Fed.Cir.1996), *cert. denied*, 520 U.S. 1115, 117 S.Ct. 1244, 137 L.Ed.2d 327 (1997).

A third position, adopted by the 1998 Federal Circuit opinion in *YBM Magnex, Inc. v. International Trade Commission*,[78] was that no *per se* rule should dictate whether subject matter included in the written description but not claimed is equivalent to the claimed invention. Proponents of this view emphasized that the doctrine of equivalents seeks to establish a just balance between providing competitors with notice of what is patented, and the judicial responsibility to avoid a "fraud on the patent" based on insubstantial changes from the patented invention. On this view, whether the accused infringement was disclosed, but not claimed in the asserted patent simply formed one of many factors to consider in the equivalency determination.

The *en banc* Federal Circuit resolved its inconsistent precedent in *Johnson & Johnston* by adopting *Maxwell* and expressly overruling *YBM Magnex*. The Federal Circuit reasoned that allowing the doctrine of equivalents to extend to disclosed, but unclaimed subject matter would conflict with the primacy of the claims in defining the scope of the patentee's exclusive right. Otherwise patent applicants would be encouraged to present a broad disclosure in the specification of the application and file narrow claims, avoiding examination of broader claims that the applicant could have filed consistent with the specification. Applying this principle to the facts of the case, the Federal Circuit concluded that R.E. Service did not infringe the Johnson & Johnston patent under the doctrine of equivalents because a steel substrate, having been disclosed but not claimed in the patent instrument, could not thereafter be considered an equivalent of an aluminum substrate.

The holding of *Johnson & Johnston* is reminiscent of a similar argument that the Supreme Court recently reviewed and rejected. In *Warner–Jenkinson v. Hilton Davis Chemical Co.*,[79] the accused infringer contended that the doctrine of equivalents should be limited to equivalents disclosed within the patent instrument. The Supreme Court expressly rejected this proposition.[80] The *Warner–Jenkinson* holding that the doctrine of equivalents is not limited to disclosed, unclaimed elements appears at odds with the *Johnson & Johnston* holding that all disclosed, unclaimed elements are not equivalents *per se*. As apparently neither party in *Johnson & Johnston* filed a petition for certiorari, this issue remains an open question.

In the wake of the *Johnson & Johnston* decision, patent applicants have been encouraged to draft claims with increasing

78. 145 F.3d 1317, 46 USPQ2d 1843 (Fed.Cir.1998), *overruled by*, Johnson & Johnston Associates, Inc. v. R.E. Service Co., 285 F.3d 1046, 62 USPQ2d 1225 (Fed.Cir.2002).

79. 520 U.S. 17, 117 S.Ct. 1040, 137 L.Ed.2d 146 (1997). *See supra* § 8.2.2.2.

80. 520 U.S. at 37.

care. Commentators have proposed that applicants draft a broad generic claim as well as more specific claims to each embodiment that can be envisioned. The Federal Circuit itself offered suggestions for parties who had not anticipated the holding of the *Johnson & Johnston* case. According to the court, if subject matter had been disclosed but not claimed, affected individuals could: (1) in cases where a patent had already issued, pursue a broadening reissue procedure; or (2) if the patent was still in prosecution at the PTO, file a continuing application or otherwise amend the claims.[81] Because the Patent Act prohibits the commencement of broadening reissue procedures more than two years after a patent has issued, however, neither of these suggestions is of much use to owners of patents that issued more than two years prior to the *Johnson & Johnston* opinion.[82] Most apparent is the Federal Circuit has introduced a significant restraint upon the doctrine of equivalents—one that will require patent applicants to craft claims with increasing precision.

8.2.2.4 The Reverse Doctrine of Equivalents

In its *Graver Tank* opinion, the Supreme Court recognized a version of the doctrine of equivalents that may act against—rather than in favor of—the interest of the patentee.[83] When an accused product or process is literally covered by the words of a patent claim, but is "so far changed in principle" that it performs in a "substantially different way," the court may reach a finding of noninfringement. The so-called "reverse doctrine of equivalents" amounts to a defense to literal infringement. Although the reverse doctrine is equitable in nature, whether an accused technology goes sufficiently outside the principles of the patented invention is a question of fact.[84]

The reverse doctrine of equivalents has been of greater interest to scholars than to the courts.[85] The Federal Circuit has termed the reverse doctrine of equivalents an "anachronistic exception, long mentioned but rarely applied,"[86] and has yet to apply this principle squarely in any of its cases. Given this paucity of precedent, it is more important to recognize situations where the reverse doctrine does not apply. One such case is where a defendant merely puts a claimed invention towards a new use.

81. 285 F.3d at 1055, 62 USPQ2d at 1231. Reissue applications are discussed *supra* at § 7.5.3, while continuing applications are taken up *supra* at § 7.2.4.

82. *See supra* § 7.5.5.3.

83. 339 U.S. at 608–09.

84. *See* SRI Int'l v. Matsushita Elec. Corp., 775 F.2d 1107, 227 USPQ 577 (Fed.Cir.1985).

85. *See* Robert P. Merges & Richard R. Nelson, *On the Complex Economics of Patent Scope*, 90 COLUM. L. REV. 839 (1990).

86. Tate Access Floors, Inc. v. Interface Architectural Resources, Inc., 279 F.3d 1357, 1368, 61 USPQ2d 1647 (Fed. Cir.2002).

For example, suppose that the Major Drug Company holds a patent claiming a chemical composition and a method of using the composition to cure hypertension. An independent researcher named Harry Hirsute discovers that the compound also prevents male pattern baldness, a previously unknown use. If Hirsute manufactures the compound, then he has undoubtedly infringed the Major Drug Company patent. The reverse doctrine of equivalents would not apply even if Hirsute intends to sell the compound only to balding men with normal blood pressure, and even if his invention is separately patentable as a process.[87]

The reverse doctrine of equivalents was instead intended to apply to extraordinary cases. It provides courts with something of an escape hatch, useful when a finding of literal infringement would work an unwarranted extension of the claims. The reverse doctrine might pertain to rapidly progressing fields of high technology, where radical subsequent advances allow predecessor patents to appropriate subject matter entirely beyond the scope of their technical contribution. Such circumstances appear so uncommon that, in its two decades of existence, the Federal Circuit has yet to encounter them.

8.2.2.5 Equivalents Under § 112 ¶ 6

Recall that the sixth paragraph of § 112 provides a mandatory procedure for interpreting functional claims.[88] Under that provision, if a claim element is drafted as a means for performing a specified function, readers must construe that claim element as covering "the corresponding structure, material, or acts described in the specification and equivalents thereof." Expressed differently, the reader must review the patent specification to find the specific structure that performs to the claimed function. The claim element should be understood to provide literal coverage of the expressly described structure along with "equivalents thereof."

The extent of the "equivalents thereof" under § 112 ¶ 6 continues to confound all who confront this issue. Not only have decades of experience failed to provide a sharp definition of the doctrine of equivalents, the patent law does not readily yield alternative conceptions of equivalency. Like the general doctrine of equivalents, § 112 ¶ 6 equivalence must focus upon the substantiality of the differences between the claimed element and a component of the accused product. Still, the Supreme Court's treatment of

87. Bear in mind that Hirsute could *get a patent* on the method of using the drug as a baldness cure. However he, and everyone else, could not *practice that method* without obtaining a license from Major Drug, because manufacturing the drug would infringe its previously issued patent.

88. *See supra* § 6.2.2.2.

§ 112 ¶ 6 in *Warner–Jenkinson* requires that some distinction exist between these two notions of equivalency.[89]

A Federal Circuit opinion subsequent to *Warner–Jenkinson*, *Al–Site Corp. v. VSI International, Inc.*,[90] presents the most thoughtful attempt to delineate the scope of § 112 ¶ 6 equivalents. There, Judge Rader identified three differences between the general common law doctrine of equivalents and § 112 ¶ 6 equivalents. The first is a matter of timing. Under *Warner–Jenkinson*, the proper time for evaluating insubstantial differences under the doctrine of equivalents is at the time of infringement. However, an equivalent under § 112 ¶ 6 cannot embrace technology developed after the time the patent issues because the PTO fixes the literal meaning of the claims at that time. Therefore, an "after-arising" technology could infringe under the doctrine of equivalents without being considered a § 112 ¶ 6 equivalent.

For example, suppose that Professor Bean obtains a patent on a new method of making artificial vanilla. Bean's patent claims in part call for "means for catalyzing" a chemical reaction. The specification of Bean's patent explains that the "means for catalyzing" should consist of Compound X, which at the time is the only chemical suitable for this purpose. Five years after the patent issues, scientists synthesize a new compound, Compound Y, which could also be used as a means for catalyzing the patented vanilla-making reaction. If one of Bean's competitors began making artificial vanilla using Compound Y, Bean would be unable to claim infringement upon § 112 ¶ 6. Instead, Bean must turn to the common law doctrine of equivalents.

Second, a § 112 ¶ 6 equivalent must perform the identical function recited in the claim element. This identity is required because § 112 ¶ 6 implicates literal infringement, and the function performed by the means-plus-function element is expressly recited in the claim. Thus, if a claim element called for "means for pushing," then the corresponding structure of the accused product must perform the function of pushing, rather than another function (such as rotating or pulling). In contrast, under the function-way-result test, the doctrine of equivalents may be satisfied when the function performed by the accused device is only substantially the same as that of the claimed invention.

Finally, the *Al–Site* court employed the term "structural equivalents" in connection with § 112 ¶ 6. This wording appears to demand an equivalency comparison that exclusively concerns physical structure. Under this view, § 112 ¶ 6 provides a scope of equivalents far more narrow than that of the doctrine of equiva-

89. *See* 520 U.S. at 27.

90. 174 F.3d 1308, 50 USPQ2d 1161 (Fed.Cir.1999).

lents. Suppose, for example, that a patent claimed a "means for securing said engine to said frame." The corresponding portion of the specification describes the use of bolts to attach the frame to the engine. Although nails and screws have the same structure as bolts, such well-known securing mechanisms as adhesives or magnets do not. Professor Mark Janis has observed that such a cramped claim coverage is little more than a subterfuge for no equivalency.[91] As the term "structural equivalents" does not appear in § 112 ¶ 6, this interpretation can also be faulted as being unfaithful to the statutory text.

91. *See* Mark Janis, *Who's Afraid of Functional Claims? Reforming the Patent Law's § 112 ¶ 6 Jurisprudence*, 15 Santa Clara Computer & High Tech. L.J. 231 (1999).

Chapter 9

REMEDIES FOR PATENT INFRINGEMENT

Table of Sections

The Patent Act sets forth the remedies a patentee may obtain upon a finding of infringement. These remedies include injunctions, monetary damages, and attorney fees. The statute also allows for damages to be increased by up to three times in exceptional cases of willful infringement. The Patent Act does not provide for criminal sanctions for violation of patent rights, nor does it allow the patentee to obtain so-called "statutory damages" in the fashion of the copyright law.

§ 9.1 Injunctions

Section 283 allows courts to "grant injunctions in accordance with the principles of equity to prevent the violation of any right secured by patent, on such terms as the court deems reasonable."[1] In practice courts routinely grant permanent injunctions to patentees that prevail in infringement litigation.[2] Logically enough, any injunction awarded under the Patent Act must end on the same

§ 9.1

1. 35 U.S.C.A. § 283 (2000).

2. *See* Richardson v. Suzuki Motor Co., 868 F.2d 1226, 9 USPQ2d 1913 (Fed.Cir.1989).

date that the patent expires.[3]

In some rare cases, however, the courts have elected not to award a permanent injunction to a prevailing patentee. In the amusingly captioned 1934 decision in *City of Milwaukee v. Activated Sludge*, the Court of Appeals for the Seventh Circuit refused to grant an injunction against infringement of a patented method for sewage treatment. Had the city of Milwaukee been prevented from using the patented invention, it would have been required to dump large quantities of raw sewage into Lake Michigan. Observing that "the health and the lives of more than half a million people are involved," the court denied the requested injunction. Because the patentee still obtained judicially determined monetary remedies against the city of Milwaukee, this outcome essentially amounted to an award of a compulsory license.

Another notable case, the 1944 decision in *Vitamin Technologists, Inc. v. Wisconsin Alumni Research Foundation*,[4] involved a patent claiming a method of irradiating foods to increase Vitamin D content. This treatment helped eliminate the debilitating Vitamin D deficiency disease called rickets. The availability of Vitamin D-enhanced margarine was particularly important to the poor, who were better able to afford margarine as compared to butter. The patentee had refused to license the patent to margarine producers, however, apparently because it was associated with the dairy industry. The Court of Appeals for the Ninth Circuit ultimately held the asserted patents invalid or unenforceable on the grounds of anticipation, claim definiteness, and laches. However, the court also discussed the concept that injunctions should be refused where they act against public health interests.

Cases like *City of Milwaukee* and *Vitamin Technologists* have been rare events in the U.S. patent law. In a contemporary world where the lay public has grown increasingly concerned with access to patented medicines, however, judicial refusals to grant permanent injunctions in cases implicating public health, safety, or environmental concerns remain an open possibility. Other courts have taken a different route by delaying the effective date of a permanent injunction rather than refusing it altogether. For example, in *Schneider (Europe) AG v. SciMed Life Systems, Inc.*,[5] the adjudicated infringer marketed a rapid-exchange catheter used by surgeons. Although the court concluded that no evidence of record supported a finding that the infringing product was more safe or objectively superior to other catheters on the market, the court recognized that

3. *See* Kearns v. Chrysler Corp., 32 F.3d 1541, 31 USPQ2d 1746 (Fed.Cir. 1994), *cert. denied*, 514 U.S. 1032, 115 S.Ct. 1392, 131 L.Ed.2d 244 (1995).

4. 146 F.2d 941, 64 USPQ 285 (9th Cir. 1944).

5. 852 F.Supp. 813 (D.Minn.1994).

some physicians did strongly prefer the infringing product.[6] The court opted to grant a permanent injunction with a delay of one year from the entry of judgment. The court reasoned that this year-long transition period would allow surgeons to switch from the infringing product with a minimum of disruption, at least in comparison with the immediate imposition of an injunction. The court further provided that the patentee would receive a 15% royalty rate during the transition period.

A patentee may also obtain a preliminary injunction against an accused infringer. Courts assess the traditional four factors when considering whether to grant such an injunction. The factors are typically stated as: (1) the probability of success on the merits; (2) the possibility of irreparable harm to the patentee if the injunction is not granted; (3) the balance of hardships between the parties; and (4) the public interest.[7]

Prior to the creation of the Federal Circuit, the trial courts were disinclined to award preliminary injunctions in patent cases. Concern over the reliability of PTO procedures was the usual reason given for their reluctance.[8] Since its creation, the Federal Circuit has eased this restrictive posture. Observing that patent terms are finite and patent litigation notoriously prolonged, the court has stated that when the patentee makes a clear showing of validity and infringement, the court should presume irreparable harm will result from denial of the injunction.[9] Contemporary district courts have also increasingly identified a strong public interest in the protection of patent rights.[10]

§ 9.2 Damages

The Patent Act succinctly provides for the award of damages "adequate to compensate for the infringement, but in no event less than a reasonable royalty for the use made of the invention by the infringer."[1] In practice, patentees seek lost profits as damages when they are able to make the required showing. Otherwise a reasonable royalty serves as the default measure of damages. If a patentee can demonstrate its entitlement to award of lost profits on some, but not all of the infringer's sales, the court may stipulate a mixed

6. *Id.* at 850–51.

7. *See* H.H. Robertson Co. v. United States Steel Deck, Inc., 820 F.2d 384, 2 USPQ2d 1926 (Fed. Cir. 1987).

8. *See* Chemical Engineering Corp. v. Marlo, Inc., 754 F.2d 331, 222 USPQ 738 (Fed.Cir.1984).

9. *See* Smith International, Inc. v. Hughes Tool Corp., 718 F.2d 1573, 219 USPQ 686 (Fed.Cir.), *cert. denied*, 464 U.S. 996, 104 S.Ct. 493, 78 L.Ed.2d 687 (1983).

10. *See, e.g.,* California Medical Prods. Inc. v. Emergency Medical Prods., Inc., 796 F.Supp. 640, 648, 24 USPQ2d 1205, 1211 (D.R.I.1992).

§ 9.2

1. 35 U.S.C.A.§ 284 (2000).

award of lost profits on the qualifying sales, with a reasonable royalty serving as the basis for compensation on the others.

The Patent Act limits monetary recovery to events occurring within the six years prior to the filing of the complaint or counterclaim for patent infringement.[2] For example, suppose that Professor Gizmo procured a patent on a method of refurbishing metal tools on April 1, 1994. Suppose further that Dr. Nefarious began using Gizmo's patented invention on March 15, 1995. Gizmo files suit for infringement on March 15, 2005. Although Nefarious has practiced the patented invention for a full decade, the period for which Gizmo may recover infringement damages commences on March 15, 1999, six years before he filed his complaint. He will be unable to secure any compensation for Nefarious's sales during the period from 1995 through 1999. Courts ordinarily award prejudgment interest in order to afford the patentee full compensation for the infringement during that six-year period, however.[3]

9.2.1 Reasonable Royalties

The patent statute provides that the award of damages to a prevailing patentee shall be no less than a reasonable royalty.[4] To determine this amount, the courts indulge in the legal fiction of a hypothetical licensing negotiation.[5] The reasonable royalty is set to the rate a willing patent owner and willing licensee would have decided upon had they negotiated the license on the date the infringement began.[6]

To determine the outcome of this fictional negotiation, the courts consider many elements. The often cited opinion in *Georgia-Pacific Corp. v. United States Plywood Corp.* provides an extensive list.[7] If the patentee has actually licensed the patent in suit to others, the actual royalty rate charged is, naturally enough, the most influential factor.[8] Other factors include the rate paid by the infringer to license a comparable patent; the effect of selling the patented invention in promoting other sales; the advantages of the patented invention; the availability of noninfringing substitutes; the infringer's expected profits; and industry licensing practices.

2. 35 U.S.C.A. § 286 (2000).

3. *See* General Motors Corp. v. Devex Corp., 461 U.S. 648, 103 S.Ct. 2058, 76 L.Ed.2d 211 (1983).

4. 35 U.S.C.A. § 284 (2000).

5. *See* Minco, Inc. v. Combustion Engineering, Inc., 95 F.3d 1109, 1119, 40 USPQ2d 1001, 1008–09 (Fed.Cir.1996).

6. *See* Unisplay, S.A. v. American Elec. Sign Co., 69 F.3d 512, 518, 36 USPQ2d 1540, 1545 (Fed.Cir.1995).

7. 318 F.Supp. 1116, 166 USPQ 235 (S.D.N.Y.1970), *modified and aff'd*, 446 F.2d 295, 170 USPQ 369 (2d Cir.), *cert. denied*, 404 U.S. 870, 92 S.Ct. 105, 30 L.Ed.2d 114 (1971).

8. *See* Unisplay, S.A. v. American Elec. Sign Co., 69 F.3d 512, 519, 36 USPQ2d 1540, 1545 (Fed.Cir.1995).

Even this brief description should indicate that the calculation of reasonable royalties is not an exact science. District courts necessarily engage in a good deal of approximation when determining a reasonable royalty rate, and the Federal Circuit affords them considerable discretion in doing so.[9] However, the rate that is ultimately chosen must be supported by evidence of record rather than amount to mere speculation.[10]

9.2.2 Lost Profits

A patentee is entitled to an award of damages equal to its lost profits if it can demonstrate a sufficient causal connection between the infringement and the unearned profits. The tests of "but for" and "proximate" causation, common to tort law, govern this inquiry. The patentee must demonstrate that "but for" the infringement, he would have earned additional profits. In addition, the infringement must have been a proximate cause of the lost profits. Generally speaking, this standard assesses whether the lost profits were a reasonably foreseeable consequence of the infringement, rather than being indirect, removed or remote.

It is important to remember that a qualifying owner of a utility patent recovers its own lost profits, rather than the profits that the infringer made. Under the 1952 Patent Act, an award of damages for infringement of a utility patent serves to compensate the patentee, rather than disgorge profits earned by the infringer.[11] However, in what can only be described as an unusual exception to this rule, the Patent Act does allow proprietors of design patents to opt for an "additional remedy" consisting of the infringer's profits.[12]

9.2.2.1 "But For" Causation

In order to demonstrate entitlement to lost profits damages, the patentee must reasonably demonstrate that, "but for" the infringement, it would have made the sales consummated by the infringer.[13] When the patentee and the infringer are the only actors in the relevant market, the courts will ordinarily infer "but for" causation.[14] Another mechanism for demonstrating causation is the

9. *See* Endress + Hauser, Inc. v. Hawk Measurement Sys. Pty. Ltd., 122 F.3d 1040, 1043, 43 USPQ2d 1849, 1852 (Fed.Cir.1997).

10. *See* King Instruments Corp. v. Perego, 65 F.3d 941, 952, 36 USPQ2d 1129, 1137 (Fed.Cir.1995), *reh'g denied*, 72 F.3d 855 (Fed.Cir.1995).

11. *See* Kori Corp. v. Wilco Marsh Buggies and Draglines, Inc., 761 F.2d 649, 654, 225 USPQ 985, 988 (Fed.Cir.), *cert. denied*, 474 U.S. 902, 106 S.Ct. 230, 88 L.Ed.2d 229 (1985).

12. 35 U.S.C.A. § 289 (2000).

13. *See* Kearns v. Chrysler Corp., 32 F.3d 1541, 1551, 31 USPQ2d 1746, 1754 (Fed.Cir.1994), *cert. denied*, 514 U.S. 1032, 115 S.Ct. 1393, 131 L.Ed.2d 244 (1995).

14. *See* Lam, Inc. v. Johns–Manville Corp., 718 F.2d 1056, 1068, 219 USPQ 670, 678 (Fed.Cir.1983).

well-known standard set forth in *Panduit Corp. v. Stahlin Brothers Fibre Works, Inc.*[15] Under *Panduit*, the patentee must show that (1) the patented product was in demand; (2) no acceptable noninfringing substitute was available; (3) the patentee or its licensees possessed the manufacturing and marketing capability to exploit the demand; and (4) the amount of profit the patentee would have made.

Patentees may satisfy the first *Panduit* factor by offering evidence from which a court can infer demand for the patented invention. Ordinarily patentees submit evidence of the infringer's sales to demonstrate demand.[16] This factor is rarely an issue during litigation. After all, if no demand existed for the patented invention, then there would be no infringement at all. The Federal Circuit has observed, however, that the method of showing demand through infringer sales presumes that the patent owner and infringer compete in the same market for the same customers.[17] In the event that the products of the patentee and infringer significantly differ in terms of price and/or product characteristics, the infringer's customers would not necessarily purchase from the patentee instead of the infringer. In this sort of case, evidence of an infringer's sales would not necessarily demonstrate demand for the patentee's product.

The second *Panduit* factor, concerning the availability of acceptable noninfringing substitutes, is of greater importance in damages trials. From a logical perspective, if there are noninfringing alternatives available in the marketplace, customers might have purchased those rather than the patented item from the patentee, thereby destroying the inference of lost profit resulting from the infringement. As a result, in order to obtain an award of lost profits, the patentee must show that there are no available noninfringing products that are acceptable substitutes for the patented invention. While weighing this factor, the Federal Circuit has stressed that the mere existence of a competing product on the market does not demonstrate that it is an acceptable noninfringing substitute. Instead, the product must have offered the beneficial attributes of the patented invention. A product that does not offer the advantages of the patented inventions, or is sold at a disparately higher price, will not be judged an acceptable noninfringing substitute.[18]

15. 575 F.2d 1152, 197 USPQ 726 (6th Cir.1978).

16. Gyromat Corp. v. Champion Spark Plug Co., 735 F.2d 549, 552, 222 USPQ 4 (Fed. Cir. 1984).

17. Bic Leisure Products v. Windsurfing Int'l, 1 F.3d 1214, 27 USPQ2d 1671 (Fed. Cir. 1993).

18. Uniroyal, Inc. v. Rudkin–Wiley Corp., 939 F.2d 1540, 1545–46, 19 USPQ2d 1432 (Fed. Cir. 1991).

Traditionally the Federal Circuit has stated that in order to be considered an acceptable non-infringing substitute, the competing product must actually be on the market at the time of the infringement. For example, in *Zygo Corp. v. Wyko Corp.*,[19] the court observed that "it is axiomatic ... that if a device is not available for purchase, a defendant cannot argue that the device is an acceptable noninfringing alternative." Under this view, a competing technology that was described in another patent or journal article, but was not sold on the market during the period of infringement, would not qualify as a non-infringing substitute.

However, the Federal Circuit's 1999 opinion in *Grain Processing Corp. v. American Maize–Products Co.*,[20] relaxed this strict posture. In that case, Grain Processing asserted that American Maize's "Lo–Dex 10" product infringed its patent on food additives. American Maize had sold Lo–Dex 10 from the time Grain Processing purchased its patent in 1979 through November 1991, the date the patent expired. However, it is important to note that American Maize employed four different production processes for manufacturing Lo–Dex 10 during this period of time. The litigants agreed that the last of these manufacturing techniques, termed "Process IV," resulted in a product that did not infringe Grain Processing's patent.

At trial, the parties disagreed whether lost profits or reasonable royalties were the most appropriate measure of damages for the Lo–Dex 10 resulting from earlier processes. Grain Processing contended that because American Maize had not employed Process IV until April 1991, Process IV should not count as an acceptable noninfringing substitute. American Maize in turn argued that it needed no new equipment to practice Process IV, and in fact required only two weeks to experiment with and perfect Process IV. The district court sided with American Maize, concluding that Process IV Lo–Dex 10 was a noninfringing substitute available the date Grain Processing purchased the patent. As a result, Grain Processing obtained a 3% royalty, rather than lost profits, as damages to compensate for American Maize's infringing sales. Grain Processing then appealed to the Federal Circuit.

In its opinion, the Federal Circuit explained that in order to obtain lost profits, the patentee must show a reasonable probability that he would have made the asserted sales "but for" the infringement. This assessment must account for alternative actions the infringer would have taken had he not infringed, according to the court. Judge Rader observed that without the infringing product or process, the infringer would likely offer an acceptable non-infring-

19. 79 F.3d 1563, 1571, 38 USPQ2d 1281 (Fed. Cir. 1996).

20. 185 F.3d 1341, 51 USPQ2d 1556 (Fed. Cir. 1999).

ing substitute, if available, rather than exit the market. As a result, a court must compare the patented invention with its next-best available alternative to determine the market value of the patent. Applying this reasoning to the case at hand, Judge Rader observed that American Maize had the ability to switch to Process IV at virtually a moment's notice. The Federal Circuit found no clear error in the district court's findings that American Maize had all the necessary materials, know-how and experience to use Process IV at any time during the life of the '194 patent. As a result, the Federal Circuit affirmed.

Following *Grain Processing*, then, to be an acceptable non-infringing substitute, a product or process must either have been available or on the market at the time of the infringement. An adjudicated infringer will have an easier time proving the availability of a substitute if it is readily available commercially. However, if the infringer can show that if all the equipment, knowledge, and expertise to produce the substitute were available in the field, then he can also avoid liability for lost profits.

The third *Panduit* factor requires the patent owner to show that it, or its licensees, possessed the manufacturing and marketing capability to exploit the demand. Simply put, the patent proprietor (plaintiff in the infringement suit), must add the infringer's sales to its own, and then demonstrate that it possessed the ability to supply the total demand had the infringement not occurred. In order to satisfy the third *Panduit* factor, the patentee has been allowed to demonstrate its ability to expand its existing capabilities by subcontracting, increasing the number of shifts in its manufacturing facilities, and by expanding its facilities to meet the heightened demand.[21]

The final factor of the *Panduit* test requires the patentee to prove the amount of profit it would have made. This is not a causation standard at all, but rather states the actual measure of the damages award itself. The most common way of determining the patentee's lost profits is to multiply (1) the number of infringing products sold by the infringer by (2) the patent owner's profit per unit on its own sales. The multiplied product of these two numbers sets the lost profits that the patentee would have made on the infringer's sales.

9.2.2.2 Proximate Causation

"But for" causation is a necessary but insufficient condition to establish entitlement to lost profits damages for patent infringe-

21. Ristvedt–Johnson, Inc. v. Brandt, Inc., 805 F.Supp. 557, 562 (N.D. Ill. 1992).

ment. Once it is established that the infringement has, in fact, been one of the causes of the patentee's lost profit damages, the question remains whether the infringer should be legally responsible for those damages. This requirement equates with the traditional tort law concept of "proximate cause."

In the patent law, the proximate cause inquiry has focused upon whether the lost profits were reasonably foreseeable, rather than indirect, removed or remote. The Federal Circuit has explained that not every injury of which the patentee complains may be the type the patent laws were designed to remedy. For example, if the patentee is so shocked to learn of the infringement that he suffers a heart attack, he is not entitled to claim damages for his medical misfortune under the Patent Act. Although this sort of harm is traceable to the infringement, the courts would find this injury too remote to justify compensation under the patent laws.[22]

In the leading decision of *Rite–Hite Corp. v. Kelley Co.*,[23] the Federal Circuit considered proximate cause concepts in awarding patent damages. The factual setting of this case was complex. Plaintiff Rite–Hite sold two sorts of "vehicle restraints," which are used to secure trucks to loading docks to prevent accidents during the loading and unloading process. Rite–Hite initially sold the "Automatic Dok–Lok Model 100," known as the ADL–100. Later, Rite–Hite introduced the Manual Dok–Lok Model 55, known as the MDL–55, which sold for about one-third the price of the ADL–100. Rite–Hite procured patents pertaining to both products. Among them was U.S. Patent No. 4,373,847, which claimed a releasable hook that was found in the MDL–55 but not in the ADL–100.

Defendant Kelley also sold a vehicle restraint under the name "Truk Stop." The Truk Stop vehicle restraint was motorized and sold for a price comparable to the ADL–100. When Rite–Hite brought an infringement suit against Kelley, however, its infringement claim was based not upon any patent pertaining to the ADL–100. Rather, Rite–Hite contended that Kelley used the releasable hook claimed by the '847 patent, and which Rite–Hite embodied in the MDL–55.

The trial court found that the '847 patent was enforceable, not invalid and infringed by Kelley. In a controversial holding, the court also held that Rite–Hite could recover profits from sales of a product not covered by the patent in suit (the ADL–100) which were lost to competition from defendant's infringing product (the Truk Stop). Kelley then appealed to the Federal Circuit, contending that the patent statute does not provide for damages based upon products not covered by the patent in suit.

22. 56 F.3d 1538, 1546, 35 USPQ2d 1065, 1069 (Fed. Cir. 1995).

23. 56 F.3d 1538, 35 USPQ2d 1065 (Fed. Cir. 1995).

Sitting *en banc*, the Federal Circuit affirmed the district court's ruling. According to the majority, claims of patent infringement are subject to the same "but for" and proximate causation standards as are other tort claims. According to Judge Lourie, these standards allowed patent proprietors to recover damages for the reasonable, objectively foreseeable consequences of an infringement. The majority observed that the ADL–100 directly competed with the infringing Truk Stop. As a result, lost sales of the ADL–100 were reasonably foreseeable, and therefore damages on those sales were necessary to provide adequate compensation to the patentee.

A strong dissent by Judge Nies took issue with the majority's holding. The dissent expressed concern over allowing a patentee to recover damages based on products not covered by the patent in suit, but supposedly covered by additional, unlitigated patents. According to Judge Nies, the patentee's property right consisted of an exclusive market in the goods embodying the invention of the litigated patent. To constitute legal injury for which lost profits may be awarded, the dissent contended, the infringer must interfere with that express property grant, not the patentee's commercial affairs more generally.

Judge Nies' reasoning is quite compelling. In terms of remedies, at least, the *Rite–Hite* holding seems to import broader notions of unfair competition law into the patent system. One also wonders whether the patentee should have been able to demonstrate the second *Panduit* factor.[24] Unless this product doesn't count because it was available only from Rite–Hite, the ADL–100 itself would serve as an acceptable noninfringing substitute to the Truk Stop. At all events, future litigation will reveal the extent to which courts will allow recovery for other "reasonably foreseeable" injuries resulting from an infringement. Increases in a patentee's advertising expenses or reductions in the patentee's selling price due to an infringing competitor are likely among the foreseeable injuries for which compensation may be sought in the future.

9.2.2.3 The Entire Market Value Rule

While showings of "but for" and proximate causation ordinarily entitle the patent owner to an award of lost profits, the courts have faced two recurring situations where they will demand additional proof. Sometimes unpatented goods are sold alongside the patented product or process. Suppose that the owner of a photocopier patent sells not just photocopiers, but the paper used in the photocopier as well. The lost paper sales may actually be more financially harmful to the patentee than the lost sales of the

24. *See supra* § 9.2.2.1.

patented photocopier. Yet since the prior art has long since prevented anyone from patenting ordinary paper, the propriety of awarding damages for these so-called "derivative sales" is questionable.[25]

A related problem occurs when the infringing technology forms but one component of a larger commercial product or process. For example, suppose that an automobile manufacturer holds a patent on a rear view mirror. If that manufacturer obtains an infringement judgment against a competitor, the court will be hard-pressed to assess damages based on the purchase price of the entire automobile. Sales made simultaneously with the patented invention are termed "convoyed sales."[26]

The courts crafted the "entire market value rule" to address such circumstances. The entire market value rule allows patentees to claim damages for unpatented products sold alongside the patented invention if three relatively strict standards are met. First, the patented feature must form the basis for customer demand for the entire product or products sold.[27] Second, the patentee must reasonably anticipate the sale of the unpatented parts along with the patented component.[28] Finally, the Federal Circuit has imposed a requirement of functional relatedness. Unless the unpatented component operates together with the patented invention in the manner of a single machine, the patentee cannot obtain a damages award based upon that unpatented component.[29]

In the *Rite-Hite* case, discussed above, the *en banc* Federal Circuit also addressed the entire market value rule. Rite–Hite and Kelley often sold unpatented "dock levelers" along with their vehicle restraints. Dock levelers bridge the gap between the truck and the loading dock so that forklifts can pass safely. In addition to damages based upon Kelly's vehicle restraint sales, the trial court awarded Rite–Hite lost profits on Kelley's sales of dock levelers.

On appeal, a plurality of the *en banc* Federal Circuit reversed the trial court's ruling, holding that Rite–Hite failed to demonstrate that sales of the dock levelers were compensable in keeping with the entire market value rule. According to six of the twelve judges, past Federal Circuit cases had awarded patentees damages for unpatented components only when "the unpatented and patented

25. *See* Carborundum Co. v. Molten Metal Equip. Innovations, Inc., 72 F.3d 872, 882 n. 8, 37 USPQ2d 1169, 1175 n. 8 (Fed.Cir.1995).

26. *Id.*

27. *See* TWM Mfg. Co. v. Dura Corp., 789 F.2d 895, 901, 229 USPQ 525, 528 (Fed.Cir.), *cert. denied*, 479 U.S. 852, 107 S.Ct. 183, 93 L.Ed.2d 117 (1986).

28. *See* King Instrument Corp. v. Otari Corp., 767 F.2d 853, 226 USPQ 402 (Fed.Cir.1985), *cert. denied*, 475 U.S. 1016, 106 S.Ct. 1197, 89 L.Ed.2d 312 (1986).

29. Rite–Hite Corp. v. Kelley Co., 56 F.3d 1538, 35 USPQ2d 1065 (Fed.Cir.), *cert. denied*, 516 U.S. 867, 116 S.Ct. 184, 133 L.Ed.2d 122 (1995).

components together were considered to be components of a single assembly or parts of a complete machine.''[30] Applying this standard, Judge Lourie observed that the dock levelers and vehicle restraints could be used independently of one another. As selling the two products together was merely "a matter of convenience or business advantage,''[31] rather than due to their operation together as a functional unit, Rite–Hite could not recover damages on the dock levelers.

Although only six of the twelve Federal Circuit judges supported this "functional relatedness" standard for convoyed goods, subsequent Federal Circuit panels have nonetheless adopted that test as the governing rule.[32] As Judge Newman observed in her dissent, however, a comparison between the *Rite-Hite* court's discussion of proximate cause concepts and the entire market value rule suggests an inconsistency. The Federal Circuit majority had previously held that Rite–Hite could obtain damages based on lost ADL–100 sales because these lost sales were reasonably foreseeable. Surely lost sales of the dock levelers were reasonably foreseeable too, as both Rite–Hite and Kelley commonly installed them in loading docks at the same time as the vehicle restraints. Yet the Federal Circuit refused to award damages based upon the mechanical particularities of the two devices. One is left with the impression that Rite–Hite would have done better to draft a patent claim expressly reciting the combination of the vehicle restraint and dock leveler, or to encourage its product designers to increase the mechanical interaction between the two devices.

9.2.3 Marking

The Patent Act encourages patentees who make or sell embodiments of their patented invention to give notice to the public of their patent rights. Section 287(a) provides that patentees and their licensees should fix the word "patent" or the abbreviation "pat.", along with the number of the patent, on patented articles.[33] If the nature of the article does not allow this notice to be placed directly upon it, a label may be placed on the article or its packaging.

There is no absolute duty to mark. If the patentee or its licensees fail to mark in the specified manner, however, then damages are available only for acts occurring after the infringer receives actual notice of the infringement. The Federal Circuit has strictly construed the requirement of actual notice. Even if the infringer is already fully aware of the patent, the patentee must affirmatively communicate a specific charge of infringement to

30. 56 F.3d at 1550, 35 USPQ2d at 1073.

31. *Id.*

32. *See* Tec Air, Inc. v. Denso Mfg. Mich. Inc., 192 F.3d 1353, 1362, 52 USPQ2d 1294, 1299 (Fed. Cir. 1999).

33. 35 U.S.C.A. § 287(c) (2000).

trigger entitlement to damages.[34] The marking statute does provide that the filing of an infringement suit suffices to provide actual notice.[35]

Patentees who do not make or sell their invention have no duty to mark.[36] The marking requirement also does not apply to process claims, which by their very nature concern intangible behavior.[37] Other patentees, concerned with the expense and inconvenience of marking or desirous of surprising competitors, make the affirmative choice not to mark.

9.2.4 Provisional Rights

The Domestic Publication of Foreign Filed Patent Applications Act of 1999 created so-called "provisional rights." Provisional rights apply only to patent applications that were published during their pendency at the PTO. Under the Act, the provisional rights are fixed at an amount equal to a reasonable royalty, starting from the date the patent application was published. They may be obtained from anyone who makes, uses, sells, offers to sell, or imports into the United States the invention as claimed in a published patent application. Congress intended provisional rights to deter potential copyists from commercially exploiting inventions that have been claimed in published patent applications.

Although provisional rights extend from the time the PTO publishes the application until the date the PTO formally grants the patent, they may be invoked only when the patent issues. In other words, the inventor may not bring a patent infringement suit against an infringer until the date the patent actually issues. If the PTO decides not to grant the patent, then the patent applicant obtains no rights at all—thus the term "provisional rights." Also, under no circumstances do inventors gain patent rights against individuals who use their inventions prior to the date of pre-grant publication.

As codified in § 154(d), provisional rights are subject to two other important qualifications. First, the claims of the published application must be substantially identical to the claims of the issued patent for provisional rights to arise. Second, the infringer must have had actual notice of the published application in order to

34. *See* Amsted Industries Inc. v. Buckeye Steel Castings Co., 24 F.3d 178, 30 USPQ2d 1462 (Fed.Cir.1994); Devices for Medicine, Inc. v. Boehl, 822 F.2d 1062 (Fed. Cir. 1987).

35. 35 U.S.C.A. § 287(a) (2000).

36. *See* Wine Railway Appliance Co. v. Enterprise Railway Equip. Co., 297 U.S. 387, 56 S.Ct. 528, 80 L.Ed. 736 (1936).

37. *See* American Medical Sys., Inc. v. Medical Eng'g Corp., 6 F.3d 1523, 1538, 28 USPQ2d 1321, 1332 (Fed.Cir. 1993), *cert. denied*, 511 U.S. 1070, 114 S.Ct. 1647, 128 L.Ed.2d 366 (1994).

face liability under the provisional rights scheme.[38] Although the statute does not further define the term "actual notice," the legislative history reveals that the mere fact that the published application is available for viewing on a publicly available database will not meet this requirement. Instead, the "published applicant must give actual notice of the published application to the accused infringer and explain what acts are regarded as giving rise to provisional rights."[39]

Published patent applicants would also be wise to include in the "actual notice" a suggestion that the notice recipient cease its activities with respect to the products or processes claimed in the published application. Recall that in cases where patent owners do not mark their patented articles, the patent statute does not allow damages to be awarded prior to the date the infringer was given "actual notice." As noted above, the Federal Circuit has interpreted "actual notice" in this context as requiring a specific charge of infringement.[40] It is possible that the court might hold similarly in this context as well. As a result, it would be prudent to include an express demand that the notice recipient halt undesired activities in a purported "actual notice" of a pre-grant publication.

A hypothetical illustrates the workings of provisional rights. Suppose that on February 10, 2004, Dr. Julius Jolt files a patent application on an automated vending machine. On May 12, 2004, Jolt becomes aware that a competitor, Andrea Ohm, has commenced sales of the identical vending machine. The PTO publishes the Jolt application on September 1, 2005. On December 24, 2005, Ohm receives a letter from Jolt that (1) states the serial number of the published patent application; (2) identifies the specific models of Ohm vending machines believed to correspond to Jolt's published patent; (3) specifically explains why Ohm's machines are covered by Jolt's published patent claims; and (4) encourages Ohm to cease selling machines within the scope of Jolt's pending application. Jolt's application matures into an issued patent that the PTO grants on March 15, 2006, with claims that are identical to those provided in the pre-grant publication.

Under these circumstances, Jolt cannot file a patent infringement lawsuit against Ohm until the patent actually issues from the PTO—in this hypothetical, on March 15, 2006. Let us assume that Jolt sues Ohm on that day, and that the court rules that Jolt's patent is not invalid and infringed on July 1, 2007. In the event Ohm continues to sell the patented vending machine during the

38. 35 U.S.C.A. § 154(d) (2000).

39. Statements on Introduced Bills and Joint Resolution, S. 1948, Section-by-Section Analysis, Congressional Record, November 17, 1999, available at http://thomas.loc.gov.

40. *See supra* § 9.2.3.

course of litigation, Jolt's damage award would consist of two components. First, Jolt would be entitled to a reasonable royalty extending from the date of actual notice to Ohm of the pending application through the date just prior to patent issuance (December 24, 2005, through March 14, 2006). Second, Jolt could obtain the normal amount of monetary damages under the Patent Act—his own lost profits, if he can demonstrate entitlement to them, or otherwise a reasonable royalty—from the date the patent issued through the date of the judgment (March 15, 2006 through July 1, 2007).

Many readers have doubtlessly observed the legend "patent pending" on a variety of products and packaging. The phrase may mean that the manufacturer has filed a patent application pertaining to that product. The mere filing of a patent application ordinarily lacks legal significance for anyone except the applicant and the PTO, however. Until the patent issues, the applicant obtains no legally enforceable rights, and of course there is some chance that the PTO will refuse to issue a patent at all. The "patent pending" phrase also will not support an award of provisional rights, for as we have seen, the Patent Act requires an applicant to provide actual notice of the pending application to qualify for provisional rights. Use of "patent pending" is essentially a form of "self help" through which applicants warn others that a patent may be in the works. The phrase "patent pending" bears no relationship to the patent marking statute and, absent special circumstances, generally has no legal ramifications at all.

9.2.5 Enhanced Damages

Section 284 provides that the court "may increase the damages up to three times the amount found or assessed."[41] An award of enhanced damages, as well as the amount by which the damages will be increased, is committed to the discretion of the trial court.[42] Although the statute does not specify the circumstances in which enhanced damages are appropriate, the courts most commonly award them when the infringer acted in blatant disregard of the patentee's rights. This circumstance is termed "willful infringement."[43]

The Federal Circuit will not ordinarily enhance damages due to willful infringement if the adjudicated infringer did not know of the patent until charged with infringement in court, or if the infringer acted with the reasonable belief that the patent was not infringed

41. 35 U.S.C.A. § 284 (2000).

42. *See* Read Corp. v. Portec, Inc., 970 F.2d 816, 23 USPQ2d 1426 (Fed.Cir. 1992).

43. *See* Beatrice Foods Co. v. New England Printing & Lithographing Co., 923 F.2d 1576, 17 USPQ2d 1553 (Fed. Cir.1991).

or that it was invalid. Federal Circuit decisions emphasize the duty of someone with actual notice of a competitor's patent to exercise due care in determining if his acts will infringe that patent. This duty may be fulfilled by obtaining and observing competent legal advice before commencing, or continuing, activity that may infringe another's patent. The best practice appears to be the commissioning of an infringement and validity opinion from a member of the patent bar who is fully conversant with the patent law; has familiarized herself with the patent, its prosecution history, and the pertinent prior art; and is knowledgeable of the products or processes that might be accused of infringement.[44]

In *Read Corp. v. Portec, Inc*,[45] the Federal Circuit explained that the most important consideration in willful infringement cases is the egregiousness of the defendant's conduct based on all the facts and circumstances. In judging whether to award enhanced damages or not, the courts consider whether the infringer investigated the scope of the patent and formed a good faith belief that it was invalid or not infringed. Prompt, competent advice from a qualified patent attorney significantly decreases the likelihood an infringement will be declared willful.[46] Other pertinent factors include whether the infringer deliberately copied from another, the infringer's behavior as a party to the litigation, the size and financial condition of the defendant, the closeness of the case, and the duration of the defendant's misconduct. Where willful infringement is found, the Federal Circuit explained, damages need not always be tripled. The trial court can increase them by a lesser amount, or not at all, depending upon the totality of the circumstances.

The wisdom of awarding enhanced damages in cases of patent infringement has been roundly debated. Critics of the policy believe that the possibility of trebled damages discourages individuals from reviewing issued patents. Out of fear that their inquisitiveness will result in multiple damages, innovators may simply avoid looking at patents until they are sued for infringement. To the extent this observation is correct, the law of willful infringement discourages the dissemination of technical knowledge, thereby thwarting one of the principal goals of the patent system. With willful infringement principles encouraging industry to seek out opinion letters of patent counsel, these developments have been likened to a "full employment act" for the patent bar. Fear of increased liability for willful

44. *See* Polaroid Corp. v. Eastman Kodak Co., 16 USPQ2d (BNA) 1481 (D. Mass. 1990), *modified*, 17 USPQ2d (BNA) 1711 (D. Mass. 1991).

45. 970 F.2d 816, 23 USPQ2d 1426 (Fed.Cir.1992).

46. *See* Underwater Devices Inc. v. Morrison–Knudsen Co., 717 F.2d 1380, 219 USPQ 569 (Fed.Cir.1983).

infringement may also discourage firms from performing the public service of challenging patents of dubious validity. Consequently some have argued that the patent system should shift to a "no-fault" regime of strictly compensatory damages, without regard to the state of mind of the adjudicated infringer.

9.2.6 Attorney Fees

Section 285 provides that the "court in exceptional cases may award reasonable attorney fees to the prevailing party."[47] As this language suggests, attorney fees are not routinely awarded to the victor of a patent infringement case. The purpose of § 285 is instead to reimburse a party who is forced to litigate an exceptional case.[48] The patentee may obtain an award of fees in cases of willful infringement, following the identical standard to that of enhanced damages.[49] Courts have also awarded attorney fees to defendants in cases where the patentee committed inequitable conduct or to either party when the opposing litigant engages in bad faith litigation.[50]

47. 35 U.S.C.A. § 285 (2000).

48. Mathis v. Spears, 857 F.2d 749, 8 USPQ2d 1551 (Fed. Cir. 1988).

49. *See* Avia Group Int'l, Inc. v. L.A. Gear California, Inc., 853 F.2d 1557, 1567, 7 USPQ2d 1548, 1556 (Fed.Cir. 1988).

50. Mahurkar v. C.R. Bard, Inc., 79 F.3d 1572, 1580, 38 USPQ2d 1288, 1292 (Fed.Cir.1996).

Chapter 10

PATENT LITIGATION

Table of Sections

Patent litigation is generally subject to the same standards that apply to all civil suits in federal courts. Such matters as discovery, exhibits, juries, motions, pleadings, presumptions, standards of proof, and witnesses are governed by broadly applicable legal principles found in sources such as the Federal Rules of Civil Procedure and the Federal Rules of Evidence. Although a detailed review of their application to patent cases would be appropriate for an advanced text on patent litigation, coverage of these materials exceeds the purposes of the overview treatment provided by this volume. The patent law has nonetheless developed a number of particularized enforcement rules based either upon patent-specific statutes or pointed judicial application of general principles within the patent context. This chapter reviews the more noteworthy of these litigation topics, including jurisdiction, venue, Federal Circuit choice of law, issue preclusion, and the defenses of laches and estoppel.

§ 10.1 Jurisdiction and Venue

10.1.1 Subject Matter Jurisdiction

28 U.S.C. § 1338(a) stipulates that the federal district courts "shall have original jurisdiction of any civil action arising under any Act of Congress relating to patents.... Such jurisdiction shall

be exclusive of the courts of the states in patent ... cases."[1] As a result, claims "arising under" the patent law may only be heard by the U.S. District Courts, which are the trial courts of the federal judicial system. It follows that such claims may not be litigated in state courts.

For the majority of cases, determining whether the cause of action "arises under" the patent laws is straightforward. A garden variety charge of patent infringement plainly arises under the Patent Act and must proceed in the federal district courts rather than in state court. Other sorts of cases may raise more difficult questions, however. For example, in the case of *Consolidated Kinetics Corp. v. Marshall, Neil, & Pauley, Inc.*,[2] the plaintiff and defendant had previously resolved a dispute by entering into a contract under which the defendant agreed not to market products covered by the plaintiff's patent. Following the formation of the contract, the defendant began to sell a new product that, in its view, did not infringe the plaintiff's patent. The patentee disagreed and ultimately filed a complaint in Washington state court claiming breach of contract.

In one sense, the dispute at hand in *Consolidated Kinetics Corp.* could be viewed as involving the interpretation of contracts. Of course, contract law is a traditional state law subject, so under this view the case was properly brought before the Washington court. However, the case could also be seen as involving important issues of federal patent law. If the defendant counterclaimed that the plaintiff's patent is invalid, the litigation could involve complex patent issues that ordinarily arise in the federal courts, such as claim interpretation and patentability standards.

To decide whether § 1338(a) applies, the courts follow the "well-pleaded complaint rule." Courts determine whether the plaintiff's complaint establishes that either (1) the federal patent law creates the cause of action, or (2) that the plaintiff's right to relief necessarily depends upon the resolution of a substantial question of federal patent law, in that patent law is a necessary element of one of the plaintiff's claims.[3] In *Consolidated Kinetics Corp.*, the Court of Appeals of Washington determined that the plaintiff had fashioned its cause of action as an alleged breach of contract. As a result, the state court had valid subject matter jurisdiction, even over such matters as patent validity. Similarly, a case concerning whether a purported assignment validly transferred certain patent applications sounds exclusively in contract law and therefore does

§ 10.1

1. 28 U.S.C. § 1338(a) (2000).

2. 521 P.2d 1209, 182 USPQ 434 (Wash. Ct. App. 1974).

3. Christianson v. Colt Indus. Operating Corp., 486 U.S. 800, 809 (1988).

not arise under § 1138(a).[4] Unless diversity jurisdiction exists, federal courts also lack jurisdiction over cases involving state antitrust laws or breach of contract claims.[5]

In contrast, a lawsuit that contested the inventorship of a particular patent would be judged to "arise under" the federal patent laws. Whether an individual qualifies as an inventor or not is an issue of substantive patent law.[6] Additionally, § 256 of the Patent Act expressly contemplates judicial correction of improper inventorship. As a result, the federal district courts possess jurisdiction over this sort of case under § 1338(a).

10.1.2 Supplemental Jurisdiction

Sometimes a plaintiff alleges both a patent law claim and additional claims based on state law. In this sort of case, the federal courts may have power to decide those additional claims under the doctrine of supplemental jurisdiction. 28 U.S.C.A. § 1338(b) provides that "the district courts shall have original jurisdiction of any civil action asserting a claim of unfair competition when joined with a substantial and related claim under the copyright, patent, plant variety protection or trade-mark laws." This provision gives the federal courts supplemental jurisdiction, but only over state claims that involve "unfair competition" and only when those claims are "related" to a federal intellectual property claim that is "substantial." While the language of this section might suggest that federal jurisdiction is mandatory when the various statutory tests are satisfied, the Federal Circuit has held that trial courts should still use discretion in determining whether or not to assume jurisdiction over an unfair competition claim.[7]

In administering this supplemental jurisdiction provision the courts have interpreted the concept of "unfair competition" broadly to include such matters as trade secret theft, conversion of intellectual property, and various forms of passing off and common law trademark infringement.[8] If the plaintiff's non-federal claims do not fall within the category of unfair competition, the plaintiff can still ask the federal court to take jurisdiction over them under the general doctrine of supplemental jurisdiction. In these circum-

4. Beghin–Say Int'l, Inc. v. Ole–Bendt Rasmussen, 733 F.2d 1568, 221 USPQ 1121 (Fed. Cir. 1984).

5. *See* Jim Arnold Corp. v. Hydrotech Sys., 109 F.3d 1567, 42 USPQ2d 1119 (Fed. Cir. 1997).

6. *See supra* § 7.3.

7. Verdegaal Bros. v. Union Oil Co., 750 F.2d 947, 950, 224 USPQ 249, 251 (Fed Cir.1984).

8. Mars Inc. v. Kabushiki–Kaisha Nippon Conlux, 24 F.3d 1368, 1372–73, 30 USPQ2d 1621, 1623 (Fed. Cir.1994) ("The common law concept of 'unfair competition' has not been confined to any rigid definition and encompasses a variety of types of commercial or business conduct considered 'contrary to good conscience,' including acts of trademark and trade dress infringement, false advertising, dilution, and trade secret theft . . . ")

stances non-federal claims must be "so related to claims in the action within such original jurisdiction that they form part of the same case or controversy...."[9] Put differently, to meet the standard of supplemental jurisdiction, the patent cause of action and the non-federal claim must both arise from a common nucleus of operative fact in order for them to be tried together.[10]

10.1.3 Personal Jurisdiction and Venue

As with other sorts of cases, in patent litigation personal jurisdiction depends upon the defendant possessing sufficient minimum contacts in the federal district in which the plaintiff brought the case. To determine whether the defendant has established minimum contacts with a forum, the Federal Circuit considers (1) whether the defendant purposefully directed activities at residents in the forum, (2) whether the cause of action or claim arises out of, or relates to, those activities, and (3) whether the assertion of personal jurisdiction in that forum is fair and reasonable.[11] This "minimum contacts" analysis rests upon general principles of constitutional law and civil procedure, the discussion of which exceeds the scope of this book.

The issue of venue raises particularized issues in patent litigation, however. That is because Congress enacted a special venue statute for patent infringement cases. Under 28 U.S.C. § 1400(b), venue is proper either: (1) in the judicial district where the defendant resides, or (2) where the defendant has committed acts of infringement and has a regular and established place of business. Individuals reside in the judicial district where they are domiciled. Prior to 1988, a corporation was viewed as residing in its state of incorporation.[12] The result was that, pre–1988, the patent venue statute was fairly restrictive, tending to move infringement litigation into the defendant's base of operations.

Following 1988 congressional amendments, venue became a much more flexible affair in patent litigation. That is because Congress adopted a new definition of "reside" as it applies to venue for corporate defendants. Under the new definition, a corporation is presumed to reside in any judicial district to which it could be subject to personal jurisdiction at the time the litigation commences. Although this change was codified in a separate provision, 28 U.S.C. § 1391, the Federal Circuit has held that this amendment should also be read into § 1400(b), the patent venue statute.[13]

9. *See* 28 U.S.C.A. § 1367 (2000).

10. *See* 3D Systems, Inc. v. Aarotech Labs., Inc., 160 F.3d 1373, 1377, 48 USPQ2d 1773, 1775 (Fed. Cir. 1998).

11. Akro Corp. v. Luker, 45 F.3d 1541, 1545–46, 33 USPQ2d 1505, 1508–09 (Fed. Cir. 1995).

12. Fourco Glass Co. v. Transmirra Prods. Corp., 353 U.S. 222 (1957).

13. VE Holding Corp. v. Johnson Gas Appliance Co., 917 F.2d 1574, 16 USPQ2d 1614 (Fed. Cir. 1990).

The result of these changes has been significant for corporate defendants, which of course constitute the great majority of defendants in patent litigation. Although § 1400(b) still governs venue in patent cases, few, if any plaintiffs rely upon the restrictive second prong of that section. Instead they base venue upon the "residence" requirement of the first prong—which now is entirely coterminous with personal jurisdiction, and which for larger corporations is likely to include every federal district in the country. For corporate defendants, then, the venue statute has essentially become superfluous, for the same standards governing personal jurisdiction also dictate whether a court is an appropriate venue or not. This, in turn, means that patent infringement plaintiffs can more often litigate in their home forum.

10.1.4 The Declaratory Judgments Act

Although of general applicability, the Declaratory Judgments Act plays a significant role in patent litigation. Under that Act:

> In a case of actual controversy within its jurisdiction, . . . any court of the United States, upon the filing of an appropriate pleading, may declare the rights and other legal relations of any interested party seeking such declaration, whether or not further relief is or could be sought. Any such declaration shall have the force and effect of a final judgment or decree and shall be reviewable as such.[14]

In the context of patents, the Act allows a potential defendant in a patent infringement suit to commence legal action, rather than wait for the patentee to file suit. The declaratory judgment action provides accused infringers with a remedy against a patentee that threatens patent infringement litigation yet never actually commences suit. Rather than suffer long periods of commercial uncertainty until the patentee takes action, the alleged infringer may take the initiative and file suit as a declaratory judgment plaintiff. Declaratory judgment actions also provide accused infringers with the strategic benefits of forum selection and control of the timing of the suit.

The key issue under the Declaratory Judgments Act is the presence of an "actual controversy." As the federal courts do not issue advisory opinions, the declaratory plaintiff must demonstrate that an actual controversy exists. The Federal Circuit pursues this inquiry through a two-part test. First, the declaratory plaintiff must actually produce or be prepared to produce an allegedly infringing product. Second, the patentee must have made an explicit threat, or otherwise engaged in conduct that created an objectively reasonable apprehension on the part of the plaintiff that the

14. 28 U.S.C. § 2201(a) (2000).

patentee will commence suit if the activity in question continues. The courts will assess these circumstances as of the time the declaratory judgment action is brought.[15]

A straightforward scenario in which an actual controversy exists is when (1) the declaratory judgment plaintiff has continuously engaged in the commercialization of an accused product or process; and (2) the patentee expressly threatens patent infringement litigation through a "cease and desist" letter specifically directed to the declaratory judgment plaintiff. In the absence of a direct threat, the courts will examine the totality of the circumstances to determine whether an objectively reasonable apprehension of suit exists. Although the decision to exercise declaratory judgment jurisdiction is highly fact specific, a large number of reported decisions suggest the key factors that the courts most often consider when making this determination. Among them are (1) patentee statements made during negotiations between the parties; (2) general announcements made by the patentee in advertisements; (3) lawsuits predicated on comparable foreign patents; (4) patentee threats or statements to the declaratory plaintiff's customers; (5) patentee suits against others for use of the same product or process used by the declaratory plaintiff; and (6) a history of litigation between the parties.[16]

Even if an actual controversy exists, the district court need not exercise declaratory judgment jurisdiction. Acceptance of jurisdiction instead remains discretionary with the court. A district court may decline to exercise declaratory judgment jurisdiction if that action would not fulfill the objectives for which the Declaratory Judgments Act was created. For example, in *EMC Corp. v. Norand Corp.*,[17] the Federal Circuit affirmed a district court's decision not to exercise jurisdiction even though an actual controversy existed between the parties. The district court found that the accused infringer had brought a declaratory judgment action in order to obtain a more favorable bargaining position in licensing negotiations with the patentee. The district court therefore concluded that exercising jurisdiction in the case would conflict with the policies of promoting private resolution of disputes and conserving judicial resources. The Federal Circuit affirmed, ruling that the existence of serious negotiations to sell or license a patent was a legitimate consideration and the district court had acted within the scope of its discretion.

15. Shell Oil Co. v. Amoco Corp., 970 F.2d 885, 23 USPQ2d 1627 (Fed. Cir. 1992).

16. *See* Lisa A. Dolak, *Declaratory Judgment Jurisdiction in Patent Cases: Restoring the Balance Between the Patentee and the Accused Infringer*, 38 Bos. Coll. L. Rev. 903 (1997).

17. 89 F.3d 807, 39 USPQ2d 1451 (Fed. Cir. 1996).

§ 10.2 Appellate Jurisdiction

Prior to 1982, patent appeals were heard by the Court of Appeals for the judicial circuit where the the district court was located. While this scheme was consistent with the rules governing all other federal litigation, it lead to the inevitable possibility of circuit splits on questions of interpretation of the patent laws. By the early 1980's, many experts had come to believe that the varying interpretations of patent issues by the differing circuit courts of appeals had become a serious problem.[1] The Federal Courts Improvement Act of 1982 attempted to rectify this problem by providing a wholly new route of appellate review in patent cases.[2] The Act created a new court, the U.S. Court of Appeals for the Federal Circuit, possessing nationwide jurisdiction to hear appeals in cases involving the patent laws.[3] Viewed by many commentators as the most significant reform to the federal judicial system in nearly a century, the creation of the Federal Circuit was motivated by a perceived need for more consistent interpretation of the patent law.[4] Congress hoped the Federal Circuit would provide more uniform and coherent guidance to innovative industry, the PTO and others impacted by the patent system.[5]

Congress accomplished this task through two principal features of the 1982 legislation. First, Congress abolished the Court of Customs and Patent Appeals ("CCPA"), a specialized tribunal that was authorized to hear appeals of PTO administrative decisions. Congress instead invested the new Federal Circuit with jurisdiction to review adverse patentability decisions from the PTO. Second, Congress stipulated in 28 U.S.C. § 1295 that "the Federal Circuit shall have exclusive jurisdiction ... of an appeal from a final decision of a district court of the United States ... if the jurisdiction of that court was based, in whole or in part, on section 1338 of this title...." By virtue of this reference to 28 U.S.C. § 1338, the same "arising under" standard that controls the original jurisdiction of the district court also governs the appellate jurisdiction of the Federal Circuit.

Some difficult jurisdictional questions arise when the plaintiff's complaint does not state a cause of action in patent law, but the defendant's answer does. The defendant's answer may include

§ 10.2

1. Howard T. Markey, *The Phoenix Court*, 10 American Pat. L. Ass'n Q. J. 227 (1982).

2. Pub.L. No. 97–164, 96 Stat. 25 (1982).

3. Thomas H. Case & Scott R. Miller, *An Appraisal of the Court of Appeals for the Federal Circuit*, 57 S. Cal. L. Rev. (1984), 301.

4. Rochelle Cooper Dreyfuss, *The Federal Circuit: A Case Study in Specialized Courts*, 64 New York University L. Rev. 1 (1989).

5. S. Rep. No. 275, 97th Cong., 1st Sess. 2, reprinted in 1982 U.S. Code Cong. & Admin. News 11, 12.

counterclaims that include a cause of action under the patent law.[6] For example, suppose that the plaintiff claims an antitrust violation in his complaint, while the defendant in turn asserts a claim of patent infringement against the plaintiff in her answer. To determine which court has appellate jurisdiction in this case—the Federal Circuit, or the relevant regional circuit—we must resolve whether the case "arises under" the patent law.

For most of its history, the Federal Circuit looked to see whether either the plaintiff's complaint or the defendant's answer asserted a cause of action based upon the patent law. If so, then the Federal Circuit took the position that it possessed jurisdiction to resolve that appeal. The Federal Circuit justified this interpretation of the statute by noting the congressional purpose to prevent forum shopping and provide consistent interpretation of the patent laws nationwide.[7]

However, in its 2002 decision in *Holmes Group, Inc. v. Vornado Air Circulation Systems, Inc.*,[8] the Supreme Court rejected the position of the Federal Circuit. The Supreme Court held that "a counterclaim—which appears as part of the defendant's answer, not as part of the plaintiff's complaint—cannot serve as the basis for 'arising under' jurisdiction."[9] The Supreme Court held that the "well-pleaded complaint rule" was of long standing and could not be converted into a "well-pleaded complaint-*or-counterclaim* rule."[10] As a result, subsequent to *Holmes v. Vornado*, appeals of cases based upon a complaints that do not state a cause of action in patent law, but nonetheless involve considerable patent issues, will be heard by the regional courts of appeals rather than the Federal Circuit.

One consequence of *Holmes v. Vornado* is a constriction of Federal Circuit jurisdiction. This ruling may well promote strategic behavior in drafting pleadings and races to the courthouse, as litigants now enjoy some ability to divert their non-patent claims to the forum of their choosing, even when they anticipate patent related counterclaims.[11] Whether this state of affairs comports with a congressional desire to establish a uniform national patent jurisprudence is questionable. On the other hand, *Holmes v. Vornado* strengthens the traditional right of plaintiffs to choose their own law and forum.[12] Moreover, Congress is free to overrule the case at

6. FED. R. CIV. PROC. 7(a).

7. Aerojet–General Corp. v. Machine Tool Works, 895 F.2d 736, 13 USPQ2d 1670 (Fed. Cir. 1990) (*en banc).*

8. 535 U.S. 826 (2002).

9. 535 U.S. at 831.

10. 535 U.S. at 832.

11. Bruce M. Wexler & Joseph M. O'Malley, Jr., *Deciding Jurisdiction in Patent Cases*, NEW YORK LAW JOURNAL (August 12, 2002).

12. James W. Dabney, Holmes v. Vornado*: A Restatement of the 'Arising Under' Jurisdiction of the Federal*

any time by clarifying that the Federal Circuit should have jurisdiction of all cases involving patent issues, whether those issues are injected by complaint or by counterclaim.

§ 10.3 Choice of Law at the Federal Circuit

As we have seen, some cases appealed to the Federal Circuit involve both patent issues and other matters over which the court lacks exclusive jurisdiction. For example, a licensing dispute could involve both patent and contract law issues. In reviewing district court judgments in patent cases, the Federal Circuit applies its own law with respect to patent law issues, but with respect to nonpatent issues the Federal Circuit generally applies the law of the circuit in which the district court sits. The Federal Circuit has reasoned that requiring trial courts to apply different standards to patent and non-patent cases would be confusing and inconvenient. However, for fields like the patent law, in which the Federal Circuit enjoys exclusive jurisdiction, the application of Federal Circuit law contributes to uniformity and certainty.[1]

The Federal Circuit also applies its own law to certain issues that are not unique to the patent law, however. Although some inconsistency exists in the case law addressing this point, the Federal Circuit has generally concluded that deference to regional circuit law is inappropriate where a substantive or procedural matter is essential to the exercise of the court's exclusive statutory jurisdiction.[2] In other words, even if a particular issue is not strictly a patent law matter, the Federal Circuit will nonetheless call for the application of its own law if doing so would promote judicial efficiency, would be consistent with the court's mandate to promote uniformity in the patent law, and would not create undue conflict and confusion among the district courts.[3]

The substantive standard for issuing a preliminary injunction against further acts of patent infringement is a good example of the application of Federal Circuit law to an issue that is not strictly a patent question. Preliminary injunctions are, of course, available in many legal disciplines other than patents. According to the Federal Circuit, however, the issuance of a preliminary injunction to enjoin patent infringement involves issues that are unique to the patent

Courts, 11 New York State Bar Ass'n Bright Ideas no. 2 (Autumn 2002), 3.

§ 10.3

1. Midwest Indus., Inc. v. Karavan Trailers, Inc., 175 F.3d 1356 (Fed. Cir. 1999). *See* Joan E. Schaffner, *Federal Circuit "Choice of Law":* Erie *Through the Looking Glass*, 81 Iowa L. Rev. 1173 (1996).

2. Biodex Corp. v. Loredan Biomedical, Inc., 946 F.2d 850, 20 USPQ2d 1252 (Fed. Cir. 1991).

3. Beverly Hills Fan Co. v. Royal Sovereign Corp., 21 F.3d 1558, 30 USPQ2d 1001 (Fed. Cir. 1994).

law.[4] As a result, the court has concluded that its own substantive standards should control. That means that a district court in California hearing a patent case must look to Federal Circuit precedents, not to those of the Ninth Circuit, in determining whether to issue a preliminary injunction.

On the other hand, the Federal Circuit has stated that as to purely procedural matters relating to the grant of a preliminary injunction—such as whether the district judge entered findings of fact and conclusions of law as required by the Federal Rules of Civil Procedure—the law of the regional circuit applies.[5]

Following these principles, the Federal Circuit has also held that regional circuit law applies to issues arising under the bankruptcy statute[6] and Copyright Act.[7] In contrast, the Federal Circuit has applied its own law to determine such issues as whether inequitable conduct before the PTO can qualify as a predicate act under the Racketeer Influenced and Corrupt Organizations Act ("RICO")[8] and whether an invention has been subject to a formal offer of sale sufficient to trigger the § 102(b) on-sale bar.[9]

§ 10.4 Issue Preclusion and the *Blonder–Tongue* Doctrine

During patent enforcement litigation, an accused infringer has the option of asserting that the patent-in-suit is invalid.[1] If the courts agree that the patent was improvidently granted, then that litigation is over. In the event that the patent proprietor later attempts to assert the same patent, there has never been a question that the same defendant could defeat the cause of action through the doctrine of issue preclusion. Where the patentee attempts to assert that same patent against persons other than the original defendant however, the situation is a bit more complex. In situations of this sort, the law has actually evolved over time.

The initial view was that a patentee could not be collaterally estopped from suing another defendant for patent infringement even though an earlier court judgment had held the patent invalid. For example, in its 1936 decision in *Triplett v. Lowell*, the Supreme

4. Reebok Int'l Ltd. v. J. Baker, Inc., 32 F.3d 1552, 1555, 31 USPQ2d 1781, 1783 (Fed. Cir. 1994).

5. Hybritech Inc. v. Abbott Laboratories, 849 F.2d 1446, 1451 n.12, 7 USPQ2d 1191, 1195 n.12 (Fed. Cir. 1988).

6. In re Cambridge Biotech Corp., 186 F.3d 1356, 51 USPQ2d 1321 (Fed. Cir. 1999).

7. Atari Games Corp. v. Nintendo of America Inc., 975 F.2d 832, 24 USPQ2d 1015 (Fed. Cir. 1992).

8. Semiconductor Energy Lab. Co. v. Samsung Elec. Co., 204 F.3d 1368, 54 USPQ2d 1001 (Fed. Cir. 2000).

9. Advanced Cardiovascular Sys., Inc. v. Medtronic, Inc., 265 F.3d 1294, 60 USPQ2d 1161 (Fed. Cir. 2001).

§ 10.4

1. 35 U.S.C. § 282 (2000).

Court observed that it "ha[d] several times held valid the claims of a patent which had been held invalid by a circuit court of appeals in an earlier suit brought by the same plaintiff against another defendant."[2] Under the *Triplett* rule, an earlier invalidity judgment in, say, the First Circuit, would not prevent the patentee from accusing a different competitor of patent infringement in the Second Circuit. While the earlier First Circuit judgment might prove persuasive, and convince the Second Circuit to rule likewise, the later accused infringer could not assert the judgment as a defense.

In its 1971 decision in *Blonder–Tongue Laboratories, Inc. v. University of Illinois Foundation*,[3] the Supreme Court overturned *Triplett* and instead embraced the doctrine of defensive non-mutual issue preclusion. The Court recognized that patent litigation was expensive and saw no indication that one particular court would issue more accurate patent judgments than another. Further, as plaintiffs, patent proprietors often enjoy considerable flexibility in choosing when, where and whom to sue. As a result, patentees should not ordinarily be unfairly surprised, or face unusual difficulties in amassing evidence, in the first litigation. The Court therefore concluded that accused infringers should not have to bear the repeat costs of defending a charge of infringement based upon a patent claim that had already been invalidated. So long as the patentee has a "full and fair chance to litigate the validity of his patent in an earlier case,"[4] then even a stranger to the earlier lawsuit may defend against a charge of patent infringement through the doctrine of issue preclusion.

Following *Blonder–Tongue*, once the courts conclusively rule that a patent is invalid, the patent proprietor effectively owns a nullity. Unless the patentee can show that it lacked a "full and fair" opportunity to litigate—an argument that, in the years since *Blonger–Tongue*, has proved spectactularly unlikely to succeed[5]—subsequent infringement suits on that patent will be summarily dismissed. A victorious patent challenger effectively acts as a "private attorney general" who strikes down the patent for all the world.

Importantly, the *Blonder–Tongue* rule is a one-way street. It bars patentees from bringing suit on patents that have been conclusively held invalid. However, alleged infringers are always free to argue that the asserted patent is invalid even though, in an earlier litigation against a different defendant, the patent survived the identical invalidity challenge.

2. 297 U.S. 638, 642 (1936).

3. 402 U.S. 313 (1971).

4. 402 U.S. at 333.

5. *See* Jerry R. Selinger & Jessica W. Young, *Suing an Infringer's Customers: Or, Life Under the Single Recovery Rule*, 31 John Marshall L. Rev. 19, 28 (1997).

The *Blonder–Tongue* doctrine presents a mixed bag for the patent law. It is hardly a unique rule for patents, as the rise of nonmutual issue preclusion commenced long before this case, and the trend has since continued in many areas of law. And as the Supreme Court observed, the prospect of patentees relitigating the same validity argument against every potential adversary seems a wasteful duplication of private and judicial resources. Yet an irony surrounds the *Blonder–Tongue* holding. Under the earlier *Triplett* rule, a successful patent challenger was the sole beneficiary of a successful lawsuit invalidating the patent. Following *Blonder–Tongue*, the challenger is forced to share the results of its efforts with everyone else, including competitors who did not bear the costs of the litigation. This legal situation creates a "public goods" problem familiar to intellectual property attorneys.[6] To put the matter concretely, why should a party spend several hundred thousand dollars to challenge a patent, when the result will be that everyone else in the industry will get to use the technology for free. A party in that posture might well prefer to simply pay a modest licensing fee and leave the patent in force. *Blonder–Tongue* may therefore actually reduce individual incentives to strike down patents. Discovering a way to encourage a socially optimal level of patent challenges, while avoiding the needless duplication of redundant patent challenges, remains an important issue for judges, legislators, legal academics, and other concerned observers of the patent system.[7]

§ 10.5 Laches and Estoppel

Although hardly unique to the patent law, the equitable defenses of laches and estoppel have recently been of considerable importance to patent litigants. In an era where patent litigation has become an increasingly lucrative endeavor, patentees have demonstrated a renewed willingness to review their portfolios in order to consider whether any claims are being infringed. Sometimes this effort results in the "dusting off" of patents that are near expiration or have in fact expired, with litigation commenced regarding alleged infringements that supposedly began years before. A review of laches and estoppel cases in the patent context therefore seems well worthwhile.

The chief Federal Circuit opinion concerning laches and estoppel is *A.C. Aukerman Co. v. R. L. Chaides Construction Co.*[1] Aukerman owned two patents relating to a "slip-form" and a

6. *See supra* § 1.3.1.

7. *See* John R. Thomas, *Collusion and Collective Action in the Patent System: A Proposal for Patent Bounties*, 2001 U. Ill. L. Rev. 305 .

§ 10.5

1. 960 F.2d 1020, 22 USPQ2d 1321 (Fed. Cir.1992) (*en banc*).

method of using that product to construct concrete highway barriers. Chaides used a slip-form product purchased from a third party, Gomaco, to manufacture concrete highway barriers. Between February and April 1979, Aukerman sent letters to Chaides accusing Chaides of infringing the patents, but offering Chaides a license under the patents. In April 1979, Chaides provided a written response stating that any responsibility was Gomaco's, and that "if Aukerman wished to sue Chaides 'for $200–$300 a year,' Aukerman should do so." The parties had no further contact for over eight years, during which time Chaides markedly increased its slip-form business.

In October 1987, prompted by a licensee's complaint about competition from Chaides, Aukerman sent a letter to Chaides advising Chaides "that litigation against another company had been resolved, and threatening litigation unless Chaides executed [a] license...." Chaides refused to enter into a license, and on October 26, 1988, Aukerman sued Chaides for infringement. The district court granted summary judgment for defendant, holding that Aukerman was barred under principles of laches and estoppel from maintaining its cause of action. On appeal, the *en banc* Federal Circuit reversed.

Turning first to laches, Chief Judge Nies listed the two elements of this defense. First, the infringer must prove that the patentee delayed filing suit for an unreasonable and inexcusable period of time, starting from the time the patentee should have known of its claim against the infringer. The court listed several possible factors that might excuse a dilatory patentee, including: other litigation, negotiations with the accused, possibly poverty and illness under limited circumstances, wartime conditions, extent of infringement, and dispute over ownership of the patent. The court also noted the possibility that laches may not apply where the infringer was guilty of particularly egregious conduct. Such conduct, which would tip the equities sharply in favor of the patentee, could include conscious copying or misrepresentations.

The second element is that the delay must have operated to the prejudice of the infringer. The court identified two sorts of prejudice, economic and evidentiary. Economic prejudice might arise where a defendant would suffer the loss of investment and business expansion due to the plaintiff's delay in filing suit. Evidentiary prejudice might arise through the death of a witness, destruction of records, or the unreliability of memories of distant events.

The court adhered to settled law that the effect of a laches defense is to bar relief on a patentee's claim only with respect to damages accumulated prior to the filing of suit. Equitable relief and claims for future damages may still be awarded in favor of the patentee even in cases where laches is applicable.

The Federal Circuit also instructed the lower courts how to allocate the burden of proof in laches cases. The defendant (who is the accused infringer) ordinarily bears both the burden of production and the burden of persuasion regarding laches. However, the court upheld the judicially created presumption that a delay of six years from the time the patentee knew of an infringement, until the time suit was filed, acted to shift the burden of production. Thus, in cases where the patentee's delay exceeded six years, the plaintiff (who is the patent owner) will bear the burden of producing some evidence to provide an adequate excuse for its delay in filing the suit. This six-year period was borrowed from 35 U.S.C.A. § 286, a statute that denies patentees the ability to obtain damages beyond six years from the time suit is filed. The court was quick to note that the presumption of laches only shifts the burden of producing evidence, not the ultimate burden of persuasion, which is always maintained by the accused infringer. Because the district court did not apply this framework in *Aukerman*, the Federal Circuit remanded the case for further consideration.

The *Aukerman* decision was generally seen as weakening the effectiveness of the laches defense in patent litigation, particularly when raised in a summary judgment motion. Some observers believe that, in practice, most patentees will have little trouble presenting reasons to excuse their delay in filing suit. Further, the infringer always maintains the burden of persuasion under the *Aukerman* framework, even though many issues in laches cases may be more readily demonstrated or disproved by evidence in the control of the patentee. That the infringer bears the burden of persuasion also means that where the trier of fact cannot decide whether the patentee's delay was reasonable or unreasonable, the patentee should prevail.[2]

The *Aukerman* court also considered the defense of estoppel, breaking the doctrine up into three elements. First, the patentee, through misleading conduct, must lead the accused infringer to believe that the patentee does not intend to enforce its patent against the alleged infringer. Such conduct could include an affirmative statement, action, inaction or even silence where there was an obligation to speak. Second, the infringer must have relied upon that conduct. Finally, the infringer must show that it has suffered material prejudice as a result of the patentee's conduct. As with laches, material prejudice would ordinarily comprise either a change in economic position or the loss of evidence. The idea here is

2. *See* Evan Finkel, *What Remains of the Laches and Estoppel Defenses After* Aukerman?, 9 Santa Clara Computer & High Tech. L.J. 1 (1993).

simple enough. If a patentee tells a competitor that it does not plan to sue, if the competitor believes that representation, and if the competitor then spends millions of dollars on a new factory to produce the product in question, it seems only fair to estop the patentee from asserting the patent when it changes its mind at some point down the road.

Applying this law to the facts before it, the court again reversed and remanded. Chief Judge Nies particularly relied upon Chaides' 1979 statement that its infringing constructions of slip-forms were extremely minimal. As one could well infer that Aukerman merely waived an infringement claim worth at most $300 per year, the grant of summary judgment of estoppel was improper. This observation proved a telling one on remand, for the district court held that Chaides could invoke neither the laches nor estoppel defense. Because Chaides had substantially increased its infringing activities after advising Aukerman that its use of the patented slip-forms was minimal, the trial court held that Chaides was itself guilty of unclean hands and thus unable to invoke these equitable defenses.[3]

3. 29 USPQ2d 1054, 1057–59 (N.D.Cal.1993).

Chapter 11

PATENT ASSIGNMENTS AND LICENSES

Table of Sections

---

§ 11.1 Basic Concepts

The Patent Act explains that "patents shall have the attributes of personal property."[1] One consequence of this characterization is that patent owners may license or sell their rights to others. Patent lawyers term the sale of a patent an "assignment." Pending patent applications may also be sold or assigned. It is also possible to assign or license the right to any invention a person may complete in the future. This situation is common for employees, who often sign employment contracts stipulating that any future work-related inventions developed by the employee will be assigned to the employer.[2]

Absent a governing employment contract or other pre-issuance transaction, the inventor named in the patent instrument is its initial owner. Those seeking to purchase or license rights under a patent should therefore contact the inventor, or an entity in a chain of title that begins with that inventor. If more than one individual qualifies as an inventor, and therefore as an owner, then these individuals are joint owners who hold the patent as tenants-in-common. As afficionados of real property may recall, under this arrangement, each joint owner owns an undivided interest in the

§ 11.1

1. 35 U.S.C. § 261 (2000).

2. *See* Robert P. Merges, *The Law and Economics of Employee Inventions*, 13 Harv. J. L. & Tech. 1 (1999).

entire property. Further, each joint owner may exploit the patent without requiring consent from the others.[3]

Suppose, for example, Groucho and Harpo are co-owners of a patent. In this situation, Groucho can use the patented invention without regard to Harpo's interests. Harpo can neither prevent Groucho from exploiting the patented invention nor claim a share of any proceeds Groucho earns. Similarly, Harpo can freely license or assign his interests to another without interference from Groucho.

To take the example further, suppose that Harpo assigned 1% of his interest in the patent to a third party, Chico. As a co-tenant, Harpo owned an undivided interest in the entire patent. Chico now owns 1% of an undivided interest in the patent—effectively making Chico another joint tenant. The Harpo–Chico deal has therefore, in effect, created a third patent owner. Chico now enjoys the same rights that Groucho and Harpo do.

There is one important exception to the general rule that joint owners may exploit a patent without regard to the others. Section 281 of the Patent Act states that: "A patentee shall have remedy by civil action for infringement of his patent."[4] Courts have interpreted this language as requiring the agreement of each of a patent's joint owners in order to enforce the patent through infringement litigation. Therefore, although a joint owner can manufacture, sell, license, or otherwise exploit a patented invention without regard to the other joint owners, permission of the other joint owners must be had prior to commencing an infringement suit.[5]

These examples illustrate the common maxim that joint owners of a patent are at each other's mercy.[6] While the conversion of laboratory collaborators into marketplace competitors may appear unseemly, the tenancy-in-common construct seeks to maximize the exploitation of patented technology. A would-be licensee need only deal with one joint owner, rather than having to risk being held up by one unconsenting joint owner. Of course, joint owners of a patent can always change their relationship by express agreement. The tenancy-in-common arrangement applies only as a default in the event the owners have not ordered their affairs otherwise, through contract.

In contrast to an assignment, a license does not transfer ownership of a patent. A license instead acts in the nature of a permission. Patents allow their owners to exclude others from

3. *See* Ethicon v. U.S. Surgical Corp., 135 F.3d 1456, 1471, 45 USPQ2d 1545, 1557 (Fed. Cir. 1998) (Newman, J., dissenting).

4. 35 U.S.C. § 281 (2000).

5. *Ethicon*, 135 F.3d at 1468, 45 USPQ2d at 1554.

6. *See* Cilco, Inc. v. Copeland Intralenses, Inc., 614 F. Supp. 431, 434, 227 USPQ 168, 170 (S.D.N.Y. 1985).

practicing the patented invention. By granting a license, the patent proprietor agrees not to exercise that right, usually in exchange for the payment of royalties.[7] Consequently, a license provides an affirmative defense in a suit for patent infringement.[8]

A patentee may limit the grant of rights awarded under a license. A licensee could, for example, obtain the right to use a patented invention but not to sell it.[9] Other common license restrictions include the stipulation of a field of use or the placement of geographical limitations upon the permitted use of the patented invention. For instance, a license might provide for the use of a patented medication only in the veterinary field, for example, or limit the sale of a patented crab pot to within the State of Maryland. Absent exceptional circumstances—such as an antitrust violation or patent misuse—the courts will uphold these restrictions. If our crab pot licensee sailed south on the Chesapeake Bay and sold some of the patented pots to crabbers within the Commonwealth of Virginia, for example, he would violate the license terms and potentially be liable for patent infringement.[10]

Some important distinctions exist between assignments and licenses. Assignments must be in writing.[11] Licenses need not be memorialized in writing, although sound business practice suggests that they should be.

Another difference between assignments and licenses concerns standing to enforce the patent right. As noted previously, the Patent Act allows only "a patentee" to bring a suit for patent infringement.[12] The courts have interpreted this language as providing standing to sue for patent infringement to assignees. Under this reasoning, an assignee of "all substantial rights" to the patent steps into the shoes of the original owner and becomes "the patentee." As a result, an assignee who is the sole owner of a patent may enforce the patent right on her own. She need not obtain the cooperation or permission of anyone else and may bring the lawsuit in her own name.

In contrast to assignees, licensees ordinarily possess no rights to enforce the licensed patent. The courts have reasoned that a licensee has merely obtained a promise not to be sued by the licensor. Although this interest may be of significant economic

7. Spindelfabrik Suessen–Schurr GmbH v. Schubert & Salzer Maschinenfabrik AG, 829 F.2d 1075, 1081, 4 USPQ2d 1044, 1048 (Fed. Cir. 1987).

8. Carborundum Co. v. Molten Metal Equipment Innovations, Inc., 72 F.3d 872, 878, 37 USPQ2d 1169, 1172 (Fed. Cir. 1995).

9. *See* Vaupel Textilmaschinen KG v. Meccnica Euro Italia SpA, 944 F.2d 870, 875, 20 USPQ2d 1045, 1049 (Fed. Cir. 1991).

10. *See* Mallinckrodt, Inc. v. Medipart, Inc., 976 F.2d 700, 24 USPQ2d 1173 (Fed. Cir. 1992).

11. 35 U.S.C. § 261 (2000).

12. 35 U.S.C. § 281 (2000).

importance to the licensee, it does not amount to an ownership interest in the patent. As a result, licensees do not qualify as "patentees" and lack legal standing to sue to enforce the licensed patent.[13]

Lying between the position of a full assignor and a mere licensee is the exclusive licensee. If a licensor promises to license the patented invention to a single licensee, and none other, then that licensee enjoys an exclusive license. In such cases the exclusive licensee receives a promise that it will be the sole individual that can make, use, sell, offer to sell, or import the patented invention in the licensed area of exclusivity. The courts have considered this exclusive interest to be tantamount to an assignment.[14]

As a result, an exclusive licensee possesses standing to sue for patent infringement directly, but only if it joins the patentee to the suit. If the patentee is unwilling to join, then Federal Rule of Civil Procedure 19 allows the exclusive licensee to compel the patentee to join as an involuntary plaintiff. Such joinder will be granted even against the patentee's will and even if the court lacks personal jurisdiction over the patentee. The results of such a litigation, including a holding of patent invalidity, will bind the patentee.[15]

§ 11.2 Recordation of Assignments

The Patent Act establishes a permissive system for recording patent assignments. The contracting parties need not record, and the assignment will generally be valid even if not recorded. As is usual with such systems, however, recordation provides protection in the event that assignor subsequently attempts to assign the same patent to another party who has no notice of the first assignment. As specified in section 261 of the Patent Act: "An assignment, grant or conveyance shall be void against any subsequent purchaser or mortgagee for a valuable consideration, without notice, unless it is recorded in the Patent and Trademark Office within three months from its date or prior to the date of such subsequent purchase or mortgage."

An example illustrates the workings of patent recordation. Assume Crooke assigns a patent to Alpha on March 1. Suppose further that Crooke enters into a second purported assignment transaction involving the same patent, this time with Omega, on April 15. Omega, in this example, knows nothing of the earlier Crooke–Alpha deal and acts entirely in good faith. Under the quoted statutory provision, if Alpha records its assignment at the

13. Rite–Hite Corp. v. Kelley Co., 56 F.3d 1538, 1552, 35 USPQ2d 1065, 1074 (Fed. Cir. 1995).

14. *Id.*

15. Intellectual Property Development, Inc. v. TCI Cablevision of California Inc., 248 F.3d 1333, 1347, 58 USPQ2d 1681, 1691 (Fed. Cir. 2001).

PTO by June 1, Alpha will have superior rights to Omega. If Alpha fails to record, however, then Omega would possess the superior rights.

§ 11.3 Security Interests

Firms often need to borrow money to operate. Many lenders will not lend money, however, unless the loan is secured by some valuable asset. In some cases, the most valuable asset owned by the borrower is its patent portfolio. It follows that in many situations, a borrower will want to use its patents as security for a loan by giving the lender a security interest in one or more patents. In effect, such an arrangement can be thought of as an "agreement to assign in the event of a default."

As students of secured transactions law are already aware, an individual seeking to "perfect" a security interest must file documents detailing the transaction with the government. This filing provides notice to other potential lenders about the true financial situation of the borrower. In particular, it advises them that they may not be able to rely on certain assets to satisfy a debt in the event of a default because those assets have already been promised to another creditor. With regard to security interests in patents, one might wonder whether the necessary filing should be made at the PTO, under the Patent Act, or whether it should be made in the relevant state office specified by the Uniform Commercial Code (UCC).

The UCC has provisions that defer to federal filing schemes where such schemes are required.[1] The relevant provision of the Patent Act, however, only deals with recordation of actual assignments, not with recordations of security interests, and in any event the federal recordation is not required even in the case of an outright assignment. The courts have therefore concluded that the Patent Act does not pertain to security interests and, as a result, that the Uniform Commercial Code continues to govern the perfection of such interests.[2] To perfect a security interest in a patent, the relevant documents should thus be filed at the relevant state office, often that of the Secretary of State.

§ 11.4 Licensee and Assignor Estoppel

Sometimes a licensee forms the belief that the licensed patent was improvidently granted. For example, the licensee may discover

§ 11.3

1. Thus under § 9–302(3)(a) of the UCC, there is an exception to the requirement of a state filing if a "statute . . . of the United States . . . provides for a national registration or . . . specifies a place of filing different from that specified in this division for filing of the security interest."

2. *See* In re Transportation Design and Technology, Inc., 48 Bankr. 635, 226 USPQ 424 (S.D. Ca. 1985).

that a prior art publication that was not available to the PTO during prosecution wholly anticipates the patented invention. Naturally, a licensee who stumbles upon such information may suddenly lose its enthusiasm for paying royalties on what it now believes to be an invalid patent. The question then arises whether the licensee may challenge the validity of the licensed patent. General rules of contract law do not allow purchasers to repudiate their promises simply because they subsequently become dissatisfied with the deal, at least without compensating the other contracting party. Traditionally courts disallowed licensee challenges to licensed patents on just this principle. This doctrine came to be known as "licensee estoppel." A companion concept, "assignor estoppel," prevented a person who assigned a patent to another from later claiming that the patent is invalid.

In the 1969 decision of *Lear v. Adkins*,[1] the Supreme Court abruptly abrogated the licensee estoppel doctrine. Here, the defendant, Lear, Inc. had hired the plaintiff, John Adkins, in order to solve a gyroscope design problem. Adkins subsequently developed an improved gyroscope design that improved the instrument's accuracy at a low cost. Lear soon incorporated Adkins' design improvements into its gyroscopes. After filing an application with the Patent Office, Adkins entered into a licensing agreement with Lear, under which Lear promised to pay Adkins royalties on its future gyroscope sales. Some time later—while the patent application was still pending—Lear refused to pay any further royalties under its license with Adkins. Lear claimed that Adkins' design was not patentable based upon an earlier patent that Lear had identified.

Once the patent issued, Adkins brought suit in a California state court on a breach of contract claim. The case eventually made its way to the California Supreme Court. Affirming a damages award to Adkins, the California Supreme Court held that the doctrine of licensee estoppel prevented Lear from challenging the validity of the Adkins patent.

The Supreme Court granted *certiorari* and vacated the decision of the California Supreme Court. Justice Harlan observed that the doctrine of licensee estoppel resulted from judicial efforts to support the sanctity of contracts. According to the Court, however, another, competing policy should enjoy a more prominent role. Justice Harlan identified a strong public interest in invalidating improvidently granted patents. Due to their desire to avoid the payment of royalties or other obligations under a license, licensees may often be the entities with the greatest economic incentives to challenge a licensed patent. Muzzling licenses through an estoppel doctrine

§ 11.4

1. 395 U.S. 653 (1969).

would undermine this compelling federal interest, the Court observed, and therefore the common law of contracts must give way. The Supreme Court therefore wholly repudiated the doctrine of licensee estoppel.

The holding of *Lear v. Adkins* has long been subject to intense criticism. It may increase bad faith licensing on the behalf of licensees. Patent licenses have to some extent become insurance policies, allowing licensees to defer their decision to litigate until such time as their potential profits on the licensed invention outweigh the costs of challenging a patent. *Lear v. Adkins* also reduces the parties' freedom to contract. Presumably, a patentee would be willing to charge a lower royalty rate if the licensee promised not to contest the patent. If the value of patent licenses has been decreased after *Lear v. Adkins*, so has the value of patents, which in turn would reduce incentives to innovate and encourage reliance upon trade secrets.[2]

The Federal Circuit seems well aware of these critiques and often strains to limit the precedential impact of *Lear v. Adkins.*[3] For example, in *Diamond Scientific Co. v. Ambico, Inc.*,[4] the Federal Circuit applied the related doctrine of assignor estoppel despite *Lear v. Adkins*. Here, a Dr. Clarence Welter invented a new gastroenteritis vaccine while working for plaintiff Diamond. Through his employment contract, Welter had assigned patent rights to Diamond. Welter assisted Diamond in preparing patent applications on the vaccine, which ultimately matured into issued patents. Welter subsequently left Diamond and formed his own company, the defendant Ambico. After Ambico commenced the manufacture and sale of gastroenteritis vaccines, Diamond sued for patent infringement. During the litigation, the trial court held that the doctrine of assignor estoppel prevented Ambico from challenging the validity of the vaccine patents.

Following an appeal, the Federal Circuit affirmed. Although the Federal Circuit declined to issue a broad reaffirmance of the assignor estoppel doctrine, the court did hold that Ambico was estopped from challenging the patents-in-suit under the facts of the case. Judge Davis observed that assignor estoppel was based on the premise that an assignor should not be able to sell something, and later to assert that what was sold is worthless, all to the detriment of assignee. The record disclosed that Welter had actively participated in preparing the patent applications, had been compensated

2. *See* Rochelle Cooper Dreyfuss, *Dethroning* Lear: *Licensee Estoppel and the Incentive to Innovate*, 72 VA. L. REV. 677 (1986).

3. *See, e.g., Foster v. Hallco Mfg. Co.*, 947 F.2d 469, 20 USPQ2d 1241 (Fed. Cir. 1991) (a consent decree concerning patent validity may bar a future patent challenge).

4. 848 F.2d 1220, 6 USPQ2d 2028 (Fed. Cir. 1988).

for the assignment of the invention, and had signed an inventor's oath declaring his belief that he was the first and sole inventor. Under these circumstance, the Federal Circuit concluded that the equities weighed heavily in favor of Diamond and refused to allow Welter to pursue his patent challenge.

Although the equities of *Diamond Scientific* are compelling, many of these factors might also arise in cases of permissible licensee challenges. The court's emphasis upon the employer-employee relationship between Welter and Diamond also suggests that this holding may not be easily applied to cases of arms-length assignments in the commercial marketplace. In attempting to distinguish assignor from licensee estoppel, the Federal Circuit further stressed that assignors did not possess the same incentives to challenge assigned patents that licensees did. In the case of a license, the Court of Appeals explained the licensee faced a continuing royalty obligation, while in the case of an assignment the assignor has already been fully paid.[5] This reasoning seems dubious. While most patent licensees probably do choose to pay a continuing stream of royalties, they just as easily could have made a one-time payment of up-front royalties. Such a licensee is free to challenge the licensed patent under *Lear v. Adkins*, while an assignor—who may now wish to compete with the patentee and therefore possesses ample incentives to challenge the assigned patent—may face estoppel issues. At all events, future litigation will reveal whether the Federal Circuit will more broadly endorse the doctrine of assignor estoppel, or whether individual assignees will be required to show that equity favors them under the facts of particular cases.

§ 11.5 Misuse, Tying, and Contributory Infringement

A patent owner commits misuse when he exploits a patent in such a manner as to exceed its lawful scope. Misuse cases often involve patentee licensing practices that the courts have disfavored. The key inquiry in patent misuse cases is whether the patentee has impermissibly broadened the scope of his patent with anticompetitive effect.[1] A successful showing of patent misuse renders the patent unenforceable. Misuse is an elusive doctrine, since there is scant statutory language explaining which activities constitute misuse and which do not. As such, patent misuse is very much a creature of the case law. Moreover, because the patent misuse

5. 848 F.2d at 1224, 6 USPQ2d at 2030.

§ 11.5

1. Windsurfing Int'l, Inc. v. AMF, Inc., 782 F.2d 995, 1001–02, 228 USPQ 562, 566 (Fed.Cir.1986).

doctrine arose in the era of anti-monopoly sentiment following the Great Depression, most of these cases are of questionable vitality today, leaving the status of the doctrine uncertain. Nonetheless, the Supreme Court has yet to overturn its misuse precedent, and it therefore remains possible that some of its dated holdings may continue to have some force in the future.

Morton Salt Co. v. G.S. Suppiger Co.[2] presents the Supreme Court's most thorough review of the misuse doctrine. Morton was the proprietor of the '645 patent, relating to a machine for depositing salt tablets. The machine was useful for adding predetermined amounts of salt to the contents of cans. Morton brought an infringement suit against Suppiger for making and leasing allegedly infringing machines. Suppiger defended on the ground that Morton had "exceeded its monopoly" by leasing its patented machines on the condition that the leasees make exclusive use of Morton's unpatented salt tablets. In other words, if a canner wanted to get a patented tablet depositing machine, it had to promise to buy all its salt from Morton. The district court agreed with Suppiger that such an arrangement was an impermissible extension of the patent monopoly, but on appeal the Seventh Circuit reversed after concluding that Morton's tying arrangement did not violate the Clayton Act.

After granting *certiorari*, the Supreme Court again reversed, concluding that Morton had misused its patent. The Court started from the proposition that the use of a patent to secure an exclusive right not granted by the Patent Office violated the constitutional goal of promoting the useful arts. Because such a "maintenance and enlargement" of the patentee's rights depended in part upon successful results in infringement litigation, the courts should withhold relief where a patent was used as a means of restraining competition in the sale of unpatented products. As a holder of an exclusive privilege granted to further a public policy, an individual who used his patent to subvert that policy could not expect to gain protection from the courts.

In keeping with *Morton Salt*, the courts have identified a number of other acts—besides tying arrangements—that could constitute patent misuse. Among them are fixing prices;[3] prohibiting the manufacture of competing products;[4] conditioning the grant of one license upon the acceptance of another license;[5] and basing

2. 314 U.S. 488, 62 S.Ct. 402, 86 L.Ed. 363, 52 USPQ 30 (1942).

3. *See* Bauer & Cie. v. O'Donnell, 229 U.S. 1, 33 S.Ct. 616, 57 L.Ed. 1041 (1913).

4. National Lockwasher Co. v. George K. Garrett Co., 137 F.2d 255, 58 USPQ 460 (3d Cir.1943).

5. American Securit Co. v. Shatterproof Glass Corp., 268 F.2d 769, 122 USPQ 167 (3d Cir.1959), *cert. denied,*

royalty payments on total sales, regardless of the extent to which the patented invention was used.[6] Judicial opinions from the *Morton Salt* era of patent misuse cases also established several core precepts concerning this doctrine. Misuse serves as an effective defense even though the accused infringer itself is not harmed by the improper practice.[7] An effective assertion of the misuse defense renders the patent unenforceable.[8] However, a patentee may purge his misuse by abandoning the improper practice. When the effects of the misuse have dissipated, then the patent may once again be enforced.[9] Activities that amounted to misuse were not required to rise to the level of antitrust violations, although they frequently did.

Two later Supreme Court opinions, *Mercoid Corp. v. Mid–Continent Investment Co*,[10] and *Mercoid v. Minneapolis–Honeywell Regulator Co.*,[11] went even further than *Morton Salt*. The patent at issue in *Mercoid* concerned a domestic heating system. Among the elements of the claimed invention was a stoker switch. Unlike the salt tablets in *Morton Salt*, which were a staple article of commerce with many uses outside the claimed invention, the stoker switch was useful only in connection with the practice of the patented heating system. When the Mercoid Corporation manufactured stoker switches without a license, the patentee brought charges of contributory infringement.

When the *Mercoid* cases at last reached the Supreme Court, the Court again concluded that the patentee was guilty of misuse. Calling the case "a graphic illustration of the evils of an expansion of the patent monopoly by private engagements," Justice Douglas relied upon the principle that the patent covered only the claimed combination, not its individual components. Under this reasoning, the attempt to suppress the sale of stoker switches also amounted to an anticompetitive restraint upon unpatented goods. The Court was unimpressed both with the fact that the patentee measured royalty rates through the sale of heating system's components and that the patentee's stoker switch formed an advance in the art that had no use outside the patented invention.

Had the *Mercoid* cases remained good law, little would have been left of the doctrine of contributory infringement. However, Congress acted to curb the misuse doctrine by incorporating

361 U.S. 902, 80 S.Ct. 210, 4 L.Ed.2d 157 (1959).

6. Zenith Radio Corp. v. Hazeltine Research, Inc., 401 U.S. 321, 91 S.Ct. 795, 28 L.Ed.2d 77 (1971).

7. Morton Salt Co. v. G.S. Suppiger Co., 314 U.S. 488, 62 S.Ct. 402, 86 L.Ed. 363, 52 USPQ 30 (1942).

8. *See* B.B. Chem. Co. v. Ellis, 314 U.S. 495, 62 S.Ct. 406, 86 L.Ed. 367, 52 USPQ 33 (1942).

9. *Id.*

10. 320 U.S. 661, 64 S.Ct. 268, 88 L.Ed. 376 (1944).

11. 320 U.S. 680, 64 S.Ct. 278, 88 L.Ed. 396 (1944).

§ 271(d) into the 1952 Act. As originally enacted, the statute declared that no misuse occurred where the patentee: (1) gained revenue from acts that would constitute contributory (as compared to direct) infringement if performed by another, (2) licensed others to perform acts that would constitute contributory (as compared to direct) infringement if performed by another, or (3) sought to enforce his patent.

The Supreme Court first interpreted § 271(d) in its 1980 opinion in *Dawson Chemical Co. v. Rohm and Haas Co.*[12] Rohm & Haas owned the '092 patent claiming a method of using an unpatented herbicide called propanil. Dawson sought a license from Rohm & Haas, but Rohm & Haas refused to license Dawson, unless Dawson agreed to purchase its propanil from Rohm & Haas. Thereafter, Dawson sold propanil to farmers along with instructions on how to apply propanil to crops—instructions that basically taught the farmers how to practice the method of the '092 patent. Eventually, Rohm & Hass sued Dawson. Because Dawson was not itself practicing the patented method, the plaintiff could not claim direct infringement. Instead, it argued that Dawson's sale of propanil along with the instructions constituted contributory infringement. In its defense, Dawson argued that Rohm & Haas had misused the '092 patent.

Under the facts of the case, propanil was not itself subject to patent protection. However, the only known use of propanil would infringe the Rohm & Haas process patent. So the essential question in this case was whether Rohm & Haas, which had identified the only valuable application for propanil, should be able to control its use. The District Court granted summary judgment on the misuse issue in favor of Dawson, but on appeal the Fifth Circuit reversed on the basis of § 271(d). The Supreme Court granted *certiorari* and affirmed the opinion of the Court of Appeals. Agreeing that Congress meant to overrule the *Mercoid* cases, the Court concluded that a patentee may "control nonstaple goods that are capable only of infringing use in a patented invention, and that are essential to that invention's advance over the prior art."

Congress augmented § 271(d) in 1988 by adding paragraphs (4) and (5), which further limited the misuse defense. Paragraph (4) states that a refusal to license or use patent rights does not constitute misuse, while paragraph (5) exempts tying practices from the patent misuse doctrine unless the patentee enjoys market power. As a result of the latter amendment, tying practices can now only constitute misuse if the patentee enjoys market power and the tied goods are staple articles of commerce.

12. 448 U.S. 176, 100 S.Ct. 2601, 65 L.Ed.2d 696 (1980).

The amendments to § 271(d) suggest the waning influence of patent misuse law, a trend that is also reflected in Federal Circuit opinions. That court's thinking regarding misuse is demonstrated by its 1992 decision in *Mallinckrodt Inc. v. Medipart Inc.*[13] Mallinckrodt held a patent on an apparatus for delivery of radioactive or therapeutic material in aerosol mist form. It sold a commercial embodiment of the claimed technology for approximately $50. Mallinckrodt marked its products with a "single use only" notice. Medipart, in disregard of that notice, refilled emptied devices and sold them for approximately $20. As you might predict, Mallinckrodt sued them for infringement. The district court held that violation of the notice was not a matter within the purview of the Patent Act. Mallinckrodt appealed and obtained a reversal from the Federal Circuit. Judge Newman began by considering whether any Supreme Court case had ever held that a patentee engaged in misuse by using any form of a limited license in selling patented products. Finding none, and rejecting analogies from price-fixing and tying cases, the Federal Circuit overturned the trial court.

The *Mallinckrodt* opinion offers two principal lessons. The first is that a patentee may limit the use of patented articles and may obtain a remedy through the patent laws if others disobey that restriction. Restraints on the repair or modification of patented equipment will be struck down only if they violate some other positive law, in particular the antitrust laws. The second is that the Federal Circuit will find misuse only when the Supreme Court has specifically declared a commercial arrangement to be a misuse, or when the conduct is demonstrably anticompetitive.[14]

More direct attacks on the misuse doctrine can be found in many law review articles, as well as in Judge Posner's thoughtful opinion in *USM Corp. v. SPS Technologies, Inc.*[15] Following a 1969 infringement suit brought by SPS against USM, the parties settled and obtained a consent judgment. Under the terms of the consent judgment, USM acknowledged the validity of the SPS patent and agreed to pay royalties. In 1974, it was USM's turn to file suit. USM urged this time that the license agreement the parties had entered into following the consent judgment constituted a patent misuse due to a differential royalty scheme.[16] The District Court

13. 976 F.2d 700, 24 USPQ2d 1173 (Fed.Cir.1992).

14. *See* Windsurfing Int'l, Inc. v. AMF Inc., 782 F.2d 995, 228 USPQ 562 (Fed.Cir.1986).

15. 694 F.2d 505, 216 USPQ 959 (Fed.Cir.1982).

16. Under the agreement in the parties' consent decree, USM was required to remit to SPS 25% of any royalties it obtained by sublicensing SPS's patent. However, if USM decided to grant a sublicense to any of four specific companies that SPS had previously licensed directly, USM was obliged to remit 75% of the royalties obtained from those parties.

held in part that the arrangement did not constitute misuse.[17] On appeal, the Seventh Circuit affirmed.

Judge Posner's opinion attacked the foundations of patent misuse doctrine. He reasoned that misuse does not extend the patent beyond the scope of the claims because, as a matter of economics, patentees are only able to charge what others will pay for use of the patent. That charge can take the form of license restrictions, such as grant-back clauses, differential royalties, measurement of the royalty by the sale of a non-patented product, or simply a higher monetary price. As he put it, "The patentee who insists on limiting the freedom of his purchaser or licensee—whether to price, to use complementary inputs of the purchaser's choice, or to make competing items—will have to compensate the purchaser for the restriction by charging a lower price for the use of the patent. If, for example, the patent owner requires the licensee to agree to continue paying royalties after the patent expires, he will not be able to get him to agree to pay as big a royalty before the patent expires."[18] On the facts of the case, Judge Posner concluded that competition policies did not prohibit the patentee's maximization of its income from the patent. Because the SPS royalty arrangement was not shown to have anticompetitive effects in the market of the patentee's customers, the defense of patent misuse could not stand.

§ 11.6 Post-Expiration Royalties

Patent licenses often call for the periodic payment of royalties during the life of the patent. This arrangement is perfectly acceptable. If, however, the licensee promises to make payments following the expiration of the patent, then troubles arise. In its 1964 decision in *Brulotte v. Thys Co.*,[1] the Supreme Court held that a patent license that provides for royalty payments beyond the life of the patent is unlawful *per se*. According to the Court, by obtaining a promise of continuing royalty payments beyond the patent's expiration date, the licensor has attempted to extend the term of the patent beyond the statutorily prescribed term. Justice Douglas reasoned that this effort amounts to an impermissible enlargement of the scope of the patent and therefore constitutes misuse. As a result, any patent license calling for the payment of post-expiration royalties is unenforceable.

Few commentators have risen to the challenge of defending the *Brulotte* rule. Starting with Justice Harlan's persuasive dissent in *Brulotte*, and continuing at least until Judge Posner's insightful

17. 453 F.Supp. at 743, 200 USPQ at 788.

18. 694 F.2d at 510–11.

§ 11.6

1. 379 U.S. 29 (1964).

2002 decision in *Scheiber v. Dolby Laboratories, Inc.*,[2] observers have in fact severely criticized *Brulotte*. It is widely agreed that post-expiration royalties cannot broaden the scope of the patent right. Whether a license calls for post-expiration royalties or not, once the relevant patent expires, the patentee no longer has the right to exclude anyone from practicing the patented invention. Post-expiration royalties are akin to a financing mechanism: presumably a license with post-expiration royalties would call for smaller payments over a longer time than a license with royalties wholly within the patent term. The *Brulotte* rule has nonetheless endured for four decades, and as yet the Supreme Court has not seen fit to overturn it.

Fifteen years after *Brulotte*, the Supreme Court issued its opinion in *Aronson v. Quick Point Pencil Co.*[3] In this case, Jane Aronson invented a keyholder and duly filed a patent application. While that application was pending at the Patent Office, she negotiated a license with Quick Point. The Aronson–Quick Point license in part called for the payment of royalties of 5% if a patent issued within five years; otherwise Quick Point would pay 2.5% of sales for as long as it sold the keyholder. After the Patent Office finally rejected Aronson's patent application, Quick Point sought a declaratory judgment action that the agreement was unenforceable. Quick Point in part argued that if Aronson had obtained a patent, then the *Brulotte* rule would have extinguished its royalty obligations upon the expiration of the patent, but that under the contract with Aronson it would be obligated to pay royalties in perpetuity.

This time the Supreme Court found no basis under federal law for invalidating the license. The Court held that enforcement of the contract would not raise concerns under the preemption doctrine, because Aronson's design entered the public domain upon the sale of the keyholders. That meant that any other party besides Quick Point was free to make the keyholder without either securing permission from Ms. Aronson or paying her a penny. Thus enforcement of the contract did not undermine the federal patent law policy that unpatented items be freely copiable by others. Chief Justice Burger also took pains to distinguish the *Brulotte* holding. As Aronson had never obtained a patent, Quick Point was unable to rely upon the doctrine of misuse. The Court also observed that the parties had expressly planned for the contingency that no patent would issue within five years, resulting in a reduced royalty payment. Under these circumstances, the Court concluded, it could not

2. 293 F.3d 1014, 63 USPQ2d 1404 (7th Cir. 2002).

3. 440 U.S. 257 (1979).

be said that Aronson had attempted to enlarge the scope of a patent impermissibly.

In a concurring opinion, Justice Blackmun explained that he had a difficult time distinguishing *Aronson* from *Brulotte*. In his view, Aronson used the leverage of her patent application to obtain perpetual royalty payments (even though the Patent Office eventually denied her application) in much the same way as the patentee in *Brulotte* used the leverage of the patent to induce the licensee to agree to post-expiration royalties. Nonetheless, Justice Blackmun agreed with the majority's holding, reasoning that although a patent application that is later denied may temporarily discourage unlicensed imitators, the degree to which competition is suppressed is less than in cases where a patentee demands post-expiration royalties.

The Supreme Court decided *Brulotte* in an era of considerable judicial hostility to patent rights. The tide has plainly turned today. Modern pro-patent trends, along with the reasoning in *Aronson* itself, render it uncertain whether the Supreme Court would reach the same result if it were asked to revisit the issue today. Nonetheless, *Brulotte* remains on the books and should be scrupulously observed. If, for example, an agreement licenses multiple patents, the patentee would be wise to stipulate a decreasing "step-down" royalty rate as each patent expires or is invalidated, lest it appear that it is demanding royalties for any one patent beyond the term of that particular patent. And, of course, if a licensee needs financing, it should go to a bank rather than the patent proprietor.

§ 11.7 Implied Licenses

A license to practice a patented invention may exist even in the absence of express contractual language. This is because a patent license may be implied in certain situations. Thorough readers of this text have already encountered a handful of circumstances where the law effectively implies a license. The exhaustion doctrine, through which a legitimate purchaser may dispose of a patented article without regard to the patent, provides an example of an implied license.[1] A legitimate purchaser also possesses an implied license to repair, although not to reconstruct, a patented product.[2] A party who successfully asserts a defense of laches or estoppel may also, in a broad sense, be viewed as enjoying an implied license.[3]

Implied licenses are not limited to these scenarios, however. As Chief Justice Taft explained in *De Forest Radio Telephone & Telegraph Co. v. United States*:

§ 11.7

1. *See supra* § 8.1.1.2.
2. *See supra* § 8.1.1.3.
3. *See supra* § 10.4.

> No formal granting of a license is necessary in order to give it effect. Any language used by the owner of a patent or any conduct on his part exhibited to another, from which that other may properly infer that the owner consents to his use of the patent in making or using it, or selling it, upon which the other acts, constitutes a license, and a defense to an action for a tort.[4]

This statement suggests that courts may imply a license in a wide variety of situations under equitable grounds, with particular focus upon the conduct of the patentee and the detrimental reliance of the accused infringer. This inquiry is conducted on a case-by-case basis and heavily depends upon the particular facts of a case. The existence of an implied license is a question of law, and the burden of proof that an implied license exists lies with the accused infringer.[5]

Although implied licenses have been found in diverse situations, a few recurring factual circumstances are worthy of note here. In some cases a patentee sells equipment that is not the subject of a product patent. The purchaser of this equipment could use the equipment in such a manner that would infringe a process patent or produce a patented product, however. The Federal Circuit has stated a two-part test to determine whether the purchaser of such equipment enjoys an implied license in these circumstances. According to the court, an implied license exists if (1) the equipment has no noninfringing uses, and (2) the circumstances of the sale must "plainly indicate that the grant of a license should be inferred."[6]

Most of the judicial opinions applying this standard focus upon the first factor. If the equipment cannot be used without infringing a patent, and the patent owner has placed no restrictions on the use of that equipment, then the Federal Circuit deems the accused infringer to have made a *prima facie* case of an implied license. The burden of proof then passes to the patentee to demonstrate the absence of one of these elements.[7] This approach certainly seems logical. The purchaser of a machine with no known use other than to practice a patented method would be more than a little shocked to learn that having paid for the machine, any use of it constituted infringement because he failed to separately negotiate a patent license.

4. 273 U.S. 236 (1927).

5. Bandag, Inc. v. Al Bolser's Tire Sales, 750 F.2d 903, 924, 223 USPQ 982, 998 (Fed. Cir. 1984).

6. 750 F.2d at 925, 233 USPQ at 998.

7. Met–Coil Systems Corp. v. Korners Unlimited, Inc., 803 F.2d 684, 687, 231 USPQ 474, 476 (Fed. Cir. 1986).

Suppose, for example, that chemists synthesized two compounds, Chemical X and Chemical Y, long ago, and any patents on these compounds expired long ago. There is no known practical use for either compound by itself. However, they may be combined to form Compound Z, a valuable pharmaceutical. Assume that the Acme Chemical Company holds a patent claiming Compound Z. Acme also sells a quantity of Compound X and Compound Y to the Beta Pharmaceutical Company, knowing that Beta will combine these chemicals to form Compound Z. Under these circumstances, Beta enjoys an implied license to combine the chemicals it purchased from Alpha into Compound Z. Because Compounds X and Y have no other use at all, and because Alpha understood Beta's intentions, then Alpha cannot assert its Compound Z patent against Beta.

The courts have also stated that an individual who assigns or licenses a patent cannot, through subsequent action, retract that grant of rights. This doctrine is sometimes termed "legal estoppel."[8] In this line of cases, the patentee typically has licensed or assigned a right, received consideration, and then sought to withdraw the right granted. In *AMP, Inc. v. United States*,[9] for example, AMP developed a wire-splicing tool under a research and development contract with the U.S. government. The contract granted the U.S. government a license to use the tool, which AMP subsequently patented. AMP only later discovered that a previously issued patent, granted to a third party, claimed one aspect of the wire-splicing tool. AMP purchased that patent and then sued the government for use of the patented invention in the Court of Claims. The court barred AMP's suit, stating the general rule that when "a person sells a patent which employs an invention which infringes a prior patent, the person selling is estopped from bringing an action against his grantee for that infringement, even though the earlier patent is acquired after the sale of the latent patent."[10] Applying this principle, the court awarded the U.S. government an implied license to prevent the patentee from using a preexisting-but-later-acquired patent to derogate from the express license negotiated under AMP's other patent.

§ 11.8 Shop Rights

The great majority of contemporary inventors create new technologies while serving as employees, usually of large corporate entities. In many of the world's patent systems, legislation provides

8. Wang Laboratories, Inc. v. Mitsubishi Electronics America, Inc., 103 F.3d 1571, 41 USPQ2d 1263 (Fed. Cir. 1997).

9. 389 F.2d 448, 156 USPQ 647 (Ct. Cl. 1968).

10. 389 F.2d at 451, 156 USPQ at 649.

such employed inventors with rights to their inventions. In the United States, however, an employed engineer or scientist will typically enter into an employment contract with her employer. Such contracts typically contain provisions expressly assigning all patent rights, in advance, to the corporate employer. Moreover, the U.S. patent law tends to favor employers over employees, regardless of whether there is an employment contract of this sort.[1] For instance, a license in favor of the employer may be implied where the employee was hired to perform a specific function that would include inventing. Even where no express agreement exists between the employee and the employer and where the employee was not hired to invent, an employer may still obtain the legal authorization to use a patented invention developed and perfected by an employee. This authorization goes by the curious name "shop right."

A "shop right" is not a machinist's tool, nor permission to go to the mall and buy new clothes, but rather an employer's entitlement to employ an invention patented by its employee without liability for infringement. This entitlement most clearly arises where an employee conceived of the invention during working hours, reduced the invention to practice using the employer's resources and allowed the invention to be incorporated into the employer's facilities.[2] Shop right cases often involve inventors who implemented improvements to an employer's manufacturing equipment. Subsequently, the inventor leaves the service of the employer and obtains a patent upon the invention. When the inventor sues his former employer for patent infringement, the shop right defense comes into play.

The leading Federal Circuit case on shop rights remains Judge Rich's instructive 1993 opinion in *McElmurry v. Arkansas Power & Light Co.*[3] The plaintiffs brought suit against Arkansas Power & Light (AP&L) for infringement of the '714 patent, which named Bowman as the inventor. Bowman had developed a patented level detector[4] while serving as a consultant to AP&L. AP&L successfully moved for summary judgment based on its possession of shop rights in the claimed level detector, and on appeal the Federal Circuit affirmed.

§ 11.8

1. *See* Jay Dratler, Jr., *Incentives for People: The Forgotten Purpose of the United States Patent System*, 16 Harv. J. Legis. 129 (1979).

2. *See* United States v. Dubilier Condenser Corp., 289 U.S. 178, 188–89, 53 S.Ct. 554, 77 L.Ed. 1114, 17 USPQ 154 (1933).

3. 995 F.2d 1576, 27 USPQ2d 1129 (Fed.Cir.1993).

4. In the course of generating electricity, coal-fired steam boilers emit gasses that contain an impurity known as "fly ash." To minimize pollution, this fly ash is removed and deposited in containers called hoppers. A level detector is a device that monitors the amount of fly ash in a hopper.

The Federal Circuit began by identifying the varying doctrinal bases for shop rights. Judge Rich noted that the courts tended to rely upon two underlying foundations for judging the existence and extent of a shop right. The first relies on a theory of an implied license.[5] This theory focuses attention upon whether the employee engaged in activities, such as using the employer's time and tools, that demand a finding the employer was impliedly licensed to use the resulting invention. The second is based upon an estoppel theory.[6] The estoppel rationale suggests that shop rights should be based upon whether the employee consented or acquiesced to an employer's use of the invention.

Declining to pick whether the implied license or estoppel theory provided the superior basis for shop rights, the court held that the proper methodology in shop right cases was "to look to the totality of the circumstances on a case by case basis and determine whether the facts of a particular case demand, under principles of equity and fairness, a finding that a 'shop right' exists." Applying this general principle to the facts of the case, Judge Rich noted that Bowman had developed the patented level detector while working at AP&L; had consented to the installation of numerous level detectors onto AP&L's equipment; and had never asserted, at least prior to this litigation, that AP&L was required to compensate him for use of the level detector. Each of these factors supported the conclusion that AP&L enjoyed a shop right in Bowman's patented invention.

Even when it is clear that a shop right is appropriate, defining the exact scope of the shop right can prove to be a perplexing task. For instance, although the very name "shop right" suggests that the employer's right to use the invention be limited to the specific site where the employee was working when she developed the invention, the courts have tended to allow employers greater flexibility. Speaking generally, the shop right has been liberally construed with an eye towards the business requirements of the employer. However, as befits an equitable doctrine, the precise extent to which the employer may expand its use of the patented invention over the life of the shop right has also been subject to a case by case determination.[7]

Fortunately, there are a few details that are clear. The case law uniformly indicates that a shop right endures through the duration of the patent.[8] A shop right remains personal to the employer and

5. *See supra* § 11.7.

6. *See supra* § 10.4.

7. *See* Kierulff v. Metropolitan Stevedore Co., 315 F.2d 839, 137 USPQ 195 (9th Cir.1963); Thompson v. American Tobacco Co., 174 F.2d 773, 81 USPQ 323 (4th Cir.1949); Pure Oil Co. v. Hyman, 95 F.2d 22, 25, 36 USPQ 306, 310 (7th Cir.1938).

8. *See* Wiegand v. Dover Mfg. Co., 292 F. 255 (N.D.Ohio 1923).

cannot be transferred,[9] except if the employer sells its entire business.[10] Finally, title to the patent remains vested in the employee-patentee, who is free to license or assign the patent to others,[11] including competitors of the employer.

9. *See* Tripp v. United States, 406 F.2d 1066, 1070, 157 USPQ 90, 161 USPQ 115 (Ct.Cl.1969).

10. Pursche v. Atlas Scraper & Eng'g Co., 300 F.2d 467, 485, 132 USPQ 104 (9th Cir.1961).

11. *See* United States v. Dubilier Condenser Corp., 289 U.S. 178, 53 S.Ct. 554, 77 L.Ed. 1114, 17 USPQ 154 (1933).

Chapter 12

PATENT LAW IN INTERNATIONAL PERSPECTIVE

Table of Sections

Globalization trends have resulted in growing international trade, burgeoning flows of information, and increasingly dispersed manufacturing facilities. One consequence of these trends is that now more than ever, innovative firms find patent protection within a single country insufficient. To provide meaningful protection, patent rights must instead be secured in multiple jurisdictions. A primary difficulty with this effort is that, under the principle of "territoriality," a U.S. patent provides its owners with rights only within the United States.[1] Furthermore, no true global patent system exists. Under current law, there is no way for an inventor to obtain an "international patent" through a single grant proceeding. The consequence is that inventors who seek patent rights overseas must file individual applications in each country or region where protection is desired.

The patent regimes of the United States and its trading partners are linked, however, through a handful of international agreements. The foundational patent treaty, the 1884 Convention of Paris for the Protection of Industrial Property, provides inventors with an "international priority" mechanism that expedites the acquisition of patent rights in many countries. The Paris Convention has been supplemented by the Patent Cooperation Treaty of 1970, which allows inventors to file a single "international patent application" that begins the patent acquisition process in over one hundred signatory nations.

By imposing an obligation of national treatment upon its signatories, the Paris Convention also made an initial effort at legal harmonization. More recent treaties have pursued this goal more aggressively. Various bilateral and regional agreements, along with the 1994 TRIPS Agreement of the World Trade Organization, require their signatories to comply with specified substantive legal standards governing such subjects as patentable subject matter, duration of rights and enforcement litigation. This effort has proven controversial. Many observers have questioned the fairness of requiring developing and least-developed countries to respect patents in light of their national needs, particularly in the field of pharmaceuticals. This Chapter takes up these topics, commencing with the Paris Convention.

§ 12.1 The Paris Convention

The foundational international agreement concerning patents, the Paris Convention, was formed in 1884.[1] As of July 15, 2003, 164 nations had signed the Paris Convention.[2] The World Intellectual Property Organization (WIPO), a specialized agency of the United Nations which is located in Geneva, Switzerland, administers this international agreement (and a number of subsequent instruments addressing intellectual property). The Paris Convention commits its signatories to the principles of national treatment and patent

1. Quality Tubing, Inc. v. Precision Tube Holdings Co., 75 F.Supp.2d 613, 619 (S.D. Tex. 1999).

§ 12.1

1. Convention of Paris for the Protection of Industrial Property, 13 U.S.T. 25 (1962).

2. To put that number in context, as of mid–2002, there were 193 sovereign nations on earth. *See,* <http://www.nationsonline.org/oneworld/states.htm>

independence. It also establishes a system of international priority that facilitates multinational patent acquisition.

12.1.1 National Treatment

Through the national treatment principle, Paris Convention signatories agree to treat foreign inventors no worse than domestic inventors in their patent laws, so long as these foreign inventors are nationals of some other Paris Convention signatory state.[3] It would be impermissible, for example, for the U.S. PTO to charge nationals of a Paris Convention signatory state a higher application fee than is required of U.S. citizens, or to provide a shorter patent term for such inventors than is given to U.S. inventors.

12.1.2 Independence of Patents

Many national patent schemes, including that of the United States, require the patentee to pay maintenance fees at various points during the life of the patent in order to retain protection throughout the patent term. If a patentee determines that an invention is not economically viable, he might decide not to pay those fees and let the patent lapse before the end of the full term of protection, rather than waste money on legal protection that provides no prospect of a market return. However, prior to the adoption of the Paris Convention, most nations applied a principle of patent dependence against foreign inventors. This meant that domestic patents would expire at the same time any foreign patent covering the same invention lapsed and that allowing one patent to lapse would amount to a global forfeiture of patent rights. In such a world, it became necessary to pay maintenance fees and otherwise vigilantly protect patent rights in every nation, even though marketing the invention might prove feasible only in some subset of them.

The Paris Convention eliminates the problem by providing for the independence of different national patents.[4] Even if patent rights lapse in one nation, they remain viable in all others where the requirements of local laws have been satisfied.

One significant consequence of the independence of national patents is that they must be enforced individually. Even different national patent instruments with identically drafted descriptions, drawings, and claims do not stand or fall together. A competitor who succeeds in invalidating one national patent may face the prospect of repeating the effort within the courts of another nation. Similarly, the successful enforcement of a patent in one forum may simply signal the start of patent litigation elsewhere.[5]

3. Paris Convention, Art. 2.

4. Paris Convention, Art. 4bis.

5. *See* Cuno Inc. v. Pall Corp., 729 F. Supp. 234, 239, 14 USPQ2d 1815, 1819–20 (E.D.N.Y. 1989).

12.1.3 International Priority

As many of us have been advised at one time or another, you can't do everything at once. For inventors seeking multinational patent protection that means that it will usually be impossible or very difficult to file patent applications in several nations simultaneously. The common practice is to file first in one's home nation, mostly for reasons of logistical convenience, and thereafter to file in other nations once the application can be translated and foreign counsel can be hired. This approach poses the risk, however, that before the foreign applications can be filed, another inventor may perfect the same invention and file an application for it in one or more other nations. The Paris Convention substantially ameliorates this problem by creating what is known as an international priority system.

Under that system, if an inventor files a patent application in any one Paris Convention signatory state, any applications filed during the next 12 months in any other Paris Convention signatory state must be treated as if they were filed on the first filing date. One critical consequence of this rule is that information that enters the public domain between the priority date and subsequent filing dates does not prejudice the later applications. The bottom line, therefore is that Paris Convention priority allows inventors to preserve their original filing dates as they make arrangements to file patent applications overseas.[6]

An example, illustrated graphically below, demonstrates the workings of the Paris Convention priority period. Suppose, for example, that inventor Dr. Snikta files a patent application at the U.S. PTO on January 19, 2004, claiming a method of making low-carbohydrate pizza dough. Snikta then files a patent application claiming the same invention in the Japanese Patent Office on January 19, 2005. As part of his Japanese application, Snikta informs the Japanese Patent Office of the earlier U.S. application. Because Japan has acceded to the Paris Convention, the Japanese Patent Office will treat Snikta's application as if it had been filed on January 19, 2004. As a result, information that entered the public domain after the U.S. filing date would not prejudice the inventor's Japanese application. Sales that begun in Japan on March 1, 2004, for example, would not limit Snikta's ability to obtain a Japanese patent.

6. *See* G.H.C. Bodenhausen, Guide to the Paris Convention for the Protection of Industrial Property (United International Bureau for the Protection of Intellectual Property, Geneva, Switzerland 1968).

MECHANICS OF THE
PARIS CONVENTION

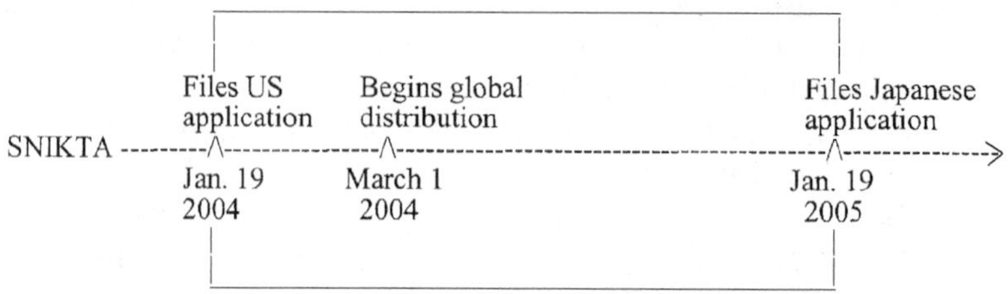

Snikta's effective filing date in Japan is January 19, 2004.

Domestically, the Paris Convention priority rule is implemented in § 119 of the Patent Act. Under that provision, the applicant must fulfill certain additional requirements in order to gain the benefit of the Paris Convention priority date. First, both the foreign and domestic applications must be filed by the same "applicant, legal representatives or assigns." Second, the applicant must formally declare his entitlement to priority at the PTO. Failure to claim priority promptly may result in a waiver of the priority right.[7] Third, the foreign application must have been for a "patent." However, certain foreign instruments such as inventor's certificates, utility model registrations, and other foreign intellectual property rights may qualify as a patent within the meaning of § 119.[8]

Finally, in order to serve as an effective priority document, the foreign application must fulfill the disclosure requirements of § 112 of the Patent Act, including enablement, written description and best mode. One decision in which a foreign applicant ran afoul of this requirement is *In re Gosteli*.[9] On May 4, 1978, Gosteli filed a U.S. patent application that included claims directed towards a generic class of antibiotic compounds. Gosteli's priority application had been filed in Luxembourg on May 9, 1977. Notably, Gosteli's Luxembourg application did not disclose the generic class that was later claimed in the United States. The examiner rejected the claims due to the disclosure of the Menard patent, which was filed in the United States on December 14, 1977. Menard disclosed two

7. 35 U.S.C.A. § 119(b)(2) (2000).

8. *See* 35 U.S.C.A. § 119(d) (2000); American Infra–Red Radiant Co. v. Lambert Indus. Inc., 360 F.2d 977, 149 USPQ 722 (8th Cir.), *cert. denied*, 385 U.S. 920, 87 S.Ct. 233, 17 L.Ed.2d 144 (1966).

9. 872 F.2d 1008, 10 USPQ2d 1614 (Fed.Cir.1989).

antibiotics that were members of the class of compounds recited in Gosteli's generic claims.

On appeal to the Federal Circuit, Gosteli attempted to rely upon the filing date of his Luxembourg application in order to antedate the Menard reference. The Federal Circuit determined that a number of differences existed between what was disclosed in the Luxembourg application and what was claimed in the United States. Alternatively, Gosteli argued that because the Luxembourg application did disclose the two compounds taught by Menard, then the Luxembourg application should at least be enough to remove Menard as a reference. The Federal Circuit disagreed—according to its reading, § 119(a) compelled a comparison between the priority application and the U.S. application, not between the priority application and the reference.

Note that § 119(a) does not limit the right of priority to Paris Convention signatories. Rather, it provides that patent applications initially filed in any country that affords "similar privileges" to applications first filed in the United States may also be awarded priority. Because Article 2 of the TRIPS Agreement requires signatories to respect Article 4 of the Paris Convention, as a practical matter any application originating in a WTO member country will be accorded priority.[10]

12.1.4 Benefits of Paris Convention Priority

Under § 119(a), a priority application has the same effect as if it had been filed in the United States. As a result, a foreign priority date allows applicants to avoid prior art rejections under § 102(a) or (g). For example, suppose that an inventor files an application in Korea on January 19, 2003, and then in the United States on January 4, 2004. The PTO examiner then cites an anticipatory article published on August 1, 2003. The applicant may point to her Korean priority date in order to antedate the reference. A foreign priority date may also be used to demonstrate a date of constructive reduction to practice in an interference under § 102(g).

Section 119(a) further specifies that if the invention had been in public use or on sale in the United States, or patented or described in a printed publication anywhere more than one year before the actual U.S. filing date, then no patent shall issue. The practical effect of this provision is that the one-year grace period provided by § 102(b) is measured from the U.S. filing date, not the foreign priority date. For example, suppose that an invention is described in a published magazine article on March 21, 2003. A German patent application directed towards that invention is filed on April 1, 2003, followed by a corresponding U.S. patent applica-

10. As of mid-2003, 146 nations were members of the WTO.

tion on March 31, 2004. In this case the March 21, 2003, publication bars the issuance of a U.S. patent even though the applicant is otherwise entitled to a priority date of April 1, 2003.

Recall that under § 102(e),[11] a granted patent has prior art effect as of its U.S. filing date, rather than its issue date, for subject matter it discloses but does not claim. Similarly, published patent applications are given prior art effectiveness as of their filing date for purposes of § 102(e). We have not yet addressed the impact of § 119 foreign priority filings upon § 102(e), however. In cases where a patent claims a foreign priority date under § 119, at least two possibilities exist: the appropriate § 102(e) date could be either (1) the foreign filing date, or (2) the actual U.S. filing date which, under the Paris Convention, may be up to twelve months later. In its infamous *Hilmer* opinions,[12] the CCPA chose the second option. The so-called *Hilmer* rule states that § 102(e) is effective only upon the date the application was filed in the United States, even where the application enjoys a foreign priority date. The following timeline displays the pertinent facts at issue in the *Hilmer* cases:

Habicht———	Files Switzerland Jan. 24, 1957	——Files United States Jan. 23, 1958	———U.S. Patent Issues Nov. 29, 1960———>
Hilmer———	Files Germany July 31, 1957	———————	Files United States July 25, 1958——>

The PTO initially conducted an interference proceeding between Habicht and Hilmer. At the time, § 104 of the Patent Act did not allow inventors to submit evidence of their dates of inventive activity that occurred outside the United States.[13] Under the facts of the case, both Habicht and Hilmer had done their inventing overseas. As a result, the earliest date that either party could rely upon was the date he had first filed a patent application in a Paris Convention signatory state. Because Habicht first filed in Switzerland about six months prior to Hilmer's German filing, Habicht handily won the interference.

The PTO then dissolved the interference and returned the Hilmer application to the examiner. All was not lost for the rather clever Hilmer, however. He then drafted a new set of claims that were somewhat different from those of the count of the interference he had just lost. Hilmer's new claims would not have been com-

11. *See supra* § 4.4.3.

12. *See* In re Hilmer, 359 F.2d 859, 149 USPQ 480 (CCPA 1966) ("Hilmer I"); In re Hilmer, 424 F.2d 1108, 165 USPQ 255 (CCPA 1970) ("Hilmer II").

13. Section 104 has since been amended to allow such evidence in some circumstances, effective January 1, 1996. *See supra* § 4.4.2.3.

pletely anticipated by the disclosure of the Habicht patent. However, Hilmer's new claims would have been obvious in view of the disclosure of the Habicht patent. The examiner quickly imposed an obviousness rejection, relying upon Habicht as prior art under § 102(e). Hilmer disagreed, asserting that priority applications under § 119 cannot be accorded prior art status under § 102(e). Hilmer lost before the Patent Office Board, but then appealed the matter to the CCPA.

The CCPA was then left to decide the point at which the disclosure of the Habicht patent served as prior art against Hilmer. Although Habicht was entitled to his Swiss filing date under § 119, the court held that the Habicht patent was effective as a prior art reference only as of its actual U.S. filing date. Section 102(e) expressly refers to patent applications "filed in the United States," the court reasoned, and priority applications under § 119 should not be read into this language. According to the court, Paris Convention priority under § 119 served only as a shield to fend off prior art references, not as a sword to defeat the applications of others. The result was that Hilmer was entitled to employ his German filling date to antedate Habicht's U.S. filing date, even though Habicht's Swiss filing predated Hilmer's German filing.

The upshot of the *Hilmer* rule is that issued U.S. patents and published U.S. patent applications are effective as prior art under § 102(e) and the *Alexander Milburn* rule only as of their actual U.S. filing date. Whether or not the patent claims a foreign priority date is irrelevant. For example, suppose that U.S.-based inventor Arthur Auralis conceives of a new kind of ear plug on November 1, 2003, and reduces it to practice on November 15, 2003. Auralis then files a U.S. patent application on March 1, 2004. During prosecution, the U.S. PTO examiner cites as a reference a published U.S. patent application. The published application, which was filed by a Dutch inventor named Oar, does not claim precisely the same ear plug as Auralis. However, given the disclosure of the Oar application, the Auralis ear plug would have been obvious. The Oar application was filed at the U.S. PTO on January 15, 2004, claiming international priority from an application filed at the Dutch Patent Office on January 30, 2003.

Under these facts, Auralis will be able to disqualify the Oar application as prior art due to the *Hilmer* rule. Auralis need simply file a Rule 131 affidavit demonstrating his actual reduction to practice prior to Oar's U.S. filing date of January 15, 2004. That Oar filed his Dutch application in early 2003—months prior to the date Auralis even thought of his own invention—is irrelevant to the analysis. Of course, had the *Hilmer* holding gone the other way, then the Oar disclosure would have prevented Auralis from obtaining a patent.

This example illustrates two consequences of the *Hilmer* rule upon U.S. patent practice. First, the U.S. PTO issues more patents as a result of *Hilmer*. The opinion in *Hilmer* itself demonstrates some of the resulting mischief, for the immediate result of that opinion was two patents with claims that were likely very similar to each other. Second, the *Hilmer* rule favors patent applicants based in the United States. Those who file their priority application elsewhere learn that their application is not accorded prior art effect until such time as they file in the United States. As a result, up to one year's worth of patent-defeating effect is lost, an eternity in many fast-moving and competitive industries.[14]

The foreign patent community continues to voice its outrage at the holdings in *Hilmer*. Most patent systems provide both priority and patent-defeating effect to the Paris Convention priority application. As a result, the winner of the race to the first patent office potentially wins exclusive rights in the disclosed invention almost everywhere in the world. In the United States, however, a subsequent applicant can obtain a patent claiming subject matter disclosed in the earlier application. Most observers consequently believe that the *Hilmer* rule violates at least the spirit of the priority mechanism of Paris Convention Article 4.[15]

12.1.5 The Future of the Paris Convention

The Paris Convention was an advanced treaty at the time of its formation in the late nineteenth century. However, many observers believed that its shortcomings have become more pronounced with the passage of time. Other than the minimal standard of national treatment, the Paris Convention does not provide substantive patent law standards for its signatories to adopt within their domestic patent systems.[16] The Paris Convention further lacks an effective enforcement mechanism. Although one member nation could commence an action against another for Paris Convention violations in the International Court of Justice, that tribunal's lack of enforcement powers made this possibility more theoretical than practical. In the long history of the Paris Convention, no such suit has ever been brought.[17]

Finally, the Paris Convention requires unanimous consent to amend. As the number of signatory states grew, such consensus became difficult to obtain. Consequently, the opportunity to advance the international patent system shifted to other vehicles,

14. *See* Richard A. Neifeld, *Viability of the Hilmer Doctrine*, 81 J. PAT. & TRADEMARK OFF. SOC'Y 544 (1999).

15. *See* Kevin L. Leffel, Comment, 26 AKRON L. REV. 355 (1992).

16. Frederick Abbott *et al.*, THE INTERNATIONAL INTELLECTUAL PROPERTY SYSTEM: COMMENTARY AND MATERIALS (Kluwer Law International, The Hague 1999), 646.

17. *Id.* at 661–62.

including the Patent Cooperation Treaty, NAFTA, and the TRIPS Agreement.

§ 12.2 The Patent Cooperation Treaty

The Patent Cooperation Treaty, or PCT, was formed in Washington, DC in 1970, and subject to significant amendments effective January 1, 2004.[1] Recognizing the needless repetition of duplicative patent examinations around the world, representatives of different patent offices agreed to a procedural framework to facilitate the often burdensome task of multinational patent acquisition. The PCT is open to any nation that has acceded to the Paris Convention, and in fact over 110 nations have currently signed the PCT. It provides for the filing of one patent application that can lead to issued patents in many countries.[2]

The PCT is a complex treaty, particularly as it allows signatory states several options as to implementing some of its finer points. A brief explanation will suffice, however, to set out treaty's basic workings as they apply to applications filed after January 1, 2004. An inventor may use the PCT if he is a national or domicile of a contracting state. U.S. inventors ordinarily commence the PCT process by filing a so-called "international application" at the U.S. PTO. Many of these applications claim priority from an earlier U.S. application under § 119—that is to say, a U.S. national application is filed first, followed by a PCT international application within twelve months. However, other inventors chose to make the international application their first filing anywhere in the world, rather than filing a U.S. application first.

No matter which of these paths is taken, an inventor who files a single "international application" is treated as if he had filed an application in each of the PCT member states.[3] Needless to say, it is much easier to file a single, English-language application at the U.S. PTO than to file over 110 patent applications in diverse languages all across the globe. Under PCT procedures, the international application is automatically published eighteen months from the earliest priority date to which it is entitled.

The PCT applicant next receives an international search report along with an "International Preliminary Report on Patentability." Because these procedures are set out in the first chapter of the PCT text itself, they are sometimes called the "Chapter I" proceedings.

§ 12.2

1. Patent Cooperation Treaty, June 19, 1970, 28 U.S.T. 7645, T.I.A.S. No. 8733.

2. Abbot *et al.* at 1430–41.

3. An applicant may expressly refrain from designating Germany, Russia and South Korea, however, as the patent laws of these countries call for the automatic withdrawal of national applications when a PCT application is also pursued on the same invention.

The search report lists citations of prior art relevant to the claims of the international patent application. In addition, a non-binding preliminary examination is made in view of this prior art, according to internationally accepted criteria of patentability, including novelty and nonobviousness. The results of the PCT Chapter I procedures, which are forwarded to the patent offices of all PCT member states, allow the applicant to learn of relevant prior art and decide whether to take further steps towards perfecting his patent rights. Applicants may amend their claims in order to account for the conclusions of the search report and preliminary examination.

Most applicants then commence acquisition procedures at the patent offices of the nations where they seek protection. In the parlance of the PCT, this option is termed the National Stage. For most PCT signatories, the applicant has up to 30 months (31 months in some countries) from the filing date of the priority application to begin local prosecution. At this time, patent examiners in each country examine the application based upon their own national laws, either allowing or rejecting the patent application.

Alternatively, the applicant may take an intermediate step under Chapter II of the PCT. This procedure permits applicants to request an additional "International Preliminary Report on Patentability." A Chapter II report is much like a Chapter I report, in that it provides a preliminary patentability assessment that does not bind the national patent offices. Applicants who received unfavorable Chapter I reports may appreciate the opportunity to receive a second report, however, as the opportunity to engage in additional dialogue with an examiner, and to enter further claim amendments, may lead to a more positive second opinion. Even if a Chapter II report is requested, the applicant must ordinarily commence prosecution in the national patent offices within 30 months (or 31 months in some countries) from the application's first filing date.

Let us try to make all this a bit more concrete with the aid of a brief hypothetical. To continue an earlier example,[4] suppose that instead of employing the Paris Convention, Dr. Snikta decided to seek multi-national patent protection for his low-carbohydrate pizza dough using the PCT. As illustrated below, Snikta should file an international application at the U.S. PTO within twelve months of his initial domestic filing date. Most PCT member states would then allow Snikta an additional 18 months before he would need to pursue acquisition procedures in individual foreign patent offices (that's because he has 30 months to begin prosecuting his applications and 12 + 18 = 30).

4. *See supra* § 12.1.3.

MECHANICS OF THE
PATENT COOPERATION TREATY

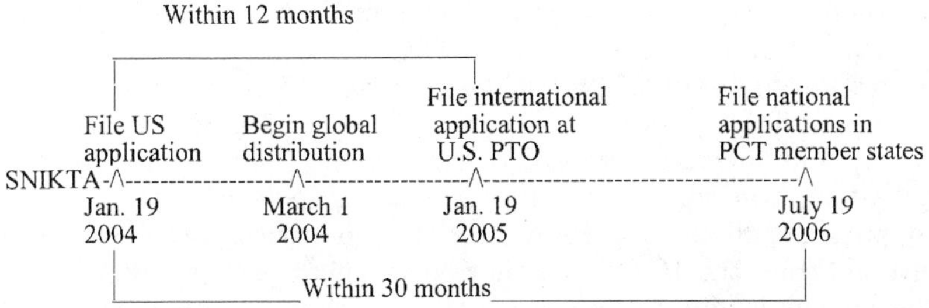

```
            Within 12 months
         ________________________________
         |                              |
         |                        File international           File national
     File US         Begin global      application at            applications in
     application     distribution      U.S. PTO                  PCT member states
SNIKTA-/\-----------------/\----------------/\----------------------------------/\
     Jan. 19          March 1          Jan. 19                          July 19
     2004             2004             2005                             2006
         |                                                              |
         |_____________________Within 30 months_________________________|
```

Effective filing date in PCT member states is January 19, 2004.

A comparison of this example with the earlier illustration involving Snikta's use of the Paris Convention demonstrates the advantages of using the PCT. Using the PCT, Snikta ordinarily obtains an additional 18 months to test his invention in the market before being required to file foreign patent applications. Snikta may also defer the preparation of foreign language translations of his U.S. application for this period. He will also be provided a search report and "International Preliminary Report on Patentability (Chapter I)." These documents may reveal that Snikta's invention is not patentable, and may allow him to abandon his international patenting efforts before devoting further resources towards the effort.

The PCT has attracted a large number of applicants, with a disproportionate share of users based in the United States. Still, the PCT has been subject to some criticism. Upon entering the national stage, many patent offices do not appear to respect fully the PCT search and patentability reports. In fact, most patent offices normally repeat the search and examination at the national phase in the same manner as for an ordinary national application. Differences in patent office practices, distinctions in the prior art definition under the world's patent laws,[5] and language barriers may account for this trend. Under the view of some observers, these redundant efforts appear to undermine much of the logic behind the PCT.[6] Resolution of some of these issues could serve as a positive step towards developing a true global patent procurement procedure.

5. *See infra* §§ 12.8.1, 12.8.2.

6. *See* Markus Nolff, *TRIPS, PCT and Global Patent Procurement*, 83 Journal of the Patent and Trademark Office Society 479 (2001).

§ 12.3 Foreign Filing Licenses

The Invention Secrecy Act—codified as part of the Patent Act—prohibits an inventor from filing a patent application in another country on an invention made in the United States unless he obtains a license from the PTO.[1] Inventors may obtain the license through one of two routes. One option is to file a petition with the PTO expressly requesting a foreign filing license. Alternatively, and far more typically, the inventor simply files a U.S. patent application, which is also deemed an application for a license to pursue patent protection in other countries. In either case, officials from the PTO and other government agencies will review the application to determine whether disclosure of the invention would be detrimental to the national security.[2] Following this review, the PTO sends a filing receipt to the applicant that indicates whether the license has been granted or not.

If the PTO grants the foreign filing license, the inventor is free to seek patent protection abroad. However, if the government concludes that disclosure of the invention would implicate national security interests, then it will deny the license and issue a secrecy order. In addition to compelling the inventor not to publish or disclose the invention to anyone not aware of the invention prior to the date of this order, the order also requires the inventor to seek PTO permission before filing applications on that invention in foreign countries. The inventor may seek compensation for damages caused by the secrecy order.[3] Government officials periodically review the secrecy order and may rescind it when disclosure of the invention is no longer deemed detrimental to national security.

Sometimes inventors fail to obtain a license before filing patent applications overseas. As a penalty, the Patent Act declares any U.S. patent on that subject matter invalid.[4] The statute does provide a liberal mechanism for curing a violation of the foreign filing license requirement. Following the 1988 Patent Law Foreign Filing Amendments Act, a license may be granted retroactively where the application was filed abroad "through error and without deceptive intent" and the application does not disclose an invention that implicated national security concerns.[5]

§ 12.4 Regional Agreements

A number of regional agreements provide for some sort of centralized examination procedure, through which an inventor can obtain multiple patents effective in each of several member nations

§ 12.3

1. 35 U.S.C.A. § 184 (2000). *See supra* § 7.2.8.
2. 35 U.S.C.A. § 181 (2000).
3. 35 U.S.C.A. § 183 (2000).
4. 35 U.S.C.A. § 185 (2000).
5. 35 U.S.C.A. § 184 (2000).

designated by the applicant. Although the United States is not a party to any of these treaties, domestic inventors frequently take advantage of these regional examination techniques when seeking patents abroad.

The European Patent Convention (EPC) is the most prominent example of a regional patent harmonization agreement.[1] The EPC established a European Patent Office based principally in Munich, Germany and the Hague, the Netherlands. An inventor may file a single patent application at the European Patent Office, which, if accepted, matures into a number of individual national patents in the European states the applicant has designated.

Significantly, the EPC does not create a unitary European patent. A European Patent Office application amounts to a group of national patent applications that are processed together but then are given individual legal effect within the appropriate jurisdictions. Once issued by the European Patent Office, these patents enjoy independent legal lives, and must be enforced and maintained separately. The nations of the EU are engaged in ongoing discussions regarding the establishment of a truly unified European patent system, through which an inventor could procure and enforce a single patent effective throughout Europe.[2]

Other regional agreements include:

- the African Intellectual Property Organization (more properly known as the Organization Africaine de la Propriete Intellectuelle or OAPI), for portions of French-speaking Africa.
- the African Regional Intellectual Property Organization (ARIPO), for portions of English-speaking Africa.
- the Eurasian Patent Convention, joined by certain former members of the Soviet Union.

§ 12.5 NAFTA

The North American Free Trade Agreement (NAFTA) became effective on January 1, 1994. This treaty, currently joined by the United States, Canada and Mexico, includes a number of intellectual property provisions.[1] NAFTA signatories have agreed to comply

§ 12.4

1. *See* Gerald Paterson, The European Patent System: The Law and Practice of the European Patent Convention (Sweet & Maxwell, London 2000).

2. *See* The EU Presidency, "Press release: Common political approach achieved on the Community Patent at the meeting of the Competitiveness Council in Brussels" (March 3, 2003) (available at http://www.eu2003.gr/en/articles/2003/3/3/2129/).

§ 12.5

1. North American Free Trade Agreement, Dec. 17, 1992, 32 I.L.M. 289; *see also* North American Free Trade Agreement Implementation Act, P. L. 103–182, 107 Stat. 2057 (1993).

with obligations that are more rigorous than either the Paris Convention or the PCT. NAFTA is notable for stipulating a number of substantive patent law measures, including term of protection, scope of rights accorded to patentees, and standards of patentability such as novelty and nonobviousness.

The patent provisions of NAFTA foreshadowed a larger project that was soon to follow. Shortly after committing to NAFTA, each of its member states also joined the World Trade Organization (WTO). One of the components of the WTO is the Agreement on Trade–Related Aspects of Intellectual Property Rights. For the most part, the "TRIPS Agreement" includes a number of provisions that are identical or similar to those found in NAFTA, but also adds some additional obligations. Given that almost 150 nations have joined the WTO, and are thus bound by TRIPS, while only three nations belong to NAFTA, global attention has focused on the patent commitments of the TRIPS Agreement. We will therefore follow the conventional practice and give NAFTA short shrift, saving ink for a more detailed discussion of the TRIPS Agreement immediately below.

It should be noted that in a few respects, however, the intellectual property obligations of NAFTA exceed those of the TRIPS Agreement. For patents, the most significant of these measures is the obligation to extend "pipeline patent protection" to pharmaceuticals and agricultural chemicals in certain circumstances. More specifically, if the NAFTA member state did not allow product patents to issue on pharmaceuticals and agricultural chemicals prior to July 1, 1991, or did not allow patents to issue on naturally occurring substances prepared or produced by, or significantly derived from, microbiological processes and intended for food or medicine, prior to January 1, 1992, then the NAFTA signatory must provide the inventor or its assignee with the means to obtain a product patent with a term equal to the unexpired term of the product patent granted in another signatory state. This obligation does not apply if the product was marketed in that NAFTA signatory state.[2] This pipeline commitment impacted both Canada and Mexico, which had placed various limitations on the availability of such patents prior to the adoption of NAFTA.

§ 12.6 The TRIPS Agreement

One component of the international agreement forming the World Trade Organization (WTO) is the so-called TRIPS Agreement, or Agreement on Trade–Related Aspects of Intellectual Property Rights.[1] The TRIPS Agreement is the most detailed and

2. NAFTA, Article 1709(4).

§ 12.6

1. *See* Agreement on Trade–Related Aspects of Intellectual Property Rights,

comprehensive multilateral agreement on intellectual property yet achieved. As every WTO member state has pledged to comply with TRIPS Agreement standards, this accomplishment is even more impressive. While the TRIPS Agreement deals with issues arising in all three branches of intellectual property, some of its most significant innovations deal with patent law, and are reviewed in the sections that follow.

12.6.1 Minimum Standards of Protection

Under Part III of the TRIPS Agreement, all WTO member countries agreed to enact patent statutes that include certain substantive provisions. In particular, each signatory agreed to allow patents to issue on inventions "in all fields of technology, provided that they are new, involve an inventive step and are capable of industrial application."[2] The TRIPS Agreement includes some exceptions to this broad principle, however. Certain methods of medical treatment, plants and animals other than microorganisms, and inventions that violate the "*ordre public* or morality" may be excluded from patentability at the option of a member state.[3] This provision is significant because many nations—especially developing nations—did not formerly permit the patenting of certain types of products, such as pharmaceuticals. Because these nations have a strong desire to join the world trading system established by the WTO, and thus gain favorable tariff treatment for their exports, they have acquiesced to the TRIPS rules concerning patentable subject matter. As a result, they will have to extend patent protection to categories of inventions that may have been traditionally outside the scope of their national patent laws. While this plainly strengthens the patent protections available to innovative companies, it is not uncontroversial, as it may increase the costs of vital medications to the poor populations of some of these nations.

WTO members also agreed that patentees shall have the right to exclude others from making, using, offering for sale, selling, or importing the patented invention.[4] The TRIPS Agreement again creates an exception to this broad principle, however, allowing member states to limit patent rights under certain circumstances. Article 30 of the TRIPS Agreement states:

> Members may provide limited exceptions to the exclusive rights conferred by a patent, provided that such exceptions do not unreasonably conflict with a normal exploitation of the patent and do not unreasonably prejudice the legitimate interests of

Apr. 15, 1994, Annex 1C, 33 I.L.M. 1197 (1994) [hereinafter "TRIPS Agreement"].

2. TRIPS Agreement, Article 27(1).

3. TRIPS Agreement, Article 27(2).

4. TRIPS Agreement, Article 28.

the patent owner, taking account of the legitimate interests of third parties.

WTO members further agreed that the term of patent protection available shall not end before the expiration of a period of 20 years counted from the filing date.[5] In addition, the TRIPS Agreement requires that member states must provide patent owners with the opportunity for judicial review of any decision to revoke or forfeit a patent.[6]

WTO members agreed that patentees should be subject to certain conditions. In particular, the TRIPS Agreement requires that WTO member states "shall require that an applicant for a patent shall disclose the invention in a manner sufficiently clear and complete for the invention to be carried out by a person skilled in the art."[7]

The TRIPS Agreement also requires its signatories to comply with certain provisions of the Paris Convention, including its foreign priority system.[8] This requirement has led to a dramatic increase in the number of Paris Convention signatories.[9] Apparently realizing that they were already obliged to respect the Paris Convention, many WTO member states that were not previously Paris Convention signatories acceded to that treaty.

The TRIPS Agreement also speaks at some length towards compulsory licenses. A compulsory license allows a competitor of the patent owner to use the patented invention without the patent owner's permission, and usually for a royalty payment established by the government.[10] Although compulsory licenses have played only a minor role in the U.S. patent system,[11] many foreign patent statutes include such provisions.[12] These statutes typically require an interested party formally to request the compulsory license from the foreign government. Competent authorities then decide whether to grant the license as well as the terms of any granted license. Grounds for granting a compulsory license include the abusive exercise of patent rights, lack of domestic manufacture of the patented product, commercialization of the patented good that does not satisfy the needs of the local market, and national emergencies.

5. TRIPS Agreement, Article 33.

6. TRIPS Agreement, Article 32.

7. TRIPS Agreement, Article 29.

8. TRIPS Agreement, Article 2. For a discussion of the Paris Convention priority rules, *see,* § 12.1.3, *supra.*

9. Keith E. Maskus, Intellectual Property Rights in the Global Economy (Washington, D.C., Institute for International Economics, 2000).

10. Robert Sherwood, *Intellectual Property and Investment Stimulation: The Ratings of Systems in Eighteen Developing Countries*, 37 IDEA (1997), 261.

11. Dawson Chemical Co. v. Rohm and Haas Co., 448 U.S. 176 n. 21, 100 S.Ct. 2601, 65 L.Ed.2d 696 (1980).

12. Gianna Julian–Arnold, *International Compulsory Licensing: The Rationales and the Reality*, 33 IDEA (1993), 349.

While some accounts suggest that formal compulsory licensing proceedings are commenced only infrequently, the mere existence of a compulsory licensing statute may do much to encourage bargaining between a foreign patentee and domestic industry, on terms favorable to local manufacturers.[13]

The TRIPS Agreement places some limits upon the ability of WTO member states to award compulsory licenses for the use of another's patented invention. Among the most detailed provisions of the TRIPS Agreement, Article 31 imposes in part the following restrictions upon the issuance of compulsory licenses:

- Each application for a compulsory license must be considered on its individual merits.
- The proposed user must have made efforts to obtain authorization from the patent owner on reasonable commercial terms and conditions and must demonstrate that such efforts have not been successful within a reasonable period of time. However, this requirement may be waived in the case of a national emergency or other circumstances of extreme urgency.
- The compulsory license must be revocable if and when its motivating circumstances cease to exist and are unlikely to recur.
- The patent owner must be paid adequate remuneration in the circumstances of each case, taking into account the economic value of the authorization.
- The legal validity of any decision relating to the authorization of such use shall be subject to judicial or other independent review.
- Any such use shall be authorized predominantly for the supply of the domestic market of the member authorizing such use.

The last of the restrictions noted above—requiring that any compulsory license be authorized predominantly for local use—proved a burdensome standard for many nations. Some countries lack the technological or financial capabilities to manufacture advanced products, including certain pharmaceuticals needed to combat AIDS or other epidemics. For many WTO members, the domestic manufacturing requirement of Article 31 rendered the entire compulsory licensing mechanism practically worthless.

13. Sarah Boseley, *Opinion: Pharmaceuticals Move Their Battleground to Brazil to Stem the Tide of Cheaper Drugs*, Irish Times (April 20, 2001), at 14.

The WTO recognized this concern and issued A "Declaration on the TRIPS Agreement and Public Health," following a WTO ministerial conference held in Doha, Qatar in 2001.[14] The result was a 2003 decision of the WTO General Council that limited the domestic supply requirement with respect to pharmaceuticals needed to address public health problems.[15] Under the 2003 decision, any "least developed country,"[15.5] as well as any other country that certifies it has insufficient manufacturing capabilities to manufacture a patented drug, may issue a compulsory license that allows for domestic public health needs to be satisfied through importation. Importantly, the 2003 decision only limits the domestic supply requirement of Article 31. All of the other requirements of Article 31 must still be satisfied for the compulsory license to be validly issued.

12.6.2 Dispute Settlement

As with other obligations imposed by the WTO, TRIPS Agreement obligations are subject to enforcement through the WTO Dispute Settlement Body (DSB).[16] If one WTO member state believes that another member state is in violation of the TRIPS Agreement, the member states may enter into consultation through the DSB. If the member states cannot resolve their dispute, the DSB will convene a panel to hear and resolve the dispute. Panel decisions are subject to review by the DSB Appellate Body. The WTO Agreement calls for compensatory trade measures in circumstances where the DSB finds a WTO member state to be in violation of the TRIPS Agreement, and the offending member state fails to amend its laws to bring them into compliance with treaty obligations.[17]

12.6.3 Effective Dates

The various patent portions of the TRIPS Agreement feature a variety of effective dates. These dates depend upon whether the WTO member state designates itself a developed, developing, or least developed country. For WTO members other than developing

14. The declaration is available at http://www.wto.org/english/thewto_e/minist_e/min01_e/mindecl_trips_e.htm.

15. The decision is available at http://www.wto.org/english/tratop_e/trips_e/implem_para6_e.htm.

15.5 The designation "least developed country" is a term of art in WTO parlance, referring to the poorest nations of the world.

16. Understanding on Rules and Procedures Governing the Settlement of Disputes, Apr. 15, 1994, WTO Agreement, Annex 2, Legal Instruments—Results of the Uruguay Round vol. 31, 33 I.L.M. 1226 (1994).

17. Mark Clough, *The WTO Dispute Settlement System—A Practitioner's Perspective*, 24 Fordham Int'l L. J. (2000), 252.

and least developed countries, the compliance date for all requirements of the TRIPS Agreement was set to January 1, 1996.[18]

For signatory states designated as developing countries, the TRIPS Agreement set the general compliance date as January 1, 2000.[19] However, there is one exception to this general date. If on January 1, 2000, a developing country did not extend patent protection to all areas of technology within the meaning of Article 27, that developing country was permitted to delay implementation of these provisions for an additional five years. Prior to the TRIPS Agreement, for example, many developing countries did not allow patents to issue on pharmaceuticals. The practical effect of this additional transition period was that developing countries need not allow patents on pharmaceuticals until January 1, 2005.[20]

Least-developed countries are entitled to a lengthier transition period in implementing TRIPS Agreement obligations. Effective dates with respect to least-developed countries are found in the TRIPS Agreement itself, as well as the 2001 "Declaration on the TRIPS Agreement and Public Health" issued following the Doha Ministerial Conference.[21] According to the text of the TRIPS Agreement, a least-developed country may delay implementing the TRIPS Agreement until January 1, 2010.[22] A showing of hardship may qualify least-developed countries for further delays and other concessions.[23] The Doha Declaration further excuses least-developed country members from granting or enforcing patents on pharmaceuticals through January 1, 2016, without prejudice to their ability to seek other extensions of these transition periods.

The TRIPS Agreement does not oblige its signatories to protect subject matter that fell into the public domain prior to the time its obligations became effective.[24] For example, suppose that a particular developed country traditionally did not allow patents to issue on pharmaceuticals. If that developed country joins the WTO, it must amend its patent law to authorize pharmaceutical patents. The TRIPS Agreement requires only that patents be allowed on new products as of January 1, 1996, however, and does not mandate that patents be granted retroactively. As a result, patent protection need not be afforded to pharmaceuticals that were known to the

18. TRIPS Agreement, Article 65.

19. The WTO does not, itself, define the concept of a "developing country." Rather, member nations announce for themselves whether they fall within this category, and other member nations may challenge any such self-designation if they think it inappropriate.

20. *Id.*

21. *See supra* notes 14–15 and accompanying text.

22. Approximately 30 of the WTO member states are classified as "least-developed." Some of the least-developed countries in the WTO include Bangladesh, Haiti, and Sierra Leone. For a full list, *see,* <http://www.wto.org/english/thewto_e/whatis_e/tif_e/org7_e.htm>.

23. TRIPS Agreement, Article 66.

24. TRIPS Agreement, Article 70.

public prior to January 1, 1996, even if those pharmaceuticals were patented elsewhere.

The TRIPS Agreement includes two other transitional measures known as pipeline protection and exclusive marketing rights. Although the TRIPS Agreement allows developing countries to delay implementing their patent law obligations, it requires that they immediately establish so-called pipeline protection for pharmaceuticals. Some sources refer to pipeline protection as the "mailbox rule."[25] Under this requirement, countries that do not allow pharmaceutical patents to issue must nonetheless accept patent applications. These patent applications will essentially be held at the national patent office until it comes time for the patent application to be considered.

Pipeline protection is valuable because it allows inventors to establish a date of priority of invention. Although many years might pass between the application's filing date and the date on which it would be examined, the inventiveness of the claimed invention must be judged as of its filing date. Pipeline protection allows inventors to obtain patents even though many years have passed between the date of filing and the date of compliance with the TRIPS Agreement.

The TRIPS Agreement also mandates that WTO member states award an Exclusive Marketing Right (EMR) to inventors in specified circumstances. The holder of an EMR concerning a particular product is designated as the only entity authorized to distribute that product within the member state. The award of EMRs provides innovators with transitional, patent-like market exclusivity in member states that do not yet offer patent protection for pharmaceuticals.

In order for an enterprise to obtain an EMR in one WTO member state, that enterprise must obtain both a patent and marketing approval on that pharmaceutical in another WTO member state. That enterprise must also take two additional steps within the jurisdiction in which an EMR is sought. First, the enterprise must obtain marketing approval for the pharmaceutical. Second, that enterprise must file a patent application claiming that pharmaceutical. Upon completing these two steps, the enterprise may obtain an EMR with a maximum duration of five years. The EMR will expire prior to the expiration of five years if either the marketed product is patented, or the local patent office rejects the enterprise's patent application.

25. John E. Guist, *Noncompliance with TRIPS by Developed and Developing Countries: Is TRIPS Working?*, 8 Indiana International and Comparative Law Review 69 (1997).

12.6.4 *Debate on the TRIPS Agreement*

The patent portions of the TRIPS Agreement have generated considerable controversy. Some commentators predict that the TRIPS Agreement will lead to large transfers of wealth from poor countries to the developed world, and in particular to the United States. Others believe that deleterious public health consequences will result from the TRIPS Agreement requirement that patents issue on pharmaceuticals. Still others have contended that the introduction of patents into the developing world restricts sustainable development and perpetuates their dependence upon developed nations.[26]

Proponents of the TRIPS Agreement instead believe that the introduction of full-fledged patent systems around the globe will provide needed incentives for investment and innovation.[27] Such efforts could promote solutions to problems that are particular to the developing world, including the provision of nutritional needs and cures for diseases not common in the developed world. Supporters also observe that the TRIPS Agreement was one component of a multi-faceted WTO agreement, and believe that the developing world obtained trade benefits in exchange for assuming obligations to protect intellectual property. At the time this book goes to press, the exchange of views about possible reforms to the TRIPS Agreement continues at a brisk pace.

§ 12.7 Free Trade Agreements

In the years following the TRIPS Agreement, the United States has entered into a number of bilateral Free Trade Agreements (FTAs) with other nations. These agreements have, to varying degrees, required their signatories to comply with patent standards that exceed the obligations of the TRIPS Agreement. For example, Article 16.7 of the 2003 Singapore–United States FTA requires that its signatories extend the term of patents to compensate for unreasonable delays in patent acquisition proceedings. The Singapore–United States FTA also places more restrictions upon the use of compulsory licenses than the TRIPS Agreement mandates.

In recent years, the United States has entered into negotiations aimed at establishing a FTA with a number of other countries. Most notable is the planned Free Trade Agreement of the Americas, which would essentially expand NAFTA into a Hemisphere-wide

26. *See* A. Samuel Oddi, *TRIPS—Natural Rights and a "Polite Form of Economic Imperialism,"* 29 Vanderbilt Journal of Transnational Law 415 (1996).

27. *See* Evelyn Su, *The Winners and the Losers: The Agreement on Trade—Related Aspects of Intellectual Property Rights and Its Effects on Developing Countries*, 23 Houston Journal of International Law 169 (2000).

agreement.[1] Future FTAs may possibly oblige their signatories to fulfill "TRIPS Plus" standards comparable to those of the Singapore FTA.

§ 12.8 Comparative Patent Law

International agreements have resulted in the growing harmonization of the world's patent systems. It is now possible to say that in every patent-issuing jurisdiction, such fundamental points as the requirements for obtaining a patent and the term of protection are substantially similar. Still, a number of important distinctions exist between the world's patent laws. The United States in particular has gone its own way in a number of significant respects, most notably by maintaining its unique "first-to-invent" priority system. The remainder of this chapter offers a brief survey of some of the notable differences between the U.S. patent system and those of other countries.

12.8.1 Priority Principle

Sometimes several persons independently develop the identical or similar invention at approximately the same time. In the United States, when more than one patent application is filed claiming the same invention, the patent will be awarded to the applicant who was the first inventor. In a so-called "interference" proceeding, applicants are allowed to submit evidence of their dates of inventive activity, such as the dates that they conceived of the invention and reduced it to practice.[1] The applicant that was the first to invent in the field is awarded the patent.[2] The U.S. priority rule is described as following the "first-to-invent" principle.

In every other patent-issuing state except the United States, priority of invention is established by the earliest effective filing date of a patent application disclosing the claimed invention. Stated differently, the first patent applicant is entitled to the patent. Whether or not the first applicant was actually the first individual to complete the invention in the field is irrelevant. This priority system follows the "first-to-file" principle.

The international patent community has witnessed an extensive and sometimes emotional debate on the relative merits of the first-to-invent versus the first-to-file principle. Supporters of the first-to-invent principle in part assert that the first-to-file system

§ 12.7

1. The text of the current working draft of this agreement can be found online at <http://www.ftaa-alca.org/FTAADraft03/Index_e.asp>. Intellectual Property issues are addressed in Chapter XX of this draft.

§ 12.8

1. 35 U.S.C. § 135 (2000).

2. *See supra* § 4.4.

creates inequities due to a "race to the Patent Office"; encourages premature and sketchy disclosures in hastily-filed patent applications; and disadvantages small entities with less resources to prepare and file patent applications quickly. Supporters of the first-to-file principle in part assert that it provides a definite, readily determined, and fixed date of priority of invention; believe that it would decrease the complexity, length, and expense associated with current USPTO interference proceedings; and observe that most of U.S. industry is already acting on this basis in order to avoid forfeiture of patent rights abroad. Although many U.S. trading partners have proposed that the United States shift to the first-to-file priority principle, there is currently no U.S. consensus on the advisability of this approach.

12.8.2 Grace Period

The U.S. patent system essentially provides inventors with a one-year period to decide whether patent protection is desirable, and, if so, to prepare an application. This is because specified activities, such as publications or sales, will bar the applicant from obtaining a patent only if they occur before the so-called "critical date," which is the day one year before the application was filed.[3] If, for example, an entrepreneur first discloses an invention by publishing an article in a scientific journal, he knows that he has one year from the publication date in which to file a patent application. If he waits longer than that, his patent will be barred, but if he applies before the one year elapses, the article will not prevent a patent from issuing. Importantly, uses, sales, and other technical disclosures by third parties will also start the one-year clock running. As a result, inventors have a broader range of concerns than merely their own behavior.[4]

In contrast, many other patent-granting states provide more limited grace periods, or no grace periods at all. In Europe, any sales or publication of an invention anywhere in the world prior to the filing date defeats the patentability of an invention.[5] The Japanese patent system includes a six-month grace period tied only to the activities of the inventor.[6] Under the patent law of Japan, any disclosures of an invention made by a third party even one day before the filing date defeats the novelty of that invention.

Much discussion has occurred over the wisdom of a grace period. Supporters of a grace period say that it assists inventors who are not sophisticated in patent matters; encourages the devel-

3. 35 U.S.C. § 102(b) (2000).

4. *See supra* § 4.3.1.

5. European Patent Convention, Article 54(2).

6. Japanese Patent Act, Article 29(1).

opment of inventions that require a certain amount of public testing before the invention can be said to be complete; and comports with norms of the academic and scientific community that call for early publication of research results. Detractors claim that grace periods increase commercial uncertainties and imply a prolongation of the patent term, and also assert that academics and scientists who wish to enter the commercial world must abide by the legal rules already established there.[7]

12.8.3 Patentable Subject Matter

The sorts of inventions that are subject to patent protection are more narrow in some foreign jurisdictions than in the United States. For example, the 1998 Federal Circuit decision in *State Street Bank* held that inventors may obtain patents on methods of doing business.[8] Recently issued U.S. patents in fields such as architecture, investment, marketing, psychological analysis, and sports methods also suggest that, in the United States, inventions from virtually any human endeavor may be the subject of proprietary rights through the patent system. In contrast, many patent systems overseas, including the harmonized European patent regime and the Japanese patent law, have been more reluctant to extend patent protection to business methods and other inventions outside the realm of traditional industry. For example, European patent law includes the requirement that an invention possess "industrial application" and expressly excludes from patentability such inventions as "schemes, rules and methods for performing mental acts, playing games or doing business."[9]

Biotechnology is also more amenable to patent protection in the United States than in some other nations. Broadly speaking, a plant or animal invention that is either a non-naturally occurring substance, or results from a substantial amount of human intervention, is patentable in the United States.[10] Both the Japanese and European systems impose additional restrictions on biotechnology patenting. According to the Japanese Patent Office, "processes in the fields of medicine, diagnosis, therapy, and pharmacology in which the human body is an indispensable element" are not patentable.[11] European patent law is still more restrictive, excluding from patentability "plant and animal varieties" and "essentially biological processes" among other inventions.[12]

7. *See supra* § 4.3.1.

8. State Street Bank & Trust Co. v. Signature Financial Group, Inc., 149 F.3d 1368, 47 USPQ2d 1596 (Fed. Cir. 1998). *See supra* § 2.7.

9. European Patent Convention, Article 52(c).

10. *See supra* § 2.3.

11. Michael North, *The U.S. Expansion of Patentable Subject Matter: Creating a Competitive Advantage for Foreign Multinational Companies?*, 18 Boston Univ. Int'l L.J. 111 (2000).

12. European Patent Convention, Article 53(b).

Much debate has proceeded about the most appropriate subject matter for patenting. Advocates of broad notions of patentable subject matter believe that patents can encourage investment, innovation, and the disclosure of new inventions in a broad range of fields.[13] Opponents of business method patents instead point to a long history of avoiding state-granted monopolies on business methods and find little evidence that patents will encourage further innovation in business practices.[14] Opponents of biotechnology patents have contended that it is inappropriate to grant property rights in living organisms and genetic materials and that such patents disrupt the norms and values of traditional agriculture.[15]

12.8.4 Deferred Examination

One distinct aspect of patent practice in some other nations is that examination is deferred following submission of an application. In contrast to the U.S. PTO, where every filed application is automatically placed into a queue for substantive examination, in many other patent-issuing states the mere filing of an application does not mean that the patent office will further consider the application. Inventors who wish their applications to mature into an issued patent must submit additional requests in order for the patent office to consider the application. Such requests must occur within a specified time and be accompanied by the appropriate fee. In Germany, an inventor may defer examination for up to seven years;[16] in Japan, the maximum deferral period was recently reduced from seven to three years.[17] If no request for examination is made in a timely fashion, the application is deemed abandoned. If a request for examination is seasonably made, the novelty and nonobviousness of the application are judged as of the application's filing date. Of course, a patent's maximum term remains 20 years from the filing date in these regimes, even where the applicant opts to defer examination.

Supporters of deferred examination regimes observe that they allow applicants the option of deciding to postpone the decision to obtain patent protection or not. Deferred examination regimes may also reduce patent office workloads. Further, since all pending applications are published approximately 18 months following their

13. *E.g.*, Jeffrey R. Kuester & Lawrence E. Thompson, *Risks Associated with Restricting Business Method and E-Commerce Patents*, 17 Georgia State Univ. L. Rev. 657 (2001).

14. John R. Thomas, *The Patenting of the Liberal Professions*, 40 Boston Coll. L. Rev. 1139 (1999).

15. *See* Paul S. Naik, *Biotechnology in the Eyes of an Opponent: The Resistance of Activist Jeremy Rifkin*, 5 Virginia Journal of Law and Technology 5 (2000).

16. Nancy J. Linck et al., *A New Patent Examination System for a New Millennium*, 35 Hous. L. Rev. 305 (1998).

17. Japanese Patent Office, *Procedures for Obtaining a Patent Right* (available at www.jpo. go.jp).

filing dates, the public has notice of the prospect of a granted patent whether examination is deferred or not. Detractors note that a deferred examination system may delay the issuance of a fully considered patent instrument and, as a result, substantially increase marketplace uncertainties.

12.8.5 Publication of Pending Applications

Most foreign patent regimes publish all pending patent applications 18 months after they have been filed. Since November 29, 2000, the U.S. PTO has published some, but not all pending applications. More specifically, U.S. patent applications will be published 18 months from the date of filing, except where the inventor represents that he will not seek patent protection abroad. If an applicant certifies that the invention disclosed in the U.S. application will not be the subject of a patent application in another country that requires publication of applications 18 months after filing, then the PTO will not publish the application.[18] It remains to be seen whether the current U.S. approach will persist, or whether it marks a transition stage to a comprehensive domestic pre-grant publication rule.

12.8.6 Oppositions

Many foreign patent regimes allow for so-called opposition proceedings. An opposition is a patent revocation proceeding that is initiated by an interested party—often a competitor of the patent owner—and is usually resolved by authorities from the national patent office. Oppositions often involve a wide range of potential invalidity arguments and are conducted through adversarial hearings that often resemble courtroom litigation.

Although the U.S. patent system does not provide for full-fledged oppositions, the U.S. patent system has incorporated a so-called "reexamination" proceeding since 1981.[19] Reexaminations are essentially a more limited form of an opposition. Although many commentators have called for the expansion of reexamination proceedings so that they more fully resemble oppositions, as of yet Congress has not yet pursued this possibility.

12.8.7 Patent Validity as an Infringement Defense

In the United States and many common law countries, courts that decide infringement matters also may review the validity of the asserted patent.[20] Accused infringers often argue that the asserted patent was improvidently granted. In some civil law nations, however, the courts that decide patent infringement matters may

18. *See supra* § 7.2.6.

19. *See supra* § 7.5.4.

20. *See* 35 U.S.C. § 282 (2000).

not rule on whether a patent is valid or invalid. Challenges to patent validity are instead exclusively considered by the national patent office or by specialized tribunals. Split proceedings allow the often technical issues of validity to be resolved by an individual with appropriate technical qualifications, rather than a lay judge or jury. Yet they can sometimes lead to delay, higher costs and the possibility of inconsistent judgments.

12.8.8 Scope of Patent Protection

A subtle but significant distinction between patent systems is the scope of protection a court will accord to an issued patent during enforcement proceedings. The extent of proprietary rights is based upon, but not limited to, the precise wording of the patent instrument. In the United States, a court may find infringement even if the accused device or method does not precisely fall within the claims of the asserted patent, so long as "insubstantial differences" exist between the patented invention and the accused infringement. U.S. courts refer to this concept as the "doctrine of equivalents."[21]

Some observers believe that the scope of protection accorded patent rights differs among the national courts. The courts of Germany and the Netherlands have, for example, been considered to accord patents more robust protection than do the U.S. courts. At the other extreme are the courts of Japan. According to a 1993 report from the U.S. General Accounting Office, "Japan has virtually no 'doctrine of equivalents' as that term is used in the United States."[22] Judicial decisions over the past decade suggest that Japanese courts are construing patents more broadly than they once did, however.[23] The U.S. Court of Appeals for the Federal Circuit appears to be moving in precisely the other direction, as its jurisprudence governing the doctrine of equivalents has exhibited a narrowing trend since the late 1990's.[24]

21. *See* Warner–Jenkinson Co. v. Hilton Davis Chemical Co., 520 U.S. 17 (1997). This doctrine is discussed in detail in § 8.2.2, *supra.*

22. General Accounting Office, *Intellectual Property Rights: U.S. Companies' Patent Experiences in Japan* (GGD–93–126) (1993).

23. Shusaku Yamamoto & John A. Tessensohn,, *Doctrine of Equivalents Adds Torque to Japanese Patent Infringement*, 81 J. Pat. & Trademark Off. Soc'y 483 (1999).

24. *See supra* § 8.2.2.

Chapter 13

STATE LAW ISSUES: TRADE SECRETS AND FEDERAL PREEMPTION

Table of Sections

Given that the patent law is the exclusive province of federal law, you might think that there would be little need for an analysis of state laws when considering proprietary rights in inventions. As the very existence of this chapter subtly suggests, you would be wrong. The patent system operates alongside a number of common law doctrines that, broadly speaking, may be used to protect innovations. Most notable is the common law of trade secrets, which protects secret, valuable commercial information from misappropriation by others. Not only is trade secret law important as an alternative source of protection for innovators, but its existence, as well as the use of unfair competition law, contract law, and specific state legislation to protect inventions has also raised issues of federal-state conflict, and the possibility of federal preemption of relevant state law. This possibility arises because, to the extent that these state laws regulate intellectual property in a manner contrary to the Patent Act, they may be invalid due to the Supremacy Clause of the U.S. Constitution. This chapter reviews trade secret law before turning to patent preemption issues.

§ 13.1 Trade Secrets

It is fairly easy to set out a concise overview of trade secret law. It protects secret, valuable business information from misappropriation by others. Subject matter ranging from marketing data to manufacturing know-how may be protected under the trade secret laws. Trade secret status is not limited to a fixed number of years, but endures so long as the information is valuable and maintained as a secret.[1] A trade secret is misappropriated when it has been obtained through the abuse of a confidential relationship or improper means of acquisition.[2] Unlike the Patent Act, trade secret law does not provide a cause of action against an individual who independently developed or reverse engineered the subject matter of the trade secret.[3]

Trade secrecy serves as the chief alternative to the patent system.[4] An inventor must either maintain a technology as a trade secret, seek patent protection from the PTO, or allow the technology to enter the public domain.[5] The regime of trade secrets is broader than this, however, for trade secret law may also be used to protect subject matter that is unpatentable. For example, although a list of valued customers does not constitute patent eligible subject matter, it is amenable to protection as a trade secret.[6]

Judicial opinions evince two distinct conceptions of the trade secret law.[7] Some courts focus on trade secrecy as an intellectual property discipline. Under this view, trade secret law creates a proprietary interest just like a copyright, patent, or trademark. In deciding whether to grant relief for misappropriation of trade secrets, these courts stress the value and secrecy of the subject matter for which trade secret status is claimed. Other courts have viewed trade secret law as less concerned with creating property than in ensuring proper conduct. In resolving trade secret cases,

§ 13.1

1. *See* United States v. Dubilier Condenser Corp., 289 U.S. 178, 186, 53 S.Ct. 554, 77 L.Ed. 1114 (1933).

2. Restatement Third, Unfair Competition § 43 (1995).

3. Restatement Third, Unfair Competition § 39 cmt. c (1995).

4. *See* David D. Friedman, et al., *Some Economics of Trade Secret Law*, 5 J. Econ. Persps. 61, 64 (1991).

5. *See* Metallizing Eng'g Co. v. Kenyon Bearing & Auto Parts, 153 F.2d 516, 68 USPQ 54 (2d Cir.), *cert. denied*, 328 U.S. 840, 66 S.Ct. 1016, 90 L.Ed. 1615 (1946).

6. *See* Courtesy Temporary Serv., Inc. v. Camacho, 222 Cal.App.3d 1278, 1287–88, 272 Cal.Rptr. 352 (1990).

7. Restatement Third, Unfair Competition § 39 cmt. a (1995).

these courts stress whether the accused misappropriator acquired the information at issue in a fair and ethical manner.

As Judge Posner noted in the leading opinion of *Rockwell Graphic Systems, Inc. v. DEV Industries, Inc.*,[8] these conceptions are entirely complementary. Trade secret law encourages industry actors to develop valuable informational resources by protecting them from improper acquisition by others. In addition, potential liability for trade secret misappropriation discourages individuals from engaging in activities that do not create wealth, but merely redistribute wealth from one individual to another.

13.1.1 Sources of Law

The modern U.S. law of trade secrets arises from the common law tradition. As far back as the early nineteenth century, English equity courts granted remedies against the misappropriation of such secret subject matter as the composition of medical compounds and dyes. Many of these cases involved breaches of confidence between partners, family members, or a master and apprentice.[9] The U.S. courts turned to this early precedent when confronted with analogous cases involving the increasingly complex commercial relationships of an industrial society.[10] Soon enough, a significant body of common law precedent existed in virtually every American jurisdiction. Even today, trade secret law continues as an adaptive area of the law, that has evolved to deal with changing technology, increasing employee mobility, and heightened entrepreneurial activity.

The American Law Institute's 1939 Restatement of Torts included two sections dealing with the law of trade secrets—one that defined the subject matter of trade secrets and a second that spelled out the elements of a trade secret misappropriation cause of action. Although this treatment was succinct, these definitions proved influential in the courts. However, trade secrets were not addressed in the 1978 Second Restatement of Torts.[11] The American Law Institute concluded that trade secret law had grown "no more dependent on Tort law than it is on many other general fields of law and upon broad statutory developments," and opted not to house trade secrets there.

The Uniform Trade Secrets Act (or UTSA) filled this gap in 1979.[12] Published by the National Conference of Commissioners on Uniform State Law, the UTSA has been enacted in the vast

8. 925 F.2d 174, 17 USPQ2d 1780 (Fed.Cir.1991).

9. I Melvin F. Jager, Trade Secret Law § 2.01 (1998).

10. *Id.* at § 2.02.

11. *Id.* at § 3.01[1].

12. 14 U.L.A. 438 (1990).

majority of states.[13] UTSA generally follows the approach of the first Restatement of Torts, but also relies upon subsequent case law to provide more useful and definitive legal standards.

The American Law Institute was not content to rest, however. In 1993, as an early phase in a project to prepare a Third Restatement of the law of Torts, the ALI published a "stand-alone" document which it labelled the Restatement (Third) of Unfair Competition. This Restatement contains a thorough treatment of trade secrets in sections 39–45, and the related commentary. The remainder of the Restatement (Third) of Unfair Competition is devoted to trademarks, misappropriation, deceptive marking, the right of publicity and related doctrines. Like the Restatement of Torts and the UTSA, the Restatement (Third) of Unfair Competition remains faithful to the case law and does not presume to be an instrument of radical legal reform.

Until recently, federal law traditionally played little role in trade secret cases. This situation changed in 1996 due to congressional enactment of the Economic Espionage Act (EEA). The EEA declares the misappropriation of trade secrets to be a federal crime in certain circumstances. Because EEA cases are prosecuted by federal government officials, rather than trade secret holders, we consider this legislation separately, in § 13.1.4 below.

That the common law has been supplemented by these additional sources of trade secrets law may seem to hold tremendous possibility for confusion. However, the substantive law of trade secrets provided in the Restatements and UTSA is largely consistent, differing only in subtle points around the margins.[14] The chief distinction is that the newer sources are worded in more familiar language and possess a greater level of detail than their predecessors. Although judicial opinions may cite to different authorities, the core precepts of trade secret law remain intact.

13. Seven states adopted the original version of the UTSA, while 37 others have adopted a version that includes amendments promulgated in 1985. At this writing legislation is pending to adopt the UTSA in at least 3 other states. For a full list of the states that have adopted the act, *see*, <http://www.nccusl.org/nccusl/uniformact_factsheets/uniformacts-fs-utsa.asp>.

14. The chief exception to this broad statement concerns the requirement of the Restatement of Torts that the trade secret be capable of "continuous use in the operation of a business." Reflecting subsequent developments in the case law, both the Restatement of Unfair Competition and Uniform Act have rejected this earlier requirement. RESTATEMENT THIRD, UNFAIR COMPETITION § 39 cmt. d (1995). In addition, unlike Restatement of Torts, the Uniform Act protects so-called "negative information" that a particular process or method does not work. Further, while the Restatement of Torts required that a trade secret afford the owner a competitive advantage, the Uniform Act requires that the continued secrecy of the trade secret possess actual or potential economic value.

13.1.2 *Eligible Subject Matter*

Perhaps due to its origins in the courts of equity, the trade secret law has never overly concerned itself with achieving an exact definition of the sorts of information that may be subjected to trade secret protection.[15] The authorities do agree that there are two principal requirements for maintaining information as a trade secret. First and foremost, the information must have been the subject of reasonable efforts to maintain secrecy. Second, the information must derive commercial value from not being generally known or readily ascertainable by others.[16]

Subject to these overriding requirements, the Restatements provide that formulae, patterns, devices, or compilations of information may be protected as trade secrets.[17] The case law reveals an enormous variety of information subject to the trade secret laws. This subject matter includes bid price information, blueprints, chemical formulas, computer programs, customer lists, manufacturing know-how, marketing data, recipes, sales forecasts, supplier lists, test records, and technical designs.[18]

13.1.2.1 *Secrecy*

The principal gatekeeper to trade secret status is that the information must have been subjected to reasonable efforts to maintain its secrecy.[19] The case law provides no precise standard as to the efforts necessary to qualify the protected subject matter as a trade secret. It is clear that a would-be trade secret holder need not erect an utterly impenetrable fortress around the information. On the other hand, the owner must make satisfactory efforts to identify the secret subject matter, notify others that it regards the subject matter as proprietary, and protect against reasonably foreseeable intrusions. In deciding whether reasonable efforts have been made to maintain secrecy, courts will balance the costs of the efforts made against the benefits obtained.[20] The courts do not require costly, burdensome safeguards that would overly disrupt the owner's usual commercial practices. However, if the owner did not engage in prudent precautions that would have yielded security benefits greater than their costs, the case for reasonable secrecy efforts is diminished.

The precautions the holder of commercially valuable information might take to maintain secrecy are legion. For example, employees, visitors, and joint venturers could be required to sign

15. Restatement Third, Unfair Competition § 39 cmt. d (1995).

16. Restatement Third, Unfair Competition § 39 (1995).

17. Restatement Third, Unfair Competition § 39 cmt. d (1995).

18. Restatement Third, Unfair Competition § 39 cmt. d (1995).

19. Uniform Trade Secrets Act § 2, 14 U.L.A. 438 (1990).

20. *See* Rockwell Graphic Sys., Inc. v. DEV Industries, Inc., 925 F.2d 174, 17 USPQ2d 1780 (7th Cir.1991).

confidentiality agreements. Signs, stamps, and legends may declare that certain subject matter is proprietary, though some have noted that this precaution may actually facilitate theft of secret information by readily identifying it to unscrupulous employees. Locked doors, alarms, and guards might deny access to individuals who do not need to know the information. Exit interviews may remind departing employees of their obligations to maintain the protected subject matter in confidence. Pertinent documents and laboratory samples could be destroyed on the premises when their commercial utility ended. Although numerous other measures should be apparent, no absolute rule governs the degree of vigilance that the putative trade secret holder must maintain. Whether a court will find the existence of a trade secret depends upon an overall balancing of the equities of particular cases.

A number of circumstances may negate secrecy. Knowledge that may be readily gained from an inspection of a commercially available product is not secret. Similarly, information that may be found in publicly available journals, texts, or other published materials may not be kept as a trade secret. Issuance of a U.S. patent or publication of a pending patent application also destroys the secrecy of any information claimed within such a document. This result holds even if the published application does not mature into a granted patent, or if the patent is later held invalid.[21]

Litigation also holds the potential of destroying a claimed trade secret. Indeed, one irony of trade secret law is that, unless the plaintiff takes precautions, enforcement of the trade secret ordinarily requires its disclosure in open court! However, Rule 26(c)(7) of the Federal Rules of Civil Procedure allows courts to mandate "that a trade secret or other confidential research, development, or commercial information not be revealed or be revealed only in a designated way." Rule 45 of the Federal Rules of Civil Procedure also allows a court to quash or modify a subpoena if it requires disclosure of a trade secret or other confidential information. Experience demonstrates that of these two options, courts strongly favor disclosure of trade secrets during discovery. The Supreme Court has recognized that "[o]rders forbidding any disclosure of trade secrets are rare. More commonly, the trial court will enter a protective order restricting disclosure to counsel or to the parties."[22]

13.1.2.2 *Economic Value*

Information must be sufficiently valuable to provide an actual or potential economic advantage over others to qualify for trade

21. Restatement Third, Unfair Competition § 39 cmt. c (1995).

22. Federal Open Market Committee v. Merrill, 443 U.S. 340, 362 n. 24, 99 S.Ct. 2800, 61 L.Ed.2d 587 (1979).

secret protection.[23] This commercial value must arise from the fact that the information is not generally known or readily ascertainable by others. Ordinarily the putative trade secret holder demonstrates value through direct evidence of the significance of the subject matter to its business, or its superiority as compared to public domain alternatives. Courts have also accepted evidence of the cost of developing the information, the willingness of others to pay for access to the trade secret, and the extent of the pains taken to protect its secrecy as evidence of value.

The courts have stressed that the economic value requirement is not as strict as patent law's novelty standard. To satisfy the novelty requirement of patent law, an invention must differ from all other earlier patents, publications, public uses, and other documents or events that qualify as prior art under the Patent Act.[24] Trade secret law imposes a less exacting standard, in that the alleged secret must merely not be a matter of public knowledge.[25] If the information could be easily obtained based upon existing knowledge, or is already generally known, then its secrecy will not impart economic value within the meaning of the trade secret law.[26] To put the same matter slightly differently, information is not a trade secret if everyone in the industry already knows about it, even if one firm purports to zealously guard that data from prying eyes.

For example, suppose that researchers employed by a particular firm synthesize a chemical process. It turns out that an obscure scientific journal, published several years earlier in a foreign language, already discloses that particular process. Assume further that the journal article, which is available only in a few libraries located overseas, has not been read by the firm's competitors. Under these facts, the journal article defeats the novelty of the chemical process for patent law purposes. A patent should not issue on that process.[27] However, the journal article would not prevent the firm from maintaining the process as a trade secret, provided the other requirements for trade secret status are met. On the other hand, if the article had been published in a U.S. periodical with wide circulation, and if the process was familiar to most of the firm's competitors, it would not qualify as a trade secret.

A combination of elements may satisfy the value requirement even though each of the elements is well-known and lies in the public domain. However, the secrecy of the particular combination

23. Restatement Third, Unfair Competition § 39 cmt. e (1995).

24. *See supra* Chapter 4.

25. SI Handling Sys., Inc. v. Heisely, 753 F.2d 1244, 1255, 225 USPQ 441, 447 (3d Cir. 1985).

26. Russell v. Wall Wire Prods. Co., 78 N.W.2d 149, 154, 111 USPQ 51, 55 (Mich. 1956).

27. *See* 35 U.S.C. § 102(b) (2000).

must afford an actual or potential competitive advantage.[28] For example, suppose that a fast-food restaurant chain develops a secret recipe for fried chicken. The recipe can qualify as a trade secret even though each of the herbs, spices, and other ingredients are commonly available at grocery stores.

Value is seldom a practical issue in trade secret cases. The high cost of enforcing intellectual property rights suggests that plaintiffs will only commence litigation concerning information of considerable value. Because the value of the information depends upon the fact that it is not generally known, the value requirement is closely related to the secrecy requirement. Many of the judicial decisions addressing value often turn on the fact that the supposed "secret" is already known or could be readily determined. For example, in *Playland Toys, Inc. v. Learning Curve Toys*,[29] the plaintiff claimed that it possessed a trade secret in the idea of cutting slits in a wooden train set in order to give the toy a "clickety clack" sound. Recognizing that the idea of notching a train track to produce a distinctive sound could be readily reverse-engineered from toy train sets already on the market, the district court concluded that the idea lacked commercial value for purposes of the trade secret law.

An intriguing series of decisions struggled with the question of whether information must not merely possess value, but economic value to qualify as a trade secret. In *Religious Technology Center v. Wollersheim*, the Church of Scientology accused a former practitioner of misappropriating secret scriptural materials that, it alleged, addressed a person's spiritual well-being.[30] The Court of Appeals for the Ninth Circuit denied the Church's trade secret claim, concluding that the value of the confidential materials were religious rather than commercial in character. The continued vitality of this analysis is questionable in light of subsequent opinions from the Ninth Circuit, however.[31] For instance, one district court concluded that the "Advanced Technology" scriptures of the Church of Scientology possessed commercial value as a matter of law because the defendant used the materials to teach a course for which she was paid.[32] It also reasoned that, like other entities, religious organizations required funds to exist. If this logic ultimately prevails, this area of law could expand to cover not merely trade secrets, but any valued secret at all.

28. Imperial Chem. Indus., Ltd. v. National Distillers & Chem. Corp., 342 F.2d 737, 742, 144 USPQ 695, 699 (2d Cir. 1965).

29. 2002 WL 391361 (N.D. Ill. 2002).

30. 796 F.2d 1076 (9th Cir.1986).

31. *See* Religious Technology Center v. Scott, 869 F.2d 1306, 10 USPQ2d 1379 (9th Cir.1989).

32. *See* Bridge Publications, Inc. v. Vien, 827 F.Supp. 629 (S.D.Cal.1993).

13.1.2.3 Identification of Trade Secrets

A key difference between patent and trade secret litigation involves the identification of the plaintiff's intellectual property. In a patent lawsuit, at least one of the parties arrives at the courthouse door with a patent instrument that specifically claims the protected invention. In the trade secret context, however, the precise information considered to be a trade secret is often not specified prior to litigation. The burden therefore falls upon the plaintiff to describe the trade secrets it claims were misappropriated.

This requirement may seem trite at first glance, and in fact many courts have been lenient in enforcing it, particularly in the early stages of a litigation.[33] Some trade secret plaintiffs nonetheless strain the limits of how vague they can be in identifying the claimed trade secret. The decision of the Court of Appeals for the Seventh Circuit in *IDX Systems Corp. v. Epic System Corp.* is a good illustration.[34] This case involved the alleged misappropriation of trade secrets used within a financial software package. Although the plaintiff submitted various documents describing the software, it made no effort to identify which information was secret and commercially valuable. For example, the plaintiff's documentation included the appearance of data-entry screens that were hardly secret—in fact, they could be readily observed by anyone passing near a computer running the software.

Given these circumstances, the trial court granted summary judgment in favor of the defendant. Complaining that the plaintiff had "buried its trade secrets in documentation," the trial court refused to speculate as to exactly which information the plaintiff sought to protect.[35] The Seventh Circuit affirmed on appeal. According to Judge Easterbrook, the plaintiff's assertion that all information about its software constituted a trade secret was neither plausible nor consistent with the legal definition of a trade secret.

There are at least two possible explanations for the curious approach of the plaintiff in a case like *IDX Systems*. On the one hand, it may be that plaintiff's claims of trade secret theft were quite speculative, and that anything but the most general definition of the secret would reveal that the defendant did not engage in any impermissible misappropriation. On the other hand, the plaintiff might have been concerned that the litigation process itself would allow its competitors to learn the details of its valuable trade secret if it opted to define it in anything but the most general terms. Of

33. *See* Lawson Products, Inc. v. Chromate Industrial Corp., 158 F.Supp. 2d 860 (N.D. Ill. 2001).

34. 285 F.3d 581, 62 USPQ2d 1278 (7th Cir. 2002).

35. 165 F.Supp.2d 812 (W.D. Wis. 2001).

course, as we have noted above,[36] the courts may issue protective orders or take other measures in order to reduce this risk, but it is a reminder that many trade secret plaintiffs must walk a tightrope in order to protect their rights without giving them away in the process.

13.1.3 Misappropriation

An enterprise possessing trade secrets will be protected against misappropriation of those trade secrets by others. Virtually all the cases can be grouped into two categories. Sometimes trade secrets are acquired by individuals with no relationship to the trade secret holder. In those cases, the dispositive legal issue is whether the trade secret was acquired by "improper means." Other trade secret cases involve parties who initially learn of the trade secret properly, usually through the voluntary disclosure by the trade secret holder, and thereafter either use the secret for their own commercial advantage or disclose it to others. Courts will grant relief in this latter class of cases where the defendant violated either an express or implied obligation of confidentiality. If we were looking for memorable, albeit pejorative, labels for these two types of trade secret misappropriators, we could call the first group spies and the second group traitors.

13.1.3.1 Improper Acquisition

A trade secret owner may claim misappropriation if the defendant acquired the trade secret by performing illegal acts. Wiretapping, bribery, fraud, and theft of personal property are examples of the types industrial espionage condemned under the trade secret law. However, trade secret protection is not limited to acts that are themselves violations of other laws. The courts have also condemned ostensibly legal activities that amount to calculated attempts to overcome reasonable efforts to maintain secrecy.

E.I. DuPont deNemours v. Christopher[37] is the leading opinion on trade secret misappropriation through improper, as compared to illegal means. The litigation involved DuPont's claims to trade secrets on methanol production methods. DuPont began construction on a new chemical plant that would make use of these trade secrets, taking various precautions to restrict access to, and views of, the plant. For a brief period in the midst of construction, however, the plant's unfinished roof allowed an overhead view of the plant's workings. This view would reveal DuPont's method of making methanol to a trained eye. At that time, an unnamed competitor of DuPont hired the Christophers to fly an airplane over

36. *See supra* § 13.1.1.1.

37. 431 F.2d 1012, 166 USPQ 421 (5th Cir.1970).

the DuPont facility and take photographs. DuPont sued the Christophers for misappropriation of trade secrets. The Christophers argued that taking aerial photographs of DuPont's plant was not in violation of any criminal law nor did it constitute trespassing.

The Court of Appeals for the Fifth Circuit agreed that the precedents before it found a trade secret misappropriation only when the defendant committed a trespass or illegal act. The court nonetheless condemned the Christophers for engaging in improper means of acquisition and affirmed the trial court's finding of misappropriation. Judge Goldberg's opinion stressed the momentary advantage the Christophers obtained over DuPont despite extensive efforts to maintain secrecy, as well as the great expenses that would be incurred in protecting the plant from aerial views. In extending the misappropriation cause of action beyond illegal activities, the court hoped to encourage efficient self-protection and investment in research and development, yet discourage extravagant security expenditures and disreputable commercial practices.

Under the approach of *DuPont v. Christopher*, distinguishing condemned industrial espionage from permissible monitoring of competitors will necessarily proceed on a case-by-case basis. The Restatement of Unfair Competition advises that courts consider the economic value of the trade secret, the availability and cost of effective precautions against such an acquisition, the foreseeability of the conduct through which the secret was acquired, and the extent to which the trade secret holder did not take reasonable precautions.[38] Plainly the court's sense of business ethics, commercial morality, and public policy will play a considerable role in the analysis.

In contrast to illegal or improper means of acquiring trade secrets, a number of appropriate methods exist to determine a trade secret. These methods include discovery by independent invention, obtaining the trade secret from published literature, observing a product embodying the trade secret in public, and "reverse engineering" by starting with a legitimately obtained product and working backwards to determine how it works.

Those new to the field of trade secrets sometimes are surprised to learn that reverse engineering is permissible. This rule makes trade secret protection much more permeable than other forms of intellectual property, and some might feel that the result is inadequate protection for innovative activity. Nonetheless, there are at least two conventional rationales for this rule. First, parties that engage in reverse engineering often discover not only the underlying trade secret, but additional methods to further improve the product. Unlike socially worthless activities such as bribery or

38. Restatement Third, Unfair Competition § 43.

theft, reverse engineering can often serve to advance the state of technology, and thus ought to be encouraged rather than penalized. Second, the risk that a trade secret might be unearthed through reverse engineering actually encourages firms to take advantage of the patent system in many cases. Driving firms to the patent system will result in a fairly prompt and fairly detailed disclosure of the invention, allowing others to build on it. Thus, the very weakness of trade secret law is often cited as an important part of the overall structure of the intellectual property enterprise.

13.1.3.2 Breach of Confidential Relationship

An individual may owe another a duty of confidence through an express promise of confidentiality. Such promises are most typically made by employees, prospective buyers, visitors to a facility, or joint venturers. For example, visitors to a manufacturing facility may be required to sign a nondisclosure agreement through which they promise not to disclose technical information disclosed or observed during the visit. Employees engaged in both research and production often have employment contracts with similar nondisclosure clauses.

Even where no express contractual provision exists, a duty of confidence may also be implied from the relationship of the parties. If the trade secret holder was reasonable in inferring that the other person consented to an obligation of confidentiality, and the other knew or should have known the disclosure was made in confidence, the court will infer that an obligation of confidentiality existed.

A representative case implying a duty of confidentiality is *Smith v. Dravo Corp.*[39] Smith was in the cargo and freight container business. Dravo expressed an interest in buying Smith's business, and the two entered into negotiations. As part of these discussions Smith showed Dravo secret blueprints and still-secret patent applications concerning its innovative cargo containers. The deal fell through and shortly thereafter Dravo began to market freight containers similar to Smith's. Smith sued Dravo for trade secret misappropriation. Although the Court of Appeals for the Seventh Circuit observed that "no express promise of trust was exacted from the defendant," it held that a relationship of trust should be implied from the facts and granted relief.

The most difficult issues regarding confidential relationships involve former employers and their ex-employees. If employees could readily transfer trade secrets to competing firms merely by accepting a new offer of employment, then employers would be discouraged from developing those trade secrets in the first instance. Enterprises might also be forced to restrict access to trade

39. 203 F.2d 369, 97 USPQ 98 (7th Cir.1953).

secrets only to a very select number of employees. A legal rule that pushes firms to an extreme, burdensome compartmentalization of information among employees could prove cumbersome, increasing the costs of production and slowing further refinement of the proprietary information.

On the other hand, post-employment restraints restrict the ability of individuals to practice their professions and earn a living. Not only may these restrictions impose an undue hardship on the employee, society may lose the services of highly skilled individuals. Labor mobility also helps employees improve their expertise by interacting with different practitioners in their fields. The potential knowledge spillovers help other firms learn blind alleys, best practices, and other valuable information, thereby improving the capabilities of the entire industry.

In addition to complex policy choices, cases between former employers and ex-employers often raise perplexing practical issues. Everyone agrees that upon termination, ex-employees should be able to use their general skills and knowledge in a new setting, provided that they do not misappropriate their former employer's trade secrets. Distinguishing proprietary knowledge from general expertise often proves difficult in individual cases, however. Ex-employees often carry their former employer's trade secrets in their heads. Even acting in the best of good faith, ex-employees may find it very difficult to avoid relying upon former employers' trade secrets in their new positions.

In addition to relying upon the common law duty of confidentiality, many employers require their employees to make an express promise of confidentiality in a nondisclosure agreement. Another, more severe mechanism is the imposition of a covenant not to compete. Absent such a covenant, an individual has no obligation not to engage in a competing business upon leaving his current employment. A covenant not to compete is a promise by the employee, under certain conditions, not to engage in a competing business following her departure from her current employer.

The law has subjected covenants not to compete to considerable scrutiny. In a minority of states, legislation severely limits covenants not to compete.[40] Even in jurisdictions where such covenants are permissible, the courts will not enforce them unless they comply with certain restrictions. Although jurisdictions vary in the precise wording of their review, they generally require courts to consider whether (1) the covenant not to compete was ancillary to an employment or other lawful contract; (2) the covenant was supported by consideration; (3) the employer has a legitimate business interest in imposing the covenant, such as protection of

40. *See* Cal. Bus. & Prof. Code § 16600 (West 1997).

the employer's trade secrets and goodwill; (4) the covenant's restrictions are reasonably related to that interest; (5) the covenant is reasonable in time, place, and scope of activity; (6) the covenant imposes an undue hardship on the ex-employee; and (7) the restraint is reasonable from the standpoint of sound public policy. The employer bears the burden of demonstrating that the covenant is enforceable.[41]

This high degree of judicial scrutiny counsels employers not to overreach when drafting covenants not to compete. Most enforceable covenants of this sort endure only for relatively brief periods of time, such as six months or a year, after which the ex-employee is free to engage in a competing business. Courts reason that this amount of time provides ample protection to the employer, especially in fields where technology progresses rapidly, and that any longer duration would impose an undue hardship on the employee. Covenants not to compete also ordinarily contain a geographic limitation on the scope of the non-competition agreement, often defined as the place where the company does business. Finally, most non-compete provisions include a limitation regarding the types of businesses that the employer considers as its competition.

The decision of the Court of Appeals for the Fourth Circuit in *Comprehensive Technologies International v. Software Artisans, Inc.* considered the propriety of a covenant not to compete under Virginia law.[42] Here, Comprehensive Technologies International (CTI) brought suit against several ex-employees, including former Vice President Dean Hawkes. CTI in part asserted that Hawkes had breached a covenant not to compete. The covenant required Hawkes, for a twelve-month period following his departure, to refrain from engaging in business in the United States that competed with the "business of CTI." This latter phrase was expressly defined as the design, marketing, and sales of two CTI electronic data interchange software programs useable on personal computers.

The district court refused to enforce the covenant on the grounds that the scope of its employment and geographic restrictions were too broad. Following an appeal by CTI, the Fourth Circuit reversed. Observing that Hawkes had been primarily responsible for the design, development, marketing, and sale of CTI software, the Court of Appeals concluded that Hawkes had intimate knowledge of every aspect of CTI's business and necessarily had acquired information he could use to compete with CTI. The covenant's restrictions, which were limited to specific software, were therefore judged reasonable. Hawkes could still work on the

41. Picker Int'l, Inc. v. Parten, 935 F.2d 257 (11th Cir. 1991).

42. 3 F.3d 730, 28 USPQ2d 1031 (4th Cir. 1993).

same type of software, so long as it was not designed to run on personal computers, and was also free to work on any other kind of software. The Fourth Circuit also found the nationwide restriction on competition reasonable, for CTI enjoyed a national market and faced competitors across the country. As a result, the covenant's restrictions were no greater than necessary to protect CTI from competition by Hawkes. The case was then remanded for a determination of whether Hawkes had violated the covenant.

In some jurisdictions, courts will apply the "blue pencil rule" to covenants not to compete. Under the blue pencil rule, if a contractual covenant contains both reasonable and excessive restrictions, the court will "scratch out" the excessive portions and enforce the remainder. Suppose, for example, that a covenant in part required that the ex-employee refrain from doing business with any of the former employer's "prospective, past or present clients." If a court found that the restrictions on doing business with prospective and past clients was unreasonable, it could disregard these provisions and enforce the remainder of the covenant with regard to "present clients."[43] It should be noted that in some jurisdictions, courts apply the blue pencil rule liberally to reform non-compete covenants that are unenforceable.[44] Others are more strict, blue penciling only when the excessive restriction may be grammatically severed from the reasonable terms based on the precise terms and phrasing used in the covenant.[45]

In some cases, where the employer has not obtained a covenant not to compete from the employee, it has attempted to invoke the "inevitable disclosure doctrine" to limit the subsequent employment options of the employee and thus prevent the potential loss of trade secrets. In this class of cases, the employer does not claim a garden variety misappropriation, in which the ex-employee attempts to transfer a specific manufacturing technology or customer list to the competitor. The former employer instead asserts that the ex-employee's new position inherently requires him to rely on its trade secrets, whether he does so consciously or not. The employer argues that even if the ex-employee does not actually intend to divulge its trade secrets, the nature of his new job ensures that he will inevitably do so. As a result, the employer seeks to enjoin the ex-employee from accepting the new position.

The well-publicized decision in *PepsiCo, Inc. v. Redmond* endorsed the inevitable disclosure doctrine.[46] Redmond was a high-

43. *See* Seach v. Richards, Dieterle & Co., 439 N.E.2d 208 (Ind. App. 1982).

44. *See* Sarasota Beverage Co. v. Johnson, 551 So.2d 503, 506 (Fla.Dist. Ct.App.1989).

45. *See* Noe v. McDevitt, 228 N.C. 242, 45 S.E.2d 121 (1947).

46. 54 F.3d 1262, 35 USPQ2d 1010 (7th Cir. 1995).

level PepsiCo employee who, in late 1994, abruptly resigned and attempted to start work for a competitor, Quaker Oats. These companies competed in the sports drink market, which included Quaker's "Gatorade" brand and PepsiCo's "All Sport" product. Redmond possessed detailed knowledge of his PepsiCo's business strategy and marketing plans. Redmond knew the contents of PepsiCo's projected 1995 strategic plan, for example, which derived much of its value from the fact that PepsiCo's competitors could not anticipate its next move. His employment contract included a promise not to disclose confidential information relating to PepsiCo's business, but no general covenant forbidding him from working for other firms in the beverage industry.

After Redmond resigned from PepsiCo and assumed the position of Vice President for Gatorade Field Operations at Quaker, PepsiCo quickly filed suit against Quaker. PepsiCo sought an injunction to prevent Redmond from disclosing PepsiCo trade secrets. The district court ruled in favor of PepsiCo and issued an injunction enjoining Redmond from commencing work at Quaker through May, 1995, and permanently enjoining him from using or disclosing any PepsiCo trade secrets.

The Seventh Circuit affirmed on appeal. The Court of Appeals recognized that Redmond's new position provided him substantial input into Gatorade pricing, marketing, packaging, and distribution. Unless Redmond possessed an uncanny ability to compartmentalize his knowledge, he would necessarily reach these decisions by relying upon his knowledge of PepsiCo trade secrets. Judge Flaum also believed these disclosures would enable Quaker to obtain a substantial advantage by knowing how PepsiCo would price, distribute, and market its drinks, and be able to respond accordingly. The Seventh Circuit rejected Redmond's argument that he would transfer to Quaker no more than his general business skills and knowledge, and found that he would necessarily reveal particularized strategic plans that were unknown to the industry.

PespsiCo, Inc. v. Redmond and the inevitable disclosure doctrine have been subject to considerable criticism. If PepsiCo wanted to limit Redmond's ability to work for a competitor, then it should have asked him to agree to a covenant not to compete. Yet PepsiCo obtained substantially the same relief by arguing he might make an "inevitable disclosure" of trade secrets. Any former employer of an individual who now works for a direct competitor would seem to be able to make the same argument, at least where the employee was a highly placed senior executive. Some commentators believe that the doctrine unfairly enjoins ex-employees even though there is no proof of any wrongdoing. On the other hand, ours is an era of considerable job mobility, growing employer reliance upon the advanced knowledge of their employees, and increasing competitive value of proprietary information. This combination suggests that an inference of an inevitable disclosure may be appropriate in cases where competitors seek to obtain specific, short-term, and commercially damaging competitor information through corporate raiding.

13.1.4 Remedies

13.1.4.1 Injunctions

Plaintiffs commonly request preliminary injunctions and temporary restraining orders in trade secrets cases. Trade secrets are fragile assets that, once publicly disclosed, lose their legal status and often their economic value as well. As one court explained, the trade secret owner cannot "slam the door of the barn after the horses are long gone."[47] In adjudicating these requests, courts employ the familiar four-factor test that generally governs the availability of preliminary relief. Courts will consider whether (1) the plaintiff has a substantial likelihood of success on the merits; (2) irreparable harm or injury will result in the absence of an injunction; (3) the harm to the moving party in the absence of an injunction outweighs the harm to the non-movant that would result from an injunction; and (4) the issuance of an injunction will serve the public interest.

The modern rule is that so-called "permanent injunctions" are appropriate only for the period of time that the subject matter of the trade secret would have remained unavailable to the defendant but for the misappropriation. This principle offers a compromise between two more extreme positions established in the older case law. One line of older cases followed the holding in *Shellmar Products Co. v. Allen–Qualley Co.*[48] and concluded that perpetual injunctions were an appropriate remedy for trade secret misappropriation on the ground that trade secrets have no set duration. On this view, the offending firm would be barred from using the technology in perpetuity even after everyone else in the industry had learned it through reverse engineering. Other opinions found more favor in Judge Learned Hand's opinion in *Conmar Products Corp. v. Universal Slide Fastener Co.*,[49] to the effect that once a trade secret entered into the public domain, the plaintiff could obtain no injunctive relief whatsoever.

47. Chem–Trend, Inc. v. McCarthy, 780 F. Supp. 458, 462, 22 USPQ2d 1458, 1462 (E.D. Mich. 1991).

48. 87 F.2d 104, 32 USPQ 24 (7th Cir.), *cert. denied*, 301 U.S. 695, 57 S.Ct. 923, 81 L.Ed. 1350 (1937).

49. 172 F.2d 150, 80 USPQ 108 (2d Cir.1949).

Each of these extreme positions is now in disfavor. Contemporary courts have reasoned that the draconian *Shellmar* rule is punitive in character and undermines the public interest in legitimate competition. On the other hand, the *Conmar* rule leads to hard results in cases where the defendant engaged in egregious conduct, particularly where he exposed the trade secret to the public himself. The compromise position of the Uniform Trade Secrets Act states that "an injunction shall be terminated when the trade secret has ceased to exist, but the injunction may be continued for an additional reasonable period of time in order to eliminate commercial advantage that otherwise would be derived from the misappropriation."[50]

As a result, successful plaintiffs in trade secret proceedings may obtain injunctions limited to the lead time advantage inappropriately gained by the misappropriator. In determining the length of this "head start," courts will weigh evidence as to the amount of time a person of ordinary skill would have required to discover independently or reverse engineer the subject matter of the trade secret. If the misappropriator can demonstrate that the trade secret holder's competitors have legitimately acquired the protected knowledge, then the court will likely decline to award an injunction at all.

13.1.4.2 Damages

Courts have demonstrated flexibility in fashioning monetary remedies for trade secret misappropriation. They will typically award an amount equal to either the loss suffered by the trade secret holder, or the gain realized by the defendant, whichever is greater. Sometimes courts award the trade secret holder the "cost avoided" by the defendant to develop the trade secret through legitimate means. Monetary damages are ordinarily limited to the time that the misappropriated information would not have been available otherwise to the defendant.[51]

An example demonstrates the remedial structure of trade secret law. Suppose that Jufi and Lojak compete in the field of photographic film. Jufi spends one million dollars to develop an improved method of making film and protects that method through adequate secrecy measures to qualify it as a trade secret. Lojak misappropriates the trade secret on May 1, 2000, and begins to produce film in competition with Jufi on September 1, 2000. Lojak earns $575,000 in net profits on film sales from September 1, 2000 through January 1, 2001. In the meantime, another market en-

50. Uniform Trade Secrets Act § 2(a), 14 U.L.A. 438 (1990).

51. *See, e.g.*, Engelhard Industries, Inc. v. Research Instrumental Corp., 324 F.2d 347, 139 USPQ 179 (9th Cir.1963), *cert. denied*, 377 U.S. 923, 84 S.Ct. 1220, 12 L.Ed.2d 215 (1964).

trant, Solanoid, purchases samples of the Jufi film and engages in extensive reverse engineering efforts. Following six weeks of work and reasonable expenditures of $200,000, Solanoid determines the steps of the Jufi process and publishes them in an industry newsletter on January 1, 2001.

Assuming a trial was held in early 2001, and Jufi produces no evidence indicating losses exceeding $575,000, Jufi may recover that amount from Lojak. Jufi may also obtain damages of $200,000, equal to the amount of reverse engineering expenses that Lojak saved. Jufi's total damages award would amount to $775,000. A court would decline to issue an injunction because the short period of time needed to reverse engineer the trade secret has already elapsed.

13.1.5 The Economic Espionage Act

Trade secrets have traditionally been the subject of state law. Prior to 1996, federal legislation concerning trade secrets was sparse. The broadly titled federal Trade Secrets Act, enacted in the 1940's, is actually of narrow application, for it forbids government employees from making an unauthorized disclosure of confidential government information, including trade secrets.[52] This legislation does not apply at all to the private sector. Of course, federal prosecutors have long been able to seek a conviction for trade secret theft under more general federal criminal legislation. This general legislation does not always present a tight fit with the facts of trade secret cases, however. Some courts have concluded that the National Stolen Property Act applies only to physical goods, for example,[53] while the mail and wire fraud statutes are inapplicable if the trade secret theft occurred through other means.[54]

Motivated by concerns over growing international and domestic economic espionage against U.S. firms, Congress enacted the Economic Espionage Act of 1996 (EEA).[55] As codified in Title 18 of the United States Code, the EEA criminalizes both "economic espionage" and the "theft of trade secrets." The "economic espionage" provision, § 1831, punishes those who knowingly misappropriate, or attempt or conspire to misappropriate, trade secrets with the intent or knowledge that the offense will benefit a foreign government, instrumentality or agent.[56] The "theft of trade secrets" prohibition of § 1832 is the more general provision. The principal elements of an EEA claim for theft of trade secrets are: (1) the intentional and/or knowing theft, appropriation, destruction, altera-

52. 18 U.S.C. § 1905 (2000).

53. 18 U.S.C. § 2314 (2000).

54. 18 U.S.C. §§ 1341, 1343 (2000).

55. Pub. L. No. 104–294, §§ 1831–1839, 110 Stat. 3488 (codified at 18 U.S.C.A. §§ 1831–39).

56. 18 U.S.C. § 1831 (2000).

tion, or duplication of (2) a trade secret placed in interstate commerce (3) with intent to convert the trade secret and (4) intent or knowledge that such action will injure the owner.[57]

The EEA provides for substantial fines and imprisonment penalties. Theft of trade secrets is punishable by a fine of up to $250,000 for individuals as well as imprisonment of up to 10 years. Organizations can be fined up to $5 million. For economic espionage, the maximum penalties increase to $500,000 for individuals and imprisonment of 15 years, or $10 million for corporations. The EEA also provides for criminal forfeiture of property[58] and court orders preserving confidentiality of trade secrets.[59]

Reflecting its concern over the theft of trade secrets by foreigners, Congress provided that the EEA potentially applies to conduct that occurs outside the United States. Section 1837 allows the United States to prosecute violations of the EEA against persons who are citizens or permanent resident aliens of the United States, or organizations formed under the laws of the United States. The EEA also applies if an act in furtherance of the offense was committed in the United States.

The jury is still out on the effectiveness of the EEA. To date, federal prosecutors have brought few cases under this statute.[60] Most of these cases have involved domestic trade secret theft under § 1832 rather than economic espionage under § 1831. This focus is unexpected given the legislative history of the EEA, which reflects significant congressional concern over economic espionage by foreign entities. Only time will tell if the EEA proves a viable mechanism for deterring the theft of trade secrets by domestic and foreign actors alike.

13.1.6 Trade Secrets and Patents

Trade secrets and patents coexist in what can be described as an uneasy relationship. A principal purpose of the patent law is the dissemination of knowledge.[61] This goal is realized through the publication of patent instruments that fully disclose the patented invention such that skilled artisans could practice it without undue experimentation.[62] A law of trade secrets that encourages the withholding of patentable inventions and the hoarding of technological insights appears fundamentally at odds with this precept.[63]

57. United States v. Hsu, 155 F.3d 189, 195–96, 47 USPQ2d 1784, 1788 (3d Cir. 1998).

58. 18 U.S.C. § 1834 (2000).

59. 18 U.S.C. § 1835 (2000).

60. The total number of cases filed as of late 2003 was approximately 25. For a table of all cases, *see,* <http://www.usdoj.gov/criminal/cybercrime/eeapub.htm>.

61. *See supra* § 1.3.1.

62. 35 U.S.C.A. § 112 (2000).

63. Joan E. Schaffner, *Patent Preemption Unlocked*, 1995 Wis. L. Rev. 1081.

This tension results in a variety of patent law doctrines that deliberately disadvantage trade secret holders. One patent law principle that deleteriously impacts trade secret holders is that a later, independent inventor may patent the subject matter of an earlier inventor's trade secret. Although this result may initially seem surprising given the "first to invent" approach of U.S. patent law, it follows from the prior art definition set out in § 102 of the Patent Act and the pertinent judicial precedents.[64] Let us assume that a trade secret holder called TraSeeCo develops a new method for purifying insulin in early 2004. TraSeeCo immediately begins to practice the method in its own, restricted access manufacturing facility. Although TraSeeCo sells purified insulin, it does not disclose how the insulin is purified. Further assume that another firm, PatCorp, develops the same method in mid–2005 through its own research, without knowledge of TraSeeCo's earlier activities. PatCorp then immediately files a patent application. TraSeeCo's activities will not constitute prior art preventing the issuance of a patent to PatCorp, because its activities do not, by definition, constitute prior art under the § 102 definition. With no prior art standing in the way PatCorp would get the patent.

Moreover, suppose that TraSee Co becomes aware of PatCorp's pending application (perhaps at the time the PTO publishes that application) and belatedly files a patent application of its own. Even though TraSeeCo was the first to invent the insulin purification method, PatCorp would be awarded the patent. This follows because TraSeeCo's own prior activities count as prior art against it—but not PatCorp—under the prevailing interpretation of § 102(b).[65] As a consequence, first inventors such as TraSeeCo may quickly transition from the status of a trade secret holder to an adjudicated patent infringer.[66] The First Inventor Defense Act of 1999 did soften this traditional principle somewhat, allowing earlier inventors an infringement defense against subsequent patentees of methods of doing business,[67] but that provision does not apply for inventions in any other fields of technology and is thus of rather narrow relevance.

This harsh treatment should not lead you to believe that the legal system disdains trade secrets. Courts have repeatedly noted that trade secrets perform a valuable role in the U.S. intellectual property scheme. Although the patent law is an increasingly expansive regime, its subject matter does not extend to the full array of

64. *See supra* §§ 4.3.2, 4.4.1.

65. *Ibid.*

66. *See* Albert C. Smith & Jared A. Stosberg, *Beware! Trade Secret Software May Be Patented By A Later Inventor*, 7 Computer Lawyer no. 11 at 15 (Nov. 1990).

67. 35 U.S.C.A. § 273 (2000). *See supra* § 4.4.2.9.

valuable information that may be the subject of a trade secret.[68] Moreover, patent rights must be affirmatively sought, and their acquisition usually entails significant costs and delays.[69] Some inventors are not well schooled in the rather rarefied patent law regime and may wait overly long before filing a patent application. Even sophisticated enterprises may not recognize the value of an invention until they too have performed acts that defeat its patentability. The trade secret law fills these gaps by providing a modicum of protection for those who take prudent measures to protect valuable information.

Inventors who do not wish to dedicate their technologies to the public domain must choose between maintaining the technology as a trade secret or pursuing patent protection. A number of factors inform this decision. Whether the inventor can keep the technology secret is the most obvious. Many mechanical inventions betray their design upon inspection, while the composition of a chemical compound may be much easier to conceal. The costs associated with acquiring and maintaining patents are another consideration. A U.S. patent provides rights only within the United States,[70] but discloses its subject matter for anyone in the world to see. An inventor should therefore also consider the expense of obtaining a patent in each jurisdiction in which he plans to do business.

The product cycle associated with the invention is also of importance. Products with a very short lifespan may be unmarketable by the time a patent issues. Inventors should also consider whether the industry in which they act is patent-intensive. If industry actors tend to invest heavily in maintaining their patent portfolios, then the inventor may well wish to patent for defensive purposes or to have a bargaining chip available if he is accused of infringement himself. Legislative enactment of the First Inventor Defense Act of 1999 introduced another element into this calculation. If the invention concerns a "method of doing business" within the meaning of the Act, then the inventor may gain an infringement defense effective against the patents of others that claim that method.[71]

The publication of a patent application or issuance of a patent will destroy trade secret status for the subject matter that it properly discloses. Nothing prevents a patentee from maintaining an invention as a trade secret until such time, however. This strategy requires the applicant to preserve secrecy until the first of

68. 35 U.S.C.A. § 101 (2000); *see supra* Chapter 2 for more on patent eligibility requirements.

69. 35 U.S.C.A. § 131 (2000); *see supra* Chapter 7 for more on patent acquisition procedures.

70. Dowagiac Mfg. Co. v. Minnesota Moline Plow Co., 235 U.S. 641, 650, 35 S.Ct. 221, 59 L.Ed. 398 (1915).

71. 35 U.S.C.A. § 273 (2000).

two events: (1) the publication of the application eighteen months following its filing date; or (2) when the PTO issues the patent, for those applications exempted from the publication requirement.

§ 13.2 Federal Preemption

Both the federal and state governments have the power to regulate intellectual property. In the event that a conflict arises between these sources of law, Article VI, clause 2 of the Constitution stipulates that the federal law "shall be the supreme Law of the Land." Under the so-called "Supremacy Clause," then, any state law that conflicts with the federal patent statute is void.

Although no provision of the Patent Act expressly preempts state law, the courts have nonetheless implied that the federal patent law has preemptive effect. In general, courts decide implied preemption cases by considering whether Congress has "occupied the field" in which the state is attempting to regulate, whether a state law directly conflicts with federal law, or whether enforcement of the state law might frustrate federal purposes.[1] Most patent preemption cases have not turned on either field preemption or direct conflicts between state and federal law, however. Instead, they rest on the more difficult determination of whether the state law conflicts with the objectives of the patent law. A review of the leading cases reveals that courts have stressed different purposes of the patent law as they have faced varying state laws, sometimes leading to results that seem hard to reconcile with one another. Still, it is possible to develop guiding principles based upon the major decisions of the Supreme Court in this area.

Two Supreme Court decisions issued on the same day, *Sears, Roebuck & Co. v. Stiffel Co.*[2] and *Compco Corp. v. Day–Brite Lighting*[3] began the modern era of patent preemption analysis. In *Sears*, plaintiff Stiffel held design and mechanical patents on a pole lamp. Soon after Stiffel began selling pole lamps, Sears put a substantially similar lamp on the market. Stiffel sued Sears for patent infringement and violation of the unfair competition laws.[4] The district court held that the two patents were invalid but found merit in the unfair competition claims. Accordingly, it awarded an injunction and damages to Stiffel, concluding that Sears had created a likelihood of consumer confusion about the source of the lamps. The Court of Appeals for the Seventh Circuit affirmed.

§ 13.2

1. *See* Joan E. Schaffner, *Patent Preemption Unlocked,* 1995 Wis. L. Rev. 1081.

2. 376 U.S. 225 (1964).

3. 376 U.S. 234 (1964).

4. The unfair competition claim essentially alleged that the shape of the pole lamp functioned as a brand-identifying symbol, analogous to a trademark, and that the use of that shape by Sears would confuse the public concerning the origin and/or source of the pole lamps.

The facts of *Compco* were similar. Plaintiff Day–Brite had obtained a design patent pertaining to the ornamental features of its flourescent lighting fixture. Although Day–Brite also sought a utility patent concerning the mechanical aspects of its invention, the Patent Office rejected its application. Once Day–Brite introduced its fixture to the marketplace, Compco began selling products with a similar appearance. As with the plaintiff in *Sears*, Day–Brite then commenced suit against Compco based upon claims of unfair competition and patent infringement. The district court held the design patent invalid but upheld the unfair competition claims, and the Court of Appeals for the Seventh Circuit again affirmed.

After granting *certiorari*, the Supreme Court reversed in both cases. The Court concluded that the state causes of action for unfair competition would stand as an obstacle to achieve the full purposes of the federal Patent Act, and as a result they were preempted. According to the Court, the patent law not only defines those innovations that are patentable, but, by negative inference, also determines which innovations remain free for all to use. Because the devices in both cases had been held ineligible for patents, the Court felt that Congress meant for them to be freely copiable by competitors. "To allow a State by use of its law of unfair competition to prevent the copying of an article which represents too slight an advance to be patented would be to permit the State to block off from the public something which federal law has said belongs to the public."[5]

The Supreme Court used broad language in its *Sears–Compco* opinions, and its implications seemed sweeping. Put succinctly, the cases seemed to hold that states could not prevent competitors from copying objects that were not patented. The Court did suggest states could regulate imitation of product designs to some degree, by mandating the use of labels or other precautionary measures, for the purposes of preventing consumer confusion.[6] However, the opinions seemed clear that the states could not prohibit, by itself, the copying of so-called "trade dress."[7]

Shortly after the decsion in *Sears–Compco*, the Supreme Court issued two decisions, *Brulotte v. Thys Co.*[8] and *Lear, Inc. v. Adkins*,[9] holding certain patent licensing practices unenforceable—effectively ruling that state contract principles would have to give way where they undermined the policies of federal patent law. In *Brulotte*, the Court refused to enforce an agreement to pay royalties on a

5. 376 U.S. at 231–32.

6. 376 U.S. at 232.

7. Product or packaging attributes that serve to identify goods or services are known as "trade dress." *See* Roger E. Schechter & John R. Thomas, Intellectual Property § 28.1 (2003).

8. 379 U.S. 29 (1964).

9. 395 U.S. 653 (1969).

patented invention beyond the term of the patent. The Court viewed the agreement as effectively extending the statutory patent term. Technically, *Brulotte* was a patent misuse case, but the Court's opinion also suggested concerns over federal preemption.[10] In *Lear, Inc. v. Adkins,* the Court held that licensees were free to challenge licensed patents even if they had agreed to refrain from doing so. According to the Court, the doctrine of "licensee estoppel" conflicted with the federal policy of invalidating improvidently granted patents. *Lear, Inc. v. Adkins* more squarely relied upon a preemption analysis, concluding that state contract laws that interfered with a federal patent policy were preempted.[11]

In light of these three decisions, the state law of trade secrets seemed ripe for the picking under a federal preemption theory. Although the patent system encourages the disclosure of inventions, individuals must conceal information in order to secure trade secret protection.[12] The patent law also reflects the policy that only new and nonobvious inventions merit proprietary patent rights. As we have seen, the value of secret information need not rise to the level of novelty for the information to be protected as a trade secret.[13] And a trade secret need not be nonobvious at all. Given these conflicts, the broad language of *Sears–Compco* seemed to provide a strong mandate for the federal preemption of trade secret law.

In *Kewanee Oil Co. v Bicron Corp.,*[14] the Supreme Court nonetheless held that the trade secret law was not federally preempted. The plaintiff in *Kewanee Oil* had developed a process for growing synthetic crystals. It maintained the process as a trade secret and required employees with access to the process to sign confidentiality agreements. When some of its employees resigned from their employment, formed their own business and allegedly began using the secret process, the plaintiff then sued for trade secret misappropriation under state law. The district court found for the plaintiff, but the Court of Appeals for the Sixth Circuit reversed, concluding that the trade secret law had been preempted by the federal patent law.

Following a grant of *certiorari,* the Supreme Court again reversed. The Court reasoned that, like the patent law, trade secret law encouraged individuals and enterprises to innovate, and as a result there was no conflict between the two legal regimes. The Court also saw no burden upon the patent law policy of preserving

10. *See supra* § 11.6.

11. *See supra* § 11.4.

12. James R. Barney, *The Prior User Defense: A Reprieve for Trade Secret Owners or a Disaster for the Patent Law?*, 82 J. Pat. & Trademark Off. Soc'y 261 (2000).

13. *See supra* § 13.1.1.1.

14. 416 U.S. 470, 94 S.Ct. 1879, 40 L.Ed.2d 315 (1974).

the public domain, for by their very nature trade secrets have not been made available to the public, and state law protection of them does not deprive competitors of something that was otherwise freely known and available.

In the most interesting part of the *Kewanee* decision, the Court also found no conflict with the public disclosure function of patent law. Chief Justice Burger envisioned that information held as a trade secrets fell into three classes: (1) inventions that did not meet the statutory subject matter, novelty, nonobviousness, and other requirements for patenting; (2) innovations of questionable patentability; and (3) patentable advances. As to trade secrets in the first category, trade secret holders—knowing that a patent was unavailable—would never apply for a patent, and even they did, no patent would ever issue. Thus trade secret protection for this category did not prevent the disclosure of information that would otherwise have been revealed through the patent system. Regarding the second category, namely trade secrets of uncertain patentability, the disclosure of the invention was of marginal social value, and thus the loss of disclosure if the innovator opted out of the patent system in favor of trade secret law would be minimal. Finally, for trade secrets that could be patented, the prospect of more robust rights through the patent system would in most cases drive the innovator to file an application at the PTO, so that again, the lost quantity of disclosure would be minimal.

Although the Court did not expressly overrule *Sears–Compco*, the *Kewanee Oil* analysis effectively ignored its reasoning. *Sears–Compco* held that everything that was not patentable was free for others to use, while *Kewanee Oil* instead concluded that only ideas in "general circulation" were public domain—a category that did not include trade secrets. The Court's analysis of the relative merits of patent and trade secret protection also seems flawed. In circumstances where a technology has a long lifespan and cannot be easily reverse engineered, trade secret protection may be much more desirable than patent rights. While the *Kewanee Oil* Court also took note of the fact that the state cause of action had been in place for many years without any congressional action to supplant it, this circumstance was also the case in *Sears–Compco*.

At least two factors allow *Kewanee Oil* to be distinguished from *Sears–Compco*, however. First, trade secrets provide a relatively weak form of intellectual property protection. Others remain free to acquire the trade secret by legitimate means, such as reverse engineering, and to invent the same subject matter independently. The Court also relied upon the fact that the trade secret law discouraged inefficient industrial espionage and maintained rights to privacy. Despite these distinguishing features, most observers, including the lower courts, walked away from *Kewanee Oil* sensing new limits upon the reasoning of *Sears* and *Compco*.[15]

The Supreme Court's next encounter with patent preemption issues occurred in *Aronson v. Quick Point Pencil Co.*[16] Here the defendant, Jane Aronson, had filed a patent application claiming a keyholder. While prosecution was ongoing at the Patent Office, she negotiated a license with Quick Point. The Aronson–Quick Point license in part called for the payment of royalties of 5% if a patent issued within five years; otherwise Quick Point would pay 2.5% of sales so long as it sold the keyholder. After the Patent Office finally rejected Aronson's patent application, Quick Point sought a declaratory judgment that the agreement was unenforceable under the preemption doctrine. According to Quick Point, enforcement of the contract under state law would conflict with the federal patent law by granting perpetual protection to an invention that had been specifically found unpatentable by the Patent Office.

In reasoning reminiscent of *Kewanee Oil*, the Court declined to invoke the federal preemption doctrine against state contract law. According to the Court, enforcement of the Aronson–Quick Point license would encourage individuals to invent and to exploit inventions that were of social value, even if they were not patentable. Enforcement also encouraged the public disclosure of the invention. Not only had Aronson's design entered the public domain upon the sale of the keyholders, competing firms had already begun to copy it.

Following *Kewanee Oil* and *Aronson v. Quick Point Pencil Co.*, some observers believed that the *Sears–Compco* analysis would play little role in future preemption cases. However, in its 1989 decision in *Bonito Boats, Inc. v. Thunder Craft Boats, Inc.*, the Supreme Court once again reasoned that "[t]o a limited extent, the federal patent laws must determine not only what is protected but also what is free for all to use."[17] In this case, the plaintiff designed a boat hull that the defendant allegedly reproduced through the use of a process called "plug molding." The plaintiff had never sought federal patent rights, instead bringing suit under a Florida state law that prohibited the use of direct molding to duplicate vessel hulls for purpose of sale. Although the Court of Appeals for the Federal Circuit had previously upheld a similar California law, the Florida Supreme Court struck down the statute on the grounds of federal preemption.

15. *See, e.g.*, SK & F, Co. v. Premo Pharm. Labs., Inc., 625 F.2d 1055, 1064, 206 USPQ 964 (3d Cir. 1980).

16. 440 U.S. 257 (1979).

17. 489 U.S. 141 (1989).

The Supreme Court granted *certiorari* and agreed that the Florida law had been preempted. Justice O'Connor initially identified a federal policy of favoring free competition in inventions that do not meet the requirements for patent protection. The Florida statute conflicted with this policy by allowing designers of unpatented boat hulls to prevent competitors from making the product in what was evidently the most efficient manner available. Not only did the Florida law block the reverse engineering of a public domain product, the Court explained, approval of this statute would create the prospect of numerous state laws offering participants in favored industries patent-like protections without the rigorous requirements for obtaining a federal patent. Justice O'Connor concluded that "the Florida statute at issue in this case so substantially impedes the public use of the otherwise unprotected design and utilitarian ideas embodied in unpatented boat hulls as to run afoul of the teaching of our decisions in *Sears* and *Compco*."[18]

Although the reasoning of *Bonito Boats* harkens back to *Sears* and *Compco*, the Court was careful not to endorse these decisions fully. Justice O'Connor in fact observed that it is inappropriate to extrapolate "a broad pre-emptive principle" from these cases.[19] In particular, the Court explained that *Sears–Compco* permits state protection against copying nonfunctional, distinctive product features when the copying is likely to lead to consumer confusion. This reasoning has the merits of preserving state "passing off" claims as they were, since the common law does not extend trade dress protection to functional product features.

As far as boat hulls are concerned, the *Bonito Boats* decision was not of lasting impact. Congress later enacted a "Vessel Hull Protection Act" that allows boat hull designers, upon securing a federal registration, to obtain protection similar to the preempted state laws.[20] *Bonito Boats* does provide important guidelines for considering future preemption cases, however. The general rule seems to be that inventions not meeting patentability standards should remain within the public domain. However, a state cause of action that restricts the copying of unpatented inventions may survive a federal preemption analysis under certain circumstances. First, the state cause of action should provide a weaker form of protection than the federal patent laws, rather than providing a competing source of intellectual property rights. Second, the state cause of action should not withdraw ideas that have entered the public domain. Third, the state cause of action should comport with congressional purposes in legislating the patent statute. Evidence

18. 489 U.S. at 157.

19. 489 U.S. at 154.

20. Pub. L. No. 105–304,112 Stat. 2860 (1998) (codified at 17 U.S.C. §§ 1301–1302).

that Congress was aware of the state cause of action and has not taken action to displace it supports the conclusion that the state law is not preempted. Finally, evidence that the state cause of action supports a legitimate state interest outside the immediate concerns of Congress when enacting the patent statute also makes a finding of federal preemption less likely.

Table of Cases

A

Abbott Laboratories v. Geneva Pharmaceuticals, Inc., 182 F.3d 1315 (Fed. Cir.1999)—§ **4.3;** § **4.3, n. 19.**

Abele, In re, 684 F.2d 902 (Cust. & Pat.App.1982)—§ **2.5;** § **2.5, n. 17.**

Abraham, Ex parte, 1868 Comm'r Dec. 59 (Comm'r Pat. 1868)—§ **2.7, n. 1.**

A.C. Aukerman Co. v. R.L. Chaides Const. Co., 960 F.2d 1020 (Fed.Cir. 1992)—§ **10.5;** § **10.5, n. 1.**

Adams v. Burke, 84 U.S. 453, 21 L.Ed. 700 (1873)—§ **8.1, n. 14.**

Adams, United States v., 383 U.S. 39, 86 S.Ct. 708, 15 L.Ed.2d 572 (1966)—§ **5.3;** § **5.3, n. 19.**

Advanced Cardiovascular Systems, Inc. v. C.R. Bard, Inc., 144 F.R.D. 372 (N.D.Cal.1992)—§ **6.2, n. 4.**

Advanced Cardiovascular Systems, Inc. v. Medtronic, Inc., 265 F.3d 1294 (Fed.Cir.2001)—§ **10.3, n. 9.**

Aerojet–General Corp. v. Machine Tool Works, Oerlikon–Buehrle Ltd., 895 F.2d 736 (Fed.Cir.1990)—§ **10.2, n. 7.**

Agawam Woolen Co. v. Jordan, 74 U.S. 583, 19 L.Ed. 177 (1868)—§ **4.3, n. 48.**

Akro Corp. v. Luker, 45 F.3d 1541 (Fed. Cir.1995)—§ **10.1, n. 11.**

Akzo N.V. v. United States Intern. Trade Com'n, 808 F.2d 1471 (Fed. Cir.1986)—§ **5.3, n. 57.**

Alappat, In re, 33 F.3d 1526 (Fed.Cir. 1994)—§ **2.5;** § **2.5, n. 21.**

Alexander Milburn Co. v. Davis–Bournonville Co., 270 U.S. 390, 46 S.Ct. 324, 70 L.Ed. 651 (1926)—§ **4.4;** § **4.4, n. 59.**

Allen, Ex parte, 2 U.S.P.Q.2d 1425 (Bd. Pat.App & Interf.1987)—§ **2.3;** § **2.3, n. 14.**

Al–Site Corp. v. VSI Intern., Inc., 174 F.3d 1308 (Fed.Cir.1999)—§ **8.2;** § **8.2, n. 90.**

American Cotton–Tie Co. v. Simmons, 106 U.S. 89, 1 S.Ct. 52, 27 L.Ed. 79 (1882)—§ **8.1, n. 42.**

American Hoist & Derrick Co. v. Sowa & Sons, Inc., 725 F.2d 1350 (Fed.Cir. 1984)—§ **5.3, n. 62.**

American Infra–Red Radiant Co. v. Lambert Industries, Inc., 360 F.2d 977 (8th Cir.1966)—§ **12.1, n. 8.**

American Medical Systems, Inc. v. Medical Engineering Corp., 6 F.3d 1523 (Fed.Cir.1993)—§ **9.2, n. 37.**

American Securit Co. v. Shatterproof Glass Corp., 268 F.2d 769 (3rd Cir. 1959)—§ **11.5, n. 5.**

Amgen, Inc. v. Chugai Pharmaceutical Co., Ltd., 927 F.2d 1200 (Fed.Cir. 1991)—§ **2.3, n. 3;** § **6.1, n. 30;** § **6.2, n. 58.**

Amgen, Inc. v. Elanex Pharmaceuticals, Inc., 1996 WL 84590 (W.D.Wash. 1996)—§ **8.1, n. 31.**

Amos, In re, 953 F.2d 613 (Fed.Cir. 1991)—§ **7.5, n. 9.**

AMP Inc. v. United States, 182 Ct.Cl. 86, 389 F.2d 448 (Ct.Cl.1968)—§ **11.7;** § **11.7, n. 9.**

Amsted Industries Inc. v. Buckeye Steel Castings Co., 24 F.3d 178 (Fed.Cir. 1994)—§ **9.2, n. 34.**

Anderson's–Black Rock, Inc. v. Pavement Salvage Co., 396 U.S. 57, 90 S.Ct. 305, 24 L.Ed.2d 258 (1969)—§ **5.3;** § **5.3, n. 20.**

Andrew Corp. v. Gabriel Electronics, Inc., 847 F.2d 819 (Fed.Cir.1988)—§ **6.2, n. 57.**

Antle, In re, 444 F.2d 1168 (Cust. & Pat.App.1971)—§ **5.3;** § **5.3, n. 34.**

Anton/Bauer, Inc. v. PAG, Ltd., 329 F.3d 1343 (Fed.Cir.2003)—§ **1.2, n. 5.**

Apotex USA, Inc. v. Merck & Co., Inc., 254 F.3d 1031 (Fed.Cir.2001)—§ **4.4, n. 50.**

Application of (see name of party)

Applied Materials, Inc. v. Advanced Semiconductor Materials America, Inc., 98 F.3d 1563 (Fed.Cir.1996)—§ **7.2, n. 19;** § **7.7, n. 10.**

Arkie Lures, Inc. v. Gene Larew Tackle, Inc., 119 F.3d 953 (Fed.Cir.1997)—§ **5.3;** § **5.3, n. 59, 60.**

B

C

D

E

Graham v. John Deere Co. of Kansas City, 383 U.S. 1, 86 S.Ct. 684, 15 L.Ed.2d 545 (1966)—**§ 5.3; § 5.3, n. 15.**

Grain Processing Corp. v. American Maize–Products Co., 185 F.3d 1341 (Fed.Cir.1999)—**§ 9.2; § 9.2, n. 20.**

Grain Processing Corp. v. American Maize–Products Co., 840 F.2d 902 (Fed.Cir.1988)—**§ 5.3, n. 26.**

Grant v. Raymond, 31 U.S. 218, 8 L.Ed. 376 (1832)—**§ 1.3, n. 3; § 7.5, n. 6.**

Graver Tank & Mfg. Co. v. Linde Air Products Co., 339 U.S. 605, 70 S.Ct. 854, 94 L.Ed. 1097 (1950)—**§ 8.2; § 8.2, n. 25.**

Grayson, Ex parte, 51 U.S.P.Q. 413 (Pat.& Tr. Office Bd.App.1941)—**§ 2.3, n. 11.**

Great Atlantic & Pac. Tea Co. v. Supermarket Equipment Corp., 340 U.S. 147, 71 S.Ct. 127, 95 L.Ed. 162 (1950)—**§ 5.3; § 5.3, n. 12.**

Greenberg v. Ethicon Endo–Surgery, Inc., 91 F.3d 1580 (Fed.Cir.1996)—**§ 6.2, n. 23.**

Griffith v. Kanamaru, 816 F.2d 624 (Fed.Cir.1987)—**§ 4.4, n. 35.**

Gulack, In re, 703 F.2d 1381 (Fed.Cir. 1983)—**§ 2.6, n. 3.**

Gyromat Corp. v. Champion Spark Plug Co., 735 F.2d 549 (Fed.Cir.1984)—**§ 9.2, n. 16.**

H

Hall, In re, 781 F.2d 897 (Fed.Cir. 1986)—**§ 4.3, n. 42.**

Halliburton Co. v. Schlumberger Technology Corp., 925 F.2d 1435 (Fed.Cir. 1991)—**§ 7.7; § 7.7, n. 4.**

Halliburton Oil Well Cementing Co. v. Walker, 329 U.S. 1, 67 S.Ct. 6, 91 L.Ed. 3 (1946)—**§ 6.2; § 6.2, n. 18.**

Harnisch, In re, 631 F.2d 716 (Cust. & Pat.App.1980)—**§ 6.2, n. 49.**

Harries v. Air King Products Co., 183 F.2d 158 (2nd Cir.1950)—**§ 5.3, n. 9.**

Hass, In re, 141 F.2d 122 (Cust. & Pat. App.1944)—**§ 5.3, n. 69.**

Heicklen, Ex parte, 16 U.S.P.Q.2d 1463 (Bd.Pat.App & Interf.1989)—**§ 3.2, n. 4.**

Heidelberger Druckmaschinen AG v. Hantscho Commercial Products, Inc., 21 F.3d 1068 (Fed.Cir.1994)—**§ 5.3, n. 40.**

Henze, In re, 181 F.2d 196 (Cust. & Pat.App.1950)—**§ 5.3, n. 69.**

Heritage, In re, 150 F.2d 554 (Cust. & Pat.App.1945)—**§ 2.5; § 2.5, n. 1.**

Hess v. Advanced Cardiovascular Systems, Inc., 106 F.3d 976 (Fed.Cir. 1997)—**§ 7.3; § 7.3, n. 5.**

Hester Industries, Inc. v. Stein, Inc., 142 F.3d 1472 (Fed.Cir.1998)—**§ 7.5, n. 17.**

Hewlett–Packard Co. v. Bausch & Lomb Inc., 909 F.2d 1464 (Fed.Cir.1990)—**§ 8.1, n. 45.**

Hewlett–Packard Co. v. Bausch & Lomb, Inc., 882 F.2d 1556 (Fed.Cir.1989)—**§ 7.5; § 7.5, n. 11.**

H.H. Robertson, Co. v. United Steel Deck, Inc., 820 F.2d 384 (Fed.Cir. 1987)—**§ 9.1, n. 7.**

Hildreth v. Mastoras, 257 U.S. 27, 42 S.Ct. 20, 66 L.Ed. 112 (1921)—**§ 4.4, n. 27.**

Hilmer, In re, 424 F.2d 1108 (Cust. & Pat.App.1970)—**§ 12.1, n. 12.**

Hilmer, In re, 359 F.2d 859 (Cust. & Pat.App.1966)—**§ 4.4, n. 66; § 12.1, n. 12.**

Hilton Davis Chemical Co. v. Warner–Jenkinson Co., Inc., 62 F.3d 1512 (Fed.Cir.1995)—**§ 8.2, n. 33.**

Holmes Group, Inc. v. Vornado Air Circulation Systems, Inc., 535 U.S. 826, 122 S.Ct. 1889, 153 L.Ed.2d 13 (2002)—**§ 10.2; § 10.2, n. 8.**

Holmwood v. Sugavanam, 948 F.2d 1236 (Fed.Cir.1991)—**§ 4.4, n. 44.**

Hormone Research Foundation, Inc. v. Genentech, Inc., 904 F.2d 1558 (Fed. Cir.1990)—**§ 6.2, n. 13.**

Hotchkiss v. Greenwood, 52 U.S. 248, 11 How. 248, 13 L.Ed. 683 (1850)—**§ 5.3; § 5.3, n. 1.**

Hotel Security Checking Co. v. Lorraine Co., 160 F. 467 (2nd Cir.1908)—**§ 2.7; § 2.7, n. 4.**

Hsu, United States v., 155 F.3d 189 (3rd Cir.1998)—**§ 13.1, n. 57.**

Hyatt, In re, 708 F.2d 712 (Fed.Cir. 1983)—**§ 6.2, n. 17.**

Hybritech Inc. v. Abbott Laboratories, 849 F.2d 1446 (Fed.Cir.1988)—**§ 10.3, n. 5.**

Hybritech Inc. v. Monoclonal Antibodies, Inc., 802 F.2d 1367 (Fed.Cir.1986)—**§ 5.3; § 5.3, n. 51; § 6.1, n. 7.**

I

IDX Systems Corp. v. Epic Systems Corp., 285 F.3d 581 (7th Cir.2002)—**§ 13.1; § 13.1, n. 34.**

Imperial Chemical Industries Limited v. National Distillers & Chemical Corp., 342 F.2d 737 (2nd Cir.1965)—**§ 13.1, n. 28.**

J

K

L

M

Q

R

T

U

V

*

Index

References are to Pages

†